THE EFFICACY
of
AUGMENTATIVE
and
ALTERNATIVE
COMMUNICATION

A Volume in the Augmentative and Alternative
Communication Perspectives Series

THE EFFICACY

of

AUGMENTATIVE

and

ALTERNATIVE

COMMUNICATION

A VOLUME IN THE AUGMENTATIVE AND ALTERNATIVE
COMMUNICATION PERSPECTIVES SERIES

Ralf W. Schlosser

Northeastern University
Department of Speech–Language Pathology and Audiology
Boston, Massachusetts

ACADEMIC PRESS
An imprint of Elsevier Science

Amsterdam   Boston   London   New York   Oxford   Paris
San Diego   San Francisco   Singapore   Sydney   Tokyo

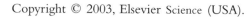
Academic Press
An imprint of Elsevier Science
525 B Street, Suite 1900, San Diego, California 92101-4495, USA
http://www.academicpress.com

Academic Press
84 Theobald's Road, London WC1X 8RR, UK
http://www.academicpress.com

Library of Congress Catalog Card Number: 2003100307

International Standard Book Number: 0-12-625667-5

PRINTED IN THE UNITED STATES OF AMERICA
03 04 05 06 07   8 7 6 5 4 3 2 1

SERIES FOREWORD

It is both a pleasure and an honor to collaborate with Academic Press in the development of the Augmentative and Alternative Communication (AAC) Perspectives Series. Academic Press has long been recognized as a major publisher of scholarly books in many of the basic areas that serve as foundations for the development of our current transdisciplinary field of AAC including acoustics, language development, linguistics, psychology, and speech and hearing sciences. During recent years, Academic Press has further developed this line of more scholarly books to include volumes appealing to more applied areas of education and speech-language pathology. It is rewarding to have such a prestigious publisher for the AAC Perspectives Series.

Some books in this series will emphasize clinical/educational practice, while others will emphasize research/basic information. All of the books will be based on the three cornerstones of evidence-based practice (EBP): research, clinical and/or educational expertise and stakeholder perspectives. They will be extensively referenced.

Books in the series will share in common the broad communication model originally proposed by Lloyd, Quist, and Windsor (1990) and subsequently discussed in other sources (e.g., Fuller & Lloyd, 1997). The series will attempt to further develop terminologic and taxonomic consistency within the field. The most commonly accepted terminology in an internally consistent manner. Terminology will be the topic of a future book (Lloyd, & Arvidson, forthcoming). Some of the books in the series will focus on emerging areas of AAC that have relevant literature but no significant books. These include topics such as efficacy and EBP (Schlosser, this volume) and literacy (Smith, forthcoming). Other books in the series will focus on topics that have been discuess in journals and books but show a need for a different perspective on AAC as, for example, the topic of assistive technology (Quist & Lloyd, forthcoming).

Although there are many critical areas in AAC, efficacy and EBP were selected for the inaugural book in the AAC Perspectives Series. During the past decade, outcomes and efficacy have emerged as critical issues in service delivery, in general, and in the provision of AAC services to individuals with the most severe disabilities, in particular. There have been a number of major publications on efficacy and outcome measures, but there has not been a major archival publication on the efficacy of AAC and EBP.

We are extremely fortunate to have Ralf Schlosser author this book. Schlosser has emerged as a leader in AAC with a strong research record on topics such as effects of specific AAC intervention approaches, symbols, and technologies. He has been a major AAC research synthesizer at the International Society for Augmentative and Alternative Communication (ISAAC) and American Speech-Language-Hearing Association (ASHA) conferences and has published a number of meta-analyses and integrative reviews in recent years. Schlosser has received several awards for his work including the *Augmentative and Alternative Communication* Editor's Award for the article entitled "Promoting Generalization and Maintenance in Augmentative and Alternative Communication: A Meta-Analysis of 20 Years of Effectiveness Research" (Schlosser & Lee, 2000) that was recognized as the most significant research article in 2000. In addition to having published numerous journal articles and chapters, Schlosser has served as a reviewer or guest reviewer for several journals, including *Augmentative and Alternative Communication, The Journal of Applied Behavior Analysis, The Journal of Speech, Language and Hearing Research* and *The Journal of Special Education Technology.* More recently, Schlosser has served as an associate editor for *Augmentative and Alternative Communication* and *The Journal of Behavioral Education.*

Schlosser has invited authors to contribute chapters in their respective areas of expertise to supplement his writing, including Jan Bedrosian, Doreen Blischak, Melinda Corwin, Erik Drasgow, Aimee Gorman, Mats Granlund, Jeff Higginbotham, David Lee, Linda Lombardino, Cecilia Olson, Rajinder Koul, Pammi Raghavendra, Mary Ann Romski, Rose Sevcik, and Jeff Sigafoos.

This inaugural book addressing the critical aspects of efficacy and EBP is intended to stimulate both researchers and practitioners and to facilitate improved AAC services for individuals with little or no functional speech. This book is designed to (1) increase the understanding and use of EBP, (2) provide efficacy information based on research that can help clinicians/educators make more informed decisions in practice, (3) serve as an extensive resource of efficacy data that can help researchers and practitioners guide stakeholders (including AAC users, family members, policy makers, administrators, and various other professionals) to make the best possible decisions that can help individuals with little or no functional speech realize optimal participation, and (4) help clinicians/educators become better consumers of research and take more active roles in the research process. We hope this book will, also, serve to improve the quality of special education and speech-language pathology personnel preparation and research programs in severe disabilities, in general, and in AAC, in particular. We anticipate that the discussion of the EBP cornerstones research, clinical/educational expertise and stakeholder perspectives in this book will serve as a valuable resource for researchers, practitioners, and stakeholders.

Lyle L. Lloyd, Ph.D., FAAMR, FASHA, CCC-A&SLP
Professor of Special Education, and
Professor of Audiology & Speech Sciences
Purdue University

REFERENCES

Fuller, D. R., & Lloyd, L. L. (1997). AAC model and taxonomy. In L. L Lloyd, D. R. Fuller and H. H. Arvidson (Eds.). *Augmentative and alternative communication: A handbook of principles and practices* (pp.25-37). Boston: Allyn and Bacon.

Lloyd, L. L., & Arvidson, H. H. (forthcoming). *AAC from A toZ*. San Diego, CA: Academic Press.

Lloyd, L. L., Quist, R. W., & Windsor, J. (1990). A proposed augmentative and alternative communication model. *Augmentative and alternative communication, 6*, 172-183.

Quist, R. W., & Lloyd, L. L. (forthcoming). *Assistive technology: Principles and applications for communication disorders and special education*. San Diego, CA: Academic Press.

Schlosser, R. W., & Lee, D. (2000). Promoting generalization and maintenance in augmentative and alternative communiction: A meta-analysis of 20 years of effectiveness research. *Augmentative and alternative communication, 16*, 208-227.

Smith, M. M., (forthcoming). *Literacy, augmentative and alternative communication*. San Diego, CA: Academic Press.

*To William Asher, who early on instilled in me
that a sustained critical evaluation of the literature in
a field can itself become an intervention in that field.*

*In memory of my beloved mother, Ruth Ingrid Schlosser (b. Kern),
1937-2000.*

CONTENTS

CHAPTER 3
Validity
Ralf W. Schlosser

CHAPTER 4
Formulating Research Questions
D. Jeffery Higginbotham

CHAPTER 5
On the Subject of Subject Selection in AAC
Jan L. Bedrosian

CHAPTER 6
Single-Subject Experimental Designs
Ralf W. Schlosser

CHAPTER 7
Group Designs
Ralf W. Schlosser

CHAPTER 8
Longitudinal Designs
Rose A. Sevcik and MaryAnn Romski

CHAPTER 9

Determining the Treatment
Integrity of AAC Interventions

Ralf W. Schlosser

CHAPTER 10
Determining the Social Validity of AAC Interventions
Ralf W. Schlosser

CHAPTER 11
Synthesizing Efficacy Research in AAC
Ralf W. Schlosser

CHAPTER 12

Toward Evidence-Based Practice in AAC

Ralf W. Schlosser and Pammi Raghavendra

CHAPTER 13

Presymbolic Communication Intervention

Cecilia Olsson and Mats Granlund

CHAPTER 14
Strategies for Beginning Communicators

Jeff Sigafoos, Erik Drasgow and Ralf W. Schlosser

CHAPTER 15
Selecting Graphic Symbols for an
Initial Request Lexicon

Ralf W. Schlosser

CHAPTER 16

Effects of AAC on Natural Speech Development

Ralf W. Schlosser

CHAPTER 17
Application of Current Literacy Theory, Efficacy Research, and Clinical Practice to AAC Users
Doreen M. Blischak, Aimee Gorman and Linda J. Lombardino

CHAPTER 18
Efficacy of AAC Intervention in Individuals with Chronic Severe Aphasia
Rajinder K. Koul and Melinda Corwin

CHAPTER 19
Roles of Speech Output in AAC
Ralf W. Schlosser, Doreen M. Blischak and Rajinder K. Koul

CHAPTER 20

Evidence-Based Strategies for Promoting
Generalization and Maintenance

Ralf W. Schlosser and David Lee

CHAPTER 21
Comparative Efficacy Studies Using
Single-Subject Experimental Designs
Ralf W. Schlosser

CHAPTER 22
Epilogue
Ralf W. Schlosser

CONTRIBUTORS

Numbers in parenthesis indicate page numbers on which authors contributions begin.

Jan L. Bedrosian (57), Western Michigan University, Department of Speech Pathology and Audiology, Kalamazoo, MI.

Doreen M. Blischak (427, 471), University of Florida, Department of Communication Sciences and Disorders, Gainesville, FL.

Melinda Corwin (449), Texas Tech University Health Sciences Center, Department of Communication Disorders, Lubbock, TX.

Erik Drasgow (323), University of South Carolina, Department of Education Psychology, Columbia, SC.

Aimee Gorman (427), University of Florida, Department of Communication Sciences and Disorders, Gainesville, FL.

Mats Granlund (299), ALA Research Foundation, Stockholm, Sweden, & Malardalen University, Vasteras, Sweden.

D. Jeffery Higginbotham (43), University of Buffalo, Department of Communicative Disorders and Sciences, Buffalo, NY.

Rajinder Koul (449, 471), Texas Tech University Health Sciences Center, Department of Communication Disorders, Lubbock, TX.

David Lee (533), Penn State University, Department of Educational and School Psychology and Special Education, Malvern, PA.

Linda J. Lombardino (427), University of Florida, Department of Communication Sciences and Disorders, Gainesville, FL.

Cecilia Olsson (299), ALA Research Foundation, Stockholm, Sweden.

Pammi Raghavendra (259), Crippled Children's Association of SA, Inc., Regency Park, Australia.

Mary Ann Romski (163), Georgia State University, Department of Communication, Atlanta, GA.

Ralf W. Schlosser (1, 13, 27, 85, 147, 181, 203, 229, 259, 323, 347, 403, 471, 533, 553, 601), Northeastern University, Department of Speech-Language Pathology and Audiology, Boston, MA.

Rose A. Sevcik (163), Georgia State University, Department of Psychology, Atlanta, GA.

Jeff Sigafoos (323), University of Texas at Austin, Department of Special Education, Austin, TX.

CHAPTER 1

Introduction

Ralf W. Schlosser
Department of Speech-Language Pathology and Audiology
Northeastern University

I. Why Was This Book Written?
II. Why Should We Care about Efficacy and EBP?
III. Organization of This Book

I. WHY WAS THIS BOOK WRITTEN?

"Protect yourself from the literature!" This is what William Asher, professor of educational psychology at Purdue University, tried to instill in his Ph.D. students in his class on research methods. As one of his students, I did not quite understand what he meant by this statement, at least at the beginning of class. Moreover, I had no idea that this statement would shape much of my approach to research and scholarship in general and this book in particular. In essence, this statement suggests that just because something is written or printed does not mean that it is accurate or to be taken at face value. As I apply this statement here, a reader of research has to be cognizant of the methodology with respect to the research question at hand as well as the conclusions to be drawn based on the ability of the study to rule out threats to internal and external validity.

During my journey in the field of augmentative and alternative communication (AAC), I found myself drawn to exploring whether AAC interventions really work (i.e., efficacy) and to methodological questions and issues related to such efficacy studies. This effort was reinforced when my adviser, Lyle L. Lloyd called for what he termed "research-based" information. To be sure, questions of methodological rigor are important in any research. In efficacy research, however, such rigor has greater bearing because we seek to separate truly effective interventions from seemingly effective interventions. Some interventions may appear effective at first glance, but once the certainty of the evidence is

1

examined from a methodological point of view, it may no longer be appropriate to consider the intervention effective.

It was not until evidence-based practice (EBP) took the fields of health care and education by storm, however, that the need to protect oneself from the literature became pertinent to the field with a renewed urgency. If EBP is defined as "the integration of best and current research evidence with clinical/ educational expertise and relevant stakeholder perspectives to facilitate decisions for assessment and intervention that are deemed effective and efficient for a given direct stakeholder" (see Chapter 12, p. 9), it is imperative that clinicians, educators, AAC users, researchers, and any other relevant stakeholders enter the literature armed with the tools to evaluate it so they may exit it with the answers they seek. It is preferable they conclude that research has not proved the effectiveness of an intervention rather than that they accept conclusions from faulty methodology. The ability to plough through relevant literature and correctly interpret the findings is essential to any attempt to act on the best and current research evidence.

The past and the current landscape of fine textbooks (Beukelman & Mirenda, 1998; Glennen & DeCoste, 1997; Lloyd, Fuller, & Arvidson, 1997; von Tetzchner & Martinsen, 1992) and other important monographs in the field of AAC (e.g., Calculator & Jorgenson, 1994; Reichle, York, & Sigafoos, 1991; Von Tetzchner & Jensen, 1996) tend, without notable exception, to proceed from research findings as stated by the authors of the original studies. Although it has not been the stated purpose of any of these works to evaluate the integrity of the research itself, any reliance on findings is a methodological acceptance of the "truth" of these findings. This book is a first step toward reconsidering to what extent our reliance on stated results of research is to be questioned due to improper implementation, design, or interpretation that led to inaccurate statements regarding what works, upon which we then relied in formulating further research and practice.

II. WHY SHOULD WE CARE ABOUT EFFICACY AND EBP?

It seems obvious that we should care about efficacy because it tells us whether an intervention is effective and efficient, and what kinds of effects were yielded. To know what interventions work is at the core of what practitioners want to accomplish—namely, to improve the communication skills of individuals who use AAC and those who support them. This book is subtitled "toward evidence-based practice." Why, then, should we care about EBP as well? Essentially, knowledge about the efficacy of an intervention is only of limited usefulness unless some mechanisms are in place to assist stakeholders in utilizing this information in a meaningful manner. EBP provides these mechanisms. To draw on an analogy, knowledge about efficacy without EBP is equivalent to having obtained a very delicious tropical fruit, without having the tools and know-how for cracking it open and eating it. The definition of EBP indicates that one needs to identify only the best and the most current research evidence and then integrate it with clinical/educational expertise and relevant stakeholder perspectives.

Practitioners should care about EBP for many reasons. First, EBP allows them to be accountable in their practice. Given the current status of the education and health care fields, accountability has become very important. Second, EBP ensures that decision making is research and data based. This is important to many funding agencies in AAC. Third, EBP attributes equal importance to clinical/educational expertise, stakeholder perspectives, and current and best research evidence; EBP does not imply that the research evidence necessarily carries more weight than the other two considerations. Thus, stakeholder perspectives need to be assessed, respected, and accounted for in order to shape the direction of decision making in light of the available evidence. This integration of stakeholder perspectives is especially important for practitioners who work in client-centered or family-centered settings. Fourth, EBP can be viewed as a viable vehicle for influencing the research agenda. If clinicians and educators disseminate their experiences in implementing EBP for answering their clinical and educational questions, as suggested in Chapter 12, researchers will be informed of major research gaps and issues.

The various stakeholders, such as the AAC user, family members, and others, should care about EBP because EBP requires that the perspectives of stakeholders be assessed, respected, and integrated with research and clinical/educational expertise. In general, EBP is relevant across stakeholder types, including direct stakeholders, indirect stakeholders, immediate community stakeholders, and extended community stakeholders (for definitions, see Chapter 10).

Researchers too should care about EBP for several reasons. Researchers, especially those with a clinical/educational applied research agenda, generally seek to shape practice. That is, they strive to see their findings influence practice. EBP has the potential to be an ideal vehicle for translating research into practice. EBP requires clinicians and educators to take into account the best and current research evidence in practical decision making. This bestows research with an immediate pertinence and the work of researchers with a renewed value. At the same time, researchers depend on practitioners as well as other stakeholders for the very direction of their research questions. EBP has created space for this to occur. To arrive at what is considered the best and most current research evidence, for example, one cannot help but to critically evaluate the certainty of the evidence. With the advent of EBP, research becomes far more open to critique than ever before, resulting in a general rise in the quality of research being carved out.

Associations such as the International Society for Augmentative and Alternative Communication (ISAAC) or the American Speech-Language Hearing Association (ASHA), Special Interest Division 12, should care about EBP for a number of reasons. For example, EBP should inform official practice documents. The recent ASHA document, titled "knowledge and skills in augmentative and alternative communication" (ASHA, 2002) lists knowledge of the hierarchy of evidence as an important factor in determining the competency of speech-language pathologists for decision making. This suggests that ASHA is beginning to care about EBP.

In summary, EBP seems to be important and relevant to many parties of the AAC enterprise. Because of this germaneness, I refer, in this book, to the *evidence-based practitioner*. The evidence-based practitioner is any individual who engages in EBP or seeks to apply principles of EBP in any sphere in AAC. As such, the evidence-based practitioner is not limited to clinicians/educators or researchers but encompasses AAC users and their families as well as other stakeholders. This book is written with all of these evidence-based practitioners in mind, and the term *practitioner* is to be understood as such. Whenever specific types of evidence-based practitioners are referred to (e.g., teachers, clinicians), they will be identified as such.

III. ORGANIZATION OF THIS BOOK

This book is arranged in three major sections. The first section lays the foundations in two related chapters. Chapter 2 tackles the notions of efficacy and efficacy research and explains how they relate to outcomes, outcomes research, and outcomes measurement. By discussing the pros and cons of some of the previous conceptualizations and definitions, a framework for conceptualizing efficacy and efficacy research is proposed for this text and for the field at large. Chapter 3 reviews and illustrates the four types of validity—internal validity, external validity and generality, social validity, and ecological validity—that form the foundation for studying and evaluating the efficacy of interventions in AAC.

The second section equips the reader with the tools and background necessary for engaging in EBP and for understanding chapters in the third section. These tools include the formulation of research questions, issues pertaining to subject selection, research designs for evaluating the efficacy of AAC interventions, the assessment of treatment integrity, methods for assessing the social validity of AAC intervention, methods for synthesizing a body of AAC efficacy studies, and a framework for EBP in AAC.

Chapter 4 focuses on a critical area of the research design process—the development of the relationship between the research question and the research investigation. This chapter examines the characteristics of a good research question, how it relates to theory, methodology, and research results, and some of the common problems associated with generating a good research question. Knowledge about these issues is critical beyond the obvious need of original researchers for research planning, implementation, and interpretation. The evidence-based practitioner needs to evaluate the internal validity of an experiment not against some arbitrary standard or an imposed standard by the reader, but rather against the research question posed by the researcher. In other words, the question is "How well did the research methods employed allow the researcher to answer the self-stated research question?" It would be neither fair nor helpful to evaluate an experiment against a purpose imposed by the evidence-based practitioner, even if that practitioner wished that the researcher had evaluated a question closer to his or her clinical concerns.

Chapter 5 tackles an often-neglected aspect of the research process, the issue of subject selection. Specifically, the author uses a 10-year review of efficacy studies published in *Augmentative and Alternative Communication* (1990 to 2000) to examine how researchers are dealing with subject selection and to identify the strengths and weaknesses of these approaches. Subject selection that is consistent with the research question is important for the researcher who is planning an efficacy study. Subject selection also bears relevance to the evidence-based practitioner who needs to evaluate whether the participants in the study were somehow biased toward the intervention or whether the findings yielded for the research participants bear generality to their clients.

Chapter 6, focused on single-subject experimental designs, initiates a trilogy of chapters on various research design strategies for evaluating the efficacy of AAC interventions. This chapter includes (1) a review of the main types of designs for evaluating behavior change, generalization, maintenance, and for comparing multiple interventions using examples from the AAC literature, (2) an illustration of common pitfalls, and (3) solutions to these pitfalls. Single-subject experiments are by far the most popular designs in evaluating AAC interventions and that is not without reason. Like many other clinical populations, the population of AAC users is very heterogeneous (Bedrosian, 1995; Iacono & Parsons, 1986). Thus, it becomes extremely difficult to create homogenous groups, even if access to a large population was given—a precondition not often met in a low-incidence field such as AAC. Second, single-subject experimental designs offer a variety of design strategies to choose from, and chances are that a researcher will find a strategy that is appropriate for the research questions. Third, single-subject experiments use the participant as his or her own control; thus, they approximate clinical or educational interventions. For researchers or students of research interested in conducting efficacy studies, it is imperative to have a thorough understanding of single-subject experimental designs. For evidence-based practitioners, an understanding of the various single-subject design options along with common pitfalls and solutions will enable an accurate evaluation of best and current research evidence.

Chapter 7 introduces the reader to group designs as a possible alternative to single-subject experimental designs. Although issues such as heterogeneity make it difficult to establish homogenous groups of individuals using AAC, some questions such as those concerned with interaction effects are best studied with group designs rather than single-subject experimental designs (Light, 1999). The group design options available are described and illustrated with examples from AAC efficacy research. The design options presented are arranged in terms of preexperimental designs, true experimental designs, and quasi-experimental designs. Although group designs are not as common in AAC intervention research, some researchers have used them even with participants with disabilities (Hodges & Schwethelm, 1984; Porter & Schroeder, 1980; Yoder & Layton, 1988). The majority of group design applications in AAC, however, have involved participants without disabilities (e.g., Mirenda & Beukelman, 1990; Schlosser & Lloyd, 1993). Group design strategies are equally prominent in the hierarchy of evidence proposed in Chapter 12. Thus, it is important that both researchers and practitioners understand the various design options along with their associated strengths and weaknesses.

Chapter 8 focuses on the role of longitudinal research designs in AAC efficacy research. Following an overview of longitudinal research designs and their use in addressing research questions, the authors illustrate how longitudinal designs may be applied in AAC intervention research by describing several of their own longitudinal research studies about augmented language development in students with developmental disabilities. Because longitudinal designs are particularly well suited for examining the broad long-term outcomes of AAC interventions, researchers and evidence-based practitioners will appreciate this chapter.

Chapter 9 is devoted to the integrity of the independent variable, an issue that is highly relevant to evidence-based practice but that has been largely ignored in the field today. To ensure that research findings guide some of the decisions involved in daily practice, practitioners need to understand what aspects contribute to the certainty of the evidence. Whereas appropriate designs, as discussed in Chapters 6 through 8, contribute to the certainty of evidence, a design alone does not ensure an accurate application of the treatment. Without information on the integrity of the treatment, serious issues as to the source of the yielded results arise. In short, the internal validity of this experiment would have to be questioned. Treatment integrity has the potential to enhance, diminish, or even destroy the certainty of evidence. Thus, evidence-based practitioners who consult original treatment studies to inform their practice may want to take a careful look at treatment integrity. Treatment integrity is relevant to AAC intervention research irrespective of the specific design type used. To introduce the field to this important topic, the author first defines treatment integrity and then summarizes reviews on treatment integrity in related fields as well as in AAC. Next, the role of treatment integrity in establishing a science of AAC intervention is discussed followed by an example of how AAC is applied in assessing treatment integrity (for a tutorial, see also Schlosser, 2002).

Chapter 10 introduces the reader to the ubiquitous role of social validation for AAC intervention research. Interventions that are socially valid in addition to being effective bear more credibility than interventions with poor or without social validity data. As such, social validation is an additional marker in decision making for evidence-based practice. This chapter presents the AAC social validity framework to assist researchers in planning, implementing, and evaluating the social validity of AAC interventions. In addition to the framework, the chapter briefly defines social validation and its methods and summarizes existing reviews of the social validation literature in related fields and AAC.

Chapter 11 evaluates three approaches to synthesizing efficacy studies: narrative reviews, quantitative reviews, and meta-analytic reviews. Among these approaches, meta-analytic reviews are high on the certainty-of-evidence hierarchy for EBP proposed in Chapter 12. For this reason, evidence-based practitioners are advised to seek out meta-analyses first related to a clinical/educational question prior to extending their search to individual efficacy studies. It is for this reason that the author illustrates the process of planning and implementing a meta-analysis rather than the other two approaches.

Chapters 2 through 11 are intended to furnish some of the most important tools or background for understanding and implementing efficacy research and evidence-based practice in the AAC field. The knowledge and information from these previous chapters are then incorporated into Chapter 12 to propose a definition of EBP in AAC and to develop a framework and principles for evaluating the research evidence in AAC. To my knowledge, such an attempt had not been made in the published AAC literature until the printing of this text. This chapter serves as a foundation for the chapters in the third section.

Chapters 13 through 21 exemplify EBP in specific content areas. Although the degree to which the framework and principles proposed in Chapter 12 are applied does vary from chapter to chapter, each of the subsequent chapters is grounded in its intent to inform practice through research and research through practice. Chapter 13 focuses on efficacy research with presymbolic communicators by tackling three decisive questions. First, what constitutes a good intervention outcome for persons who interact at a presymbolic level? Second, how are decisions made about which outcomes to prioritize in intervention? Third, what methods are used in communication intervention focused on interaction between presymbolic communicators and their partners? This content area is characterized by only a limited number of intervention studies that inform EBP. The authors have reviewed what can be inferred from the literature thus far, and their preliminary conclusions can serve as a framework both for future research and for implementations in practice.

Chapter 14 reviews the evidence concerning the efficacy of AAC intervention for beginning communicators. In reviewing this literature, the authors provide evidence-based guidelines for many of the decisions faced by clinicians and educators. After considering the characteristics of beginning communicators and EBP, the chapter is organized around the types of questions that a practitioner might ask when starting AAC interventions with beginning communicators, including the following: Are beginning communicators ready for AAC? What AAC mode and system are best for beginning communicators? What should I teach first? How do I teach requesting? How do I teach rejecting? Can I teach other communicative functions? How can I ensure appropriate use of newly acquired communication skills? What about maintenance? These are indeed crucial clinical/educational questions that many practitioners and other stakeholders face in working with beginning communicators.

Chapter 15 is also related to beginning communicators in that it addresses the selection of graphic symbols for an initial request lexicon. Specifically, the existing research evidence is reviewed in terms of its certainty of evidence and the degree to which the research base speaks to those variables pertinent to the decision-making process in selecting graphic symbols for an initial request lexicon. This chapter also illustrates how EBP may be used to assist practitioners in selecting graphic symbols for an initial request lexicon.

Chapter 16 is concerned with the role of AAC in facilitating or hindering natural speech development. This has been a long-standing issue for many parents and other family members who are contemplating whether or not to introduce AAC to their children. This chapter summarizes the best and current research evidence on the effects of AAC intervention on natural speech development, highlights methodological issues, and provides directions for future research. Finally, the author portrays how this research evidence may be used, through EBP, to inform decision making for a practical question concerned with this very issue.

Chapter 17 tackles the content area of literacy development in learners using AAC. The authors discuss models of typical reading development, identification and treatment of children at risk for reading disability, and research to date involving literacy assessment and intervention with individuals who use AAC. (Based on the review completed by these authors, this area is challenging for evidence-based practitioners because of an inadequate research base from which to inform one's practice. Therefore, these authors resorted to what is known as typical reading development to inform their decision making relative to the case illustration of Michael.) It is not surprising that this chapter ends with a considerable number of research questions to be addressed through future research.

Chapter 18 is the only content chapter in this volume that is solely focused on people with acquired disorders. The authors deliver an overview of the current repertoire of AAC options available and evaluate the literature on the efficacy of AAC intervention in individuals with chronic, severe, or global aphasia. Similar to Chapter 17, this represents an area that is challenging for the evidence-based practitioner. The authors state that the current AAC efficacy research in persons with aphasia is characterized not only by a lack of data but by data that are seriously compromised due to internal validity concerns. Therefore, the authors are able to offer only preliminary conclusions and call for future research using sound research designs and procedures.

Chapter 19 focuses on the effects of speech output. Specifically, this chapter synthesizes the extant knowledge base concerning the effects of speech output on learners, on communication partners, and on learner-partner dyads and offers directions for future research. This narrative synthesis is then used as the basis for an illustration of EBP related to decision making involving speech output. Although more research is clearly needed, this content area, in comparison to some of the others addressed in this volume, offers the evidence-based practitioner a substantial research base.

Chapter 20 addresses an issue that is relevant across content areas and intervention approaches in AAC: How do we best promote generalization and maintenance of the skills taught during intervention? Using a recent meta-analysis (Schlosser & Lee, 2000) as the foundation for their EBP illustration, the authors consider it premature to herald individual strategies as the most effective strategies. In fact, the meta-analysis data call for training of evidence-based practitioners in the breadth of available strategies and how these strategies may be incorporated into treatment planning. Thus, through vignettes of published examples, this chapter illustrates the repertoire of strategies and their potential role in intervention planning and implementation.

Chapter 21 deals with a special type of efficacy: comparative efficacy. In comparative efficacy studies, two or more intervention approaches are directly compared to one another. Comparative efficacy evaluations provide data-based arguments for choosing one intervention over another intervention. Comparisons are made not only in terms of whether one intervention works as well as the other in producing effective behavioral change, but also in terms of efficiency (e.g., rate of learning, error rate, cost). In times of scarce resources, efficiency seems to be the most crucial index of efficacy. Comparative efficacy studies can be invaluable for the practitioner applying EBP principles. To name but a few choice scenarios that require "the integration of best and current research evidence with clinical/educational expertise and relevant stakeholder perspectives" (Chapter 12), practitioners may need to decide between (1) a gestural mode and a graphic mode, (2) a graphic mode and traditional orthography, (3) picture exchange and direct selection, (4) scanning method A and scanning method B,

(5) direct instruction and activity-based intervention, and (6) speech-generating devices and nonelectronic communication boards (Schlosser, 1997). Evidence from comparison studies are deemed especially helpful for target behaviors for which there is an array of intervention options and the practitioner is hard-pressed to choose one over the other. In addition to discussing how comparative studies can inform EBP, the author provides a narrative review of comparative efficacy studies using single-subject experimental designs.

From the body of work reviewed in this book, it is clear that the field has made considerable progress in evaluating the efficacy of its interventions. However, research needs to be intensified in existing as well as in new areas, taking into account methodological rigor and the four types of validity discussed in the Section II (internal validity, external validity, social validity, ecological validity). Chapter 22 offers directions for the next-generation of efficacy research. As far as EBP is concerned, we are only in the beginning of a long and exciting journey. Important first steps have been made, and I hope the reader is as excited as I am about going on this journey and working together to make the effort viable for the field. This chapter offers numerous directions for enhancing our field to move further toward EBP.

REFERENCES

American Speech-Language-Hearing Association. (2002, April 16). Augmentative and alternative communication: Knowledge and skills for service delivery. *ASHA Leader, 7 (Suppl. 22)*, 97–106.

Beukelman, D. R., & Mirenda, P. (1998). *Augmentative and alternative communication: Management of severe communication disorders in children and adults.* Baltimore: Paul H. Brookes.

Calculator, S. N., & Jorgensen, C. M. (1994). *Including students with severe disabilities in schools: Fostering communication, interaction, and participation.* San Diego, CA: Singular Publishing Group.

Bedrosian, J. L. (1995). Limitations in the use of nondisabled subjects in AAC research. *Augmentative and Alternative Communication, 11,* 6–10.

Glennen, S. L., & DeCoste, D. C. (1997). *The handbook of augmentative and alternative communication.* San Diego, CA: Singular Publishing Group.

Hodges, P., & Schwethelm, B. (1984). A comparison of the effectiveness of graphic symbol and manual sign training with profoundly retarded children. *Applied Psycholinguistics, 5,* 223–253.

Iacono, T. A., & Parsons, C. L. (1986). A comparison of techniques for teaching signs to intellectually disabled individuals using an alternating treatments design. *Australian Journal of Human Communication Disorders, 14,* 23–34.

Light, J. C. (1999). Do augmentative and alternative communication interventions really make a difference?: The challenges of efficacy research. *Augmentative and Alternative Communication, 15,* 13–24.

Lloyd, L. L., Fuller, D. R., & Arvidson, H. (1997), *Augmentative and alternative communication: A handbook of principles and practices.* Needham Heights, MA: Allyn & Bacon.

Mirenda, P., & Beukelman, D. R. (1990). A comparison of intelligibility among natural speech and seven speech synthesizers with listeners from three age groups. *Augmentative and Alternative Communication, 6,* 61–68.

Porter, P. B., & Schroeder, S. R. (1980). Generalization and maintenance of skills acquired in Non-Speech Language Initiation Program training. *Applied Research in Mental Retardation, 1,* 71–84.

Reichle, J., York, J., & Sigafoos, J. (Eds.) (1991). *Implementing augmentative and alternative communication: Strategies for learners with severe disabilities*. Baltimore: Paul H. Brookes.

Schlosser, R. W. (2002). On the importance of being earnest about treatment integrity. *Augmentative and Alternative Communication, 18,* 36–44.

Schlosser, R. W. (1997, November). *"Which AAC Intervention works better?" Methodologic issues in comparative efficacy evaluations*. Invited paper presented at the Panel "Efficacy Research Issues in Augmentative and Alternative Communication" at the Annual Convention of the ASHA, Boston, MA.

Schlosser, R. W., & Lee, D. (2000). Promoting generalization and maintenance in augmentative and alternative communication: A meta-analysis of 20 years of effectiveness research. *Augmentative and Alternative Communication, 16,* 208–227.

Schlosser, R. W., & Lloyd, L. L. (1993). Effects of initial element teaching in a storytelling context on Blissymbol acquisition and generalization. *Journal of Speech and Hearing Research, 36,* 979–995.

Von Tetzchner, S., & Jensen, M. H. (1996). *Augmentative and alternative communication: European perspectives*. London: Whurr.

Von Tetzchner, S., & Martinsen, H. (1992). *Introduction to symbolic and augmentative communication*. London: Whurr.

Yoder, P., & Layton, T. (1988). Speech following sign language training in autistic children with minimal verbal language. *Journal of Autism and Developmental Disabilities, 18,* 217–229.

CHAPTER 2

Efficacy and Outcomes Measurement in Augmentative and Alternative Communication

Ralf W. Schlosser
Department of Speech-Language Pathology and Audiology
Northeastern University

I. INTRODUCTION

What is efficacy, and how does it relate to outcomes and outcomes measurement? What is efficacy research, and what is outcomes research? These are some of the questions that will be tackled in this chapter. After discussing the pros and cons of some of the previous conceptualizations and definitions, a framework for conceptualizing efficacy and efficacy research for use in this text and, perhaps, for the field at large will be proposed.

II. OUTCOMES DEFINED

For the purposes of this text, *outcomes* will be defined as the changes attributed to an augmentative and alternative communication (AAC) intervention. These changes may be positive (i.e., in the desired direction), negative (i.e., in a direction opposite to the one desired), or unplanned (i.e., not anticipated) (Schlosser, 1999b; Wolf, 1978). If one were to consider functional communication training, for example, increased requesting through appropriate communicative behaviors and decreased requesting through challenging behaviors would be considered positive outcomes (Durand, 1993). Conversely, increased requesting through challenging behaviors would be considered a negative outcome. Further, changes in the attitudes of caregivers as a result of successful functional communication training might be considered unplanned, albeit welcome, outcomes.

III. A DISCUSSION OF VARIOUS CONCEPTUALIZATIONS OF EFFICACY RESEARCH

The link between efficacy research and outcomes research has not always been clear and warrants examination. Four different conceptualizations for evaluating changes emerged from the previous two decades of research in AAC and related fields. The first conceptualization distinguishes *efficacy research* from *outcomes research* (Granlund & Blackstone, 1999). The second classification differentiates *efficacy* from *effectiveness* (Blockberger, 1994 as cited in Blackstone (1995); Robey & Schultz, 1998). The third conceptualization defines *efficacy* as an umbrella term that encompasses *effectiveness*, *efficiency*, and *effects* or *outcomes* (Calculator, 1991; Fawcett, 1991; Kendall & Norton-Ford, 1982; Olswang, 1990; Schlosser, 1999a; Schlosser & Braun, 1994). The fourth conceptualization views *outcomes measurement* as an umbrella term for *efficacy research* and *outcomes research* (Frattali, 1999). In the following pages, we consider each of these conceptualizations in terms of its strengths and weaknesses before proposing a new conceptualization. This new conceptualization will form part of the basis for evaluating the research base on the efficacy of AAC interventions. The key terms of this new conceptualization, adopted for this text, are summarized in Table 2.1. Before arriving at this conceptualization, however, it is useful to review the strengths and weaknesses of the existing conceptualizations.

A. EFFICACY RESEARCH VERSUS OUTCOMES RESEARCH

This conceptualization distinguishes efficacy research from outcomes research. Granlund and Blackstone (1999) defined these concepts as follows:

Table 2.1

Key Definitions from Efficacy Research to Outcomes Research Adopted for This Text

Construct	Definition
Outcomes	Changes attributed to an AAC intervention. These changes may be positive (i.e., in the desired direction), negative (i.e., in a direction opposite to the one desired), or unplanned (i.e., not anticipated).
Outcomes measurement in AAC	A process designed to index differences between observations made prior to an intervention and observations made during or after an intervention, ranging on a continuum of conditions from efficacy research to outcomes research.
Efficacy research in AAC	The process of demonstrating, under ideal conditions, the (1) acquisition, maintenance, and generalization of behavior change (i.e., effectiveness), (2) comparative effectiveness of at least two interventions in terms of one or more criteria such as time, cost, error rate, and so forth (i.e., efficiency), or (3) demonstrated links of specific components of the intervention to specific changes. Results speak to the probability of benefit to individuals in a defined population from AAC intervention applied for a given communication problem under ideal conditions of use.
Outcomes research in AAC	The process of demonstrating, under average or less-than-average conditions, the (1) acquisition, maintenance, and generalization of behavior change (i.e., effectiveness), (2) comparative effectiveness of at least two interventions in terms of one or more criteria such as time, cost, error rate, and so forth (i.e., efficiency), or (3) demonstrated links of specific components of the intervention to specific changes. Results speak to the probability of benefit to individuals in a defined population from AAC intervention applied for a given communication problem under average or less-than-average conditions of use.
Efficacy	An umbrella term that encompasses "effectiveness," "efficiency," and "effects."
Effectiveness	The demonstration of behavior change as a direct result of intervention.
Efficiency	A comparison of at least two effective interventions in terms of one or more criteria such as time, cost, and error rate, and so forth.
Effects	The demonstrated links of specific components of the intervention to specific changes.

In these studies [i.e., efficacy research studies, added by this author] the desired outcome of intervention is defined by the researcher in relation to a specific research question or theory rather than by a specific stakeholder (e.g., user, family member or clinician). In contrast, outcomes research focuses on the evaluation of everyday AAC interventions and their results in relation to the outcomes desired by different stakeholder groups. (p. 207)

According to this conceptualization, only studies that evaluate the effectiveness of everyday interventions as perceived by various stakeholder groups would be considered outcomes research. Further, this conceptualization of efficacy research does not accommodate intervention studies in which the desired outcomes originally defined by researchers are *also* socially validated (Schlosser, 1999b) (see also Chapter 12). In other words, the terms *efficacy research* and *outcomes research*, as used by Granlund and Blackstone (1999), are not necessarily mutually exclusive because of stakeholder involvement. Even though the classification by Granlund and Blackstone (1999) distinguishes everyday AAC interventions from those designed by researchers, it does not adequately accommodate the breadth of AAC efficacy research—That is, some of the intervention research designed by researchers is also socially validated by various stakeholders (see Chapter 10).

B. Efficacy Research versus Effectiveness Research under the Umbrella of Outcomes Research

The classification of efficacy research versus effectiveness research under the umbrella of outcomes research was first brought to the AAC field by Blockberger (1994) who presented a paper at the First AAC Outcomes Conference in Monterey, California, as cited by Blackstone (1995).[1] Based on the field of epidemiology, Blockberger highlighted the need for more AAC intervention research under typical circumstances while introducing a distinction between efficacy research (i.e., under ideal situations) and effectiveness research (i.e., under average situations). The clinical outcomes literature at large seems to have adopted this distinction, which is based on definitions put out by the Office of Technology Assessment in 1978. Efficacy is defined as follows: "The probability of benefit to individuals in a defined population from a medical technology applied for a given medical problem under *ideal* conditions of use" [italics added for emphasis] (Office of Technology Assessment, 1978, p. 16).

Thus, efficacy research is conducted under ideal intervention conditions, using optimally selected and trained clinicians, optimally selected clients, optimally delivered treatments (i.e., treatments having high treatment integrity), optimally structured conditions for delivering treatment, optimal measures or indices of change, and so forth. As Robey and Schultz (1998) pointed out, the outcome

---

[1]The same conceptualization was proposed by Robey and Schultz (1998), who defined outcomes research as a process designed to index differences between observations made prior to an intervention and observations made after an intervention. This definition seems to be based largely on measurements in group studies that tend to compare results from pretests and posttests. Differences may also be indexed between observations made prior to an intervention and observations made *during* an intervention, as is the case when data are collected in time-series format.

of an efficacy study indexes *possible* benefits given optimal operational conditions for transforming a treatment from ideal to real terms. In other words, efficacy research does not index *actual* benefits. Effectiveness, on the other hand, is defined as follows: "The probability of benefit to individuals in a defined population from a medical technology applied for a given medical problem under *average* conditions of use" [italics added for emphasis] (Office of Technology Assessment, 1978, p. 16). Thus, effectiveness research is conducted under average intervention conditions, using average or typical clinicians, typical clients, and so forth. Robey and Schultz (1998) have posited that the outcome of an effectiveness study, unlike the outcome of an efficacy study, indexes actual benefits given average conditions.

In proposing a model for conducting clinical outcomes research in aphasiology, Robey and Schultz (1998) convincingly argued that both types of research ought to be viewed as outcomes research and that there is a contingent relationship between the two types of research. In fact, their model calls for a progression from intervention research under ideal conditions to intervention research under average conditions. This progression is intuitively appealing and inherently logical and could productively inform the AAC field.

An example from the AAC intervention literature illustrates the relevance of the distinction between intervention research under ideal conditions and under average conditions. It has been suggested that augmented input, also known as aided language stimulation (Goossens' & Crain, 1986; Wood, Lasker, Siegel-Causey, Beukelman, & Ball, 1998), may facilitate the learning of graphic symbol-referent relationships (e.g., Romski & Sevcik, 1993; Romski, Sevcik, Robinson, Mervis, & Bernard, 1995; Schlosser, Belfiore, Nigam, Blischak, & Hetzroni, 1995). Augmented input shall be defined here as the pointing to graphic symbols as the partner talks with the AAC user.

Research under ideal conditions may examine this question with the provision of augmented input on every occasion a graphic symbol is introduced or reintroduced. In other words, the experimenter demonstrates 100% (or as close as possible to 100%) treatment integrity (the degree to which a treatment is carried out as planned, see Chapter 9) for providing augmented input to the learner. Such hypothetical research may very well indicate that augmented input promotes graphic symbol learning under ideal conditions—indexing *possible* benefits of augmented input. It would be unclear, however, whether augmented input promotes graphic symbol learning under average conditions as well. Of course, the question arises as to what constitutes average conditions for providing augmented input. Fortunately, the literature provides some insight in this regard.

Sevcik, Romski, Watkins, and Deffebach (1993) examined the quantity and quality of augmented input provided to children with intellectual disabilities who had little or no functional speech. They found that only 10% of the partners' overall spoken communicative utterances directed to the children included augmented input. Assuming that 10% represents average conditions for providing augmented input, a systematic replication of this study with 10% input would result in a greater understanding how things operate under everyday conditions. Results of such a study would then index the actual benefits of augmented input for graphic symbol learning. Thus, the determination of average and ideal conditions itself becomes a crucial and urgent area of intervention research.

Sometimes, though, interventions in communication disorders in general and AAC interventions in particular take place under neither ideal nor average conditions but rather under below-average conditions. Therefore, it seems only logical to expand the definition of effectiveness from the Office of Technology Assessment (1978) to reflect this condition and read as follows: The probability of benefit to individuals in a defined population from a medical technology applied for a given medical problem under average or *less than average* conditions of use.

Thus, the outcome of an effectiveness study conducted under less-than-average conditions indexes *actual* benefits given below-average conditions. To relate this definition to the earlier example, studies on the role of augmented input may need to be conducted with a treatment integrity of less than 10% for providing augmented input. Results of such research might generate a closer understanding of how well AAC interventions (here augmented input) work when conditions are below average.

The example of augmented-input research illustrated the potential value of adopting the distinction between research under ideal conditions (i.e., efficacy research) and research under average conditions (i.e., effectiveness research) for the AAC field. This distinction seems to be suited in accommodating the breadth of AAC intervention research. Both of the terms used to denote this distinction (i.e., *efficacy* and *effectiveness*) are, however, already in use with different definitions as discussed in the next section. Altering the meaning of these terms at this point would create nothing but confusion.

C. EFFICACY AS AN UMBRELLA TERM

The third conceptualization includes efficacy as an umbrella term that encompasses effectiveness, efficiency, and effects (Calculator, 1991; Fawcett, 1991; Kendall & Norton-Ford, 1982; Olswang, 1990; Rosen & Proctor, 1981; Schlosser, 1999a; Schlosser & Braun, 1994). This classification was first introduced to the field of communication disorders by Olswang (1990), who borrowed it from clinical psychology (Kendall & Norton-Ford, 1982; Rosen & Proctor, 1981), a field that has a long-standing history addressing accountability. Calculator (1991) and subsequently Schlosser and Braun (1994) proposed this taxonomy of efficacy for the AAC field.

1. Effectiveness

Effectiveness has been defined as the demonstration of behavior change as a direct result of intervention (Schlosser & Braun, 1994). Essentially, research that documents the acquisition of behavior change, the maintenance of behavior change, and the generalization of behavior change may be considered effectiveness research. Studies that evaluate the acquisition of behavior change examine intervention effectiveness. The field is replete with studies demonstrating intervention effectiveness involving a range of AAC interventions (see Schlosser & Lee, 2000). Studies that evaluate the maintenance of behavior change are concerned with maintenance effectiveness—that is, effectiveness over time (i.e., after treatment is terminated). Finally, studies that evaluate the generalization of behavior change are examining generalization effectiveness or the degree to which the behavior change generalizes to conditions beyond those used in instruction. Studies evaluating maintenance effectiveness or generalization effectiveness are available as well, albeit to a lesser degree. (For a meta-analysis of effectiveness studies that evaluated intervention effectiveness and generalization or maintenance effectiveness, see Schlosser & Lee, 2000).

2. Efficiency

Efficiency refers to a comparison of at least two effective interventions in terms of one or more criteria such as time, cost, or error rate (Schlosser & Braun, 1994). Goodman and Remington (1993), for example, compared two reinforcement strategies on expressive signing in four children with severe intellectual disabilities. In the first condition, nonspecific reinforcement was provided—that is, participants received a reinforcer unrelated to the signs produced. In the second condition, specific reinforcement was provided—that is, participants received the visual referent for the signs produced. Although both conditions were effective, the specific reinforcement strategy produced faster acquisition of expressive signing than the nonspecific strategy for three of the participants. Efficiency studies serve a crucial function in separating treatments that are each effective in their own right but differ nonetheless in terms of time, cost, and error rate. Therefore, efficiency is an important construct in these times of scarce resources and accountability (Schlosser, 1999a) and evidence-based practice. For further examples of efficiency studies, see Schlosser (1999a) and Chapter 21.

3. Effects

Effects refer to the demonstrated links of specific components of the intervention to specific changes (Rosen & Proctor, 1981; Schlosser & Braun, 1994). Even though other classifications of effects have been discussed in the literature (Fawcett, 1991; Schlosser, 1999b), the classification by Rosen and Proctor (1981) is adopted for this volume because it is inherently logical in describing the links of specific intervention components to specific changes for individual stakeholders. Depending on their role in the treatment process, *intermediate effects* are distinguished from *instrumental effects* and *ultimate effects* as defined by Rosen and Proctor (1981).

Intermediate effects are changes that (1) facilitate continued intervention or (2) serve as preconditions for the use of other interventions. Adequate and suitable positioning, for example, may be considered a precondition to implementing a subsequent intervention such as facilitating the use of a communication board (Angelo & Goldstein, 1990).

Instrumental effects are changes that result in effects other than those specifically targeted for further intervention. McEwen (1992), for example, showed that adequate assistive positioning resulted in the effects of improvements in social-communicative interactions between students with profound multiple disabilities and classroom staff. Beukelman (1986) also noted the importance of identifying change that would support future improvement in other aspects of performance. He described the case of a child whose use of a two-switch-scanning technique led to steadily improved spelling and written expression. These changes were perceived as instrumental for later use of a Morse Code–based system.

Ultimate effects are changes that reflect goals and objectives toward which intervention efforts are directed. Once ultimate effects are achieved, intervention may be terminated. For example, once a student with severe intellectual disabilities has learned to use a speech-generating device effectively and efficiently across a variety of communication partners and settings, pragmatic intervention may be discontinued.

D. OUTCOMES MEASUREMENT AS AN UMBRELLA TERM

Outcomes measurement has been conceptualized as an umbrella term for both efficacy research and outcomes research (Frattali, 1999). This makes sense intuitively because both efficacy research and outcomes research are concerned with the measurement of outcomes. Therefore, this conceptualization is considered in the proposed conceptualization that follows.

IV. A PROPOSED CONCEPTUALIZATION OF EFFICACY RESEARCH IN AAC

A. THE PROPOSED CONCEPTUALIZATION

To understand efficacy, one must understand the conditions under which outcomes these measures are obtained. In addition to ideal and average conditions (Robey & Schultz, 1998), it is necessary to consider less-than-average or marginal conditions. The terms of efficacy and effectiveness used by Robey and Schultz (1998) for describing ideal and average conditions are already occupied with other functional meaning within the highly logical taxonomy of efficacy as an umbrella term, encompassing effectiveness, efficiency, and effects. Moreover, the useful distinctions between the constructs underlying the terms of effectiveness, efficiency, and effects are not covered in any of the other classifications reviewed. Specifically, the simple distinction of outcomes attained under ideal versus average conditions does not specify whether the outcomes demonstrate effectiveness, efficiency, or effects. On the other hand, each of the terms (*effectiveness*, *efficiency*, or *effects*) readily allows the interventionist or consumer of research to specify the conditions under which they were studied. Therefore, the following schematic conceptualization for efficacy research in AAC is displayed in Figure 2.1.

The relation between efficacy research and outcomes research may be viewed on a continuum of outcomes measurement (this is why the lines sepa-

Efficacy	Outcomes Measurement		
	Efficacy research	Outcomes research	
	Ideal conditions	Average conditions	Marginal conditions
Effectiveness			
Efficiency			
Effects			

Figure 2.1 A schematic conceptualization of outcomes measurement in AAC.

rating the columns are dashed), consistent with Frattali's (1999) understanding of outcomes measurement. Both efficacy research and outcomes research are concerned with the measurement of outcomes. Therefore, using outcomes measurement as an umbrella term makes intuitive sense. *Outcomes measurement in AAC* is a process designed to index differences between observations made prior to an intervention and observations made during or after an intervention, ranging on a continuum of conditions from efficacy research to outcomes research.

Research conducted under ideal conditions is called efficacy research. *Efficacy research in AAC* may be defined as the process of demonstrating, under ideal conditions, (1) the acquisition, maintenance, and generalization of behavior change (i.e., effectiveness), (2) the comparative effectiveness of at least two interventions in terms of one or more criteria such as time, cost, or error rate (i.e., efficiency), or (3) demonstrated links of specific components of the intervention to specific changes. Borrowing from the definition of the Office of Technology Assessment (1978), the results of efficacy research speak to the probability of benefit to individuals in a defined population from AAC intervention applied for a given communication problem under ideal conditions of use.

As one moves along the continuum from ideal conditions to more average conditions, this type of research may be referred to as outcomes research. *Outcomes research in AAC* may be defined as the process of demonstrating, under average or less-than-average conditions, (1) the acquisition, maintenance, and generalization of behavior change (i.e., effectiveness), (2) the comparative effectiveness of at least two interventions in terms of one or more criteria such as time, cost, or error rate (i.e., efficiency), or (3) the demonstrated links of specific components of the intervention to specific changes. Borrowing from the definition of the Office of Technology Assessment (1978), the results of outcomes research speak to the probability of benefit to individuals in a defined population from AAC intervention applied for a given communication problem under average or less-than-average conditions of use.

Regardless of whether individual AAC studies investigate effectiveness, efficiency, or effects, they fall somewhere on this continuum. This proposed conceptualization allows the distinction of the conditions under which outcomes research is being conducted while maintaining such useful and previously defined constructs as effectiveness, efficiency, and effects. For instance, the evidence-based practitioner will be able to determine whether the demonstration of behavior change as a direct result of an AAC intervention (effectiveness) has occurred under ideal conditions, average conditions, or less-than-average conditions. The conceptualization reinforces the notion that a demonstration of effectiveness is as important a goal in efficacy research as it is in outcomes research. Similarly, the efficiency (i.e., demonstration of comparative effectiveness of at least two interventions in terms of one or more criteria) of one intervention over another may occur under ideal conditions or under average or less-than-average conditions.

Once the effectiveness of two everyday interventions has been established, a study comparing the two interventions in terms of efficiency may be called for. The efficiency yielded under ideal conditions may or may not be the same, and an AAC intervention may have yielded instrumental effects only under ideal conditions. Put another way, the constructs of effectiveness, efficiency, and effects, which have been associated primarily with efficacy research, bear relevance for outcomes research as well.

The borders of these conditions are fluid rather than a reflection of clearly separate entities. This fluidity is particularly applicable to the border between efficacy research and outcomes research. The specific conditions under which a particular study is being conducted may comprise some factors that represent ideal conditions and other factors that represent average conditions. For example, while an effectiveness study conducted in group home settings may have selected participants that maximize the success of a treatment (reflective of ideal conditions), direct care staff rather than experimenters implemented the treatment perhaps less stringently than planned (reflective of average conditions).

For the evidence-based practitioner or any other interested reader of AAC intervention research, this schematic conceptualization bears important implications. Once the location (in the matrix) most closely resembling the conditions for which efficacy research or outcomes research data are sought has been defined, the research base may be examined accordingly. In turn, studies identified as applicable for a given clinical question can be categorized by placing the question in its appropriate location in the matrix. This process affords a visual representation of the potential generality of the findings for the situation addressed through the clinical questions (see also Chapter 12).

B. From Efficacy Research to Outcomes Research

Robey and Schultz (1998) proposed a natural progression of research under optimal conditions to research under typical conditions. The underlying assumption is that an intervention is likely not going to work under less-than-ideal conditions if it had previously failed to work under ideal conditions. Applied to the conceptualization at hand, the effectiveness, efficiency, or effects of AAC interventions should first be evaluated under ideal conditions before pursuing evaluation under average or even less-than-average conditions. In other words, efficacy research should precede outcomes research. As one moves along the continuum from efficacy research to outcomes research, it would be expected to be more difficult to (1) minimize threats to internal validity through adequate designs and to (2) ensure that the treatment was applied as intended (i.e., treatment integrity). Outcomes research, however, cannot abandon these important cornerstones of treatment research if is to achieve its objectives.

V. SUMMARY

This chapter discussed the various conceptualizations of efficacy in terms of their pros and cons, to distinguish efficacy from other related terms such as outcomes measurement and outcomes research and to derive a conceptualization that serves as the foundation for this text.

The resulting framework includes the use of efficacy as an umbrella term, including effectiveness, efficiency, and effects. The effectiveness, efficiency, and effects of AAC interventions may be studied under various conditions, from ideal to average to less-than-average. As one moves from outcomes measurement under ideal conditions to typical and less-than-typical conditions, one moves from efficacy research to outcomes research. Different implications may be drawn for the probability of benefit from an intervention, depending on whether the intervention was studied in efficacy research or outcomes research.

REFERENCES

Angelo, D. H., & Goldstein, H. (1990). Effects of a pragmatic teaching strategy for requesting information by communication board users. *Journal of Speech and Hearing Disorders, 55*, 231–243.

Beukelman, D. R. (1986). Evaluating the effectiveness of intervention programs. In S. W. Blackstone (Ed.), *Augmentative communication: An introduction* (pp. 423–445). Rockville, MD: American Speech-Language-Hearing Association.

Blackstone, S. (1995). Outcomes in AAC. *Augmentative Communication News, 7*, 1–8.

Calculator, S. N. (1991). Evaluating the efficacy of AAC intervention for children with severe disabilities. In J. Brodin, & E. Björck-Åkesson (Eds.), *Methodologial issues in research in augmentative and alternative communication. Proceedings from the First ISAAC Research Symposium* (pp. 22–31). Stockholm, Sweden: The Swedish Handicap Institute.

Durand, V. M. (1993). Functional communication training using assistive devices: Effects on challenging behavior and affect. *Augmentative and Alternative Communication, 9*, 168–176.

Fawcett, S. B. (1991). Social validity: A note on methodology. *Journal of Applied Behavior Analysis, 24*, 235–239.

Frattali, C. M. (1999). Outcomes measurement: Definitions, dimensions and perspective. In C. Frattali (Ed.), *Measuring outcomes in speech-language pathology* (pp. 1–27). New York: Thieme.

Goodman, J., & Remington, B. (1993). Acquisition of expressive signing: Comparison of reinforcement strategies. *Augmentative and Alternative Communication, 9*, 26–35.

Goossens', C., & Crain, S. (1986). *Augmentative communication intervention resource.* Lake Zurich, IL: Don Johnston Development Equipment.

Granlund, M., & Blackstone, S. (1999). Outcomes measurement in AAC. In F. Loncke, J. Clibbens, H. H. Arvidson, & L. L. Lloyd (Eds.), *AAC: New directions in research and practice* (pp. 207–227). London: Whurr.

Kendall, P., & Norton-Ford, J. (1982). Therapy outcome research methods. In P. Kendall & J. Butcher (Eds.), *Handbook of research methods in clinical psychology* (pp. 429–460). New York: John and Sons.

McEwen, G. R. (1992). Assistive positioning as a control parameter of social-communicative interaction between students with profound multiple disabilities and classroom staff. *Physical Therapy, 72*, 634–647.

Office of Technology Assessment (1978). *Assessing the efficacy and safety of medical technologies.* OTA-H-75 (Washington, DC: U.S. Government Printing Office).

Olswang, L. B. (1990). Treatment efficacy: The breadth of research. In L. B. Olswang, C. K. Thompson, S. F. Warren, & N. J. Minghetti (Eds.), Treatment efficacy research in communication disorders. *Proceedings of the American Speech-Language-Hearing Foundation's National Conference on Treatment Efficacy* (pp. 99–103). San Antonio, TX: ASHA.

Robey, R. R., & Schultz, M. C. (1998). A model for conducting clinical-outcome research: An adaptation of the standard protocol for use in aphasiology. *Aphasiology, 12,* 787–810.

Romski, M. A., & Sevcik, R. A. (1993). Language comprehension: Considerations for augmentative and alternative communication. *Augmentative and Alternative Communication, 9,* 281–285.

Romski, M. A., Sevcik, R. A., Robinson, B. F., Mervis, C. B., & Bernard, J. (1995). Mapping the meaning of novel symbols by youth with moderate or severe mental retardation. *American Journal on Mental Retardation, 100,* 391–402.

Rosen, A., & Proctor, E. (1981). Distinctions between treatment outcomes and their implications for treatment evaluation. *Journal of Consulting and Clinical Psychology, 49,* 418–425.

Schlosser, R. W. (1999a). Comparative efficacy of interventions in augmentative and alternative communication. *Augmentative and Alternative Communication, 15,* 56–68.

Schlosser, R. W. (1999b). Social validation of interventions in augmentative and alternative communication. *Augmentative and Alternative Communication, 15,* 234–247.

Schlosser, R. W., Belfiore, P. J., Nigam, R., Blischak, D., & Hetzroni, O. (1995). The effects of speech output technology in the learning of graphic symbols. *Journal of Applied Behavior Analysis, 28,* 537–549.

Schlosser, R. W., & Braun, U. (1994). Efficacy of AAC interventions: Methodologic issues in evaluating behavior change, generalization, and effects. *Augmentative and Alternative Communication, 10,* 207–223.

Schlosser, R. W., & Lee, D. (2000). Promoting generalization and maintenance in augmentative and alternative communication: A meta-analysis of 20 years of effectiveness research. *Augmentative and Alternative Communication, 16,* 208–227.

Sevcik, R. A., Romski, M. A., Watkins, R. V., & Deffebach, K. P. (1993). *A descriptive analysis of augmented linguistic input to nonspeaking children with mental retardation.* Unpublished manuscript, Georgia State University.

Wolf, M. M. (1978). Social validity: The case for subjective measurement, or how applied behavior analysis is finding its heart. *Journal of Applied Behavior Analysis, 11,* 203–214.

Wood, L. A., Lasker, J., Siegel-Causey, E., Beukelman, D. R., & Ball, L. (1998). Input framework for augmentative and alternative communication. *Augmentative and Alternative Communication, 14,* 261–267.

CHAPTER 3

Validity

The Foundation for Evaluating the Efficacy of Interventions

Ralf W. Schlosser
Department of Speech-Language Pathology and Audiology
Northeastern University

I. INTRODUCTION

At least four types of validity form the foundation for studying and evaluating the efficacy of interventions in augmentative and alternative communication (AAC). These types of validity include (1) internal validity, (2) external

The Efficacy of Augmentative and Alternative Communication

Table 3.1

Types of Validity Relevant for Studying and Evaluating the Efficacy of AAC Interventions

Type of Validity	Definition
Internal validity	The extent to which changes in the dependent variable can be attributed to the independent variable rather than to extraneous variables.
External validity/ generality	The extent to which conclusions of a research study can be extended to other participants, variables, and conditions.
Social validity	The extent to which the goals, methods, and outcomes are socially significant.
Ecological validity	The extent to which the settings, treatment agents, and materials are valid as measured by what is considered appropriate for the experimental context or the environment in which the skill is expected to be performed.

validity and generality, (3) social validity, and (4) ecological validity. Each type of validity will be reviewed and illustrated with examples from AAC research. Table 3.1 provides the definitions for each type of validity at a glance.

II. THREATS TO INTERNAL VALIDITY

This section describes the essential ingredients of intervention studies rated high in terms of internal validity, including but not limited to (1) operational definitions of dependent and independent variables, (2) use of valid instruments (if applicable), (3) interobserver agreement of the dependent variable, (4) interobserver agreement of the independent variable (i.e., treatment integrity), (5) experimental control, and (6) control of extraneous variables. The seminal work of Campbell and Stanley (1966) on experimental validity becomes essential here.

Internal validity refers to the degree to which obtained results are valid within the context of a particular study. Thus, internal validity evaluates the extent to which changes in the dependent variable can be attributed to the independent variable rather than to extraneous variables (Campbell & Stanley, 1966; Kazdin, 1992; Scruggs, 1992). Experimenters want to know whether the manipulation of certain elements (i.e., the independent variable) can be shown to impact the changes observed (i.e., the dependent variable). Problems with the internal validity of an experiment may potentially compromise a clear interpretation of the results and open the door for alternative explanations. Campbell and Stanley (1966) offered a taxonomy of potential threats to internal validity that researchers and evidence-based practitioners may encounter. Those threats that bear particular relevance to efficacy research in AAC are (1) maturation and history, (2) order effects and carryover effects, (3) interobserver agreement for the dependent variable, (4) treatment integrity, (5) instrumentation and testing, (6) regression, and (7) Hawthorne effects and novelty effects. How significant these threats to internal validity really are may depend, in part, on the type of design used to study the efficacy of AAC interventions—that is, threats to internal validity may be different with single-subject experimental designs, quasi-experimental group designs, small n designs, and longitudinal designs.

A. Maturation and History

Maturation may constitute a threat to internal validity when outcomes are confounded with the normal developmental process. Maturation may become an issue when AAC intervention is applied over an extensive period of time as, for example, when a study initiated as part of an early intervention program extends through the preschool years. It may complicate the ability of the experimenter to rule out maturation as a possible explanation for any outcomes obtained. A threat to internal validity due to history is said to occur when outcomes are compromised by an event that occurs outside the context of the experiment at a time that coincides with the onset of intervention. History may be of relevance, for example, when examining the efficacy of a requesting intervention in a child with profound intellectual disabilities and no functional speech. Incidentally, the parents of the participant may have signed up for a training program aimed at teaching parents to create more opportunities for their child to communicate. As a result, they begin providing their child with more opportunities to engage in requesting behavior at home at the same time that the formal requesting intervention is going on in the classroom. This increased awareness by the parents, resulting in an altered interaction with their child, may, in turn, enhance requesting skills in the classroom that cannot be solely attributed to the intervention designed in the experiment.

In single-subject experimental research, maturation and history can be controlled via multiple-baseline designs and their variants or reversal designs. With multiple-baseline designs and their variants, maturation and history could show their influences on the untreated baselines before the introduction of treatment. With reversal designs, maturation and history could demonstrate their influences when returning to baseline after treatment. For example, if maturation or history were at work, the return to baseline would be less pronounced or would not take place at all. If, however, the return to baseline is consistent with the expectations of treatment removal, it is assumed that the independent variable is responsible for changes (Tawney & Gast, 1984). With group designs, a control group that does not receive treatment may control history and maturation. If the control group does not change, it is assumed that history and maturation did not influence the outcome. Therefore, they can be ruled out as sources of variation (Hegde, 1994). As Kerlinger (1973) pointed out, the longer the time interval of intervention, the greater the possibility that maturation and history may confound treatment outcomes.

B. Order Effects and Carryover Effects

Order effects may occur when outcomes are confounded by treatment order. That is, the problem of order effects arises whenever one intervention is followed by a different intervention and conclusions are drawn about the effectiveness of this second intervention in isolation (Scruggs, 1992). In single-subject experimental research, order effects may become an issue with the following designs: ABC or ABB', interactional designs (e.g., A-B-BC-B-BC), adapted alternating treatments designs, and parallel treatments designs.

Parsons and La Sorte (1993) studied the effects of synthetic speech output from computers on spontaneous communication in children with autism via an interactional design. They used both additive designs (A-B-BC-B-BC) and reductive/subtractive designs (A-BC-B-BC) to examine the role of additional speech output. With the additive design, speech output was added to a computer following the B phase. Based on the additive design alone, one could argue that speech output was only effective because it followed B. In an attempt to control for order effects, these authors then employed a reductive design with other participants whereby speech output was taken away from an initial BC phase. Some of the study participants were assigned to the additive design, whereas others were assigned to the reductive design. Whether or not this strategy is sufficient to control order effects is discussed in more detail in Chapter 6.

Order effects may become a threat to internal validity with group designs as well when more than one treatment is involved. The problem of an order effect arises when two or more interventions are applied in a single, fixed order to all the participants. Fuller and Lloyd (1992) studied the effects of configuration (superimposed versus nonsuperimposed) on the learning of Blissymbols in nondisabled preschoolers using a within-subjects design. Had the authors presented the two types of configurations in a particular order to all of their participants, they would have been unable to rule out that order effects (rather than configuration per se) were responsible for the results obtained. However, the sequence of presenting the 30 stimuli (containing 15 superimposed and 15 nonsuperimposed symbols) was appropriately randomized across the four trials. This allowed these authors to attribute differential learning effects to configuration. In addition to randomization, order effects may be controlled through counterbalancing the different sequences. For example, in a study involving three treatments, one could assign groups to the following orders using a Latin square design: ABC, ACB, BAC, BCA, CAB, and CBA. In such a case, the greater the number of treatments involved the more difficult it is to counterbalance the order.

While order effects signify that the effectiveness of an intervention can be altered due to the position in which a given intervention appears, carryover effects specify the type of influence a preceding intervention has on the effectiveness of a succeeding intervention (Hegde, 1994; Kazdin, 1982). For example, the succeeding intervention may be stronger (compared to implementation by itself) due to the influence of the preceding intervention. In this situation, this carryover effect would be labeled as a *positive* carryover effect. In the event that the succeeding intervention appears weaker than it is, this carryover effect would be called a *negative* carryover effect.

In group designs, carryover effects may be identified by using a completely counterbalanced design in which each intervention precedes and follows every other intervention more than once (see Hegde, 1994). A positive carryover effect would be indicated if the effect for a treatment is typically larger when it follows a certain intervention and smaller when it precedes the same intervention. A negative carryover effect would be indicated if the effect for a given intervention is typically smaller when it follows a certain intervention and larger when it precedes the same intervention. This will be discussed further in Chapter 7.

In single-subject experimental designs, carryover effects may be controlled by counterbalancing the sequence of interventions and by enhancing the discriminability among the interventions for the participant (Barlow & Hersen, 1984; Kazdin, 1982; Kazdin & Hartmann, 1978). A number of single-subject experimental design studies illustrate the control of carryover effects (e.g., Schlosser, Belfiore, Nigam, Blischak, & Hetzroni, 1995; Schlosser, Blischak, Belfiore, Bartley, & Barnett, 1998). This is discussed in more detail in Chapter 6.

C. INTEROBSERVER AGREEMENT FOR THE DEPENDENT VARIABLE

Interobserver agreement data for the dependent variable are essential for at least three reasons (see Kazdin, 1982). First, assessment of the dependent variable is only useful to the extent that it can be done with some consistency. In other words, if the recording of the number of requests by a child differs depending on who is observing, it will be difficult to know the child's actual performance. Second, interobserver agreement reflects that the biases individual observers might have are minimal. Using an independent second observer may counteract changes in the primary observer's definition of behavior over time. Using more than one observer may provide a useful partial check on the consistency with which response definitions are applied over time. Finally, the collection of inter-observer agreement data provides insights into whether the response definitions were sufficiently objective, clear, and complete.

Kazdin (1982) and Johnston and Pennypacker (1980) pointed out that interobserver agreement is not equivalent to accuracy but is rather an indicator of *believability*. Equating the two concepts is rooted in the belief that if observers record the same behaviors, their data probably reflect what the participant is doing. We need to keep in mind, however, that this assumption is not justified in all situations. For example, it is quite possible for two observers to agree on a response that was inaccurate in the first place. This would yield high inter-observer agreement data on a behavior that did not occur as such. Johnston and Pennypacker (1980) provided demonstrations of the fallacy of this assumption. How is the field doing in terms of assessing interobserver agreement of the dependent variable? The meta-analysis by Schlosser and Lee (2000) showed that interobserver agreements for dependent measures were reported with decreasing percentages for intervention (92.7%), generalization (70.9%), and maintenance (28.4%). Encouraging is the increased used of interobserver agreement in these studies compared to studies in Udwin's (1987) earlier review of the efficacy literature. Udwin (1987) indicated that among the studies published between 1980 and 1984, only 49% reported adequate interobserver agreement data.

D. TREATMENT INTEGRITY

Traditionally, along with fields such as applied behavior analysis and special education, the AAC field has paid more attention to the reliable recording of the dependent variable than it has to the independent variable (also known as treatment integrity) (Schlosser, 2002). Treatment integrity, however, cannot be taken for granted (Yeaton, 1980). In fact, poor implementation or failures to ensure planned implementation are considered a major threat to internal validity. That is, one cannot assume that the treatment was necessarily implemented as planned by the interventionist and as described. An accurate and detailed description (i.e., an operational definition) of the independent variable is a necessary precursor for treatment integrity assessments to take place. Without an accurate and detailed description, procedural steps will be unclear and impossible to observe. Further, it will be impossible for researchers to replicate a study and impossible for the evidence-based practitioners to adopt the procedures for daily practice (see the discussion of external validity presented later in this chapter). Unfortunately, the independent variable is not always clearly described in AAC intervention re-search (Schlosser, Clifford, & Blischak, 2001). Strategies to enhance treatment integrity in AAC interventions are described in Chapter 9.

E. INSTRUMENTATION AND TESTING

While instrumentation has been addressed as far as human observers are concerned (see interobserver agreement of the dependent variable and treatment integrity), problems of instrumentation may also arise from measuring instruments such as machines or devices. Attempts have recently been initiated to use automated performance monitoring to study device use (Hill, 2001). If data from automated performance monitoring are to be used in decision making, it is essential that the monitoring instruments work reliably. In general, threats to internal validity due to instrumentation can be avoided by ensuring that instruments are carefully calibrated and repeatedly checked prior to and during a study.

Testing represents another threat to internal validity (Campbell & Stanley, 1966). Testing is said to occur when the dependent variable changes simply as a result of repeated measurement, possibly due to increased familiarity with the testing format or conditions under which the test is being taken. There are several avenues for minimizing the effects of testing. For example, one may try to avoid reactive measures altogether. Hegde (1994) suggested that whenever possible it is better to measure behavior directly rather than relying on opinion or perspectives about behavior because indirect measures tend to be more reactive. For example, instead of asking parents to fill out a questionnaire on their use of prompts in interacting with their daughter, it may be better to observe the parents interacting with their daughter directly and then record the frequency of prompting behavior.

In general, single-subject designs may be less prone than group designs to threats of testing because they typically rely on observable behavior rather than variables from which behaviors are inferred (e.g., attitudes). Testing effects may be counteracted in single-subject experimental designs by using well-established baseline measures. This allows the researcher to demonstrate that improvement through testing has not occurred or that changes have stabilized prior to the onset of intervention (Scruggs, 1992). Alternatively, one may consider using a multiple probe design rather than a multiple baseline design to avoid too many exposures to testing (see Chapter 6). In group designs, testing effects may be controlled by employing an additional group that does not receive the pretest (see Hegde, 1994).

F. REGRESSION

Scruggs (1992) noted that regression effects have been a continuous concern in group-experimental research with special populations. According to the statistical phenomenon known as regression toward the mean, a group that is preselected based on extreme test scores could be predicted to score closer to the mean in a second testing, without being given the treatment. Using random assignment of the group to experimental and control conditions can control this threat to internal validity.

In single-subject experimental research, regression can play out somewhat differently (Scruggs, 1992) and is most likely to occur when using the response-guided method for selecting the intervention onset (Todman & Dugard, 1999). A researcher, for example, may observe an extreme score in baseline that runs opposite the desired direction. This is then taken as an excellent point for initiating intervention with the next data point as it likely allows for the demonstration of strong treatment effects. The statistical phenomenon regression toward the mean suggests that this first intervention data point is likely to revert back to the mean. That is, the data point will likely be in the anticipated direction of the treatment effect. According to Todman and Dugard (1999), intervention effects are most credible when intervention phases are initiated at a predetermined, randomly selected point in time. If a researcher has collected a sufficient number of data points and no trends are evident in the data, the researcher may randomly select one data point to represent the exact onset of intervention.

G. Hawthorne Effects or Novelty Effects

The Hawthorne effect describes a situation in which the participant responds to the additional personal attention provided along with the independent variable, rather than to the independent variable alone. Novelty effects may occur when the participant responds positively to a new intervention simply because it represents a welcome change in daily routine. Both effects are more likely to occur in single-subject experiments with a no treatment baseline that involves little or no attention from the experimenter (Scruggs, 1992). In some studies on the effects of speech-generating devices (SGDs), participants were presented with a device only during the intervention phase and not during baseline (e.g., DiCarlo & Banajee, 2000; Schepis & Reid, 1995). During baseline, the participants were using their typical modes of communication in interacting with communication partners. Both novelty and Hawthorne effects are difficult to rule out in such situations. Novelty effects may have occurred because the device was something new and exciting and that was not available during baseline. Hawthorne effects may have played a role because the participants received more staff attention during intervention than during baseline because of the presence of a device. Thus, Hawthorne effects may interact with the independent variable. One might argue that the presence of a Hawthorne effect is acceptable from a clinical or educational point of view. If the presence of the device does recruit additional attention, so be it. Why not capitalize on this function? From an experimental point of view, however, it becomes difficult to separate the effects of the independent variable from the Hawthorne effect. What are some solutions to this potential threat to internal validity? Instead of using a no-treatment baseline, one could make the device available during baseline. This should reduce some of the novelty and possibly the differential in staff attention between baseline and intervention.

III. EXTERNAL VALIDITY AND GENERALITY

Generality refers to the extent to which conclusions of a research study can be extended (Hegde, 1994). The concept of generality is of significant importance because evidence-based practitioners often wish to know whether a given intervention will be equally effective under different circumstances such as an intervention delivered by other clinicians in others settings. As Hegde (1994) has pointed out, in essence, when considering generality issues, of interest is the range of conditions under which a demonstrated cause-effect relationship holds good. This section discusses the necessary condition for establishing the generality of research findings, including the notion of systematic and direct replications (Sidman, 1988). Sidman (1988) distinguished several types of generality.

A. Subject Generality

Sidman (1988) defined subject generality as the representativeness of a given experimental result with a given type of participant or other participants of the same type. For example, an experimental finding that iconicity promotes graphic-symbol learning for nouns in children with cerebral palsy and little functional speech may or may not be representative for other children with cerebral palsy and little functional speech. In group experiments, which strive to select a sample of participants representative of the larger population, generality may be evaluated by asking how representative the mean value is of all the participants. In single-subject experiments, subject generality may be evaluated by asking whether the experimental effect was demonstrated across a sufficient number of individual participants. Subject generality may also relate to participants of another type. For example, would the iconicity findings with children with cerebral palsy and little functional speech generalize to children with autism and little functional speech? This subject generality cannot be evaluated on the basis of one experiment but rather must be gathered from a synthesis of studies examining the same issue across several experiments with different participants.

B. Variable Generality

Variable generality is concerned with the relevance of a given variable or class of variables outside the confines of a particular experiment. An example of evaluating variable generality would occur when asking whether the iconicity hypothesis (i.e., iconic symbols are learned more readily than opaque symbols) has generality beyond a labeling response task (e.g., "Point to _____") to, for example, the initiation of a request (e.g., "I want the _____").

C. Condition Generality

In addition to the generality of subjects and variables, evidence-based practitioners may be interested in the generality of conditions as described in Chapter 2. Does an intervention conducted under ideal or optimal conditions bear generality under more typical conditions? For example, is a SGD as effective in a noisy classroom as it is in a semiquiet area in supporting spelling?

D. Role of Replication in Establishing Generality

Generality may be established through the process of direct or systematic replication (Sidman, 1988). Direct replication is the "repetition of a given experiment by the same investigator" (Sidman, 1988, p. 73). Direct replication may be done by repeating the same experiment with new participants, so-called intersubject replication, or by retaining the same participants, so-called intrasubject replication. Systematic replication helps establish the generality of findings by changing the conditions of the original experiment. For instance, an experiment may have indicated that teaching with augmented input (pointing to graphic symbols, stating the referent with natural speech, and activating the SGD) resulted in more efficient graphic-symbol learning than teaching without augmented input. In a systematic replication, the researcher may replicate this experiment using augmented input less frequently (25% of occasions) than it was provided in the original experiment (100%). Results from this experiment would extend the generality of the importance of providing augmented input to circumstances that may be more representative of daily practice. Schlosser and Blischak (2002) have replicated a preliminary experiment with one student with autism on the role of speech feedback and print feedback on spelling (Schlosser *et al.*, 1998). The procedures are identical across experiments with the exception that the current study does not include the provision of finger-spelled input by the experimenter. As such, this meets the criteria of systematic replication. Direct and systematic replications are scant in the AAC field as of yet, but they are essential toward establishing a science of AAC intervention research. To build a replicative history, however, it is essential that researchers assess and document treatment integrity data. Without such information it is impossible to accurately replicate procedures and therefore to establish generality.

IV. SOCIAL VALIDITY

Intervention research in AAC should be evaluated in terms of social validity (Schlosser, 1999). In other words, are AAC interventions socially valid? Social validity is established through the process of *social validation*, defined as the process of assessing the social significance of goals, methods, and outcomes (Kazdin, 1977; Wolf, 1978). This process may be implemented through the methods of *subjective evaluation* and *social comparison*.

A. SUBJECTIVE EVALUATION

Subjective evaluation refers to soliciting the opinions of persons who have a special position due to their expertise or their relationship to a client (Kazdin, 1977; 1982; Kazdin & Matson, 1981; Wolf, 1978). It is the consumers or stakeholders of interventions who should engage in this process, the results of which constitute measures of social validity: "If we aspire to social importance, then we must develop systems that allow our consumers to provide feedback about how our applications relate to their values" (Wolf, 1978, p. 210).

> Are consumers satisfied with the results, all of the results [positive or negative], including those that were unplanned? Behavioral treatment programs are designed to help someone with a problem. Whether or not the program is helpful can be evaluated only by the consumer. Behavior analysts may give their opinions, and these opinions may even be supported with empirical objective behavioral data, but it is the participants and other consumers who want to make the final decision about whether a program helped solve their problems. (Wolf, 1978, p. 210)

B. SOCIAL COMPARISON

Social comparison refers to the comparability of performance with a group of individuals whose behavior is considered to be typical, desirable, or normal (Kazdin, 1977; 1982; Kazdin & Matson, 1981; Wolf, 1978). See Chapter 10 for further details on implementing the methodologies of subjective evaluation and social comparison.

Presumably, goals, methods, and outcomes that are socially valid in addition to being objectively valid are the ones that are most likely to be adopted by stakeholders and that will result in more widespread dissemination (Winett, Moore, & Anderson, 1991). Interventionists and those involved in the provision of AAC need to target goals for change in order to focus an intervention. Likewise, evidence-based practitioners need to evaluate whether the goals targeted in research studies were socially valid. The focus selected may or may not represent a target that is considered (1) significant by consumers (via subjective evaluation) or (2) comparable with a group of typical individuals (via social comparison). To ensure that a selected target is socially important, the process of social validation becomes paramount. In addition to goals, interventionists and evidence-based practitioners need to determine or evaluate the methods for implementing the intervention. Again, these methods may or may not be considered of social value or considered comparable to the methods used with typical individuals. To increase the potential that stakeholders will adopt interventions, steps need to be taken to ensure that stakeholders find the methods to be important and acceptable. Even though data may have indicated that an intervention was efficacious, results observed in an experimental situation do not always imply that stakeholders perceive a change as efficacious or that the changes are comparable to behaviors yielded with typical individuals. Thus, interventionists and evidence-based practitioners need to assess the social validity of outcomes. Chapter 10 provides a framework for evaluating the social validity of AAC interventions.

V. ECOLOGICAL VALIDITY

This section addresses ecological validity as a concept for evaluating AAC intervention research. Ecological validity is closely related to social validity. Some authors assimilate social validity under the umbrella of ecological validity; others blend the two concepts (e.g., Banaji & Crowder, 1989; Gannon, 1986). In this text, ecological validity will be treated as a concept different from, but related to, that of social validity. Whereas the notion of social validity is concerned with the social significance of goals, methods, and outcomes as measured by perspectives of stakeholders or comparisons with a normative group, ecological validity is primarily concerned with the validity of settings, treatment agents, and materials as measured by what is considered appropriate for the experimental context or the environment in which the skill is expected to be performed.

Related to the ecological validity of treatment agents (e.g., clinicians, educators, research assistants, and parents), for example, it is of interest whether the person who implemented the training would also apply the training in typical daily practice? Clearly, trained research assistants may be excellent for yielding superior treatment integrity, but they are not likely to be ecologically valid treatment agents. The work by Light and Binger (1998) is exemplary in that classroom teachers rather than research assistants were trained to implement strategies aimed at improving communicative competence of their students.

Ecological validity has also been brought to bear on experimental decisions involving what possibly should (or could) be expected of communication partners. To be ecologically valid, communication partners in experimental situations should be expected to do what communication partners in everyday interactions would do. Sigafoos, Laurie, and Pennell (1996) reduced the amount of time given for a child to make a request from 30 seconds to 10 seconds to increase the ecological validity of the request. These authors argued that it seemed inappropriate to expect listeners to wait a full 30 seconds for a person to make a request in response to the instruction "Let me know if you want something." Ecological validity may play a decisive role in specifying treatment procedures.

Ecological validity may also be of concern when preparing or evaluating materials for AAC intervention studies. This author is currently involved in planning research into the effects of digitized speech output versus no speech output on requesting in beginning communicators (Schlosser, Blischak, Sigafoos, Ferrier, & Manuel, 2001–2003). Ideally, digitized messages should be recorded in a quiet area (preferably using a remote microphone that plugs into the SGD to decrease recording of machine noise) at a distance in accordance with the manufacturer's suggestions (Blischak & Schlosser, 2002). Yet in thinking about how teachers and other direct service providers may program these devices, it is likely that the recordings will contain some level of background noise and not be recorded at the optimum distance. Therefore, researchers need to address whether they wish to study digitized speech output under ecologically valid conditions or optimal conditions. There is no correct answer to this dilemma. The researcher needs to balance ecological validity with the independent variable on the continuum between ideal or typical conditions.

VI. SUMMARY

Internal validity, external validity, social validity, and ecological validity represent the foundations for studying and evaluating the efficacy of interventions in AAC. This chapter explained and illustrated each of these concepts with examples from AAC research. The chapters on the various methodologies for studying the efficacy of AAC interventions (Chapters 6 through 8) rely heavily on these types of validity, with particular emphasis on internal validity. Some of the constructs discussed, such as treatment integrity and social validity, are elaborated on in Chapters 9 and 10, respectively. Each type of validity plays a critical role in understanding and implementing evidence-based practice as discussed in Chapter 12 and infused throughout subsequent chapters.

REFERENCES

Banaji, M. R., & Crowder, R. G. (1989). The bankruptcy of everyday memory. *American Psychologist, 44*, 1185–1193.

Barlow, D. H., & Hersen, M. (1984). *Single-case experimental designs: Strategies for studying behavior change.* New York: Pergamon Press.

Blischak, D. M., & Schlosser, R. W. (2002). *Selection and use of speech output for communication and learning: What does the research tell us?* Manuscript submitted for publication.

Campbell, D. T., & Stanley, J. C. (1966). *Experimental and quasi-experimental designs for research.* Chicago: Rand McNally.

DiCarlo, C., & Banajee, M. (2000). Using voice output devices to increase initiations of young children with disabilities. *Journal of Early Intervention, 23*, 191–199.

Fuller, D. R., & Lloyd, L. L. (1992). Effects of configuration on the paired-associate learning of Blissymbols by preschool children with normal cognitive abilities. *Journal of Speech and Hearing Research, 35*, 1376–1383.

Gannon, P. M. (1986). Research with moderately, severely, profoundly retarded and autistic individuals (1975 to 1983): An evaluation of ecological validity. *Australia and New Zealand Journal of Developmental Disabilities, 12*, 33–53.

Hegde, M. N. (1994). *Clinical research in communicative disorders* (2nd ed.). Austin, TX: PRO-Ed.

Hill, K. (2001). *The development of a model for automated performance measurement and the establishment of performance indices for augmented communicators under two sampling conditions.* Unpublished doctoral dissertation. University of Pittsburgh, Pittsburgh.

Johnston, J. M., & Pennypacker, H. S. (1980). *Strategies and tactics of human behavioral research.* Hillsdale, NJ: L Erlbaum.

Kazdin, A. E. (1977). Assessing the clinical or applied significance of behavior change through social validation. *Behavior Modification, 1*, 427–452.

Kazdin, A. E. (1982). *Single-case research designs: Methods for clinical and applied settings.* New York: Oxford University Press.

Kazdin, A. E. (1992). *Research design in clinical psychology* (2nd ed.). New York: MacMillan.

Kazdin, A. E., & Hartmann, D. P. (1978). The simultaneous-treatment design. *Behavior Therapy, 9*, 912–922.

Kazdin, A. E., & Matson, J. L. (1981). Social validation in mental retardation. *Applied Research in Mental Retardation, 2*, 39–53.

Kerlinger, F. N. (1973). *Foundations of behavioral research.* New York: Holt, Rinehart, & Winston.

Light, J., & Binger, C. (1998). *Building communicative competence with individuals who use augmentative and alternative communication.* Baltimore: Paul H. Brookes.

Parsons, C. L., & La Sorte, D. (1993). The effect of computers with synthesized speech and no speech on the spontaneous communication of children with autism. *Australian Journal of Human Communication Disorders, 21*, 12–31.

Schepis, M. M., & Reid, D. H. (1995). Effects of a voice output communication aid on interactions between support personnel and an individual with multiple disabilities. *Journal of Applied Behavior Analysis, 28*, 73–77.

Schlosser, R. W. (1999). Social validation of interventions in augmentative and alternative communication. *Augmentative and Alternative Communication, 15*, 234–247.

Schlosser, R. W. (2002). On the importance of being earnest about treatment integrity. *Augmentative and Alternative Communication, 18*, 36–44.

Schlosser, R. W., Belfiore, P. J., Nigam, R., Blischak, D., & Hetzroni, O. (1995). The effects of speech output technology in the learning of graphic symbols. *Journal of Applied Behavior Analysis, 28*, 537–549.

Schlosser, R. W., & Blischak, D. M. (2002). *Effects of synthetic speech and print feedback on spelling in learners with autism*. Manuscript submitted for publication.

Schlosser, R. W., Blischak, D., M., Belfiore, P. J., Bartley, C., & Barnett, N. (1998). The effects of synthetic speech output and orthographic feedback on spelling in a student with autism: A preliminary study. *Journal of Autism and Developmental Disorders, 28*, 319–329.

Schlosser, R. W., Blischak, D. M., Sigafoos, J., Ferrier, L., & Manuel, S. (2001–2003). *Role of speech output for beginning communicators*. Grant funded by the Department of Education. CFDA 84.327A Steppingstones of Technology Innovation for Students with Disabilities.

Schlosser, R. W., Clifford, M., & Blischak, D. M. (2001, November). *Treatment integrity in augmentative and alternative communication*. Poster presented at the Annual Convention of the American Speech-Language and Hearing Association, New Orleans, LA.

Schlosser, R. W., & Lee, D. (2000). Promoting generalization and maintenance in augmentative and alternative communication: A meta-analysis of 20 years of effectiveness research. *Augmentative and Alternative Communication, 16*, 208–227.

Scruggs, T. E. (1992). Single-subject research methodology in the study of learning and behavioral disorders: Design, analysis, and synthesis. In T. E. Scruggs, & M. A. Mastropieri (Eds.), *Advances in Learning and Behavioral Disabilities* (Vol. 7, pp. 223–248). Greenwich, CT: JAI Press.

Sidman, M. (1988). *Tactics of scientific research: Evaluating experimental data in psychology*. Boston: Authors Cooperative.

Sigafoos, J., Laurie, S., & Pennell, D. (1996). Teaching children with Rett Syndrome to request preferred objects using aided communication: Two preliminary studies. *Augmentative and Alternative Communication, 12*, 88–96.

Tawney, J. W., & Gast, D. L. (1984). *Single subject research in special education*. Columbus, OH: Merrill.

Todman, J., & Dugard, P. (1999). Accessible randomization tests for single-case and small-n experimental designs in AAC research. *Augmentative and Alternative Communication, 15*, 69–82.

Udwin, O. (1987). Analysis of the experimental adequacy of alternative and augmentative communication training studies. *Child Language Teaching and Therapy, 3*, 18–39.

Winett, R. A., Moore, J. F., & Anderson, E. S. (1991). Extending the concept of social validity: Behavior analysis for disease prevention and health promotion. *Journal of Applied Behavior Analysis, 24*, 215–230.

Wolf, M. M. (1978). Social validity: The case for subjective measurement, or how applied behavior analysis is finding its heart. *Journal of Applied Behavior Analysis, 11*, 203–214.

Yeaton, W. H. (1982). A critique of the effectiveness of applied behavior analysis research. *Advances in Behavior Research and Therapy, 4*, 75–96.

CHAPTER 4

Formulating Research Questions[1]
Linking Theory to the Research Process

D. Jeffery Higginbotham
Department of Communicative Disorders and Sciences
University at Buffalo

I. INTRODUCTION

The area of augmentative and alternative communication (AAC) is perhaps unique for several important reasons. First, it is one of only a few fields that relates to many aspects of the human condition, which are influenced by several

---

[1]Parts of this chapter were presented at the Research Symposium of the International Society for Augmentative and Alternative Communication (ISAAC) held in Washington, D.C., in August 2000, and they were subsequently published in its proceedings: Higginbotham (2001). Constructing research questions in augmentative and alternative communication. In S. von Tetzchner & J. Clibbens (Eds.), *Understanding the theoretical and methodological bases of augmentative and alternative communication* (pp. 119–122). Toronto: International Society for Augmentative and Alternative Communication.

distinct scientific fields (e.g., computer science, engineering, cognitive science, psychology, linguistics and cultural anthropology, special education, speech-language pathology). Second, it is a small field made up of relatively few researchers and clinicians. Finally, AAC is primarily an applied field. There is a conscious focus on solving real and pressing problems. Scientific investigation, particularly research that focuses on basic issues, typically takes a back seat to solving immediate problems: the practical supersedes the theoretical. These factors—a large problem space, relatively few researchers, and a practical focus—can create problems for making scientific progress. In particular, it complicates the conception of appropriate research questions that AAC should pursue.

The motivation for this chapter is based primarily on the experience with a contemporary situation concerning the use of language-performance monitoring via automated data logging (Hill, 2001; Hill & Romich, 2001). This language-performance monitoring involves the automated collection and analysis of output from speech-generating devices (SGDs). Although this type of performance monitoring could provide important clinical evidence regarding communication performance and treatment efficacy, fundamental questions regarding the validity and the reliability of data collection and analysis must be resolved before it can be considered valid and ethical. Without a concerted effort to ask appropriate questions in a rigorous manner, an opportunity to move the AAC field forward could be missed.

This chapter focuses on a critical area of the research design process: developing the relationship between the research question and the research investigation. Issues regarding the characteristics of a good research question—how it relates to theory, methodology, and research results—and some of the common problems associated with generating a good research question are addressed. The chapter also introduces and addresses two contemporary theoretical perspectives on communication with respect to the measures relying on the automated analysis of language performance.

II. RELATIONSHIP OF THEORY TO RESEARCH

In any field, theory is a systematized body of related facts about the phenomenon under study. A theory is organized to provide a coherent description of the phenomenon, explain how it works, or make predictions about its behavior. Theory achieves its credibility by being tied to a preexisting body of research whose results support the tenets of the theory. Theory structures observed facts by guiding empirical evidence and principled arguments regarding the behavior of the phenomenon in question.

One way to represent the impact of theory is to construct a model. A model is a constructed representation of a theory, which focuses on how a phenomenon functions. When specified in sufficient detail, a theory or model can be tested systematically by disturbing some aspect of the phenomenon, then hypothesizing how that disturbance will affect the phenomenon (e.g., observing communication using the same device in two different contexts or using a single AAC device in a controlled context). Observations can also be made without altering the phenomenon. In this case, the observer's goal is to detail the constitution and dynamics of the phenomenon in its natural context. The results of these studies can be used to assess the validity of the theory—the reasonableness of the explanation.

Without scientifically based theory, individuals typically rely on common-sense notions about how the phenomenon should operate, which can be described as a naive theory (Norman, 1988). Although individuals conduct much of their everyday lives based on this type of sense making, it is typically covert, hard to elaborate explicitly, not based on observable fact, and often laden with emotion and opinion.

Another difficulty arises when research problems are justified by appealing to the work of authority figures without presenting the details of their work. Citing popular historical or contemporary authorities is a common rhetorical strategy and can be important in orienting the reader to a content area. This rhetorical style, however, becomes problematic when the writer makes sweeping, emotionally appealing claims without discussing specifics. Problems associated with naive theory and rhetorical appeals to authority can be avoided by constructing research questions that articulate with theory and methodology.

III. RELATIONSHIP OF THEORY AND THE RESEARCH PROCESS TO THE RESEARCH QUESTION

A research question is centered on testing the hypothesis developed to explain the phenomenon being studied. The initial motivation for the research question may stem from a practical problem (e.g., Is Benny's language becoming more complex?), previous research, or theoretical perspectives (e.g., language complexity increases as a result of input efficiency). Structurally, a research question should be in the form of a testable proposition that contains elements that link theory with methodology. Underlying any question (e.g., "Did language performance improve?") are assumptions about conditions in which performance was measured, measurement techniques, measurement criteria, and the theory that drives the importance and implication of the research question. A well-constructed research question unifies these different elements, reflecting the investigator's thoughtful engineering of the research design. Typically, the research question is narrowly focused so that the results of the study are not ambiguous. Poorly constructed research questions do not integrate with these elements, only partially responding to the underlying theory (if at all), thus defeating the goal of the project. The formulation of strong research questions has direct bearing on the progress of the field.

The research question reflects the research methodology by providing the criteria that must be attained before the question can be adequately answered. Subject selection, testing methods, instrumentation and analysis techniques all need to link with the research question. In practice, integrating research questions with theory and methodology is a dialectical process. That is, during the development of a research investigation, the research question and the methodology are progressively restructured through back-and-forth discussion and pilot testing. A successful match between theory, research question, and methodology minimizes threats to internal validity (see Chapter 3) and establishes construct validity and credibility (Abelson, 1995; Mitchell & Jolley, 2001). The research question should address the following methodological issues:

- How does the phenomenon under study relate to existing theory?
- What predictions does the theory make regarding the behavior of the phenomenon?
- Can the phenomenon be measured accurately by the chosen research method?
- Does the research method meet the constraints of the theory as it is proposed?
- How do subject selection and instruction articulate with the theory as it is proposed?
- How do the research techniques affect the phenomenon being studied?

When a close link between theory, research question, and methodology is achieved, the results of a study should answer the research question clearly. The discussion provides an interpretation of the study. A clear research question can provide a sound structure for relating results to the theory being tested. To provide a frame of reference for this discussion, the application of two models of language processing on the problem of implementing automated language analyses is examined.

IV. LANGUAGE MEASURES OBTAINED THROUGH AUTOMATED DATA LOGGING AND OBJECTIVE MEASURES

Automated data logging (ADL) involves the collection of human and device activities into a log or data file that can be analyzed quantitatively (Hill,

2001; Hill & Romich, 2001). Historically, ADL has been used primarily for research and clinical practice. One use of ADL is to quantify human-device interaction. From these data, researchers are beginning to investigate various measures to index human communication performance. Among those measures with a clinical appeal is mean length of utterance (MLU). Derived from child-language study, MLU has been used extensively in both the research and clinical domains as a measure of language development (Paul, 2001) and has been shown to be a reliable correlate to both cognitive and syntactic development during childhood. MLU has also been found to reliably discriminate typical from disordered language development and has been used as a descriptive measure of adult language (Shadden, 1998). Measures of utterance length have been used to a lesser extent with adults with extreme MLU scores (both high and low) associated with language problems. In the AAC area, Romski and Sevcik (1996) employed MLU to inspect early augmented language productions. Similar measures involving utterance length have been employed to document communication performance of clinical populations and the effects of communication device features on conversation (Chapanis, Parrish, Ochsman, & Weeks, 1977; Farrier, 1991; Higginbotham, 1989; Stoll, Hoecker, Krueger, & Chapanis, 1976)

One attractive feature of MLU is that it can be computed using ADL techniques. For example, Hill (2001) has shown that with the language activity monitor (LAM), MLU can be reliably collected, transcribed, and analyzed within a relatively short time. Although MLU can be obtained with relative ease, it is not clear what it signifies from an AAC perspective. An augmented speaker must operate a piece of technology to speak, and so the question arises as to what extent utterance length is affected by the technology itself. Previous human factors research has shown that changes in communication media (speech, writing, typing) have a pronounced effect on the length and structural complexity of communication (Chapanis, 1976; Clark & Brennan, 1991). Another issue arises around ADL's inability to capture the gesture, vocalizations, interlocutor activity or contextual information and their contributions to utterance production. For these reasons, Nelson (1992) questioned the clinical validity of MLU for measuring the language performance of augmented speakers.

Undoubtedly, a reliable and valid measure of child language development or device use would be a valuable tool for both selecting devices and monitoring progress. Determining the validity and utility of MLU takes on increased importance because of the potential use for determining eligibility for a communication aid. Without clear, empirical demonstration of the relationship between MLU, language development, and device use, it would be inappropriate and dangerous if clinicians and insurers used such measures to recommend or deny AAC devices and services. The better way to determine whether MLU (or any other measure) could address these issues is to understand what the measure actually reflects with respect to contemporary theories of communication and interaction.

To illustrate the relationship of theory and the research question, two models of language will be introduced. The first (Levelt, 1993) focuses on the cognitive processes associated with utterance generation. The second (Clark, 1996) accounts for language use during conversation. Both models depict communication in real time and can be used to assess the impact of AAC technologies on utterance production.

A. Language Processing

Models of language production processing are concerned with the manner in which spoken language is produced, from thought and intention through articulation. Levelt's (1993) model of spoken language processing portrays the cognitive processes and processing constraints involved in real-time language production. Levelt's model consists of three sequential stages of processing: the conceptualizer, the formulator, and the articulator (see Figure 4.1).

At the first stage (conceptualizer), the speaker utilizes his background knowledge of the situation and discourse to generate a preverbal form of his intended utterance. He then submits it to the formulator component of his language generation system. Within the formulator, the preverbal utterance is encoded with grammatical, lexical, and phonetic information and then is submitted as a phonetic plan to the articulatory component of the system, which then articulates the utterance. Processing modules exist independently of stored information. If there is not enough information at the formulator stage to produce a grammatical chunk, processing pauses until sufficient information is received from the conceptualizer.

This model possesses the following characteristics. Each stage provides information to the next stage for processing. Language processing components are distinct from storage of language materials. Each stage is encapsulated—that is, each stage processes information independently from the other stages. Finally, the speaker can benefit from feedback during the course of language processing (not shown in the model). Levelt argued that normally speakers have no conscious access to language encoding or articulation. For most speakers, language production is relatively effortless.

Levelt's language processing model has several implications for the relationship of AAC technologies to the speaking process (see Figure 4.1).

1. In order to adapt slow-paced output during conversation, at the conceptualizer stage, the augmented speaker may need to pay specific attention to the current status of common ground and social contingencies. The longer the

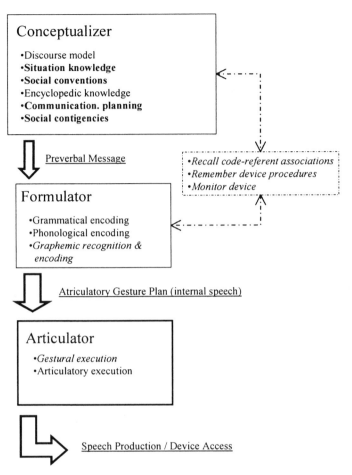

Figure 4.1 Model of speaking production for natural and augmented communicators (based on Levelt, 1993). Processes specific to AAC are italicized. Processes emphasized by AAC are bolded. Dashed lines and arrows suggest possible connections between components. © D. Jeffery Higginbotham, 2000.

delay between the initial conceiving and finalizing of the utterance, the harder it is for the speaker to keep the individual constituents in mind.

2. To issue an utterance, the user must consciously retrieve vocabulary from his or her device by recalling communication codes or monitor his or her device for the target prediction or selection. This is markedly different from speech production that is largely unconscious. These processes are represented in a separate box in Figure 4.1.

3. It is not clear how the formulator is involved in augmented utterance production. Given the conscious generation of individual lexical items (word by word, letter by letter, etc.), coupled with the slowness of utterance production, some augmented speakers may circumvent the automatic grammatical processing associated with the formulator and rely, instead, on the conceptualizer stage for utterance construction. Another possibility is that the utterances are first constructed through an interaction between the conceptualizer and formulator components, then submitted to the AAC component for coding into the particular symbol or alphabetic sequence. Being conscious and volitional, these strategies may demand significantly more attentional resources than speaking and could result in shorter utterances, depending on the processing demands placed on the speaker by his or her device and situation.

From a language-processing point of view, Levelt's model highlights the extra processing burdens faced by augmented speakers during utterance production. Based on this model, utterance generation appears overtly conscious, tactical, and difficult for many augmented speakers. Given this model, MLU does not appear to be simply a product of an augmented speaker's language competence but may be fundamentally related to device constraints and the particular speaking task.

To illustrate how one could productively probe Levelt's theory, ask the following question: Under varying levels of temporal pressure (quick completion, no limit to completion time), how do different production options or modes (e.g., spelling, word prediction, icon encoding, natural speech) impact on utterance production (rate, vocabulary diversity, MLU, etc.)?

B. Joint Action

One of the most compelling models of communication was developed by Herbert Clark (Clark, 1992, 1996) to account for language use during conversational interaction. According to Clark, the primary use of language is to converse. Language is a joint activity with one's interlocutor to achieve understanding, which Clark talks about as establishing common ground (Clark, 1996; Clark & Brennen, 1991). During conversation, interactants are busy getting their stated business accomplished, transacting the procedural issues of communication, managing the face or interpersonal aspects of the communication, as well as meeting their private communication agendas. To accomplish conversation in real time, speakers must find ways to coordinate their actions to ensure that their addressees are interpreting them correctly.

Clark proposed a four-level process of interactive production and comprehension, which he termed the "joint action ladder" (Clark, 1994, 1996)

Level	Speaker (A)	Addressee (B)
4	Proposes a joint project to B	Considers the proposal from A
3	Signals a meaning for B	Recognizes the meaning from A
2	Presents the signal to B	Identifies the signal from A
1	Executes a behavior for B	Attends to the behavior from A

Figure 4.2 Joint action ladder (adapted from Clark, 1996).

(Figure 4.2). Successful communication depends on the ability of interactants to coordinate their production and comprehension activities across four different levels. Each level of production is linked to a specific level of comprehension.

During successful communication, movement up and down the ladder is instantaneous. When communication is problematic, movement on the ladder is stopped and moves forward a step at a time until the communication is fulfilled. Problems occurring during interaction can be located on the ladder and are recognized as such by the interactants, who work to resolve them. Thus, the ladder has diagnostic significance and can be used to identify joint action problems involved in speaking, listening, and turn taking. Similar models have been proposed to account for the cognitive processing stages involved in human machine interaction (Norman, 1988; Schneiderman, 1997).

The tactics that interactants take to ensure mutual understanding (i.e., progress through the joint action ladder) are influenced by the communication medium employed to transact the interaction (Clark, 1996; Clark & Brennan, 1991). For example, the differences between face-to-face conversation (speech, visual, real-time, etc.) and e-mail (electronic text, typing production constraints, delayed time, etc.) affect the shape of the interaction (frequency of exchange, turn length, how referencing is accomplished, etc.). There are particular costs for communicating in the particular medium (e.g., increased chance of misunderstanding, different prevention and repair strategies, relative ease). Clark argued that departures from face-to-face conversation result in predictable adaptations and problems. When communicative aims and constraints of the medium are at cross-purposes (e.g., using typing to try to achieve fast interactive communication, such as on Microsoft messenger), problems are likely to arise. Research by Chapanis and colleagues (Chapanis, 1976; Chapanis *et al.*, 1977; Stoll *et al.*, 1976) has long demonstrated the effects of communication media on various aspects of interaction. Recently, Hancock and Dunham (2001) empirically tested Clark's joint action ladder model and found it to have diagnostic significance in the design of interactive computer-mediated technologies.

For Clark, timing is critical to joint action success. Conversation is produced in real time and participants coordinate their actions—simultaneously and sequentially—to advance common ground. Examples of events that depend on precise timing and the continuity of action include turn regulation, the use of referents, responses and back channels (Clark, 1996, p. 42). Clark also noted that in face-to-face interaction, speakers are under considerable social pressure to communicate without hesitation. The temporal imperative to communicate without delay results in the observation that the standard maximum tolerance for silence during conversation among English speakers is about one second (Clark, 1996, p. 268; Jefferson, 1989).

Clark's model of language has significant implications for AAC performance and the validity.

1. This model recognizes that the primary context of language use is conversation, which is interactive, multimodal, and emerges from joint actions produced by the participants, the situation, and the communication medium—in real time (Clark, 1994, 1996).

2. The model emphasizes the inclusion of gesture as part of language use versus a unimodal solitary sentence construction approach, and it refocuses our attention on communication performance and the socially coordinated actions required for the establishment and progression of common ground. Gesture becomes an inseparable part of the performance of the utterance (Clark, 1996; Goodwin, 1981; Higginbotham & Wilkins, 1999). AAC devices can be seen as a specific medium—or several varieties of related media—that specifically affects language use. The medium-related properties of these devices combined with the augmented speaker's physical and communication skills affect the sequential and temporal flow of communication. To establish and move ground during augmented conversations, participants find alternative joint action tactics, such as message co-construction and listener dis-attention, addressee questioning, and so forth (Blau, 1987; Higginbotham & Wilkins, 1999; Mueller & Soto, 2000; Sweidel, 1991/1992).

3. Clark argues that all interaction is situated—consisting of a particular constellation of participants, settings, personal agendas, and communication goals. These issues must be considered, particularly in experimental situations, as they bear directly on the ways participants construct common ground and assign relevance to each other's actions. The situation combines with the medium to shape conversation.

Viewed from Clark's theory of language use, MLU must be regarded as a product of the situation, participants, communication task, and the medium involved in the communication. This could have significant impact on the variability of MLU. The AAC medium may place considerable constraints on the interactants, compelling the augmented communicator—irrespective of his or her linguistic competence—to make tactical decisions about what and how many words to use to communicate within an appropriate frame of time. Moreover, augmented speakers may choose to split their utterance into linguistic, gestural, and co-constructional units, which make the definition of utterance—and therefore MLU—difficult to apply.

The notion that all communication is situated also poses MLU sampling problems for choosing appropriate participants and settings and providing instructions to augmented speakers. Do augmented speakers and their addressees behave differently in a clinical context than they do in a nonclinical setting? For example, the temporal imperative that is operative during most interactions may be altered or suspended during clinical language sampling. That is, the clinician does not hold the AAC speaker accountable for slow output. Task instructions (e.g., "tell me the whole story") or the augmented speaker's perceptions of what the clinician expects (long utterances) may have a facilitating influence on utterance length.

In the context of clinical language sampling (and perhaps other situations as well), augmented utterance production may resemble a writing task more than a speaking task. Writing carries with it different expectations and temporal demands compared to speaking, which could affect utterance length, grammaticality, and word choice. For example, if augmented communication in these situations was regarded as a narrative writing task, the need to be brief and succinct would not be operative, although it clearly is during face-to-face conversation (Clark, 1996).

Selecting subjects naive to the purposes of the study would be necessary in testing Clark's model. It is reasonable to assume that the knowledge that one's language was being monitored for utterance length could produce longer utterances in order to display one's competencies or to please the investigator.

Finally, utterances produced by the augmented speaker may consist of a combination of device output, gesture, and the coordinated verbal contributions by the augmented speaker's addressee. Methods for collecting and analyzing utterance productions may need to take these information sources into account. Because ADL is not equipped to collect this type of data, it becomes crucial to empirically determine what kind of effect this would have on computing MLU. It is likely the MLU measure will be affected by these influences, which would have to be controlled in order to use this measure in a productive manner.

To illustrate how one could productively probe Clark's theory, ask the following question (with the participant naive to the purpose of the study and communicating in a natural setting): How do language analyses that take into account gesture, co-constructed talk, and device output differ from those that only analyze device output with respect to various utterance characteristics (e.g., MLU, structural, and prepositional complexity)?

V. CONCLUSION: ASKING THE RIGHT QUESTIONS ABOUT MLU

This chapter demonstrated the importance of linking theory with research and the formulation of research questions. Without background information or an empirical basis of comparison, language assessment and analysis problems may appear simple to solve. However, validity is not dependent on the ease or consistency of the analysis technique, but on what it reveals about language performance and its utility as an index of communication competence. Objective findings are, by themselves, insufficient support for an evidence-based approach. Data must be tied to explanations of the phenomenon being studied. To show how theory can link with the research question, the chapter examined two theories about language processing. Each theory differed according to its focus and methodological requirements. Levelt's speaking model is based on psycholinguistic processes and lends itself to an experimental methodology. Clark's joint action model provides attention to context and requires a naturalistic approach to assess the model.

REFERENCES

Abelson, R. (1995). *Statistics as principled argument.* Hillsdale, NJ: Erlbaum.

Blau, A. F. (1987). *Communication in the back-channel: Social structural analyses of nonspeech/speech conversations.* Unpublished doctoral dissertation, City University of New York, New York.

Chapanis, A. (1976). Interactive human communication: Some lessons learned from laboratory experiments. *Johns Hopkins University Department of Psychology Technical Report, 3.*

Chapanis, A., Parrish, R. N., Ochsman, R. B., & Weeks, G. D. (1977). Studies in interactive communication: II. The effects of four communication modes on the linguistic performance of teams during cooperative problem solving. *Human Factors, 19,* 101–126.

Clark, H. H. (1992). *Arenas of language use.* Chicago: University of Chicago Press.

Clark, H. H. (1994). Managing problems in speaking. *Speech Communication, 15,* 243–250.

Clark, H. H. (1996). *Using language.* New York: Cambridge University Press.

Clark, H. H., & Brennan, S. E. (1991). Grounding in communication. In L. B. Resnick & J. M. Levine (Eds.), *Perspectives on socially shared cognition* (pp. 127–149). Washington, DC: American Psychological Association.

Farrier, L. (1991). Clinical study of a dysarthric adult using a Touch Talker with Words Strategy. *Augmentative and Alternative Communication, 7,* 266–274.

Goodwin, C. (1981). *Conversational organization: Interaction between speakers and hearers.* New York: Academic Press.

Hancock, J., & Dunham, P. J. (2001). Language use in computer-mediated communication: The role of coordination devices. *Discourse Processes, 31,* 91–110.

Higginbotham, D. J. (1989). The interplay of communication device output mode and interaction style between nonspeaking persons and their speaking partners. *Journal of Speech and Hearing Disorders, 54,* 320–333.

Higginbotham, D. J., & Wilkins, D. P. (1999). Title slipping through the timestream: Social issues of time and timing in augmented interactions. In D. Kovarsky, J. F. Duchan, & M. Maxwell (Eds.),

Constructing (in)competence: Disabling evaluations in clinical and social interaction (pp. 49–82). Mahwah, NJ: Erlbaum.

Hill, K. (2001). *The development of a model for automated performance measurement and the establishment of performance indices for augmented communicators under two sampling conditions.* Unpublished doctoral dissertation, University at Pittsburgh, Pittsburgh.

Hill, K., & Romich, B. (2001). *AAC clinical summary measures for characterizing performance.* Conference Proceedings from the 2001 Computer S University of Northridge Conference on Disabilities, March 21–24, 2001, Los Angeles, CA. http://www.prentrom.com/assessment/aac%20selection%20rate%20measurement.pdf

Jefferson, G. (1989). Preliminary notes on a possible metric which provides for a "standard maximum" silence of approximately one second in conversation. In D. Roger, P. Bull, *et al.* (Eds.) *Conversation: An interdisciplinary perspective* (pp. 166–196). Clevedon, UK: Multilingual Matters.

Levelt, W. (1993). *From intention to articulation.* Boston: MIT Press.

Mitchell, M., & Jolley, J. (2001). *Research design explained.* Philadelphia: Harcourt College Publishers.

Mueller, E., & Soto, G. (2001). Capturing the complexity of aided interactions: A conversation analysis perspective. In S. von Tetzchner & J. Clibbens (Eds.), *Understanding the theoretical and methodological bases of augmentative and alternative communication* (pp. 64–83). Toronto: International Society for Augmentative and Alternative Communication.

Nelson, N. (1992). Performance is the prize: Language competence and performance among AAC Users, *Augmentative and Alternative Communication, 8,* 3–18.

Norman, D. A. (1988). *The psychology of everyday things.* New York: Basic Books.

Paul, R. (2001). *Language disorders from infancy through adolescence: Assessment and intervention* (2nd ed.). St. Louis, MO: Mosby.

Romski, M., & Sevcik, R. A. (1996). *Breaking the speech barrier, language development through augmented means.* Baltimore: Paul H. Brookes.

Schneiderman, B. (1997). *Designing the user interface: Strategies for effective human-computer interaction.* Boston: Addison-Wesley.

Shadden, B. (1998). Sentential/surface level analysis. In B. S. L. R. Cherney & C. A. Coelho (Eds.), *Analyzing discourse in communicatively impaired adults* (pp. 35–64). Gaithersburg, MD: Aspen.

Stoll, F. C., Hoecker, D. G., Krueger, G. P., & Chapanis, A. (1976). The effects of four communication modes on the structure of language used during cooperative problem solving. *Journal of Psychology, 94,* 13–26.

Sweidel, G. (1991/1992). Management strategies in the communication of speaking persons and persons with a speech disability. *Research on Language and Social Interactions, 25,* 195–214.

CHAPTER 5

On the Subject of Subject Selection in AAC[1]
Implications for Planning and Interpreting Efficacy Research

Jan L. Bedrosian
Department of Speech Pathology and Audiology
Western Michigan University

[1]Parts of this paper were presented at the Research Symposium of the International Society for Augmentative and Alternative Communication (ISAAC) held in Washington, D.C., in August 2000, and they were subsequently published in its proceedings: Bedrosian, J. (2001). Who is who in augmentative and alternative communication research: Issues in subject selection. In S. von Tetzchner & J. Clibbens (Eds.), *Understanding the theoretical and methodological bases of augmentative and alternative communication* (pp. 93–102). Toronto: International Society for Augmentative and Alternative Communication.

The Efficacy of Augmentative and Alternative Communication

I. INTRODUCTION

In our field, there has been only limited research to establish the efficacy of augmentative and alternative communication (AAC) interventions. Recent attention to this topic has revealed a multitude of methodological issues that have yet to be resolved in conducting efficacy research with individuals who require AAC systems (Bedrosian, 1999a, 1999b; Calculator, 1999; Granlund & Olsson, 1999; Light, 1999; Schlosser, 1999; Sevcik, Romski, & Adamson, 1999; Todman & Dugard, 1999). One such issue deals with the selection of the individuals themselves. Who are the participants in AAC efficacy research? Which participant variables are important to consider? How are these participants selected? What impact does participant selection have on establishing external validity or the generality of findings? This chapter addresses these and other pertinent questions pertaining to participant selection in AAC efficacy research.

The type of efficacy research of interest is that involving single-subject experimental designs where the independent variable(s) is systematically manipulated, as opposed to case studies (Barlow & Hersen, 1984). Group research designs will not be considered due to the difficulty in obtaining a large enough sample of homogeneous AAC participants (Remington, 1991). Additionally, only efficacy research involving disabled participants who require the use of AAC as opposed to nondisabled participants will be addressed, based on the questionable nature of generalizing findings from nondisabled to disabled participants (Bedrosian, 1995; Higginbotham & Bedrosian, 1995).

A 10-year review of the efficacy studies published in *Augmentative and Alternative Communication* from 1990 to 2000, which met these criteria, was conducted to form the basis of the discussion. The goals of this review were to examine how researchers are dealing with participant selection and to identify the strengths and weaknesses of these approaches. The journal *Augmentative and Alternative Communication* alone, as opposed to the inclusion of other journals, was selected for the review because this is the official research journal of the International Society for Augmentative and Alternative Communication (ISAAC) and is easily accessible to all of its members. A brief overview of these studies will begin our discussion.

II. OVERVIEW OF AAC EFFICACY STUDIES

From the period covering January of 1990 to March of 2000, 22 efficacy studies meeting the previously specified criteria were published in *Augmentative and Alternative Communication* (see Table 5.1). Of these studies, 20 involved child or adult participants with congenital disorders, while the remaining two (Koul & Harding, 1998; Lasker, Hux, Garrett, Moncrief, & Eischeid, 1997) involved adult participants with acquired disorders. Of the total number of studies, 16 were conducted with multiple participants (range of two to five participants per study), while the remaining 6 were conducted with a single participant. A variety of AAC target areas, single-subject experimental designs, and intervention proce- dures are represented across the studies. An overview of this information is pre- sented in Table 5.1, along with the following additional participant-related units of information: (1) reported participant variables, (2) the use of an explicit par- ticipant selection criteria, (3) the consistency of results across participants within multiple-subject studies, and (4) participant variables contributing to mixed results. This table will be referred to throughout the remainder of the chapter.

III. WHO ARE THE PARTICIPANTS IN AAC EFFICACY RESEARCH?

It is widely recognized that individuals who require the use of AAC systems constitute a heterogeneous population. According to Higginbotham and Bedrosian (1995) and others, heterogeneity appears to be "the rule rather than the exception" (Romski & Sevcik, 1988, p. 90). There is a remarkable range of differences across AAC system users with respect to cognitive, linguistic, and physical variables alone. These differences, coupled with other subject variables such as sensory status and AAC intervention history, add to the difficulty of the task of finding homogeneous-like subjects for participation in efficacy research. Indeed, homogeneity is a necessary condition for determining the effectiveness of the independent variable (i.e., the intervention procedures) (Barlow & Hersen, 1984). Fortunately, when using single-subject experimental designs, large samples of participants are not an issue.

Kiesler (1966), in his discussion of the patient uniformity myth, indicated that we have been misled to believe that all patients with the same etiology/medical diagnosis are alike. Instead, he noted that these individuals are really more different than they are alike. When participants in a given efficacy study are heterogeneous, "no meaningful conclusions regarding the types of patients for whom therapy was effective or ineffective are possible" (Kiesler, 1966, p. 111).

Who are the participants, then, who have participated in AAC efficacy research? Which participant variables have and have not been reported? We can begin to address these questions by examining the columns in Table 5.1 per- taining to age/disability of participants and participant variables reported.

Across the efficacy studies reviewed, reported disabilities involving children or adults with congenital disorders (20 studies) included those with Down syndrome, cerebral palsy, autism, Rett syndrome, verbal apraxia, sensory or dual sensory impairments, and those with cognitive impairments of unknown

Table 5.1

Overview of Efficacy Studies Published in the AAC Journal from January of 1990 to March of 2000 (Arranged by Year of Publication)

Author(s)/Year	AAC Target Area(s)	#/Age/Disability of Subject(s)	Subject Variables Reported	Subject Selection Criteria
Hunt, Alwell, & Goetz (1991)	Turn-taking via pictures in a communication book	3 children with severe cognitive impairment (1 with Down syndrome)	—Chronological age —Gender —Etiology —Cognitive level —Educational placement —Language production —Language comprehension	Yes —Speech intelligibility 50% —Level of syntactic production restricted to simple sentences —Initiated interactions but did not maintain beyond 2 to 3 turns
Buzolich, King, & Baroody (1991)	Commenting via communication device	3 children with cerebral palsy	—Chronological age —Gender —Etiology —Sensory impairments —Educational placement —Ambulation —History of AAC —Type of communication device, access, # of messages —Language comprehension —Communicative functions —Reading/Spelling level —Math level	No
Kozleski (1991)	Request for objects via photographs on a communication board	2 children with severe cognitive and physical impairments	—Chronological age —Gender —Etiology —Cognitive level —Vision/hearing —Educational placement —Ambulation —Communication modes —Language comprehension	No
McGregor, Young, Gerak, Thomas, & Vogelsberg (1992)	Functional use of a communication device	1 adult with cerebral palsy and moderate cognitive impairment	—Chronological age —Gender —Etiology —Cognitive level —Educational placement —Ambulation —Type of communication device, access —Communication modes —Pragmatic skills	No
O'Keefe & Dattilo (1992)	Response-recode via communication board/device	3 adults with cognitive impairments (1 with cerebral palsy)	—Chronological age —Gender —Etiology —Cognitive level	Yes —Age —Etiology —Degree of

Single–Subject Experimental Design	Intervention Procedures	Consistency of Results Across Subjects	Variables Possibly Contributing to Mixed Results
—Multiple baseline design across subjects —Multiple probe design	Prompting	No —Differences with respect to generalization	Subject —Language levels
Multiple baseline design across subjects	Prompting	No —Differences with respect to: • Length of treatment phases • Types of prompts responded to • Extent of spillover effects • Generalization	Subject —Cognitive levels —Multiple disabilties —Language levels
Multiple probe design	Expectant time delay	No —Differences with respect to rate of learning	Subject —Cognitive levels
Multiple baseline design across settings	—Preinstruction —Natural environmental teaching	—	—
Multiple baseline design across subjects	Levels of instruction	No —Differences with respect to: • Ability to meet training criterion • Amount of training time required	Subject —No formal language/cognitive measures reported for the subject who exhibited

(*continues*)

Table 5.1 (*continued*)

Author(s)/Year	AAC Target Area(s)	#/Age/Disability of Subject(s)	Subject Variables Reported	Subject Selection Criteria
			—Vision/hearing —Residential placement —Ambulation —Type of communication device, access, symbol systems —Language production —Communication modes —Language comprehension	cooperation —Ability to understand instructions, questions, commands —Access to device for making requests and demands —No use of target
Schweigert & Rowland (1992)	Microswitch technology to develop early communication	3 children with dual sensory impairments (2 with cerebral palsy)	—Chronological age —Gender —Etiology —Vision/hearing —Educational placement —Orthopedic impairment —Seizure activity —Communication skills —Language comprehension	No
Hamilton & Snell (1993)	Use of symbols in a communication book	1 adolescent with autism and severe cognitive impairment	—Chronological age —Gender —Etiology —Cognitive level —Educational placement —Type of communication book, # of symbols —Communication modes —Challenging behaviors	No
Goodman & Remington (1993)	Sign production	4 children with severe cognitive impairment (1 with Down syndrome)	—Chronological age —Gender —Etiology —Cognitive level —Vision/hearing —Language production —Sign vocabulary —Language comprehension	No
Remington & Clarke (1993a) (2-part study)	—Sign production —Speech comprehension	4 children with severe cognitive impairment (2 with Down syndrome; 1 with Phenylketonuria) (Part 1); 2 children with severe cognitive impairment (1 with Down syndrome) (Part 2)	(Parts 1 and 2) —Chronological age —Gender —Etiology —Cognitive level —Vision/hearing —Educational placement —History of sign training —Language production —Language comprehension —Vocal imitation	No
Remington & Clarke (1993b)	—Sign production —Speech comprehension	5 children with severe cognitive impairment (3 with Down syndrome)	—Chronological age —Gender —Etiology —Cognitive level	No

Single-Subject Experimental Design	Intervention Procedures	Consistency of Results Across Subjects	Variables Possibly Contributing to Mixed Results
		• Average rate of using target • Generalization	performance differences
—ABA for 2 subjects —BABCD for 1 subject	Levels of instruction	Unable to determine as targets/ designs varied across subjects	—
Changing criterion design within a multiple probe across settings	—Expectant time delay —Mand-model	—	—
—Alternating treatment design	—Imitation —Simultaneous communication —Prompting	No —Differences with respect to: • Rate of learning • Performance in relation to each treatment condition • Generalization • Post-intervention maintenance	Subject —Cognitive levels —Language levels
—Alternating treatment design and multiple probe design (Part 1) —Alternating treatment design and multiple baseline design across subjects (Part 2)	Prompting	No (Part 1) —Differences with respect to ability to meet criterion for one of the treatment conditions No (Part 2) —Differences with respect to rate of learning	Subject (Parts 1 and 2) —Cognitive levels —Language levels
—Alternating treatment design —Multiple probe design	Prompting	No —Differences with respect to: • Rate of learing in each treatment condition	Subject —Cognitive levels —Language levels

(*continues*)

Table 5.1 (*continued*)

Author(s)/Year	AAC Target Area(s)	#/Age/Disability of Subject(s)	Subject Variables Reported	Subject Selection Criteria
			—Vision/hearing —Educational placement —History of sign training —Language production —Language comprehension —Vocal imitation	
Durand (1993)	Functional communication training (challenging behaviors) via communication device	3 children with moderate or severe cognitive impairment (2 with cerebral palsy)	—Chronological age —Gender —Etiology —Cognitive level —Educational placement —Language production —Communication modes —Challenging behaviors —History of behavior intervention	Yes —Presence of frequent challenging behaviors —Demonstrated need for a communication device
Iacono, Mirenda, & Beukelman (1993)	Two-word semantic productions via speech, signs, &/or communication device	2 children with cognitive impairment (1 with Down syndrome)	—Chronological age —Gender —Etiology —Cognitive level —Educational placement —Language production —Language comprehension —Symbolic play —Symbol—object matching abilities	Yes —Hearing thresholds 20 dB —Normal vision —No functional spoken language —Minimum # of signs in vocabulary
McNaughton & Tawney (1993)	Spelling via communication device	2 adults with cerebral palsy	—Chronological age —Gender —Etiology —Vision/hearing —Upper extremity mobility —Type of communication device —Typing rate —Language production —Language comprehension —Spelling skills	No
Vaughn & Horner (1995)	Functional communication training (challenging behaviors) via photographs	1 adult with autism and cognitive impairment	—Chronological age —Gender —Etiology —Adaptive behavior —Residential placement —Language production —Communication modes —Medication —Challenging behaviors	No
Iacono & Duncum (1995)	Single-word production via signs, or signs	1 child with cognitive impairment (Down syndrome)	—Chronological age —Gender —Etiology	No

Single–Subject Experimental Design	Intervention Procedures	Consistency of Results Across Subjects	Variables Possibly Contributing to Mixed Results
		• Speech comphrension performance • Visual stimulus control • Overselective responding • Other post-intervention performance	
Multiple baseline design across subjects (Author reported misuse of this design with respect to the length of baseline for each subject)	—Prompting —Fading	No —Differences with respect to initial response to treatment	Subject (uncertain) —Baseline performance
—Multiple baseline design across behaviors —Alternating treatment design	Prompting	No —Differences with respect to: • Effectiveness of the 2 treatments • Rate of learning • Communication mode preference	Subject —Cognitive levels —Possibly language comprehension levels
Alternating treatment design	—Copy-write-compare instruction —Student-directed cueing instruction	No —Differences with respect to: • Rate of learning for each treatment method • Time needed to complete instruction • # of correctly spelled words	Subject —Language levels —Spelling levels
ABA'B	Instruction	—	—
Alternating treatment design	—Models —Reinforcement	—	—

(*continues*)

Table 5.1 (*continued*)

Author(s)/Year	AAC Target Area(s)	#/Age/Disability of Subject(s)	Subject Variables Reported	Subject Selection Criteria
	with communication device		—Hearing —Educational placement —History of language intervention —Type of communication device —Language comprehension —Communication modes —Symbolic play	
Horn & Jones (1996)	Selection techniques: scanning and direct selection	1 child with cerebral palsy	—Chronological age —Gender —Etiology —Cognitive level —Vision/hearing —Educational placement —Ambulation, upper extremity mobility —Language production —Communication modes —Language comprehension	No
Harris, Skarakis-Doyle, & Haaf (1996)	Syntactic production via a Unicorn keyboard	1 child with developmental verbal apraxia	—Chronological age —Gender —Etiology —Cognitive level —Hearing —Adaptive behavior —Language production —Communication modes —Language comprehension	No
Heller, Allgood, Davis, Arnold, Castelle, & Taber (1996)	Conversational skills via dual communication boards	3 young adults with cognitive and sensory impairment(s) (1 with Down syndrome; 2 with cerebral palsy)	—Chronological age —Gender —Etiology —Cognitive level —Sensory impairment(s) —Vocational placement —Communication modes —Conversational skills via ASL	Yes —Used dual communication boards for minimum of 1 year —No functional speech —Use of ASL for conversation —Minimal interaction with co-workers —Age —Cognitive and sensory impairments
Sigafoos, Laurie, & Pennell (1996)	Request for objects via symbol on a	2 children with Rett syndrome (Parts 1 and 2)	(Parts 1 and 2) —Chronological age —Gender	No

Single-Subject Experimental Design	Intervention Procedures	Consistency of Results Across Subjects	Variables Possibly Contributing to Mixed Results
Alternating treatment design	Prompting	—	—
Multiple baseline design across contexts	Scaffolding	—	—
Multiple baseline probe design across subjects	Prompting	No —Differences with respect to: • Rate of learning • Topic maintenance skills	Subject —Cognitive levels —Possible etiology
Multiple probe across subjects (Parts 1 and 2)	—Reinforcement and prompting (Part 1)	No (Parts 1 and 2) —Differences with respect to % of requesting	Subjects (Parts 1 and 2) —No specific cognitive/language levels were reported

(*continues*)

Table 5.1 (*continued*)

Author(s)/Year	AAC Target Area(s)	#/Age/Disability of Subject(s)	Subject Variables Reported	Subject Selection Criteria
(2-part study)	communication board (Part 1) and/or a switch (Part 2)		—Etiology —Met AAMR criteria for mental retardation —Ambulation —Adaptive behavior —Language production —Language comprehension —No requesting	
Lasker, Hux, Garrett, Moncrief, & Eischeid (1997)	Written choice to enhance communication	3 adults with severe aphasia	—Chronological age —Gender —Etiology —Type/severity of aphasia —Type of CVA —Time post CVA —Hearing/vision —Years of education —History of intervention —Communication modes/ performance —Reading comprehension —Language comprehension	No
Koul & Harding (1998)	Identification and production of graphic symbols	5 adults with severe or global aphasia	—Chronological age —Gender —Etiology —Type/severity of aphasia —Type of CVA —Time post CVA —Years of education —Residential placement —History of speech-language intervention —No previous exposure to computer-based AAC intervention —Reading comprehension —Language comprehension	Yes —Ability to select symbols using a trackball or mouse —Adequate visual skills determined by ability to match symbols that are identical
Sigafoos & Roberts-Pennell (1999)	Rejecting via gesture or communication device	2 children with severe cognitive impairment	—Chronological age —Gender —Cognitive impairment (but no measures reported) —Educational placement —No history of AAC intervention —Language production —No use of appropriate rejecting —Language comprehension	No

Single-Subject Experimental Design	Intervention Procedures	Consistency of Results Across Subjects	Variables Possibly Contributing to Mixed Results
	—Reinforcement, shaping, and prompting (Part 2)		—Stage of Rett syndrome (Part 2)
Alternating treatment design	Written choice strategy varying visual/auditory information	No —Differences with respect to responses to the 3 written choice formats	Subject —Language comprehension skills —Reading skills
Multiple baseline design across behaviors	—Instruction —Feedback	No —Differences with respect to • % of symbols correctly identified and produced • Rate of learning symbols for particular grammatical categories • Ease of symbol production	Subject —Type/severity of aphasia —Language skills
Multiple baseline design across subjects	Prompting	No —Differences with respect to: • Baseline performance • Generalization	—Subjects appeared closely matched although no cognitive measures were reported —Authors attributed differences to methods

etiology. For the most part, researchers conducting these studies were careful to identify or report a number of participant variables, frequently including: (1) chronological age (all 20 studies); (2) gender (all 20 studies); (3) etiology (all 20 studies); (4) cognitive impairment (15 studies), although degree of impairment was not always specified; (5) educational placement (13 studies); (6) language production (all 20 studies); and (7) language comprehension (15 studies), although developmental levels of production and comprehension were not always specified.

A critical aspect of efficacy research in AAC is the inclusion of detailed information about the participants so that the findings can be more easily interpreted with respect to for whom the intervention will be most successful (Sevcik et al., 1999). The previously specified participant variables appear to lend themselves to this goal. However, other participant variables may also be important to consider. A less frequently reported participant variable in these studies involved AAC intervention history (e.g., previous experience/exposure to AAC technology). In fact, of the 20 efficacy studies conducted with individuals with congenital disorders, only five provided information pertaining to the particpants' history of using AAC (Buzolich, King, & Baroody, 1991; Iacono & Duncum, 1995; Remington & Clarke, 1993a, 1993b; Sigafoos & Roberts-Pennell, 1999). According to Sevcik et al. (1999), a consideration of intervention history is important in conducting efficacy research, especially in light of the increasing number of children who have had early exposure to AAC. The performance patterns of these children may be different from those who have had later exposure to AAC technologies.

Surprisingly, another infrequently reported particpant variable involved vision and hearing status. Only half (10 out of 20) of the studies pertaining to users with congenital disorders provided this information. Two others provided information only pertaining to hearing, excluding vision (Harris, Skarakis-Doyle, & Haaf, 1996; Iacono & Duncum, 1995). Given the fact that AAC systems involve visual symbols, whether aided or unaided, information pertaining to the visual status of AAC participants is critical.

Although information pertaining to the language comprehension of these participants was provided in 15 of the 20 studies reviewed, this is a participant variable that should be reported in each AAC efficacy study. Information about language production is not enough. Language production cannot predict language comprehension, especially when considering the population of augmented language learners (Nelson, 1992). Other reasons for including comprehension as a participant variable will be provided later in this chapter (in the section dealing with variables contributing to mixed findings across participants within studies).

Unfortunately, one participant variable was not reported in any of the reviewed efficacy studies involving participants with congenital disorders. This variable deals with the ethnicity of the participating participants. Most likely, it is to be assumed that all of the participating participants were white. In future efficacy studies, it will be important to identify AAC interventions that will be sensitive and effective with respect to the ethnic and cultural diversity of the population of AAC system users (Soto, Huer, & Taylor, 1997).

The discussion of one last issue related to participant variables in users with congenital disorders is warranted. This issue deals with the etiology or disability type of the participants. In each of the studies, researchers were careful to identify the disability type (e.g., cognitive, physical, visual) of the participants. This practice should continue in future efficacy research, as it contributes to more detailed descriptions of the participants, which could facilitate interpretation of the findings (Sevcik *et al.*, 1999). However, it is the opinion of Granlund and Olsson (1999), at least with respect to presymbolic communicators, that disability type has a weak to moderate impact on the outcome of communication intervention; whereas the communication status of the communicators, regardless of disability type, has a strong impact on outcomes. Other researchers have suggested that what is most important is "determining which individuals can best fulfill the particular requirements posed by the research question, not the disability status of the individuals studied" (Higginbotham & Bedrosian, 1995, pp. 11–12) (see also Chapter 4). In debate of this view, I would like to add that in my own experience conducting AAC efficacy research in the area of literacy, the disability type of the participants has had an impact on aspects of the intervention procedures or approaches selected. For example, intervention procedures employed with children who have severe speech impairments associated with cerebral palsy have been modified to include more structured teaching when employed with children who have severe speech impairments associated with autism. It is my belief that we cannot yet rule out the effect of participant disability type in AAC efficacy research until more data are available.

Of the 22 efficacy studies reviewed, only two involved adult participants with acquired disorders (Koul & Harding, 1998; Lasker *et al.*, 1997). The reported disability of these participants involved aphasia. Researchers conducting these studies were careful to identify and report a number of participant variables, including (1) chronological age, (2) gender, (3) type or severity of aphasia, (4) type of cerebrovascular accident (CVA), (5) time post CVA, (6) years of education, (7) history of intervention, (8) reading comprehension, (9) auditory comprehension, and (10) language production. Only one of the studies reported the hearing and vision status of the participants (Lasker *et al.*, 1997), and neither identified the ethnic background of the participants (again, requiring us to assume that all participants were white).

IV. WHAT IS THE NATURE OF THE ASSESSMENT TOOLS USED TO MEASURE LANGUAGE AND COGNITIVE PERFORMANCE IN THE PARTICIPANTS?

A variety of norm-referenced tools for measuring language and cognitive performance was employed across the studies reviewed pertaining to children and adults with congenital disorders. Examples of language comprehension tests included the *Peabody Picture Vocabulary Test-Revised* (*PPVT-R*) (Dunn & Dunn, 1981) and the *Test for Auditory Comprehension of Language-Revised* (*TACL-R*) (Carrow-Woolfolk, 1985). Language production tests included the *Expressive One Word Picture Vocabulary Test* (*EOWPVT*) (Gardner, 1990), and measures of cognition/intelligence included the *Weschler Intelligence Scale for Children-Revised* (*WISC-R*) (Weschler, 1974). When considering the norm-referenced tests employed, we are reminded of the importance of examining the characteristics of the population samples on which these tests were normed and determining if these characteristics are similar to those represented by our small samples of AAC system users. For the most part, the available cognitive and language assessment tools are not normed on individuals with severe speech or physical impairments, thereby possibly making their use inappropriate with these individuals. We also need to make certain that language tests normed on children are not given to the population of AAC adults with intellectual disabilities. Years ago, Calculator and Bedrosian (1988) cautioned researchers to avoid this practice. Research focusing on the development of appropriate norm-referenced assessment tools measuring language and cognitive performance of AAC system users is warranted.

It is important to point out, however, that some of the efficacy studies dealing with participants with congenital disorders did employ informal assessment methods (e.g., spontaneous language samples) for examining the language production of aided messages such as length and syntactic complexity, size of symbol lexicon, semantic functions, communicative functions, turn taking, and topic initiations/maintenance. The continued use of informal methods is critical for attaining a more representative picture of the language performance of these participants. When possible, it will be important for researchers to attach developmental levels to this performance so that it will be easier to interpret the findings in relation to the participants. This practice was not always performed in the studies reviewed.

Another assessment issue that was apparent in the studies involving participants with congenital disorders pertained to the reported information about cognitive performance. The majority of these studies was conducted with participants exhibiting some degree of cognitive impairment. In some cases, the researchers did not have access to scores from standardized tools for assessing cognitive performance. Rather, they reported that school records indicated that their participants had intellectual disabilities. Without providing information pertaining to the degree of cognitive impairment (through either reported IQ levels or developmental levels), it is again difficult to interpret the findings in relation to the participants.

A final assessment issue pertaining to AAC participants with congenital disorders, as well as those with acquired disorders, is that, frequently, obtained scores or measures are indicative of minimal levels of performance rather than optimal levels. Common participant factors negatively influencing performance include fatigue, unknown sensory deficits, and inappropriate response modes. The presence of any one of these factors could affect the reliability and validity of test performance. Cultural biases of assessment tools must also be considered.

The assessment tools employed in those studies focusing on adults with acquired disorders involving aphasia included the *Western Aphasia Battery* (Kertesz, 1980) and the *Boston Assessment of Severe Aphasia* (Helm-Estabrooks, Ramsberger, Morgan, & Nicholas (1989). These tools were appropriate for the participants.

V. HOW ARE PARTICIPANTS IN AAC EFFICACY RESEARCH SELECTED?

When conducting AAC efficacy research, participants should be selected based on the consideration of some type of criteria. The participant selection criteria must be clearly specified in order to foster accurate interpretation and generalization of the findings (i.e., external validity) (Bedrosian, 1999b). According to Higginbotham and Bedrosian (1995),

> When AAC users are incorporated in research without stringent subject-selection criteria, investigators frequently are presented with a highly diverse set of performance-related factors (e.g., sensory, perceptual, and physical status; language and cognitive skills; educational level) making the results difficult to interpret and generalize. . . . Even when such studies produce statistically or clinically significant findings, it is difficult to relate these findings to other individuals, particularly if they do not share the same characteristics of the subjects studied. (p. 11)

In some cases, the selection criteria may be narrow (e.g., a specific chronological age, a specific developmental level of language comprehension), whereas in other cases, they may be broader (e.g., a range of chronological ages, a range of developmental levels of language comprehension) (Bedrosian, 1999b). Likewise, in some cases "participants are matched on one or more inclusionary criteria or all include the same participant selection criteria" (Sevick *et al.*, 1999, p. 41). Sometimes researchers specify exclusionary criteria indicating participant variables excluded from the selection process (e.g., excluded were partcipants who exhibited: cognitive impairments, more than 10 intelligible spoken words). In any event, the participants' characteristics in relationship to the criteria need to be fully documented. Again, such criteria are critical to establishing external validity (this topic will be further discussed later in this chapter). Without specifying a selection criterion, even for those studies involving a single participant, it becomes difficult for others to determine the type of client for whom the intervention will be successful.

With this information in mind, let us now turn to the efficacy studies under review. How were the participants in these studies selected? Of the 22 studies reviewed, it was surprising to find that only six specified a participant selection criteria (see the participant selection criteria column in Table 5.1) (Durand, 1993; Heller, Allgood, Davis, Arnold, Castelle, & Taber, 1996; Hunt, Alwell, & Goetz, 1991; Iacono, Mirenda, & Beukelman, 1993; Koul & Harding, 1998; O'Keefe & Dattilo, 1992). All six of these studies were conducted with multiple participants, and all but one (Koul & Harding, 1998) was conducted with AAC users with congenital disorders. The number of participant variables listed in the selection criteria reported across studies ranged from two to six (mean of 3.83 variables per study). These variables included (1) degree of speech intelligibility (Heller *et al.*, 1996; Hunt *et al.*, 1991; Iacono *et al.*, 1993); (2) level of syntactic production (Hunt *et al.*, 1991); (3) turn-taking or interaction performance (Heller *et al.*, 1996; Hunt *et al.*, 1991); (4) chronological age (Heller *et al.*, 1996; O'Keefe & Dattilo, 1992); (5) etiology or type of disability (O'Keefe & Dattilo, 1992); (6) comprehension of instructions, questions, or commands (O'Keefe & Dattilo, 1992); (7) communication device type, need, or accessibility (Durand, 1993; Heller *et al.*, 1996; O'Keefe & Dattilo, 1992); (8) presence or absence of communication or target behaviors (Durand, 1993; O'Keefe & Dattilo, 1992); (9) hearing or vision status (Heller *et al.*, 1996; Iacono *et al.*, 1993; Koul & Harding, 1998); (10) size or type of symbol lexicon (Heller *et al.*, 1996; Iacono *et al.*, 1993); (11) cognitive status (Heller *et al.*, 1996); and (12) AAC selection technique (Koul & Harding, 1998).

Although the investigators of these studies should be commended for having included participant selection criteria, there are some notable problems. What is apparent from the data is the vagueness or lack of specificity and thoroughness of the variables used in the selection criteria across studies. This problem relates back to that discussed previously with respect to participant variables that are infrequently reported (e.g., hearing and vision status). It may be that some researchers are not yet certain about which participant variables are important to include in the selection criteria. This may be a reasonable explanation in light of the fact that AAC is still a relatively new science. However, research intuition would tell us that at least some participant variables absolutely must be included in selection criteria such as vision and hearing status and the degree of presence or absence of the target behavior(s) in baseline performance. As we shall see in a discussion that follows (which deals with specific variables contributing to mixed findings across participants within each study), certain cognitive and language variables must also be considered in the selection criteria of future AAC efficacy studies. These participant variables could act as guidelines in establishing valid selection criteria. Another surprising finding was that of the seven studies employing multiple baseline designs across participants (see the single-subject experimental design column in Table 5.1), four of them included a participant selection criteria (Durand, 1993; Heller et al., 1996; Hunt et al., 1991; O'Keefe & Dattilo, 1992), and three did not (Buzolich et al., 1991; Remington & Clarke, 1993a; Sigafoos & Roberts-Pennell, 1999). When using this particular single-subject experimental design, it is critical for the participants to be matched as closely as possible. McReynolds and Kearns (1983) stated, with respect to multiple baseline designs across participants, that "because a number of subjects are used to achieve control, subject characteristics take on greater importance" (p. 74). With this design, the effectiveness of the treatment variable is demonstrated when changes occur only in those participants receiving treatment, with no changes in the untreated participants, presuming that all of the participants are exposed to identical experimental conditions. Should no changes occur in one or more treated participants, it would be difficult to separate whether this is due to the lack of treatment effectiveness or differences in participant characteristics (R. Schlosser, personal communication, July 2000), especially if the participants displayed different characteristics from the onset. Thus, the use of participant selection criteria for this type of design may help to minimize sources of variability.

If participant selection criteria were only used in 6 of the 22 efficacy studies under review, how were the participants in the remaining studies selected? Probably the most common response to this question would relate to the availability of participants, given the low incidence of AAC users in the general population. To the credit of many of these researchers, however, variables on which the participants were matched were often reported, but appeared to be done as an afterthought. It would have been advisable for these researchers to consider these variables upfront in establishing selection criteria.

VI. WHAT IMPACT DOES PARTICIPANT SELECTION HAVE ON ESTABLISHING EXTERNAL VALIDITY?

Although fewer participants are needed for single-subject experimental designs as opposed to group designs, external validity, or generality of findings, is still a necessary component of these designs. External validity in single-subject research can be achieved through replication, of which there are generally two categories: direct and systematic (McReynolds & Kearns, 1983). Each of these types of replication will be discussed in relation to issues of participant selection. The efficacy studies under review will then be incorporated into each discussion.

A. DIRECT REPLICATION

Direct replication is essential for demonstrating the reliability and effectiveness of treatment for a given population (Barlow & Hersen, 1984). According to Sidman (1960), there are two types of direct replication: repetition of the same experiment on the same participant and repetition of the same experiment on more than one participant. Our attention will be directed toward the latter involving generality of findings across participants, as it occurs most frequently in single-subject experimental research. More specifically, "direct replication in applied research refers to administration of a given procedure by the same investigator or group of investigators in a specific setting . . . on a series of clients homogeneous for a particular behavior disorder" (Barlow & Hersen, 1984, p. 326). An experiment successfully conducted with one participant and successfully replicated across three more similar participants is sufficient for establishing external validity (Barlow & Hersen, 1984).

Of critical importance is that the participants must be as homogeneous as possible with respect to aspects of the target behavior as well as other relevant/background variables (Barlow & Hersen, 1984). If the participants are not homogeneous, two possible interpretations arise (Sidman, 1960). First, if the intervention is effective across heterogeneous participants, then there is "evidence of generality broader than would have been obtained if participants had been matched closely. Results would indicate that the treatment is not limited to a small, homogeneous group of clients, but applies to a larger, diverse group" (McReynolds & Kearns, 1983, p. 111). A problem occurs, however, when the participants are heterogeneous and the findings of the research are mixed—that is, some participants improve and others do not, or all participants improve but differ in their degree or rate of improvement. Specifically, if this happens, it is difficult to determine which of the participant variables was responsible for the differences, assuming that the treatment procedure was uniformly administered across participants by the same investigator(s). In such cases, according to McReynolds and Kearns (1983), participant characteristics provide a reasonable explanation for differences in performance.

The next step, then, would involve searching for the source of inter-participant variability (Sidman, 1960). This could be accomplished by examining or identifying characteristics that differentiate successful from unsuccessful participants (McReynolds & Kearns, 1983), and then bringing these participant variables under experimental control by systematically exploring their effects. According to Sidman (1960), "every time we discover and achieve control over a factor that contributes to variability, we increase the likelihood that our data will be reproducible with new participants and in different situations" (p. 152). Repeated measurement of the dependent variable along with changing and altering experimental designs can be used to search for variability (Barlow & Hersen, 1984).

Attempting to search for homogeneous participants for purposes of direct replication, then, is an important component of conducting AAC efficacy research. Granted, it is impossible in applied research to match participants on all variables (Barlow & Hersen, 1984), especially considering the heterogeneous population of AAC system users. Nevertheless, it is our challenge to figure out which participant variables are important to consider, to match participants on these variables, and to relinquish a match on variables of less importance (McReynolds & Kearns, 1983). Therefore, it is highly recommended that AAC researchers consistently employ participant selection criteria so that we can begin to sort through some of these issues. As long as it involves relevant participant variables, selection criteria may help to foster interpretation and generalization of the findings.

Having now addressed participant selection issues pertinent to direct replication, let us return to the AAC efficacy studies under review, specifically those involving multiple participants. Refer to the columns labeled consistency of results across participants and variables possibly contributing to mixed results in Table 5.1. The goals of this discussion are to (1) determine if the participants in these studies were homogeneous, (2) to look for the presence of mixed results as an indication of participant heterogeneity, and (3) to begin to identify participant variables possibly contributing to mixed results so that guidelines for inclusion of relevant participant selection variables can be established.

Of the 14 studies conducted with multiple participants involving children or adults with congenital disorders, none of them reported consistent findings across participants. It is important to point out, however, that each study reported that intervention was effective across all participants. Nevertheless, many differences were found in the performance across participants within each of these studies. Some of these differences were indicated by the researchers themselves, whereas other differences were detected through my own analysis of the data. Differences across participants were found with respect to a number of performance areas, most frequently involving (1) differences in generalization performance (Buzolich et al., 1991; Goodman & Remington, 1993; Hunt et al., 1991; O'Keefe & Dattilo, 1992; Sigafoos & Roberts-Pennell, 1999), (2) differences in the rate of using the target behavior after the onset of intervention (Durand, 1993; O'Keefe & Dattilo, 1992; Sigafoos, Laurie, & Pennell, 1996), and (3) differences in the rate of learning (including differences in the length of treatment phases or the amount of training time required) (Buzolich et al., 1991; Goodman & Remington, 1993; Heller et al., 1996; Iacono et al., 1993; Kozleski, 1991;

McNaughton & Tawney, 1993; O'Keefe & Dattilo, 1992; Remington & Clarke, 1993a, 1993b). Interestingly, these differences were apparent even in those few studies employing a participant selection criteria, perhaps suggesting that the criteria were either not specific enough or did not include relevant participant variables. In either case, the participants in these studies may not have been as homogeneous as we were led to believe.

Which variables may have contributed to these performance differences? Again, if researchers were consistent in the way the intervention methods were administered across participants, then participant variables provide a reasonable explanation (McReynolds & Kearns, 1983) for these differences. In some of the studies, participant variables possibly contributing to the mixed findings were indicated by the researchers themselves, whereas in other studies, potentially relevant participant variables were detected through my own analysis of the data. Overall, it appears that differences across participants with respect to their language and cognitive levels contributed to the mixed findings. Frequently, the lowest functioning participant in these studies exhibited the slowest rate of learning or the weakest generalization. In a few cases, this analysis is less certain as researchers did not always present specific cognitive and language levels of the participants. Recall that in some of the studies, information pertaining to the language comprehension of the participants was not provided.

How close, then, should cognitive and language levels be matched across such AAC participants so that the effects of language or communication intervention will be more consistent? Which participant variables should be included in the selection criteria? Unfortunately, these are difficult questions. An attempt is made here to offer a few guidelines or suggestions. First, for participants with congenital disorders functioning in sensorimotor stages of cognitive development or slightly higher, great care must be taken to more closely match language levels, for both comprehension and production, across participants. A gap of even as much as 6 months in these developmental levels across participants could have an impact on the effects of intervention. This was, in fact, the case in some of the studies reviewed. As cognitive and language levels extend beyond the sensorimotor period, larger gaps in language levels across participants may be more permissible. Second, we should attempt to report participant levels of language comprehension and closely match participants with respect to this variable. Information about language production is not enough. In any event, we should at least specify a minimum level of language comprehension as a selection criterion. Third, it may be important to also specify a minimum level of language production (e.g., length of aided/unaided message production, size of aided/unaided lexicon) as a selection criterion so that participants are more carefully matched. Finally, as previously discussed, variables pertaining to intervention history, sensory status, and the degree of presence or absence of the target behavior during baseline should also be included in the criteria.

Neither of the two studies conducted with multiple participants involving adults with acquired disorders (Koul & Harding, 1998; Lasker *et al.*, 1997) reported consistent findings across participants. It is important to point out, however, that each study reported that the intervention was effective across all participants. Nevertheless, differences were found in the performance across participants within each of these studies. In the Lasker *et al.* (1997) study, differences with respect to participant responses to each of the treatment conditions were found; while in the Koul and Harding (1998) study, differences with respect to the rate of learning and the rate of using the target behaviors were found despite the use of a selection criteria. The criteria in this latter case, however, may not have been specific or relevant enough. The suggested participant variables contributing to the performance differences across participants in these studies, just as in those studies with participants having congenital disorders, involved language skills and, in one case (Lasker *et al.*, 1997), literacy skills. Even though participants may have been matched according to the type and degree of aphasia, they may have represented "individuals with widely divergent residual skills" (Lasker *et al.*, 1997, p. 115). In the case of adults with acquired disorders, then, variables pertaining to expressive and receptive language should be considered in participant selection criteria, along with literacy skills when appropriate to the target behavior, intervention history, sensory status, and the presence or absence of the target behavior in baseline.

B. Systematic Replication

According to Hersen and Barlow (1976), systematic replication involves "exploring the effects of different settings, therapists or clients on a procedure previously demonstrated as successful in a direct replication series" (p. 62). With systematic replication, then, the researcher intentionally varies one or more of these variables to determine if treatment continues to be effective (McReynolds & Kearns, 1983). It is important to emphasize that direct replication should occur before systematic replication.

Unlike direct replications where participants are required to be closely matched, systematic replications allow and sometimes encourage participant heterogeneity (McReynolds & Kearns, 1983). Recall that direct replication with other participants who are closely matched (i.e., who meet the selection criteria) will establish the validity of the results for that specific population of AAC users with greater certainty. In contrast, systematic replication with a wider range of AAC participants will begin to establish the generality of results to other individuals who use AAC with different characteristics.

In this examination of the efficacy studies under review, the author may have unfairly assumed that the studies involving multiple participants were all attempts at direct replication. It is possible, based on the heterogeneity of the participants in these studies, that they were actually intended as systematic replications. Because the researchers in these studies do not directly specify them as direct or systematic replications, it is impossible to know for certain. Unfortunately, there are no guidelines to determine to what degree the participants should differ from each other to qualify as a systematic replication (McReynolds & Kearns, 1983). Nevertheless, with either direct or systematic replications, the arguments surrounding interpretations when mixed findings are obtained still apply.

When viewing the AAC field and its heterogeneous populations, it appears that it would be much easier to conduct efficacy studies involving systematic replications as opposed to direct replications, even though direct replications should occur prior to systematic replications. Of overriding importance is that the participants should be described in enough detail, including all relevant participant variables in a selection criteria, so that we will be able to accurately determine the type of AAC users for whom intervention will be effective.

VII. CLOSING COMMENTS

This chapter addressed several issues pertinent to participant selection in AAC efficacy research. Because of the heterogeneity inherent in the population of AAC users, our task in appropriately selecting participants is not an easy one. However, our future AAC efficacy research efforts with respect to participant selection will be strengthened if we can begin to (1) employ selection criteria, even if only a single participant is used, in order to foster accurate interpretations and generalizations of the findings, (2) recognize that we do have some preliminary data suggesting which participant variables are important to consider, and (3) develop appropriate language and cognitive assessment tools. We should work together as an international community of researchers and evidence-based practitioners to set higher standards for the efficacy research conducted in our field. We must strive to go beyond participant selection based solely on availability.

REFERENCES

Barlow, D. H., & Hersen, M. (1984). *Single case experimental designs: Strategies for studying behavior change* (2nd ed.). New York: Pergamon Press.

Bedrosian, J. L. (1995). Limitations in the use of nondisabled subjects in AAC research. *Augmentative and Alternative Communication, 11*, 6–10.

Bedrosian, J. L. (1999a). AAC efficacy research: Challenges for the new century. *Augmentative and Alternative Communication, 15*, 2–3.

Bedrosian, J. L. (1999b). Efficacy research issues in AAC: Interactive storybook reading. *Augmentative and Alternative Communication, 15,* 45–55.

Buzolich, M. J., King, J. S., & Baroody, S. M. (1991). Acquisition of the commenting function among system users. *Augmentative and Alternative Communication, 7,* 88–99.

Calculator, S. N. (1999). AAC outcomes for children and youths with severe disabilities: When seeing is believing. *Augmentative and Alternative Communication, 15,* 4–12.

Calculator, S. N., & Bedrosian, J. L. (1988). *Communication assessment and intervention for adults with mental retardation.* Austin, TX: Pro-ed.

Carrow-Woolfolk, E. (1985). *Test for Auditory Comprehension of Language-Revised (TACL-R).* Austin, TX: Pro-Ed.

Dunn, L. M., & Dunn, L. M. (1981). *Peabody Picture Vocabulary Test-Revised (PPVT-R).* Circle Pines, MN: American Guidance Services.

Durand, V. M. (1993). Functional communication training using assistive devices: Effects on challenging behavior and affect. *Augmentative and Alternative Communication, 9,* 168–176.

Gardner, M. (1990). *Expressive One Word Picture Vocabulary Test-Revised (EOWPVT-R).* Austin, TX: Pro-ed.

Goodman, J., & Remington, B. (1993). Acquisition of expressive signing: Comparison of reinforcement strategies. *Augmentative and Alternative Communication, 9,* 26–35.

Granlund, M., & Olsson, C. (1999). Efficacy of communication intervention for presymbolic communicators. *Augmentative and Alternative Communication, 15,* 25–37.

Hamilton, B. L., & Snell, M. E. (1993). Using the milieu approach to increase spontaneous communication book use across environments by an adolescent with autism. *Augmentative and Alternative Communication, 9,* 259–272.

Harris, L., Skarakis-Doyle, E., & Haaf, R. (1996). Language treatment approach for users of AAC: Experimental single-subject investigation. *Augmentative and Alternative Communication, 12,* 230–243.

Heller, K. W., Allgood, M. H., Davis, B., Arnold, S. E., Castelle, M. D., & Taber, T. A. (1996). Promoting nontask-related communication at vocational sites. *Augmentative and Alternative Communication, 12,* 169–178.

Helm-Estabrooks, N., Ramsberger, G., Morgan, A. R., & Nicholas, M. (1989). *Boston Assessment of Severe Aphasia.* Austin, TX: Pro-ed.

Hersen, M., & Barlow, D. H. (1976). *Single case experimental designs: Strategies for studying behavior change.* New York: Pergamon Press.

Higginbotham, D. J., & Bedrosian, J. L. (1995). Subject selection in AAC research: Decision points. *Augmentative and Alternative Communication, 11,* 11–13.

Horn, E. M., & Jones, H. A. (1996). Comparison of two selection techniques used in augmentative and alternative communication. *Augmentative and Alternative Communication, 12,* 23–31.

Hunt, P., Alwell, M., & Goetz, L. (1991). Interacting with peers through conversation turntaking with a communication book adaptation. *Augmentative and Alternative Communication, 7,* 117–126.

Iacono, T. A., & Duncum, J. E. (1995). Comparison of sign alone and in combination with an electronic communication device in early language intervention: Case study. *Augmentative and Alternative Communication, 11,* 249–259.

Iacono, T., Mirenda, P., & Beukelman, D. (1993). Comparison of unimodal and multimodal AAC techniques for children with intellectual disabilities. *Augmentative and Alternative Communication, 9,* 83–94.

Kertesz, A. (1980). *Western Aphasia Battery.* London, Ontario: University of Western Ontario.

Kiesler, D. J. (1966). Some myths of psychotherapy research and the search for a paradigm. *Psychological Bulletin, 65,* 110–136.

Koul, R. K., & Harding, R. (1998). Identification and production of graphic symbols by individuals with aphasia: Efficacy of a software application. *Augmentative and Alternative Communication, 14,* 11–23.

Kozleski, E. B. (1991). Expectant delay procedure for teaching requests. *Augmentative and Alternative Communication, 7*, 11–19.

Lasker, J., Hux, K., Garrett, K. L., Moncrief, E. M., & Eischeid, T. J. (1997). Variations on the written choice communication strategy for individuals with severe aphasia. *Augmentative and Alternative Communication, 13*, 108–116.

Light, J. C. (1999). Do augmentative and alternative communication interventions really make a difference?: The challenges of efficacy research. *Augmentative and Alternative Communication, 15*, 13–24.

McGregor, G., Young, J., Gerak, J., Thomas, B., & Vogelsberg, T. (1992). Increasing functional use of an assistive communication device by a student with severe disabilities. *Augmentative and Alternative Communication, 8*, 243–250.

McNaughton, D., & Tawney, J. (1993). Comparison of two spelling instruction techniques for adults who use augmentative and alternative communication. *Augmentative and Alternative Communication, 9*, 72–82.

McReynolds, L. V., & Kearns, K. P. (1983). *Single-subject experimental designs in communicative disorders.* Baltimore: University Park Press.

Nelson, N. W. (1992). Performance is the prize: Language competence and performance among AAC users. *Augmentative and Alternative Communication, 8*, 3–18.

O'Keefe, B. M., & Dattilo, J. (1992). Teaching the response-recode form to adults with mental retardation using AAC systems. *Augmentative and Alternative Communication, 8*, 224–233.

Remington, B. (1991). Why use single subject methods in AAC? In J. Brodin & E. Bjorck-Åkesson (Eds.), *Methodological issues in research in augmentative and alternative communication. Proceedings from the First ISAAC Research Symposium* (pp. 74–78). Stockholm, Sweden: The Swedish Handicap Institute.

Remington, B., & Clarke, S. (1993a). Simultaneous communication and speech comprehension. Part I: Comparison of two methods of teaching expressive signing and speech comprehension skills. *Augmentative and Alternative Communication, 9*, 36–48.

Remington, B., & Clarke, S. (1993b). Simultaneous communication and speech comprehension. Part II: Comparison of two methods of overcoming selective attention during expressive sign training. *Augmentative and Alternative Communication, 9*, 49–60.

Romski, M., & Sevcik, R. (1988). Augmentative and alternative communication systems: Considerations for individuals with severe intellectual disabilities. *Augmentative and Alternative Communication, 4*, 83–93.

Schlosser, R. W. (1999). Comparative efficacy of interventions in augmentative and alternative communication. *Augmentative and Alternative Communication, 15*, 56–68.

Schweigert, P., & Rowland, C. (1992). Early communication and microtechnology: Instructional sequence and case studies of children with severe multiple disabilities. *Augmentative and Alternative Communication, 8*, 273–286.

Sevcik, R. A., Romski, M. A., & Adamson, L. B. (1999). Measuring AAC interventions for individuals with severe developmental disabilities. *Augmentative and Alternative Communication, 15*, 38–44.

Sidman, M. (1960). *Tactics of scientific research: Evaluating experimental data in psychology.* New York: Basic Books.

Sigafoos, J., Laurie, S., & Pennell, D. (1996). Teaching children with Rett syndrome to request preferred objects using aided communication: Two preliminary studies. *Augmentative and Alternative Communication, 12*, 88–96.

Sigafoos, J., & Roberts-Pennell, D. (1999). Wrong-item format: A promising intervention for teaching socially appropriate forms of rejecting to children with developmental disabilities? *Augmentative and Alternative Communication, 15*, 135–140.

Soto, G., Huer, M. B., & Taylor, O. (1997). Multicultural issues. In L. L. Lloyd, D. R. Fuller, & H. H. Arvidson (Eds.), *Augmentative and alternative communication: A handbook of principles and practices* (pp. 406–413). Needham Heights, MA: Allyn & Bacon.

Todman, J., & Dugard, P. (1999). Accessible randomization tests for single-case and small-n experimental designs in AAC research. *Augmentative and Alternative Communication, 15,* 69–82.

Vaughn, B., & Horner, R. H. (1995). Effects of concrete versus verbal choice systems on problem behavior. *Augmentative and Alternative Communication, 11,* 89–92.

Wechsler, D. (1974). *Wechsler Intelligence Scale for Children-Revised (WISC-R).* San Antonio, TX: The Psychological Corporation.

CHAPTER 6

Single-Subject Experimental Designs[1]

Ralf W. Schlosser
Department of Speech-Language Pathology and Audiology
Northeastern University

[1]Small portions of this chapter were presented at the Research Symposium of the International Society for Augmentative and Alternative Communication (ISAAC) in Washington D.C., in August 2000 and were published in its proceedings: Schlosser, R. W. (2001). Common pitfalls and solutions in designing and interpreting single-subject experiments. In S. von Tetzchner & J. Clibbens (Eds.), *Understanding the theoretical and methodological bases of augmentative and alternative communication* (pp. 112–118). Toronto: International Society for Augmentative and Alternative Communication. The writing of this chapter was made possible through support from a Distinguished Switzer Fellowship (H133F010010) from the National Institute on Disability and Rehabilitation Research.

The Efficacy of Augmentative and Alternative Communication

I. INTRODUCTION

Single-subject experimental designs can provide a sound basis for determining the efficacy of interventions in augmentative and alternative communication (AAC). In this chapter (1) the main types of designs for evaluating behavior change, generalization, and maintenance and for comparing multiple interventions using examples from the AAC literature are reviewed; (2) common pitfalls are illustrated, and (3) solutions are offered. Readers who wish to learn about single-subject experimental designs beyond the scope of this chapter may consult any of the texts available in the fields of applied behavior analysis, special education, and psychology (e.g., Barlow & Hersen, 1984; Franklin, Allison, & Gorman, 1997; Julius, Schlosser, & Goetze, 2000; Kazdin, 1982; McReynolds & Kearns, 1983; Tawney & Gast, 1984; Todman & Dugard, 2001). Intervention research typically follows a progression from evaluating the efficacy of *one* intervention to evaluating the comparative efficacy of *multiple* interventions. Therefore, this chapter is organized to follow this progression.

II. EVALUATING BEHAVIOR CHANGE IN AAC INTERVENTIONS

When evaluating behavior change, the researcher is interested in determining whether a particular AAC intervention resulted in the behavior change targeted. "Targeted" is the operative word here. It is the taught behavior that is of relevance rather than some generalized instance of that skill. For example, a practitioner teaching an individual to use automatic linear scanning with a set of four line drawings would evaluate whether this person is able to scan these same four line drawings. The following section first examines, the role of the preexperimental AB design in AAC intervention research. Next, designs are introduced that lend themselves to an evaluation of behavior change resulting from one AAC intervention, including the ABA design, the ABAB design, the multiple-baseline design, and the multiple-probe design.

A. EVALUATING BEHAVIOR CHANGE IN ONE AAC INTERVENTION

1. AB Design

In an AB design, an initial baseline is followed by an intervention phase and the data are analyzed by visually comparing the data between the two phases (see Figure. 6.1). Occasionally, AB designs also include a follow-up phase or maintenance phase (Kazdin, 1982).

A common pitfall is to utilize an AB design for evaluating behavior change without recognizing its limitations. When using an AB design, one cannot be

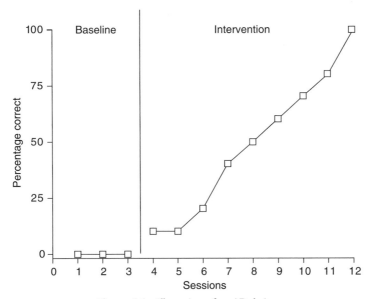

Figure 6.1 Illustration of an AB design.

sure whether the behavior would have changed in the desired direction even without introducing the intervention. That is why, among other reasons, AB designs are considered preexperimental. Basically, they do not allow the evidence-based practitioner to rule out the commonly encountered threats to internal validity discussed in Chapter 3, such as maturation, history, and so forth. AB designs have been used to some degree in the AAC field (e.g., Calculator & Dollaghan, 1982; Glennen & Calculator, 1985; Locke & Mirenda, 1988; Spiegel, Benjamin, & Spiegel, 1993).

Glennen and Calculator (1985), for example, used an AB design, replicated across two subjects, to examine the effects of using a treatment package (consisting of expected delay along with structured communicative events and modeling and imitation) on the requesting of objects. The increases in observed requesting during the intervention phase across participants were considered an indicator of the effectiveness of the intervention. The limitations of the design and how that would affect the conclusions to be drawn concerning the effectiveness of the treatment, however, need to be taken into account. As indicated in Chapter 12, such awareness of the limitations imposed by the use of a preexperimental design is essential for implementing evidence-based practice. Should the setting or specific circumstance allow only for the use of an AB design, it is nonetheless important that the limitations of this design be discussed in terms of their implications for concluding its effectiveness. Even though AB designs are preexperimental, they can generate interesting hypotheses and avenues for future research. As such they are similar to many case studies (see McEwen & Karlan, 1990, for a discussion of case studies). Another solution to this situation, if the circumstances permit, is to avoid using an AB design altogether, considering its shortcomings. Instead, the clinician may explore other design options such as multiple-baseline designs (discussed later) or withdrawal designs, which will be discussed next.

2. ABA Design

To yield results with a greater degree of internal validity than possible with an AB design, one has to add at least one more experimental phase, which will result in an ABA design. The ABA design constitutes the most basic experimental design for evaluating the efficacy of an intervention. This design involves a baseline (A), followed by intervention (B), and a return to baseline (A) (see Figure 6.2 for a hypothetical example). The intervention is considered effective when the behavior changes in the desired direction in the B phase, and the behavior changes again in the following A phase in the direction of the original baseline. The ABA design is superior to the AB design because it demonstrates some experimental control through introducing and later withdrawing treatment. Accordingly, the data in Figure 6.2 suggest that the intervention had an effect.

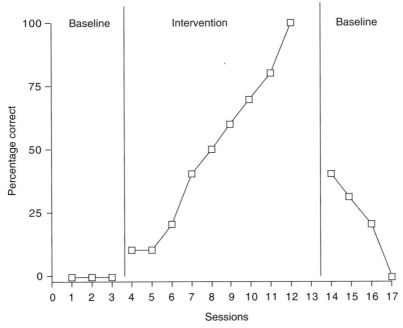

Figure 6.2 Illustration of an ABA design.

ABA designs are not as common in the AAC literature although they are used on occasion (e.g., Schweigert, 1989; Schweigert & Rowland, 1992), possibly because they invoke ethical issues due to ending the intervention on a non-treatment phase. This design may be a difficult sell because many stakeholders, such as parents of an AAC users, are understandably not as concerned as are scientists about demonstrating the efficacy of an intervention in a manner that is consistent with scientific principles. Rather, they are interested in interventions that help the recipient of the intervention. Thus, taking away something that seemingly works is difficult to explain in these terms. Another reason for the infrequent use of this design may pertain to the type of behaviors typically taught in AAC interventions. It can be argued that many of these behaviors are not susceptible to changes on withdrawal of treatment. For example, once a learner has managed to request preferred activities, it is unlikely that the learner will discontinue requesting these same activities just because the treatment is withheld. Similarly, once a learner has learned to spell target words, it is questionable whether this learner will forget how to spell the words once the training is withdrawn. On the other hand, someone who is taught to request through appropriate means rather than engaging in challenging behavior may very well be susceptible to the withdrawal of treatment (e.g., withdrawal of contingent social attention). This may particularly hold true in the initial stages of functional communication training where it is especially important to reinforce every appropriate communicative attempt (Durand, 1990). In summary, withdrawal designs may not be as applicable to many AAC interventions or, at the very least, they need to be carefully selected.

Thus, a possible pitfall is to choose a withdrawal design for behaviors that are not susceptible to changes upon withdrawing the treatment, accompanied by the potentially erroneous conclusion that the treatment was not effective. Behaviors that are not susceptible to treatment withdrawal are those that cannot be unlearned such as those mentioned earlier. A potential solution is for the clinician to determine a priori whether or not the behavior is going to be susceptible to treatment withdrawal. If so, withdrawal designs are an option. Whenever possible, the clinician may find it useful to consult previous research to assist with this a priori determination. If withdrawal designs are not an option, the clinician may want to explore the feasibility of a multiple-baseline design (discussed later).

3. ABAB Design

The ABAB design extends the ABA design by reintroducing the intervention. In doing so, the ABAB design circumvents one of the major ethical shortcomings of the ABA design, which is the ending on a nontreatment phase. By ending on an intervention phase, the study can be ended on a more positive note, especially in studies where the intervention appears to work well. Figure 6.3 provides a fictitious example of an ABAB design.

As Figure 6.3 illustrates, this design works similarly to the ABA design with the additional return to an intervention phase. The logic of the ABAB design suggests that for an intervention to be considered effective, the behavior will not only change in the desired direction during the first B phase, but also return to that level in the second B phase. From an experimental point of view, the ABAB design allows for the demonstration of experimental control three times (A to B, B to A, and A to B).

The ABAB design has been used on several occasions to study the efficacy of AAC interventions (e.g., Kouri, 1988; Rotholz, Berkowitz, & Burberry, 1989; Schweigert, 1989; Vaughn & Horner, 1995). Vaughn and Horner (1995) examined the effects of using concrete (i.e., via graphic symbols plus spoken words) versus verbal modes by the instructor on choice-making and challenging behaviors in Karl, an adult with autism and severe intellectual disabilities. During baseline, the A phase, Karl's meal choices were offered verbally by staff. During intervention, the B phase, his meal choices were presented via photographs in addition to spoken words. Subsequently, in the second A phase, Karl's choices were pre-

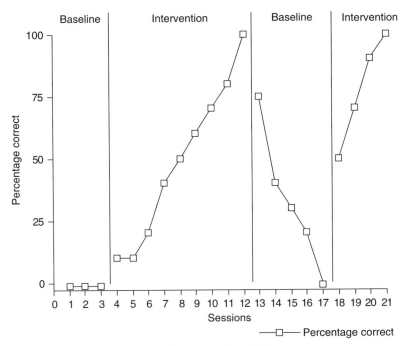

Figure 6.3   Illustration of an ABAB design.

sented again only verbally analogous to baseline. Finally, the intervention was reinstated in the second B phase. Results indicate that the presentation via photographs and spoken words resulted in more acceptances by Karl and less challenging behaviors. Rotholz *et al.* (1989) studied two communication modes in terms of the percentage of successful requests for ordering fast food in two students with autism. The ABAB design was combined with a multiple-baseline design across two subjects. During baseline, the A phase, the participants requested their choices using manual signs—their existing mode. Subsequently, during the B phase, the students were introduced to the use of communication boards and taught how to point to graphic symbols to communicate their request. Next, the intervention was withdrawn to return to the second A phase. Finally, the intervention was reinstated in the second B phase. Results indicated that the use of communication boards resulted in more successful requests than signing with both participants in this community setting.

The authors in both cases described their research as comparison studies between two modes. Is this justifiable? Although it is one of the hallmarks of evaluating effectiveness in single-subject experiment designs to compare an intervention phase with a baseline phase in a given participant, ABAB designs have serious limitations for truly serving as a comparison design. For one thing, ABAB designs are limited in their conclusion only to a specific sequence of events—that is, they do not allow the ruling out of order effects. In other words, it remains an unknown whether communication boards are really more effective than signing or whether this is simply an artifact of the particular sequence in which the two modes were studied (i.e., communication board use followed manual signing). Moreover, in both of these studies, the effects of *existing* communication modes were monitored during baseline before introducing new modes of communication that were deemed more effective. This is quite different from comparing two interventions (one with signing and one with communication boards).

In summary, the ABAB design bypasses some of the ethical shortcomings of an ABA design while demonstrating great potential for studying the functional relation between an independent variable and a dependent variable. As such, the ABAB design has considerable application potential in AAC. Frequently, however, viewing the results from this design as comparisons often causes authors to overstate the implications of their findings without sufficient regard to internal validity considerations.

4. Multiple-Baseline Designs

Previously discussed design options for evaluating the effectiveness of one intervention involved the withdrawal or reversal of an intervention in order to demonstrate experimental control. Although this may be desirable from an experimental perspective, many clinicians, educators, and parents may feel uncomfortable with such a strategy because it means that treatment is taken away even after it appears to have been working.

The multiple-baseline design (MBD) (and its variants to be discussed later), first introduced in the applied behavior analysis literature by Baer, Wolf, and Risley (1968), offers an alternative (Barlow & Hersen, 1984). As its name indicates, the MBD includes multiple baselines with the baselines being extended sequentially from the first to the second baseline, the second to the third baseline, and so forth. Accordingly, the intervention is introduced sequentially rather than simultaneously across the multiple baselines. In general, MBDs may be run across (1) settings, (2) behaviors, or (3) subjects. Table 6.1 offers published examples of AAC intervention research that employed MBDs, categorized with respect to MBD type. Each of the three basic MBD types is illustrated using selected examples from the research listed in Table 6.1.

a. Multiple-Baseline Design across Settings

In the MBD across settings, the intervention may be introduced in the school setting first while baselines are extended and monitored in the group

Table 6.1

Examples of Multiple-Baseline Designs from AAC Intervention Research

Author(s)	Type of MBD	Participants
Alberto, Briggs, Sharpton, & Goldstein (1981)	Across behaviors (response dimensions of "yes" and "no")	One child with severe intellectual disabilities and cerebral palsy
Angelo & Goldstein (1990)	Across behaviors (information request types)	Four children with developmental disabilities
Buzolich et al. (1991)	Across subjects (students)	Three students with physical disabilities
Carr et al. (1978)	Across behaviors (objects)	Four children with autism
Carr & Kologinsky (1983)	Across subjects (students) (combined with a reversal design)	Three children with developmental disabilities
Ducker & Moonen (1986)	Across behaviors (signs)	Three children with Down syndrome
Duker & Michielsen (1983)	Across behaviors (signs)	Three children with severe intellectual disabilities
Duker & Morsink (1984)	Across behaviors (instructions)	Two adults with intellectual disabilities (experiment one); two children with intellectual disabilities (experiment 2)
Durand (1993)	Across subjects (students)	Three students with severe disabilities and challenging behaviors
Gobbi, Cipani, Hudson, & Lapenta-Neudeck (1986)	Across behaviors (food and drink referents)	Two students with severe intellectual disabilities
Harris, Skarakis, Doyle, & Haaf (1996)	Across settings (discourse contexts)	One young child with developmental verbal apraxia
Hunt, Alwell, Goetz, & Sailor (1990)	Across subjects (students)	Three students with severe disabilities
Iacono et al. (1993)	Across behaviors (types of two-word combinations) combined with ATD	Two young children with intellectual disabilities
Kaiser, Ostrosky, & Alpert (1993)	Across subjects (triads of teacher, target child, and generalization child)	Three teachers; three target nonspeaking preschoolers with developmental disabilities; three generalization children
Kotkin, Simpson, & Desanto (1978)	Across behaviors (verbal lablels)	Two children with Down syndrome

(continues)

Table 6.1 (*continued*)

Author(s)	Type of MBD	Participants
Light *et al.* (1992)	Across subjects (learner-facilitator dyads)	Two young adults with severe motor and speech impairments and three facilitators
McGregor *et al.* (1992)	Across settings	One young adult with physical disabilities
O'Keefe & Dattilo (1992)	Across subjects	Three adults with intellectual disabilities
Reid & Hurlbut (1977)	Across subjects (adults)	Four adults with multiple disabilities
Remington & Clarke (1983)	Across behaviors (signs) (combined with ATD)	Two children with autism
Rotholz *et al.* (1989)	Across subjects (combined with ABAB)	Two students with autism
Schuebel & Lalli (1992)	Across behaviors (objects)	One adult with intellectual disabilities
Sigafoos *et al.* (1996)	Across subjects	Two girls with Rett syndrome
Soto *et al.* (1993)	Across settings (combined with ATD)	One young adult with profound intellectual disabilities

home and community. Then, after several sessions, the intervention is introduced in the group home, while baseline continues to be monitored in the community. Finally, intervention is introduced in the community as well. The term "setting" is to be understood in its broadest sense, including locations such as school and community, activities such leisure and household activities, contexts such as discourse or instructional formats, and so forth. Figure 6.4 illustrates the structure of the MBD across settings.

The logic of the MBD works such that the experimenter or evidence-based practitioner is expected to see desired changes in the setting where the intervention is introduced while observing no changes in the yet untreated baselines. Specifically, when intervention is introduced in the school, the evidence-based practitioner is to expect changes only in the school and not in the group home or the community until intervention is introduced in these settings as well. Similarly, once intervention is introduced in the group home, changes are to be expected in the group home settings without observing changes in the yet untreated community setting. It is the marked areas of overlap among the first intervention phase and the yet untreated baselines (see Figure 6.4) that constitute the window of opportunity for extraneous variables (i.e., variables other than the intervention) to display their influence. An intervention is considered effec-

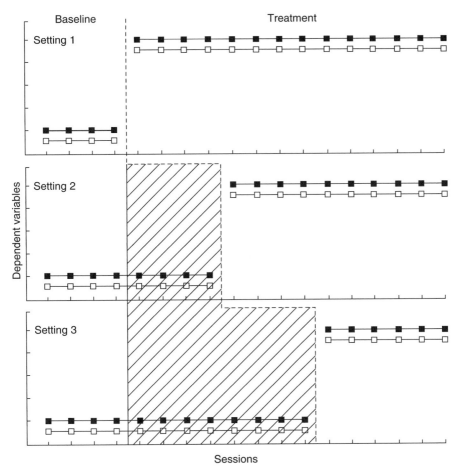

Figure 6.4   Illustration of the MBD across settings.

tive if desired changes are consistently observed in the treated baselines only once the intervention is introduced, rather than before the intervention is introduced. Alternatively, an intervention is considered ineffective if the desired changes in the treated baselines are not observed or the changes occur in the as of yet untreated baselines.

Several examples of MBDs across settings are available in the extant AAC intervention literature (e.g., Buzolich, King, & Baroody, 1991; McGregor, Young, Gerak, Thomas, & Vogelsberg, 1992; see also Table 6.1). McGregor *et al.* (1992) evaluated the effectiveness of preinstruction and natural-environment teaching on the functional use of a speech-generating device (SGD) across three school settings. Because desirable changes were observed once intervention was introduced in each setting and there were no notable changes in the untreated baselines, the authors appropriately concluded that the intervention was effective. In other applications of the MBD across settings, however, considerable changes were noted in some of the *untreated* baselines. In the study by Buzolich *et al.* (1991), for example, the intervention was reported to be effective when, in fact, the influence of extraneous variables cannot be ruled out due to changes in the untreated baselines (this is discussed further in Section III, "Evaluating Generalization").

b. Multiple-Baseline Design across Behaviors

The same logic described for MBDs across settings also applies to MBDs across behaviors. In the MBD across behaviors, the clinician applies the same treatment to separate target behaviors in a single participant. Figure 6.4 applies with the exception that the settings would be replaced with behaviors. The term "behaviors" refers to a wide variety of behaviors, including but not limited to referents, symbols, information request types, word combinations, and so forth. Regardless of which type of behavior it is, the target behaviors selected should be independent of each other, but otherwise related. The selection of *independent* behaviors is important in order to minimize the danger that treatment of one behavior will influence performance of the yet untreated behaviors. This would render an equivocal demonstration of effectiveness. This is not always practiced in the field as demonstrated in the next paragraphs. Selecting independent behavior is an important step, but it is not the only necessary step to a fruitful application of the MBD across behaviors. At the same time, the behaviors selected need to be *related* to one another. This requirement is crucial because the behaviors need to be susceptible to *one and the same* treatment—it is not legitimate within the MBD to apply different treatments to different behaviors (or settings and subjects for that matter) as the application of the same treatment ensures a replication function. The design cannot serve this function if different treatments are applied. Thus, the interventionist needs to walk a fine line between independent yet related behaviors.

The MBD across behaviors has been implemented extensively in the field (see Table 6.1 for a list of examples). Angelo and Goldstein (1990), for example, evaluated the effectiveness of a pragmatic teaching strategy on children's ability to initiate requests for information using the MBD across three types of requests for information (i.e., who, what, where). Treatment was first introduced to teach information requests for "who" while monitoring baselines for "what" and "where." Sequentially, treatment was applied to "what" and last to "where." In this successful application of the MBD, it is clear that the behaviors are related (they are all types of information requests), yet they are independent of one another. There is no scientific basis to assume that the acquisition of the "who" request type will assist a learner to acquire the "what" type without training. The last group of MBDs is the MBD across subjects.

c. Multiple-Baseline Design across Subjects

Again, the same underlying logic applies to this type of MDB. The MBD across subjects may be implemented with (potential) AAC users, parents, teachers, or any other communication partners. In essence, anyone who is the intended recipient of an intervention (also known as a direct stakeholder, see Chapter 10) could conceivably participate in MBDs across subjects. As such, MBDs across subjects may involve dyads of interactants should the dyad be the target of the intervention as was the case in a study on facilitator training (Light, Dattilo, English, Gutierrez, & Hartz, 1992). Here, dyads involving two young adults and their three facilitators served as the participants. Data were monitored for both, learner behavior and facilitator behavior. Table 6.1 presents further applications of the MBD across subjects.

5. Nonconcurrent Multiple-Baseline Design

When participants are available only in succession rather than concurrently, Watson and Workman (1981) proposed the use of the nonconcurrent MBD. With this design, the experimenter determines a priori the lengths of each of several baselines (e.g., 5, 10, 15 days) and when a given participant becomes available, this participant is randomly assigned to one of the predetermined baseline lengths. Todman and Dugard (2001) recommended a strategy for randomly determining when to end baseline and when to start the first intervention session. This approach might be useful in particular with the nonconcurrent MBD.

Some reasons for participants being available only sequentially include the following. First, the target behavior of interest may not be available across a sufficiently large number of clients. Second, there may not be a large enough pool of subjects displaying amenability to the particular intervention in need of efficacy evaluation. Third, there may not be enough subjects displaying a certain rare syndrome (e.g., Angelman's syndrome). Typical AAC service delivery systems may be confronted with such situations repeatedly. Therefore, the nonconcurrent MBD may represent a viable option for evaluating the efficacy of AAC intervention in typical service delivery situations. The nonconcurrent MBD has not been applied in AAC as far as this author can tell. As Chapter 3 indicates, however, the ability to minimize history as a threat to internal validity is greatly diminished because the participants are not assessed concurrently (Barlow & Hersen, 1984). Thus, whenever possible, the standard MBD is preferred over the nonconcurrent MBD.

6. Multiple-Probe Design

Whereas the previously discussed MBD requires continuous data collection, the multiple probe design (MPD) permits noncontinuous data collection. In general, continuous data collection is preferred because it provides the clinician with a complete rather than an erratic picture of a participant's performance. MPDs have been used extensively in the field (Culatta & Blackstone, 1980; Dattilo & Camarata, 1991; Fitzgerald, Reid, Schepis, Faw, Welty, & Pyfer, 1984; Hamilton & Snell, 1993; Hetzroni & Belfiore, 2000; Hinderscheit & Reichle, 1987; Hunt, Alwell, & Goetz, 1991a; Light, 1993; Reichle, Barrett, Tetlie, & McQuarter, 1987; Reichle, Rogers, & Barrett, 1984; Schepis & Reid, 1995; Sigafoos, Laurie, & Pennell, 1996; Sigafoos & Reichle, 1992; Sommer, Whitman, & Keogh, 1988; Stephenson & Linfoot, 1995; Sternberg, McNerney, & Pegnatore, 1987; Sternberg, Pegnatore, & Hill, 1983; Turner & Carter, 1994). Given this extensive utilization, when is it appropriate to use the MPD, or rather are there situations where it is inappropriate?

a. When Should One Use the Multiple Probe Design?

Frequently, MPDs are chosen without the provision of any rationale. This leaves the reader with the notion that perhaps the only reason for an author to have chosen the MPD was its resource efficiency. "Less effort," however, is not one of the accepted reasons for determining when the use of the MPD is appropriate (Horner & Baer, 1978). So what are some of the legitimate rationales for using the MPD according to Horner and Baer (1978)? One reason is when repeated measurement required by continuous data collection could result in reactivity—that is, the behavior would change simply from being observed repeatedly rather than from the treatment. Here it may be advisable to use the MPD to minimize potential reactivity effects. Another situation may be when continuous data collection is not feasible due to the setting or behavior observed. For example, in a recent study, Schlosser, McGhie-Richmond, Blackstien-Adler, Mirenda, Antonius, and Janzen (2000) evaluated a student's participation in the classroom during literacy and math activities using the MPD across instructional formats. Using the MBD was not feasible because the specific activities targeted did not occur on a continuous and regular basis. The research design had to follow the curriculum rather than the curriculum following the research design. A third situation for using the MPD might be presented when an a priori assumption of stability can be made. For example, if a practitioner were to introduce Lexigrams to a beginning communicator (e.g., Van Acker & Grant, 1995), it would be safe to assume that the baseline is going to be stable and at zero regardless of whether continuous or noncontinuous data are collected. This is based on the common knowledge that Lexigrams are opaque and impossible to guess.

In summary, researchers and evidence-based practitioners should first consider using the MBD due its strength of continuous data collection before contemplating the use of the MPD. Only when that seems impossible should interventionists carefully evaluate whether or not any of the legitimate rationales for choosing a MPD outlined are indicated. If so, the rationale for using the MPD should be stated in the manuscript. A common pitfall relates to the interpretation of findings yielded by certain applications of MPDs or of MBDs.

b. How Many Data Points Are Needed?

Typically, *at least* three data points are required to determine a potential trend in the data. This convention has been accepted in various texts on designing single-subject experimental designs (e.g., Barlow & Hersen, 1984; Kazdin, 1982). When this convention is applied irrespective of the design chosen, however, the consequences may be severe. Especially severe may be the consequences when it comes to the use of designs that ask for noncontinuous data collection such as the MPD. Recently, this author and several collaborators were confronted with this very same issue by a reviewer who questioned the number of data points collected for the MPD across instructional formats (group, individual, small group) (Schlosser *et al.*, 2000). Essentially the reviewer noted that "a multiple probe design requires a minimum of three data points be established immediately prior to the application of the treatment" under each tier and that this application fails to meet this requirement.

This author proceeded to consult the original source for MPDs to determine the accuracy of this proposed "requirement." In illustrating the difference between a MBD and a MPD, Horner and Baer (1978) provided their Figure 2 (p. 194). It turns out that two of the four baselines contained fewer than three baseline data points. Given this original source for the MPD and its publication in *Journal of Applied Behavior Analysis*—the premier journal for single-subject experimental research—this application appeared to be well within accepted standards concerning the number of data points needed for baselines in the MPD.

Although three data points seem to be generally the number for establishing a trend in single-subject designs, this number should not be applied indiscriminately without considering the specific design at hand. As discussed earlier, the main point for using the MPD rather than the MBD relates to a good rationale for not collecting continuous data. Thus, a reduction in the number of data points is inherent in choosing the MPD. With MPDs, the strategic location of the baseline data points is more important than the mere number of data points. Examining Figure 2 in Horner and Baer (1978), and Figure 1 in Schlosser *et al.* (2000, p. 38) one can clearly see that baseline data points are placed in each of the untreated baselines when treatment in a preceding baseline was introduced. For example, there is a baseline data point in the second baseline (individual format) at the same time the intervention in the first baseline (group format) was introduced, and there is a baseline data point in the untreated third baseline (small group format) while treatment in the second baseline (individual format) was introduced. The logic of MPDs says that changes in behavior should occur *only* when introducing treatment. That is, there should be no changes in the untreated baselines as a result of introducing treatment in a preceding baseline. The strategic location of baseline data points in this window of opportunity (i.e., the overlap of a treated baseline with an untreated baseline) in the Schlosser *et al.* (2000) study clearly demonstrated that changes only occurred when treatment was introduced in a given baseline.

III. EVALUATING GENERALIZATION

In addition to demonstrating behavior change, generalization is highly desirable for evaluating the efficacy of AAC interventions. After all, successful generalization means that instruction has been maximized beyond what was directly trained to the demonstration of instrumental effects—effects that occur without direct intervention (see Chapter 20 for strategies to maximize generalization). To arrive at an accurate evaluation of generalization effectiveness, however, sound design options must be employed. According to Schlosser and Lee (2000), the use of sound design options for evaluating generalization continues to be a problem in the field as indicated in a recent meta-analysis on the effectiveness of AAC interventions: "Many of the designs chosen make it impossible to attribute generalization or maintenance effectiveness unequivocally to the treatment" (p. 220). Therefore, in this section various design options are contemplated so that readers may position themselves better for an unequivocal demonstration of generalization effectiveness.

A. EVALUATING GENERALIZATION VIA MULTIPLE BASELINE DESIGNS AND ITS VARIANTS

Although generalization may be assessed via reversal designs, many AAC interventions cannot be readily unlearned or reversed as discussed earlier. Thus, the design options provided by the variants of the MBD have greater applicability to AAC and will be emphasized here. Readers interested in the use of reversal designs to assess generalization may consult Barrios and Hartmann (1988). Each variant of the MBD/MPD affords the possibility for a demonstration of generalization across two general dimensions. The two dimensions depend

Table 6.2

Types of Generalization Assessment Possible via MBDs or MPDs

| MBDs/MPDs across | Stimulus generalization | | | | Response generalization |
| | Setting generalization | Person generalization | | | |
		AAC users	Communicative Partners	Facilitators	Behavior generalization
Settings	★				
Subjects:					
— AAC users		★			
— Communicative Partners			★		
— Facilitators				★	
Behaviors					★

★This factor is being used to demonstrate experimental control. Thus, it cannot be used as a dimension across which generalization is being evaluated. With permission adapted from Schlosser and Braun (1994, p. 212).

on the factor being used to show therapeutic control over the target behavior (Barrios & Hartman, 1988). Table 6.2 illustrates this logic.

Unfortunately, this central logic has been violated in studies in related fields (Hagiwara & Myles, 1998) and some AAC studies (e.g., Buzolich et al., 1991; Hinderscheit & Reichle, 1987) where changes in the untreated baseline have been attributed to generalization effectiveness rather than a threat to internal validity. Buzolich et al. (1991), for example, spoke of changes in the untreated baselines as "spillover effects," which are deemed positive. Hinderscheit and Reichle (1987) taught an 18-year-old women to use a direct select color encoding strategy. The intervention was evaluated using the MPD across four sets of vocabulary items. The authors concluded that "encoding maintained and generalized to untrained exemplars" (p. 137). An inspection of Figure 6.5, however, may lead the researcher or evidence-based practitioner to draw a different conclusion. It appears that the changes in the untreated baselines of sets 2 through 4 occur as soon as the vocabulary items in set 1 are beginning to be acquired.

In fact, training in sets 3 and 4 was no longer necessary because the participant seemingly generalized encoding. As alluded to earlier, the factor that is used for demonstrating experimental control cannot be used to evaluate generalization at the same time. This study clearly violates this principle because sets of vocabulary items are used to demonstrate experimental control *and* to evaluate generalization. Also, the logic of the MBD/MPD requires that changes occur only in treated baselines, whereas untreated baselines do not change in the desired

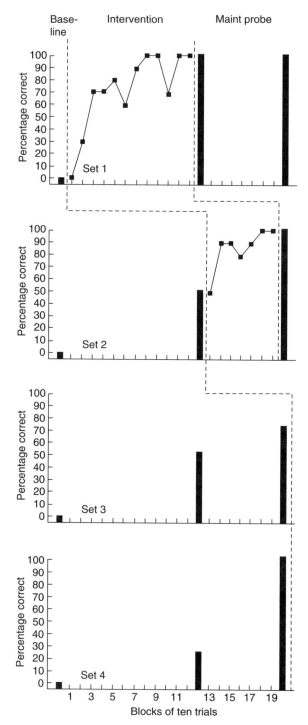

Figure 6.5 Example of the MPD (Hinderscheit & Reichle, 1987) that violates the rules for evaluating generalization. With permission from ISAAC.

direction. This study falls short on this aspect as well, thus making it difficult to rule out threats to internal validity. To avoid these misapplications, researchers and evidence-based practitioners should consult Table 6.2 to ensure that the central logic remains intact when planning evaluations of generalization effectiveness or when evaluating the soundness of generalization demonstrations in the literature.

B. Choosing an Appropriate Generalization Design

In addition to following the internal logic of MBDs/MPDs, the evidence-based practitioner and researcher is faced with the task of choosing an appropriate generalization design. Barrios and Hartmann (1988) proposed a six-step process for a persuasive demonstration of generalization:

> The first two steps are intended to guarantee that there is a treatment to be generalized and involve (1) repeated measurement of the target response and (2) demonstration of covariation of this response with sequential application and removal of the treatment. To ensure that it is generalization and not merely further training that is taking place, (3) the untrained response must be isolated from the treatment that has been applied to the trained response; (4) the untrained response also must be isolated from other agents or factors that might plausibly be invoked to account for changes produced in the target behavior. The final steps in the demonstration require (5) continuous measurement of the untrained response and (6) covariation of this response with the trained-response. (pp. 13–14)

Specifically, Barrios and Hartmann (1988) distinguished and appraised three principal designs for assessing generalization, including single-generalization probes, multiple-generalization probes, and continuous-generalization probes. Their description of these designs is not sufficiently detailed to exemplify many of the specific designs found in the literature. Therefore, Schlosser and Braun (1994) adapted many of the definitions and included the designs corresponding to the respective principal assessment strategies. This resulted in eight design options that will be discussed later. An appraisal of these designs, as well as hypothetical data are provided in Table 6.3. For each of these methods, AAC literature is exemplified in the text.

1. Single-Generalization Probes

Single-generalization probes refer to those strategies that use a single assessment of the nontargeted response(s) in a given phase of an experiment (i.e., pretreatment, within-treatment, posttreatment). Thus, theoretically, the single-generalization probe strategy may entail three substrategies and various combinations thereof. Only the more common strategies, however, will be addressed.

Table 6.3

A Summary of Principal Strategies and Substrategies in Single-Subject Research for Assessing Generalization

Principal strategies	Substrategies	Description	Appraisal
Single-generalization probes	Posttreatment	A single measure of a nontargeted behavior, person (i.e., subject, experimenter, communicative partner), or setting is taken *upon* demonstration of therapeutic control over the targeted response(s) via a reversal design, a PTD (Gast & Wolery, 1988) (only across persons and settings) or MBD across behaviors, persons, or settings. A graphic illustration is presented in Figure 6.6.	This strategy does not allow us to infer with any confidence the generality of therapeutic effects. We cannot legitimately infer from a single measure of nontargeted response the level of that response prior to treatment, nor can we attribute its current level to the treatment.
	Pre- and posttreatment	A single measure of a nontargeted behavior, person, or setting is taken *before* and *upon* demonstration of therapeutic control over the targeted response(s) via a reversal design, a PTD (Gast & Wolery, 1988) (only across persons and settings) or MBD across behaviors, persons, or settings. A graphic illustration is presented in Figure 6.7.	This strategy does not allow us to infer with any confidence the generality of therapeutic effects. We cannot attribute the level of that response to the absence of treatment. From a single measure of a nontargeted response upon demonstration of therapeutic control, we cannot attribute its current level to the treatment.
Multiple-generalization probes	Posttreatment	Repeated measurement of a nontargeted response or responses is carried out *only upon* demonstration of therapeutic control over the target response via either the MBD across settings or behaviors. A graphic illustration is presented in Figure 6.8.	This strategy does not allow us to infer with any confidence the generality of therapeutic effects over either behaviors or settings. From the repeated measures of the nontargeted response(s), we cannot legitimately infer the level of responding prior to treatment, nor can we attribute the current level to the treatment.
	Pre- and posttreatment	Repeated measurement of a nontargeted response or responses is carried out *before* and *upon* demonstration of therapeutic control over the target response via either the MBD across settings or behaviors. A graphic illustration is presented in Figure 6.9.	This strategy does not allow us to infer with any confidence the generality of therapeutic effects over either behaviors or settings. Although we can infer the level of responding prior to treatment to some degree, the absence of continuous data does not allow us to attribute the current level of responding to the treatment.

Pre- and within-treatment	Repeated measurement of a nontargeted response or responses is carried out *before* and *within* treatment via either the MBD across settings or behaviors. A graphic illustration is presented in Figure 6.10.	Although we can infer to some degree the level of generalization responding prior to and during treatment, the lack of continuous data precludes any definite conclusions.
Pre-, within-, and posttreatment	Repeated measurement of a nontargeted response(s) is carried out *before* treatment, *within* treatment, and *upon* demonstration of therapeutic control over the target response via either the MBD across settings or behaviors. A graphic illustration is presented in Figure 6.11.	This strategy does not allow us to infer with any confidence the generality of therapeutic effects over either behaviors or settings. Although we can infer the level of responding prior to treatment and during treatment to some degree, the absence of continuous data does not allow us to attribute the current level of responding to the treatment.
Continuous-generalization probes	Across *regular* (1) phase lengths or (2) intervals	(1) Concurrent measurement of targeted and nontargeted responses across *regular* phase lengths vis-à-vis a reversal design. For a graphic illustration of this strategy, see Barrios and Hartmann's (1988) Figure 1.2 (p. 18).	This strategy does not allow for an unequivocal demonstration of either response or subject (experimenter, communicative partner) generality. The strategy gives rise to two equally plausible accounts for systematic fluctuations in targeted and nontargeted responding; the treatment and a recurrent historical event. However, the strategy does not enable us to choose one of these explanations over the other; thus it does not allow us to attribute fluctuations in targeted and nontargeted responding to the treatment.
	(2) Concurrent measurement of targeted and nontargeted responses with *regular* intervals between successive administration of treatments vis-à-vis a PTD (Gast & Wolery, 1988) (only across persons and settings) or MBD across behaviors, persons, or settings. A graphic illustration is presented in Figure 6.12.	The strategy does not allow for an unequivocal demonstration of either response or person generality. The strategy gives rise to two equally plausible accounts for systematic fluctuations in targeted and nontargeted responding; the treatment and a recurrent historical event. However, the strategy does not enable us to choose one of these explanations over the other; thus it does not allow us to attribute fluctuations in targeted and nontargeted responding to the treatment.

(continues)

105

Table 6.3 (*continued*)

Principal strategies	Substrategies	Description	Appraisal
	Across *irregular* (1) phase lengths; or (2) intervals	(1) Concurrent measurement of targeted and nontargeted responses across *irregular* phase lengths vis-à-vis a reversal design. For a graphic illustration, see Barrios and Hartmann's (1988) Figure 1.4 (p. 22).	This strategy allows for a demonstration of both therapeutic control and generality of therapeutic effects across behaviors, subjects (experimenters, communicative partners), and settings. Systematic fluctuation in targeted and nontargeted responding can be legitimately attributed to the treatment since the lack of orderliness to the design's repeated presentation-and-removal of treatment allows us to eliminate recurrent historical events as a competing interpretation of covariation. A demonstration of setting generality is possible insofar as the treatment is conceptualized as being present merely by being operative in the targeted situation.
		(2) Concurrent measurement of targeted and nontargeted responses across *irregular* intervals between successive administration of treatments vis-à-vis a PTD (Gast & Wolery, 1988) or MBD across behaviors, subjects (experimenters, communicative partners), or settings. Graphic illustrations are presented in Figures 6.13 and 6.14.	With this strategy, variants of the MBD allow for demonstrations of various types of generalization (see Table 6.2). Systematic fluctuations in targeted and nontargeted responding can be legitimately attributed to the treatment since the lack of orderliness to the design's sequential administration across three or more independent behaviors, subjects (experimenters, communicative partners), or settings allows us to eliminate recurrent historical events as a competing interpretation of covariation.

Adapted with permission from Barrios and Hartmann (1988).

106

a. Posttreatment Single-Generalization Probes

This strategy involves a single assessment of the nontrained behavior carried out *upon* demonstrating that the treatment controls the target behavior. Figure 6.6 provides hypothetical data of this strategy in conjunction with the MBD across subjects. As a result of several shortcomings, this strategy fails to persuasively infer generalization (a number of the above-mentioned steps are omitted). Causal change cannot be deduced from this strategy either, as there is no assessment of the untreated behavior prior to intervention. Thus, a baseline under

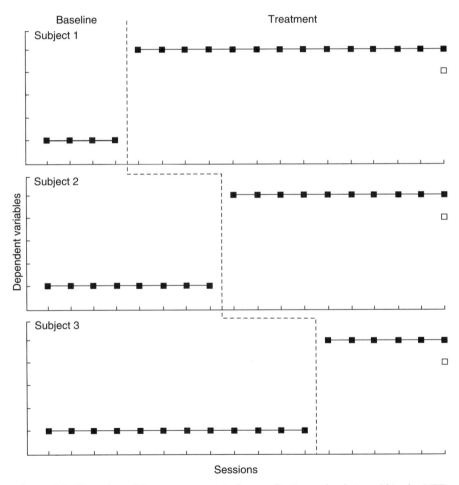

Figure 6.6 Illustration of the posttreatment single-generalization probe design within the MBD across subjects. Solid squares represent target responses; open squares represent responses in a nontarget setting.

generalization conditions is required (Barlow & Hersen, 1984; Hughes, 1985). Evaluating stimulus generalization across settings, for example, necessitates the collection of baseline data in the novel setting. Despite these glaring shortcomings, this strategy continues to be used in AAC intervention research (e.g., Kozleski, 1991) as evident from the meta-analysis of intervention research (Schlosser & Lee, 2000). Barrios and Hartmann (1988) submitted two reasons for the continued use of this strategy over other more sound strategies: (1) pure convenience and (2) faulty logic in interpreting this design.

b. Pre- and Posttreatment Single-Generalization Probes

This strategy involves a single assessment of the nontrained behavior carried out *before* and *upon* demonstrating that the treatment controls the target behavior. Figure 6.7 provides hypothetical data of this strategy in conjunction with the MBD across subjects. Although this strategy provides one baseline data point under generalization conditions, the level before treatment cannot be attributed to the absence of treatment with only one data point. Several threats to internal validity (e.g., maturation, history, selection) remain uncontrolled with only one data point. Similar to the previously discussed strategy, one data point upon demonstration of therapeutic control does not permit the researcher to attribute the current level of responding to the treatment. This strategy has not been used much in AAC intervention research (Schlosser & Lee, 2000).

2. Multiple-Generalization Probes

Multiple-generalization probes refer to strategies that use more than one data point in any phase of the study (i.e., pretreatment, within-treatment, posttreatment).

a. Posttreatment Multiple-Generalization Probes

Barrios and Hartmann (1988) defined this strategy as the repeated measurement of untreated responses *upon* demonstration of treatment control without the measurement of untreated responses during the baseline. Post-treatment multiple-generalization probes confound generalization with maintenance (i.e., generalization over time). Multiple-generalization probes may be incorporated into the MBD across behaviors, for instance, to measure setting generalization. Thus, treatment is sequentially applied to different behaviors and results in sequential changes in the target behaviors for each of these behaviors. Once this treatment control has been established, the targeted behavior is measured repeatedly across a nontargeted setting (see Figure 6.8). If generalization is to be assessed across more than one setting, the target behaviors are measured consecutively in the nontargeted settings rather than simultaneously.

In absence of a generalization baseline, little can be concluded regarding generalization, although this strategy meets the required demonstration of treat-

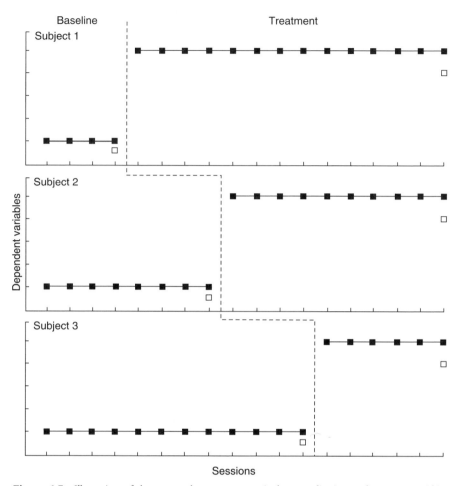

Figure 6.7 Illustration of the pre- and posttreatment single-generalization probe strategy within the MBD across subjects. Solid squares represent target responses; open squares represent responses in a nontarget setting.

ment control (Barrios & Hartmann, 1988). Thus, this strategy is similar to the single-generalization probe in its inability to demonstrate generalization. Another multiple-generalization probe strategy to assess generalization (i.e., response generalization) appraised by Barrios and Hartmann (1988) is the use of multiple-generalization probes via the MBD across settings. This strategy is considered similar to previous ones in terms of strengths and weaknesses. Again, little can be concluded regarding generalization effects due the absence of an assessment of the behavior in the novel setting prior to treatment. Despite its inherent short-comings, this is by far the most frequently used design option in the AAC inter-

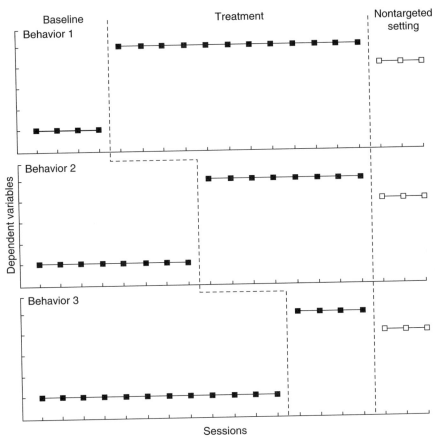

Figure 6.8   Illustration of the post-treatment multiple-generalization probe design within the MBD across behaviors. Solid squares represent target responses; open squares represent responses in a non-target setting.

vention literature (Schlosser & Lee, 2000). For an example, see Soto, Belfiore, Schlosser, and Haynes (1993).

b. Pre- and Posttreatment Multiple-Generalization Probes

Neither of Barrios and Hartmann's (1988) principal generalization assessment strategies accommodate designs that involve the use of probes *before* treatment under generalization conditions *and* the repeated measurement of the untreated response *upon* demonstration of treatment control (see Figure 6.9). Hence, their listing and appraisal were adapted accordingly (see Table 6.3). Pre-

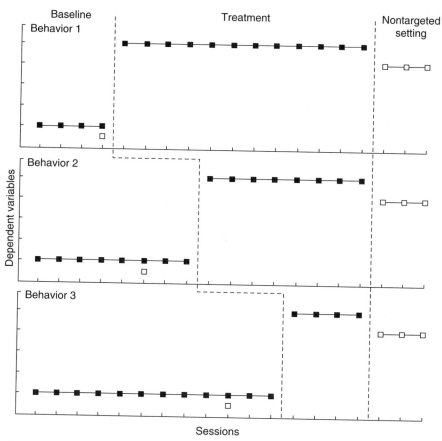

Figure 6.9 Illustration of the pre- and posttreatment multiple generalization probe design within a MBD across behaviors. Solid squares represent target behaviors in a nontarget setting.

treatment and posttreatment multiple probes are superior to the previously described strategy in allowing some degree of inference of the responding level *before* treatment. However, in the example depicted in Figure 6.9, this inference would have been stronger if the baseline data had been continuous. Nonetheless, despite the assessment of responding before treatment, this strategy has serious shortcomings as well. Because there is no concurrent measurement of the treated and untreated settings at all times, the changes in the untreated setting cannot be attributed to the treatment with certainty. The appraisal of this strategy would be analogous when used to assess response and subject generalization. Despite this weakness, this strategy has been used in the AAC generalization literature (e.g., Sternberg *et al.*, 1983).

c. Pre- and within-Treatment Multiple-Generalization Probes

This design strategy involves multiple-generalization probes implemented *before* and *within* the treatment phase (see Figure 6.10). Although we can infer to some degree the level of generalization responding before and during treatment, the lack of continuous data precludes any definite conclusions. Nonetheless, this strategy was applied in several AAC interventions studies (e.g., Carr, Binkoff, & Kologinski, & Eddy, 1978; experiment 2 by Carr & Kologinsky, 1983; Duker & Michielsen, 1983; Duker & Morsink, 1984).

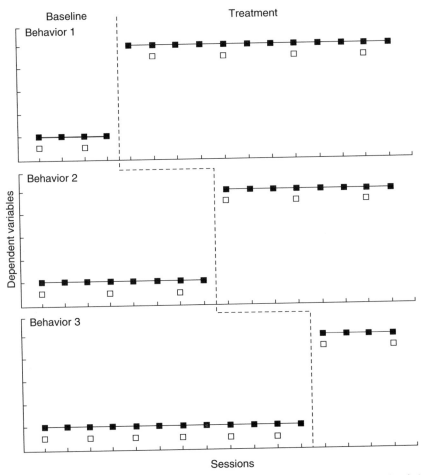

Figure 6.10 Illustration of the pre- and within-treatment multiple generalization probe design within a MBD across behaviors. Solid squares represent target behaviors in a nontarget setting.

d. Pre-, Within-, and Posttreatment Multiple-Generalization Probes

Neither of the principal generalization assessment strategies described by Barrios and Hartmann (1988) accommodates designs that involve the use of multiple probes *before* treatment, *during* treatment, and *subsequent* to treatment (see Figure 6.11). Hence, their listing and appraisal were adapted accordingly (see Table 6.3). This strategy allows some degree of inference of responding levels before and during treatment, although the lack of continuous data does not permit that the posttreatment level of responding is attributable to the treatment. This strategy was used by Angelo and Goldstein (1990), who assessed setting and experimenter generalization of a pragmatic teaching strategy using the MBD across wh-interrogative use. The appraisal of this strategy would be analogous when used to assess response and subject generalization.

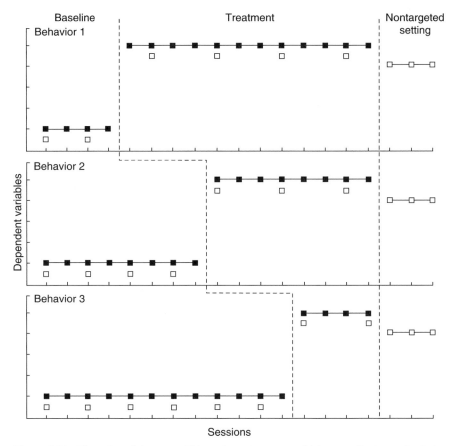

Figure 6.11 Illustration of the pre-, within, and posttreatment multiple-generalization probe design within a MBD across behaviors. Solid squares represent target behaviors in a nontarget setting.

3. Continuous-Generalization Probes

Continuous-generalization probe designs represent the most sophisticated design options available for an unequivocal demonstration of experimental control and generalization effectiveness. Yet these design options are severely underutilized in the AAC intervention literature (Schlosser & Lee, 2000).

a. Continuous-Generalization Probes across Regular Intervals

This refers to a group of designs that employ concurrent measurement of the targeted and nontargeted responses throughout a given study whereby the sequential administration of treatment across tiers that represent behaviors (settings, persons) is orderly—that is, the sequential administration follows a regular interval. Generalization across behaviors (responses) assessed with the MBD across settings, for example, requires that the target behavior be measured repeatedly over three or more settings while the nontargeted response is monitored concurrently over the same settings (see Figure 6.12).

These hypothetical data illustrate an example of a continuous generalization probe strategy involving response generalization with both behaviors increasing (target behaviors such as tacts and nontreated behaviors such as mands; see Sigafoos & Reichle, 1992, for further information on tacts and mands). Barrios and Hartmann (1988) submitted that a pattern of covariation between target behaviors and the nontargeted behaviors, as shown in Figure 6.12, leads to two competing inferences: (1) treatment control and generalization and (2) a periodic, attendant event (see Cook & Campbell, 1979). If there is an orderliness (i.e., equal intervals such as every fifth session in Figure 6.12, between successive application of the treatment across settings) to the treatment's application across settings, the latter is said to become the more plausible inference.

While some AAC intervention research seems to adequately narrow the interpretation to these two competing inferences (e.g., Carr, & Kemp, 1989; Keogh, Whitman, Beeman, Halligan & Starzynksi, 1987; Sommer et al., 1988), this design option does little to reduce the possibility of periodic events unrelated to the treatment being responsible for changes of treated and nontreated participants, behaviors, or settings.

b. Continuous-Generalization Probes across Irregular Intervals

To unequivocally demonstrate generalization, the strategy must not only provide continuous and concurrent probes but also administer treatments on an irregular basis. Here, the technique proposed by Todman and Dugard (2001) for randomly determining the onset of intervention on an a priori basis may be useful. Using irregular intervals as a design approach has been suggested as a control to the threat of periodic events unrelated to the treatment being responsible for

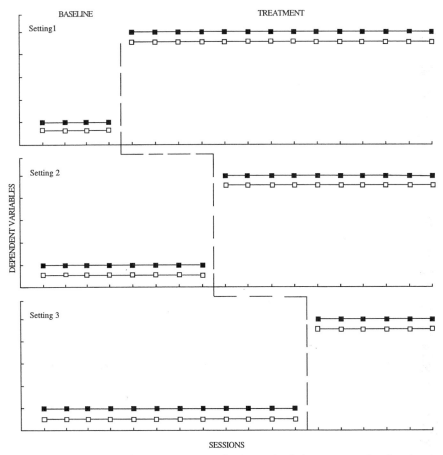

Figure 6.12 Illustration of a continuous-generalization probe design across regular phase lengths involving response generalization with increases in both behaviors. The strategy exemplified is based on the MBD across settings. Solid squares represent target responses; open squares represent nontarget responses.

treatment and generalization changes (Barrios & Hartmann, 1988). Figure 6.13 illustrates another MBD across settings to measure response generalization with both behaviors increasing after successive application of treatment. In contrast to Figure 6.12, however, there is no orderliness to the successive application of treatment from one setting to the next. Thus, it is unlikely that treatment and generalization changes are a result of a recurrent historical event unrelated to treatment.

This strategy may also be used in the MBD across subjects to investigate response generalization. Figure 6.14 illustrates hypothetical data involving response generalization with increases in requesting and pointing (R2) and

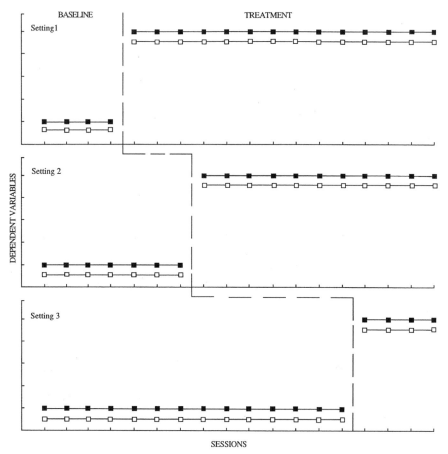

Figure 6.13 Illustration of a continuous-generalization probe design across irregular phase lengths involving response generalization with increases in both behaviors. The strategy exemplified is based on the MBD across settings. Solid squares represent target responses; open squares represent nontarget responses.

decreases in self-injurious behavior and autistic leading (R1) upon application of treatment across settings. The MBD across subjects was used in experiment I by Carr and Kologinsky (1983) to examine response generalization involving manual signing (R2) and self-stimulation (R1).

C. SUMMARY

MBDs and MPDs afford the possibility for evaluating generalization effectiveness in AAC. To do so, however, evidence-based practitioners and researchers need to (1) abide by the internal logic of the MBDs or MPDs and (2) choose

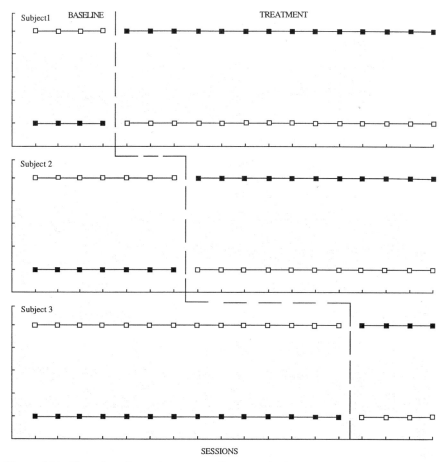

Figure 6.14 Illustration of a continuous-generalization probe design across irregular phase lengths involving response generalization with one behavior increasing and the nontarget behavior decreasing. The strategy exemplified is based on the MBD across subjects. Solid squares represent target responses; open squares represent nontarget responses.

an appropriate generalization design. The internal logic of the MBD/MPD mandates that the factor used to demonstrate treatment control cannot be used to assess generalization within the same design. Table 6.2 offers a matrix to assist with the adherence to this logic. An appropriate generalization design allows for an unequivocal demonstration that the generalization results obtained are due to the treatment rather than extraneous variables. Table 6.3 offers an appraisal of the various design strategies beginning with poor design choices leading to more and more sophisticated design options. It is suggested that evidence-based practitioners and researchers in AAC consider more continuous probe designs as the generalization design option of their choice and ensure that the interval between successive administrations of treatments is kept less regular.

IV. EVALUATING MAINTENANCE

A. CONCEPTUALIZING MAINTENANCE EVALUATION

Maintenance may be viewed as another instance of generalization—that is, generalization over time. Maintenance is, however, conceptually different from the evaluation of generalization across behaviors, persons, or settings as discussed in Section III. How does it differ? In evaluating generalization, changes observed in nontraining conditions should be attributed to the treatment. This problem is solved by demonstrating that changes under nontraining conditions systematically covary with changes in the treatment condition. Barrios and Hartmann (1988) accurately pointed out that this solution is not possible for the evaluation of maintenance because the nontraining condition is essentially the same as the training condition with the exception of two important differences: (1) the absence of treatment and (2) the location of nontraining in time following the termination of treatment. Thus, researchers are faced with the difficulty of needing to show that responding is a result of treatment that is no longer in operation. This same withdrawal of treatment, however, is expected to result in a return toward baseline when demonstrating experimental control via intervention designs such as the ABAB design discussed in Section II. Should not this same line of reasoning apply to maintenance evaluation? That is not the case, because a lack of change after withdrawing treatment is now attributed to the effectiveness of the treatment (which is no longer in operation). Why are the data not expected to return to baseline here? Barrios and Hartmann (1988) put it eloquently: "The rules of the game are reversed" (p. 29). Any maintenance design to be discussed next needs to address this fundamental dilemma.

B. CHOOSING AN APPROPRIATE MAINTENANCE DESIGN

Light (1999) highlighted the need for more maintenance data in the efficacy literature, in particular the effects of AAC interventions on long-term maintenance. To do so, it is essential that adequate design options be employed. Despite the substantial logical issues surrounding maintenance evaluations, several design strategies have been proposed to evaluate the maintenance of intervention effects. These design strategies may be grouped into (1) follow-up probes, (2) withdrawal strategies, and (3) comparative designs (Barrios & Hartmann, 1988; Rusch & Kazdin, 1981).

1. Follow-up Probes

Follow-up probes constitute the primary design option chosen for evaluating maintenance in AAC. The synthesis of maintenance effectiveness by Schlosser and Lee (2000) indicated that except for a negligible few data series, all other studies involved the use of follow-up probes. Follow-up probes are implemented at the end of a successful demonstration of treatment effectiveness by removing treatment, letting a specified time elapse, and then measuring responding again. With single follow-up probes, the posttreatment measure is taken only once and with multiple follow-up probes the measure is applied more than once. In the AAC literature, examples of single follow-up probes are numerous (e.g., Soto *et al.*, 1993), and so are applications of the multiple follow-up strategy (e.g., Angelo & Goldstein, 1990; Reid & Hurlbut, 1977; Sommer *et al.*, 1988).

Performance during the follow-up probe that is comparable with that observed during the treatment phase is considered to be an indication of maintenance effectiveness. As described earlier, this logic is flawed and it thus becomes questionable what role, if any, these follow-up probes serve. Because of the unreliability of one-shot measurements (i.e., this is the reason why at least three data points are needed to establish a trend), a single follow-up probe may serve no useful purpose (O'Leary & Drabman, 1971). Multiple follow-up probes, however, may yield useful information as argued by Barrios and Hartmann (1988). A change in behavior toward baseline, for instance, may call for the provision of booster treatments or for other changes in the participant's environment. Angelo and Goldstein (1990) took such an approach by instituting "review sessions" subsequent to the maintenance phase in which performance declined. Therefore, the researchers reinstated the prompt conditions of the pragmatic teaching strategy in order to strengthen the effects of training. Improved performance during maintenance, on the other hand, may allow for a fruitful examination of "delayed treatment effects" or unprogrammed ameliorative events.

2. Withdrawal Strategies

Rusch and Kazdin (1981) proposed three other strategies for evaluating maintenance, including (1) sequential-withdrawal, (2) partial-withdrawal, and (3) partial-sequential withdrawal.

a. Sequential-Withdrawal Designs

In this design the experimenter is first required to demonstrate experimental control of a multicomponent treatment via the MBD or MPD or a withdrawal design such as an ABAB design. Subsequently, one treatment component after another is sequentially withdrawn until the entire treatment is removed, while the target behavior is monitored throughout. Barrios and Hartmann (1988) offer an

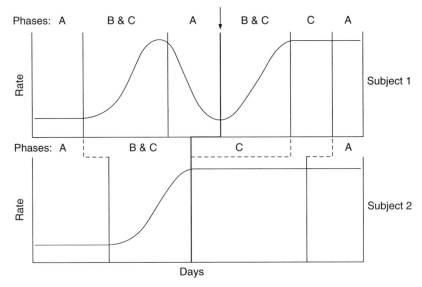

Figure 6.15 Illustration of withdrawal strategies for investigating maintenance. Subject 1 illustrates sequential withdrawal following demonstration of control using the MBD across subject. The combination of subjects 1 and 2 illustrates partial-sequential withdrawal following a demonstration of control using the MBD across subjects. Source: Figure 1.7 (p. 33) in Barrios, B. A., & Hartmann, D. P. (1988). Recent developments in single-subject methodology: Methods for analyzing generalization, maintenance, and multicomponent treatments. In M. Hersen, R. M. Eisler, & P. M. Miller (Eds.), *Progress in behavior modification: Vol. 22* (pp. 11–47). Newbury Park, CA: Sage. Copyright (c) 1988 by Sage Publications, Inc. Reprinted by Permission of Sage Publications, Inc.

excellent illustration of this design in Figure 6.15 (see subject 1). In this example, the treatment was no longer effective once both components were withdrawn (see second A phase) so both components were reinstated (see B and C phases). The experimenter then removed only the B component of the treatment while performance maintained and then decided to remove the C component as well. It is unclear, however, whether the effects would have been maintained if the components were withdrawn in reverse order or if both components had been withdrawn together. Another option is to use the partial-withdrawal design.

b. Partial-Withdrawal Designs

This design is to be used only in conjunction with the MBD or MPD. Upon demonstrating experimental control, the experimenter removes part or all of the treatment from one of the baselines while leaving the other baseline intact. The partial-withdrawal design is indicated in Figure 6.15 up to the bold line (indicated by the arrow). Because the withdrawal of both treatment components (A phase) resulted in a lack of maintenance in subject 1, this investigator would be wise to choose an alternative approach with subject 2. Applying the logic of the MBD/MPD, there should be no changes (in the same direction as in the altered baseline) in the unaltered baseline for subject 2 during the overlapping period. A visual analysis indicates that this is the case here, suggesting that the withdrawal of both treatment components was responsible for the decline in performance.

c. Partial-Sequential-Withdrawal Designs

This third withdrawal design strategy is a combination of the previous two strategies. The partial-sequential-withdrawal design can be used with a reversal design (e.g., ABAB design) or the MBD/MPD. Upon demonstrating experimental control, part or all of a treatment is withdrawn from one baseline while the other baselines remain unaltered. After monitoring performance in the altered baseline for some time, treatment is withdrawn sequentially from the remaining baseline. Figure 6.15, in its entirety, illustrates this approach. After the removal of both treatment components resulted in a loss of maintenance, the investigator sequentially removes first treatment component B and then C from subject 2. The application of this design suggests that the withdrawal of both treatment components resulted in a loss of treatment effects, whereas the sequential withdrawal of one component after the other did not. This holds true only with the caveat that the sequential withdrawal needs to occur in the exact sequence as tested here (i.e., first B and then C). Whether the reverse order would have resulted in the same maintenance effectiveness is unknown.

The use of withdrawal designs for examining maintenance is rare in AAC intervention studies (Schlosser & Lee, 2000). McGregor *et al.* (1992), however, offered a fitting illustration of the partial-sequential-withdrawal design in their study on teaching the functional use of SGDs. Upon demonstrating experimental control of the treatment package consisting of preinstruction and natural-environment teaching via the MBD across settings, the investigators employed a partial-sequential-withdrawal design to determine maintenance without preinstruction. During intervention, preinstruction consisted of training operational competence pertaining to the location of five task-related keys. During the maintenance phase, the researchers first discontinued the modeling and identification of each of the five task-related keys in the classroom (see withdrawal 1 in Figure 6.16), while monitoring performance in the vocational training room and the speech room. Next, modeling and identification was discontinued in the vocational training room and later in the speech room. Because the participant maintained performance across settings despite the withdrawal of the first preinstruction component, the researchers decided to withdraw all preinstruction (see withdrawal 2 in Figure 6.16). Unfortunately, this second withdrawal was implemented in peculiar fashion as preinstruction was first withheld in the vocational training room (second setting), followed by the speech room (third setting), and last the classroom. Even though the participants' performance

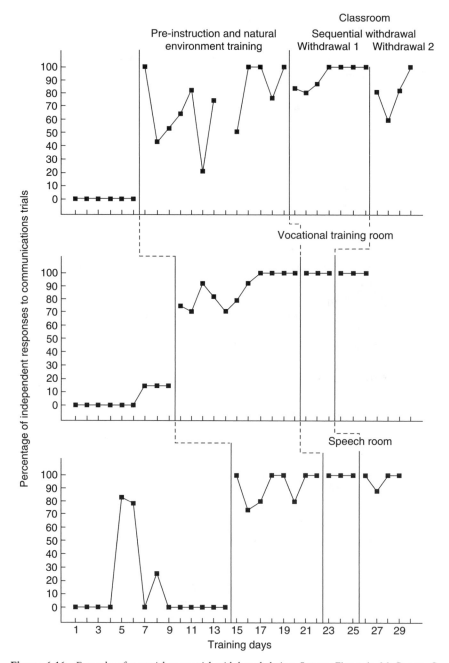

Figure 6.16 Example of a partial–sequential withdrawal design. Source: Figure in McGregor, G., Young, J., Gerak, J., Thomas, B., & Vogelsberg, R. T. (1992). Increasing functional use of an assistive communication device by a student with severe disabilities. *Augmentative and Alternative Communication, 8,* 243–250. Copyright (c) by ISAAC. Reprinted by Permission of ISAAC.

maintained at high levels, the role of the second preinstruction component could have been more clearly demonstrated, had it been implemented analog to the first withdrawal—that is, first in the classroom, followed by the vocational training room and the speech room.

In summary, three withdrawal design strategies are available to examine maintenance effectiveness via single-subject experimental designs. Despite considerable complexity and their ability to dismantle a treatment, Barrios and Hartmann (1988) remind us that withdrawal designs do not solve the basic maintenance dilemma alluded to earlier.

3. Comparative Designs

Comparative designs such as alternating-treatments designs, adapted alternating-treatments designs and parallel-treatment designs (see Section V for a complete description) offer potential alternatives to the evaluation of maintenance effectiveness. By comparing two or more maintenance procedures to one another as well as to their respective acquisition procedures, comparative designs allow the researcher to sidestep the previously described major interpretive obstacle to an assessment of maintenance. This is possible only, however, if two or more maintenance procedures are compared. If treatment is withdrawn completely, these designs face the same interpretive quagmire as the previous design options. The next section is devoted entirely to comparative designs. Therefore, no further details shall be provided here.

V. COMPARING THE EFFICACY OF TWO OR MORE INTERVENTIONS

With the exception of the comparative design options to the evaluation of maintenance, the designs discussed thus far focused on evaluating the efficacy of *one* intervention. This type of efficacy evaluation is what the field has been primarily concerned with in its research (Schlosser & Lee, 2000). Although it is rather typical and essential for any evolving field to first establish whether a *particular* intervention is working, Schlosser (1999) offered at least three sets of reasons for evaluating which intervention is working better. These sets of reasons include (1) the current state of the AAC field, (2) the increased accountability in health care and education, and (3) practitioners as decision makers. The following section raises some of the methodological decision-making points for planning and implementing comparative single-subject experimental designs.

A. FORMULATING THE RESEARCH QUESTION

Research questions are a pivotal part of any research endeavor (Chapter 4; see also Light, 1999). All subsequent aspects of the research process (e.g., participants, design, procedures, results, discussion, and implications of the results) have to be consistent with the question. In formulating a research question involving a comparison of interventions, the independent variables of interest need to be carefully identified and examined. If the interest pertains, for example, to determining the effects of speech output as added auditory stimuli to communication boards, the comparison should include a condition in which speech output is present and another condition in which speech output is not present (Koul, Schlosser, Corwin, & Sims, 1997; Schlosser, Belfiore, Nigam, Blischak, & Hetzroni, 1995). Thus, the materials should allow for everything else to be constant across conditions, except speech output. This would allow researchers to draw conclusions concerning the effects of speech output. The researcher cannot, however, extend these conclusions beyond speech output to the relative efficacy of SGDs versus communication boards. After all, SGDs differ from communication boards not only with respect to speech output. If, on the other hand, the research question entails a comparison of SGDs and a communication board (see Soto *et al.*, 1993), researchers can draw conclusions only concerning the effectiveness of these two means to transmit. They cannot, however, attribute differences to the presence or absence of speech output alone because other variables could have, in concert with speech output or by themselves, accounted for the results. This highlights the need for a carefully phrased research question when comparing interventions.

B. Choosing an Appropriate Design

Choosing the appropriate experimental design is crucial for examining the stated research questions. A number of design options are available for comparing the effectiveness and efficiency of two or more interventions, including the ABACA/ACABA design, the alternating-treatments design, the adapted alternating-treatments design, and the parallel-treatments design.

1. ABACA/ACABA Design

Koul *et al.* (1997) used an ABACA/ACABA design (McReynolds & Kearns, 1983) to examine the effects of speech output feedback (SPEECH) versus no speech output (NO SPEECH) on the learning of symbol-referent relations high and low in translucency. Following an initial baseline (A), participant 1 received speech output (B) followed by a second baseline (A) and instruction without speech output (C). The reverse order was received for participant 2. Although the results suggest speech output does enhance the learning of symbols low in translucency, they need to be viewed cautiously for at least two reasons. First, this design requires the use of the same symbols in both conditions (SPEECH,

NO-SPEECH) (i.e., the design selection is linked to the materials issue). This may result in so-called order effects whereby performance in one condition influences performance in the other condition. In other words, participant 1 may have learned more symbols with speech output because speech output followed the condition without speech output using the same symbols. On the other hand, it could be argued that if order effects were indeed present, the performance of both participants would have differed from the results obtained. This is clearly not the case. Participant MA learned more low-translucency symbols in the SPEECH condition with the SPEECH condition presented first followed by the NO-SPEECH condition, while participant JQ also learned more low-translucency symbols in the SPEECH condition receiving the reverse order of conditions. Nonetheless, it cannot be ruled out that this could have occurred by chance because there is only one participant each associated with a particular order of interventions. Thus, although counterbalancing across participants provides some level of control over order effects, the degree of control is unknown and order effects cannot be ruled out. Therefore, the results are rendered only suggestive. To this author's knowledge, the study by Koul *et al.* (1997) represents the only AAC application using this particular design.

2. Alternating-Treatments Design

An alternating-treatments design (ATD) involves the application of two or more interventions to the same set of stimuli or behaviors, usually following an initial baseline (Barlow & Hayes, 1979). Sometimes, the more effective or efficient intervention is applied alone in the third phase. ATDs have been applied in several AAC studies (e.g., Goodman & Remington, 1993; Horn & Jones, 1996; Iacono & Duncum, 1995; Soto *et al.*, 1993).

Soto *et al.* (1993), for example, used an ATD to evaluate the effects of a SGD versus a communication board. This particular ATD was embedded into the MBD across two settings. The participant was taught the same symbols for requesting with the SGD and with the communication board in the group home where he resided and later in the community-based workshop where he worked. The conditions were counterbalanced across sessions to control for order effects. Counterbalancing of conditions within the same participant rather than across participants allows for superior handling of order effects compared to the ABACA/ACABA design. Had there been enough opportunities for alternating the treatments, an alternative procedure for minimizing order effects would have been to randomize the order of treatment introduction.

As evident, comparisons of interventions pose a special design challenge. Although order effects can be controlled in the ATD through counterbalancing or randomization, carryover effects are not controlled as readily because the same symbols and referents were taught in both conditions. Even though procedural safeguards were put in place to enhance discriminability of the conditions, one cannot rule out the possibility that the learning of a symbol in one condition affected the performance in the other condition. Similar problems would occur in comparing two or more AAC interventions for teaching manual signs, spelling, and scanning. That is, whenever the focus is instruction rather than reinforcement contingencies, carryover effects are a serious threat to internal validity when the interventions are applied to the same set of stimuli. A design solution that controls these carryover effects would be beneficial. The adapted ATD and the parallel-treatments design represent two such solutions.

3. Adapted Alternating Treatments Design

The adapted alternating-treatments design (AATD) differs from the standard ATD in that each intervention is assigned to a unique set of instructional items (Sindelar, Rosenburg, & Wilson, 1985). This requires the identification of two (or as many as there are treatments) equivalent and functionally independent instructional sets. If done appropriately, those potential carryover effects resulting from the same set of instructional items are eliminated. Carryover effects resulting from other reasons, however, are potentially as prevalent in the AATD as in the ATD. Using different instructional sets may also enhance the perceived discriminability of conditions by participants. As in the ATD, order effects in AATDs are controlled through counterbalancing or randomizing the order of interventions (Sindelar et al., 1985).

The vast majority of AAC comparisons applications have relied on using an AATD (Conaghan, Singh, Moe, Landrum, & Ellis, 1992; Dalrymple & Feldman, 1992; Hurlbut, Iwata, & Green, 1982; Iacono, Mirenda, & Beukelman, 1993; Linton & Singh, 1984; McNaughton & Tawney, 1993; Remington & Clarke, 1983, 1993a, 1993b; Schlosser, Blischak, Belfiore, Bartley, & Barnett, 1998). Even though many of these authors referred to the use of an ATD, the characteristics they described are consistent with those of an AATD as detailed by Sindelar et al. (1985). For example, an AATD was used to compare the effectiveness and efficiency of three feedback conditions on spelling (Schlosser et al., 1998) (see Figure 6.17).

Three equivalent, but independent sets of words were selected (see the discussion of equivalency presented later) and assigned to three feedback conditions: auditory, auditory-visual, and visual. The equivalence of the words was demonstrated through equal performance during baseline. A learning criterion was set. To reach criterion for a particular set of words, the participant had to spell each of the four words in a set correctly over two consecutive probes. The training for a particular set of words continued until the criterion was reached with all sets of words. Assuming that the criterion is reached with each intervention, all interventions involved in an AATD comparison are equally effective. Differences

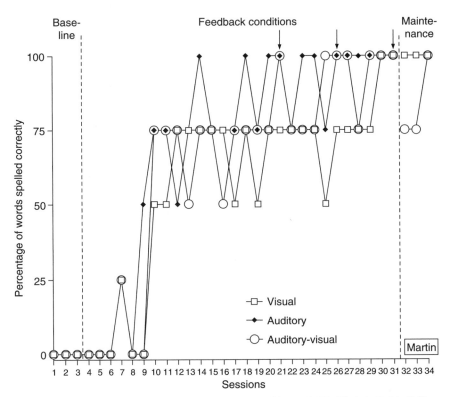

Figure 6.17 Example of an AATD. Source: Figure 1 in Schlosser, R. W., Blischak, D. M., Belfiore, P. J., Bartley, C., & Barnett, N. (1998). The effects of synthetic speech output and orthographic feedback on spelling in a student with autism: A preliminary study. *Journal of Autism and Developmental Disorders, 28,* 319–329. Copyright (c) by Plenum Press. Reprinted by Permission of Plenum Press.

in an AATD, however, are determined through a comparison of efficiency indicators. That is, differences could be demonstrated when acquisition in one set is more rapid than in other sets (Sindelar *et al.,* 1985). In the study at hand, the participant reached the criterion first in the auditory-visual condition, followed by the auditory condition, and finally the visual condition. A comparison of training errors could serve as an efficiency indicator.

4. Parallel-Treatments Design

The parallel-treatments design (PTD) (Gast & Wolery, 1988) offers a second potential design solution that permits the control of carryover effects. Two or more conditions are introduced to two or more different instruction sets as in the AATD. However, with the PTD the conditions are subsequently applied to the remaining instructional sets in a sequential order. This sequential order requires repeated baselines on untrained sets and repeated maintenance probes on previously trained sets. The design also requires that the first sets per condition are trained to criterion before initiating training on the second sets and so forth. This allows for later efficiency comparisons between the conditions. Whereas the AATD involves the teaching of one set per condition (Sindelar *et al.*, 1985), the PTD involves within-subject replications across multiple sets similar to two concurrently implemented multiple probe designs. Figure 6.18 shows an example of a PTD.

Because these multiple sets allow for the demonstration of the effect across behaviors, the PTD has the potential to strengthen the conclusions relative to an AATD (Gast & Wolery, 1988). However, there is also a cost to be paid in that the length of data collection may be considerable and the risk for participant attrition is high. The risk of lengthy data collection is compounded by the requirement to train each successive set to meet the criterion in each condition. Sometimes, one condition may not be effective at all and a decision needs to be made whether or not to give up and discontinue teaching of this particular set in this condition.

Considering its strength, the PTD is considerably underused in AAC. A recent synthesis of intervention research in AAC (Schlosser & Lee, 2000) indicated only two published experiments that used a PTD (Bennett, Gast, Wolery, & Schuster, 1986; Schlosser *et al.*, 1995). Schlosser *et al.* (1995) used a PTD to study the effects of speech output on symbol learning with three individuals who had severe to profound intellectual disabilities. The SPEECH and NO-SPEECH conditions were concurrently applied to two equivalent sets of Lexigram-referent relations. The learning criterion was set at 100% correct in 11 out of 12 consecutive trials. Once the criterion was reached on both of these first sets, baseline probes were collected on the other sets before training was initiated on the second two sets in both conditions. This was repeated until all four sets in each condition were trained to the criterion. As in the spelling study, the sequence of conditions was counterbalanced across time of day (morning, afternoon) to control for sequence effects. Differences in a PTD are determined by comparing efficiency indicators. That is, differences could be demonstrated when acquisition in one set is more rapid or is achieved with fewer errors than in other sets. Conditions are considered equally effective if the criterion is reached in both conditions consistently across multiple instructional sets and participants. In the study discussed earlier, both conditions were equally effective for two of three participants because they reached the criterion across sets in both conditions. The results for one of the participants are displayed in Figure 6.18. The third participant reached criterion only when provided with speech output. Efficiency comparisons could be made only for the two participants who reached

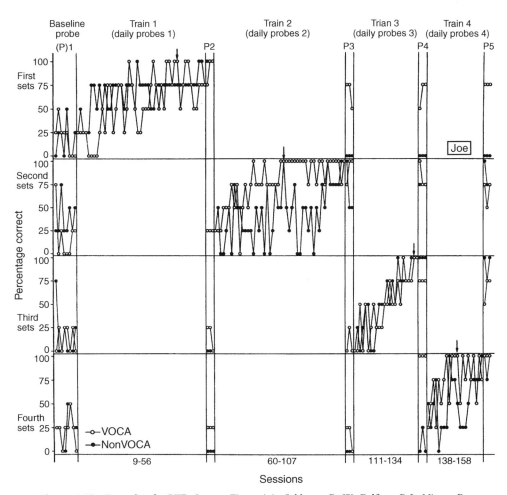

Figure 6.18 Example of a PTD. Source: Figure 1 in Schlosser, R. W., Belfiore, P. J., Nigam, R., Blischak, D., & Hetzroni, O. (1995). The effects of speech output technology in the learning of graphic symbols. *Journal of Applied Behavior Analysis*, *28*, 537–549. Copyright (c) by JABA. Reprinted with permission by JABA.

the criterion in both conditions. Both of these participants required fewer sessions to reach the criterion and made fewer training errors to the criterion when provided with speech output.

In the study by Bennett *et al.* (1986), a PTD was employed in a similar fashion to determine differences between time delay and the system of least prompts on manual sign production in three children with multiple disabilities. Unlike the Schlosser *et al.* (1995) study, they incorporated review trials on previously taught signs in each session in order to monitor maintenance. This additional procedure may have assisted their subjects in maintaining manual sign production throughout the study on all eight signs.

C. Setting a Learning Criterion versus a Teaching Criterion

1. Learning Criterion

A learning criterion, defined as a predetermined measurable level of performance that indicates mastery, serves important functions in comparative efficacy studies. First, a learning criterion has multiple implications for the termination of training. One potential implication is that training will be terminated only if the criterion was reached while training in the other condition continued (e.g., Goodman & Remington, 1993; Horn & Jones, 1996). Another implication is that training in *all* conditions is terminated when one of the conditions attained criterion. Subsequently, the more effective condition is then applied to the stimuli in the other conditions during a third design phase (e.g., Barrera, Lobato-Barrera, & Sulzer-Azaroff, 1980; Conaghan et al., 1992; Iacono et al., 1993; Linton & Singh, 1984). Although this is a widespread practice, it has serious ramifications for comparing interventions in terms of efficiency (discussed later). When the criterion is reached in one condition, some researchers will discontinue training only in that condition while monitoring performance through continuous probes until training in the other condition is at the criterion level as well. For example, the PTD requires probing beyond criterion attainment (i.e., maintenance probes) until the criterion in the other condition for the parallel stimuli set has been met and until the criterion on subsequent sets has been met (Bennett et al., 1986; Schlosser et al., 1995). Studies using the AATD would benefit from continued probing until the criterion is reached across conditions as well (e.g., Schlosser et al., 1998).

A second important function of a learning criterion is that it permits an unequivocal demonstration of effectiveness for the condition in which the criterion is attained. Although behavior change may be demonstrated through a visual analysis of level or slope changes from baseline to intervention as well (Parsonson & Baer, 1992), the attainment of the criterion is clearly a more convincing indicator of effectiveness.

Third, a learning criterion can set the stage for efficiency comparisons—that is, interventions can be compared in terms of (1) trials to criterion, (2) training errors to criterion, (3) cost to criterion, and so forth. With a few exceptions (Iacono & Duncum, 1995; Iacono et al., 1993; Sigafoos & Reichle, 1992), the majority of comparisons included in this chapter and Schlosser (1999) chose to set a learning criterion. To engage in efficiency comparisons legitimately, however, the criterion has to be attained in all conditions. This may be preempted from occurring because of (1) questionable design decisions (e.g., terminating training in all conditions whenever the criterion is reached in one condition; as noted earlier) or (2) the ineffectiveness of a particular condition for a given participant. Sam, one participant in Schlosser *et al.* (1995), for example, reached the criterion in the SPEECH condition but failed to reach the criterion without the provision of speech output. Therefore, we were unable to compare the two conditions in terms of efficiency for this participant. In summary, setting a learning criterion serves important functions in comparative efficacy evaluations. As such, a learning criterion is an essential ingredient of internally valid comparison studies. Researchers and evidence-based practitioners, however, may also want to consider using a teaching criterion given the previously stated negative implications when a learning criterion is not attained.

2. Teaching Criterion

A teaching criterion may be defined as a predetermined maximum number of teaching trials or sessions. Setting a teaching criterion permits the termination of training even when the learning criterion has not been attained for a particular intervention. This could be a useful safeguard in situations where investigators plan to take performance to the criterion in all conditions, but have little data to predict that this will actually occur. For example, Dalrymple and Feldman (1992) continued training until both trained signs met 100% correct across two consecutive sessions (learning criterion) or 160 trials (teaching criterion), whichever came first. As such, a teaching criterion may prove particularly useful with designs such as the PTD where learning criteria across conditions need to be achieved for parallel sets of instructional items before moving on to training of the next sequential sets of items. In the previous example of Sam, for whom the condition without speech output failed to attain the criterion, a preset teaching criterion would have been advantageous in hindsight. It would have saved us numerous discussions regarding the economic and ethical aspects of continuing training in one condition seemingly *forever* by providing us an a priori defined signal for when to move on to training the next instructional sets.

Considering its potential utility, the teaching criterion is severely underused as an additional criterion. Exceptions are studies by Dalrymple and Feldman (1992), Iacono and Duncum (1995), and McNaughton and Tawney (1993). The attainment of a teaching criterion by itself without attainment of a learning criterion, however, does not permit legitimate efficiency comparisons. After all, efficiency comparisons require demonstrated effectiveness.

D. Choosing Appropriate Materials

The materials selected for a comparative efficacy study need to support the type of comparison. For example, the studies on the effects of speech output versus no speech output required the selection of materials that differed only in the presence or absence of speech output. The researches decided to use a SGD across conditions (Schlosser *et al.*, 1995). In one condition, the speech was turned on, whereas in the other condition it was turned off. An inactive SGD allowed the simulation of a nonelectronic communication board while controlling for the effects of antecedent stimuli (e.g., overall appearance) and consequent stimuli (e.g., proprioceptive stimuli) other than synthetic speech.

E. Creating Equivalent Instructional Sets

The logic of the AATD (Sindelar *et al.*, 1985) and the PTD (Gast & Wolery, 1988), the designs posited as most useful for AAC, rests on the construction of equivalent sets. In principle, any universe of items that can be identified and divided into equivalent sets is appropriate to study with the AATD or PTD (Gast & Wolery, 1988; Sindelar *et al.*, 1985). Equivalence can be based on different methods, including those that are (1) informal, (2) factual, or (3) objective. Either source of information begins with a logical analysis of the universe of items (from which the stimuli will be drawn) for factors that are known to contribute to item acquisition. For example, the learning of symbol–referent associations is influenced, among other factors, by the degree of iconicity (Lloyd & Fuller, 1990), at least for learners with receptive knowledge of the referent (Sevcik, Romski, & Wilkinson, 1991). To compare the effects of two conditions on symbol learning, it is crucial to equate the sets of symbol–referent associations for the degree of iconicity and for receptive understanding of the referent. Similarly, the acquisition of manual signs may be influenced by the reinforcement value of the referent, transparency of the signs, and performance difficulty (Doherty, 1985).

1. Informal Methods

Using informal ways to "equate" conditions often involves the consultation of experts by asking them to equate sets based on their perceptions of levels of contributing factors (Barrera *et al.*, 1980; Conaghan *et al.*, 1992; Dalrymple & Feldman, 1992). These factors may be predetermined or left at the discretion of the expert. Conaghan *et al.* (1992) asked sign language instructors to equate manual sign sets in terms of performance difficulty. Barrera *et al.* (1980) asked four language specialists to rate 50 nouns in terms of pronunciation difficulty, number of syllables, and difficulty in signing. Linton and Singh (1984) had three sets of manual signs checked by a specialist teacher for ease of sign production and importance of the word/sign to the participant. Although the informal method of equating sets is probably superior to no method at all, it has serious limitations comparable to relying on any other anecdotal information in the research process. For example, is the number of respondents large enough and randomly selected in order to be representative of the population of sign language instructors or language specialists? For this reason, more "objective" ways of generating equal sets are preferred.

2. Factual Methods

Matching sets based on factual information represents a second avenue some authors chose to use (e.g., Bennett *et al.*, 1986; Schlosser *et al.*, 1998). This factual information is derived from a logical analysis of the universe of potential stimulus items. For example, in Bennett *et al.* (1986), the authors paired signs with similar topographies to equate for difficulty. In the study on spelling (Schlosser *et al.*, 1998), equally difficult word sets were created by equating for factors known to contribute to spelling performance, including the following: (1) mean length, (2) the mean percentage of possible correct letter sequences, (3) the mean percentage of correct letter sequences during preassessment, (4) the mean number of syllables, and (5) grade levels associated with the words. All of these factors were readily determined by using procedures documented elsewhere such as by observing the percentage of letter sequences or by consulting published lists for grade-level difficulty and the number of syllables of instructional words. Sometimes sets can be assumed to be equivalent without engaging in the process of matching but by virtue of the materials used. For example, we have selected Lexigrams for both conditions (SPEECH, NO-SPEECH) because they are arbitrary and known to be opaque. Therefore, with a high degree of confidence, iconicity was ruled out as a variable that would influence the learning of graphic symbols in a different way across conditions (Schlosser *et al.*, 1995). Equating sets based on factual information is preferable to relying on subjective methods. If researchers and evidence-based practitioners document the procedures for the particular factor they wish to equate (e.g., "How is similar topography determined?"), factual equating allows at least for the potential to be objective.

3. Objective Methods

"Objective," as used in this chapter, is defined as the gathering of data that are publicly verifiable and reliable. This leads to the third method for equating sets. Objective data collection for equating sets should be accompanied by interobserver agreement data in much the same way as the application of the independent variable and the dependent variable (discussed later). For example,

Goodman and Remington (1993) asked 32 children to rate the transparency and performance difficulty of manual signs. Pretest data sorted out which word referents were receptively known and which were unknown. These data allowed a close matching of conditions. Baseline data may also be used to ensure that the sets are indeed equally difficult (e.g., Schlosser et al., 1998).

An issue that is frequently raised in the planning of comparative single-subject studies is the creation of equal sets by counterbalancing the sets across participants rather than within participants. Hurlbut et al. (1982), for instance, assigned five words to iconic graphic symbols and five other words to Blissymbols with Randy, while Tom was assigned Blissymbols to the first five words and iconic graphic symbols to the second five words. Although this counterbalancing across students seems an elegant solution to equate sets in terms of difficulty, it actually has serious shortcomings as discussed previously in regards to the ABACA/ACABA design. It could be argued that Randy learned to associate iconic graphic symbols more readily because the first five words lend themselves more to a graphic depiction than the second five words assigned to iconic graphic symbols for Tom. Counterbalancing across participants is an appropriate strategy to equate for difficulty if the number of participants is large enough for what is essentially a group design strategy. With only two or three participants, however, such counterbalancing cannot ensure that the sets are indeed equally difficult. Whenever possible, the more elegant and effective strategy within the single-subject design tradition is to equate for difficulty within participants. Returning to the example by Hurlbut et al. (1982), the words could have been assigned to the two types of graphic symbol according to referent variables that are known to be associated with the learning of symbols as discussed earlier.

In summary, the internal validity of comparisons rests to a large degree on the creation of equivalent instructional sets based on the knowledge of contributing factors at the time of study planning. Three methods for creating equating sets were discussed with the objective method being portrayed as the preferred method. As evident, the creation of equal sets does not always occur with the full consideration of all the contributing factors at the time of study planning. For example, it has been known for a long time that the receptive status of words (known or unknown) contributes to the ease of acquiring manual signs (Clarke, Remington, & Light, 1986; Light, Remington, Clarke, & Watson, 1989). Yet a number of studies dated after 1986 have failed equating sets for receptive status (e.g., Conaghan et al., 1992; Dalrymple & Feldman, 1992). Even when equivalent sets are created under consideration of all contributing factors at the time of study planning, the internal validity of comparisons may be time limited. Efficacy research published at a later date may show that acquisition of an AAC system is under the control of factors that were previously unknown. Therefore, some comparative studies may need to be replicated in the future under full consideration of an updated list of contributing factors for equating instructional sets.

In addition to creating equivalent sets, comparisons via the AATD and PTD also require the creation of sets that are functionally independent.

F. Creating Functionally Independent Sets

To ensure that the sets are independent of one another, those items need to be selected whose acquisition does not aid the acquisition of other items in the study. For example, suppose we taught a participant to spell the word "bath" in one condition and the word "bathroom" in the other condition. Logical reasoning and research on spelling would tell us that the participant might spell "bathroom" more efficiently because of learning how to spell "bath." Similarly, if the purpose of the study were to teach a certain rule that can be applied to items in the other set, the logic of the AATD and PTD would be compromised.

G. Minimizing Carryover Effects

Carryover effects are almost always due to the inability of the participant to discriminate between two interventions (Barlow & Hersen, 1984). In addition to counterbalancing as part of the design, the following procedures may help the participants discriminate the conditions. First, the interventions can be separated from one another by a time interval. Second, the speed of alternations should be appropriate for the participant to facilitate discrimination. Third, some participants may just need to be told which treatment they are getting (Kazdin & Hartmann, 1978). Depending on the receptive skills of the participants, "telling" may take various forms and visual supports. For example, the speaker of the device was covered with a piece of colored paper in the NO-SPEECH condition and the participants were told that "the device is broken, it doesn't speak" while pointing out the covered speaker (Schlosser et al., 1995).

H. Keeping Procedures Constant across Conditions Except for the Independent Variable

In comparative efficacy studies, only the procedures that are associated directly with the independent variable should differ across conditions, which should otherwise remain identical. For instance, the general teaching approach in the Schlosser et al. (1998) study on spelling was copy-cover-compare (Schlosser et al., 1998). This teaching method was applied across conditions in the same manner. The only difference across conditions was the presence or absence of speech output or visual output. In the other study, symbol-referent associations in both conditions were taught by asking the participants to point to a symbol (e.g., "Point to _____."), which was immediately followed by modeling the correct response to the participant. Again, the only difference was the presence or absence of speech output (Schlosser et al., 1995).

I. COLLECTING TREATMENT INTEGRITY DATA

In addition to interobserver agreement for the dependent measure, it is essential to collect and report interobserver agreement data for the application of the independent variable—treatment integrity (see Chapter 9). In comparative studies, the lack of treatment integrity affects not only the determination of effectiveness of each intervention in its own right, but also the comparison of the interventions in terms of effectiveness and efficiency. Satisfactory (or at least comparable) treatment integrity data for both interventions are required in order to compare the interventions to one another. Unfortunately, more than half of the comparison studies reviewed by Schlosser (1999) failed to report treatment integrity data (see also Chapter 21). For positive examples the reader may consult the following studies (Bennett et al., 1986; Connaghan et al., 1992; Iacono & Duncum, 1995; Schlosser et al., 1995; 1998; Sigafoos & Reichle, 1992).

J. INTERPRETING THE RESULTS IN TERMS OF EFFECTIVENESS AND EFFICIENCY

Evaluating the effectiveness of each intervention may differ depending on the exact design employed. For example, in an ATD or AATD, effectiveness is evaluated on the basis of whether a change occurs in the dependent measure when intervention is introduced. When the ATD or AATD is combined with the MPD/MBD or in the PTD, effectiveness is determined on the basis of whether the dependent measure changes only when intervention is introduced and not before. This is consistent with the logic of MBDs and MPDs. In these situations, effectiveness is determined by the consistency of the effects across the instructional sets and tiers (Gast & Wolery, 1988). Obviously it helps to compare interventions for which functional control has been established in previous research (Sindelar et al., 1985). If this is not so, it is advisable to include a no-training control condition in order to demonstrate that interventions were responsible for behavior changes rather than extraneous variables.

If learning criteria have been established and are attained in each condition, most interventions will be equally effective in producing behavior change because instructional sets will be trained until the criterion is reached in both conditions. Should the criterion be reached in only one condition, however, only this condition can be considered effective. This, of course, is not the desired result, because efficiency comparisons are only possible when the criterion is reached across conditions. As mentioned earlier, a criterion is the standard of comparison among interventions. Differences in efficiency with the AATD and PTD are demonstrated when the instructional sets in one condition are acquired more rapidly (i.e., fewer trials/sessions to the criterion), with fewer errors to the criterion, less instructional time to the criterion, and less material preparation time to the criterion. In a PTD, one intervention would be considered more efficient than the other if the sum of these measures were consistently higher or lower within (i.e., across sequential sets) and across participants (Gast & Wolery, 1988).

K. SUMMARY

The issues and solutions presented in this chapter are intended to assist researchers and evidence-based practitioners in producing comparative evaluations and in becoming informed consumers of comparative efficacy evaluations. To assist with this process, a checklist was prepared for planning and evaluating of comparative studies using single-subject experimental designs (see the appendix). This checklist is intended to help with identifying issues that are deemed essential to the conduct and internal validity of comparative studies. Twenty evaluation items, grouped into five categories, are rated on a 4-point scale. Based on the ratings of each item, an overall rating can be derived. Comparative studies assist in the development of data-based recommendations about which interventions are not only effective but also efficient. To derive such sound recommendations from comparative studies, however, close attention to methodological issues is essential.

VI. SUMMARY

Single-subject experimental designs are the most prevalent and popular experimental designs in the AAC field today. Their popularity may be partially explained by their flexibility in terms of the number of participants needed to engage in single-subject experimental research. In fact, most available designs only require one participant. To strive toward greater generality, however, one participant is obviously not sufficient. Nonetheless, often researchers can initiate a preliminary study with only one participant and make it available in the peer-reviewed literature for later replication. The widespread acceptance of single-subject experimental designs in AAC may also be due to their flexibility in accommodating participants that are very heterogeneous in terms of characteristics (Light, 1999). To successfully plan, implement, and evaluate single-subject experimental designs, it is necessary to understand the main types of designs. Using examples from the AAC literature, the chapter illustrated the main design types for evaluating behavior change, generalization, and maintenance, and for comparing multiple interventions. The common pitfalls and solutions to these problems as presented in this chapter will facilitate the sound application and evaluation of these designs.

REFERENCES

Alberto, P., Briggs, T., Sharpton, W., & Goldstein, D. (1981). Teaching a non-verbal YES/NO response to severely handicapped students. *Journal of Childhood Communication Disorders, 5*, 90–103.

Angelo, D. H., & Goldstein, H. (1990). Effects of a pragmatic teaching strategy for requesting information by communication board users. *Journal of Speech and Hearing Disorders, 55*, 231–243.

Baer, D. M., Wolf, M. M., & Risley, T. R. (1968). Some current dimensions of applied behavior analysis. *Journal of Applied Behavior Analysis, 1*, 91–97.

Barlow, D. H., & Hayes, S. C. (1979). Alternating treatments design: One strategy for comparing the effects of two treatments in a single subject. *Journal of Applied Behavior Analysis, 12*, 199–210.

Barlow, D. H., & Hersen, M. (1984). *Single-case experimental designs: Strategies for studying behavior change* (2nd ed.). New York: Pergamon Press.

Barrera, R. D., Lobato-Barrera, D., & Sulzer-Azaroff, B. (1980). A simultaneous treatment comparison of three expressive language training programs with a mute autistic child. *Journal of Autism and Developmental Disorders, 10*, 21–37.

Barrios, B. A., & Hartmann, D. P. (1988). Recent developments in single-subject methodology: Methods for analyzing generalization, maintenance, and multicomponent treatments. In M. Hersen, R. M. Eisler, & P. M. Miller (Eds.), *Progress in behavior modification: Vol. 22* (pp. 11–47). Newbury Park, CA: Sage.

Bennett, D. L., Gast, D. L., Wolery, M., & Schuster, J. (1986). Time delay and system of least prompts: A comparison in teaching manual sign production. *Education and Training of the Mentally Retarded, 21*, 117–129.

Buzolich, M. J., King, J. S., & Baroody, S. M. (1991). Acquisition of the commenting function among system users. *Augmentative and Alternative Communication, 7*, 88–99.

Calculator, S. N., & Dollaghan, C. (1982). The use of communication boards in a residential setting. *Journal of Speech and Hearing Disorders, 14*, 281–287.

Carr, E. G., Binkoff, J. A., Kologinsky, E., & Eddy, M. (1978). Acquisition of sign language by autistic children I: Expressive labeling. *Journal of Applied Behavior Analysis, 11*, 489–501.

Carr, E. G., & Kemp, D. C. (1989). Functional equivalence of autistic leading and communicative pointing: Analysis and treatment. *Journal of Autism and Developmental Disorders, 19*, 561–578.

Carr, E. G., & Kologinsky, E. (1983). Acquisition of sign language by autistic children II: Spontaneity and generalization effects. *Journal of Applied Behavior Analysis, 16*, 297–314.

Clarke, S., Remington, B., & Light, P. (1986). An evaluation of the relationship between receptive speech skills and expressive signing. *Journal of Applied Behavior Analysis, 19*, 231–239.

Conaghan, B. P., Singh, N., Moe, T. L., Landrum, T. J., & Ellis, C. R. (1992). Acquisition and generalization of manual signs by hearing-impaired adults with mental retardation. *Journal of Behavioral Education, 2*, 177–205.

Cook, T. D., & Campbell, D. T. (Eds.). (1979). *Quasi-experimentation: Design and analysis issues for field settings*. Chicago: Rand McNally.

Culatta, B., & Blackstone, S. (1980). A program to teach non-oral communication symbols to multiple handicapped children. *Journal of Childhood Communication Disorders, 4,* 29–55.

Dalrymple, A. J., & Feldman, M. A. (1992). Effects of reinforced directed rehearsal on expressive sign language by persons with mental retardation. *Journal of Behavioral Education, 2,* 1–16.

Dattilo, J., & Camarata, S. (1991). Facilitating conversation through self-initiated augmentative communication treatment. *Journal of Applied Behavior Analysis, 24,* 369–378.

Doherty, J. (1985). The effects of sign characteristics on sign acquisition and retention: An integrative review of the literature. *Augmentative and Alternative Communication, 1,* 108–121.

Ducker, P. C., & Moonen, X. M. (1986). The effect of two procedures on spontaneous signing with Down's syndrome children. *Journal of Mental Deficiency Research, 30,* 355–364.

Duker, P. C., & Michielsen, H. M. (1983). Cross-setting generalization of manual signs to verbal instructions with severely retarded children. *Applied Research in Mental Retardation, 4,* 29–40.

Duker, P. C., & Morsink, H. (1984). Acquisition and cross-setting generalization of manual signs with severely retarded individuals. *Journal of Applied Behavior Analysis, 17,* 93–103.

Durand, v. M. (1990). *Severe behavior problems: A functional communication training approach.* New York: Guilford Press.

Durand, v. M. (1993). Functional communication training using assistive devices: Effects on challenging behavior and affect. *Augmentative and Alternative Communication, 9,* 168–176.

Fitzgerald, J. R., Reid, D. H., Schepis, M. M., Faw, G. D., Welty, P. A., & Pyfer, L. M. (1984). A rapid training procedure for teaching manual sign language skills to multidisciplinary institutional staff. *Applied Research in Mental Retardation, 5,* 451–469.

Franklin, D. B. Allison, & B. S. Gorman (1997). *Design and analysis of single-case research.* Hillsdale, NJ: Erlbaum.

Gast, D. L., & Wolery, M. (1988). Parallel treatments design: A nested single subject design for comparing instructional procedures. *Education and Treatment of Children, 11,* 270–285.

Glennen, S. L., & Calculator, S. N. (1985). Training functional communication board use: A pragmatic approach. *Augmentative and Alternative Communication, 1,* 134–142.

Gobbi, L., Cipani, E., Hudson, C., & Lapenta-Neudeck, R. (1986). Developing spontaneous requesting among children with severe mental retardation. *Mental Retardation, 24,* 357–363.

Goodman, J., & Remington, B. (1993). Acquisition of expressive signing: Comparison of reinforcement strategies. *Augmentative and Alternative Communication, 9,* 26–35.

Hagiwara, T., & Myles, B. S. (1999). A multimedia social story intervention: Teaching skills to children with autism. *Focus on Autism and Other Developmental Disabilities, 14,* 82–95.

Hamilton, B. L., & Snell, M. E. (1993). Using the milieu approach to increase spontaneous communication book use across environments by an adolescent with autism. *Augmentative and Alternative Communication, 9,* 259–272.

Harris, L., Skarakis Doyle, E., & Haaf, R. (1996). Language treatment approach for users of AAC: Experimental single-subject investigation. *Augmentative and Alternative Communication, 12,* 230–243.

Hetzroni, O. E., & Belfiore, P. (2000). Preschoolers with communication impairments play shrinking kim: An interactive computer storytelling intervention for teaching Blissymbols. *Augmentative and Alternative Communication, 16,* 260–269.

Hinderscheit, L. R., & Reichle, J. (1987). Teaching direct select color encoding to an adolescent with multiple handicaps. *Augmentative and Alternative Communication, 3,* 137–142.

Horn, E. M., & Jones, H. A. (1996). Comparison of two selection techniques used in augmentative and alternative communication. *Augmentative and Alternative Communication, 12,* 23–31.

Horner, R. D., & Baer, D. M. (1978). Multiple-probe technique: A variation of the multiple baseline design. *Journal of Applied Behavior Analysis, 11,* 189–196.

Hughes, D. L. (1985). Measurement of generalization. In D. L. Hughes (Ed.), *Language Treatment and Generalization—A Clinician's Handbook* (pp. 15–36). San Diego, CA: College-Hill Press.

Hunt, P., Alwell, M., & Goetz, L. (1991a). Establishing conversational exchange with family and friends: Moving from training to meaningful communication. *Journal of Special Education, 25*, 305–319.

Hunt, P., Alwell, M., Goetz, L., & Sailor, W. (1990). Generalized effects of conversation skill training. *Journal of the Association for Persons with Severe Handicaps, 15*, 250–260.

Hurlbut, B. I., Iwata, B. A., & Green, J. D. (1982). Nonvocal language acquisition in adolescents with severe physical disabilities: Blissymbol versus iconic stimulus formats. *Journal of Applied Behavior Analysis, 15*, 241–257.

Iacono, T. A., & Duncum, J. E. (1995). Comparison of sign alone and in combination with an electronic communication device in early language intervention: Case study. *Augmentative and Alternative Communication, 11*, 249–259.

Iacono, T., Mirenda, P., & Beukelman, D. (1993). Comparison of unimodal and multimodal AAC techniques for children with intellectual disabilities. *Augmentative and Alternative Communication, 9*, 83–94.

Julius, H., Schlosser, R. W., & Goetze, H. (2000). *Kontrollierte Einzelfallstudien: Eine Alternative für die sonderpädagogische und klinische Forschung.* Goettingen, Bern, Toronto, Seattle: Hogrefe.

Kaiser, A. P., Ostrosky, M. M., & Alpert, C. L. (1993). Training teachers to use environmental arrangement and milieu teaching with nonvocal preschool children. *Journal of the Association for Persons with Severe Handicaps, 18*, 188–199.

Kazdin, A. E. (1982). *Single-case research designs: Methods for clinical and applied settings.* Oxford, England: Oxford University Press.

Kazdin, A. E., & Hartmann, D. P. (1978). The simultaneous treatment design. *Behavior Therapy, 9*, 912–922.

Keogh, D., Whitman, T., Beeman, D., Halligan, K., & Starzynski, T. (1987). Teaching interactive signing in a dialogue situation to mentally retarded individuals. *Research in Developmental Disabilities, 8*, 39–53.

Kotkin, R. A., Simpson, S. B., & Desanto, D. (1978). The effect of sign language on picture naming in two retarded girls possessing normal hearing. *Journal of Mental Deficiency Research, 22*, 19–25.

Koul, R. Schlosser, R. W., Corwin, M., & Sims, S. (1997, November). *Effects of speech output on graphic symbol learning.* Paper presented at the Annual Convention of the American Speech-Language and Hearing Association, Boston.

Kouri, T. A. (1988). Effects of simultaneous communication in a child-directed treatment approach with preschoolers with severe disabilities. *Augmentative and Alternative Communication, 4*, 222–232.

Kozleski, E. B. (1991). Visual symbol acquisition by students with autism. *Exceptionality, 2*, 173–194.

Light, J. (1993). Teaching automatic linear scanning for computer access: A case study of a preschooler with severe physical and communication disabilities. *Journal of Special Education Technology, 7*, 125–134.

Light, J. C. (1999). Do augmentative and alternative communication interventions really make a difference?: The challenges of efficacy research. *Augmentative and Alternative Communication, 15*, 13–24.

Light, J., Dattilo, J., English, J., Gutierrez, L., & Hartz, J. (1992). Instructing facilitators to support the communication of people who use augmentative communication systems. *Journal of Speech and Hearing Research, 35*, 865–875.

Light, P., Remington, B., Clarke, S., & Watson, J. (1989). Signs of language? In I. Leudar, M. Beveridge, & G. Conti-Ramsden (Eds.), *Language and communication in the mentally handicapped* (pp. 56–79). London: Chapman and Hall.

Linton, J. M., & Singh, N. N. (1984). Acquisition of sign language using positive practice overcorrection. *Behavior Modification, 8*, 553–566.

Lloyd, L. L., & Fuller, D. R. (1990). The role of iconicity in augmentative and alternative communication symbol learning. In W. I. Fraser (Ed.), *Key issues in mental retardation research* (pp. 295–306). London: Routledge.

Locke, P. A., & Mirenda, P. (1988). A computer-supported communication approach for a child with severe communication, visual, and cognitive impairments: A case study. *Augmentative and Alternative Communication, 4*, 15–22.

McEwen, & Karlan, G. R. (1990). Case studies: Why and how? *Augmentative and Alternative Communication, 6*, 69–75.

McGregor, G., Young, J., Gerak, J., Thomas, B., & Vogelsberg, R. T. (1992). Increasing functional use of an assistive communication device by a student with severe disabilities. *Augmentative and Alternative Communication, 8*, 243–250.

McNaughton, D., & Tawney, J. (1993). Comparison of two spelling instruction techniques for adults who use augmentative and alternative communication. *Augmentative and Alternative Communication, 9*, 72–82.

McReynolds, L. V., & Kearns, K. P. (1983). *Single-subject experimental designs in communicative disorders.* Baltimore: University Park Press.

O'Keefe, B. M., & Dattilo, J. (1992). Teaching the response-recode form to adults with mental retardation using AAC systems. *Augmentative and Alternative Communication, 8*, 224–233.

O'Leary, K. D., & Drabman, R. (1971). Token reinforcement programs in the classroom: A review. *Psychological Bulletin, 75*, 379–398.

Parsonson, B. S., & Baer, D. M. (1992). The visual analysis of data, and current research into the stimuli controlling it. In T. R. Kratochwill & J. R. Levin (Eds.) *Single-case research design and analysis: New directions for Psychology and Education* (pp. 15–40). Hillsdale, NJ: Erlbaum.

Reichle, J., Barrett, C., Tetlie, R., & McQuarter, R. J. (1987). The effect of prior intervention to establish a generalized requesting on the acquisition of object signs. *Augmentative and Alternative Communication, 3*, 3–11.

Reichle, J., Rogers, N., & Barrett, C. (1984). Establishing pragmatic discriminations among communicative functions of requesting, rejecting, and commenting in an adolescent. *Journal of the Association for Persons with Severe Handicaps, 9*, 31–36.

Reid, D. H., & Hurlbut, B. (1977). Teaching nonvocal communication skills to multihandicapped retarded adults. *Journal of Applied Behavior Analysis, 10*, 591–603.

Remington, B., & Clarke, S. (1983). Acquisition of expressive signing by autistic children: An evaluation of the relative effects of simultaneous communication and sign-alone training. *Journal of Applied Behavior Analysis, 16*, 315–328.

Remington, B., & Clarke, S. (1993a). Simultaneous communication and speech comprehension. Part I: Comparison of two methods of teaching expressive signing and speech comprehension skills. *Augmentative and Alternative Communication, 9*, 36–48.

Remington, B., & Clarke, S. (1993b). Simultaneous communication and speech comprehension. Part II: Comparison of two methods of overcoming selective attention during expressive sign training. *Augmentative and Alternative Communication, 9*, 49–60.

Rotholz, D. A., Berkowitz, S. F., & Burberry, J. (1989). Functionality of two modes of communication in the community by students with developmental disabilities: A comparison of signing and communication books. *Journal of the Association for Persons with Severe Handicaps, 14*, 227–233.

Rusch, R. R., & Kazdin, A. E. (1981). Toward a methodology of withdrawal designs for the assessment of response maintenance. *Journal of Applied Behavior Analysis, 14*, 131–240.

Schepis, M. M., & Reid, D. H. (1995). Effects of a voice output communication aid on interactions between support personnel and an individual with multiple disabilities. *Journal of Applied Behavior Analysis, 28*, 73–77.

Schlosser, R. W. (1999). Comparative efficacy of interventions in augmentative and alternative communication. *Augmentative and Alternative Communication, 15*, 56–68.

Schlosser, R. W., Belfiore, P. J., Nigam, R., Blischak, D., & Hetzroni, O. (1995). The effects of speech output technology in the learning of graphic symbols. *Journal of Applied Behavior Analysis, 28,* 537–549.

Schlosser, R. W., Blischak, D. M., Belfiore, P. J., Bartley, C., & Barnett, N. (1998). The effects of synthetic speech output and orthographic feedback on spelling in a student with autism: A preliminary study. *Journal of Autism and Developmental Disorders, 28,* 319–329.

Schlosser, R. W., & Braun, U. (1994). Efficacy of AAC interventions: Methodologic issues in evaluating behavior change, generalization, and effects. *Augmentative and Alternative Communication, 10,* 207–223.

Schlosser, R. W., & Lee, D. (2000). Promoting generalization and maintenance in augmentative and alternative communication: A meta-analysis of 20 years of effectiveness research. *Augmentative and Alternative Communication, 16,* 208–227.

Schlosser, R. W., McGhie-Richmond, D., Blackstien-Adler, S., Mirenda, P., Antonius, K., & Janzen, P. (2000). Training a school team to integrate technology meaningfully into the curriculum: Effects on student participation. *Journal of Special Education Technology, 15,* 31–44.

Schuebel, C. L., & Lalli, J. S. (1992). A program for increasing manual signing by a nonvocal adult within the daily environment. *Behavioral Residential Treatment, 7,* 277–282.

Schweigert, P. (1989). Use of microswitch technology to facilitate social contingency awareness as a basis for early communication skills. *Augmentative and Alternative Communication, 5,* 192–198.

Schweigert, P., & Rowland, C. (1992). Early communication and microtechnology: Instructional sequence and case studies of children with severe multiple disabilities. *Augmentative and Alternative Communication, 8,* 273–286.

Sevcik, R. A., Romski, M. A., & Wilkinson, K. (1991). Roles of graphic symbols in the language acquisition process for persons with severe cognitive disabilities. *Augmentative and Alternative Communication, 7,* 161–170.

Sigafoos, J., Laurie, S., & Pennell, D. (1996). Teaching children with Rett Syndrome to request preferred objects using aided communication: Two preliminary studies. *Augmentative and Alternative Communication, 12,* 88–96.

Sigafoos, J., & Reichle, J. (1992). Comparing explicit to generalized requesting in an augmentative communication mode. *Journal of Developmental and Physical Disabilities, 4,* 167–188.

Sindelar, P. T., Rosenberg, M. S., & Wilson, R. J. (1985). An adapted alternating treatments design for instructional research. *Education and Treatment of Children, 8,* 67–76.

Sommer, K. S., Whitman, T. L., & Keogh, D. A. (1988). Teaching severely retarded persons to sign interactively through the use of a behavioral script. *Research in Developmental Disabilities, 9,* 291–304.

Soto, G., Belfiore, P. J., Schlosser, R. W., & Haynes, C. (1993). Teaching specific requests: A comparative analysis on skill acquisition and preference using two augmentative and alternative communication aids. *Education and Training in Mental Retardation, 28,* 169–178.

Spiegel, B., Benjamin, B. J., & Spiegel, S. A. (1993). One method to increase spontaneous use of an assistive communication device: Case study. *Augmentative and Alternative Communication, 9,* 111–118.

Stephenson, J., & Linfoot, K. (1995). Choice-making as a natural context for teaching early communication board use to a ten year old boy with spoken language and severe intellectual disability. *Australia and New Zealand Journal of Developmental Disabilities, 20,* 263–286.

Sternberg, L., McNerney, C. D., & Pegnatore, L. (1987). Developing primitive signalling behavior of students with profound mental retardation. *Mental Retardation, 25,* 13–20.

Sternberg, L., Pegnatore, L., & Hill, C. (1983). Establishing interactive communication behaviors with profoundly mentally handicapped students. *TASH Journal, 8,* 39–46.

Tawney, J. W., & Gast, D. L. (1984). *Single subject research in special education*. Columbus, OH: Merrill.

Todman, J. B., & Dugard, P. (2001). *Single-case and small-n experimental designs*. Hillsdale, NJ: Earlbaum.

Turner, R., & Carter, M. (1994). Establishing a repertoire of requesting for a student with severe and multiple disabilities using tangible symbols and naturalistic time delay. *Australia and New Zealand Journal of Developmental Disabilities, 19*, 193–207.

Van Acker, R., & Grant, S. (1995). An effective computer-based requesting system for persons with Rett Syndrome. *Journal of Childhood Communication Disorders, 2*, 31–38.

Vaughn, B., & Horner, R. H. (1995). Effects of concrete versus verbal choice systems on problem behavior. *Augmentative and Alternative Communication, 11*, 89–92.

Watson, P. J., & Workman, E. A. (1981). The non-concurrent multiple baseline across-individuals design: An extension of the traditional multiple baseline design. *Journal of Behavior Therapy and Experimental Psychiatry, 12*, 257–259.

Evaluation Checklist for Planning and Evaluating Comparative Efficacy Studies

Instructions: This evaluation checklist is intended to guide in the planning and evaluation of comparative efficacy studies using single-subject designs. The checklist helps identify those issues that are deemed important to the conduct and internal validity of comparative studies. The individual ratings should serve as the basis for the overall rating. Use check marks.

Evaluation Items	P^a F^b G^c E^d
Introduction	
1. The effectiveness literature pertaining to each condition is thoroughly and accurately reviewed.	
2. There is a logical and convincing rationale presented for the comparison to be made.	
3. The research question or purpose statement accurately reflects the conditions to be compared.	
Subjects	
4. The participants are not biased toward a particular condition due to previous experiences.	
Materials	
5. The materials support the comparison to be made.	
Design	
6. The design offers adequate control of sequence effects.	
7. The design provides adequate control of carryover effects.	
8. The design allows for within-subject replication of effects.	
Procedures	
9. Carryover effects are minimized through procedural safeguards.	
10. A learning criterion *and* teaching criterion were set; training in a condition continued until whichever criterion was attained first.	
11. The equivalence of instructional sets is based on current knowledge of contributing factors to equivalency.	
12. The equivalence of instructional sets is demonstrated.	
13. Treatments are randomly assigned to instructional sets.	
14. The functional independence of sets is demonstrated.	
15. Interobserver agreement data for the *dependent* measure(s) is adequate for the particular target behaviors.	
16. Interobserver agreement data for the *independent* variable are adequate and comparable across conditions.	
17. Procedures are held constant except for differences across conditions, which are to be examined.	

(continues)

Evaluation Items	P[a]	F[b]	G[c]	E[d]
Results 18. Effectiveness of conditions is demonstrated unequivocally through the attainment of a learning criterion. 19. Efficiency comparisons are based on attainment of an a priori learning criterion for all conditions compared. 20. Results are reported to facilitate comparisons.				
Overall Rating	P	F	G	E

[a]Poor.
[b]Fair.
[c]Good.
[d]Excellent.

CHAPTER 7

Group Designs

Ralf W. Schlosser
Department of Speech-Language Pathology and Audiology
Northeastern University

I. INTRODUCTION

Chapter 6 addressed single-subject experimental designs as a means for evaluating the efficacy of augmentative and alternative communication (AAC) interventions. Although these designs are the most frequently used designs involving learners with disabilities in AAC, there are other options to consider. This

The Efficacy of Augmentative and Alternative Communication

chapter is devoted to group designs as a potential alternative to single-subject experimental designs. Group designs may be categorized into (1) preexperimental designs, (2) true experimental designs, and (3) quasi-experimental designs (Hegde, 1994).

II. PREEXPERIMENTAL DESIGNS

Among the group design strategies, the preexperimental designs are commonly used in AAC intervention research. Because of their relatively frequent use, it is important that researchers and evidence-based practitioners understand their limitations relative to demonstrating the efficacy of an AAC intervention.

A. THE ONE-SHOT CASE STUDY

With this design an existing group is selected and receives an intervention. After the intervention is complete, a posttest is applied. No control group is involved. This design does not permit any valid judgments concerning the efficacy of an intervention for the following reasons. First, the absence of a pretest makes it difficult to evaluate the posttest data. In fact, it is impossible to attribute the posttest data to the intervention. Moreover, the lack of a control group adds additional difficulties to the interpretation of the source that produced the posttest data. In short, the one-shot case study is unable to rule out most threats to internal validity discussed in Chapter 3. Dowden, Beukelman, and Lossing (1986) used the one-shot case study design to examine outcomes for an intact group of 50 nonspeaking patients in an acute care setting. The percentage of communication needs met by the communication approaches that had been recommended was used an outcomes measure. Consistent with this design, there was no pretest and no control group. Results indicated that the mean percentage of communication needs met in these categories ranged from approximately 10% to about 80%, with multiple system intervention generally meeting a greater percentage of needs than a single intervention. These results offer interesting avenues for future research, but they need to be viewed cautiously due to their preexperimental nature.

B. THE ONE-GROUP PRETEST-POSTTEST DESIGN

The one-group pretest-posttest design is very similar to the one-shot case study, except that this design does involve a pretest. Differences between the pretest and the posttest are typically attributed to the intervention. Again, there is no control group. Although this design is an improvement over the previous design, it still does not permit an unequivocal attribution of changes in the posttest to be attributed to the treatment. Threats to internal validity such as history, maturation, testing, and regression to the mean go uncontrolled due to a lack of a control group (see Chapter 3 for further discussion of threats to internal validity).

C. THE STATIC-GROUP COMPARISON

This design includes the term "static" because one of the two existing groups has already received treatment and is not flexible in that respect. The other group has not received treatment and is selected to serve the function of a "control" group. Because no pretest was possible for the "experimental" group, no pretest is being implemented for the "control" group either. Differences in posttest scores between the two groups are attributed to the treatment. This, however, is an erroneous conclusion given that the design does not rule out subject selection bias as the major threat to internal validity (see Chapter 3). That is, subjects were not randomly assigned to the two groups, and there was no pretest to begin with. Therefore, it becomes difficult to argue that the groups, were equal prior to intervention.

D. SUMMARY

Preexperimental designs have serious limitations in their potential to demonstrate that an AAC intervention is effective. Analog to case studies in single-subject designs (see Chapter 6), preexperimental group designs should be considered exploratory in nature. Nonetheless, they may be useful for generating interesting hypotheses for future research.

III. TRUE EXPERIMENTAL DESIGNS

From an experimental point of view, true experimental designs lend themselves very well to evaluating the efficacy of AAC interventions because they are more apt in controlling threats to internal validity. True experimental designs include (1) the pretest-posttest control group design, (2) multigroup pretest-posttest design, (3) posttest-only control group design, (4) multigroup posttest-only design, (5) the Solomon-four group design, and (6) factorial designs.

A. THE PRETEST-POSTTEST CONTROL GROUP DESIGN

This is the prototypical group design, involving one experimental group and one control group. The experimental group receives treatment, whereas the control group does not. Both groups are presented with a pretest, intervention, and a posttest. To ensure appropriate inferences, it is necessary that the two groups are equal in the beginning along parameters central to the purpose of this study. True experimental designs require the participants to be randomly selected from the population randomly assigned to the two groups. This design controls all threats to internal validity for as long as the participants were randomly assigned to the two groups. If matching is used, on the other hand, this design is unable to rule out subject selection bias (Campbell & Stanley, 1966; Hegde, 1994).

B. MULTIGROUP PRETEST-POSTTEST DESIGN

The previously described design involves one experimental group and one control group. In clinical research such as AAC, one often wonders about the effectiveness of one treatment over another. For example, is the exchange of a card with a graphic symbol more effective than the mere pointing to a graphic symbol in teaching requesting to children from the Autism Spectrum Disorder? A multigroup pretest-posttest design would allow the experimenter to add additional treatment groups. Hegde (1994) noted that the use of the control group is optional given that the researcher would be more interested in the relative effects of the various treatments rather than its absolute effects. The use of a control group would, however, enhance the studies internal validity and allow the researcher to draw conclusions concerning the absolute *and* relative effects of the treatments.

C. THE POSTTEST-ONLY CONTROL GROUP DESIGN

This is essentially the same design as the pretest-posttest control group design, except no pretest is given. Some researchers (Campbell & Stanley, 1966) have argued that pretests are not necessary when participants are drawn randomly from the population because randomization ensures that they are equal to begin with. In addition, having a pretest may actually result in a threat to internal validity due to pretest sensitization. Hegde (1994), however, cautioned that randomization may work well in theory but is often not possible in clinical research. AAC certainly is an area of clinical research and would thus fit that argument. Having a pretest in designs other than true experimental designs at least allows researchers to check for equivalence prior to the initiation of treatment.

D. MULTIGROUP POSTTEST-ONLY DESIGN

This is the same design as discussed in the previous paragraph with one or more additional treatment groups added. Its strengths and weaknesses are analogous to the posttest-only control group design.

E. THE SOLOMON FOUR-GROUP DESIGN

Should pretest sensitization remain an issue of concern, researchers have the option, at least at a theoretical level, to use the Solomon four-group design. This design is identical to the pretest-posttest control group design, except that it includes one additional control group and one additional experimental group. These additional groups do not get a pretest unlike the other two groups. This permits an examination into the role of pretest sensitization, if any, by comparing those groups with a pretest to groups without a pretest. While theoretically very appealing, the low incidence of the population of AAC users makes it unlikely that our field will have the luxury of exploring such questions. Even when nondisabled individuals serve as participants, researchers need to carefully weigh the "cost" of recruiting to extra groups relative to the "magic" in return.

F. FACTORIAL DESIGNS

"Factor" is another term for independent variable. Factorial designs have at least one active independent variable possibly combined with an assigned variable. Assigned variables such as subject characteristics may affect the results but cannot be manipulated (Hegde, 1994). The active independent variable in factorial designs has a minimum of two levels such as presence versus absence, technique A versus B, or high intensity versus low intensity. Hegde (1994) distinguished randomized block designs from the completely randomized factorial designs.

1. Randomized Block Design

In a basic randomized block design, there is at least one active independent variable and one assigned variable with two levels each. Treatments would qualify as an active variable that the investigator can manipulate. The participant's level of intelligence, adaptive behavior, receptive knowledge of referents, and the like could serve as assigned variables. The following is an example of a randomized block design, adapted from the quasi-experimental work of Mirenda and Beukelman (1987). Three different synthesizers plus one natural voice were com-

Treatment	Age levels		
	26–40	10–12	6–8
Echo II+			
Votrax			
DECtalk			
Natural			

Figure 7.1 Randomized block design.

	Augmented input	
	Present	Absent
Paired-associate		
Semantic-structural		

Figure 7.2 Completely Randomized Block Design.

pared in terms of their intelligibility with listeners from three age groups. The type of voice served as the independent variable manipulated by the experimenter, whereas the age level served as the nonmanipulated assigned variable. The resulting design is illustrated in Figure 7.1.

To qualify as a randomized block design, it is important that for each level of the assigned variable, the participants are drawn randomly and assigned to the treatments. This design permits an evaluation of the main effects of the treatment as well as the interaction effects of treatment levels with age groups. The actual design used by Mirenda and Beukelman (1987) differs in terms of selection of participants and assignment to treatment conditions (discussed later).

2. Completely Randomized Block Design

In a completely randomized block design, all of the factors are active rather than just one of them as in the randomized block design. For example, a study could be comparing two general teaching approaches (paired-associate, semantic-structural; Schlosser & Lloyd, 1997) with augmented input and without augmented input. Here, both the teaching approaches and augmented input are actively manipulated (see Figure 7.2).

G. Summary

True experimental designs are ideal for controlling threats to internal validity. Therefore, they are highly desirable from a research point of view. True experimental designs require random selection of participants from the population and random allocation of the participants to conditions. In clinical/educational research areas such as AAC, the first criterion is rarely met for practical considerations. This is where quasi-experimental designs come in.

IV. QUASI-EXPERIMENTAL DESIGNS

When nondisabled preschoolers or college students serve as subjects, for example, it would be cost-prohibitive to select these from the population of preschoolers or the population of college students. Thus, investigators often draw the sample from various preschools or sometimes from the same university within the same community. For individuals with disabilities, researchers may sometimes study students in a self-contained classroom—an intact group rather than a group specifically formed for research purposes. These decisions, which are fueled by practical constrains, undoubtedly raises questions as to how representative the data are in terms of the population at large. Quasi-experimental designs are therefore weaker than true experimental designs. Quasi-experimental designs may be grouped into (1) nonequivalent control group designs, (2) separate sample pretest-posttest design, and (3) time-series designs (see Hegde, 1994).

A. Nonequivalent Control Group Designs

The nonequivalent control group design is similar to the pretest-posttest control group design discussed earlier. It involves a pretest and a control group. The exception, however, is that there is no random selection or assignment in the nonequivalent control group design. This design permits the comparison of multiple treatment groups rather than a control group. Hegde (1994) pointed out that this design does not assure preexperimental equivalence of groups, which could be presumed, based on random selection. Nonetheless, this does not mean that the experimenter is not expected to do everything possible to approximate equivalence of the groups (based on mechanisms other than random selection). Because the groups cannot be presumed to be equal to begin with, subject selection bias and statistical regression to the mean constitute serious threats to internal validity with this design.

B. Quasi Multigroup Pretest–Posttest Design

Although Hegde (1994) did not list this design, it does fit the characteristics of many quasi-experimental group studies in AAC. Many group designs used in the AAC field tend to use a nonrandom selection of participants but allocate the participants randomly to conditions or use matching in an attempt to achieve equivalence. It is argued that there is no reason to assume the absence of equivalence if pretest data show equivalence. Therefore, the quasi-experimental design should be viewed as almost as powerful as the true experimental multigroup pretest posttest design. The theoretical argument against it, however, is that equivalence based on pretests equates only for known variables. Although there may be a theoretical difference, in practical terms the two designs should be treated as equivalent. Some authors even go as far as to say, for all practical reasons, that as long as a pretest indicates equivalence of intact groups, there should be little difference between the outcomes of a study using this design and a study using a design with random allocation participants to conditions. Mizuko (1987), for example, used this design. Thirty-six 3-year-old children were drawn from a group of normally developing children (nonrandom). Each participating child was randomly assigned to one of three experimental conditions (i.e., Blissymbols, Picture Communication Symbols, and Picsyms).

C. Separate Sample Pretest–Posttest Design

Unlike the nonequivalent control group design, this separate sample pretest-posttest design does use the random procedure for allocation of participants to experimental conditions. Therefore, sampling equivalence can be assumed. In this design only one group, the control group, is pretested and then presented with a treatment of which the results have no bearing on the conclusions of the study. The experimental group is not pretested and then receives the actual treatment followed by a posttest. The rationale for these decisions is based on the assumption that the experimental group's behavior would change due to pretest sensitization if group members received a pretest. Therefore, the pretest is given to the equivalent control group instead. This design is best illustrated with a hypothetical example that is based on the research interests of this author.

Suppose you wanted to find out what variables practitioners in a particular school district consider in selecting graphic symbols for their AAC caseload prior to introducing a training program on important selection considerations. Assume you also wanted to determine whether clinicians would change their selection behavior based on the training they receive. However, you also needed to be mindful of pretest sensitization. That is, once the clinicians are being asked what factors they consider during the pretest they may be sensitized to the following treatment and any behavior changes may be due to this sensitization rather than to the training itself. Therefore, you randomly select two subgroups of clinicians within the district and randomly assign the groups to the experimental and the control conditions. The control group is pretested on the variables they consider in selecting graphic symbols. They subsequently receive a presentation on the selection considerations one should take into account, whose effects are being ignored. The experimental group, in the absence of the pretest, receives the same training. The posttest evaluates any changes in the clinicians' inclination to use the newly introduced selection considerations.

Hegde (1994) noted that this design does not adequately control for the threats of history, maturation, and differential subject attrition. Thus, when possible a more robust design is preferred. It is also important to distinguish this design from the Solomon-four group design described earlier. First of all, the separate pretest-posttest design is quasi-experimental, whereas the Solomon-four group design is a true experimental design. Second, the Solomon-four group design is specifically concerned with determining the effects of pretesting, whereas this design is not. Its primary concern rests with minimizing sensitization to treatment by the experimental group through exposure to a pretest.

D. TIME-SERIES DESIGNS

With time-series designs, the dependent measure is systematically tracked over time both before and after treatment rather than only twice, as is typical with the designs discussed thus far. Hegde (1994) distinguished single-group time-series designs from multiple-group time-series designs.

1. Single Group-Time Series Designs

As its name indicates, single-group time-series designs involve only one group that is observed several times before and after treatment. This design allows for several variations. For example, the treatment may continue during some observations after the first administration of treatment, leaving only some of these observations to be true posttreatment observations. In some time-series designs, only one pretest may occur followed by several observations during posttreatment. When introducing novel symbols to some groups of participants, for example, it may be appropriate to assume that there would not be much variation across pretests and therefore only one measure would suffice. Other applications of the single-group time-series design do not include a pretest. Fuller and Lloyd (1992), for example, studied the effects of symbol configuration (superimposed versus nonsuperimposed) on symbol learning in a group of 20 nondisabled preschoolers. The students were exposed to all 30 symbols (including 15 superimposed and 15 nonsuperimposed) in random order for a total of four trials. The experimenter would point to each symbol and announce the name of the referent. After each training session, the child was tested. Specifically, the child was asked to point to the correct symbol following the experimenter calling out the name of the referent. Thus, a total of four observations for each child entered the analysis. Repeated measures on the trials indicated that the children learned more symbols with each successive trial. Results also indicated that the children learned more superimposed symbols than nonsuperimposed symbols.

2. Multigroup Time-Series Designs

When more than one group is involved, the design is referred to as the multigroup time-series design. Typically, these designs cannot rely on sampling equivalence because the participants are not randomly drawn from the population. Again, this design has numerous variations, and not all of them can be described here. In one variation, one of the groups serves as a control group, whereas the other serves as an experimental group. This design is very similar to the previously described nonequivalent control group design, except that repeated measures are involved rather than one pretest and one posttest. As mentioned previously, in clinical research investigators are often more concerned with the relative effects of different treatments rather than the absolute effects of one treatment over a control group. Schlosser and Lloyd (1993, 1997) used the multigroup time-series design in their research on the relative effectiveness of various approaches to the teaching of Blissymbols. In the Schlosser and Lloyd (1997) study, 39 preschoolers were assigned to one of three teaching methods: (1) paired-associate learning with referent-relevant comments, (2) symbol explanations, and (3) symbol explanations within a storytelling context. The groups were matched on relevant participant characteristics, and the teaching method to which a group was assigned was randomly determined. Following pretests, each of the groups was first taught semantic elements comprising the subsequently taught compound symbols. Both elements and compounds were taught over two sessions each and tested after each session. Results indicated that there were no differences across groups in terms of element comprehension, compound comprehension (acquisition and retention), and compound production. However, the group receiving the symbol explanations within a storytelling context generalized elements to novel combinations significantly better than the other two groups.

E. WITHIN-SUBJECTS DESIGNS

Thus far, the design strategies discussed established experimental control by using one group that receives treatment and another group that does not receive treatment. Differences in the dependent measure are attributed to the treatment. Alternatively, two groups may be used in which one group is exposed to treatment A and the other group to treatment B. Thus, these strategies all share one common feature—the use of between-group designs. There is an alternative to the use of different groups, commonly referred to as the within-subject design. Within-subject designs figure prominently in the landscape of AAC efficacy research. According to Hegde (1994), within-subject designs may be grouped into (1) basic within-group designs, (2) crossover designs, (3) complex counterbalanced designs, and (4) latin square designs.

1. Basic Within-Group Design

The most basic form of this design involves one treatment and a no-treatment control. The group is divided into two subgroups. The first subgroup is first exposed to the treatment followed by the no-treatment condition. The second subgroup receives the reverse order. By using a reverse order across the two subgroups and both subgroups receiving both conditions, experimenters can control for order effects while determining the effects of the treatment. Within-subject designs using a no-treatment control are scant in AAC intervention research.

2. Crossover Design

The crossover design, whereby *two treatments* (rather than one treatment and one control) are being compared with two subgroups appears to be more common. In the standard crossover design, a group of participants is selected and divided into two randomly formed groups. Both groups first receive a pretest. Next, the order of treatments is randomly determined. If subgroup I receives treatment A first followed by B, subgroup II should receive the reverse order. This allows for the control of order effects. In addition to the pretest, the standard design requires another test before the treatments are being crossed over and after they have been crossed over. In a within-group design with two treatments, it is not sufficient to vary the order from participant to participant. For example, Levine, Gauger, Bowers, and Khan (1986) compared the use of mouthstick and Morse Code as a means of input in six able-bodied participants. To control for order effects, they varied the input method between participants. The question arises, how exactly was the input method varied? Was it done at random or counterbalanced? Order effects need to be taken seriously in within-group designs.

The study by Fuller and Lloyd (1992) discussed earlier, could have been conducted as a crossover design. Rather than presenting superimposed and non-superimposed symbols in random order to all subjects (as done by these authors), a crossover design would have required the participants to be divided into two groups. One group would first receive superimposed symbols followed by non-superimposed symbols. The second group would receive the reverse order. The design chosen by these authors, however, is equally appropriate.

3. Complex Counterbalanced Designs

The crossover design described previously is rather simple in terms of its configuration because only two treatments are involved. As soon as one adds more treatments, counterbalancing becomes infinitely more complex. By adding just one more treatment, the three treatments A, B, and C, combine into six possible sequences: ABC, ACB, BAC, BCA, CAB, and CBA. Thus, a group of participants would need to be randomly assigned to one of the six sequences to achieve a counterbalanced design. If one were to investigate four treatments, a total of 24 sequences are required ($1 \times 2 \times 3 \times 4 = 24$), and so forth. Such complete counterbalancing may not always be practical due to its complexity. Perhaps it is therefore not surprising that many of the group studies in AAC do not employ crossover designs in a strict sense. For example, Mirenda and Beukelman (1990) employed a within-subject design involving four different voices (synthesizers, natural voices). They recruited seven persons in each of three age groups. Each of the age groups listened to all of the voices, which were presented in random order. Counterbalancing the order would have required many more participants because within each age group, one subgroup would need to be assigned to one particular order. Given that there were seven synthesizers and one natural voice involved, this would have required 40,320 subgroups for 40,320 sequences ($1 \times 2 \times 3 \times 4 \times 5 \times 6 \times 7 \times 8 = 40,320$). Clearly, that is not feasible, and therefore randomization is a legitimate tool to assume that order did not influence the results of the study. An alternative to complex counterbalanced designs and randomization are latin square designs.

4. Latin Square Designs

A latin square design represents a unique type of crossover design that reduces the complexity of other counterbalanced designs. Instead of having all conditions precede or follow each other in all sequences or in equal numbers (as in the complex counterbalanced design), each treatment in each position appears only once in each group (Hegde, 1994; Winer, Brown, & Michels, 1991).

Hupp and Mervis (1981) used a repeated measures latin square design to evaluate the acquisition of generalized concepts in learners with severe disabilities. Each learner received instruction in labeling two categories of objects within three experimental conditions. In the first condition (GE1), the students were taught two manual signs using one good exemplar to represent each of the two categories. The second condition was identical to the first except that the students were taught three good exemplars (GE3). In the third condition, the student was taught two manual signs using one good exemplar, one moderate exemplar, and a poor exemplar (ALL). The six participating learners were divided into three pairs with each pair receiving a different order of conditions. Learners 1 and 5 received GE3 first, followed by GE1 and ALL. Learners 2 and 3 received GE1 first, followed by ALL and GE3. And Learners 4 and 6 received ALL first, followed by GE3 and GE1. Teaching with representative exemplars resulted in generalization above chance levels, whereas teaching with moderate exemplars or nonrepresentative exemplars did not result in generalization above chance levels. Moreover, teaching with three good exemplars was more effective than teaching with only one good exemplar.

This author is currently pursuing research into the role of graphic symbols on concept formation for which a latin square design was selected (Schlosser, 2002). It is hypothesized that teaching Blissymbols results in greater generalization to novel exemplars than teaching Picture Communication Symbols (PCS). Moreover, it is hypothesized that teaching three typical exemplars (TE3) will be more effective than teaching one typical exemplar (TE1) regardless of the graphic symbol set/system. In TE3, for example, the basic-level categories PANTS, SHIRT, and DRESS will be taught for clothing. In TE1, only the most typical exemplar (e.g., PANTS) will be taught. ALL involves the most typical exemplar (e.g., PANTS), one exemplar of medium typicality (e.g., SHOES) and one atypical exemplar (e.g., WRISTWATCH).

These hypotheses required a design that permits between-graphic system-set comparisons and within-graphic system/set comparisons while guarding against order effects. A repeated-measures latin square design meets these requirements. The 12 participants will be divided into six pairs, and the six pairs will be counterbalanced for gender. Three pairs will be assigned to Blissymbols, and three pairs will be assigned to PCS. Each pair in each of the graphic symbol media will receive a different order of the three experimental conditions, TE3, TE1, and ALL. The experimental design is presented in Figure 7.3. With this arrangement, this design allows not only for comparisons between Blissymbolics and PCS, but also controls for order effects using only a minimum number of participants.

Participants (#)		Phase		
Blissymbolics	PCS	1	2	3
		Clothing	Vehicle	Furniture
1, 5	7, 11	TE3	TE1	ALL
2, 3	8, 9	TE1	ALL	TE3
4, 6	10, 12	ALL	TE3	TE1

Figure 7.3 Latin-square design to be used in Schlosser (2002).

V. CONCLUSIONS

Group designs serve an important function in the landscape of design options for evaluating the efficacy of AAC interventions. Unlike single-subject experimental designs, group designs allow for a more fruitful examination of interaction effects (Light, 1999). They also afford the possibility for researchers to compare multiple treatments, even when it is difficult to create equal sets of stimuli (as would be required in comparative single-subject experimental designs). To date, group designs have been applied only to a limited extent with individuals with disabilities in AAC (Hodges & Schwethelm, 1984; Porter & Schroeder, 1980; Yoder & Layton, 1988). Practical barriers, such as a low-incidence field and heterogeneity among AAC users, are contributing factors. With the advent of multicenter trials, however, it should be increasingly feasible to use the group design strategy with AAC users as well. Group designs already serve an important function in studying the efficacy of AAC interventions with nondisabled participants. These efforts should continue while reminding those who are interpreting the findings of the questionable generality of the results for people with disabilities. This chapter highlighted the importance of selecting designs that are both feasible along practical considerations and have the potential to minimize threats to internal validity. Quasi-experimental designs appear the most promising design options for AAC. But even within the quasi-experimental design strategy, not all designs are created equal (see Chapter 12). Researchers and evidence-based practitioners need to be aware of design differences and apply them in their efforts to advance the field in terms of science and practice.

REFERENCES

Campbell, D. T., & Stanley, J. C. (1966). *Experimental and quasi-experimental designs for research*. Chicago: Rand McNally.

Dowden, P., Beukelman, D. R., & Lossing, C. (1986). Serving nonspeaking patients in acute care settings: Intervention outcomes. *Augmentative and Alternative Communication, 2*, 38–44.

Fuller, D. R., & Lloyd, L. L. (1992). Effects of configuration on the paired-associate learning of Blissymbols by preschool children with normal cognitive abilities. *Journal of Speech and Hearing Research, 35*, 1376–1383.

Hegde, M. N. (1994). *Clinical research in communicative disorders: Principles and strategies* (2nd ed.). Austin, TX: Pro-Ed.

Hodges, P., & Schwethelm, B. (1984). A comparison of the effectiveness of graphic symbol and manual sign training with profoundly retarded children. *Applied Psycholinguistics, 5*, 223–253.

Hupp, S. C., & Mervis, C. B. (1981). Development of generalized concepts by severely handicapped students. *TASH Journal, 6*, 14–21.

Levine, S. P., Gauger, J. R. D., Bowers, L. D., & Khan, K. J. (1986). A comparison of mouthstick and morse code text inputs. *Augmentative and Alternative Communication, 2*, 51–55.

Light, J. C. (1999). Do augmentative and alternative communication interventions really make a difference?: The challenges of efficacy research, *Augmentative and Alternative Communication, 15*, 13–24.

Mirenda, P., & Beukelman, D. R. (1987). A comparison of speech synthesis intelligibility with listeners from three age groups. *Augmentative and Alternative Communication, 3,* 120–128.

Mirenda, P., & Beukelman, D. R. (1990). A comparison of intelligibility among natural speech and seven speech synthesizers with listeners from three age groups. *Augmentative and Alternative Communication, 6,* 61–68.

Mizuko, M. (1987). Transparency and ease of learning of symbols represented by Blissymbols, PCS, and Picsyms. *Augmentative and Alternative Communication, 3,* 129–136.

Porter, P. B., & Schroeder, S. R. (1980). Generalization and maintenance of skills acquired in Non-Speech Language Initiation Program training. *Applied Research in Mental Retardation, 1,* 71–84.

Schlosser, R. W. (2002). *Roles of graphic symbols in concept formation.* Research in progress.

Schlosser, R. W., & Lloyd, L. L. (1993). Effects of initial element teaching in a storytelling context on Blissymbol acquisition and generalization. *Journal of Speech and Hearing Research, 36,* 979–995.

Schlosser, R. W., & Lloyd, L. L. (1997). Effects of paired-associate learning versus symbol explanations on Blissymbol learning and use. *Augmentative and Alternative Communication, 13,* 226–238.

Winer, B. N. J., Brown, D. R., & Michels, K. M. (1991). *Statistical principles in experimental design* (3rd ed.). New York: McGraw-Hill.

Yoder, P., & Layton, T. (1988). Speech following sign language training in autistic children with minimal verbal language. *Journal of Autism and Developmental Disabilities, 18,* 217–229.

CHAPTER 8

Longitudinal Designs

Measuring the Outcomes of AAC Interventions[1]

Rose A. Sevcik
Georgia State University

MaryAnn Romski
Georgia State University

I. Introduction
II. Longitudinal Research Designs
III. Longitudinal Designs in AAC Research
   A. The System for Augmenting Language (SAL)
   B. Issues for Longitudinal Research Designs in AAC
IV. Evaluating Longitudinal Designs in Evidence-Based Practice
V. Summary and Conclusions

I. INTRODUCTION

Knowledge about augmentative and alternative communication (AAC) and its use with both children and adults who present with diverse profiles has expanded substantially over the past three decades (e.g., Beukelman & Mirenda, 1998). At present, there are many choices about modes of communication, from manual signs and communication boards to speech–generating devices (SGDs). Selection of an appropriate communication mode is just the beginning of the intervention process, which then must be focused on the development of functional language and communication skills through an alternative mode. As stakeholders and practitioners deliberate about the choice of an intervention program,

[1]This chapter draws on two earlier publications by Sevcik, Romski, and Robinson (1996) and Sevcik, Romski, & Adamson (1998) as a foundation. The preparation of this manuscript was supported by NIH grant nos. DC-03766 and DC-03799. Thanks to our staff and students for their assistance with the literature review for this manuscript: Andrea Barton, Tanya Kobek, Mia Liagon, Ebony Patton, and Ashlyn Smith.

data-based evidence about the outcomes from different interventions must be considered. One type of evidence is derived from research studies that evaluate the effects of AAC interventions.

Evidence-based practices result from an examination of research and clinical practice and require at least a basic understanding of the types of research designs and methods that may be employed in studies addressing efficacy. Borrowing from clinical psychology (Abrahamson, 2001; Kendall & Norton-Ford, 1982; Rosen & Proctor, 1981), Olswang (1990) and others (Calculator, 1991; Schlosser & Braun, 1994) have argued that treatment efficacy is an umbrella term that incorporates the effectiveness, the effects, and the efficiency of different treatments or interventions (also see Chapter 2). The effectiveness of an intervention addresses whether or not the intervention actually has produced a result, whereas the effects of an intervention focus on its precise impact on changing behavior. Questions of efficiency are comparative in nature and are directed to whether one effective intervention produces a better outcome than another effective intervention for the same type of individual and at what rate and cost in terms of time and benefit. The design of the study is critical to an examination of treatment efficacy.

This chapter focuses on the role longitudinal research designs play in AAC efficacy research. First, the chapter presents an overview of longitudinal research designs and their use in addressing research questions. Second, the authors describe three of their own longitudinal research studies about augmented language development in children and youth with developmental disabilities to illustrate how longitudinal research designs may be applied within AAC intervention research. Third, issues related to the conduct of longitudinal research designs in AAC are discussed. Finally, the field's ability to assess the role of longitudinal designs in AAC interventions is considered.

II. LONGITUDINAL RESEARCH DESIGNS

One type of research design used in efficacy studies is the longitudinal design. These designs are chosen based on the research question or questions of interest and are always employed in conjunction with a wide range of research methods taking into account the major variables to be addressed. Longitudinal designs study a group of participants repeatedly at different points in time and changes are noted in the participants over a defined period of time (Janson, 1981). When group designs are the method of choice, longitudinal approaches are often contrasted with cross-sectional designs. Cross-sectional designs focus on groups of people differing on some variable (e.g., age) studied at the same point in time. In a sense, cross-sectional group research designs permit investigators to gain a series of single snapshots showing different AAC users at different points in time (see Crabtree, Mirenda, & Beukelman, 1990; Bruno & Goehl, 1991, for illustrations of AAC cross-sectional studies). In contrast, extending this analogy, longitudinal designs can be a more powerful tool for certain types of research questions than cross-sectional designs by offering the opportunity to create a documentary videotape of a group of AAC users' functioning over a specified time period (see Rowland & Schweigert, 2000, for an illustration of a longitudinal design used in AAC intervention research).

Longitudinal designs represent a well-established, though relatively under-utilized, approach that has been employed in behavioral science research for more than two centuries. These designs can address a range of issues from the cumulative impact of multiple independent variables to an understanding of variables that show small, but important, changes. Longitudinal designs can also highlight the interrelationships between variables, the patterns of individual differences as well as the mechanisms underlying the described change or changes (see Gallagher, Ramey, Haskins, & Finkelstein, 1976, for a discussion). These designs have been applied to the study of age-related changes in development such as Roger Brown's (1973) classic study that carefully mapped the expressive language acquisition of three typically developing children from 16 to 50 months. Gowen, Johnson-Martin, Goldman, and Hussey (1992) studied the development of object play and exploration by children with and without cognitive disabilities across time through the use of a longitudinal design. More recently, Lederberg and Everhart (1998) employed a longitudinal design to evaluate communication between deaf children and their hearing mothers from 22 to 26 months of age. The issues longitudinal research designs can address seem particularly applicable to questions about AAC intervention outcomes because AAC interventions are focused on describing change and patterns of individual variation.

III. LONGITUDINAL DESIGNS IN AAC RESEARCH

How can longitudinal designs be employed in the research agenda of the AAC field? Historically, some of the most important information our young field has gained has been derived from multiyear case study data or single-subject experimental research designs. Light, Beesly, and Collier's (1988) 3-year case study of an adolescent's transition through multiple AAC systems during her recovery from a head injury, for example, provided insights into the changing role AAC systems played in the regaining of her spoken communication skills. While case study approaches obviously have an important place in an applied discipline such as the AAC field, they are preexperimental and do not permit one to rule out extraneous variables and demonstrate experimental control (McEwen & Karlan,

1990). Single-subject experimental designs have been the most commonly employed research design in AAC (see Chapter 6). They offer an experimental approach to studying small samples of participants and evaluate the effects of intervention. Iacono and Duncum (1995), for example, used an alternating-treatments design to assess the effects of two interventions, sign alone and sign plus an electronic device on the single word productions of a preschool child with Down syndrome. They found that sign plus an electronic device was more effective than sign alone.

Sevcik, Romski, and Robinson (1996) argued that as a relatively young yet rapidly developing field, longitudinal designs were used all too infrequently in AAC research endeavors. Further, they suggested that longitudinal designs deserved serious consideration as they could serve an important function in the development and refinement of our field's empirical knowledge base. These designs offer us an opportunity to transition from a reliance on the case study approach and single-subject designs with small sample sizes to the implementation of a powerful research method for studying groups of individuals over time. One particular strength of longitudinal designs is their ability to address the issue of individual differences by uncovering meaningful long-term patterns of behaviors within cohorts of participants. During the 1990s, some AAC researchers employed longitudinal designs (see, for example, Björck-Åkesson, 1990, 1992; Romski & Sevcik, 1996; Rowland, 1990; Schweigert & Rowland, 1992). Schweigert and Rowland (1992) demonstrated that over a 3-year period, three subgroups of children with dual sensory and orthopedic impairments were all able to use microtechnology to communicate, even though they began the intervention with diverse skills. In a recent follow-up study, Rowland and Schweigert (2000) studied the use of tangible symbols by 41 children with a variety of handicapping conditions over a 3-year period. More recently, Sandberg (2001) described a longitudinal study of the reading and spelling abilities of seven school-aged children with severe speech impairments.

A. The System for Augmenting Language (SAL)

For more than two decades, the authors' research team has been studying the communication development of children and youth with developmental disabilities who do not speak. In the large majority, longitudinal designs were employed because they have permitted an examination of changes in the development of communication skills in children who have not typically demonstrated such skill when they were provided with an augmented language intervention, such as the SAL. Table 8.1 provides a capsule summary of the three longitudinal research studies undertaken by the authors to date, including research questions, participants, timespan, measures, and outcomes.

Table 8.1

Longitudinal Studies Using the System for Augmenting Language (SAL)

Study and questions of interest	Participants	Time span	Measures	Outcomes
Romski & Sevcik (1996) (1) To explore the use of the SAL (2) To determine if instructional environment affects communication development (3) To describe the language and communication gains over the 2-year period	13 school-aged youth w/ moderate or severe intellectual disabilities Mean CA = 12 yrs., 8 mos.	24 months of SAL use at home and at school; pre–post assessments	(1) Communication use probes (2) Vocabulary assessment measures (3) Parent–teacher questionnaires	Development of symbol vocabularies in all 13 youth Communicative use of symbol vocabularies w/ adults and peers Development of intelligible word approximations and printed word recognition
Romski, Sevcik, & Adamson (1999) (1) To characterize the communication development of toddlers with a range of disabilities who were not speaking (2) To explore the use of an augmented language intervention on communication development with toddlers	10 toddlers w/ developmental disabilities Mean CA = 33 mos.	12 months of SAL use pre–post assessments	(1) Communicative symbol use (2) Comprehension of symbols (3) Comprehension of speech (4) Production of speech	(1) Increase in speech comprehension skills (2) Increase in speech production skills in 5 children (3) Development of symbol vocabularies in all 10 children
Romski, Sevcik, & Adamson (2001) (1) To develop a fine-grained longitudinal description of the communication development (2) To compare the relative effects of three interventions on the communication skills, adaptive behavior, and educational placement of the toddlers	60 toddlers w/ developmental disabilities and significant difficulty w/ speech development CA = 24–36 months of age at the onset of their participation in the study	3-month intervention, pre–post assessment follow-up at 3, 6, 12 months post-intervention	(1) Speech and symbol comprehension and production (2) SICD, MCDI, Parent–child interaction	Ongoing

1. School-Aged Participants—Study 1

As illustrated in Table 8.1, the first study described in detail is Romski and Sevcik (1996). This study examined and described changes in the communication skills of 13 school-aged participants with moderate or severe intellectual disabilities (mean chronological age = 12 years, 8 months) from baseline through two years of intervention at home and school using the System for Augmenting Language (SAL). Each participant had an expressive vocabulary of less than 10 spoken words and had at least a documented 2-year unsuccessful history learning to communicate via speech and other means prior to participating in this study.

The SAL intervention was designed to supplement the participants' natural, albeit severely limited, language abilities and to facilitate their ability to communicate in a conventional manner in everyday environments, most notably home and school (Romski, Sevcik, Robinson, & Bakeman, 1994). It consists of five integrated components that functioned in concert: (1) a speech-generating device (SGD), (2) an individualized symbol vocabulary using arbitrary visual-graphic symbols placed on the SGD, (3) naturalistic communicative experiences throughout the day that provided arranged opportunities for the participant to use the SGD for communication, (4) adult partner augmented communicative input using speech plus symbols during communicative interactions, and (5) a resource and feedback mechanism for the parents and teachers administered by the investigators (see Romski & Sevcik, 1996, for a detailed description).

A longitudinal research design was employed with two instructional groups (home and school). The participants' communication skills were assessed at the onset of the study and their progress was tracked over time using two sets of measures described later. Given the participants' cognitive and communicative profiles, the authors were confident that any changes that might be observed were not due to maturational changes because of their chronological ages. The participants were matched in pairs and randomly assigned one participant to each group (home or school). During the first year of the study, the participants assigned to the home group used the SAL at home and those assigned to the school group used the SAL at school. In year 2 of the study, all participants used the SAL at home and at school.

Two aspects of communicative achievement were measured during the course of the longitudinal study: communication use and vocabulary mastery. To measure communication use, nonparticipant observers coded the participants' communications during daily interactions at home and school during regular intervals throughout the 2 years of the study. The Communicative Use Probes consisted of live coded observations (using the Communication Coding Scheme) with accompanying audiotapes of communicative interactions. The codes and audiotapes were compiled into a language transcript (using the Systematic

Analysis of Language Transcripts; Miller & Chapman, 1985). The result was a rich transcript of the communicative interaction that permitted us to extract information about the participants' and their partners' communications. The four-digit cross-classified event-based Communication Coding Scheme reliably coded five types of information: (1) the participant's partner (adult, peer), (2) the individual participant's role in the communication (initiation, response), (3) the mode of the communication (symbol, gesture, vocalization, word, physical manipulation), (4) the function of the communication (e.g., greeting, answering, commenting, requesting), and (5) the success of the communication. After coding the transcripts using the Communication Coding Scheme, the effectiveness, defined in terms of how the partner responded to the SAL user's communication (see Romski, Sevcik, Robinson, *et al.*, 1994, for a description of the coding scheme), and vocabulary focus (see Adamson, Romski, Deffenbach, & Sevcik, 1992, for a description on the coding scheme) were coded subsequently.

Vocabulary mastery provided a measure of the participants' comprehension and production of the symbols they were using apart from the contextual framework in which they were used. The Vocabulary Assessment Measures, which is a series of 10 structured tasks (four comprehension tasks and six production tasks including one measuring speech production and one measuring printed English word recognition) were designed to determine what the participants had learned about the symbols. Each task was administered by an investigator at school in a one-to-one assessment format outside of the communicative use settings (see Romski & Sevcik, 1996, for a full description of the Communicative Use Probes and the Vocabulary Assessment Measures).

The youth integrated the use of their SGD into their extant vocal and gestural repertoires (Romski, Sevcik, Robinson, *et al.*, 1994). The result was a rich multimodal means of communication that they employed to communicate both successfully and effectively with adults (Romski, Sevcik, Robinson, *et al.*, 1994) and peers (Romski, Sevcik, & Wilkinson, 1994). Individual participant achievements ranged from the communicative use with adults of a modest set of 20 to 35 symbols to the use of more than 100 symbols to convey referential and social-regulative symbolic messages in varied daily contexts (Adamson, Romski, Deffebach, *et al.*, 1992) with familiar and unfamiliar adult and peer partners. Some youth also developed combinatorial symbol skills (Wilkinson, Romski, & Sevcik, 1994) as well as the production of intelligible spoken words and rudimentary reading skills (Romski & Sevcik, 1996).

This descriptive longitudinal approach permitted us to detail the achievements of a relatively small number of participants (actually a substantial number given the typical number reported in the AAC literature) across a relatively lengthy period of time. While these findings indicated that the 13 participants developed substantial skills communicating with adults and peers using their vocabulary over this 2-year period (Romski & Sevcik, 1996; Romski, Sevcik, Robinson, *et al.*, 1994;

Romski, Sevcik, & Wilkinson, 1994), each participant had served as his own control by comparing his performance at the onset of the study with his performance across the 2 years of the study. A traditional control group design (see Chapter 7) was not employed. Consequently, the authors were not able to assert that the use of the SAL was better than no intervention at all because we did not use an experimental design that permitted us to address this question.

To determine if broader conclusions about the effects of the SAL could be drawn, three additional cross-sectional studies were conducted (see Sevcik, Romski, & Adamson, 1999, for a discussion). The contrast group design permitted a confirmation of the authors' initial hypothesis that the use of the SAL intervention was better than no intervention at all. In fact, SAL experience enhanced the communication skills of the 13 original participants so that they functioned more like individuals with developmental disabilities who speak than those who do not speak in interactions with familiar as well as unfamiliar partners. The studies fulfilled at least one aspect of efficacy as an umbrella term—that is, making explicit the *effectiveness* of the SAL intervention.

With some AAC populations, such as children with severe cognitive disabilities, the acquisition and use of an AAC system is a process that emerges slowly and thus can necessitate the employment of a longitudinal design. Studying the AAC development of 13 youth with cognitive disabilities and little or no functional speech for a 2-year time period permitted the authors to gain a broad spectrum of information about their learning patterns and subsequent long-term achievements (Romski & Sevcik, 1996). If a cross-sectional design had been employed instead, the authors would have likely concluded that 4 of our 13 participants could not readily learn to use the SGD they were given to communicate, because their learning occurred more slowly and, initially, in a different domain (comprehension rather than production) than the remaining 9 participants.

2. Exploratory Study of SAL Use with Toddlers—Study 2

The successful outcomes from the SAL intervention led the authors to explore adapting the SAL to younger children with similar developmental profiles. After conducting a pilot case study to determine if this adaptation was feasible (see Romski & Sevcik, 1996, for a description), the authors undertook an exploratory study of SAL use by 10 toddlers with severe communication disabilities. This study, also described in Table 8.1, spanned a 12-month period of time. The original research plan was to use a quasi-experimental control group design (see also Chapter 7 for more information on this type of design) by asking parents to select the augmented language intervention or a nonaugmented language intervention. We anticipated that some parents would choose not to augment their child because they wanted to focus exclusively on speech production and we would have a natural control group. Unfortunately, this prediction was incorrect, and all of our parents selected the SAL intervention. Instead, their comprehension and production symbol and speech skills were assessed pre-post intervention.

All ten toddlers were using symbols to communicate at the end of the year. Five toddlers were speaking at the end of 1 year and five toddlers were still not talking (Romski, Sevcik, & Adamson, 1999). These findings suggest that there may be two profiles that emerge in these toddlers. Yet without further research, this exploratory study cannot rule out the role of development or other threats to internal validity (see Chapters 3 and 7) in the findings.

3. Contrasting Early Communication Interventions with Toddlers—Study 3

The findings from the exploratory study strongly suggested that the intervention protocol had to be modified for young children. Also, the children needed to be randomly assigned to treatment to ensure that the interventions could be contrasted. Ongoing as this chapter is written is a third longitudinal study. Also included in Table 8.1, Sevcik, Romski, and Adamson (2001) are comparing three interventions for these very young children using a design that includes random assignment to intervention. Random assignment to intervention condition is particularly important in this study as it permits control for the potential effects of development or maturation because of the chronological age of the participants (see also Chapters 3 and 7 for these design issues). This type of experimental control was not accomplished in the exploratory toddler study. Recruiting 60 toddlers is a major task, and it will be a few years before the results of this investigation can be shared.

4. Summary

In sum, the authors have employed longitudinal studies to examine the effects of augmented interventions on communication development from school-aged children and youth to toddlers. The authors' program of research provides one example of how longitudinal research can be used to explore the communication development of children with severe disabilities.

B. Issues for Longitudinal Research Designs in AAC

What issues are investigators confronted with when contemplating the use of longitudinal designs to answer AAC research questions? Some of these issues are unique to longitudinal research, whereas others may be applicable to the broader range of research designs addressed in this volume. First and foremost, the research question or questions to be addressed via the design must be articulated. Bakeman and Gottman (1986) argued that the research question drives the design and methods employed (also see Chapter 4).

Once the question is linked to the study design, a number of methodological issues must be addressed when undertaking a longitudinal study. Four broad areas of concern are addressed: (1) design issues; (2) participant issues: selection and attrition; (3) data collection issues: measurement of change, study duration, and treatment integrity; and (4) data management: data summary, data analyses, and statistical applications.

1. Design Issues

In a field where change is evaluated in the context of the provision of an intervention, it is critical to consider the impact of development or spontaneous recovery in the design of a study. Traditional experimental approaches employ some type of control group to examine the issues of development or recovery. The traditional concept of control groups who receive no intervention obviously presents ethical challenges for the AAC field. What alternative mechanisms are available in longitudinal research? There are no methodological reasons why longitudinal designs cannot integrate single-subject experimental design methodology (see Chapter 6 for a review). Single-subject experimental designs permit each participant to serve as his or her own control with change measured against the participant's own baseline performance. The introduction of an intervention can be staggered across participants (e.g., multiple-baseline design across subjects) with some participants remaining in baseline for a longer period of time to control for development or recovery. Another approach is to employ a contrast group rather than a traditional control group. In the authors' ongoing intervention study, all children receive an intervention. One group of children receives what is defined as the current standard of care intervention rather than an experimental augmented language intervention. In this case, however, safeguards are built in to ensure that all families are advised if one of the interventions is far exceeding another in results. Another concern in longitudinal research is the notion of a cohort effect or difference. If some children begin the intervention in year 1 and others in year 2 or year 3, will there be differences based on when they receive the intervention rather than the intervention itself? These issues must be considered in the planning of the study.

2. Participant Issues

Two participant issues that emerge with respect to longitudinal designs are participant selection and participant attrition.

a. Participant Selection

By definition, in studies of low-incidence populations, recruiting a sufficient number of participants who share a common feature is often a difficult task (see Iacono, 1992, and Rowland, 1992, for a discussion of small *n* designs). For longitudinal studies, careful delineation of the common feature that binds the group together, regardless of the number of participants, is essential to the success of the study. The delineation of a common feature is important because results are usually reported for the group, not the individual. In the school-aged study described earlier, for example, a criterion of less than 10 intelligible spoken words was employed. Even using this criterion, the communication profiles of the participants varied. If the group is not clearly defined, the results could be obscured or extremely difficult to interpret (see also Chapter 5). For some populations, such as individuals with specific degenerative neurological disorders, the common feature may be easily discernible though clearly there is variability. For other populations, like children with severe disabilities, the variables that are included and excluded in the composition of a cohort are often arbitrary and dependent on the investigator's questions(s) of interest. In the ongoing toddler intervention study, the authors' have excluded children with certain diagnoses from our sample because the exploratory toddler study showed that other factors affected the successful participation of these youngsters in the intervention process.

b. Participant Attrition

Participant attrition is another practical concern that is somewhat unique to longitudinal research even though some single-subject experimental designs are faced with similar issues (see Chapter 6). How do we maintain the participation of a participant group over a defined period of time? Some attrition, for example, family relocation, is unavoidable. In some cases, the investigator can still follow a family even though they are no longer in the local area. Other types of attrition, such as the participant or her family choosing not to continue to participate, may be averted. In the authors' research with school-aged children and youth, an ongoing resource and feedback mechanism was employed, including a questionnaire to maintain biweekly interactions with the participants' teachers and families. This resource permitted the authors to maintain regular contact with families and teachers and sustain their own interest in the study and its outcomes (see Romski & Sevcik, 1996). In the ongoing toddler intervention study, the following serve as strategies to avert attrition: flexible intervention session times, makeup sessions, paid parking or public transportation, child care for siblings, a standard report of the child's assessment performance, and a range of supports for the families. These additional supports help the authors to ensure that every family has the opportunity to succeed in completing the intervention protocol and the follow-up assessments. It is important, however, that every family in all three interventions be provided with the same opportunities for support so that there is no bias toward any one condition.

3. Data Collection Issues

A number of considerations are related to the collection of data, including measurement, study duration, treatment integrity, and ecological validity.

a. Measurement

One important issue, influenced by the research question or questions of interests is how to measure the target behaviors of interest as they change over time. For example, if the target behavior is the overall communicative use of an AAC device, what is the measure? Is it how many times the individual requests an item using a symbol during a specific activity? Requesting would be a very narrow measure of overall communication use. The device used may change over time due to improvements in technology, age, or disrepair. The measure of overall communicative use must be broad enough to encompass all the different devices that may be employed over the course of the study. For AAC, this often includes the development of new tools for capturing data. For economic and logistical reasons, there is often a necessity for limitations on the types and amount of data to be collected in a longitudinal study. Careful planning at the onset of the study is needed to determine which measurement tools will be most helpful in answering the questions to be addressed. Planning should include examining the range of measurement tools available and choosing ones that permit the capture of the broadest outcomes.

b. Study Duration and Costs

What role should duration play in longitudinal studies? In a field that is rapidly changing in terms of information and technology, the longer the duration of the study to be conducted, the more difficult it may be to maintain comparable experiences and equipment across participants. The duration of longitudinal studies also makes them costly endeavors, both in terms of financing and personnel utilization. Longitudinal studies require additional resources, both personnel and financial, to maintain the participants in the study over time and thus reduce or eliminate attrition. Because there are multiple data collection points, there is extra cost to collect all the data and manage a database of considerable size. These studies may require external funding from federal agencies (e.g., Department of Education, National Institutes of Health) or private foundations.

c. Treatment Integrity

Another issue exacerbated by the duration of the study is the integrity of the intervention. The longer the study is, the more likely it will be that more than one person will implement the intervention. In fact, in the authors' ongoing study, two interventionists are employed at one time so that the effect of one interventionist on the outcome of the interventions can be ruled out. Thus, it is important to consider the reliability of the implementation over time. Two approaches can facilitate treatment integrity. First, interventionists must receive a standard instruction program to ensure that the intervention protocol is administered correctly and consistently. Second, frequent systematic checks throughout the study duration are important to ensure that the treatment is being implemented in a consistent manner across time and interventions. In the ongoing study, a standard treatment integrity checklist was developed to ensure that each intervention is administered as intended. These checks occur on a randomly determined subset of the intervention sessions by coders naive to the children and the interventions. If the implementation of the treatment drifts, the investigator must take measures (i.e., additional instruction) to ensure that integrity is maintained (see Schlosser, 2002, and Chapter 9 for other strategies for ensuring treatment integrity).

d. Ecological Validity

Rapid changes in AAC computer technology may modify the way in which an individual communicates or the way in which one is perceived by others. Developments in the area of digitized or synthesized speech, for example, can change the quality of the speech an AAC user employs, thus perhaps altering how one is perceived by others. A change in a communication device can also affect how an individual communicates. For instance, in the longitudinal study by Romski and Sevcik (1996), the SGD that was originally provided to the participants was outdated before the end of the study's second school year. For experimental control, the authors chose to purchase a new device for all of the participants and assess the transfer of symbol knowledge from one device to the other to ensure a comparable experience for all participants. With respect to technology, in the ongoing study, the authors have chosen to use devices with similar features rather than a specific product (e.g., direct selection versus auditory scanning). Measurement tools must be developed to assess communication and other skills across time in an ecologically valid way (see also Chapter 3 for other ecological validity issues). The caution here is that in these studies, particular measurement tools were developed to answer a specific question. They may be applicable to other issues and questions but it is important to remember that they were developed for a specific purpose. Sometimes, tools are criticized for what they have not done. But it is important to evaluate the tool in the context of what it has been developed to do.

4. Data Management Approaches

At least three issues emerge in relation to data management: data summary, statistical approaches to data analyses, and data sharing.

a. Data Summary

In longitudinal studies, the size of the database can, at times, be overwhelming. The implementation of data management systems becomes an important consideration to the integrity of the data set. Care must be taken to ensure that data are entered into the database in a consistent and reliable manner. Errors can occur in a number of places along the data entry and summary path. Carefully laid out procedures for the process with frequent checks are critical to avoiding error.

b. Statistical Approaches to Data Analyses

With respect to longitudinal databases, at least two relatively new analysis approaches may be employed. First, Bakeman and Robinson (1997) described two approaches for the scientific scrutiny of data collected from a small number of participants that facilitate the examination of research questions beyond simple mean difference tests. They suggest that graphic presentation of data (Tukey, 1977) provides an approach to understanding variability. The use of conditional probabilities is another approach they propose for small sample sizes.

More recently, the use of hierarchical linear models to estimate individual and group growth curves is expanding (e.g., Campbell, Pungello, Miller-Johnson, & Burchinal, 2001). Hierarchical linear models are used to describe patterns of change over time and factors associated with those patterns. This method permits examination of regression relationships among dependent and predictor variables and the ways in which these relationships vary over time. It offers a statistical approach by which to analyze change over time.

c. Data Sharing

Given the richness of some longitudinal databases, they may also be an invaluable resource, not only for the individual investigator, but for the field in general. The development of an archive for databases may be a consideration for our field. How can such resources be preserved? In the field of child language acquisition, language transcript databases can be stored through CHILDES, an international computer-based resource that is available to a broad audience of researchers (MacWhinney & Snow, 1985). However, a number of confidentiality and ethical issues are related to the sharing of data sets beyond the original investigators.

IV. EVALUATING LONGITUDINAL DESIGNS IN EVIDENCE-BASED PRACTICE

Longitudinal designs may be particularly well suited for examining the broad long-term outcomes of AAC interventions. They can be employed, in concert with single-subject experimental designs, to build the foundation for evidence-based practice. The evaluation of longitudinal research designs is a complex undertaking but shares some commonalties with the evaluation of other research designs (see Chapter 12).

The first question that must be addressed by researchers and evidence-based practitioners alike, regardless of the type of design employed, is how well the study answered the question that the investigators asked. Sometimes an individual evaluating a study expects that it will address a different question than the authors of the study intended. In this regard, it is important that the study be evaluated with respect to the question the authors asked, not the question the reader expects the study will address.

How well did the study minimize threats to internal validity? Here is where the reader would review issues regarding data collection including treatment measures, reliability measures, and the integrity of the intervention protocol itself over time (see also Chapters 3 and 12). For longitudinal designs, it is critical to examine how well the study minimizes threats to internal validity over the course of the study. Another concern the researcher and evidence-based practitioner must consider is the size of the sample. If it is a small sample study, then the generalizability of the findings must be interpreted cautiously. A complete description of the research participants is also important especially when employing information from research studies to make decisions about clinical practice (see Chapter 5 for more information on subject description).

V. SUMMARY AND CONCLUSIONS

Longitudinal research designs offer one approach for examining the outcome of interventions. The challenges discussed in this chapter highlight some of the issues we must address as the AAC field pursues questions of treatment efficacy. Although longitudinal designs are costly endeavors, both in terms of financing and personnel utilization, they provide the AAC field with a powerful design by which to understand the efficacy of AAC interventions for a range of children and adults who employ AAC systems. The increased use of longitudinal research designs in AAC research, coupled with other qualitative and quantitative research methods, will serve not only to advance our empirical knowledge base but, more important, the data on which our clinical practice should be based.

REFERENCES

Abrahamson, D. (2001). Treatment efficacy and clinical utility: A guidelines model applied to psychotherapy research. *Clinical psychology: Science and practice, 8*, 176–179.

Adamson, L. B., Romski, M. A., Deffebach, K., & Sevcik, R. A. (1992). Symbol vocabulary and the focus of conversations: Augmenting language development for youth with mental retardation. *Journal of Speech and Hearing Research, 35*, 1333–1343.

Bakeman, R., & Gottman, J. (1986). *Observing interaction: An introduction to sequential analysis.* Cambridge, MA: MIT Press.

Bakeman, R., & Robinson, B. F. (1997). When Ns do not justify means: Small samples and scientific conclusions. In L. B. Adamson & M. A. Romski (Eds.) *Communication and language acquisition: Discoveries form atypical development* (pp. 49–74). Baltimore: Paul H. Brookes.

Baltes, P., & Nesselroade, J. (1979). History and rationale of longitudinal research. In J. Nesselroade & P. Baltes (Eds.), *Longitudinal research in the study of behavior and development* (pp. 1–38). New York: Academic Press.

Beukelman, D. R., & Mirenda, P. (1998). *Augmentative and alternative communication: Management of severe communication disorders in children and adults* (2nd ed.). Baltimore: Paul H. Brookes.

Björck-Åkesson, E. (1990, August). *Communicative interaction of young nonspeaking children and their parents.* Paper presented at the biennial meeting of the International Society for Augmentative and Alternative Communication, Stockholm, Sweden.

Björck-Åkesson, E. (1992). Longitudinal research in AAC. In D. J. Gardner-Bonneau (Ed.), *Methodological issues in research in augmentative and alternative communication: Proceedings of the Second ISAAC Research Symposium* (pp. 80–86). Toronto, Canada: ISAAC.

Brown, R. (1973). *A first language.* Cambridge, MA: Harvard University Press.

Bruno, J., & Goehl, H. (1991). Comparison of picture and word association performance in adults and preliterate children. *Augmentative and Alternative Communication, 7*, 70–79.

Calculator, S. N. (1990). Evaluating the efficacy of AAC intervention for children with severe disabilities. In J. Brodin & E. Björck-Åkesson (Eds.), *Methodological issues in research in augmentative and alternative communication. Proceedings from the First ISAAC Research Symposium* (pp. 22–31). Stockholm, Sweden: The Swedish Handicap Institute.

Campbell, F., Pungello, E., Miller-Johnson, S. & Burchinal, M. (2001). The development of cognitive and academic abilities: Growth curves form an early childhood educational experiment. *Developmental Psychology, 37*, 231–242.

Crabtree, M., Mirenda, P., & Beukelman, D. (1990). Age and gender preferences for synthetic and natural speech. *Augmentative and Alternative Communication, 6*, 256–261.

Gallagher, J., Ramey, C., Haskins, R., & Finkelstein, N. (1976). Use of longitudinal research in the study of child development. In T. Tjossem (Ed.), *Intervention strategies for high risk infants and young children* (pp. 161–186). Baltimore: University Park Press.

Gowen, J., Johnson-Martin, N., Goldman, B. D., & Hussey, B. (1992). Object play and exploration in children with and without disabilities: A longitudinal study. *American Journal on Mental Retardation, 97,* 21–38.

Iacono, T. (1992). A step back from small "N" designs to view the total picture. In D. J. Gardner-Bonneau (Ed.), *Methodological issues in research in augmentative and alternative communication: Proceedings of the Second ISAAC Research Symposium* (pp. 12–16). Toronto, Canada: ISAAC.

Iacono, T. A., & Duncum, J. E., (1995). Comparison of sign alone and in combination with an electronic communication device in early language intervention: Case study. *Augmentative and Alternative Communication, 11,* 249–259.

Janson, C. (1981). Some problems of longitudinal research in the social sciences. In F. Schulsinger, S. Mednick, & J. Knop (Eds.), *Longitudinal research: Methods and uses in the behavioral sciences* (pp. 19–55). Boston: Martinus Nijhoof Publishing.

Kendall, P., & Norton-Ford, J. (1982). Therapy outcome research methods. In P. Kendall & J. Butcher (Eds.), *Handbook of research methods in clinical psychology* (pp. 429–460). New York: John Wiley and Sons.

Lederberg, A., & Everhart, V. (1998). Communication between deaf children and their hearing mothers: The role of language, gesture, and vocalizations. *Journal of Speech and Hearing Research, 39,* 518–533.

Light, J., Beesly, M., & Collier, B. (1988). Transition through multiple augmentative and alternative communication systems: A three-year case study of a head-injured adolescent. *Augmentative and Alternative Communication, 4,* 2–14.

MacWhinney, B., & Snow, C. (1985). The Child Language Data Exchange System. *Journal of Child Language, 12,* 271–296.

McEwen, I., & Karlan, G. (1990). Case studies: Why and how? *Augmentative and Alternative Communication, 6,* 69–75.

Miller, J., & Chapman, R. (1985). *Systematic analysis of language transcripts.* Madison, WI: Waisman Center on Mental Retardation and Human Development.

Olswang, L. B. (1990). Treatment efficacy: The breadth of research. In L. B. Olswang, C. K. Thompson, S. F. Warren, & N. J. Minghetti (Eds.), *Treatment efficacy research in communication disorders: Proceedings of the American Speech-Language-Hearing Foundation's National Conference on Treatment Efficacy* (pp. 99–103). San Antonio, TX: American Speech-Language and Hearing Association.

Romski, M. A., & Sevcik, R. A. (1996). *Breaking the speech barrier: Language development through augmented means.* Baltimore: Paul H Brookes.

Romski, M. A., Sevcik, R. A., & Adamson, L. B. (1999). Communication patterns of youth with mental retardation with and without their speech-output communication devices. *American Journal on Mental Retardation, 104,* 249–259.

Romski, M. A., Sevcik, R. A., Robinson, B. F., & Bakeman, R. (1994). Adult-directed communications of youth with mental retardation using the system for augmenting language. *Journal of Speech and Hearing Research, 37,* 617–628.

Romski, M. A., Sevcik, R. A., & Wilkinson, K. M. (1994). Peer-directed communicative interactions of augmented language learners with mental retardation. *American Journal on Mental Retardation, 98,* 527–538.

Rosen, A., & Proctor, E. (1981). Distinctions between treatment outcomes and their implications for treatment evaluation. *Journal of Consulting and Clinical Psychology, 49,* 418–425.

Rowland, C. (1990). Communication in the classroom for children with dual sensory impairments: Studies of teacher and child behavior. *Augmentative and Alternative Communication, 6,* 262–274.

Rowland, C. (1992). Small "N" studies: The case for more and better data. In D. J. Gardner-Bonneau (Ed.), *Methodological issues in research in augmentative and alternative communication: Proceedings of the Second ISAAC Research Symposium* (pp. 17–22). Toronto, Canada: ISAAC.

Rowland, C., & Schweigert, P. (2000). Tangible symbols, tangible outcomes. *Augmentative and Alternative Communication, 16,* 61–78.

Sandberg, A. (2001). Reading and spelling, phonological awareness, and working memory in children with severe speech impairments: A longitudinal study. *Augmentative and Alternative Communication, 17,* 11–26.

Schlosser, R. W. (2002). On the importance of being earnest about treatment integrity. *Augmentative and Alternative Communication, 18,* 36–44.

Schlosser, R. W., & Braun, U. (1994). Efficacy of AAC interventions: Methodologic issues in evaluating behavior change, generalization, and effects. *Augmentative and Alternative Communication, 10,* 207–223.

Schweigert, P., & Rowland, C. (1992). Early communication and micro-technology: Instructional sequence and case studies of children with severe multiple disabilities. *Augmentative and Alternative Communication, 8,* 273–286.

Sevcik, R. A., Romski, M. A., & Adamson, L. B. (1999). Measuring AAC interventions for individuals with severe developmental disabilities. *Augmentative and Alternative Communication, 15,* 38–44.

Sevcik, R. A., Romski, M. A., & Adamson, L. B. (2001, March). Toddlers with developmental disabilities who are not speaking: Receptive language skills and augmented language intervention outcomes. In C. Kasari & M. A. Romski (Chair). Early communication development in young children with developmental delays. Symposium conducted at The Annual Gatlinburg Conference on Research and Theory in Intellectual and Developmental Disabilities, Charleston, SC.

Sevcik, R. A., Romski, M. A., & Robinson, B. W. (1996). Longitudinal research: Considerations for augmentative and alternative communication. *Augmentative and Alternative Communication, 12,* 272–276.

Tukey, J. W. (1977). *Exploratory data analysis.* Reading, MA: Addison-Wesley.

Wilkinson, K. M., Romski, M. A., & Sevcik, R. A. (1994). Emergence of visual-graphic symbol combinations by youth with moderate or severe mental retardation. *Journal of Speech and Hearing Research, 37,* 883–895.

CHAPTER 9

Determining the Treatment Integrity of AAC Interventions[1]

Ralf W. Schlosser

Department of Speech-Language Pathology and Audiology
Northeastern University

[1]Sections of this chapter have been published as an abbreviated tutorial as referenced in the bibliography (Schlosser, 2002). The writing of this chapter was made possible through support from a Distinguished Switzer Fellowship (H133F010010) from the National Institute on Disability and Rehabilitation Research.

I. INTRODUCTION

Traditionally, the field of augmentative and alternative communication (AAC) has paid relatively close attention to the reliability of its dependent measures. In fact, it is rare to find intervention studies published in AAC's flagship journal *Augmentative and Alternative Communication*, and other journals with AAC content, that do not report interobserver agreement data for the dependent measures used (see Schlosser & Lee, 2000). This situation is also the case in related fields such as applied behavior analysis (Peterson, Homer, & Wonderlich, 1982). The reliability of the independent variable, also known as treatment integrity, however, presents a drastically different scenario, which this chapter will examine. Specifically, in this chapter treatment integrity is defined, reviews of treatment integrity in related fields as well as AAC are summarized, and the role of treatment integrity for establishing a science of AAC intervention research is discussed. In addition, the author presents an AAC application example for assessing treatment integrity. The chapter concludes with recommendations for planning, implementing, and evaluating intervention research in terms of treatment integrity.

II. TREATMENT INTEGRITY DEFINED

The degree to which an independent variable is implemented as intended has come to be known as treatment integrity (Gresham, 1997; Gresham, Gansle, & Noell, 1993a; Peterson *et al.*, 1982; Vermilyea, Barlow, & O'Brien, 1984; Yeaton & Sechrest, 1981). Others have used the terms "procedural reliability" (Billingsley, White, & Munson, 1980) or "treatment fidelity" (Moncher & Prinz, 1991) to describe the same concept (Billingsley *et al.*, 1980) or a similar concept.

III. REVIEWS OF TREATMENT INTEGRITY

Several reviews have been conducted in related fields to evaluate the degree to which studies assessed the implementation of interventions. In absence of a systematic review that focuses on this topic in the AAC field, a summary of reviews conducted in related fields may help us in preparing a review of treatment integrity in the AAC field and in planning treatment integrity assessments of AAC interventions.

A. REVIEWS FROM RELATED FIELDS

Several authors in related fields have reviewed the treatment integrity literature (Billingsley *et al.*, 1980; Gresham, 1989; Gresham *et al.*, 1993a; Gresham, Gansle, Noell, Cohen, & Rosenblum, 1993b; Moncher & Prinz, 1991; Peterson *et al.*, 1982; Yeaton, 1982).

1. Billingsley *et al.* (1980)

These authors reviewed research reports published in the *Journal of Applied Behavior Analysis (JABA)* (1977 and 1978) and *Behavior Modification* (1978 and the January issue of 1979). In total, 79 articles were published in the *JABA* and 29 articles in *Behavior Modification*. Of these studies, 89% reported data concerning the reliability of the dependent measure, whereas only 5.6% included any assessment of treatment integrity. Unfortunately, this review provides only a small slice of activity (only 2 years), and the question arises as to the representativeness of the data for these two journals. Also, the criteria for inclusion of studies are unclear and so are the coding categories. There is also no mention of interobserver agreement on the inclusion of studies and the coding of studies (see Chapter 11).

2. Yeaton (1982)

In his critique of the effectiveness of applied behavior analysis research, Yeaton reviewed Volume 10 of the *JABA*. He found that only 16 of the 59 regular research articles (27%) "supplied data monitoring the degree of implementation of the independent variable" (p. 92). Of the 16 studies that did monitor treatment integrity, 11 studies provided actual data for the implementation of treatment. In addition to the rather narrow time frame of included studies and the focus on only one journal, the criteria for inclusion as well as the procedures for reviewing these studies, however, were not reported. It should be noted though that a review of treatment integrity was not the main purpose of this article. The subsequently reviewed paper by Peterson *et al.* (1982) was aimed at just that.

3. Peterson *et al.* (1982)

In this seminal paper, Peterson *et al.* (1982) reviewed experimental articles published in the *JABA* between 1968 (Volume 1, Number 1) to 1980 (Volume 13, Number 3). "Experimental" was defined as any article longer than three pages of text that included a method section. This permitted the exclusion of brief reports, which may have gathered integrity data but failed to report them due to space limitations imposed by the journal. Two observers rated the articles; the primary observer rated every article, whereas the secondary observer rated only one issue per year (25%). It is unclear from this report whether or not this particular issue was selected at random. The observers coded the articles in terms of (1) ratings of independent variable assessment and the (2) occurrence of an independent variable operational definition.

The rating of independent variable assessment included three coding options: A "yes" was selected when the article reported some form of assessment of the independent variable, including informal assessment (e.g., "observers agreed on all but one instance of the treatment variable application" [p. 484]), a statistical estimate of reliability between two observers, or calibration (i.e., a check by the experimenter to ensure that the actual occurrence matched the description in the method section). The "no, low risk" category was marked if assessment was not reported but the application of the independent variable was judged to be low risk for inaccuracy as might be the case with mechanically defined treatments. The "no, high risk" category was coded if independent variable checks were not reported and they were necessary. The occurrence of an independent variable operational definition also included three coding choices: A "yes" was marked when an explicit operational definition was included. The code "no, not needed" was selected when a definition was not included but was unnecessary because it was mechanical, very simplistic, had been defined previously, or had a citation to a source describing it. The code "no, needed" was selected if no definition was supplied and it was not exempt due to situations described under the previous category.

Interobserver agreement results showed reasonable levels of agreement with Kappa $K = .80$ and $K = .82$ for the rating of independent variable assessment and the occurrence of an operational definition, respectively. Results indicated that the majority of articles (e.g., 68% in 1968) did not report independent variable assessments even when the risk of inaccuracy was high. In addition, there was no trend toward improvement over the 12 years noted. The majority of articles did report operational definitions when needed, although in a sizable number of cases (10–50%) operational definitions were not reported when necessary.

Except for the lack of interobserver agreement checks for the inclusion of articles, Peterson *et al.* (1982) offer a systematic review with solid operational definitions for the coding categories employed. In summary, the data show that the majority of articles published in *JABA* did not use necessary treatment integrity data and a sizable minority of article failed to provide operational definitions of the independent variable. In my opinion and that of others (Gresham *et al.*, 1993a), the data on the lack of treatment integrity are probably underestimating the actual extent to which these assessments are missing, given the rather liberal acceptance of "informal assessments" as part of this category. To accept an author's statement that an intervention was effective without actual treatment integrity data is analogous to accepting an author's claim that the intervention was effective without showing us the necessary data.

4. Gresham *et al.* (1993a)

These authors examined the treatment integrity of applied behavior analysis studies with children published in *JABA* between 1980 and 1990. Even though they exclusively focused on interventions targeting children, to some extent their review serves as a follow-up to the Peterson *et al.* (1982) review. Except for the age limitation (under age 19) and the different years of publication (1980 to 1990), the inclusion criteria were consistent with those of Peterson *et al.* (1982).

Studies were coded in terms of (1) the operational definition of the independent variable and the (2) treatment integrity. In terms of operational definition, the independent variable was considered as operationally defined *only* if its specific verbal, physical, temporal, and spatial parameters were described. Otherwise, the category was marked as "no." Gresham *et al.* (1993a) are quick to point out that their definition differs from Peterson *et al.* (1982) because the latter included a "no-unnecessary" category for independent variables that apparently do not require operational definitions, and they believe that all independent variables require operational definitions. Studies that referred to more extensive sources (e.g., technical manual) for an operational definition were marked as "yes." It is, however, unclear whether those sources were actually examined by the reviewers in order to arrive at this judgement. In terms of treatment integrity, studies were coded as "yes," "no," or "monitored." Studies with reported treatment integrity percentages were marked as "yes." Studies that made no mention of treatment integrity and did not report data to that effect were marked as "no." Studies that claimed to have assessed treatment integrity or provided a treatment protocol or manual but failed to provide a numerical index were classified as "monitored."

Three advanced doctoral students who served as primary raters rated the studies and one additional doctoral candidate rated 10% of randomly selected studies for interobserver agreement. Percent agreement was 81% for operational definition and 93% for integrity assessment. Results indicated that only 34.2% (54 studies) provided an operational definition of the independent variable and only 15.8% (25 studies) reported treatment integrity data. In summary, the findings by Gresham *et al.* (1993a) indicate that there has not been any improvement in treatment integrity assessment since the call by Peterson *et al.* (1982) for increased attention to the measurement of independent variable application.

B. Reviews of the AAC Intervention Literature

To date, no systematic synthesis of treatment integrity applications in the AAC field has been conducted. One such effort is currently in progress (Schlosser, Clifford, & Blischak, 2001). In the absence of such data, we will draw from reviews whose primary purpose was often larger or different from a specific focus on treatment integrity (Udwin, 1987; Schlosser & Lee, 2000).

1. Udwin (1987)

Udwin's (1987) review, for example, focused on the experimental adequacy of AAC intervention studies. Although the studies were not coded in terms of the monitoring of integrity per se, only 50% of studies provided an adequate description of training procedures (i.e., defined as sufficient detail for replication). Given that an operational definition of procedures is a precondition to treatment integrity assessments (see Gresham, 1993a), this finding is noteworthy.

2. Schlosser and Lee (2000)

Schlosser and Lee (2000) synthesized single-subject experimental studies examining generalization or maintenance in AAC published between 1976 and 1995. Treatment integrity was assessed in 40.6% of data units stemming from 12 studies (24% of the studies). Thus, although the percentage of data series with treatment integrity assessments seems fairly large, these data series were drawn from a considerably smaller percentage of studies. This suggests that only a few authors tend to assess treatment integrity and do so for all experiments and data series within a given study. It should be kept in mind, however, that the Schlosser and Lee (2000) synthesis excluded group studies along with single-subject studies that did not examine generalization or maintenance. Therefore, they are not representative of the entire AAC intervention data set. Nonetheless, they provide some preliminary insights, suggesting that the same double-standard existing in other fields also seems to plague the AAC field: while interobserver agreements for the dependent measures are commonplace, the standards in our field do not appear to require monitoring of the independent variable. Clearly, the results of the systematic review that is currently in progress (Schlosser *et al.*, 2001) are needed to substantiate these preliminary data.

IV. TREATMENT INTEGRITY AND ITS ROLE IN ESTABLISHING A SCIENCE OF AAC INTERVENTION RESEARCH

Poor treatment integrity or failure to monitor treatment integrity has profound implications for various types of experimental validity distinguished by Cook and Campbell (1979), including the following, which shall be examined here: internal validity of experiments, the establishment of the external validity of an intervention through the process of replication, and the construct validity of interventions (e.g., Gresham, 1997; Moncher & Prinz, 1991).

A. Internal Validity

If internal validity refers to the extent to which changes in the dependent variable can be attributed to the independent variable rather than to extraneous variables (see Chapter 3), data concerning the implementation of AAC interventions become indispensable. According to Billingsley *et al.* (1980), the monitoring of the dependent variable alone will allow unambiguous conclusions about changes in the dependent variable, even though it will not permit conclusions about the source of these changes. Gresham's (1997) description of the relationships between treatment integrity and changes in the dependent variable is helpful as a basis for discussing the interpretive consequences of low or absent treatment integrity data.

Essentially, Gresham described four possible scenarios concerning the evaluation of treatment integrity and its relation to the dependent variable. Two of these possible scenarios present with high treatment integrity. In the first scenario, a treatment is implemented as planned, and changes in the dependent variable are observed. In the second scenario, a treatment is carried out as planned, but there are few or no changes in the dependent variable. Neither of these scenarios causes any reason for interpretive concern because the treatment integrity is high. The following scenarios with no treatment integrity, however, cause considerably more difficulty for interpretation. In the third scenario, there is no documentation as to how well the treatment was implemented, yet changes in the dependent variable are noted. This scenario is representative of most behavioral research (Billingsley *et al.*, 1980; Gresham *et al.*, 1993a; Peterson *et al.*, 1982; Yeaton, 1982) and possibly AAC research as well. Without documentation as to how well the intervention was implemented, it is impossible to attribute the observed changes to the independent variable. Even though many authors of such intervention research operate under the assumption that the independent variable did indeed cause the changes to occur (i.e., because they conclude that the treatment was effective), this assumption is, at best, tenuous because the accuracy of implementation remains an unknown. Treatment agents (e.g., teachers, speech-language pathologists, parents, peers, or research assistants) may or may not have implemented the treatment as planned (Gresham, 1997). If the treatment integrity happens to be documented but is low, it is unlikely that the treatment, as planned, caused the changes in the dependent variable. In fact, the review by Schlosser and Lee (2000) indicated that the more consistent the application of treatment the more positive were the outcomes.

The fourth scenario presents with low or no integrity data and no changes in the dependent variable. This scenario is likely to be rare in the published AAC literature, assuming that the AAC field is no different from other social science fields that face publication bias toward positive effects (Begg, 1994; Light & Pillemer, 1984; Rosenthal, 1979). Regardless, this does not exclude its occurrence in daily practice and therefore warrants discussion. Some evidence-based practitioners and researchers may be inclined to conclude that the intervention was simply not effective when changes were not observed. Is this conclusion necessarily accurate, however, in the absence of integrity data? Alternatively, the intervention may not have been implemented as planned, and that is why no effects occurred. Thus, no or poor integrity may cause the field to reject or discount potentially effective treatments as ineffective (Gresham, 1989; Peterson *et al.*, 1982; Yeaton & Sechrest, 1981). According to Moncher and Prinz (1991), for clinical psychology, such an action may prove costly to the field in the long run.

Given the established importance of treatment integrity to internal validity, an approach such as "given X% of treatment integrity, the following results were yielded" seems healthy, logical, and conducive to establishing a science of AAC intervention research. Using this approach also lends itself to study varying degrees of a priori defined treatment integrity as an independent variable. For example, the role of augmented input (Wood, Lasker, Siegel-Causey, Beukelman, & Ball, 1998) may be studied under ideal conditions with augmented input being provided with 100% of the utterances directed to the learner. Under more typical conditions, however, augmented input is not provided as consistently. In fact, Sevcik, Romski, Watkins, and Deffebach (1993) examined the quantity and quality of augmented input provided to nonspeaking children with intellectual disabilities in classrooms. They found that only 10% of the partners' overall spoken communicative utterances directed to the children included augmented input. Thus, it may be beneficial to study the effects of augmented input with varying degrees of treatment integrity to understand the role of augmented under a range of conditions, from ideal to typical (see Chapter 3). In general, studying the effects of treatment integrity as an independent variable may help distinguish the efficacy of AAC interventions, depending on the location of a study on the optimal-typical continuum of conditions.

A specific situation is presented for treatment integrity when two or more treatments are compared to one another in an AAC intervention study (Schlosser, 1999) (see also Chapters 6 and 21). Here, it is absolutely essential that each treatment is implemented as planned (see also Yeaton, 1982). Otherwise, it will be next to impossible to attribute differences in the dependent variable to the different treatments rather than differences in treatment integrity. Next, the implications of poor treatment integrity or failure to monitor treatment integrity are discussed in terms its implication for external validity.

B. External Validity

The external validity of AAC interventions has to be established through the process of replication (see Chapter 5). Johnston and Pennypacker (1980) defined replication as the degree to *which equivalent environmental manipulations* (i.e., the independent variable) associated with earlier observations are duplicated. This duplication may occur through direct replication or systematic replication (Sidman, 1960). Direct replication may be accomplished by performing the same experiment with new participants or by making repeated observations on the same participants. Systematic replication involves some procedural variation or participant variation in order to extend the generality of the findings from the original experiment. The failure to provide operational definitions of the independent variable and to document treatment integrity not only delimits the internal validity of experiments but also compromises the science of building a replicative history (Gresham, 1997; Moncher & Prinz, 1991). After all, it is impossible to replicate (directly or systematically) something that is unknown in the first place. Next, the implications of poor or absent treatment integrity are discussed in terms of construct validity.

C. Construct Validity

Whereas internal validity involves the demonstration that the independent variable was responsible for changes in the dependent variable, construct validity "addresses the presumed cause or the explanation of the causal relation" (Kazdin, 1992, p. 39). Because the internal validity of an experiment needs to be established prior to engaging in a discussion of its construct validity, the lack of treatment integrity data or inadequate data may also interfere with its construct validity. Without treatment integrity data, one cannot know which parts of the construct underlying the treatment were provided at all or at what level of consistency they were provided. To minimize threats to construct validity, it is essential to include all of those procedural steps in the assessment of treatment integrity that are reflective and representative of the construct that aims to explain the causal relation between the independent variable and the dependent variable (e.g., the quality of contingent praise rather than just the provision of praise per se; a variable ratio 20 reinforcement schedule as opposed to a variable ratio 2 schedule). Without construct-guided inclusion of procedural steps, treatment integrity assessments can be an inadequate representation of the construct and therefore may constitute a threat to the construct validity of AAC interventions.

In summary, poorly defined and idiosyncratically implemented interventions and the failure to assess the integrity of AAC interventions can limit various types of experimental validity (internal, external, and construct) and therefore restrict the certainty of conclusions concerning the efficacy of AAC interventions. In light of this established importance, it is crucial to examine how well the AAC field and related fields have been documenting the treatment integrity of their interventions.

V. ASSESSING TREATMENT INTEGRITY—AN AAC EXAMPLE

Planning an assessment of AAC treatment integrity involves the following steps: (1) defining the independent variable operationally, (2) deciding procedural steps, (3) determining an assessment method, (4) preparing data collection sheets, (5) ascertaining the number of observations, (6) minimizing the reactivity of observations, (7) minimizing experimenter bias, (8) calculating treatment integrity, and (9) reporting treatment integrity data. This section is devoted to an application example for assessing the integrity of AAC interventions, using these steps, drawn from the work of the author and his colleagues. In addition, a checklist was developed (see Appendix 9A) to assist evidence-based practitioners as well as producers of research with the assessment of some of the steps in evaluating and planning treatment integrity. An abbreviated tutorial is available elsewhere (see Schlosser, 2002).

A. DEFINING THE INDEPENDENT VARIABLE OPERATIONALLY

The example is taken from an intervention study on the effects of speech output and orthographic feedback on spelling in a student (referred to as Martin) with autism (Schlosser, Blischak, Belfiore, Bartley, & Barnett, 1998). Specifically, the student's spelling performance was compared under three feedback conditions: (1) auditory (with synthetic speech output), (2) visual (with print output), and (3) auditory-visual (with synthetic speech output *and* print output). First, the training procedures are described while dissecting the procedures for the parameters that are deemed essential for considering the independent variable as operationally defined according to Gresham *et al.* (1993a), including its specific verbal, physical, temporal, and spatial parameters:

> Using the copy-cover-compare method, the experimenters presented an index card with the printed word [*physical dimension, added by author*], pronounced the word [*verbal*], fingerspelled the word [*verbal*], pronounced the word again [*verbal*], and told Martin to spell the word twice on the device ("Spell _____ [word]") [*verbal*]. If necessary, he was instructed to activate the Enter key upon completing the word. After 40 sec had elapsed or when Martin completed the second spelling of the word [*temporal dimension*], the experimenter removed the index card [*physical*] and asked him again to "Spell _____ [word]" [*verbal*]. After 20 sec had elapsed or when the word was completed [*temporal*], the experimenter presented the index card with the printed word [*physical*] and instructed Martin to compare his spelling with that on the index card by pointing to the Enter key [*physical*] while saying "Check your work" [*verbal*]. After 5 sec [*temporal*], the experimenter asked whether the spelling is correct ("Is it correct?") [*verbal*]. Martin was expected to nod or say "yes" if it was correct or shake his head or sign "no" within 5 sec [*temporal*]. If he identified a correct spelling as correct [*physical or verbal*], he was told "That's correct" [*verbal*]. If he identified an incorrect spelling as correct [*physical*], the experimenters said, "No, this is not correct" [*verbal*] and asked Martin to correct it ("Fix it") [*verbal*]. No further feedback was provided. Either way, after 3-sec intertrial interval (ITI) [*temporal*], he was presented with the index card again [*physical*], and subsequent steps were repeated once for a total of two trials. (Schlosser *et al.*, 1998, p. 313)

The procedures, as described, appear to have all the dimensions necessary to be considered an operational definition, with the exception of the spatial dimension. The spatial dimension, however, applies here only in describing the location of the device relative to Martin and the position of the experimenter relative to the device and Martin. This dimension is only implicitly evident in the description of the setting and the speech-generating device with dual displays (one for the learner and one for the listener [here, the experimenter]). Although it is probably obvious that the student was seated opposite the experimenter with the device placed for easy learner access and within sufficiently close distance to allow the reading of the partner display, this could have been made more explicit as part of the procedures. Because these procedures needed to be implemented in the same manner for each of the three feedback conditions, it is necessary to know how the conditions differed in order to arrive at a complete operational definition of the independent variable. This is defined in the "procedures" section:

> In the Auditory condition, Martin received auditory feedback from synthetic speech output for each letter selected (letter feedback) and for each word (whole word feedback) entered. In the Auditory-Visual condition, Martin received auditory feedback as well as visual (i.e., orthographic) feedback from the liquid crystal display (LCD) for each letter entered and word entered. In the Visual condition, Martin received no auditory feedback—only orthographic feedback from the LCD for each letter selected and words entered (Schlosser *et al.*, 1998, p. 313).

B. Deciding Procedural Steps

The next step involves deciding on the procedural steps in need of treatment integrity assessment. Once the experimenter has thoroughly defined the independent variable, these procedural steps should unfold easily from this definition. In our example, independent observer data were collected on the following behaviors:

> (a) Presentation of index card with printed word, (b) provision of spoken word, (c) finger spelling of the word, (d) delivery of the instructional cue ("Spell _____ [word]"), (e) latency of 20 sec, (f) removal of index card, (g) delivery of instructional cue ("Check your work"), (h) latency of 5 sec; (i) delivery of instructional cue ("Check your work; is it correct?"), (j) provision of corrective feedback, and (k) adherence to a 3-sec ITI (Schlosser *et al.*, 1998, p. 314).

To ensure that the experimenter applied the condition correctly (auditory, auditory-visual, visual), the data sheets were color coded and the experimenter was asked to self-monitor by using a check mark if the device had been prepared consistent with the respective condition. For example, in the visual condition, instructions on the top of the sheet said "Turn voice off, cover and point out the loudspeaker and say 'it doesn't talk.'" A box was available next to the statement for the experimenter to check it. In hindsight, it would have been beneficial to collect independent observer data on this procedural aspect as well, rather than relying only on self-monitoring.

C. Determining an Assessment Method

The next step requires the selection of a method for assessing treatment integrity. Gresham (1997) distinguished direct assessment from indirect assessment. Direct assessment involves behavioral observations of the occurrence and nonoccurrence of the steps to be followed. Indirect assessments include rating scales, self-monitoring, self-report, and behavioral interviews. In the example by Schlosser *et al.* (1998), a combination of direct observation and self-monitoring was used. First, the experimenter used self-monitoring while administering the procedures. The procedural steps were made available in a task-analysis fashion on the data recording sheet so that the experimenter could use check marks to monitor herself as she administered the intervention. Second, an independent rater observed the steps to be followed. From these direct observations, the level of treatment integrity can be obtained in multiple ways (see "Calculating Treatment Integrity").

D. Preparing Data Recording Sheets

The next step is to develop a data recording sheet that is conducive to the assessment of treatment integrity. In the example at hand, the same type of data sheet was used for the experimenter (i.e., the primary observer) and the independent observer. This approach was consistent with the use of self-monitoring and direct observation (by an independent observer) as methods to integrity assessment. In addition to each of the target words, each of the procedural steps required for teaching the words was provided. The experimenter and independent observer simply needed to use check marks for those procedural steps that were indeed implemented as planned. Figure 9.1 provides an example of a data collection sheet used in the reported example. In addition to each of the target spelling words, each of the procedural steps required for teaching the words is provided.

E. ASCERTAINING AN ADEQUATE NUMBER OF OBSERVATIONS

The interventionist also needs to decide how many observation sessions are sufficient. This question is not unique to treatment integrity assessments but also applies when assessing interobserver agreement of the dependent measure. The issue of sufficiency relates directly to the need for the observations to be representative of the entire data set (Foster & Cone, 1986; Johnston & Pennypacker, 1980). In other words, are data collected during treatment integrity assessments reflective of the experimenter's behavior when he or she is not observed? Obviously, the greater the number of observations the greater the representativeness of the data set. Extrapolating from recommendations for gathering interobserver agreement data for the dependent variable, treatment integrity observations during 20 to 40% of all sessions seem appropriate. Perhaps more important than the mere percentage may be the distribution of assessment sessions, such that they are approximately equal across all study phases. The observations need to be conducted approximately equal across all study phases (e.g., baseline, intervention, maintenance, generalization) and, if applicable, equally across conditions. In the presented example, assessments were implemented during baseline, intervention, and maintenance. During the intervention phase, for example, integrity assessments were implemented for 36.7% in the visual condition, 30% in the auditory-visual condition, and 36.7% in the auditory condition (Schlosser *et al.*, 1998).

F. MINIMIZING THE REACTIVITY OF OBSERVATIONS

In addition to increasing the representativeness of the treatment integrity observations through increasing the number of observations, the representativeness may also be jeopardized by reactivity. Reactivity is a common threat to internal validity of all observations (Johnson & Pennypacker, 1980). Relative to treatment integrity, reactivity is said to occur when the treatment agent behaves

Training (Auditory-Visual)

Name: _____ Date: _____

Before you start:

1. Randomly determine the order of conditions	
2. Make visual display available	
3. Turn on speech output	
4. Say "the device is working"	

Word	Pre-sent card	Say work	Say "Spell ___"	Pro-vide 20s	+ or –	Error spelling	Say "Spell ___"	Pro-vide 20s	+ or –	Error spelling	Re-move card	Say "Spell ___"	Pro-vide 20s	+ or –	Error spelling	Pre-sent card	Say "Check your work"	Say 5s: "Is the word correct?"	Say "That's correct" or "Fix it"	Pro-vide 20s	+ or –	Error spelling	Pro-vide 3s ITI	Pro-vide 5min
1																								
2																								
3																								
4																								
1																								
2																								
3																								
4																								

Figure 9.1 Sample data collection sheet for assessing treatment integrity used in Schlosser *et al.* (1998).

differently when the independent observer is present compared to when the observer is not present. Although this difference in treatment agent behavior may be in the desired direction in that the treatment protocol is followed more closely when being observed (e.g., during 30% of sessions), the treatment may be less effective or ineffective when applied less stringently during the other sessions (e.g., during the remaining 70% of sessions).

Gresham (1997) suggested several procedures that may ameliorate reactive effects: (1) observers can "spot check" by observing on a random schedule so that the interventionist never knows whether or not the observer is going to be there; (2) the observer can try to be as unobtrusive as possible so that the interventionist "hardly" feels the observer's presence, in the hope that the interventionist would behave as without the observer being present; and (3) the observer simply does not communicate the purpose of the observations to the treatment agent.

In the example by Schlosser *et al.* (1998), each of these procedures played some role, but, as noted by Gresham (1997), these procedures are far from perfect. The first safeguard procedure, the use of spot checks, assumes that the observer is going to follow procedures more closely when observer presence is predictable. This assumption, however, may not be warranted. Because it is inappropriate for the observer to join in the middle of a session, the treatment agent knows at the beginning of the session whether or not she is going to be observed, unless the observer is behind a one-way mirror. As a result, experimenters may adjust their behavior accordingly. The second suggested mechanism, the use of unobtrusive observations, might be more feasible, although it is unknown to what degree a treatment agent can actually "forget" the presence of an observer. Finally, the third strategy, concealing the purpose of the observation works only when the treatment agent follows the protocol in a perfect or near-perfect manner. Otherwise, independent observers are obligated to provide feedback after a session as to how the interventionist might be able to improve his or her performance; at that point, the purpose of the observations will become obvious. Even though there are no perfect solutions to control for reactivity, these measures are useful in minimizing reactivity, at least to some degree.

G. Minimizing Experimenter Bias

Experimenter bias represents another threat to internal validity of much intervention research. In terms of treatment integrity, Peterson *et al.* (1982) argued that integrity observations are more susceptible to experimenter bias than dependent variable observations because the treatment variable is predefined and an experimenter or an informed observer might simply report what the experimenter was supposed to do rather than what actually occurred. Given this threat to internal validity, it is clear that treatment integrity assessments cannot rely on self-monitoring methods alone.

H. CALCULATING TREATMENT INTEGRITY

Treatment integrity may be calculated in a number of ways. One approach is to calculate the percentage of treatment components implemented according to an independent observer who monitors the interventionist. Billingsley *et al.* (1980) provides such an example; integrity was calculated by multiplying the number of teacher behaviors emitted in correspondence with the plan times 100, divided by the total number of behaviors that could have been emitted in accord with the plan. So if the plan called for "praise" following each correct response, and the student made 10 correct responses but the teacher only praised 7 of these responses, it would yield a percentage correct of $7 \times 100/10 = 70\%$. The strength of this approach is that it delivers what has been called the most relevant measurement principle in evaluating treatment integrity—that is, accuracy. Accuracy has been defined as the correspondence between measured behavior and the value prespecified by the experimenter (Gresham, 1997). The weakness of this approach is the reliance on the perspective of one observer, albeit one who is independent.

The calculation of treatment integrity is more valid if it is implemented analogous to that of interobserver agreement for the dependent measure. When calculating interobserver agreement, researchers first report the performance data as observed by the primary observer. Next, a percent agreement (or correlation coefficient) is calculated between the primary observer's recording of performance data and that of an independent observer (Johnston & Pennypacker, 1980). The percentage of correct data reported previously (i.e., 70%) represent only the first part of this procedure—the experimenter's performance data as observed by the primary observer. If that primary observer is the experimenter, these data also describe self-monitoring performance. In addition to these data, treatment integrity ideally requires the calculation of interobserver agreement. In Schlosser *et al.* (1998), we chose to calculate the percentage agreement between the experimenter, who recorded her own behavior as part of self-monitoring, and the independent observer, who monitored the implementation of each treatment component at the same time. An agreement was scored when the experimenter and the observer both recorded the same response. Interobserver agreement was then determined by calculating the number of agreements divided by the number of agreements plus disagreements and multiplying by 100. The resulting interobserver agreement data represent an estimate of the reliability of treatment implementation. This approach remedies the weakness of the earlier one by comparing the coding among at least two observers, analog to interobserver agreement for the dependent measure.

I. Reporting Treatment Integrity Data

Treatment integrity data may be reported in a number of ways. In the Schlosser *et al.* (1998) example, the mean percentage agreement scores were reported along with ranges, where applicable, for each condition: "Mean results were 100% for the Visual condition, 99.1% (range, 99–100%) for the Auditory-Visual condition, and 100% for the Auditory condition" (p. 314). These means per condition may be called *overall integrity*—that is, the integrity of all treatment components across sessions. Gresham (1997) advocated that interventionists also report data on component integrity and session integrity: *Component integrity* is defined as the integrity of each treatment component across sessions, whereas *session integrity* refers to the integrity of all treatment components within one session. It may very well be that failure to find treatment effects can be attributed to poor component integrity over time or poor daily integrity across components. Thus, reporting of treatment integrity data in terms of overall integrity, component integrity, and session integrity is essential to credibility, replicability, and ultimately to the trustworthiness of the research record.

In summary, the assessment of treatment integrity involves several steps beginning with an operational definition of the independent variable and ending with the reporting of treatment integrity data. The example chosen involved a highly structured intervention with the intent of assisting with the ease of illustration. Treatment integrity assessments are, however, as readily accomplished (and as important) when less structured interventions are involved. Hamilton and Snell (1993), for example, assessed treatment integrity for the application of milieu teaching—an approach that tends to be less structured and occurs in the learners' natural environment. When planning and implementing treatment integrity assessments for less structured interventions, the first two steps of defining (1) the independent variable operationally and (2) the procedural steps are admittedly somewhat more difficult and less obvious but are nonetheless both doable and necessary.

VI. TREATMENT INTEGRITY AND THE EVIDENCE-BASED PRACTITIONER

What is the relevance, if any, of the notion of treatment integrity for the clinician or educator in the trenches of daily practice? Despite many parallels between clinicians and clinical researchers (Hegde, 1994), the situation of the practicing clinician or educator is sufficiently different from a clinical researcher to warrant a close look. At least the following two roles that practitioners need to fulfill distinguish the clinician from the researcher: (1) implementing evidence-based practice and (2) evaluating the outcomes of daily interventions (rather than tightly controlled interventions).

A. IMPLEMENTING EVIDENCE-BASED PRACTICE

For research findings to guide some of the decisions involved in daily practice, the evidence-based practitioner needs to understand what aspects contribute to the certainty of the evidence. From the information presented in this chapter, it is very clear that treatment integrity is an important aspect, perhaps even the most important aspect to be considered when evaluating the evidence. Because Chapter 12 is devoted to evidence-based practice, the role of treatment integrity for evidence-based practice will be discussed in more detail in that chapter.

B. EVALUATING THE OUTCOMES OF DAILY INTERVENTIONS

Evidence-based practitioners have a strong interest in determining whether their daily interventions are responsible for the observed changes. Given that it is impossible to attribute observed changes to the intervention without documentation as to how well the intervention was implemented, there is no question that practitioners ought to monitor the integrity of their treatments. Rather, the question is how the suggested steps can be adapted so that they are consistent with the realities of daily practice. To summarize, the steps for planning and implementing treatment integrity assessments are as follows: (1) defining the independent variable operationally, (2) deciding procedural steps, (3) determining an assessment method, (4) preparing data collection sheets, (5) ascertaining the number of observations, (6) minimizing the reactivity of observations, (7) minimizing experimenter bias, (8) calculating treatment integrity, and (9) reporting treatment integrity data.

It is essential that practitioners define their interventions in observable terms including all necessary parameters such as verbal, physical, temporal, and spatial parameters. Without operational definitions it would be difficult to implement the intervention consistently over time or to train others in applying the intervention as planned. If the intervention has been carefully defined, the procedural steps should unfold relatively easily from the definition. Many clinicians and educators are used to performing a task analysis and will find this to be a familiar process. The steps identified are important in that they describe the sequence of events that need to be implemented. Thus far, the practitioner would do essentially the same as a researcher. The next step involves determining an assessment method. Analog to the measurement of dependent variables, it is important that practitioners attempt to get the best measure that is practically possible for independent variables as well. Although it would be desirable to use direct assessments such as observations by another party, this may not be feasible because of the extra resources involved. Indirect assessments such as self-monitoring or self-report are much more conducive to the assessment of treatment integrity in daily practice. The development of data collection sheets in daily practice provides the tools that make self-monitoring possible. As a result of the likely use of self-monitoring as an assessment method, ascertaining the number of observation sessions is only relevant to the number of self-monitoring sessions. Because self-monitoring lends itself to be part of treatment implementation, it could be used in most if not all sessions.

Observer reactivity is unlikely to be an issue in daily practice when self-monitoring is used. Should direct observations be used, the same principles apply as those outlined for clinical research. As discussed previously, the use of self-monitoring is prone to experimenter bias or "practitioner bias." In other words, the practitioner may simply record what he or she was supposed to do rather than what was actually done.

VII. CONCLUSIONS

This chapter substantiated the crucial role of treatment integrity in (1) establishing a science of AAC intervention research and (2) helping practitioners to engage in evidence-based practice and to evaluate the outcomes of everyday interventions. In doing so, an attempt was made to illustrate the importance of adequate treatment integrity to the trustworthiness of the research record. As illustrated, inadequate or missing data can pose numerous threats to the internal validity, external validity, and construct validity of AAC treatment research and therefore restrict the conclusions concerning the efficacy of AAC interventions.

Despite its significance, preliminary surveys of our intervention research indicate that the AAC field appears to be no different from related fields in its neglect to assess treatment integrity. To assist consumers of research as well as producers of research with the assessment of treatment integrity, an evaluation/planning checklist was developed (see Appendix 9A). This checklist, along with the strategies described in the text, may be helpful in moving the field from neglect of the issue to a place of prominence that it deserves. If practice is to be informed through best evidence, treatment integrity assessments must become an integral part of planning, implementing, and evaluating intervention research in AAC. In terms of evaluating AAC intervention research, several projects have incorporated treatment integrity considerations into determining the certainty of evidence evaluated (Millar, Light, & Schlosser, 2000; Schlosser & Lee, 2000; Schlosser & Sigafoos, 2002). Although these are steps in the right direction, more such efforts need to be undertaken. Given its importance to the trustworthiness of the research record, the assessment of treatment integrity in intervention studies needs to be given considerable weight in publication decisions. Only then will the field succeed in developing a science of AAC intervention research. It is hoped that this chapter will serve toward that end.

REFERENCES

Begg, C. B. (1994). Publication bias. In H. Cooper & L. V. Hedges (Eds.), *The handbook of research synthesis* (pp. 399–409). New York: Russell Sage Foundation.

Billingsley, F. F., White, O. R., & Munson, R. (1980). Procedural reliability: A rationale and an example. *Behavioral Assessment, 2,* 229–241.

Cook, T., & Campbell, D. (Eds.) (1979). *Quasi-experimentation: Design and analysis issues for field settings.* Chicago: Rand McNally.

Foster, S., & Cone, J. (1986). Design and use of direct observation. In A. Ciminero, K. Calhoun, & H. Adams (Eds.), *Handbook of behavioral assessment* (2nd ed., pp. 253–324). New York: Wiley Interscience.

Gresham, F. M. (1989). Assessment of treatment integrity in school consultation and prereferral intervention. *School Psychology Review, 18,* 37–50.

Gresham, F. M. (1997). Treatment integrity in single-subject research. In R. D. Franklin, D. B. Allison, & B. S. Gorman (Eds). *Design and analysis of single-case research* (pp. 93–117). Hillsdale, NJ: L Earlbaum.

Gresham, F. M., Gansle, K., & Noell, G. (1993a). Treatment integrity in applied behavior analysis with children. *Journal of Applied Behavior Analysis, 26,* 257–263.

Gresham, F. M., Gansle, K., Noell, G., Cohen, S., & Rosenblum, S. (1993b). Treatment integrity of school-based behavioral intervention studies: 1980–1990. *School Psychology Review, 22,* 254–272.

Hamilton, B. L., & Snell, M. E. (1993). Using the milieu approach to increase spontaneous communication book use across environments by an adolescent with autism. *Augmentative and Alternative Communication, 9,* 259–272.

Hegde, M. N. (1994). *Clinical research in communicative disorders* (2nd ed.). Austin, TX: Pro-Ed.

Johnston, J., & Pennypacker, H. (1980). *Strategies and tactics of human behavioral research.* Hillsdale, NJ: L Erlbaum.

Kazdin, A. (1992). *Research design in clinical psychology* (2nd ed.). New York: MacMillan.

Light, R. J., & Pillemer, D. B. (1984). *Summing up: Science for reviewing research.* Cambridge, MA: Harvard University Press.

Millar, D., Light, J., & Schlosser, R. (2000). The impact of AAC on natural speech development: A meta-analysis. In *Proceedings of the 9th biennial conference of the International Society for Augmentative and Alternative Communication* (pp. 740–741). Washington, DC: ISAAC.

Moncher, F., & Prinz, R. (1991). Treatment fidelity in outcome studies. *Clinical Psychology Review, 11,* 247–266.

Peterson, L., Homer, A. L., & Wonderlich (1982). The integrity of independent variables in behavior analysis. *Journal of Applied Behavior Analysis, 15,* 477–492.

Rosenthal, R. (1979). The "file drawer problem" and tolerance for null results. *Psychological Bulletin, 86,* 638–641.

Schlosser, R. W. (1999). Comparative efficacy of interventions in augmentative and alternative communication. *Augmentative and Alternative Communication, 15,* 56–68.

Schlosser, R. W. (2002). On the importance of being earnest about treatment integrity. *Augmentative and Alternative Communication, 18,* 36–44.

Schlosser, R. W., Blischak, D. M., Belfiore, P. J., Bartley, C., & Barnett, N. (1998). Effects of synthetic speech output and orthographic feedback on spelling in a student with autism: A preliminary study. *Journal of Autism and Developmental Disorders, 28,* 309–319.

Schlosser, R. W., Clifford, M., & Blischak, D. (2001, November). *Treatment fidelity in augmentative and alternative communication.* Poster presented at the Annual Convention of the American Speech-Language and Hearing Association.

Schlosser, R. W., & Lee, D. (2000). Promoting generalization and maintenance in augmentative and alternative communication: A meta-analysis of 20 years of efficacy research. *Augmentative and Alternative Communication, 16,* 208–226.

Schlosser, R. W., & Sigafoos, J. (2002). Selecting graphic symbols for an initial request lexicon: An integrative review. *Augmentative and Alternative Communication, 18,* 102–123.

Sevcik, R. A., Romski, M. A., Watkins, R. V., & Deffebach, K. P. (1993). *A descriptive analysis of augmented linguistic input to nonspeaking children with mental retardation.* Unpublished manuscript, Georgia State University.

Sidman, M. (1960). *Tactics of scientific research: Evaluating experimental data in psychology.* Boston: Authors Cooperative.

Udwin, O. (1987). Analysis of the experimental adequacy of alternative and augmentative communication training studies. *Child Language Teaching and Therapy, 3,* 18–39.

Vermilyea, B. B., Barlow, D. H., & O'Brien, G. T. (1984). The importance of assessing treatment integrity: An example in anxiety disorders. *Journal of Behavioral Assessment, 6,* 1–11.

Wood, L. A., Lasker, J., Siegel-Causey, E., Beukelman, D. R., & Ball, L. (1998). Input framework for augmentative and alternative communication. *Augmentative and Alternative Communication, 14,* 261–267.

Yeaton, W. H. (1982). A critique of the effectiveness of applied behavior analysis research. *Advances in Behavior Research and Therapy, 4,* 75–96.

Yeaton, W. H., & Sechrest, L. (1981). Critical dimensions in the choice and maintenance of successful treatments: Strength, integrity, and effectiveness. *Journal of Consulting and Clinical Psychology, 49,* 156–167.

APPENDIX 9A

Evaluation Checklist for Planning and Evaluating Treatment Integrity Assessments

Instructions: This checklist aims to guide the planning and evaluation of treatment integrity. The items identify those issues that are important to the assessment of integrity and its consequences to validity (internal, external, and construct). Individual ratings serve as the basis for the overall rating.

	Evaluation/Planning Items	P[a]	F[b]	G[c]	E[d]
1	IV is operationally defined, including necessary parameters.				
2	All observable procedural steps are decided and described.				
3	Direct approaches are chosen at least as one assessment method.				
4	Data-collection sheets are consistent with direct approaches.				
5	The number of observations indicates representativeness.				
6	Reactivity of observations is minimized.				
7	Experimenter bias is minimized.				
8	Provides percentage accuracy *and* percentage agreement on occurrences/nonoccurrence.				
9	Results are reported in terms of (a) component, (b) session, and (c) overall.				
10	Integrity results support the treatment efficacy results.				
	Overall rating	P	F	G	E

[a]Poor.
[b]Fair.
[c]Good.
[d]Excellent.

CHAPTER 10

Determining the Social Validity of AAC Interventions

Ralf W. Schlosser
Department of Speech-Language Pathology and Audiology
Northeastern University

Are consumers satisfied with the results, all of the results [positive or negative], including those that were unplanned? Behavioral treatment programs are designed to help someone with a problem. Whether or not the program is helpful can be evaluated only by the consumer. Behavior analysts may give their opinions, and these opinions may even be supported with empirical objective behavioral data, but it is the participants and other consumers who want to make the final decision about whether a program helped solve their problems.

Wolf, 1978, p. 210

I. INTRODUCTION

Generally, interventions in augmentative and alternative communication (AAC) have been found effective as far as objective behavior change is concerned

The Efficacy of Augmentative and Alternative Communication

(Schlosser & Lee, 2000). The preceding quote eloquently states, however, that empirical and objective data are only one piece to the puzzle. That is, stakeholders' perspectives on the outcomes attained are of vital importance in any science involved with human behavior. The process to reveal these stakeholder perspectives is commonly referred to as social validation. Due to this importance, it is not surprising that social validity represents one of several established parameters for evaluating intervention research in general and AAC intervention research in particular (see Chapter 3). Moreover, interventions that are socially valid in addition to being effective bear more credibility than interventions that lack social validity data. As such, social validation is used as an additional marker in decision making for evidence-based practice (EBP) (see Chapter 12). Given its ubiquitous nature, this chapter presents the reader with the AAC Social Validity Framework to assist researchers and evidence-based practitioners in planning, implementing, and evaluating the social validity of AAC interventions. Before introducing the framework, the chapter presents the definitions of social validation and social validation methods and summarizes existing reviews of the social validation literature in related fields and AAC.

II. SOCIAL VALIDATION DEFINED

Social validation is the process of assessing the social significance of goals, methods, and outcomes (Kazdin, 1977; Wolf, 1978; Schlosser, 1999). This process may be implemented through the methods of (1) subjective evaluation and (2) social comparison. Subjective evaluation refers to the soliciting of opinions of persons who have a special position due to their expertise or their relationship to the client (Kazdin, 1977; 1982; Kazdin & Matson, 1981; Wolf, 1978). It is the stakeholders of interventions who should engage in this process, the results of which constitute measures of social validity: "If we aspire to social importance, then we must develop systems that allow our consumers to provide feedback about how our applications relate to their values" (Wolf, 1978, p. 475). Social comparison refers to the comparability of performance with a group of individuals whose behavior is considered to be typical, desirable, or normal (Kazdin, 1977; 1982; Kazdin & Matson, 1981; Wolf, 1978).

Presumably, goals, methods, and outcomes that are socially valid in addition to being objectively valid are the ones that are most likely to be adopted by consumers and will result in more widespread dissemination (Winett, Moore, & Anderson, 1991). Interventionists involved in the provision of AAC need to target goals for change in order to focus an intervention. The focus selected, however, may or may not represent a target that is considered (1) significant by consumers (via subjective evaluation) or (2) comparable with a group of typical individuals (via social comparison). To ensure that a selected target is socially valid, the process of social validation becomes paramount. In addition to goals, interventionists need to determine the methods for implementing the intervention. Again, these methods may or may not to be considered of social value or considered comparable to the methods used with typical individuals. To increase the potential that stakeholders will adopt interventions, steps need to be taken to ensure that consumers find the methods to be important and acceptable. Similarly, to ensure that the steps are comparable to individuals who are considered typical, researchers need to engage in social comparisons. Although data may have indicated that an intervention was efficacious, such results do not always imply that stakeholders also perceive a change as efficacious or that the changes are comparable to behaviors yielded with typical individuals. Thus, interventionists need to assess the social validity of outcomes. Before presenting a framework for evaluating the social validity of interventions in AAC, we will examine several reviews of social validation in related fields.

III. REVIEWS OF THE SOCIAL VALIDATION LITERATURE

Several reviews have been conducted in related fields to evaluate the degree to which studies assessed the social validity of interventions. In absence of a systematic review that focuses on this topic in the AAC field, a summary of reviews conducted in related fields may help in preparing a review of social validation in the AAC field and in planning social validation assessments of AAC interventions.

A. REVIEWS FROM RELATED FIELDS

In fields related to AAC, several comprehensive reviews of the social validation literature have been conducted (Kennedy, 1992; Storey & Horner, 1991; Test, 1994). The review by Fuqua and Schwade (1986) was selective with a methodological focus, and therefore it does not enter the section that follows.

1. Kennedy (1992)

This author presented a content analysis of social validity measures used for more than 20 years in articles published in the *Journal of Applied Behavior Analysis* (1968–1990) and *Behavior Modification* (1977–1990). Social validity was evaluated in terms of the (1) type of assessment, (2) focus of assessment, and (3) time of assessment. The type of assessment is consistent with the term "method of evaluation" used in this chapter and refers to the methodologies of subjective evaluation and social comparison. The focus of assessment refers to the three aspects of the intervention process, namely the goals, procedures, and outcomes. Last, the time of assessment focuses on its use as a pre- versus postintervention measure. Kennedy (1992) reviewed the literature in terms of 12 possible combinations as far as time of assessment is concerned. An independent coder rated 20% of the articles included, resulting in an overall interrater agreement for occurrences of 94% and nonoccurrences of 99%.

Results indicated that at the time of publication, approximately 20% of studies in both journals included social validity assessments. Social comparison was rarely used as a method of evaluation, suggesting that subjective evaluation has become the almost exclusive method for assessing social validity in these journals. In terms of subjective evaluation, postintervention assessments were used more frequently than preintervention assessments. Most of the preintervention assessments were concerned with the evaluation of goals. Perceptions of procedures or outcomes were rarely assessed prior to intervention. The majority of postintervention assessments (96%) aimed at the evaluation of outcomes. Subjective evaluations of procedures and goals were the most prominent forms. Social comparison data displayed a similar pattern as the subjective evaluation results. The use of multiple measures such as the combined use of either multiple types of subjective evaluation or normative comparison or both was found to be scant (10%).

Based on his review, Kennedy (1992) called for a distinction of applied research that requires social validation and research that may not necessitate such data. Research that aims to remedy societal problems, for example, would strongly benefit from social validity data. In AAC, research that aims to improve the communicative competence of learners (e.g., Light & Binger, 1998) would be more convincing if social validity data were gathered. On the other hand, research designed to study basic behavioral functions and processes may not call for social validity data. Horner and Day (1991), for instance, studied the effects of response efficiency on problem behaviors by manipulating the (1) schedule of reinforcement, (2) physical effort (e.g., key word signing versus sentence signing), and (3) time delay. Because this study aimed to examine the role of these three variables rather than a mere replacement in challenging behaviors, social validation data are not necessary. Kennedy (1992) also suggested that current trends in social validity might be a reflection of the insensitivity of current measures to the "ecological" variables of interest. Likert type scales may not capture the social importance of an intervention. Similarly, social comparison is perhaps not useful if we have to compare normative rates of one population in one particular context and time with another population and another context and time. Thus, Kennedy (1992) argued for the development of more meaningful and sensitive measures of social validity.

2. Storey and Horner (1991)

This review provided a critical comprehensive review of the social validation literature involving persons with disabilities. It included studies published through 1988 and involved a handsearch of 15 journals along with an ancestry search. These authors presented satisfactory levels of interobserver agreement both in terms of inclusion of articles and coding of articles. Results revealed a substantial upward trend in the number of articles using social validation procedures. Unlike Kennedy's (1992) review, however, the percentage of studies with social validation as compared to those without is not reported. The majority of studies consulted only a few members of *one* stakeholder group to validate the social significance of outcomes. Subjective evaluation findings have correlated positively with objective measurements, suggesting that stakeholders are able to detect important changes in behavior. Social comparison efforts for determining optimal levels of performance revealed that 96% of the studies compared persons with disabilities to nondisabled individuals and about 5% compared the participants with other individuals with disabilities. In terms of the subjective evaluation of goals, each of the reported studies found the goals to be significant. None of the studies reviewed, however, reported interobserver agreement data. In terms of procedures, different groups of raters rank-ordered the appropriateness of the procedures fairly consistently.

This review raised several methodological concerns of the social validity literature. First, the majority of social validation efforts failed to offer indices of reliability regardless of whether subjective evaluation or social comparison was used. Second, the measures used are often based on their face validity as the sole validity criterion. Third, questionnaires are typically developed without following guidelines for questionnaire or survey construction. Fourth, the selection of videotape segments usually does not occur at random, which increases chances of bias. Fifth, raters/evaluators are few and often selected from only one stakeholder group. Last, social validity assessments rarely map onto experimental designs used to evaluate treatment efficacy.

3. Test (1994)

This author reviewed the social validation literature in the area of supported employment using the Social Validity Matrix. This matrix includes Schwartz and Baer's (1991) four types of stakeholders combined with Fawcett's (1991) nine categories of social validity data to yield a 4×9 matrix. This matrix was used to systematically assess the social validity in supported employment. In addition to a handsearch of six journals, Test (1994) also used an ancestry search. To be included, studies needed to report (1) empirical or quantifiable data, (2) primary findings collected from any of the four types of stakeholder groups, and (3) data pertaining to the nine categories of social validity. Thirty studies met the criteria of inclusion. Interrater observer agreement yielded 100% agreement for the type of consumer and 86.7% for the level of social validity.

Test (1994) offers numerous recommendations for future research. Only the most pertinent to the cause of the AAC field shall be summarized as follows. First, since the majority of assessments consulted stakeholders other than direct stakeholders, more efforts need to be directed to solicit the opinions of direct stakeholders, in particular those with severe disabilities. Second, the field must explore the use of alternative methods for assessing social validity, including behavioral correlates of satisfaction, quality of life measures, and measures of integration. Third, systematic procedures of collecting and using social validity data need to be established. Fourth, ease of use is a major consideration for ensuring the use of social validation measures in everyday practice.

B. REVIEWS IN AAC

Systematic reviews of social validation in AAC are not available at this time. The existing cursory data, however, seem to suggest that social validation is not commonplace in many AAC intervention studies. Schlosser (1999) coded single-subject experiments published in *Augmentative and Alternative Communication* in terms of their presence or absence of social validity assessments. This informal content analysis revealed that only 12.5% of the surveyed studies included social validation procedures (i.e., Hamilton & Snell, 1993; Heller, Allgood, Davis, Arnold, Castelle, & Taber, 1997; McNaughton & Tawney, 1993; O'Keefe & Datillo, 1992). Thus, the AAC field appears to be struggling with similar issues as applied behavior analysis in terms of the overall lack of social validation evaluation (Kennedy, 1992). The AAC Social Validity Framework may assist researchers and evidence-based practitioners in planning, implementing, and evaluating the social validation of AAC interventions and reviewing the social validation literature in AAC.

IV. THE AAC SOCIAL VALIDITY FRAMEWORK

In conducting a credible evaluation or planning of social validity, the reader should examine how the three main components of the AAC Social Validity Framework have been addressed as defined in Table 10.1 (for an explanation of the derivation of this matrix, refer to Schlosser, 1999).

This framework consists of intersections among stakeholders (the "who" of social validation), intervention components (the "what"), and methods (the "how") (see Table 10.1 for definitions). Based on the work of Schwartz and Baer

Table 10.1

Categories, Components, and Definitions of the Social Validity Matrix for AAC Interventions[a]

Categories	Components	Definitions
Stakeholders	Direct	Primary recipients of an intervention
	Indirect	Persons who are strongly affected by the targeted change
	Immediate community	Persons who interact with the direct or indirect stakeholders on a regular basis either professionally or socially
	Extended community	(a) Persons who live in the same community but who probably do not know or interact with the direct and indirect stakeholders, or
		(b) Experts in the field of study
Intervention goals	Topography	Broad social goals: value base that underlies AAC
		Behavioral categories: hypothesized subcategories of broad social goals
		Discrete responses: specific behaviors make up the behavioral categories
Intervention goals	Level	Anticipated performance that indicates a goal has been achieved
Intervention methods	Materials	Articles used for the preparation or implementation of intervention
	Procedures	Type: the specific intervention strategy used during intervention
		Form: the "how" of intervention implementation
Intervention outcomes	Proximal	Perceived changes that are directly related to intervention
	Instrumental	Perceived changes presumed to lead to other outcomes without further intervention
	Intermediate	Perceived changes in total "quality of life" as a result of intervention
	Distal	Perceived changes for stakeholders as a group
Validation methods	Subjective evaluation	Soliciting of opinions of persons who have a special position due to their expertise or their relationship to the client
	Social comparison	Comparability of performance with a group of individuals whose behavior is considered to be "typical," "desirable," or "normal"

[a]With permission from ISAAC taken from Schlosser, R. W. (1999). Social validation in augmentative and alternative communication. *Augmentative and Alternative Communication, 15.* 234–247.

(1991), the stakeholders of AAC interventions ("who") will be grouped into direct stakeholders, indirect stakeholders, immediate community stakeholders, and extended community stakeholders. Each of these stakeholders may be asked to validate three components of intervention ("what"), including the goals, methods, and outcomes (Fawcett, 1991; Kazdin, 1977, 1982; Schlosser & Braun, 1994; Wolf, 1978). This validation may be accomplished through the methods ("how") of subjective evaluation or social comparison (Kazdin, 1977; 1982; Kazdin & Matson, 1981; Wolf, 1978). Clinical examples and studies that exemplify the intersections of this AAC Social Validation Framework are presented in Table 10.2.

Table 10.2

Intersections of the AAC Social Validation Framework: Illustrative examples[a]

Intervention Components ("What")	Sub-components	Perspectives ("Who")/Methods ("How")	
		Direct Stakeholder Subjective Evaluation	Indirect Stakeholders Subjective Evaluation
Goals	Topography	Individuals who used AAC (as appropriate) and their facilitators validated target skills as appropriate intervention goals for enhancing communicative competence through discussion and problem solving (Light et al., 1999). [pretreatment]	Dowden et al. (1986) employed subjective evaluation with nursing staff and family members of AAC users to select the broad social goals and behavioral categories of clinical intervention. [pretreatment]
Methods	Materials	Based on Hamilton and Snell (1993), the participant with autism could have been asked whether he thought the pictures on his communication book were working well for him. [posttreatment]	The parents of an adolescent boy with autism, who served as trainers in using the milieu approach, were surveyed at the end of the intervention to determine whether the pictures in the child's communication book seemed to meet most of their child's communication needs (Hamilton & Snell, 1993). [posttreatment]
	Procedures	Following request training in two conditions (SGD, manual communication board), the participant with profound mental retardation was asked to choose whether he wanted to continue using the SGD or the communication board. He consistently selected the SGD (Soto et al., 1993).[posttreatment]	The parents of an adolescent boy with autism were taught to serve as trainers to implement the milieu approach with their child. Subsequent to intervention, the parents were surveyed to determine their understanding of the milieu approach, and its ease of use (Hamilton & Snell, 1993). [posttreatment]
Outcomes	Proximal	In a study on the effects of facilitator training, structured interviews were conducted with two participating AAC users and their facilitators to determine the social importance of proximal outcomes (Light et al., 1992). [posttreatment]	Using a questionnaire, family members and caregivers of three participants were asked for perceived changes as a result of teaching the response-recode form. The changes were perceived as observable, valuable and lasting (O'Keefe & Dattilo, 1992). [posttreatment]

Immediate Community Stakeholders		Extended Community Stakeholders	
Subjective Evaluation	Social Comparison	Subjective Evaluation	Social Comparison
Light *et al.* (1999) held extensive discussions with expert users of AAC and with experienced professionals in AAC to determine what skills they believed contributed to the attainment of communicative competence. *[pretreatment]*	Researchers could examine the communicative competence of highly successful AAC users to determine the focus of intervention for less successful AAC users. *[pretreatment]*	Researchers met to establish consensus on a research agenda in AAC for the next decade (Beukelman & Ansel, 1995). *[pretreatment]*	Researchers could examine the communicative competence of laypersons, matched on relevant characteristics to the recipients of intervention, to determine the discrete responses to be taught in intervention. *[pretreatment]*
Based on Schlosser's (1995) study on instructional methods to Blissymbol teaching, story narratives could have been validated by soliciting the opinions of the participants' preschool teachers. *[pretreatment]*	Based on Schlosser's (1995) study on instructional methods to Blissymbol teaching, peers of participants could have been presented with two types of story boards and asked to choose the boards they preferred. *[pretreatment]*	In a study on the instructional methods to Blissymbol teaching, story narratives were validated by soliciting the opinions of four experts in story grammar in terms of the stories' adherence to established story grammar components (Schlosser, 1995). *[pretreatment]*	Based on Schlosser's study (1995) on methods to Blissymbol teaching, children who did not know the participants could have been presented with two types of story boards and asked to choose the boards they preferred. *[pretreatment]*
In a study on the effects of speech output and orthographic feedback on spelling in a student with autism, the participant's teacher was surveyed to baseline to determine procedures such as (a) type of spelling instruction, (b) latency required to spell a word, and (c) level of speech output feedback most beneficial (Schlosser, *et al.* 1998). *[pretreatment]*	Based on the work of Schlosser *et al.* (1998), nondisabled peers of the student with autism could have been presented with the same spelling task under two conditions: one SGD that provided letter-level feedback, and one SGD that provided word-level feedback. Observational data could have been recorded to determine the peers' procedural preferences. *[pretreatment]*	In a study on Blissymbol teaching within a story-telling context, Blissymbol instructors validated the symbol instructions to be used in terms of their adherence to best practices of instruction (Schlosser & Lloyd, 1993). *[pretreatment]*	Based on the Schlosser *et al.* (1998) study, nondisabled students, age matched to the student with autism but unfamiliar with this particular student, could have been presented with the same spelling task under two SGD conditions: one that provided letter-level feedback, and another that provided word-level feedback. Observational data could have been recorded to determine the procedural preferences of the peers. *[pretreatment]*
Based on Angelo's and Goldstein's (1990) study involving four AAC users exposed to a pragmatic teaching strategy, independent raters who were professionals with regular contact with the participants could have been shown pre- and post-treatment videotapes to rate outcomes. *[posttreatment]*	Based on Angelo and Goldstein (1990), several communication tasks, identical to those used in later experiments with AAC users, could have been administered to nondisabled peers to determine (a) whether nondisabled children would request information using wh-interrogative forms in naturally structured activities, and (b) their levels. The levels of wh-information requests by AAC users during follow-up could be found comparable to that of nondisabled individuals. *[pretreatment]*	In a study on facilitator training, pre- and post-treatment videotapes of three dyads were shown to four independent raters who were experts in the field but blind to the status of the videotapes. The experts noted differences on the target behaviors (Light *et al.*, 1992). *[posttreatment]*	Based on Angelo and Goldstein (1990), several communication tasks (based on milieu teaching), identical to those used in later experiments with AAC users, could have been administered to *nondisabled preschoolers* (roughly matched for mental age) to determine (a) whether nondisabled children would request information using wh-interrogative forms in naturally structured activities, and (b) their levels. The levels of wh-information requests by AAC users during follow-up could be found comparable to those of nondisabled individuals. *[pretreatment]*

(continues)

Table 10.2 (*continued*)

Intervention Components ("What")	Sub-components	Perspectives ("Who")/Methods ("How")	
		Direct Stakeholder Subjective Evaluation	Indirect Stakeholders Subjective Evaluation
	Instrumental	Bower Hulme, Bain, Hardin, McKinnon, and Waldron, (1989) found that assistive positioning improves vocalizations and diversity in speech sounds among nonspeaking children with cerebral palsy. The children could have been asked whether they feel more like talking. *[posttreatment]*	McEwen (1992) found that changes in positioning in students with severe disabilities resulted in improved communication without further intervention. Caregivers could have been interviewed to determine whether they also perceived changes in communication. *[posttreatment]*
	Intermediate	Based on Datillo and Camarata (1992), the two participating AAC users could have been interviewed to determine whether they perceived themselves as more active conversation participants. *[posttreatment]*	Following self-initiated conversation treatment with two AAC users, Datillo and Camarata (1991) interviewed friends of the users to determine the validity of outcomes. The friends felt that John was a more active conversation participant and more assertive in managing his own needs. The friends found Carl to use less aversive vocalization and to be more involved in a greater variety of leisure activities. *[posttreatment]*
	Distal	AAC user participants in a national outcome study could be surveyed to understand their perceptions of positive, negative, and unplanned outcomes. *[posttreatment]*	The parents and other family members of the participants in a national outcome study could be surveyed to determine their perceptions regarding positive, negative, and unplanned outcomes. *[posttreatment]*

[a]With permission from ISAAC, adapted from Schlosser, R. W. (1999). Social validation in Augmentative and Alternative Communication. *Augmentative and Alternative Communication, 15.* 234–247.

Immediate Community Stakeholders		Extended Community Stakeholders	
Subjective Evaluation	Social Comparison	Subjective Evaluation	Social Comparison
McEwen (1992) found that changes in positioning in students with severe disabilities resulted in improved communication without further intervention. Professionals who interact with the children on a regular basis could have been interviewed to determine whether they also perceived changes in communication. [posttreatment]	McEwen (1992) found that changes in positioning in students with severe disabilities resulted in improved communication without further intervention. Successful AAC user peers in adapted seating arrangements could have been presented with similar tasks to determine their rates of communication. These rates could haven been compared to those achieved for the students with severe disabilities [posttreatment].	Reid and Hurlbut (1977) assessed the validity of instrumental effects of a training program for teaching direct selection of communication boards in four participants with severe physical disabilities. Upon completing training, the participants were placed in situations with strangers and asked to indicate what they wanted to do, first without the board, then with the board. It was felt that, if access training was indeed socially valid, the strangers should be able to interpret the message and escort the subjects to the requested activity area. Results indicated the social validity of outcomes. [posttreatment]	In a fictitious study on functional communication training, a child was taught to request attention with a buzzer instead of engaging in disruptive behavior. Children in a regular classroom could have been observed to determine whether the target child's level of disruptive behavior was comparable to children not in need of functional communication training [posttreatment].
Following self-initiated conversation treatment with two AAC users, Datillo and Camarata (1991) interviewed trainers and caregivers to determine the validity of outcomes. Both found John to be a more active conversation participant and more assertive in managing his own needs. Carl was found to use his device more to signal caretakers, and to use less of aversive vocalizations. [posttreatment]	Loosely based on the work of Kozleski and Sands (1992), researchers could have examined the effects of AAC intervention on communication and quality of life. Results could have indicated that post-training quality of life in the AAC users was comparable to that of nondisabled peers, and a group of successful AAC users. [posttreatment]	Based on the work of Light et al. (1992) on facilitator training, videotapes outside the structured dyad activities could have been shown to independent raters who were experts in the field but blind to the purpose of the study. The facilitators could have been asked whether they noted changes in the AAC users' quality of life and/or membership as a result of intervention. [posttreatment]	Loosely based on the work of Kozleski and Sands (1992), researchers could have examined the effects of AAC intervention on communication and quality of life. Results could have indicated that post-training quality of life in AAC users was comparable to a representative group of nondisabled children in the same state. [posttreatment]
The teachers and peers of the participants in a national outcome study could be surveyed to determine their perceptions regarding positive, negative, and unplanned outcomes. [posttreatment]	Researchers could gather standards on various outcome behaviors from successful AAC users, matched on relevant parameters to the participants in the national outcome study. These standards could then be compared to those outcomes obtained for the AAC users. [posttreatment]	Laypersons, unfamiliar with the AAC user participants in a national outcomes study, could be shown videotapes before and after intervention and could be asked to rate whether they noted positive, negative, or unplanned outcomes. [posttreatment]	Researchers could gather standards on various outcome behaviors from nondisabled children nationwide, matched on relevant parameters to the participants in the national outcome study. These standards could then be compared to those outcomes obtained for the AAC users. [posttreatment]

A. The Who

1. The Who in Subjective Evaluation

The method of subjective evaluation relies on the soliciting of opinions of those who have a special position to the client in terms of their expertise or relationship. Typically, these individuals are named "consumers" (see preceding quotes). Schlosser (1999) adopted the term *stakeholder* from Blackstone (1995) when referring to the range of individuals who have an investment in the intervention, due to the strong history of association of the term "consumer" in the AAC field, primarily with individuals who use AAC (DeRuyter, 1995).

Researchers may consult a variety of stakeholder types to socially validate AAC interventions via subjective evaluation, including direct stakeholder, indirect stakeholders, immediate community stakeholders, and extended community stakeholders (see Table 10.1 for definitions and examples). Informed readers are well advised to ask themselves whether the stakeholder types consulted are indeed appropriate for the research at hand, and researchers in the process of designing an intervention study may also ask themselves who would be appropriate stakeholders to consult for their project. To that end, it is important that interventionists are provided with guidelines for selecting those individuals that have a relevant investment in evaluating a particular intervention or intervention component.

Schlosser (1999) provided the following guidelines to AAC interventionists for selecting stakeholders that should validate a particular intervention: First, while all individuals involved in the AAC field do "hold a stake" at some level and it is desirable to include persons beyond the immediate AAC user, not all of these individuals always hold the same "investment" in a given intervention. In fact, the four conceptually distinct types of stakeholders may evaluate the social validity of AAC interventions differently depending on the directness of their investment in the AAC intervention. In fields related to AAC there is no consensus as to what type of stakeholders should be involved. There is, however, some agreement that those stakeholders should be included who, directly or indirectly, control the feasibility of the intervention (Fawcett, 1991; Schwartz & Baer, 1991).

As the recipients of AAC interventions, direct stakeholders would be appropriate to include in any subjective evaluation efforts. When it comes to selecting the specific individuals as the direct stakeholders, we have to be careful not to assume that the direct stakeholder is always going to be the AAC user. True, AAC users are the primary recipients of many interventions for which they control its feasibility. For example, an AAC user may be taught to combine icon sequences as in semantic compaction to retrieve phrases from a communication device. In many other instances, however, partners (i.e., clinicians, parents, peers) are the recipients of AAC interventions such as partner training (e.g., Light, Dattilo, English, Gutierrez, & Hartz, 1992). In those situations, partners would be the most appropriate direct stakeholders to be consulted in subjective evaluation efforts.

The question arises as to the circumstances for selecting stakeholder types beyond the direct stakeholders. By definition, there seems to be a notable decrease in the extent to which stakeholders are affected by changes as a result of AAC interventions as we move from the direct stakeholders to indirect stakeholders to immediate and extended community stakeholders (Table 10.1). Which stakeholder type to select, however, depends largely on the nature of the particular AAC intervention. For example, interventions for beginning communicators may be hypothesized to affect not only the communication of the learners but also the behaviors of indirect stakeholders such as teachers or parents. Whether or not these interventions are feasible depends to a large degree on partner behaviors such as providing for opportunities for communication to occur (see Sigafoos, 1999). For AAC interventions that aim to improve community inclusion of learners through improved communication, immediate community stakeholders, such as the cashier at the learner's favorite fast-food restaurant, may be appropriate to socially validate the intervention (despite the fact that they are not strongly affected by the change). Finally, studies on interventions targeting improved communicative competence may want to solicit the opinions of laypersons (i.e., extended community stakeholders) as "ultimate judges" so to speak. In many cases, experts are also considered extended community stakeholder even though they are quite different from other extended community stakeholders (Light, personal communication, June 25, 2001). That is, experts may not necessarily interact with the targeted participants on a regular basis, but they may have some degree of familiarity with the population from which the participants are drawn or they may be knowledgeable about AAC and its application relative to the intervention. Experts may be consulted for some social validation purposes such as the validation of materials. In Schlosser and Lloyd (1993), for example, story grammar experts were consulted to validate that the stories used in the study adhered to the rules of story grammar elements.

2. The Who in Social Comparison

Whereas the methodology of subjective evaluation is concerned with the consultation of appropriate stakeholders, the method of social comparison struggles with the selection of an appropriate group of individuals who are considered typical. One of the most prominent examples of social comparison in the AAC field to date occurs within the Participation Assessment Framework (Beukelman & Mirenda, 1998). In completing the Activity Standards Inventory that is part of this framework, the practitioner is asked to compare the level of and barriers to participation of a target student (i.e., the learner using AAC) with that of a nondisabled peer within the same activity. This process facilitates the identification of barriers and intervention development toward removing these barriers with the aim of achieving participation patterns comparable to the nondisabled peer. In applying this process we have successfully increased the participation levels of a 10-year-old student in an inclusive class so that they are closer to the levels of his comparison peers (Schlosser, McGhie-Richmond, Blackstien-Adler, Mirenda, Antonius, & Janzen, 2000). Fuqua and Schwade (1986) have cautioned that social comparison evaluations need to select a comparison sample that is functioning in the same context as the target participants in order to be valid. In other words, "consideration must be given to selecting normative groups and standards so that the criterion is representative of the environment in which persons with handicaps are expected to function" (Storey & Horner, 1991, p. 359; Thurman & Fiorelli, 1979). The use of nondisabled peers within the Activity Standard Inventory is a prime positive example because the peers selected are not only from the same classroom environment but are also performing the same activity as the target student. Although striving toward participation comparable to nondisabled peers in inclusive environments is essential to focus our efforts, there may be situations where this may not be warranted. Storey and Horner (1991) argued that individuals with disabilities have been shown to perform within performance levels of nondisabled individuals—an argument in support of using nondisabled persons as comparison groups. They further argued, however, that this might depend entirely on whether the skill areas assessed for academic performance have yielded differences between the groups.

Schlosser (1999) offered some guiding considerations for selecting a comparison standard. It is important to avoid overlap between the comparison sample and the clinical population studied. Although this could be accomplished by using nondisabled individuals as in the preceding example, it sometimes may be paramount to take into account the rules that should be adapted to circumvent the constraints of AAC strategies and techniques and the context of the intervention. As such, the comparison data may be more realistically collected from a more restricted sample of peers matched on certain characteristics of the participants in the study (e.g., chronological age, cognitive level, educational level, gender, language background, physical and sensory disabilities, race, school placement, or socio-economic status). For example, one could select a distinct comparison group of age- and gender-matched peers with cerebral palsy who are successful AAC users but are not receiving the target AAC intervention. The comparison group's performance in a given task could then be compared to pre- and postintervention performance of AAC users who do the same task with communication boards. This approach is an experimental attempt to ensure that there is no overlap with the clinical population and "to identify individuals who are functioning well or optimally and who despite certain disabilities are not judged to be in need of treatment" (Goldstein, 1990, p. 92).

B. THE WHAT: VALIDATING RELEVANT INTERVENTION ASPECTS

Social validation is often thought of as the validation of outcomes only. This perception is not surprising given that outcomes validation is overwhelmingly the most prominent focus of social validation efforts (Kennedy, 1992). This focus is also intuitively comprehensible given the impact associated with successful outcomes. Outcomes, however, are not created in a vacuum but rather stem from the setting of appropriate goals (goals are nothing but desired outcomes) and the use of appropriate materials and procedures. Thus, although outcomes are arguably the most important aspect of our efforts, social validation should also be directed at the goals targeted and the methods to be applied (Kazdin, 1982; Wolf, 1978). Goal validation may involve the topography of the goal or the anticipated level (i.e., desired outcome). Methods validation may pertain to the materials and the procedures to be applied. Related to the acceptability of treatment procedures, Kazdin (1982) suggested that "treatments that are viewed as more acceptable may be more readily sought, initiated, and adhered to than those viewed as less acceptable. Hence, acceptability may have direct implications for dissemination and utilization of treatments" (p. 494).

It is essential for the evidence-based practitioner and the planner of future research alike to determine what intervention aspects should have been or should be socially validated. In my opinion, it is not essential that all efficacy research in AAC be socially validated. In fact, social validation becomes increasingly more essential as one moves along the continuum from clinical outcomes research under ideal circumstances to clinical outcomes research under typical conditions (see Chapter 2 for a discussion of ideal versus typical conditions).

C. THE HOW: USING APPROPRIATE MEASUREMENT TECHNIQUES

Social validity may be assessed via subjective evaluation or social comparison. As mentioned earlier, the method of subjective evaluation relies on soliciting the opinions of those who have a special position to the client in terms of their expertise or relationship. Social validation measures are exposed to the same threats of internal and external validity as other measurements. Fuqua and Schwade (1986) stated that if social validation data are important, "they should be collected with the same methodological rigor and subject to the same level of scrutiny as other behavioral research data" (p. 289). In their critical review, they raised several methodological issues concerning the use of appropriate measurement techniques in social validation. These issues are summarized, enhanced with contributions to the methodological debate from others (e.g., Finney, 1991; Kennedy, 1992; Storey & Horner, 1991), and exemplified with references to the AAC literature.

1. Validity and Reliability

Questionnaires are frequently employed to assess the social validity of goals, methods, and outcomes, yet researchers have most often solely relied on their face validity rather than their construct validity or predictive validity (Fuqua & Schwade, 1986; Storey & Horner, 1991). In terms of predictive validity, for example, a researcher may solicit the opinions of regular education teachers to determine the kinds of behaviors of AAC users and nondisabled peers that would enhance the probability for successful inclusion. Let us assume that the researcher's aim is to select treatment goals for AAC user training and peer training based on the responses to the questionnaires. In the absence of data to attest to the predictive validity of the questionnaire data, we must assume that the regular education teachers can accurately select specific behaviors from a complex situation that are functionally related to the probability of successfully including AAC users. This seems a tenuous assumption in the absence of supporting data. Fuqua and Schwade (1986) rightfully make the point that social comparison methods are not immune to the notion of predictive validity either. Current social validation efforts often lack interobserver agreement data (Storey & Horner, 1991). This is in stark contrast to the care with which dependent measures are typically defined and evaluated in many AAC intervention studies. Social validity data are no different from other behavioral data and as such require interobserver agreement data.

2. Experience of the Respondents

In selecting respondents, interventionists should consider those individuals and stakeholder groups that bear a relevant investment in evaluating a particular intervention or intervention component (Schlosser, 1999). When assessing the acceptability of *methods*, for example, it is vital that the respondents selected have experienced the treatment themselves. In other words, although it may be appropriate to consult indirect and other stakeholders, it is absolutely important to select direct stakeholders for this purpose. In their critical review, Fuqua and Schwade (1986) noted that many of the stakeholder respondents to questionnaires designed to assess the acceptability of procedures have never experienced the treatments themselves. Test's (1994) review also supports this lack of data from direct stakeholders, in particular from individuals with severe disabilities. Whether this is the case in the AAC literature as well has not been determined.

3. Anonymous Collection of Responses

Whereas it is a given in survey research methodology that questionnaires should be collected anonymously, this is typically not specified in applied behavior analysis studies reporting on the collection of social validation data via questionnaires (Fuqua & Schwade, 1986). This severely limits the possibility of ruling out bias and reactivity effects for the data obtained. How common this practice is in the AAC literature has not been addressed.

4. Time between Treatment and Administering Social Validation

The timing of social validation assessments may yield differing information and hold different implications as a result of the specific timing used. Fuqua and Schwade (1986) noted that the points in time at which the *procedures* are validated, for example, may prove important in clarifying the alleged relationship between procedural acceptability and treatment initiation, adherence to the treatment regimen, and effectiveness. Their suggestions of time between treatment and social validation assessment go beyond the review of much published social validation research, which indicated that investigators do not seem to utilize the breadth of options for assessing social validity (Kennedy, 1992). Among the 12 possible times of social validation assessment, there appears to be a clear dominance of preintervention assessment for goal validation and of postintervention assessment of outcomes. Table 10.2 lists the time of assessment for each example in parentheses (e.g., posttreatment). Further, Table 10.3 provides an overview of the 12 social validation assessments depending on the time of assessment relative to treatment along with relevant AAC examples.

Procedural validation may be assessed prior to baseline, after completion of baseline but prior to treatment, after the initiation of treatment, immediately upon completion of treatment, and well after completion of treatment. A procedural validation implemented at these various points in time would permit a close analysis into the relationship of acceptability of procedures and treatment initiation and adherence. For instance, using subjective evaluation, a stakeholder may have rated a proposed treatment as acceptable prior to baseline and after completion of baseline. At that time the direct stakeholder may have seemed eager to initiate the treatment and therefore adhered closely to the protocol. Further into the treatment, the assessment may indicate that the direct stakeholder found the treatment no longer acceptable. At that time, the adherence to the treatment regimen may be found greatly reduced.

Generally, social validation measures should be viewed similarly to other measures commonly used in AAC intervention research such as generalization probes (see Chapter 6). That is, social validation measures are exposed to similar threats of internal and external validity. For instance, a *posttreatment* subjective

Table 10.3

Time (and Type) of Social Validation Assessment, Descriptions, and AAC Application

Social validation assessment		Description	Published or fictitious AAC applications
Pretreatment subjective evaluation	Goals	What behavior(s) should be changed	Dowden *et al.* (1986) used subjective evaluation with nursing staff and family members of AAC users to select the *focus* of clinical intervention.
	Methods	What procedures or materials should be used	Schlosser and Lloyd (1993) asked Blissymbol experts to evaluate the teaching procedures proposed, including the age appropriateness of the symbol explanations.
	Outcomes	What a desirable target level for behavior change should be	Staff in an immediate care facility are surveyed regarding desirable levels of reductions in self-injurious behavior and increases in request behavior to be expected following functional communication training.
Pretreatment social comparison	Goals	Determine prevalent type(s) and form(s) of behavior(s) to determine target behavior(s)	Interventionists assessed the strategies used by nondisabled peers in a third-grade classroom to determine the competitive academic participation strategies to be taught to an AAC user who is to be fully included.
Pretreatment social comparison	Methods	Evaluate treatment typologies and strategies to select procedures and materials	Interventionists surveyed parents as to what strategies they typically use to interact successfully with their child in order to determine the procedures to be used in an intervention study.
	Outcomes	Determine typical levels of target behavior(s) to specify whether the participants reached these levels or when intervention is to be terminated	Angelo and Goldstein (1990) administered 15 communication tasks (based on milieu teaching and time delay) identical to those used in later experiments with AAC users to nondisabled preschoolers (roughly matched for mental age) to determine (1) whether nondisabled children would request information using wh-interrogative forms in naturally structured activities and (2) their levels. The levels of wh-information requests by AAC users during follow-up was then found comparable to that of nondisabled individuals.
Posttreatment subjective evaluation	Goals	Answer: "Should this (these) behavior(s) have been chosen as a goal(s) for intervention?"	Caretakers of AAC users were asked whether the teaching of a generalized request ("want") was a valuable focus to be addressed through intervention.

(continues)

Table 10.3 (*continued*)

Social validation assessment		Description	Published or fictitious AAC applications
	Methods	The subjective value of the procedures and materials used during intervention	Blissymbol experts are surveyed regarding their satisfaction with the paired-associate paradigm used to teach Blissymbols in an examination of Blissymbol learning.
	Outcomes	Perceived changes in behavior as a result of intervention	Light *et al.* (1992) used two subjective evaluation strategies in a study examining facilitator training: (1) pre- and post-treatment videotapes of three dyads were shown to four independent raters and the raters were blind to the status of the videotapes; (2) structured interviews were conducted with the two AAC users and the three participating facilitators. Results of both assessments confirmed the efficacy of facilitator instruction.
Posttreatment social comparison	Goals	Typicality of the type and form of behavior(s) that had (have) been selected for intervention	After teaching an AAC user the use of slang in social situations, the interventionist observes nondisabled same-age peers to determine whether the goals of instruction were actually typical of the age group.
	Procedures	Typicality of the procedures applied compared to those applied by others	Interventionists surveyed parents as to what strategies they typically use to successfully interact with their child in order to determine whether the procedures used during interventions are actually typical.
	Outcomes	Typicality of the levels of target behavior(s) obtained	This approach is similar to its pretreatment counterpart (see Angelo & Goldstein, 1990). After teaching AAC users to request information using wh-interrogatives, nondisabled preschoolers (roughly matched for mental age) were subjected to the same task to determine whether their levels of wh-interrogatives are comparable to those of the AAC users after treatment.

evaluation of *procedures* cannot unequivocally demonstrate the acceptance of the procedures even though the direct stakeholder provided a positive evaluation. Confounding variables other than the treatment may have accounted for the stakeholders' rating (e.g., bias and reactivity effects on the measure). In the absence of a pretest of a stakeholder's acceptability of an impending treatment, it may be impossible to determine if a positive evaluation after completion of treatment represents a preformed opinion that was altered by exposure to the treatment or a favorable change in opinion engendered by the treatment (Fuqua & Schwade, 1986). Only a comparison of pretreatment measures (prior to baseline or after completion of baseline but prior to treatment) with posttreatment measures may allow changes in stakeholder acceptance to be attributed to the relevant treatment procedures. Ideally speaking, to isolate the impact of a prospective target behavior on social judgments, social validation should definitely occur prior to the clinical intervention (Fuqua & Schwade, 1986).

Posttreatment subjective evaluations of outcomes may also be confounded by the bias of the stakeholders. Kazdin and Matson (1981), for example, presented a scenario whereby global ratings changed even when more objective measures indicated that no change has occurred. The stakeholders surveyed are obviously aware that intervention has been completed and they assume that performance will improve with training. This threat to internal validity can be circumvented by having the stakeholders observe videotapes of performance before and after treatment without disclosing the status of the segments (e.g., Light *et al.*, 1992). Thus, this elegant solution actually keeps the stakeholders blind to whether this is a pre- or a posttreatment evaluation.

To minimize threats to internal validity, social validation assessments should be mapped onto the experimental designs used to demonstrate treatment efficacy (Storey & Horner, 1991). For it is only under these conditions that we can unequivocally attribute social validity data to AAC interventions rather than extraneous variables. For example, a multiple-baseline design across subjects may include social validation assessments pre- and posttreatment for each of the participants. Further, an ABAB design may incorporate social validation assessments in each of the phases or, at the very least, in the first A phase and the last B phase (Storey & Horner, 1991). Another issue pertains to the specificity of the requested rating, discussed next.

5. Specificity of the Requested Rating and Vagueness of Items

Fuqua and Schwade (1986) noted that most stakeholder satisfaction surveys request a global rating concerning the treatment program without asking specific aspects of what may be a complex multicomponent therapy program. Along these lines, many statements on satisfaction scales are sufficiently vague (e.g., "were you satisfied" "was . . . acceptable?") as to render interpretation of these statements and corresponding answers questionable. What does "satisfied" mean to different respondents? Fuqua and Schwade (1986) called for the use of more precise terms, such as "*difficulty* of implementation" [italics added] in developing questionnaires. Another problem with the questions arises from the fact that the experimenters develop many questions for their own study. This may cause the questions to be leading without intending them to be leading. Thus, it may be helpful to have someone else qualified develop the social validation questions. In summary, rating scales and question phrases may differ widely between studies, making comparisons of the results across studies difficult.

6. Social Validation as a Dynamic Process

With particular relevance to the social validation of goals and methods, Finney (1991) proposed that social validations should be a dynamic rather than a static process whereby feedback from respondents is used to further refine goals or methods. Schlosser and Lloyd (1993, 1997) employed such a dynamic approach to social validation. In one study, examining the efficacy of two strategies for teaching Blissymbols, Schlosser and Lloyd (1997) repeatedly solicited the opinions of story grammar experts concerning the story narratives used during teaching. Specifically, the experts were surveyed in terms of the adherence of the narratives to established story grammar components, including setting, beginning, development, and ending. Once the experts provided input, the investigators revised the narratives and presented those to the experts again. The symbol instructions used to explain the derivation of Blissymbols were also validated repeatedly by a group of certified Blissymbol instructors (Schlosser & Lloyd, 1993, 1997). Social validation as a dynamic process also bears on the validation of outcomes (Test, 1994). Negative feedback by stakeholders concerning the outcomes of an AAC intervention should be utilized to modify the intervention accordingly. The outcomes of the revised application can then be validated again and it is hoped that the stakeholders are satisfied with the outcomes attained this time around. At a service delivery level, procedures must be put into place to use social validation outcomes data to improve service delivery to direct stakeholders. Especially in client-centered or family-centered service delivery systems, there must be a visible link between collecting social validation data and improving service delivery.

V. CONCLUSIONS

Social validation can help the AAC field to not only demonstrate efficacy but also acceptability in the eyes of those who care the most: direct stakeholders and other relevant stakeholders. Social validation is important for researchers and evidence-based practitioners to consider in planning, implementing, or evaluating the efficacy of AAC interventions. As limited as existing reviews of the social validation literature in AAC are at this time, it is already fairly certain that we need to conduct more efficacy studies that also include social validation assessments of goals, methods, or outcomes. Clearly, a comprehensive review of the social validation literature, using the AAC Social Validation Matrix as a framework, is essential to guide our future social validation efforts. Also, the matrix presented in this chapter is intended to assist researchers and evidence-based practitioners alike in planning and implementing social validation assessments. In implementing EBP, the availability of favorable social validation data serves as a distinguishing criterion that helps separate an effective treatment with social validity from another effective treatment without social validity (see Chapter 12). Social validation bears relevance on the continuum of efficacy research from research under optimal conditions to research under typical conditions (see Chapter 2), perhaps increasingly so as we move toward outcome measurement under typical conditions. Conceptually, care must be taken to sample subjective evaluations from relevant stakeholders for a given AAC intervention or to select adequate comparison samples for our social comparison efforts. This chapter presented several considerations along these lines. In addition, the field must be cognizant of the intervention components in need of social validation data. Despite the understandable focus on outcomes validation, outcomes do not occur in a vacuum but are targeted through goals and met with certain treatment methods including procedures and materials. In terms of methodology, the field has to ensure that social validation data are collected with the same detail toward minimizing the threats to internal validity as we do with primary data. The Social Validation Checklist in Appendix 10A should be helpful toward these ends. Social validation is as relevant to researchers and evidence-based practitioners (who integrate research with their practice) as it is to practitioners in general. Appendix 10B provides an avenue for evidence-based practitioners and researchers to evaluate the certainty of social validation evidence. What could be more important than ensuring that treatment goals, procedures, and outcomes of everyday interventions are considered significant by direct stakeholders and other relevant stakeholders? It has been said that applied behavior analysis is finding its heart through social validation (Wolf, 1978). To use an analogy, social validation refers to how the efforts directed toward studying the efficacy of AAC interventions are finding their soul.

REFERENCES

Angelo, D. H., & Goldstein, H. (1990). Effects of a pragmatic teaching strategy for requesting information by communication board users. *Journal of Speech and Hearing Disorders, 55*, 231–243.

Beukelman, D. R., & Mirenda, P. (1998). *Augmentative and alternative communication: Management of severe communication disorders in children and adults* (2nd ed.). Baltimore: Paul H. Brookes.

Blackstone, S. (1995). AAC Stakeholders: It's all relative. *Augmentative Communication News, 8*, 4.

Carpenter, C. D., Bloom, L. A., & Boat, M. B. (1999). Guidelines for special educators: Achieving socially valid outcomes. *Intervention in School and Clinic, 34*, 143–149.

DeRuyter, F. (1995). Evaluating outcomes in assistive technology: Do we understand the commitment? *Assistive Technology, 7*, 3–16.

Dowden, P., Beukelman, D. R., & Lossing, C. (1986). Serving nonspeaking patients in accute care settings: Intervention Outcomes. *Augmentative and Alternative Communication, 2*, 38–44.

Fawcett, S. B. (1991). Social validity: A note on methodology. *Journal of Applied Behavior Analysis, 24,* 235–239.

Finney, J. W. (1991). On further development of the concept of social validity. *Journal of Applied Behavior Analysis, 24,* 245–249.

Fuqua, R. W., & Schwade, J. (1986). Social validation of applied behavioral research: A selective review and critique. In A. D. Poling & R. W. Fuqua (Eds.), *Research methods in applied behavior analysis* (pp. 265–292). New York: Plenum Press.

Goldstein, H. (1990). Assessing clinical significance. In L. B. Olswang, C. K. Thompson, S. F. Warren, & N. J. Minghetti (Eds.), *Treatment efficacy research in communication disorders. Proceedings of the American Speech-Language-Hearing Foundation's National Conference on Treatment Efficacy* (pp. 91–98), San Antonio, TX: American Speech-Language and Hearing Association.

Gresham, F. M., & Lopez, M. F. (1996). Social validation: A unifying concept for school-based consultation research and practice. *School Psychology Quarterly, 11,* 204–227.

Hamilton, B. L., & Snell, M. E. (1993). Using the milieu approach to increase spontaneous communication book use across environments by an adolescent with autism. *Augmentative and Alternative Communication, 9,* 259–272.

Heller, W. K., Allgood, M. H., Davis, B., Arnold, S. E., Castelle, M. D., & Taber, T. A. (1996). Promoting non-task related communication at vocational sites. *Augmentative and Alternative Communication, 12,* 169–180.

Horner, R. H., & Day, H. M. (1991). The effects of response efficiency on functionally equivalent competing behaviors. *Journal of Applied Behavior Analysis, 24,* 719–732.

Kazdin, A. E. (1977). Assessing the clinical or applied significance of behavior change through social validation. *Behavior Modification, 1,* 427–452.

Kazdin, A. E. (1980). Acceptability of alternative treatments for deviant child behavior. *Journal of Applied Behavior Analysis, 13,* 259–273.

Kazdin, A. E. (1982). *Single-case research designs: Methods for clinical and applied settings.* New York: Oxford University Press.

Kazdin, A. E., & Matson, J. L. (1981). Social validation in mental retardation. *Applied Research in Mental Retardation, 2,* 39–53.

Kennedy, C. H. (1992). Trends in the measurement of social validity. *The Behavior Analyst, 15,* 147–156.

Light, J. L., & Binger, C. (1998). *Building communicative competence with individuals who use augmentative and alternative communication.* Baltimore: Paul H. Brookes.

Light, J. L., Binger, C., Agate, T. L., & Ramsey, K. N. (1999). Teaching partner-focused questions to individuals using augmentative and alternative communication to enhance their communicative competence. *Journal of Speech and Hearing Research, 42,* 251–255.

Light, J., Dattilo, J., English, J., Gutierrez, L., & Hartz, J. (1992). Instructing facilitators to support the communication of people who use augmentative communication systems. *Journal of Speech and Hearing Research, 35,* 865–875.

Lloyd, J. W., & Heubusch, J. D. (1996). Issues in social validation in research serving children with emotional or behavioral disorders. *Behavior Disorders, 22,* 8–14.

McNaughton, D., & Tawney, J. (1993). Comparison of two spelling instruction techniques for adults who use augmentative and alternative communication. *Augmentative and Alternative Communication, 9,* 72–82.

O'Keefe, B., & Dattilo, J. (1992). Teaching the response-recode form to adults with mental retardation using AAC systems. *Augmentative and Alternative Communication, 8,* 224–233.

Schlosser, R. W. (1995). Effectiveness of three teaching strategies on Blissymbol learning, retention, generalization, and use. (Doctoral dissertation, Purdue University, 1994). *Dissertation Abstracts International, 56(038),* 892.

Schlosser, R. W. (1999). Social validation of interventions in augmentative and alternative communication. *Augmentative and Alternative Communication, 15,* 234–247.

Schlosser, R. W., Blischak, D. M., Belfiore, P. J., Bartley, C., & Barnett, N. (1998). The effects of synthetic speech output and orthographic feedback on spelling in a student with autism: A preliminary study. *Journal of Autism and Developmental Disorders, 28*, 319–329.

Schlosser, R. W., & Braun, U. (1994). Efficacy of AAC interventions: Methodologic issues in evaluating behavior change, generalization, and effects. *Augmentative and Alternative Communication, 10*, 207–223.

Schlosser, R. W., & Lee, D. (2000). Promoting generalization and maintenance in augmentative and alternative communication: A meta-analysis of 20 years of effectiveness research. *Augmentative and Alternative Communication, 16*, 208–227.

Schlosser, R. W., & Lloyd, L. L. (1993). Effects of initial element teaching in a story-telling context on Blissymbol acquisition and generalization. *Journal of Speech and Hearing Research, 36*, 979–995.

Schlosser, R. W., & Lloyd, L. L. (1997). Effects of paired-associate learning versus symbol explanations on Blissymbol learning and use. *Augmentative and Alternative Communication, 12*, 226–238.

Schlosser, R. W., McGhie-Richmond, D., Blackstien-Adler, S., Mirenda, P., Antonius, K., & Jantzen, P. (2000). Training a school team to integrate technology meaningfully into the curriculum: Effects on student participation. *Journal of Special Education Technology, 15*, 31–44.

Schlosser, R. W., Quist, R. W., & Lloyd, L. L. (1990, August). *The effects of element vs. whole teaching approaches in Blissymbol learning and generalization: Social validation.* Paper presented at the European Bliss Affiliate Meeting, Östhammar, Sweden.

Schwartz, I. S., & Baer, D. M. (1991). Social validity assessments: Is current practice state of the art? *Journal of Applied Behavior Analysis, 24*, 189–204.

Sigafoos, J. (1999). Creating opportunities for augmentative and alternative communication: Strategies for involving people with developmental disabilities. *Augmentative and Alternative Communication, 15*, 183–190.

Sobsey, D., & McDonald, L. (1988). Special education. Coming of age. In B. L. Ludlow, A. P. Turnbull, & R. Luckasson (Eds.), *Transition to adult life for people with mental retardation—Principles and practices* (pp. 21–44). Baltimore: Paul H. Brookes.

Storey, K., & Horner, R. H. (1991). An evaluative review of social validation research involving persons with handicaps. *The Journal of Special Education, 25*, 352–401.

Test, D. W. (1994). Supported employment and social validity. *Journal of the Association for Persons with Severe Handicaps, 19*, 116–129.

Thurman, S. K., & Fiorelli, J. S. (1979). Perspectives on normalization. *The Journal of Special Education, 13*, 339–346.

Van Houten, R. (1979). Social validation: The evolution of standards of competency for target behaviors. *Journal of Applied Behavior Analysis, 12*, 581–591.

White, D. (1986). Social validation. In F. R. Rusch (Ed.), *Competitive employment issues and strategies* (pp. 199–213). Baltimore: Paul H. Brookes.

Winett, R. A., Moore, J. F., & Anderson, E. S. (1991). Extending the concept of social validity: Behavior analysis for disease prevention and health promotion. *Journal of Applied Behavior Analysis, 24*, 215–230.

Wolf, M. M. (1978). Social validity: The case for subjective measurement, or how applied behavior analysis is finding its heart. *Journal of Applied Behavior Analysis, 11*, 203–214.

Evaluation Checklist for Planning and Evaluating Social Validation Assessments

Instructions: This checklist aims to guide the planning and evaluation of social validation. The items identify those issues that are important to the assessment of social validation and its consequences to validity. Individual ratings serve as the basis for the overall rating.

Evaluation/Planning Items	P[a]	F[b]	G[c]	E[d]
1. Assesses relevant categories (e.g., goals) and components (e.g., level).				
2. Consults multiple stakeholder types (e.g., direct) as appropriate.				
3. Selects stakeholders that (are thought to) control intervention viability.				
4. Matches comparison sample to target along pertinent characteristics.				
5. Engages comparison sample in the same activity/setting as the target.				
6. Utilizes multiple subject evaluation methods (e.g., focus groups).				
7. Develops questionnaire based on principles of survey construction.				
8. Develops questionnaire by someone independent of the project.				
9. Supports questionnaire data with predictive validity.				
10. Minimizes threats to internal validity via appropriate designs.				
11. Minimizes threats to internal validity via interobserver agreement.				
12. Utilizes a dynamic approach to assessment when appropriate.				
Overall Rating	P	F	G	E

Notes:
[a]Poor.
[b]Fair.
[c]Good.
[d]Excellent.

Appraising the Certainty of Social Validation Evidence

In determining the certainty of the social validation evidence, take into account the social validation design, the instruments used, and interobserver agreement data. Whether or not adequate stakeholder types or comparison samples are used is an external validity issue and thus not relevant here.

Certainty	Characteristics
Inconclusive	Establishes that certain social validation results are *not* plausible. The study's flaws preclude any conclusions that the results are due to the intervention: • Exhibits fatal flaws in social validation design such as use of a pretest measure only (posttest measure only) (irrespective of interobserver agreement and instruments).
Suggestive	Certain social validation results are plausible and are within the realm of possibility: • *Minor flaws* in design such as a pre- *and* posttest design, which is not mapped onto an appropriate intervention design, with inadequate instruments or inadequate interobserver agreement.
Preponderant	Certain social validation results are not only possible, but also they are more likely to have occurred than they have not: • *Minor flaws* in design such as a pre- *and* posttest design (i.e., not mapped onto an appropriate intervention design), adequate instruments, and interobserver agreement, or • *Strong* social validation design with *questionable* interobserver agreement or *questionable* instruments.
Conclusive	Certain social validation results are unequivocally the result of the intervention: • *Strong* design (i.e., mapped onto an appropriate intervention design); • *Adequate* (or better) instruments (e.g., survey constructed using principles of questionnaire construction). • Adequate (or better) interobserver agreement.

CHAPTER 11

Synthesizing Efficacy Research in AAC[1]

Ralf W. Schlosser
Department of Speech-Language Pathology and Audiology
Northeastern University

Two decades ago, the actual mechanics of integrating research usually involved covert, intuitive processes taking place inside the head of the synthesist. Meta-analysis made these processes public.

Cooper & Hedges, 1994, p. 11

[1]The writing of this chapter was made possible through support from a Distinguished Switzer Fellowship (H133F010010) from the National Institute on Disability and Rehabilitation Research.

I. INTRODUCTION

The previous chapters in this section have dealt with various methodologies for evaluating the efficacy of interventions in augmentative and alternative communication (AAC). These methodologies have in common that they lend themselves to evaluate the efficacy of one intervention or a comparison of more than one intervention in a single study. Although a single study may allow us to draw tentative conclusions regarding the effectiveness of an AAC intervention, more definite statements must be based on a synthesis of a body of individual studies (Cooper & Hedges, 1994). Not too long ago, it was difficult to respond to the question "What makes a review a good review?" This changed with the publication of Jackson's (1980) seminal paper. Accordingly, syntheses need to meet the following criteria in order to be systematic: (1) the topic has to be carefully defined and delimited so that the inclusion and exclusion of studies can be replicated; (2) previous reviews need to be described and distinguished from the current synthesis; (3) the procedures for obtaining studies must be detailed, including the search strategies used and the time frame to which the search was delimited; (4) the degree to which the studies share the same dependent and independent variables must be reported; (5) the criteria used to arrive at judgments of effectiveness should be stated so that the reader can replicate the analyses and draw the same conclusions; (6) the covariation of study outcomes with study characteristics must be examined; and (7) the conclusions of the synthesis need to be supported by the data from the studies reviewed.

There are essentially three approaches to synthesize efficacy research in general and AAC in particular. These include narrative literature reviews, quantitative literature reviews, and meta-analyses. The purpose of this chapter is twofold: (1) to evaluate these three approaches (narrative, quantitative, and meta-analysis) by holding them to Jackson's (1980) standard of a systematic review and (2) to illustrate the process of planning and implementing a meta-analysis.

II. THREE APPROACHES TO THE SYNTHESIS OF EFFICACY RESEARCH

A. NARRATIVE REVIEWS

> However, despite growing interest in this area, a review of the empirical literature pertaining to symbol research revealed only one focused study that incorporated participants from a non-European American linguistic community. (Huer, 2000, p. 180)

This example illustrates the use of a narrative review to establish the need for an empirical study that followed this statement. But how did Huer search the literature to arrive at this judgment? Unfortunately, the sources used to identify studies were not described. Second, the search terms used were not documented. Third, the principles for including and excluding studies are left unspecified. It is, therefore, not surprising that at least one study involving symbol research with African-American preschoolers appears to have been missed (Burroughs, Albritton, Eaton, & Montague, 1990). There may be more, but this study was known to this author without engaging in a thorough review. Alternatively, it is possible that this study did not meet the criteria for inclusion, which, unfortunately, are not made known to the reader. Narrative reviews appear to be the most prevalent approach to synthesizing the efficacy literature in AAC to date. Without having engaged in systematic review of the extant database, several narrative reviews have been published in the AAC field (e.g., Bryen & Joyce, 1985; Doherty, 1985; Kiernan, 1977; Lancioni, O'Reilly, & Basili, 2001; Lloyd & Fuller, 1990; Schlosser & Sigafoos, 2002).

1. Doherty (1985)

In her review of the effects of sign characteristics on sign acquisition, Doherty (1985) reviewed the literature in each of the following categories of sign characteristics: (1) phonological parameters, (2) motoric dimensions, and (3) conceptual features. The topic appears fairly well defined in that only literature pertaining to each of these three categories of sign characteristics is reviewed. Even though some previous reviews are described (e.g., Dennis, Reichle, Williams, & Vogelsberg, 1982), they are not clearly distinguished from this effort. The procedures for obtaining studies, the search strategies employed, and the time frame of the search are not reported. The degree to which independent variables are shared is evident from the three categories that are used to structure the review. That is, it can be assumed that the studies reviewed under "phonological parameters," for example, share phonological parameters as independent variables. The review is explicit in that its focus is on "sign acquisition and retention" as a dependent variable. Therefore, it can be assumed that all studies included shared this dependent variable. The criteria used to arrive at judgments of effectiveness, however, are not specified. The conclusions drawn by the authors of the original studies concerning effectiveness are, it would seem, adopted at face value. This review does, however, distinguish whether statements are based on empirical research, inferred from basic research, or reasonable conjecture. The covariation of study outcomes (e.g., effectiveness of phonological parameters) with study characteristics (e.g., type of participants) is not examined. The conclusion of the synthesis based on empirical research is as follows: "These recommendations can be implemented simultaneously by including highly translucent, one-handed contact signs among the first five signs taught, and by including symmetric, two-handed contact signs among signs to be taught thereafter" (p. 119). This integrated conclusion is supported by individual studies as follows—thus, Doherty (1985) does substantiate synthesis conclusions with individual study outcomes (even though references are not provided in this section, each of the statements is based on a reviewed study cited earlier):

> Strategies of the first group derive directly from empirical research on the dimension of production mode, handedness, symmetry, and iconicity. From this research, it can be recommended that: contact signs be selected over noncontact signs; symmetric signs over asymmetric signs; translucent signs over nontranslucent signs for signs produced with one hand; and one-handed signs over two-handed signs for signs high in translucency. (p. 119)

2. Summary

Similar shortcomings can be found in other narrative reviews (Bryen & Joyce, 1985; Schlosser & Sigafoos, 2002), but limited space does not warrant a detailed analysis of each review. Nonetheless, the reading of narrative literature reviews on the efficacy of AAC reflects the critique raised by several authors: narrative reviews are typically at risk for (1) subjectively determining the inclusion and exclusion of studies and (2) subjectively evaluating and interpreting individual study outcomes along with their covariation with study characteristics (Hunter, Schmidt, & Jackson, 1982; Schlosser & Goetze, 1992; Scruggs, 1992; Wolf, 1986). These weaknesses have been systematically documented, for example, in narrative reviews on the treatment of self-injurious behavior (Schlosser & Goetze, 1992). Several reviews on the effectiveness of interventions to reduce self-injurious behaviors were analyzed in terms of the specific studies included during the years overlapping the reviews. This indicated that several studies were included in some but not in other reviews, supporting subjective criteria for inclusion of studies typically found in narrative reviews.

B. QUANTITATIVE REVIEWS

Quantitative reviews are typically more systematic in terms of delimiting the topic, making the search criteria explicit, applying the parameters of the review, and evaluating the outcomes along with the covariation of study outcomes. Essentially, quantitative reviews employ vote count procedures to arrive at quantified judgments of effectiveness or they employ meta-analytic techniques (see Section II.C for quantitative reviews using meta-analytic techniques). Quantitative reviews are scant in AAC, but a few are available (Mirenda, 1997; Udwin, 1987). These review studies will be examined in terms of adherence to Jackson's (1980) criteria.

1. Udwin (1987)

Udwin engaged in a systematic review of 133 AAC training studies in terms of nine criteria of adequate research design. Although this review has many positive aspects, several shortcomings were uncovered based on the application of Jackson's (1980) criteria for a systematic review.

The topic was defined as "reports of sign and symbol training in adult language impaired populations appearing in the literature" (p. 20). The author excluded studies involving persons who were deaf unless they also had intellectual or physical disabilities as well as studies that were surveys. It is unclear whether preexperimental studies satisfied the criteria for inclusion or whether only experiments were included. Although one review is somewhat described (Kiernan, 1977), it is not distinguished from Udwin's own synthesis. Although Udwin's stated attempt was "to be as comprehensive as possible to include all published reports . . . up to December 1984" (p. 20), the reader is left in the dark regarding the actual procedures for obtaining studies. Unpublished papers were considered as well as long as they could be traced. In its current form, it would be difficult to replicate the search. The degree to which the studies shared the same dependent variables is unclear and perhaps understandably so, since the focus of the review was on methodological adequacy. Udwin was interested in whether the outcome data were specified (1) as formal assessments, (2) as anecdotal, or (3) as partially formal. The degree to which independent variables were shared is unclear as well. Again, the primary concern was to provide an adequate description of treatment, which meant that "the details [had to] allow for full replication of the study and time involved" (p. 21) (see also Chapter 9 for a more concise definition of treatment integrity). In this review, judgments were not made on effectiveness but rather on the methodological adequacy of the studies. The criteria used to do so is best described as the vote-count method. That is, six methodological criteria were assigned a vote of +, −, or +/− with definitions specified for each of the criteria (see, for example, the preceding discussion on vote count as an outcome measure). Several of these definitions, such as the one for scoring treatment integrity, are inadequate to allow for adequate replications. The covariation of study outcomes with study characteristics is not applicable here because no attempt was made to synthesize the efficacy of the study. Although descriptive summary data supported the conclusions of the synthesis, individual studies were not referenced to support these conclusions.

2. Mirenda (1997)

In her quantitative literature review, Mirenda (1997) aimed to summarize the extant research on functional communication training (FCT) involving AAC "in an accessible format and to identify areas for future research" (p. 207). The

topic is well delimited with a clear focus on studies using FCT with AAC techniques, defined as "both the assessment of the function of the problem behavior
and the teaching of a more appropriate form that serves the same function"
(Durand, 1990, p. 23). It is also made clear that studies involving FCT with individuals who primarily rely on natural speech were not included. It is unspecified whether studies that involve FCT in combination with another approach
such as punishment or extinction were eligible for inclusion as well. Typically,
the dependent variables that qualify for inclusion need to be operationalized. In
this case, the specified use of FCT and AAC automatically renders the dependent variable as challenging behavior, regardless of its specific topography. The
type of the studies to be included is not specified. Previous reviews were not
described and distinguished from the current effort. The procedures for obtaining studies are described in detail: a database search was implemented using the
key words "functional communication training" and "functional equivalence."
Here, it would have been beneficial to specify the names of the databases that
were consulted. Although a handsearch was conducted of all issues from 1985 to
1996 of the *Journal of Applied Behavior Analysis*, the *Journal of the Association for
Persons with Severe Handicaps*, and *Augmentative and Alternative Communication*,
rationales for the selection of these journals and the cutoff year, 1985, were
not offered.

This review offers explicit and detailed information concerning the degree
to which included studies shared the same independent variable (i.e., FCT using
AAC techniques). This identification of the independent variable as FCT using
AAC implies that the dependent variable was challenging behavior. The criteria
used to arrive at judgments of effectiveness were not reported. Even though terms
such as "immediate substantial reduction (ISR) in frequency of the target behavior" and "gradual reduction (GR)" were used to quantify and summarize the
outcomes of studies, it is unclear how these measures were operationalized. For
example, what was considered to be "immediate" as measured by the number of
data points (e.g., 5 data points or 10 data points)? Likewise, the term "substantial" remains subjectively determinable. Table 3 in Mirenda (1997) lists studies
with an outcome of an ISR ranging from "to zero," "to 8% of baseline," "to 95%
of baseline." Given this wide range, an operational understanding of the term
"substantial" is not possible. The reported result that "the FCT/AAC intervention resulted in an immediate and substantial reduction in the frequency of the
target behavior for 44 of the 55 participants (85%)" (p. 222) needs to be recon-
sidered, given the lack of operational definitions and the range of ISR.

The covariation of study outcomes with study characteristics was reported
in a very limited anecdotal manner and not on statistical grounds. One study
that was found to bear only a gradual reduction in challenging behavior was
deemed the result of poor treatment integrity. The authors of the original study
included in the review had suggested this explanation. For another study with
similar outcomes, the reader is referred to several hypotheses offered by the

authors of the respective original study. Thus, it is fair to say that the covariation of study outcomes with study characteristics was not examined in a systematic manner.

Finally, the last of Jackson's (1980) criteria states that the conclusions of the synthesis should be supported with the data from the studies reviewed. This criterion is met to some extent. The conclusion that "it is clear that FCT/AAC is a promising practice for the reduction of severe behavior problems, at least on a short-term basis" (p. 222) is clearly based on the outcome data reported for the percentage of participants who experienced an immediate and substantial reduction in target behaviors (keeping in mind the aforementioned limitations of this measure). On the other hand, however, the author provides no data to support the following conclusions:

> Overall, the research reviewed suggests that both generalization and mainte-
> nance of new communicative behaviors can be enhanced by the use of the following
> practices: (a) natural settings for instruction, (b) distributed practice trials, and (c) selec-
> tion of FCT/AAC behaviors that are efficient, acceptable, and recognizable by others.
> On the other hand, FCT/AAC interventions are less likely to be successful over time
> in environments that (a) are homogenous (e.g., classrooms designed specifically for
> students with challenging behaviors), (b) de-emphasize the importance of choice
> and control in the lives of the people supported, and (c) do not work within a
> collaborative (i.e., team) model of intervention (p. 222; also see Carr *et al.*, 1994;
> Durand, 1990)

The conclusions in syntheses should be *directly supported* with data from the review. In this case, no data are provided that contrast the generalization and maintenance of new communicative behaviors in (1) natural settings versus con-trived settings, (2) distributed practice trials versus massed trials, and (3) FCT/AAC behaviors that are efficient versus inefficient, acceptable versus unacceptable, recognizable versus opaque. Although it is appropriate to support one's findings with conclusions reached by other synthesists, it is so only when the current syn-thesis has arrived at the same or different conclusions based on the data reviewed.

3. Summary

In summary, quantitative syntheses are typically more systematic than nar-rative reviews, in particular related to the search strategies used and the criteria for inclusion. Although quantitative reviews often attempt to quantify outcomes, vote count methods often fall short on adequate operational definitions.

C. META-ANALYTIC REVIEWS

Meta-analytic reviews or meta-analyses are a specific instance of quantita-tive reviews. The main difference between a meta-analysis and other types of quantitative reviews is the application, in the case of the former, of an objective quantitative effectiveness measure and the subsequent application of statistics to determine efficacy across studies in meta-analysis. Meta-analyses in the field are still severely underutilized (Correa & Nye, 2001; Millar, Light, & Schlosser, 2000; Schlosser & Lee, 2000). This section briefly summarizes how the meta-analysis by Schlosser and Lee (2000) measures up to Jackson's (1980) criteria. This meta-analysis was chosen rather than any other because of the author's degree of familiarity with this review and because it is the only published meta-analysis in the field.

1. Schlosser and Lee (2000)

This meta-analysis determined the effectiveness of AAC intervention with particular emphasis on strategies that induce generalization or maintenance. For an experiment to be included, it needed to address training in AAC, which is defined as an "area of clinical practice that attempts to compensate (either temporarily or permanently) for the impairment and disability patterns of persons with severe expressive communication disorders (i.e., people with severe communication impairments)" (American Speech-Language-Hearing Association, 1989, p. 107). In addition, several other criteria were used to determine the inclusion or exclusion of experiments. For example, manual signing intervention with persons whose only disability is due to a hearing impairment did not qualify. Also, the target behavior needed to serve a communicative function. Further, the target of the intervention had to be a person with disability or a communication partner. In addition, there were several other requirements pertaining to design issues. For example, only single-subject experimental designs (see Chapter 6) were included. Finally, the experiment had to be published in English between 1976 and 1995. English was chosen as the only language due to its international importance and the limitations of the authors in reading research in many other languages. The cutoff year of 1976 was chosen due to a convergence of historical factors during that time. As per Jackson's first requirement, the definition and delineation of the topic permit a replication of the inclusion and exclusion of studies.

Previous reviews were not only described but also distinguished from the current synthesis in terms of focus, synthesis methodology, and rigor. This allowed the researchers to clearly establish the need for this meta-analysis. The meta-analysis described the procedures for obtaining studies, such as the search strategies used and the time frame to which the search was delimited. We used three techniques, including computerized searches, handsearches, and footnote chasing (for a rationale see the discussion that follows). Databases searched included ERIC, PsycINFO, Psychological Abstracts, and Dissertations Abstract International. Forty-six journals were handsearched as well. In terms of footnote chasing, the reference list of included articles, topical bibliographies, and previous reviews were searched. As far as the independent variable is concerned, all studies needed to pertain to AAC intervention as specified in the topic delimitation. In addition, the intervention was coded in terms of the strategies used to promote generalization and maintenance. The dependent variable had to be classifiable as a communicative function.

Effectiveness was determined through the percentage of nonoverlapping data (PND) (Scruggs, Mastropieri, & Casto, 1987a) or the percentage of overlapping data (POD). "The PND method requires the calculation of nonoverlap between baseline and successive intervention phases (or generalization phases) by identifying the highest data point in baseline and determining the percentage of data points during intervention (or generalization) that exceed this level (Schlosser & Lee, 2000, p. 210). POD was used to calculate the percentage of maintenance data points within or above the last three intervention data points.

The covariation of study outcomes with study characteristics was examined in multiple ways. A comparison of studies examining generalization across a single dimension with those across multiple dimensions (e.g., partners, settings), for example, yielded that generalization across a single dimension is more efficacious. Second, differences were also found depending on the intervention designs used. Third, a moderate relationship was found between treatment integrity and intervention effectiveness, suggesting that more consistent application of treatment resulted in more positive outcomes.

The conclusions of the synthesis were supported by the data from the studies reviewed. The conclusion that the use of strategies is considerably unbalanced in favor of train and hope approaches was supported with descriptive summary data (91.2%) and examples of individual studies (e.g., Duker & Morsink, 1984). The conclusion that generalization may be accomplished more effectively when only a single dimension is altered rather than multiple dimensions was also supported by results of individual studies that attested to it (e.g., Hunt, Alwell, & Goetz, 1991; Kratzer, Spooner, Test, & Koorland, 1993). Finally, many of the methodological issues discussed were substantiated with references to individual studies (see also Chapter 20).

III. PLANNING AND IMPLEMENTING A META-ANALYSIS IN AAC

There are essentially five stages involved in planning and implementing a research synthesis: (1) problem formulation, (2) data collection, (3) data evaluation, (4) analysis and interpretation, and (5) public presentation (Cooper & Hedges, 1994). This section describes these stages and illustrates them using the author's experience in planning and implementing meta-analyses (Millar *et al.*, 2000; Schlosser & Goetze, 1991; Schlosser & Lee, 2000).

A. THE PROBLEM FORMULATION STAGE

The only major constraint on problem formulation in research synthesis is the availability of a body of primary studies. In determining whether a review is needed, the number of primary studies available is secondary to whether or not a review would generate new insights (Cooper & Hedges, 1994). In the case of Schlosser and Lee (2000), intervention studies had been published for more than 20 years. In addition, AAC users had been reported to have difficulty generalizing newly acquired skills (e.g., Calculator, 1988). Other scholars in and outside the AAC field have insisted that generalization and maintenance needs to be viewed proactively by employing strategies that help learners to generalize and to maintain (e.g., Reichle & Sigafoos, 1991). Several strategies had been proposed and studied in primary research in AAC and related fields. Thus, it was only a logical extension to pose the question regarding which strategies do effectively promote generalization or maintenance in AAC through a synthesis of primary intervention research. Other fields had engaged in similar efforts (e.g., Scruggs & Mastropieri, 1994a; White *et al.*, 1988).

It is in the problem formulation stage when the synthesist needs to delimit the topic and determine criteria for inclusion and exclusion of studies. Delimiting the topic requires considerable knowledge of the content area as is illustrated next. The Schlosser and Lee (2000) synthesis specified several content requirements pertaining to participants, interventions, and dependent variables. For example, participants whose only disability was due to a hearing impairment were not included, even if they were taught unaided methods. This was considered an important requirement because the review was to be concerned with the field of AAC rather than that of deaf education. Also, studies that trained communication partners were eligible for inclusion. This was chosen as a requirement because AAC is often viewed as a transactional process involving the learner and his or her communication partner; sometimes change in the learner is best accomplished by changing the behaviors of communication partners. Communication-based approaches to challenging behaviors were excluded, even if they used AAC as part of FCT. This exclusion criterion was deemed important because such studies require other outcome measures and other authors had already implemented a meta-analysis on challenging behaviors (e.g., Carr *et al.*, 1999). The dependent variables needed to serve a communicative function—match-to-sample procedures, for example, were excluded. For the purposes of this synthesis, the authors were interested in synthesizing research that evaluated functional communication skills. In addition, the dependent variables needed to include data on generalization or maintenance. This criterion was put in place because it directly related to the author's desire to study strategies that induce generalization or maintenance rather than behavior change per se.

Examples of content variables that would lead to exclusion are extremely helpful for readers to replicate a later synthesis. Methodological considerations may also be necessary to specify as inclusion criteria. Several methodological considerations were specified, including the type of experiments to be included (only single-subject experiments), the need for a baseline, and time-series data depicted in graphic form. Finally, temporal considerations (1976 to 1995) and language constraints (English only) were specified to round out our inclusion criteria.

B. The Data Collection Stage—Formulating a Search Strategy

A sound search strategy is absolutely essential in fields such as AAC where the literature is not tied to a few journals. It is fair to say that AAC intervention literature is a scattered literature (see Chapter 12). The search conducted in Schlosser and Lee (2000), for example, yielded relevant articles in 22 journals. These journals span fields such as speech-language pathology, special education, and applied behavior analysis. A quick look at the abstracts from other journals published in *Augmentative and Alternative Communication* gives us an appreciation of how widespread our literature really is. This places a considerable burden on the synthesist and anyone who wishes to engage in evidence-based practice (see Chapter 12). Therefore, a solid search strategy is a must in meta-analysis, especially in AAC.

Cooper (1987) and White (1994) identified five major modes of searching, consisting of 15 techniques for retrieving research literature. Each procedure, if applied alone, results in a biased sample of studies. For instance, computerized database searches underrepresent the most recent research and unpublished research. Alternately, using the reference lists of journal articles ("ancestor search") overrepresents those operations or results that are compatible with the research paradigm that ties the particular journal to its journal network (for these issues see also Cook *et al.*, 1992). Footnote chasing may reinforce the homogeneity of one's findings (White, 1994). A multifaceted search strategy in which varied or differential search strategies complement one another ameliorates systematic bias. To this end, Schlosser and Lee (2000) used a combination of computerized database search, handsearches, and ancestry searches. The handsearch strategy, for example, permits a systematic search of relevant professional journals, including those that may not be indexed by any of the databases considered. A handsearch does not rely on key word indices provided by the journals; the accuracy of these indices depends on the judgment of the individual authors, reviewers, or editors regarding the accuracy and appropriateness of selected key words. In addition, earlier contributions might have studied AAC, but used different key words at that time (auxiliary communication, simultaneous communication, total communication, etc.). A handsearch, on the other hand, involves a systematic search of the table of contents for relevant titles of each issue. Should titles appear relevant, the abstract can be examined for relevance. Whereas an ancestry research goes into the past to retrieve relevant studies, a forward citation search takes an existing reference and seeks later (i.e., future) sources that cite this reference. According to White (1994), this method has the potential to bring substantive or methodological links between studies into the open and often crosses disciplinary boundaries.[2]

The use of key words plays a crucial role in computerized database searches because you get what you ask for. Generally, we distinguish natural language terms from controlled-vocabulary terms (White, 1994). Natural language terms are used by authors to write abstracts and titles. Controlled-vocabulary terms are assigned to the bibliographic record by libraries, which index articles in an attempt to bring together articles that may otherwise be scattered through authors' use of idiosyncratic terms. Sometimes, controlled-vocabulary terms may also backfire by making an article less accessible to an audience. For example, one article on Blissymbolics (Schlosser & Lloyd, 1993) was assigned the controlled-vocabulary term "artificial languages," which is unlikely to be used by those interested in AAC. In addition to descriptors, searchers for evidence may also find it helpful to use additional identifiers such as "experiments" or "single-subject experiment." It may be appropriate to delimit the search temporally by stating a cutoff year. The synthesist may also want to impose language constraints as part of the search by specifying a language. In our case we made it clear that only English works would be included. Although this action may exclude valuable research published in other languages, the reader is not led to believe that the review is complete in that respect.

A solid search strategy, one that minimizes the danger of missing relevant articles outside one's regular purview (White, 1994), allows the meta-analyst to address two of the hallmarks of a "good" review. First, it offers the reader information on *domain* by describing all the sources used to identify studies (including sources that failed to yield items though they seemed plausible at first). Second, it states information concerning the *scope* of the review by listing subject

---

[2]Although I have not used a forward citation search for purposes of meta-analyses, I have relied on it to strengthen documents for promotion and tenure. I was truly surprised that some of my work was cited in fields I did not anticipate. This method is worthwhile exploring for meta-analysts.

headings or other search terms used along with geographic, temporal, and language constraints (Bates, 1992; White, 1994).

C. THE DATA EVALUATION STAGE

Data evaluation is concerned with a number of decisions. Most of these decisions are related to the questions of (1) what to code and (2) how to code (Cooper & Hedges, 1994).

1. What to Code?

In deciding what to code, the synthesist has to make a number of decisions about the classes of variables that are of interest to the reviewer. In general, Cooper and Hedges (1994) consider the following classes of variables: (1) quality judgments, (2) variables that predict effectiveness, (3) potential mediators of effectiveness, and (4) differences in how outcomes are conceptualized and therefore measured. Another category is that of "demographic contextual variables." This category is discussed first.

a. Demographic Contextual Variables

These variables provide the necessary context for the synthesis data. For example, in which settings are AAC interventions typically implemented? What is the age of the participants? What is their classification? Are persons with disabilities or their communication partners the primary recipients of the interventions? These are the variables we coded for in Schlosser and Lee (2000).

b. Quality Judgments

Regarding quality judgments, two basic views can be distinguished: the exhaustive view and the best evidence view. In the author's opinion, these views are not necessarily mutually exclusive, although others disagree (see Slavin, 1986). According to the *exhaustive view*, all studies should be included that meet the criteria and undergo a quality evaluation; this quality rating will then be considered in the subsequent covariation analysis of study outcomes with study characteristics (i.e., quality in this case) (Scruggs, 1992). According to the *best evidence view*, only studies that meet predefined quality indicators should be included (Slavin, 1986). In the author's opinion, it is important to arrive at decisions first based on the *exhaustive* evidence while taking into account quality. Meta-analysis has the potential to uncover methodological gaps and strengthen future research by pointing these out (Eagly & Wood, 1994). This would not be possible if the weaker evidence were excluded upfront. Thus, in Schlosser and Lee (2000) we decided to first include all studies that met our criteria regardless of their quality. In terms of quality, we coded for the type of design, treatment integrity, and interobserver agreement for the dependent variable. Essentially, quality indicators may pertain to the internal validity of a study or its relevance and acceptability (see Wortman, 1994, for further reading). There are, however, benefits to also identifying the pool of studies that meet best evidence criteria. Thus, Schlosser and Lee (2000) decided to then eliminate studies that failed to meet predefined rigid quality indicators. These included the following: (1) certain design requirements for intervention, generalization, and maintenance (to rule out threats to internal validity); (2) interobserver agreement and treatment integrity above 80%; (3) a stable baseline; and (4) sufficient data points to calculate a PND or POD. This resulted in a significant reduction in the number of studies/data series, which had repercussions for data analysis (discussed later).

c. Variables that Predict Effectiveness

The synthesist may also consider coding for variables that seem to predict effectiveness. In the synthesis at hand, the most obvious predictor variables were the generalization or maintenance strategies used in original studies. Also, the type of prompt intervention strategy employed was coded to determine whether it might predict intervention effectiveness. Obviously, the type of variables that predict effectiveness will depend on the specific independent variables and dependent variables studied.

d. Potential Mediators of Effects

These are variables that potentially have an influence on the magnitude of the effects yielded. Schlosser and Lee (2000) considered the AAC system and the instructional format to be such potential mediator variables. Even if these variables fail to operate as mediators, they provide, at the very least, the necessary context for the effectiveness of data obtained.

e. Differences in How Outcomes Are Conceptualized

Outcomes may be conceptualized in a number of ways in the original treatment literature. Therefore, it is incumbent on the synthesist to select effectiveness measures that can accommodate the various outcomes. In synthesizing studies using group designs, the measure used is called "effect size." For further information on the possible derivations of the effect size measure, see Cooper and Hedges (1994).

In Schlosser and Lee (2000), intervention effectiveness, generalization effectiveness, and maintenance effectiveness needed to be addressed within single-subject experimental designs. Several quantitative techniques have been proposed for integrating single-subject research studies through some sort of effect size measure. These methods include the d statistics (e.g., White, Rusch, Kazdin, & Hartmann, 1989), the "Percentage of Nonoverlapping data (PND)" (Scruggs, Mastropieri, & Casto, 1987a), regression procedures (e.g., Center, Skiba, & Casey, 1985–1986), and expanded regression-based approaches (Allison & Gorman, 1993; Hershberger, Wallace, Green, & Marquis, 1999).

Schlosser and Lee (2000) chose the PND (Scruggs *et al.*, 1987a) to integrate studies in terms of intervention effectiveness, generalization effectiveness, and maintenance effectiveness. The PND method requires the calculation of nonoverlap between baseline and successive intervention phases (or generalization phases) by identifying the highest data point in baseline and determining the percentage of data points during intervention (or generalization, or maintenance) that exceed this level. For instance, when 80% of intervention data points exceed the highest data point in the baseline, the PND is 80.

To integrate studies in terms of maintenance effectiveness, Schlosser and Lee (2000) also used the percentage of overlapping data (POD) by calculating the percentage of maintenance data points within or above the last three intervention data points. The PND and POD provide a meaningful metric of treatment effectiveness that is easy to interpret (see Section III.D, "The Analysis and Interpretation Stage"). In addition, the PND is a nonparametric statistic not affected by problems of heterogeneous variances or nonlinearity. Finally, the PND is the method that has been field-tested most widely in syntheses of single-subject research, including such issues as generalization (Scruggs & Mastropieri, 1994a), conduct disorders (Scruggs, Mastropieri, Cook, & Escobar, 1986), developmental functioning (Scruggs, Mastropieri, & McEwen, 1988), language interventions (Scruggs, Mastropieri, Forness, & Kavale, 1988), problem behavior (Didden, Duker, & Korzilius, 1997; Scotti, Evans, Meyer, & Walker, 1991), self-injurious behavior (Schlosser & Goetze, 1991; 1992), social skills training (Mathur, Kavale, Quinn, Forness, & Rutherford, 1998), and social withdrawal (Mastropieri & Scruggs, 1985–1986).

The PND metric, however, has not been without controversy (e.g., Allison, & Gorman, 1993, 1994; Busk & Serlin, 1992; Salzberg, Strain, & Baer, 1987; Scruggs & Mastropieri, 1994b; Scruggs, Mastropieri, & Casto, 1987b, 1987c; White, 1987; White *et al.*, 1989). It has been argued that the PND (1) erroneously represents effects when outliers are present in baseline, the treatment has a detrimental effect, trend is present in the data; (2) ignores changes in slope; and (3) has an expected value that changes as a result of the number of data points in a graphic display (as n increases, the PND decreases).

With adequate coding conventions, however, the noted shortcomings are manageable. In Schlosser and Lee (2000), data series with a baseline with isolated floor or ceiling effects in relation to the goal of intervention were excluded. A baseline floor effect is operationalized as one or more baseline data points that are located at the floor (e.g., 0 occurrence) when the goal of intervention is to decrease behavior. A baseline ceiling effect is operationalized as one or more baseline data points that are located at the ceiling (e.g., 100% correct) when the goal is to increase behavior. Floor and ceiling effects, as related to the goal of intervention, are problematic when the effectiveness metric (e.g., percent of nonoverlapping data or PND) is applied; these floor or ceiling instances will automatically yield a score representing "ineffectiveness," although only one or two data points of all of the baseline points may be located at the floor or the ceiling. To the knowledge of this author, there has been only one meta-analysis of single-subject research on the reduction of challenging behavior that included floor effects in synthesizing studies (Scotti et al., 1991) despite the risks of misrepresenting effectiveness data. However, several conceptual papers (e.g., Scruggs, 1992; Scruggs et al., 1987a) and the majority of meta-analyses opted for the conservative solution and excluded these data series (Mastropieri & Scruggs, 1985–1986; Schlosser & Goetze, 1991, 1992; Scruggs & Mastropieri, 1994a; Scruggs et al., 1986; Scruggs et al., 1988; Scruggs, Mastropieri, Forness, & Kavale, 1988). For experimental designs with several baselines (e.g., between-series designs such as multiple baseline designs), a ceiling/floor effect will result in the exclusion of only the particular tier with the effect, not the entire experiment.

In reviewing the various techniques to synthesize single-subject research, Scruggs and Mastropieri (1998) convincingly answered these criticisms in this author's opinion and that of others (Kavale, Mathur, Forness, Quinn, & Rutherford, 2000). Other techniques were not utilized, as they tend to require an extensive number of data points. Typically, an extensive number of data points are not available in published single-subject experimental research. In addition, the large effect size values associated with these techniques cannot be easily reconciled with those obtained in syntheses of group studies (see Kavale et al., 2000; Scruggs & Mastropieri, 1998).

For intervention designs, the conventions established by Scruggs et al. (1987a) were followed for commonly used designs. A multiple-baseline design, for example, involved a comparison of intervention with its corresponding baseline in each of the tiers; the resulting PNDs for each tier were then added and divided by the number of tiers to derive a PND for intervention effectiveness. For generalization designs, conventions were developed for each design strategy described in Chapter 6 (see also Schlosser & Braun, 1994). For maintenance designs, conventions were developed for each of the design options described by

Barrios and Hartmann (1988). Once what to code is decided, the next step is to resolve how the coding will be done.

2. How to Code?

a. Constructing Coding Forms and Books

Now that the prerequisites to full-scale coding are resolved, the meta-analyst can begin with the construction of coding forms and a code book. In the Schlosser and Lee (2000) synthesis, a coding protocol, a coding form, and a coding book were used as part of a comprehensive manual (Schlosser & Lee, 1998). The "AAC Generalization and Maintenance Coding Protocol" included the variable (abbreviated for computer entry; e.g., SET-I), the format (the number of digits; e.g., *nn*), the variable name (spelled out; e.g., Setting-Intervention), and the definition with a numerical code for each category (e.g., 11 = Segregated School/Classroom). The "AAC Generalization and Maintenance Coding Form" included the abbreviated variable names, blank boxes to fill in the numerical code, and a computational worksheet for calculating outcome measures. The "AAC Generalization and Maintenance Coding Manual—Definitions" provides operational definitions and conventions for arriving at coding decisions. Tables 11.1 to 11.3 offer excerpts of each of these documents.

In hindsight, it might have proved more efficient to combine our form and protocol into one, analogous to examples provided by Stock (1994). An attempt to do this for the excerpts presented earlier can be found in Table 11.4. In addition to eliminating one piece of paper from the data management process, this approach also facilitates data entry into statistical software packages.

Coding forms should be developed through an iterative process allowing the author for revisions (as and) when required. Our coding protocol underwent a number of revisions as various articles were coded and through the feedback from independent raters who were being trained for coding. Stock (1994) suggests that various workers in the field could be asked for their input for additional coding categories or revisions of existing ones.

b. Minimizing Bias in the Coding Process

Part of determining how to code pertains to carrying out the actual coding and ensuring the trustworthiness of this process. One way of minimizing bias is to use multiple effectiveness measures for the same construct. The original Schlosser and Lee (2000) manuscript submitted for publication used PND measures and vote count measures. The reviewers of the manuscript, however, encouraged us to remove the vote count results from the study, in part due to difficulties with reconciling the results obtained with the two measures. Schlosser and Lee

Table 11.1

AAC Generalization and Maintenance Coding *Protocol*—**Excerpt Schlosser & Lee (1998)**

Variable	Format	Variable Name	Definition

STRATEGY	nn	Strategies— Generalization or maintenance	Enter one of the following two-digit classification codes:
			10 *Non*strategies
			  11 Train and hope
			  12 Train to criterion and hope
			20 *Setting*-related strategies
			  21 Natural settings
			  22 Sequential modification
			  23 Modification of the environment
			30 *Consequence*-related strategies
			  31 Contact/recruit natural consequences
			  32 Make consequences less discriminable
			  33 Train to generalize
			  34 Reinforce unprompted generalization
			40 *Antecedent*-related strategies
			  41 Program common stimuli
			  42 Train sufficient exemplars
			  43 Multiple exemplars
			  44 General case programming/instruction
			50 *Other* strategies
			  51 Train loosely
			  52 Mediate generalization
			  53 Functional equivalence training
			  54 Other single strategies
			  55 Multiple strategies

FOCUS	n	Focus of generalization	Enter one of the following one-digit classification codes:
			  1 Behavior
			  2 Stimuli
			  3 Persons
			  4 Setting
			  5 Instructional format
			  6 Combination

(2000) also used two PND measures for evaluating generalization effectiveness; one was based on a comparison with the generalization baseline and the other with the intervention baseline. Two measures were also used for evaluating maintenance; one measure relied on a comparison with the intervention baseline whereas the other measured the overlap with the last three intervention data points.

Second, selection of primary coders with experience not only in the topic area but also in the methodology can enhance trustworthiness. Third, an independent coder should be used both to determine the inclusion of articles and to code an adequate percentage of studies. Similar to observational research, the independent rater should be trained up to a criterion prior to coding the actual data. Another step to minimize bias, which was not taken in Schlosser and Lee (2000), is the use of *blind* independent coding (Cook *et al.*, 1992). Ratings of study characteristics can be influenced by knowledge of the study results. To eliminate this potential bias, results and methodological characteristics should be coded independently by separating the procedure section of the article from the results section and by coding the two at different times.

Table 11.2

AAC Generalization and Maintenance Coding *Form*—**Schlosser & Lee (1998)**

| | | ID# | | Data Series # | |

| YEAR | | SUBJ# | | TARGET | |

| CA | | CLASSF | |

SET-I		SET-G		SET-M	
AAC-I		AAC-G		AAC-M	
FORMAT-I		PROMPT-I	

| DV | |

| STRATEGY | | FOCUS | | DIM | |
| DESIGN-I | | DESIGN-G | | DESIGN-M | |

| PROCED | | REL-I | | REL-G | | REL-M | |
| %PROC | | %REL-I | | %REL-G | | %REL-M | |

| BASELINE | |

| IVOTE | | GVOTE | | MVOTE | |

| IPND | | GPND-IB | | MPND-IB | |
| | | GPND-GB | | MPOD-I | |

(continues)

Table 11.2 (*continued*)

Computational Worksheet

IPND

ENTER DATA or
VALUE HERE

TI = Total number of intervention data points	
IND = Number of intervention nonoverlapping data points (i.e., number above highest baseline point)	
IPND = IND/TI	

GPND-IB

ENTER DATA or
VALUE HERE

TG = Total number of generalization data points	
GND-IB = Number of generalization nonoverlapping data points (i.e., number above highest *intervention baseline* point)	
GPND-IB = GND-IB/TG	

GPND-GB

ENTER DATA or
VALUE HERE

TG = Total number of generalization data points	
GND-GB = Number of generalization nonoverlapping data points (i.e., number above highest *generalization baseline* point)	
GPND-GB = GND-GB/TG	

MPND-IB

ENTER DATA or
VALUE HERE

TM = Total number of maintenance data points	
MND-IB = Number of Maintenance nonoverlapping data points (i.e., number above highest *intervention baseline* point)	
MPND-IB = MND-IB/TM	

MPOD-I

ENTER DATA or
VALUE HERE

TM = Total number of maintenance data points	
MOD-I = Number of maintenance overlapping data points (i.e., number within or above the **last three** *intervention baseline* points)	
MPOD-I = MOD-I/TM	

Table 11.3

Dear Coder,

This manual contains operational definitions for those variables that are not self-evident or self-explanatory. Please consult this manual while coding any experiments. Questions or needed clarifications should be directed to the first author.

STRATEGY—10 NONSTRATEGIES

Strategies to promote generalization/maintenance: These strategies were taken from the Stokes and Baer article in *JABA*, a study by White *et al.* (1989), a chapter by Stokes & Osnes (1988), and others. Strategies will be described and, if available, illustrated with an example from the literature. Sometimes experimenters attempt two different strategies of training with two groups of subjects or try more than one strategy with a single subject. In these cases, you will need to code each type of intervention that occurred. *Warning!* Do not rely on the authors' phrase for the procedures used, but code this item only after a careful examination of the methodology. Often authors do not refer to a strategy with a particular name.

11—Train and Hope

Actually, this is not a method of programming generalization. Generally, this category means that the authors utilized an intervention method that they hoped would generalize, and then they collected data to see if they obtained generalization. If authors do not cite specific references to generalization in reporting why procedures were chosen, it is probably a train-and-hope method.

Example: Three preschool boys who were blind and severely or profoundly retarded were taught to reach for noise-making toys always presented at midline. None of the boys generalized to objects presented on the right or left (Correa, Poulson, & Salzberg, 1984).

12—Train to Criterion and Hope

This is identical to number 11 except that the researchers trained behavior to a criterion hoping that the behaviors will generalize.

STRATEGY—20 *SETTING*-RELATED STRATEGIES

21—Natural Settings

Does the training or generalization occur in a setting where the response can be normally be expected to occur? Training is conducted directly in at least one type of setting in which the skill will be used. Generalization is then probed in other nontraining settings.

Example: The social interaction skills of several individuals with severe handicaps were trained in the classroom and courtyard during class breaks (Gaylord-Ross & Holvoet, 1985).

22—Sequential Modification

This is not really a method of programming either, but rather a sequence of a train-and-hope method applied to different settings. Training is provided in one setting, and generalization is probed in other settings. If necessary, training is conducted sequentially in more and more settings until generalization to all desired settings is observed. In general, if the methodology is training in setting 1, no generalization in setting 2, training in setting 2, no generalization in setting 3, training in setting 3, etc., it is sequential modification.

Example: One girl with moderate handicaps needed articulation training in three settings before generalizing to all remaining situations of interest: a second girl only required training in two situations before generalizing (Murdock, Garcia, & Hardman, 1977).

[a]References to citations supplied in this manual are available upon request from the author.

(continues)

Table 11.3 (*continued*)

STRATEGY—40 *ANTECEDENT*-RELATED STRATEGIES

41—Program Common Stimuli

This strategy involves selecting a salient, but not necessarily task-related, stimulus from the situation to which generalization is desired and including that stimulus in the training program. Common stimuli may be physical or social in nature. (1) The availability of physical stimuli (e.g., furniture) in both intervention and generalization may serve as a discriminative function because they assume a salient role in intervention. The presence of the same physical stimuli in generalization settings may facilitate generalization. (2) Available common social stimuli may have discriminative properties to facilitate generalization (e.g., peers). The social discriminative function of such stimuli is included in nontraining situations (e.g., peer mediators).

44—General Case Instruction/Programming

The universe to which generalization is desired is analyzed and representative examples of positive stimuli (stimuli in the presence of which the skill should be used), negative stimuli (stimuli in the presence of which the skill should not be used), and irrelevant stimuli (stimuli that should not affect skill use but might inappropriately do so) are selected for training.

Example: Six young men with moderate or severe retardation were trained on three vending machines that reflect the range of machine-types found in the community. Good generalization was obtained to 10 untrained machines in the community (Sprague & Horner, 1984).

STRATEGY—50 OTHER STRATEGIES

51—Train Loosely

Settings, cues, prompts, materials, response definition, and other features of the training situation (e.g., have distractions occurred sometimes but not always) are purposely varied to avoid a ritual, highly structured, invariant program that might inhibit generalization. This would include *making antecedents less discriminable* by purposefully introducing variety into the conditions of training so the individual will not readily identify performance with a particular set of conditions or circumstances.

Example: Mothers were taught to vary the type of stimuli and reinforcers they used in working with their children's motor skills. All children learned their skills quickly and generalized well to another setting (Filler & Kasari, 1981).

FOCUS

This factor refers to the focus of generalization or the dimension that the target individual is expected to generalize without direct training.

1—Behavior

The behavior (response) in intervention is different from the behavior (response) in generalization. Behaviors include AAC systems, communicative functions (requesting/manding, labeling/tacting), and selection techniques (e.g., scanning).

2—Stimuli

The stimuli in intervention are different from the stimuli in generalization but the same behavior (response) is exhibited.

3—Persons

The persons in intervention are different from the persons in generalization.

4—Settings

The intervention setting differs from the generalization setting.

5—Instructional Format

The instructional format (one to one, small group, large group) in intervention differs from that in generalization.

6—Combination

A combination of foci that differ from intervention to generalization.

Table 11.4

Generalization and Maintenance Items

ID No. _____

15. Strategies:

    10 *Non*strategies
        11 Train and hope
        12 Train to criterion and hope
    20 *Setting*-related strategies
        21 Natural settings
        22 Sequential modification
        23 Modification of the environment
    30 *Consequence*-related strategies
        31 Contact/recruit natural consequences
        32 Make consequences less discriminable
        33 Train to generalize
        34 Reinforce unprompted generalization
    40 *Antecedent*-related strategies
        41 Program common stimuli
        42 Train sufficient exemplars
        43 Multiple exemplars
        44 General case programming/instruction
    50 *Other* strategies
        51 Train loosely
        52 Mediate generalization
        53 Functional equivalence training
        54 Other single strategies
        55 Multiple strategies

16. Focus:

    1 Behavior
    2 Stimuli
    3 Persons
    4 Setting
    5 Instructional format
    6 Combination

Margin boxes: $\overline{15}$, $\overline{16}$

D. THE ANALYSIS AND INTERPRETATION STAGE

Once the primary data are evaluated and coded, the next stage involves analysis and interpretation. One of the most important tasks at this stage is the estimation of the magnitude of an effect. This estimation is typically called "effect size," defined as "the degree to which the phenomenon is present in the population, or the degree to which the null hypothesis is false" (Cohen, 1988, pp. 9–10). In group studies, the effect size is often derived by establishing the difference between the mean of experimental and control group criterion variables, divided by the standard deviation of the variable; effect sizes vary from −3.00 to zero to +3.00 (Lauer & Asher, 1988).

In our meta-analysis of single-subject experimental designs, the PND or POD was used as an effect size measure. First, a process of data reduction was initiated by examining the two PND measures for generalization to determine whether they would yield the same results statistically. Because they did, the PND measure that used the intervention baseline as a comparison was chosen for subsequent analyses due to greater availability in the data set. Data series were aggregated by creating a mean PND or POD across data series. Criteria established by Scruggs et al. (1986) were used to interpret effectiveness of mean PND data: a mean PND greater than 90% is considered highly effective, a PND between 70% and 90% is considered fairly effective, a PND between 50% and 70% is considered of questionable effectiveness, and a PND below 50% reflects unreliable treatments. Inferential statistical analyses were used to evaluate the following variables: differential effectiveness of generalization and maintenance strategies, generalization dimensions, prompt intervention strategies, instructional formats, AAC systems, and experimental designs. Mean PND/POD measures were viewed as dependent variables, whereas the variables listed here were considered independent or predictor variables.

At this stage, the synthesist also needs to decide whether to engage in exhaustive inclusion inferential analyses only or in best evidence analyses as well. There are limitations to the exhaustive inclusion analysis in that evidence-based practitioners would find it difficult to determine which interventions are effective *and* at the same time are of good quality. After all, the mean effect size data would be based on all the studies; knowing about a covariation with study quality does not necessarily help the practitioner in this regard. Thus, Schlosser and Lee (2000) decided to engage in a best-evidence analysis using predefined, rigid quality indicators. These included the following: (1) certain design requirements for intervention, generalization, and maintenance (to rule out threats to internal validity); (2) interobserver agreement and treatment integrity above 80%; (3) a stable baseline; and (4) sufficient data points to calculate our effect size measure. This resulted in a significant reduction in the number of studies/data series to the point where the planned best-evidence inferential analyses could not be implemented due to small *n*. Noteworthy was the decline of eligible data series, particularly for generalization and maintenance.

E. THE PUBLIC PRESENTATION STAGE

This is the final stage where the synthesist needs to place the results in context. This stage is similar to the typical discussion section of a primary research study. Essentially, the synthesist will need to remember the reasons for conducting a meta-analysis in the first place and address those reasons. One of the reasons for having completed a synthesis may be to contribute to theory development. Another reason may be to provide directions for future research, both in terms of methodological considerations and content. Finally, a synthesist may have intended to inform evidence-based practice (EBP) through recommendations as to which treatments are effective and which treatments are not. This was one of Schlosser and Lee's (2000) original intents for conducting the synthesis; these authors aimed to identify those strategies that are effective in promoting generalization and maintenance in AAC and communicate those to practitioners and clinical researchers. Due to the prominence of the train-and-hope approach and the lack of best-evidence data for generalization and maintenance, this was rendered an impossible task. Instead, Schlosser and Lee (2000) focused on methodological gaps and offered directions for future research. Methodological gaps involved a lack of adequate designs for evaluating generalization and maintenance effectiveness unequivocally and a lack of treatment integrity data.

IV. CONCLUSIONS

An examination of narrative literature reviews demonstrates that narrative reviews are typically at risk for (1) subjectively determining the inclusion and exclusion of studies and (2) subjectively evaluating and interpreting individual study outcomes along with their covariation with study characteristics. Quantitative reviews are typically more explicit in terms of inclusion and exclusion criteria than narrative reviews. Also, even though study outcomes are often quantified through vote-count methods, the underlying operational definitions for "votes" tend to be rather subjective. The discussion in this chapter indicates that meta-analysis potentially offers a more systematic and objective means of synthesizing efficacy literature in AAC. It is for this reason that evidence from meta-analyses ranks very high in terms of the hierarchy of evidence considered in EBP (see Chapter 12). The AAC field is only beginning to utilize research synthesis via meta-analysis. It is hoped that this chapter stimulates interest in implementing meta-analyses because they serve such an important function in practice as well as in the research enterprise. The description of the planning and implementing of a meta-analysis along with illustrations from the author's experiences are intended to facilitate this process. On a cautionary note, however, meta-analysis is not a foolproof technique. As with any other methodology, some meta-analyses are well implemented, whereas others are of questionable quality (see Schlosser & Goetze, 1992). However, thoughtfully planned and scrupulously implemented meta-analyses provide a way of reviewing vast quantities of studies and evaluating them with regard to specific, predetermined aspects consistent with the criteria for a systematic review. Other review methods do not have this capacity.

REFERENCES

Allison, D. B., & Gorman, B. S. (1993). Calculating effect sizes for meta-analysis: The case of the single case. *Behaviour Research and Therapy, 31,* 621–631.

Allison, D. B., & Gorman, B. S. (1994). "Make things as simple as possible, but no simpler." A rejoinder to Scruggs and Mastropieri. *Behaviour Research and Therapy, 31,* 885–883.

American Speech-Language-Hearing Association (1989). Competencies for speech-language pathologists providing services in augmentative communication. *Asha, 31,* 107–110.

Barrios, B. A., & Hartmann, D. P. (1988). Recent developments in single-subject methodology: Methods for analyzing generalization, maintenance, and multicomponent treatments. In M. Hersen, R. M. Eisler, & P. M. Miller (Eds.), *Progress in behavior modification: Vol. 22* (pp. 11–47). Newbury Park, CA: Sage.

Bates, M. J. (1992). Rigorous systematic bibliography. In H. D. White, M. J., Bates, & P. Wilson (Eds.), *For information specialists: Interpretations of reference and bibliographic work* (pp. 117–130). Norwood, NJ: Ablex.

Bryen, D., & Joyce, D. G. (1985). Language intervention with the severely handicapped: A decade of research. *Journal of Special Education, 19,* 7–39.

Burroughs, J., Albritton, E., Eaton, B., & Montague, J. (1990). A comparative study of language delayed preschool children's ability to recall symbols from two symbol systems. *Augmentative and Alternative Communication, 6,* 202–206.

Busk, P. L., & Serlin, R. C. (1992). Meta-analysis for single-case research. In T. R. Kratochwill & J. R. Levin (Eds.). *Single-case research design and analysis: New directions for psychology and education* (pp. 187–212). Hillsdale, NJ: Erlbaum.

Calculator, S. N. (1988). Promoting the acquisition and generalization of conversational skills by individuals with severe disabilities. *Augmentative and Alternative Communication, 4,* 94–103.

Carr, E. G., Horner, R. H., Turnbull, A. P., Marquis, J. G., McLaughlin, D. M., McAtee, M. L., Smith, C. E., Anderson Ryan, K., Ruef, M. B., & Doolabh, A. (1999). *Positive behavior support for people with developmental disabilities: A research synthesis.* Washington, DC: American Association on Mental Retardation.

Carr, E. G., Levin, L., McConnachie, G., Carlson, J. I., Kemp, D. C., & Smith, C. E. (1994). *Communication-based intervention for problem behavior: A user's guide for producing positive change.* Baltimore: Paul H. Brookes.

Center, B. A., Skiba, R. J., & Casey, A. (1985–1986). A methodology for the quantitative synthesis of intra-subject design research. *Journal of Special Education, 19,* 387–400.

Cohen, J. (1988). *Statistical power analysis for the behavioral sciences* (2nd ed.). Hillsdale, NJ: Erlbaum.

Cook, T. D., Cooper, H., Cordray, D. S., Hartmann, H., Hedges, L. V., Light, R. J., Louis, T. A., & Mosteller, F. (1992). *Meta-analysis for explanation: A casebook.* New York: Russell Sage Foundation.

Cooper, H. M. (1987). Literature searching strategies of integrative research reviewers: A first survey. *Knowledge, 8,* 372–383.

Cooper, H. M., & Hedges, L. V. (1994). *The handbook of research synthesis.* New York: Russell Sage Foundation.

Correa, N., & Nye, C. (2001, November). *Sign language and autism: A quantitative synthesis of single-subject research.* Poster presented at the Annual Convention of the American Speech-Language and Hearing Association, New Orleans, LA.

Dennis, R., Reichle, J., Williams, W., & Vogelsberg, T. (1982). Motoric factors influencing the selection of vocabulary for sign production programs. *Journal of the Association for Persons with Severe Handicaps, 7,* 20–33.

Didden, R., Duker, P. C., & Korzilius, H. (1997). Meta-analytic study on treatment effectiveness for problem behaviors with individuals who have mental retardation. *American Journal on Mental Retardation, 4,* 387–399.

Doherty, J. (1985). The effects of sign characteristics on sign acquisition and retention: An integrative review of the literature: *Augmentative and Alternative Communication, 1,* 108–121.

Duker, P. C., & Morsink, H. (1984). Acquisition and cross-setting generalization of manual signs with severely retarded individuals. *Journal of Applied Behavior Analysis, 17,* 93–103.

Durand, V. M. (1990). *Severe behavior problems: A functional communication training approach.* New York: Guilford Press.

Eagly, A. E., & Wood, W. (1994). Using research syntheses to plan future research. In H. M. Cooper & L. V. Hedges (Eds.), *The handbook of research synthesis* (pp. 485–500). New York: Russell Sage Foundation.

Hershberger, S. L., Wallace, D. D., Green, S. B., & Marquis, J. G. (1999). Meta-analysis for single-case designs. In R. H. Hoyle (Ed), *Statistical strategies for small sample research.* Newbury Park, CA: Sage.

Huer, M. B. (2000). Examining perceptions of graphic symbols across culture: Preliminary study of the impact of culture/ethnicity. *Augmentative and Alternative Communication, 16,* 180–185.

Hunt, P., Alwell, M., & Goetz, L. (1991). Establishing conversational exchange with family and friends: Moving from training to meaningful communication. *Journal of Special Education, 25,* 305–319.

Hunter, J., Schmidt, F. L., & Jackson, G. B. (1982). *Meta-analysis: Cumulating research findings across studies.* Beverly Hills, CA: Sage.

Jackson, G. B. (1980). Methods for integrative reviews. *Review of Educational Research, 50,* 438–460.

Kavale, K. A., Mathur, S. R., Forness, S. R., Quinn, M. M., Rutherford, R. B. (2000). Right reason in the integration of group and single-subject research in behavioral disorders. *Behavioral Disorders, 25,* 142–157.

Kiernan, C. (1977). Alternatives to speech: A review of research on manual and other forms of communication with mentally handicapped and other noncommunicating populations. *Journal of Mental Subnormality, 23,* 6–28.

Kratzer, D. A., Spooner, F., Test, D. W., & Koorland, M. A. (1993). Extending the application of constant time delay: Teaching a requesting skill to students with severe multiple disabilities. *Education and Treatment of Children, 16,* 235–253.

Lancioni, G. E., O'Reilly, M. F., & Basili, G. (2001). Use of microswitches and speech output systems with people with severe/profound intellectual or multiple disabilities: A literature review. *Research in Developmental Disabilities, 22,* 21–40.

Lauer, J. M., & Asher, J. W. (1988). *Composition research: Empirical designs.* New York: Oxford University Press.

Lloyd, L., & Fuller, D. (1990). The role of iconicity in augmentative and alternative communication symbol learning. In W. Fraser (Ed.), *Key issues in mental retardation research* (pp. 295–306). London: Routledge.

Mastropieri, M. A., & Scruggs, T. E. (1985–1986). Early intervention for socially withdrawn children. *Journal of Special Education, 19,* 429–441.

Mathur, S. R., Kavale, K. A., Quinn, M., Forness, S. R., & Rutherford, R. B. (1988). Social skills interventions with students with emotional and behavioral problems: A quantitative synthesis of single-subject research. *Behavioral Disorders, 23*, 193–201.

Millar, D., Light, J., & Schlosser, R. W. (2000, August). *The impact of AAC on natural speech development: A meta-analysis.* Paper presented at the Biennial Conference of the ISAAC, Washington, D.C.

Mirenda, P. (1997). Supporting individuals with challenging behavior through functional communication training and AAC: A research review. *Augmentative and Alternative Communication, 13*, 207–225.

Reichle, J., & Sigafoos, J. (1991). Establishing spontaneity and generalization. In J. Reichle, R. J. York, & J. Sigafoos (Eds.). *Implementing augmentative and alternative communication: Strategies for learners with severe disabilities* (pp. 157–172). Baltimore: Paul H. Brookes.

Salzberg, C. L., Strain, P. S., & Baer, D. M. (1987). Meta-analysis for single-subject research: When does it clarify, when does it obscure? *Remedial and Special Education, 8*, 43–48.

Schlosser, R. W., & Braun, U. (1994). Efficacy of AAC interventions: Methodologic issues in evaluating behavior change, generalization, and effects. *Augmentative and Alternative Communication, 10*, 207–223.

Schlosser, R. W., & Goetze, H. (1991). Selbstverletzendes Verhalten bei Kindern und Jugendlichen mit Geistiger Behinderung: Eine Meta-Analyse zur Effektivität von Interventionen. *Sonderpädagogik, 21*, 138–154.

Schlosser, R. W., & Goetze, H. (1992). Effectiveness and treatment validity of interventions addressing self-injurious behavior: From narrative reviews to meta-analysis. In T. E. Scruggs & M. A. Mastropieri (Eds.), *Advances in Learning and Behavioral Disabilities* (Vol. 7, pp. 135–175). Greenwich, CT: JAI Press.

Schlosser, R. W., & Lee, D. (1998). *Augmentative and alternative communication: Generalization and maintenance coding manual.* Unpublished manuscript, Northeastern University.

Schlosser, R. W., & Lee, D. (2000). Promoting generalization and maintenance in augmentative and alternative communication: A meta-analysis of 20 years of effectiveness research. *Augmentative and Alternative Communication, 16*, 208–227.

Schlosser, R. W., & Lloyd, L. L. (1993). Effects of initial element teaching in a storytelling context on Blissymbol acquisition and generalization. *Journal of Speech and Hearing Research, 36*, 979–995.

Schlosser, R. W., & Sigafoos, J. (2002). Selecting graphic symbols for an initial request lexicon: An integrative review. *Augmentative and Alternative Communication, 18*, 102–123.

Scotti, J. R., Evans, I. M., Meyer, L. H., & Walker, P. (1991). A meta-analysis of intervention research with problem behavior: Treatment validity and standards of practice. *American Journal on Mental Retardation, 96*, 243–256.

Scruggs, T. E. (1992). Single subject research methodology in the study of learning and behavior disorders: Design, analysis, and synthesis. In T. E. Scruggs & M. A. Mastropieri (Eds.), *Advances in Learning and Behavioral Disabilities* (Vol. 7, pp. 223–248). Greenwich, CT: JAI Press.

Scruggs, T. E., & Mastropieri, M. A. (1994a). The effectiveness of generalization training: A quantitative synthesis of single-subject research. In T. E. Scruggs & M. A. Mastropieri (Eds.), *Advances in learning and behavioral disabilities* (Vol. 8, pp. 259–280). Greenwich, CT: JAI Press.

Scruggs, T. E., & Mastropieri, M. A. (1994b). The utility of the PND statistic: A reply to Allison and Gorman. *Behaviour Research and Therapy, 32*, 879–883.

Scruggs, T. E., & Mastropieri, M. A. (1998). Summarizing single-subject research. *Behavior Modification, 22*, 221–243.

Scruggs, T. E., Mastropieri, M. A., & Casto, G. (1987a). The quantitative synthesis of single-subject research: Methodology and validation. *Remedial and Special Education, 8*, 24–33.

Scruggs, T. E., Mastropieri, M. A., & Casto, G. (1987b). Reply to Owen White. *Remedial and Special Education, 8*, 49–52.

Scruggs, T. E., Mastropieri, M. A., & Casto, G. (1987c). Response to Salzberg, Strain, and Baer. *Remedial and Special Education, 8*, 49–52.

Scruggs, T. E., Mastropieri, M. A., Cook, S. B., & Escobar, C. (1986). Early intervention for children with conduct disorders: A quantitative synthesis of single-subject research. *Behavioral Disorders, 11*, 260–271.

Scruggs, T. E., Mastropieri, M. A., Forness, S. R., & Kavale, K. A. (1988). Early language intervention: A quantitative synthesis of single-subject research. *Journal of Special Education, 22*, 259–283.

Scruggs, T. E., Mastropieri, M. A., & McEwen, I. (1988). Early intervention for developmental functioning: A quantitative synthesis of single-subject research. *Journal for the Division of Early Childhood, 12*, 359–367.

Slavin, R. E. (1986). Best-evidence synthesis: An alternative to meta-analytic and traditional reviews. *Educational Researchers, 15*, 5–11.

Stock, W. A. (1994). Systematic coding for research synthesis. In H. Cooper & L. V. Hedges (Eds.), *The handbook of research synthesis* (pp. 125–138). New York: Russell Sage Foundation.

Udwin, O. (1987). Analysis of the experimental adequacy of alternative and augmentative communication training studies. *Child Language Teaching and Therapy, 3*, 18–39.

White, D. M., Rusch, T. R., Kazdin, A. E., & Hartmann, D. P. (1989). Applications of meta-analysis in individual-subject research. *Behavioral Assessment, 11*, 281–296.

White, H. D. (1994). Scientific communication and literature retrieval. In H. Cooper & L. V. Hedges (Eds.), *The handbook of research synthesis* (pp. 42–55). New York: Russell Sage Foundation.

White, O. R. (1987). Some comments concerning "The quantitative synthesis of single-subject research." *Remedial and Special Education, 8*, 34–39.

White, O. R., Liberty, K. A., Haring, N. G., Billingsley, F. F., Boer, M., Burrage, A., Conners, R., Farman, R., Federochak, G., Leber, B. D., Liberty-Laylin, S., Miller, S., Opalski, C. Phifer, C., & Sessoms, I. (1988). Review and analysis of strategies for generalization. In N. G. Haring (Ed.), *Generalization for students with severe handicaps—Strategies and solutions* (pp. 15–51). Seattle: University of Washington Press.

Wolf, F. M. (1986). *Meta-analysis: Quantitative methods for research synthesis*. Beverly Hills, CA: Sage.

Wortman, P. M. (1994). Judging research quality. In H. Cooper & L. V. Hedges (Eds.). *The handbook of research synthesis* (pp. 97–109). New York: Russell Sage Foundation.

CHAPTER 12

Toward Evidence-Based Practice in AAC

Ralf W. Schlosser
Department of Speech-Language
  Pathology and Audiology
Northeastern University

Pammi Raghavendra
Crippled Children's Association of SA,
  Inc.
Regency Park, Australia

The Efficacy of Augmentative and Alternative Communication

I. INTRODUCTION

Evidence-based practice (EBP) has taken various health care fields by storm. To name but only a few, discussions about EBP have occurred in medicine (Sackett, Richardson, Rosenberg, & Haynes, 1997), physical therapy (Helewa & Walker, 2000), occupational therapy (Law & Baum, 1998; Lloyd-Smith, 1997), family therapy (Carr, 2000), clinical psychology (Hunsley, Dobson, Johnston, & Mikail, 1999), and gerontology (Olson, 1996). Recently, the then president of the American Speech-Language and Hearing Association, Logeman (2000), presented speech-language pathologists with the notion of EBP by posing the question "Why should we care?" She then proceeded with several compelling reasons as to why the field of communication disorders better seriously think about EBP. What are, if any, some of the reasons why augmentative and alternative communication (AAC) as a field and area of clinical practice should care about EBP? One reason may be related to the frequently documented research-practice gap in health care fields (e.g., Nutbeam, 1996). EBP may serve as a vehicle for translating research into practice and vice versa. A second reason is that in today's health care environment as well as in education, there are increasing demands for accountability, and AAC is no exception (Schlosser, 1999a). Funding agencies and insurers are asking questions such as "Why do we do what we do?" EBP is a way of ensuring that research evidence is considered in making decisions about what is being done in daily practice. This chapter is grounded in the firm belief that research evidence, where available, can and should play a crucial role in helping practitioners arrive at decisions in planning and implementing AAC assessments and interventions.

Although various health care fields have engaged in critical dialogue about what EBP means to them, discussions about how it should be conceptualized and what it takes to move their fields toward implementing EBP have not yet occurred in the AAC field. Thus, in this chapter a definition of EBP in AAC is proposed and a framework for evaluating the research evidence in AAC is developed. The chapters that follow exemplify EBP in specific content areas. Although the degree to which the principles proposed here are applied does vary from chapter to chapter, they are grounded in their intent to inform practice through research and research through practice.

II. EVIDENCE-BASED PRACTICE DEFINED

In thinking about a suitable definition for the AAC field, it may be helpful to consider definitions of specific instances of EBP from related health care fields.

A. Definitions of EBP in Other Fields

1. Evidence-Based Medicine

EBP grew out of evidence-based medicine (Egan, Dubouloz, Zweck, & Vallerand, 1998), so due to its long-standing history, evidence-based medicine may be a good starting point in our search for a viable definition. EBP has been defined several ways depending on the sources consulted. Rosenberg and Donald (1995), for example, defined EBP as intervention guided by the results of the most scientifically sound research relevant to that intervention. Sackett *et al.* (1997), on the other hand, defined evidence-based *medicine* as "the integration of best research evidence with clinical expertise and patient values" (p. 1). Unlike the definition by Rosenberg and Donald (1995), this definition emphasizes the role of clinical expertise as well as patient values and stresses that these need to be *integrated* with the best research evidence. Another field with a more recent tradition of EBP is occupational therapy.

2. Evidence-Based Occupational Therapy

Evidence-based occupational therapy practice occurs when an occupational therapist "uses research evidence together with clinical knowledge and reasoning to make decisions about interventions that are effective for specific clients" (Law & Baum, 1998, p. 131). This definition emphasizes the integration of research evidence and clinical expertise for a particular client in terms of intervention. Other workers in occupational therapy also included consensus expert opinion, in addition to research, as an acceptable basis for guiding intervention (Egan *et al.*, 1998).

B. Decision Making in AAC Today

Both of the preceding definitions emphasize the importance of research evidence, clinical knowledge and reasoning, and client needs or values in clinical decision making. Just how are decisions being made in the AAC field today? The answer to this question is based more on speculation, extrapolation, and anecdotal accounts rather than scientific data. First, the early support for facilitated communication, for example, has clearly shown that many clinical decisions are made in the absence of research evidence (e.g., Jacobson, Mulick, & Schwartz, 1995). Thus, to emphasize the role of research in AAC decision making may pose some challenges and barriers. Second, through the work of Fried-Oken and Bersani (2000), researchers in the field have learned that direct stakeholders are often excluded from the decision-making process. This is in sharp contrast to the emphasis placed on client values and needs in the EBP definitions of medicine and occupational therapy. Mitchell (1999) was quite pessimistic that the EBP process will truly respect the perspectives of direct stakeholders, even though the definitions and process descriptions of EBP say otherwise. Clearly, existing practices of excluding direct stakeholders from decision making will need to change if EBP is to succeed. Other practitioners might rely on other sources for decision making, such as habit or expedience (Zarin, Seigle, Pincus, & McIntyre, 1997). A practitioner who uses Picture Communication Symbols with a given child just because they are on his or her bookshelf would be following the principle of expedience rather than other more pertinent factors. Clearly, habit or expedience would be unacceptable sources for decision making in EBP. Although it is a high priority to conduct research on exactly how decisions are being made in AAC, these extrapolated issues need to be taken into account when proposing a definition of EBP in the AAC field and for contemplating its implementation.

C. A Proposed Definition for AAC

1. Desirable Features of an EBP Definition for the AAC Field

The preceding definitions from various health care fields reveal several desirable ingredients for defining the term EBP for AAC. First, the definition should speak of research evidence and its desired quality or certainty. Researchers in the AAC field have been discussing methodological issues such as those contributing to quality and certainty during Biennial Research Symposia and elsewhere (e.g., the special *AAC* issue on efficacy in March 1999). "Scientifically sound research," as stated in the definition by Rosenberg and Donald (1995), or "best research evidence," as stated in the Sackett *et al.* (1997) definition, speak to the quality or certainty of evidence. In a subsequent section, a process will be proposed for evaluating the certainty of the evidence.

Second, the perspectives of relevant stakeholders need to be considered as part of the decision-making process. Depending on the nature of the intervention at hand, relevant stakeholders may be direct stakeholders, indirect stakeholders, immediate stakeholders, or extended community stakeholders (Schlosser, 1999b). Definitions for each of these stakeholder groups will be provided later in this chapter.

Third, clinical or educational expertise is essential to the definition because evidence from research (even if that evidence is considered "best evidence") and an account of stakeholder perspectives do not automatically translate into meaningful decisions for a given client. Clinical or educational expertise includes skills, reasoning, intuition, and innovation. The clinician or educator needs to use reasoning in integrating the research evidence with the stakeholder perspectives and rely on intuition and innovation in this process when the research evidence is insufficient for directly facilitating decisions about assessment or intervention for a given direct stakeholder.

These definitions also reveal inadequately represented issues for the needs of the AAC fields. First, the definition from occupational therapy, for example, states that decisions will be derived from EBP for implementing *interventions*. Although there are many decision-making points in AAC interventions, decision making is also necessary during the assessment process. For example, a clinician working with a person whose challenging behavior is possibly communicative will need to make decisions about what assessment methods (direct, indirect) or tools (e.g., the Motivation Assessment Scale such as Durand, 1990) he or she is going to use. In fact, researchers are increasingly recognizing that assessment and intervention in AAC are intertwined as exemplified by concepts such as "dynamic assessments" or "ongoing assessments" (e.g., Calculator & Jorgenson, 1994).

Further, the definition from occupational therapy states that decisions are made about interventions that are deemed effective. In addition to the need for being effective, it may be possible to select some interventions that are also efficient. Efficiency has been defined as a comparison of at least two effective interventions in terms of one or more criteria such as time, cost, or error rate (see Chapter 3). Evidence-based teams, including stakeholders, may need to choose between two interventions that are both effective. In these situations, the efficiency of each intervention may serve as a useful distinguishing characteristic to select one intervention over the other.

2. Proposed Definition

Given these desirable features, the following working definition of EBP in AAC is proposed: Evidence-based practice is defined as the integration of best and current research evidence with clinical/educational expertise and relevant stakeholder perspectives to facilitate decisions for assessment and intervention that are deemed effective and efficient for a given direct stakeholder. Given this definition, it is clear that EBP does not mean giving up clinical reasoning or incorporating stakeholder perspectives (DiCenso, Cullum, & Cilisika, 1998). The three elements influence each other for the benefit of making the best possible decision with a given direct stakeholder. Each of the elements of this definition shall be described as follows:

a. Defining "Integration"

By *integration* we mean the joining or the synthesis of current best research evidence, clinical/educational expertise, and stakeholder perspectives to create a coherent conclusion that informs practice. Integration is said to be accomplished when the process renders the recommendation of a decision in assessment or intervention.

b. Defining "Best and Current Evidence"

Best and current research evidence is defined as current verified and replicated data that also rank as high as possible on the hierarchy of the evidence continuum proposed later. Although some dated evidence may meet the requirements of best evidence, it is desirable to seek out best evidence that is also more current.

c. Defining "Clinical/Educational Expertise"

Clinical expertise is defined as reasoning, intuition, knowledge, and skills related to the following clinical roles, as delineated by the American Speech–Language and Hearing Association (ASHA, 2002):[1] (1) assessing of individuals whose impairments preclude their use of natural speech or writing as a primary means of communication, as well as their communication partners and the various environments in which communication occurs; (2) determining AAC methods, components, and strategies to maximize functional communication by individuals; (3) developing and implementing intervention plans that maximize functional communication between individuals who use AAC and their communication partners; (4) evaluating functional communication outcomes of the intervention plan; (5) evaluating the effectiveness and usefulness of current AAC devices; (6) advocating for increased responsiveness from community, regional, governmental, and educational agencies to the communication and funding needs of individuals who can benefit from AAC; (7) collaborating with individuals who use AAC in the provision of in-service training to medical and allied health professionals, educators, and family members about how AAC can enhance the quality of life of individuals in various settings; and (8) coordinating AAC services.

Educational expertise is defined as reasoning, intuition, knowledge, and skills related to the following educational roles, as delineated by Locke and Mirenda (1992) based on a survey of special education teachers: (1) adapting the curriculum, (2) identifying needed vocabulary, (3) preparing and maintaining of student progress, (4) writing goals and objectives, and, (5) assessing cognitive abilities.

---

[1]We recognize that professionals from disciplines other than speech-language pathology (e.g., occupational therapy, physical therapy, regular education) may have different roles and responsibilities. We have listed the ones for speech-language pathologists and special educators for illustrative purposes and because we are unaware that other such AAC knowledge and skills documents exist for other disciplines.

d. Defining "Relevant Stakeholder Perspectives"

Relevant stakeholder perspectives are defined as the viewpoints, cultural beliefs, preferences, concerns, and expectations relative to aided and unaided approaches, intervention strategies, symbols, and devices of those stakeholders that control the viability of an assessment or intervention either directly or indirectly. As mentioned previously, stakeholders may be grouped into direct stakeholders, indirect stakeholders, immediate community stakeholders, and extended community stakeholders (see also Chapter 10 for stakeholder issues).

The person who is, or will be, using AAC is considered the *direct stakeholder* in many situations because this person is the direct recipient of the assessment or intervention. Exceptions are assessments or interventions targeting facilitator behaviors; here, the facilitator is considered the direct stakeholder. Given that direct stakeholders have to live with whatever the outcomes might be as the *direct* recipients of assessments or interventions, evidence-based practitioners should hold paramount the perspectives of direct stakeholders. In fact, the EBP process must be centered on the direct stakeholder, even when the direct stakeholder wishes to pursue avenues that differ from the best and current research evidence or clinical/educational expertise (Bennett & Bennett, 2000).

Indirect stakeholders are strongly affected by the change in communicative behavior of the direct stakeholder and may thus indirectly influence the feasibility of assessments or interventions. Family members of AAC users who are receiving assessments or intervention often are considered indirect stakeholders, if not already direct stakeholders through participation in a facilitator training program. Services that pride themselves to be family centered, in particular, need to ensure that any evidence is reconciled with the viewpoints of the family. Other indirect stakeholders involved may include caregivers and friends.

Immediate community stakeholders may influence the feasibility of assessments or interventions indirectly through regular professional or social interactions (or lack thereof) with direct and indirect stakeholders. Unlike indirect stakeholders, immediate community stakeholders are not as strongly affected by the results of assessments or the targeted intervention changes. Examples include supervisors of AAC users in supported employment situations who had been targeted for intervention, such as those who teach participants about requesting assistance, prospective regular education teachers, and nondisabled peers of an AAC user whose participatory strategies in group activities were targeted for intervention. The following example illustrates when it may be appropriate to consult immediate community stakeholders in EBP: A learner is about to be taught to place an order in a fast-food restaurant and the practitioner is exploring what AAC system may be most beneficial for this learner. After reviewing the research evidence and assessing the preferences of the learner (i.e., direct stakeholder) and her family (i.e., indirect stakeholder), the practitioner interviews several clerks in local fast-food restaurants to determine what they think might be the most recognizable communication modes.

Extended community stakeholders do not interact with direct or indirect stakeholders on a regular basis and often do not even know them personally. Extended community stakeholders may be drawn from two groups with possibly quite distinct perspectives (Light, personal communication, June 25, 2001): (1) experts in the field of study and (2) laypersons. Experts may not necessarily interact with the targeted participants on a regular basis, but they may have some degree of familiarity with the population from which the participants are drawn or they may be knowledgeable about AAC and its application relative to the intervention. Although the viewpoints of experts can add important perspectives to decision making using EBP, it is the extended community stakeholder group of laypersons that has been heralded as the ultimate judges of communicative competence (Light, 1989). Compared to experts, laypersons generally do not have the same knowledge base of the field or experience in interacting with people with disabilities that may increase their interaction skills or modify their expectations. At the same time, experts may be influenced in their perspectives by the "stake" they hold in a field's success. Some experts may hold higher expectations in terms of communicative form, whereas strangers may not care as much about form for as long as they understand what has been communicated. Thus, there are distinct differences between these two groups of extended community stakeholders to warrant a careful selection process. Next, we will discuss the nature of evidence and offer a framework for evaluating the research evidence in AAC toward EBP.

III. THE NATURE OF EVIDENCE—DEVELOPING A HIERARCHY FOR AAC

Several related fields have developed a hierarchy of evidence that allows for a critical evaluation of the certainty of evidence for a particular intervention and for the sharing of the results with practitioners and stakeholders. In the AAC field, Raghavendra (2000) recently raised an important question, "What should be *our* gold standard [emphasis added]?" To stimulate thinking in the field along these lines, several challenges and issues that may affect the answer to this question were brought up, including the following: the heterogeneity of the population, the complexity of AAC systems and interventions, and the dynamic nature of the communication process. The aim of this section is to engage in a critical evaluation of these existing hierarchies in order to propose a framework that seems to make sense for the AAC field.

A. Hierarchies of Evidence in Related Fields

Lloyd-Smith (1997) proposed a hierarchy of evidence for the field of occupational therapy with meta-analysis of randomized control trials (RCTs) heralded as the gold standard (see Table 12.1). Other fields such as occupational therapy have a used a hierarchy very similar or identical to this one (e.g., Law & Baum, 1998). This hierarchy offers a clear progression from more experimental designs (or synthesis thereof) that permit excellent control over extraneous variables to designs that allow for a lesser degree of control over extraneous variables or no designs at all. Does this progression, however, fit the needs of the AAC field? The next several paragraphs address this question.

B. Recognizing Shortcomings of Existing Hierarchies for AAC

Any hierarchy proposed for the AAC field should take into account the shortcomings of the previous hierarchy as well as the needs of the AAC field. First, the breadth of quasi-experimental group designs will be discussed. Next, the role of single-subject experimental designs will be addressed, followed by the role of syntheses.

C. The Role of RCTs and the Breadth of Quasi-Experimental Group Designs

As pointed out by Raghavendra (2000) and noted by Schlosser and Lee (2000), there appear to be next to no group studies to date involving individuals with disabilities in the AAC field. In the review conducted by Iacono (in press) of the journal *Augmentative and Alternative Communication*, only 13 of the 105 studies were group studies. Among the few group studies, none met the criteria of an RCT. An RCT is "a trial in which subjects are randomly assigned

Table 12.1

Hierarchy of Evidence by Lloyd-Smith (1997)

1a. Meta-analysis of RCTs
1b. One RCT
2a. One well-designed non-RCT
2b. Well-designed quasi-experimental study
3a. Nonexperimental descriptive studies—case studies
3b. Respectable opinion

to two groups: one (the experimental group) receives the intervention that is being tested, and the other (the control group) receives a standard or placebo treatment. The two groups are followed up to see if there are any differences and so establish the effectiveness of the intervention" (Lloyd-Smith, 1997, p. 476). What are some of the reasons for the dearth of RCTs in the AAC field? For one, AAC is a low-incidence field, and it is often difficult to recruit a sufficiently large number of participants. Another reason is that AAC users present as a very heterogeneous group of individuals. It becomes difficult to recruit a group that is homogenous enough to allow the forming of any group, but it is particularly difficult to permit randomizing of participants to conditions. Moreover, even when participants with disabilities are randomly assigned to groups, usually these designs involve a contrast group (receiving somewhat of a "lesser" treatment) rather than a standard or placebo control group. This renders these designs to be more of the multigroup pretest-posttest design type rather than an RCTs. For these combined reasons, the authors have chosen to exclude RCTs from the proposed hierarchy for participants with disabilities (see Table 12.2). Should, however, researchers manage to conduct an RCT with people with disabilities in the future, despite the existing barriers, this evidence would rank at tier 2, right below meta-analyses. Similar concerns have been raised in the field of occupational therapy; due to the individualized nature of treatments and heterogeneity in the client groups, Ottenbacher (1990) and others argued that many questions concerning effectiveness are more suited to quasi-experimental group designs or single-subject experimental designs (Johnston, Ottenbacher, & Reichardt, 1995).

For AAC efficacy research involving nondisabled participants, however, RCTs are indeed feasible and should be considered in the design hierarchy (see Table 12.3). In fact, in order to demonstrate the effectiveness of a particular intervention with nondisabled individuals, it is essential to include a standard or placebo control group.

True experiments, as defined in Chapter 7, require that participants be randomly drawn from the population. Quasi-experiments, on the other hand, do not have this requirement. Unlike true experiments, quasi-experimental designs cannot ensure that the participants are representative of the population at large. There are those researchers who argue that the differences between designs with random selection from a population and those without are negligible for as long as the subjects are randomly allocated to the conditions (Asher, personal communication, December 4, 2001). Therefore, the characteristic of random allocation of participants to conditions should carry considerable weight in any design hierarchy, regardless of whether the design is quasi-experimental in nature or a true experiment (in AAC efficacy research involving participants with disabilities, true experiments are not used). For quasi-experimental designs, however, the same design should rank higher if random allocation of participants to conditions was used compared to a design without random allocation.

Table 12.2

Participants with Disabilities: Proposed Design Hierarchy for Efficacy Research

1. Meta-analysis of (a) single-subject experimental designs (Schlosser & Lee, 2000), (b) quasi-experimental group designs[a]

2a. One well-designed non-RCT	2b. One single-subject experimental design—one intervention	2c. One single-subject experimental design—multiple interventions
i. Multigroup pretest-posttest design without control group (Layton, 1988; Yoder & Layton, 1988)	i. Multiple baseline design (e.g., Reid & Hurlbut, 1977; Sigafoos et al., 1996)	i. Parallel treatments design (e.g., Bennett, Gast, Wolery, & Schuster, 1986; Schlosser et al., 1995)
ii. Basic within-group design, crossover design, complex counterbalanced design	ii. Multiple probe design (e.g., Schlosser et al., 2000)	ii. Adapted alternating treatments design (e.g., Schlosser et al., 1998)
iii. Multigroup time-series designs	iii. ABAB design (e.g., Vaughn & Horner, 1995)	iii. Alternating treatments design (e.g., Remington & Clarke, 1993)
iv. Factorial designs	iv. ABA design (Schweigert & Rowland, 1992)	iv. ABACA/ACAB design (e.g., Koul, Schlosser, Corwin, & Sims, 1997)
v. Latin square designs (Hupp & Mervis, 1981)	v. Nonconcurrent multiple baseline design	v. A-B-BC-B-BC/A-BC-B-BC design (Parsons & LaSorte, 1993)
vi. Posttest-only control group design, multigroup posttest-only design		vi. ABAB design (e.g., Rotholz, Berkowitz, & Burberry, 1989)
vii. Single-group time-series design		
viii. Separate sample pretest-posttest design		

3. Quantitative reviews that are non-meta-analytic (Mirenda, 1997)

4. Narrative reviews (Doherty, 1985; Schlosser & Sigafoos, 2002)

5. Preexperimental group designs (e.g., one-shot case study, one-group pretest-posttest design, and the static group comparison) and single-case studies (e.g., AB designs, case studies) (Blischak, 1995; Dowden, Beukelman, & Lossing, 1986; Glennen & Calculator, 1985)

6. Respectable opinion (Augmentative Communication News, Perspectives, ISAAC Bulletin, opinions of expert presenters, textbook authors)

[a]RCTs are heralded as the most superior type of design among group designs. Group designs in general, however, are rare in the AAC field, especially with participants who have disabilities. In terms of RCTs specifically, the authors are not aware of a single RCT involving people with disabilities. This has at least three explanations. First, AAC is a low-incidence field and it is often difficult to recruit a sufficiently large number of participants. Second, AAC users are a very heterogeneous group of individuals and it becomes difficult to recruit a group that is homogenous enough to allow the forming of any group, but it is particularly difficult to permit randomizing of participants to conditions. Third, even when participants with disabilities are randomly assigned to groups, usually these designs involve a contrast group (receiving somewhat of a lesser treatment) rather than a no-treatment control group. These therefore become more of a multigroup pretest-posttest design type rather than an RCT. For these combined reasons, the authors have chosen to exclude RCTs from this hierarchy. Should, however, researchers manage to conduct an RCT with people with disabilities in the future, despite the existing barriers, this evidence would rank at tier 2, right below meta-analyses.

Table 12.3

Nondisabled Participants: Proposed Design Hierarchy for Efficacy Research

1. Meta-analysis of RCTs
2. Meta-analysis of non-RCTs,
3. One RCT
4. One well-designed non-RCT
    a. Multi-group pretest-posttest design without control group (Mizuko, 1987)
    b. Basic within-group design, crossover design, complex counterbalanced (Levine, Gauger, Bowers, & Khan, 1986)
    c. Multigroup time-series designs (Schlosser & Lloyd, 1993)
    d. Factorial designs (Mirenda & Beukelman, 1987)
    e. Latin square designs (Schlosser, 2002b)
    f. Posttest-only control group design, the multigroup posttest-only design
    g. Nonequivalent control group design
    h. Single-group time series design (Fuller & Lloyd, 1992)
    i. Separate sample pretest-posttest design (see hypothetical example in Chapter 7)
5. Quantitative reviews that are non-meta-analytic
6. Narrative reviews
7. Preexperimental group designs (e.g., one-shot case study, one-group pretest-posttest design, and the static group comparison)
8. Respectable opinion (Augmentative Communication News, Perspectives, ISAAC Bulletin, opinions of expert presenters, textbook authors)

As indicated in Chapter 7, some group designs lend themselves more to a demonstration of experimental control than do other designs, based on design characteristics other than random allocation of conditions. These differences need to be recognized in a proposed hierarchy. The hierarchy from the field of occupational therapy (Table 12.2), for example, does not distinguish various quasi-experimental designs. Instead all quasi-experimental designs rank the same among the other design options. In a field such as AAC whose landscape of group designs is so heavily dominated by quasi-experimental designs, it becomes important to distinguish those designs that more effectively control for threats to internal validity from others that do so less effectively. The proposed hierarchy in Table 12.2 attempts to do just that. Readers may wish to consult Chapter 7 for a rationale as to why some designs are ranked higher than others.

1. The Role of Single-Subject Experimental Designs

In an initial examination, Iacono (2002) categorized the evidence that is available in AAC based on study design or research type. The research was reviewed within the World Health Organization's classification of impairments, activity limitation, and participation (ICIDH-2). As mentioned earlier, out of 105 identified articles, 58 were case studies and 34 were single-subject experimental designs. Given their prominent role in AAC intervention research, it is clear that we must include single-subject experimental designs in any hierarchy proposed for the AAC field. Heterogeneity among subjects does appear to be the rule in the AAC field rather than the exception (Bedrosian, 1995). This makes it difficult for investigators to form homogenous groups. Further, AAC is a low-incidence field. This makes it often impossible to create large-scale group studies. This may, at least in part, not only explain the few group designs involving people with disabilities (e.g., Hodges & Schwethelm, 1984; Porter & Schroeder, 1980; Yoder & Layton, 1988), but also the popularity and role of single-subject experimental designs for evaluating interventions in AAC (e.g., Schlosser, 2001; Schlosser & Braun, 1994; Schlosser & Lee, 2000; see also Chapter 6). These findings and rationales support the need for including single-subject designs within a hierarchy of evidence for research involving participants with disabilities in the AAC field. For AAC research involving nondisabled participants, single-subject experimental designs do not seem to play a role. Therefore, there is no need to include single-subject experimental designs in a design hierarchy involving nondisabled participants.

Single-subject experimental designs are quasi-experimental in nature analogous to quasi-experimental group designs. Single-subject experimental designs may be used to evaluate the efficacy of one particular intervention or to compare the efficacy of at least two interventions. Within each of these groups of single-subject experimental designs, it is noteworthy that not all single-subject experimental designs are equally apt to control for threats to internal validity (see Chapter 6). Any hierarchy among single-subject designs needs to take this into account. For a rationale as to why some designs are ranked higher than others, the reader is referred to Chapter 6. Also, even though they are not listed separately in the hierarchy, some specific designs can be implemented with a differential number of within-subject replications. For example, the multiple-baseline design may be used across as few as two behaviors or as many as five behaviors or more. The design with more within-subject replications ranks higher than the same design with fewer replications because a larger number of replications enhances the internal validity of the evidence. Evidence-based practitioners using this hierarchy should be mindful of these consequential differences.

2. The Role of Syntheses

It has been stated repeatedly in this text that the efficacy of an intervention is best judged based on not only one single-subject experiment or one quasi-experimental group study but rather on a synthesis of several experiments (see Chapter 11). Systematic reviews use rigorous methods to locate, access, and synthesize the results of individual studies (Glanville & Lefebvre, 2000; Jackson, 1980). Given the popularity of single-subject experimental designs, it is therefore not surprising that meta-analysis of single-subject research has gained increasing momentum in intervention research in general (e.g., Scruggs & Mastropieri, 1998) and AAC intervention research in particular (Millar, Light, & Schlosser, 2000; Schlosser & Lee, 2000). Thus, it is important to include meta-analysis of single-subject experimental research as well as meta-analysis of quasi-experimental designs in any design hierarchy of evidence for AAC. Meta-analysis is an objective and highly desirable method for synthesizing efficacy research. In addition to meeting all the necessary criteria for a systematic review, meta-analysis also minimizes type II errors stemming from original experiments with small n and lack of precise measures (e.g., Lauer & Asher, 1988). Nonetheless, meta-analysis constitutes only one synthesis method. As discussed in Chapter 11, quantitative reviews and narrative reviews represent other synthesis methods and need to be included in any hierarchy proposed for the AAC field. In comparison to meta-analyses, quantitative reviews tend to meet fewer of the seven criteria necessary for a review to be considered systematic. In turn, narrative reviews tend to meet fewer of the criteria than quantitative reviews (see Chapter 11).

D. A PROPOSED HIERARCHY FOR THE AAC FIELD

Based on the shortcomings of existing hierarchies as well as the needs of the AAC field, two hierarchies are proposed for AAC, one for efficacy research involving participants with disabilities (see Table 12.2) and another for research involving nondisabled participants (see Table 12.3). The hierarchy, recognized in Table 12.2., recognizes the important role of single-subject experimental designs and meta-analysis of single-subject experimental studies, along with the important function of meta-analyses of quasi-experimental designs, given the prevalence of quasi-experimental designs in AAC. Further, the hierarchy aims to distinguish among quasi-experimental designs and among single-subject experimental designs in terms of their capacity for controlling threats to internal validity. Finally, the proposed hierarchy creates space for syntheses methods other than meta-analyses (e.g., quantitative reviews and narrative reviews). The hierarchy proposed for efficacy research involving nondisabled participants accommodates both RCTs and non-RCTs and distinguishes the ability of various quasi-experimental group designs to rule out threats to internal validity. Moreover, the hierarchy separates the contributions of various synthesis methodologies.

IV. LIMITATIONS OF HIERARCHIES BASED ON DESIGN ONLY: A PROPOSED FRAMEWORK

The hierarchy presented by Lloyd-Smith (1997) and applied in fields such as occupational therapy (Law & Baum, 1998; Tickle-Degnen, 1998) and the hierarchies proposed for the AAC field are primarily sequenced in terms of how well certain designs lend themselves to control threats to internal validity. Although there is no question that the type of design used does impact the conclusions that are permitted (Hegde, 1994), it is also clear that other factors contribute to the certainty of research evidence. For example, just because a certain design was used, does not necessarily mean that the study was well conducted or that the results generalize to the clinical situation in which the evidence-based practitioner finds herself. A framework is proposed for evaluating the evidence in terms of its internal validity and external validity. Table 12.4 provides a suggested sequence of questions for several dimensions of EBP in AAC along with suggested actions. Each of the proposed dimensions are discussed in this section.

A. Treatment Integrity as a Contributor to Internal Validity

There are issues, other than design, that speak to the internal validity of intervention research including treatment integrity and interobserver agreement. A study may have employed a well-designed quasi-experimental design and thus rank highly on the Lloyd-Smith (1997) hierarchy or the proposed hierarchy for the AAC field. Yet it turns out that the report under evaluation does not state the degree to which the independent variable was applied as intended. This lack of treatment integrity raises serious issues as to the source of the yielded results. That is, the internal validity of this experiment would have to be questioned. Treatment integrity has the potential to enhance, diminish, or even destroy the certainty of evidence (for a detailed discussion, please consult Chapter 9 and Schlosser, 2002a). Thus, published treatment studies need to be evaluated in terms of treatment integrity if they are to inform practice in a meaningful manner. An evaluation of the evidence based on design issues alone seems inaccurate and perhaps trivializes the complexity of solid intervention research. This may result in erroneous conclusions concerning the certainty of the evidence before us. Likewise, a lack of sufficient interobserver agreement for the dependent measures raises questions of internal validity as well.

B. Recognizing External Validity Issues in EBP

The degree to which studies bear external validity seems to have been used as a secondary criterion for sequencing the designs in the hierarchy used in the field of occupational therapy as well as that proposed here for AAC. A meta-analysis of RCTs, for example, may bear a greater degree of external validity than one RCT and therefore is considered better evidence. Similarly, single-

Table 12.4

Proposed Critical Appraisal Dimensions for Establishing the Validity and Transportability of a Study's Results

Dimensions and Actions		Questions about research evidence	Evaluating the Certainty of the Evidence
Internal Validity: Select studies with designs that maximize control of extraneous variables	Design	To what degree does the design rule out threats to internal validity?	*INCONCLUSIVE:* Establishes that certain outcomes are *not* plausible. The study's flaws preclude any conclusions that symbol acquisition is the result of the IV: • *Fatal* flaws in the design (irrespective of IA—DV *or* IV). *SUGGESTIVE:* Certain requesting outcomes are plausible, and are within the realm of possibility: • *Minor flaws in design, or adequate (or better) design with inadequate* IA (DV *or* IV). *PREPONDERANT:* Certain requesting outcomes are not only possible, but also they are more likely to have occurred than they have not: • *Minor flaws in design with adequate (or better)* IA (DV *and* IV); or • *Strong* design with one *questionable* IA indicator (and the other *adequate* [or better]) *CONCLUSIVE:* Certain requesting outcomes are undoubtedly the result of the IV: • *Strong* design along with *adequate (or better)* IA (DV *and* IV).
	Treatment integrity	To what degree have the procedures been followed as intended? (IA–IV)	
	Interobserver agreement	To what extent are the dependent measures reliable? (IA–DV)	
Select treatments whose outcomes, methods, and goals have been found socially significant	Social Validity —Outcomes	To what extent are the outcomes socially significant as determined by relevant stakeholders and/or social comparison samples?	*INCONCLUSIVE:* Establishes that certain results are *not* plausible. The study's flaws preclude any conclusions that the results are due to the intervention: • Exhibits fatal flaws in social validation design such as use of a pretest measure only (posttest measure only) (irrespective of interobserver agreement and instruments). *SUGGESTIVE:* Certain results are plausible, and are within the realm of possibility: i. *Minor design flaws* (e.g., pre- *and* post design that is not mapped onto an appropriate intervention design), with inadequate instruments or interobserver agreement. *PREPONDERANT:* Certain social validation results are not only possible, but also they are more likely to have occurred than they have not:
	Social Validity —Methods	To what extent are the methods acceptable as determined by relevant stakeholders and/or social comparison samples?	
	Social Validity —Goals	To what extent are the goals social significant as determined by	

		relevant stakeholders and/or social comparison samples?	• *Minor design flaws* such as a pre- *and* post design (i.e., not mapped onto an appropriate intervention design), adequate instruments & interobserver agreement; or • *Strong design* with *questionable* interobserver agreement or instruments CONCLUSIVE: Certain results are unequivocally the result of the intervention: • *Strong design* (i.e., mapped onto an appropriate intervention design); • *Adequate* (or better) instruments (e.g., survey constructed using principles of questionnaire construction), and adequate (or better) interobserver agreement.
External Validity	Design: Select meta-analysis over single studies	Is there a meta-analysis available on the clinical problem?	A synthesis of several studies using the same or similar type of intervention enhances the external validity of the outcomes of only one study. The larger the number of studies and the larger the effect size, the more certain the evidence.
	Ideal-typical generality: Select studies with ecologically valid conditions	How close are the conditions under which the experiment was conducted to the conditions to which you seek to apply the findings?	Evaluate the closeness of the study conditions to those of your practical situation in terms of setting, selection of subjects, level of experimenter training, delivery of treatments (i.e., high treatment integrity), structure of conditions for delivering treatment, measures or indices of change, stakeholders, comparison samples, and so forth.
	Subject generality: Select replicated treatments	Have the results been replicated across a sufficient n of the same type of participants?	SUGGESTIVE: Less than 3 participants and consistent findings. PREPONDERANT: Between 3 and 6 participants and consistent findings. CONCLUSIVE: More than 6 participants and consistent findings
Select socially valid outcomes, methods, and goals that will translate to practice	Social Validity —Outcomes	To what degree would the stakeholders' perceived effectiveness translate to the practical situation?	Does the treatments' goals, methods, and outcomes fit in with the direct stakeholder's values and preferences? In addressing the ideal-typical generality, the evidence-based practitioner has determined that the stakeholders in the study are of the same type as those relevant to his/her situation?
	Social Validity —Methods	To what degree would the stakeholders' acceptability of methods translate to the practical situation?	
	Social Validity —Goals	To what degree would the stakeholders' acceptability of goals translate to the practical situation?	

subject experiments replicated across a larger number of participants bear more external validity than studies replicated with fewer participants, provided that the results were consistent. The American Psychological Association took these factors into account when it established evidence categories for treatments on specific childhood syndromes (Chambless, *et al.*, 1996; Lonigan, Elbert, & Johnson, 1998). To be considered a "well-established" treatment, "two or more studies must show that it is superior to medication, placebo, or an alternative treatment or that it is equivalent to an already established treatment, or nine single-subject case studies must be conducted to establish its equivalence or superiority" (Hoagwood, Burns, Kiser, Ringeisen, & Schoenwald, 2001, p. 1180). For a treatment to be classified as "probably efficacious," "two or more studies must show it to be superior to a wait-list control condition or one experiment must meet the criteria for a well-established treatment, or three single-case studies must be conducted" (p. 1180). For AAC, such criteria had not been established. Therefore, the following criteria are proposed. For an AAC intervention to be considered well-established, two or more quasi-experimental designs must show that it is superior to a contrast group or an alternative treatment or that it is equivalent to an already established treatment, or well-designed single-subject experimental designs replicated across at least six participants must show its superiority relative to a baseline condition or alternative treatment.

For an AAC intervention to be considered probably efficacious, one quasi-experimental design must show that it is superior to a contrast group, wait-list control condition, or an alternative treatment or well-designed single-subject experimental design replicated between three and six participants must show its superiority relative to a baseline condition or alternative treatment. For treatments to be considered either well-established or probably efficacious, it is important that the studies report acceptable levels of treatment integrity (see Chapter 9) and that relevant stakeholders have found the treatment to be efficacious as well (see Chapter 10).

Some of the issues pertaining to external validity, which also should be taken into account when implementing EBP, shall be discussed in more detail as follows, including the generality of (1) conditions, (2) subjects, (3) communication partners, (4) settings, (5) treatment agents, and (6) materials.

1. The Generality of Conditions

The conditions of intervention research may vary on a continuum ranging from optimal (ideal) to typical (average) to less than typical (below average) (Chapters 2 and 3). According to Robey and Schulz's (1998) model, intervention research should follow a natural progression beginning with evaluation under optimal conditions and leading to a subsequent evaluation under typical conditions. An intervention that has undergone this scrutiny may bear considerable generality to the conditions under which the practitioner seeks to implement a treatment. On the other hand, an intervention that has been found effective under optimal conditions may not generalize to the conditions of daily practice. In fact, Hoagwood *et al.* (2001) questioned the underlying presupposition of EBP that the development of the evidence-base has taken into account the fit between the treatment and the context of delivery in daily practice. Arguably, this fit is rarely taken into account.

That is why it is important for evidence-based practitioners to evaluate the exact fit between the research conditions and the conditions of their practical situation. The closer the fit between the study conditions and the conditions for which the practitioner is evaluating evidence, the more informative the research evidence for decision making. The concept of ecological validity might aid the practitioner in making these generality assessments. As a concept, ecological validity is different from, but related to, social validity (social validity is discussed later in this chapter). The word "conditions" serves as an umbrella term for components such as subjects, communication partners, treatment agents, and materials that do make up the conditions and render them optimal or typical. Each of these components is addressed separately later. Ecological validity is primarily concerned with the validity of these components as measured by what would be appropriate for the environment where the skill is expected to be performed and the degree to which this has been applied in the experimental situation (see Chapter 3).

2. The Generality of Subjects

The conditions of the research evidence and the conditions in practice may differ, for example, in terms of the *subjects* selected. Because practitioners do not have the luxury to work only with direct stakeholders of the exact same type (if there is such a phenomenon) as the participants in published studies, they will be interested in knowing whether the findings generalize to different types of participants. In other words, will the results obtained in research work for my client even if this client might differ from the study participants in a number of characteristics? Under ideal conditions, subjects are often selected to maximize the effectiveness of an intervention. In our study on the effects of speech output on spelling, for instance, we selected a participant without prior exposure to speech output (Schlosser, Blischak, Belfiore, Bartley, & Barnett, 1998). Thus, the effects of speech output may have been exacerbated due to the possibility of a "novelty" effect working by itself or alongside the "true" effect of speech output. Making the device available during baseline (and not just intervention) has helped to minimize this possible novelty effect, but it cannot be ruled out entirely (for further discussions of novelty effects in AAC, see Chapter 3). In practice though, a clinician may work with a child who has had some exposure to speech output prior to the assessment. Thus, the clinician will need to make an informed judgment call to determine the extent to which this prior experience may or may not modify the effects of speech output for this client. Issues such as these need to be considered when evaluating the generality of subjects in research to the direct stakeholders in practice.

3. The Generality of Communication Partners

Evidence-based practitioners should evaluate what possibly should (or could) be expected of communication partners in a given clinical situation and to what degree this is consistent with the communication partners in published experiments. To be ecologically valid, communication partners in experimental situations should be expected to do what is consistent with what typical listeners in everyday interactions would be inclined to do. Sigafoos, Laurie, and Pennell (1996) reduced the amount of time given for a child to make a request from 30 seconds to 10 seconds to increase the ecological validity of the request. These authors argued that it seemed inappropriate to expect listeners to wait a full 30 seconds for a person to make a request in response to the question "Let me know if you want something." Put another way, typical communication partners would not wait that long. Another generality question pertains to that of settings.

4. The Generality of Settings

Intervention research under optimal conditions is often conducted in *settings* that are highly conducive to the study of a particular treatment. To maximize the effects of speech output on graphic symbol learning of young adults with intellectual disabilities (Schlosser, Belfiore, Nigam, Blischak, & Hetzroni, 1995), for example, the experiment could have been conducted in a soundproof room to eliminate extraneous noise. This would have allowed us to study the role of speech output under optimal conditions. These optimal conditions, however, are not consistent with the settings in which young adults with developmental disabilities may use speech-generating devices. Therefore, we opted to implement the experiment in a small room adjacent to the participants' workroom. This semi-quiet area allowed for a setting that is more closely related to the participants' daily work environment while maintaining some control for visual and auditory distractions. Evidence-based practitioners need to take into account how close the fit is between the setting in the research study and the setting in which clients are being served.

5. The Generality of the Treatment Agent

Closely related to the issue of setting is the level of *training of the interventionists*. Intervention research under optimal conditions generally relies on optimally trained clinicians as experimenters such as master clinicians in university-based lab schools. Optimally selected and trained clinicians are likely to implement treatment with a high degree of treatment integrity (noted earlier). Clearly, trained research assistants may be excellent for yielding superior treatment integrity, but they are not likely to be ecologically valid treatment agents. In fact, intervention research under more typical conditions may need to rely on clinicians whose training has been more on the average side. Here, the work by Light and Binger (1998) is exemplary in that typical classroom teachers rather than research assistants were trained to implement strategies aimed at improving the communicative competence of students. Practitioners need to determine whether the treatment agents in a published experiment, for example, are the kind of treatment agents encountered by a specific client. In other words, would the kind of person who implemented the training in the study also apply the training in typical daily practice? If the evidence-based practitioner is going to implement an intervention herself, she will need to engage in a sort of self-evaluation to determine how her level of training corresponds to that of the clinician in the research study. Another generality issue relates to the materials used in research.

6. The Generality of Materials

The *materials* used in research may also bear on the generality of the study to conditions of daily practice. In our study on the effects of speech output on graphic symbol learning, we selected Lexigrams as the symbols because they are opaque and were likely to maximize the benefit of speech output (Schlosser *et al.*, 1995). This decision was based on the hypothesis that opaque symbols do not allow learners to rely on iconicity to help them build a relation between symbol and referent and therefore learners may use the auditory stimuli to a greater extent than they would with more iconic symbols. Although this may be a plausible hypothesis, it may not have been the most ecologically valid symbol choice. In fact, practitioners may be more interested in the benefits of speech output for introducing iconic graphic symbols such as Picture Communication Symbols.

To present another example, this author is currently involved in planning research into the effects of digitized speech output versus no speech output on requesting in beginning communicators. Ideally, digitized messages are to be recorded in a quiet area (ideally, one should use a remote microphone that plugs into the speech-generating device to decrease recording of machine noise) and with adequate distance in accordance with manufacturer suggestions (Blischak & Schlosser, 2002). Yet in thinking about how teachers and other direct service providers may actually program these devices, it is likely that they will not exactly observe adequate distance and that the recordings will contain some level of background noise. These conditions would be considered ecologically valid because they may represent typical practice. Researchers need to decide whether they wish to study digitized speech output under ecologically valid conditions or optimal conditions. There is no correct answer to this dilemma; the researcher needs to balance the independent variable on the continuum between optimal and typical conditions. The evidence-based practitioner, on the other hand, needs to determine which way the researcher decided to lean. This has ramifications whether the materials used in the experiment were ecologically valid relative to the clinical situation at hand. In summary, practitioners need to determine how close the fit is between the materials in the study and the materials involved in their daily practice.

C. Acknowledging the Role of Social Validity in EBP

Definitions of EBP in related fields along with the definition proposed for AAC emphasize the importance of reconciling or integrating research evidence with stakeholder perspectives. Stakeholder perspectives are not only important, however, in implementing EBP with actual clients, but also when evaluating the certainty of the research evidence. That is, practitioners need to know whether published interventions also bear social validity. Social validity is evaluated through social validation—the process of assessing the social significance of goals, methods, and outcomes (Kazdin, 1977). The social significance of the goals, methods, and outcomes may be assessed by soliciting the opinions of persons who have a special position due to their expertise or their relationship to the client (Wolf, 1978). The individuals who hold a stake in the success of an intervention should engage in this process, the results of which constitute measures of social validity: "If we aspire to social importance, then we must develop systems that allow our consumers to provide feedback about how our applications relate to their values" (Wolf, 1978, p. 475). Although interventions may be supported through empirical objective data with a high degree of internal validity,[2] it is the relevant stakeholders who will make the final decisions as the whether a particular intervention was indeed useful. Thus, it becomes important for practitioners

---

[2]It is important to realize that social validation becomes relevant only to evidence-based practitioners when the intervention was objectively effective in the first place.

to know whether relevant stakeholders have found the published intervention outcomes, methods, and goals to be socially significant. Schlosser (1999b) offered suggestions as to what stakeholders may be considered relevant for a particular intervention. Let us assume that an AAC intervention's efficacy is indeed supported by objective data with a high degree of internal validity. What differential recommendations might be in store for a practitioner depending on the nature of the social validation results?

1. If the Intervention Is Found Objectively Effective

Practitioners strive to consider effective treatments (for a clinical situation) with favorable subjective evaluation *outcomes* that have been obtained with a high degree of internal validity and also bear external validity. The social validation of outcomes in original studies may be implemented pretreatment, posttreatment, or both. Pretreatment social validation provides information concerning desired outcomes. Posttreatment evaluation provides information as to whether there are differences in the outcomes yielded in comparison to the situation prior to treatment. Pretreatment evaluation of outcomes alone offers little information to the practitioner. Posttreatment evaluation, on the other hand, has the potential to offer valuable insights if done with appropriate steps to minimize threats to internal validity. If stakeholders were asked to compare posttreatment performance to pretreatment performance, for example, the internal validity rests on the assumption that the respondents did indeed remember the pretreatment performance accurately. This may be a tedious assumption. It would be more sound to ask the stakeholder to rate the current performance and then have the researchers compare these ratings with the same stakeholders' pretreatment rating. An even more elegant solution is to present the stakeholders with a participant's record of pretreatment and posttreatment performance via videotapes, for example, without disclosing the status of particular segments (i.e., baseline or intervention) (e.g., Light, Dattilo, English, Gutierrez, & Hartz, 1992). Even though this has to occur posttreatment (only after treatment can we provide posttreatment segments of performance), it is in essence a pre- and posttreatment assessment of social validation. In summary, it is prudent that the social validity of outcomes can be unequivocally attributed to the intervention rather than to extraneous variables. Outcomes that are found favorable in the preceding terms are strengthened even further when the methods and goals have been found socially acceptable as well. Such data, from published studies offer the practitioner a context in which these favorable outcomes and social validation data have been obtained.

Practitioners strive to consider treatment *methods* for a clinical situation that have been found acceptable in addition to yielding socially significant outcomes. If the social validation of outcomes was not assessed but the treatment was objectively effective, the social validity of methods would still be taken into account. Methods may have been evaluated pretreatment, posttreatment, or both. Pretreatment evaluation of an impending treatment method may provide some helpful information about preconceived expectations of stakeholders. It is unknown, however, whether the experience of treatment implementation could have altered the stakeholders' perspectives. If a treatment method was accepted prior to treatment, then the practitioner might consider it tentatively positive with the appropriate amount of skepticism. When pretreatment evaluations yield negative perspectives, the practitioner should examine whether this resulted in revisions to the methods followed by another pretreatment evaluation, eventually resulting in positive perspectives.

A posttreatment evaluation of methods cannot unequivocally demonstrate the acceptance of the methods either. Confounding variables such as bias and reactivity effects on the measure may have accounted for the stakeholders' rating, rather than the treatment itself. In the absence of a pretest of stakeholder acceptability of an impending treatment, it may be impossible to determine if a positive evaluation after completion of treatment represents a preformed opinion that was altered by exposure to the treatment or a favorable change in opinion engendered by the treatment. Preferably, the practitioner would want to have bias and other threats to internal validity ruled out in order to attribute the social validity of the methods to the treatment. Thus, only a comparison of pretreatment measures with posttreatment measures may allow changes in stakeholder acceptance to be attributed to the relevant treatment procedures.

Practitioners may consider adopting the *goals* (for intervention development in a clinical situation) that have been found acceptable to relevant stakeholders. Goals that were found acceptable and, in addition, were targeted with socially significant methods yielding socially significant outcomes would be preferred. Goals may be evaluated pretreatment, posttreatment, or both. Evaluating goals during pretreatment may provide some helpful information about preconceived expectations of stakeholders. Specifically, these expectations existed prior to knowing whether the goals were actually attained and prior to having had any experience with the methods to be used to achieve these goals. In other words, it is unknown whether the experience of the treatment or the yielding of certain outcomes could have altered the stakeholders' perspective on the importance of goals. Because of these limitations, socially accepted goals based on a pretreatment evaluation might be considered tentatively positive but with a healthy amount of skepticism. When pretreatment evaluations of goals yield negative stakeholder perspectives, practitioners should examine whether this information was used for revising the goals prior to treatment implementation followed by another pretreatment evaluation until the perspectives were eventually positive.

A posttreatment evaluation of goals cannot unequivocally demonstrate the acceptance of the goals either. Confounding variables such as bias and reactivity effects on the measure may have accounted for the stakeholders' rating instead of the treatment. In the absence of a pretest of stakeholder acceptability of the goals, it is difficult to determine if a positive evaluation represented a preformed opinion that was altered by exposure to the treatment or a favorable change in opinion engendered by the treatment. Thus, only a comparison of pretreatment measures with posttreatment measures may allow changes in stakeholder acceptance of goals to be attributed to the relevant treatment or outcomes.

Once the practitioner has determined that the outcomes, methods, or goals were socially validated in a sound manner and with favorable results, the practitioner is ready to ask whether the social validity bears generality to the clinical situation. For example, the stakeholders surveyed in the research may or may not closely match those who are relevant stakeholders for an intervention under a given practical situation. Thus, the practitioner may need to evaluate whether the findings bear generality beyond the stakeholders of the research. An intervention study may have solicited the input from parents of a young AAC user to determine their perceptions of the outcomes of an intervention targeting beginning communicators. In the educational situation presented to the practitioner, however, the clinician may be more interested in the perceptions of the child's teacher, since the intervention would be implemented primarily in the classroom. A favorable generality evaluation may cause the practitioner to seriously consider a particular intervention for a given clinical situation. Although it increases the likelihood that the given stakeholders in a particular situation may think of an intervention similarly as those in the research study, this generality evaluation cannot and should not replace the soliciting of the perspectives of relevant stakeholders in the practical situation at hand (see Chapter 10). Thus far, the discussion concerning the role of social validity in EBP has been based on interventions that were found objectively effective. What is the role of social validity, if any, when an intervention was ineffective?

2. If the Treatment Is Found Objectively Ineffective

Let us assume a scenario where the social validation of outcomes is positive contrary to the objective data. Researchers would need to explore the testing of possible hypotheses for this unexpected finding in future research. Using EBP, practitioners would not further consider this intervention until such explanatory data become available. On the other hand, one could argue that perception is everything, so why not adopt an intervention that is believed to work? To do so, however, may have dangerous ramifications. Facilitated communication, for example, was at one point attributed a great deal of "social validity" from various stakeholder types including parents and some researchers. This social validity persisted and perpetuated the continued use of facilitated communication without sufficient objective data to back up the authorship of messages by the individuals using the devices. Such a treatment would not be adopted by an evidence-based practitioner regardless of its perceived social validity. In other words, although perception is clearly important, it is not everything in EBP.

If a treatment is found ineffective in objective terms, the social validity of the methods would not be a likely consideration for the practitioner—perhaps the researcher may find directions for researching plausible explanations for the lack of effectiveness. How would the social validity of goals inform EBP when faced with an ineffective treatment? To assume that failed attainment of goals (i.e., outcomes that are objectively poor or socially invalid) renders the evaluation of goal validation irrelevant for the practitioner is tedious at best. After all, it could be that the treatment was not appropriate for achieving the goals, which were considered socially significant. Thus, under these circumstances the practitioner might still decide to adopt the goals, not the intervention.

In summary, the social validity of outcomes, methods, and goals plays an important role in evaluating the research evidence to inform EBP. The exact role may differ depending on the effectiveness of the intervention studied. Both internal validity and external validity consideration are of relevance when evaluating the social validity of intervention research to inform EBP. In addition to acknowledging the role of social validity in EBP, ecological validity may serve another important function. Ecological validity considerations have been discussed as part of evaluating the external validity of the findings from research studies.

V. THE PROCESS OF EBP IN AAC

As Tickle-Degnen (2000) has stated, "EBP provides tools for (a) organizing evidence around central clinical tasks such as assessment and intervention planning, (b) evaluating the evidence for how current and valid it is, and (c) using the best evidence to accomplish the clinical tasks in such a manner as to achieve optimal outcomes" (p. 538). To realize these tools, there is a process involved in assisting practitioners engaged in EBP, including the following steps (Sackett et al., 1997): (1) asking an answerable question, (2a) selecting evidence sources, (2b) executing the search strategy, (2c) examining the evidence, and (3) applying the evidence. These basic steps are undisputed, even though several variations have been proposed for other health care fields. In occupational therapy, for example, Tickle-Degnen (2000) highlighted the communication with clients and colleagues about the evidence as evaluation and intervention decisions are being made as part of the phase "application of the evidence." In addition, she included a final step to evaluate and revise the EBP recommendations.

Both of these additions to the original steps described by Sackett et al. (1997) are consistent with current practices in AAC. Therefore, these steps were included here either as part of the existing steps (i.e., communicating with stakeholders) or as a separate step (i.e., evaluating the evidence application). Additionally, a step was added to describe the need for disseminating the findings of EBP. These additions/modifications resulted in the following steps for AAC: (1) asking an answerable question, (2) selecting evidence sources, (3) executing the search strategy, (4) examining the evidence, (5) applying the evidence, (6) evaluating the application of the evidence, and (7) disseminating the findings. This section describes each of the steps in general terms as a way of introduction.

A. Asking a Well-Built Question

The question to be asked needs to be well built and answerable through a systematic search of the relevant evidence. This step is extremely important to the process, because the nature of the question will determine the direction of the other steps involved. In AAC, the questions are likely to be drawn from the roles pertaining to the "knowledge and skills" described earlier.

Such questions contain at least the following essential components: they (1) describe the direct stakeholder and her or his capabilities relevant to the clinical problem, (2) explain the direct stakeholders' current (and possibly future) environment and relevant other stakeholders, (3) make explicit the clinical/educational problem to be solved (this may or may not include a comparison), and (4) specify the expected clinical/educational outcomes. It is important that relevant stakeholder perspectives are solicited in formulating a question. This is analogous to the social validation of goals via stakeholder input (see Schlosser, 1999b and Chapter 10). Stakeholder perspectives are particularly crucial for making the clinical/educational problem explicit as seen by the stakeholders. So-called "foreground" questions ask for specific knowledge and skills about managing direct stakeholders or relevant other stakeholders (Sackett *et al.*, 1997). Prior to asking this question it may sometimes be appropriate to ask "background" questions—they demand general knowledge about direct stakeholders as a group (see Chapter 17 for an example).

B. Selecting Evidence Sources

Naturally, evidence sources are first sought for the background question; a foreground question becomes relevant only if the answer to the background question is affirmative or at least hopeful.

1. The Role of Textbooks

As a first source, one may find it useful to consult the subject index of one of the textbooks in the field (e.g., Beukelman & Mirenda, 1998; Glennen

& DeCoste, 1998; Lloyd, Fuller, & Arvidson, 1997). Textbooks, however, are typically outdated by the time they are published (Sackett *et al.*, 1997), and the most recent ones available in AAC are dated 1998. This means that the most recent studies included are from 1997, but most likely are older than that. In addition, it is unclear whether these textbooks have engaged in an exhaustive search of the relevant literature.

To illustrate this concern, the respective reference lists of three standard textbooks in AAC were searched for the studies included in a recent meta-analysis of the effectiveness of AAC interventions (Schlosser & Lee, 2000). Because the studies included ranged in publication year from 1976 to 1995, there is the expectation that all of the references of the studies included in Schlosser and Lee (2000) should be included in the textbooks given that the meta-analysis is focused on AAC intervention studies.

Table 12.5 clearly demonstrates that this is not so, regardless of the particular textbook consulted. Thus, when it comes to their utility as a source of evidence, textbooks are not exhaustive and tend to suffer from subjective inclusion of literature. This is by no means a criticism of AAC textbooks in general (as we have been consistently relying on them for other purposes), but rather a pointed statement that they do have limitations as a tool for EBP. Sackett *et al.* (1997) went so far as to say "burn your (traditional) textbooks" (p. 30) and called for three criteria for a textbook to survive in the modern era: (1) it should be frequently revised (at least once a year), (2) it should be heavily referenced, and (3) the evidence in support of a statement should be selected according to explicit principles of evidence. Although we would not advocate burning our existing textbooks, we do agree with the importance of his suggested three criteria for improving the textbooks if they are to be useful for EBP. Therefore, practitioners in AAC still need to engage in their own systematic search. The existing AAC texts further have a tendency to accept the findings of research at face value in that they agree with what the authors of original research say. Thus, no explicit principles of evidence evaluation are typically applied.

2. The Role of Database Searches

A database search may allow the practitioner to gather more recent evidence in a more systematic manner. MEDLINE®, for example, delivers numerous studies on AAC by using the descriptor "augmentative communication." It should be noted, however, that MEDLINE does not index articles published in *Augmentative and Alternative Communication* and may therefore underrepresent what is actually available. Other databases with AAC content are CINHAL (Cumulative Index of Nursing and Allied Health), PsycINFO®, and ERIC (Educational Resources Information Center). Instead of consulting each of these databases separately, practitioners or researchers could access the OVID database

Table 12.5

Studies	B & M (1998)	G & D (1998)	L et al. (1998)
Acker & Grant (1995)			
Alberto, Briggs, Sharpton, & Goldstein (1981)			
Alwell, Hunt, Goetz, & Sailor (1989)	✓		
Angelo & Goldstein (1990)			
Barrera, Lobato-Barrera, & Sulzer-Azeroff (1980)	✓		
Buzolich, King, & Baroody (1991)	✓		✓
Carr & Kologinsky (1983)	✓		✓
Carr, Binkoff, Kologinsky, & Eddy (1978)	✓		
Conaghan, Singh, Moe, Landrum, & Ellis (1992)			
Culatta & Blackstone (1980)			
Dalrymple & Feldman (1992)			
Dattilo & Camrata (1991)	✓		
Duker & Moonen (1986)			
Duker & Michielsen (1983)			
Duker & Morsink (1984)			
Francis & Williams (1983)			
Gobbi, Cipani, Hudson, & Lapenta-Neudeck (1986)			
Goodman & Remington (1993)	✓	✓	
Hamilton & Snell (1993)	✓		✓
Heller, Ware, Allgood, & Castelle (1994)	✓		
Hunt, Alwell, & Goetz (1991a)	✓		
Hunt, Alwell, & Goetz (1991b)	✓		✓
Hunt, Alwell, Goetz, & Sailor (1990)			✓
Hurlbut, Iwata, & Green (1982)	✓	✓	✓
Iacono, Mirenda, & Beukelman (1993)	✓	✓	✓
Kaiser, Ostrosky, & Alpert (1993)	✓		
Keogh, Whitman, Beeman, Halligan, & Strazynski (1987)			
Kotkin, Simpson, & Desanto (1978)			
Kratzer, Spooner, Test, & Koorland (1993)			
Light, Dattilo, English, Gutierrez, & Hartz (1992)	✓	✓	
Locke & Mirenda (1988)	✓		✓
Mirenda & Santogrossi (1985)	✓		✓
O'Keefe & Dattilo (1992)	✓		✓
Oliver & Halle (1982)	✓	✓	
Reichle & Brown (1986)	✓		✓
Reichle & Ward (1985)	✓		
Reichle, Barrett, Tetlie, & McQuarter (1987)			
Reichle, Rogers, & Barrett (1984)	✓		
Reid & Hurlbut (1977)			
Remington & Clarke (1983)			
Rothholz, Berkowitz, & Burberry (1989)	✓		✓
Schepis & Reid (1995)			✓
Schuebel & Lalli (1992)			
Sigafoos & Reichle (1992)	✓		
Sommer, Whitman, & Keogh (1988)			
Soto, Belfiore, Schlosser, & Haynes (1993)			✓
Spiegel (1983)			
Sternberg, McNerney, & Pegnatore (1987)			
Sternberg, Pegnatore, & Hill (1983)			
Turnell & Carter (1994)	✓		
Total Yield:	25	5	14

(www.ovid.org), which allows access to each of these and many other databases. OVID also offers the evidence-based medicine reviews (EBMR) database to meet the unique needs of the practicing clinician. EBMR builds and aggregates information resources that enable doctors, nurses, and other allied health professionals to get bottom-line summary information on clinical topics to aid decision making at the point of care. In addition to the Cochrane Controlled Trials Register (CCTR), EBMR combines three other leading evidence-based medicine sources: (a) the Cochrane Database of Systematic Reviews, produced by the Cochrane Collaboration; (b) the ACP Journal Club, produced by the ACP; and (c) the Database of Reviews of Effectiveness (DARE), produced by the National Health Services' Centre for Reviews and Dissemination (NHS CRD) at the University of York in the United Kingdom. To date, these services are of limited value to AAC practitioners, however, because AAC is not yet represented as an area of clinical practice. Efforts are currently under way to develop a Center for Evidence-Based Practice in AAC (Schlosser, 2002c). This would allow practitioners access to similarly useful information when engaging in EBP in the field of AAC.

3. The Role of Hand Searches

One may also handsearch the annual author or key word index of *Augmentative and Alternative Communication* to retrieve recent studies on a given topic. Alternatively, one may search the journal's content on CD-ROM available from the International Society of Augmentative and Alternative Communication (ISAAC). This avenue permits the search for key words or phrases not only in the title or abstract, but also the body of the text of articles. Handsearches of other journals may be relevant as well, depending on the topic of interest. A practitioner interested in early intervention, for example, may do a handsearch of specific journals such as *Topics in Early Childhood Special Education* or the *Journal of Early Intervention.*

Sometimes we have found it also fruitful to consult the proceedings (if available) or abstracts of recent conferences such as the ISAAC Biennial Conference, the Annual Convention of the American Speech-Language and Hearing Association, or the European Conference on the Advancement of Rehabilitation Technology. This method permits one to gather information that has not been published yet but might be published in the near future.

C. Executing the Search Strategy

Once the sources to be targeted have been identified, a search strategy needs to be formulated. Essentially this step is asking the practitioner to identify key words and combinations therefore that yield evidence in the most efficient manner. Naturally, we would want to identify the best evidence first. To do so it is a good idea to retrieve research syntheses first. Preferably, those that use a quantitative approach to synthesizing the efficacy studies such as meta-analysis (De Vet, de Bie, van der Heijden, Verhagen, Sijpkes, & Knipschild, 1997; Tickle-Degnen, 2000). Even research syntheses that do not use a quantitative effectiveness measure but are based on systematic searches may be a useful first stop for gathering a large body of evidence (see also Chapter 11). The key words to be entered will depend on the specific database used. Generally, we distinguish natural language terms from controlled-vocabulary terms (White, 1994). Authors of articles in abstracts and titles use natural language terms. Controlled-vocabulary terms are assigned to the bibliographic record by libraries, which index articles in an attempt to bring together articles that may otherwise be scattered through authors' use of idiosyncratic terms. Sometimes, controlled-vocabulary terms may also backfire in making an article less accessible to an audience. For example, an article by the first author on Blissymbolics (Schlosser & Lloyd, 1993) was assigned the controlled-vocabulary term "artificial languages," which is unlikely to be used by those interested in AAC.

In addition to descriptors, searchers for evidence may also find it helpful to use additional identifiers such as "review," "integrated review," or "meta-analysis." As mentioned in Chapter 11 and as stated earlier in this chapter, high-quality systematic reviews are of great value to practitioners because they use rigorous techniques to accurately summarize available evidence. The NHC Centre for Reviews and Dissemination of the University of York (http://www.york.ac.uk/inst/crd/) provides useful search strategies to identify reviews and meta-analyses in MEDLINE (see also Boynton, Glanville, McDaid, Lefebvre, 1998) and CINHAL (see also the University of Rochester Medical Center Web site).

Other useful descriptors in absence of high-quality systematic reviews are "experiment," "single-subject experiment," or "randomized control trial." After all, evidence-based practitioners are not interested in retrieving all there is on a given topic, but evidence of preferably high quality. At any rate, it is beneficial to have a high degree of familiarity with such tools as the *Thesaurus of ERIC Descriptors*, the *Medical Subject Headings*, or the *Thesaurus of Psychological Index Terms*, or, if available through your library, the search strategies available through OVID.

D. EXAMINING THE EVIDENCE

Once the search strategy has been executed, the next step involves an examination of the obtained evidence. Here, the evidence-based practitioner evaluates the evidence in terms of its internal validity, external validity, and social validity using the guiding questions listed in Table 21.3. We do suggest that the broad dimensions of internal validity and external validity should be addressed in the sequence presented for logical reasons. There is little point in contemplating the external validity or the social validity of evidence, for example, if the internal validity is poor in the first place. Likewise, it is futile to evaluate the social validity of the evidence if the external validity would make it impossible to apply the evidence to the circumstances in which practitioner finds herself or himself.

E. Applying the Evidence

Once the practitioner has determined that the evidence is valid internally, externally, and socially, it is time to discuss the findings with relevant stakeholders from relevant stakeholder groups. Relevant stakeholders may hold viewpoints, preferences, concerns, or expectations concerning the recommendations stemming from the evidence that affect its implementation. Now is the time to integrate these viewpoints, before applying the evidence. In integrating these components it is possible that families, for example, might hold perspectives that contradict the evidence. Especially in organizations or centers where family-centered practice forms one of the core philosophies, practitioners may have to address situations where what the evidence shows and what the family wants might be in contradiction. Several scenarios are possible. Two of these scenarios are discussed next.

1. Stakeholder Perspectives Differ from Evidence

The first situation may be presented with evidence that an intervention is effective, but the family has serious concerns about implementing this intervention. The impact of AAC on the child's ability to develop speech might be such a plausible area of discrepancy. A practitioner identifies a recent meta-analysis, which shows that the use of AAC with individuals who have developmental disabilities does *not* hinder the development of natural speech (Millar *et al.*, 2000). Further, the review does identify several studies where natural speech seemed to improve, even though disclaimers are made concerning the poor internal validity of these studies. The practitioner shares these findings with the family and suggests that AAC be introduced to provide the child with a functional means of communication. The family who has a child with developmental apraxia, however, may not want to introduce AAC for another 2 years until their child has been given a "fair chance" to develop speech. This practitioner may have to rely on clinical reasoning skills. These clinical reasoning skills may be used to educate the family with the respective advantages of "communication versus speech" and assurances that AAC is multimodal and includes natural speech input to the child, emphasizing that this is not an either-or decision. The family may still feel strongly that they would like to put off using AAC and may prefer other interventions that are aimed at facilitating natural speech directly. The practitioner will need to respect this decision, knowing that she or he has provided all the evidence that allowed the family to make an informed choice.

2. Stakeholders Prefer a Scientifically Invalid Treatment

Stakeholders may prefer to try out a treatment even though the scientific evidence has found the treatment to be invalid. The use of facilitated communication might be a case in point. The practitioner may have shared the overwhelming evidence against facilitated communication (i.e., indicating that messages are authored by the facilitator rather than the learner) (Biermann, 2000; Nussbeck, 2000) with a family of a teenager with autism. The family, however, may still want to give facilitated communication a chance because nothing else, in their minds, has worked to their satisfaction and, perhaps, it could work for their child. Although the evidence-based practitioner may feel dissatisfied with their decision, it is important that the practitioner recognizes that he or she has done what is expected—shared the scientific evidence with stakeholders so that they can make an informed decision. Perhaps the family is receptive to the suggestion of testing the validity of facilitated communication directly with their child and to use these results to guide decision making.

The application of the evidence will lead the evidence-based practitioner to take a certain direction as far as intervention development or intervention implementation is concerned. Theoretically, the application of the evidence may bear relevance for any of the decision-making points necessary to fulfill the clinical roles described by ASHA (2002) for speech-language pathologists or other roles and responsibilities of other professional disciplines involved in the provision of AAC services. Applying the evidence as it pertains to selecting graphic symbols for an initial request lexicon in individuals with developmental disabilities (see Chapter 14), for example, will yield decisions as to what kinds of graphic symbols should be selected for individuals with developmental disabilities (see Chapter 15).

F. EVALUATING THE EVIDENCE APPLICATION

Once the decisions are made and the evidence has been applied, the next logical step is to evaluate the chosen evidence-based implementation and to revise accordingly (Tickle-Degnen, 2000). This step, if you will, is where EBP comes full circle, because we are using *further* evidence-gathering results to evaluate the success of the decisions as based on already existing research evidence. How may this be accomplished? The evidence-based practitioner may draw from a variety of methodologies, including single-subject experimental designs, group designs, and longitudinal designs. Many of these methodologies will be explained and reviewed in Section II of this text. Alternatively, methods that are conducive to more typical conditions may be applied as well, including Goal Attainment Scaling or the Activity Standards Inventory (Beukelman & Mirenda, 1998; Schlosser, McGhie-Richmond, Blackstien-Adler, Mirenda, Antonius, & Janzen, 2000). Regardless of the methodology chosen, it is pertinent that we engage in the social validation of outcomes by relevant stakeholders because they are *the* judges as to whether the applied evidence and intervention really worked (Schlosser, 1999b). For further information on how to validate the social significance of EBP and AAC interventions, refer to Chapter 10. No one, however, has stated this as eloquently as Wolf (1978):

> Are consumers satisfied with the results, all of the results [positive or negative], including those that were unplanned? Behavioral treatment programs are designed to help someone with a problem. Whether or not the program is helpful can be evaluated only by the consumer. Behavior analysts may give their opinions, and these opinions may even be supported with empirical objective behavioral data, but it is the participants and other consumers who want to make the final decision about whether a program helped solve their problems. (p. 210)

G. Disseminating the Findings

EBP is not complete, however, unless evidence-based practitioners disseminate their experiences. Only through dissemination at professional conferences or in journals can others benefit from attempts to implement EBP. In this case, "others" are other evidence-based practitioners and researchers. Only when our experiences are documented in public can we influence how EBP might be practiced in the future and what kind of research is being conducted in the future. Bennett and Bennett (2000) noted that if gaps in available research are identified and fed back to the profession, a more directed research agenda can be established. The journal *Augmentative and Alternative Communication* always invites researchers to submit to a section concerned with intervention development and implementation, titled "Intervention Notes." This would appear to be an excellent forum for publishing experiences in implementing EBP. We also look forward to many sessions at professional conferences where practitioners share their experiences, good and bad, in implementing EBP.

VI. SUMMARY

This chapter proposed a definition of EBP in AAC and developed a framework for evaluating the research evidence in AAC. In comparison to other health care fields, the field of AAC is still in its infancy as far as EBP is concerned. This represents both a challenge to catch up and an opportunity to avoid mistakes made in other fields. A first step in capitalizing on this opportunity is to propose a working definition of EBP for the AAC field. Further, before pursuing other implementation issues, it is essential that practitioners agree upon a framework for evaluating the research evidence in AAC. An initial framework was proposed here, and reactions and discussions thereof are necessary and welcomed. Illustrative EBP application examples are presented in subsequent chapters.

REFERENCES

American Speech-Language-Hearing Association. (2002, April 16). *Augmentative and alternative communication: Knowledge and skills for service delivery*. ASHA Leader, 7 (Suppl. 22), 97–106.

Bedrosian, J. L. (1995). Limitations in the use of nondisabled subjects in AAC research. *Augmentative and Alternative Communication*, *11*, 6–10.

Bennett, S., & Bennett, J. W. (2000). The process of evidence-based practice in occupational therapy: Informing clinical decisions. *Australian Occupational Therapy Journal*, *47*, 171–180.

Bennett, D. L., Gast, D. L., Wolery, M., & Schuster, J. (1986). Time delay and system of least prompts: A comparison in teaching manual sign production. *Education and Training of the Mentally Retarded*, *21*, 117–129.

Beukelman, D. R., & Mirenda, P. (1998). *Augmentative and alternative communication: Management of severe communication disorders in children and adults* (2nd ed.). Baltimore: Paul H. Brookes.

Biermann, A. (2000). *Gestützte Kommunikation im Widerstreit. Empirische Aufarbeitung eines umstrittenen Ansatzes*. Berlin, Germany: Wissenschaftsverlag Spiess.

Blischak, D. M. (1995). Thomas the writer: Case study of a child with severe physical, speech, and visual impairments. *Language, Speech, and Hearing Services in Schools*, *26*, 11–20.

Blischak, D. M., & Schlosser, R. W. (2002). *Roles of speech output in augmentative and alternative communication and learning*. Manuscript in preparation.

Boynton, J., Glanville, J., McDaid, D., Lefebvre, C. (1998). Identifying systematic reviews in MEDLINE: developing an objective approach to search strategy design. *Journal of Information Science*, *24*, 137–157.

Calculator, S. N., & Jorgenson (1994). *Including students with severe disabilities in schools: Fostering communication, interaction, and participation*. San Diego, CA: Singular.

Carr, A. (2000). Evidence-based practice in family therapy and systemic consultation: I Child-focused problems. *Journal of Family Therapy*, *22*, 29–60.

Chambless, D. L., Sanderson, W. C., Shohman, V., Bennett Johnson, S., Pope, K. S., Crits-Christoph, P., Baker, M., Johnson, B., Woody, S. R., Sue, S., Beutler, L., Williams, D. A., McCurry, S. (1996). An update on empirically validated therapies. *Clinical Psychologist*, *49*, 5–18.

De Vet, C. W. H., de Bie, R., van der Heijden, G., Verhagen, A., Sijpkes, P., & Knipschild, P. (1997). Systematic reviews on the basis of methodological criteria. *Physiotherapy*, *83*, 284–289.

DiCenso, A., Cullum, N., & Ciliska, D. (1998). Implementing evidence-based nursing: Some misconceptions. *Evidence-Based Nursing*, *1*, 38–40.

Doherty, J. (1985). The effects of sign characteristics on sign acquisition and retention: An integrative review of the literature: *Augmentative and Alternative Communication, 1,* 108–121.

Dowden, P., Beukelman, D. R., & Lossing, C. (1986). Serving nonspeaking patients in acute care settings: Intervention outcomes. *Augmentative and Alternative Communication, 2,* 38–44.

Durand, V. M. (1990). *Severe behavior problems.* New York: Guilford Press.

Egan, M., Dubouloz, C.-J., Zweck, C. v., & Vallerand, J. (1998). The client-centred evidence-based practice of occupational therapy. *Canadian Journal of Occupational Therapy, 65,* 136–143.

Fried-Oken, M., & Bersani, H. A. (2000). *Speaking up and spelling it out.* Baltimore: Paul H. Brookes.

Fuller, D. R., & Lloyd, L. L. (1992). Effects of configuration on the paired-associate learning of Blissymbols by preschool children with normal cognitive abilities. *Journal of Speech and Hearing Research, 35,* 1376–1383.

Glanville, J., & Lefebvre, C. (2000). Identifying systematic reviews: Key resources. *Evidence-Based Medicine, 5,* 68–69.

Glennen, S. L., & Calculator, S. N. (1985). Training functional communication board use: A pragmatic approach. *Augmentative and Alternative Communication, 1,* 134–142.

Glennen, S., & DeCoste, D. (1998). *Handbook of augmentative and alternative communication.* San Diego, CA: Singular.

Hegde, M. N. (1994). *Clinical research in communicative disorders: Principles and strategies.* Austin, TX: PRO-ED.

Helewa, A., & Walker, J. M. (2000). *Critical evaluation of research in physical rehabilitation: Towards evidence-based practices.* Philadelphia: WB. Saunders Company.

Hoagwood, K., Burns, B. J., Kiser, L., Ringeisen, H., & Schoenwald, S. K. (2001). Evidence-based practice in child and adolescent mental health services. *Psychiatric Services, 52,* 1179–1189.

Hodges, P., & Schwethelm, B. (1984). A comparison of the effectiveness of graphic symbol and manual sign training with profoundly retarded children. *Applied Psycholinguistics, 5,* 223–253.

Hunsley, J., Dobson, K. S., Johnston, C., & Mikail, S. F. (1999). Empirically supported treatments in psychology: Implications for Canadian professional psychology. *Canadian Psychology, 40,* 289–302.

Hupp, S. C., & Mervis, C. B. (1981). Development of generalized concepts by severely handicapped students. *TASH Journal, 6,* 14–21.

Iacono, T. (in press). Evidence-based practice in AAC. In S. Reiley, A. Perry, & J. Douglas (Eds.), *Evidence-based practice in speech pathology.* London: Whurr.

Jackson, G. B. (1980). Methods for integrative reviews. *Review of Educational Research, 50,* 438–460.

Jacobson, J. W., Mulick, J. A., & Schwartz, A. A. (1995). A history of facilitated communication. *American Psychologist, 50,* 750–765.

Johnston, M. V., Ottenbacher, K. J., Reichardt, C. S. (1995). Strong quasi-experimental designs for research on the effectiveness of rehabilitation. *American Journal of Physical and Medical Rehabilitation, 74,* 383–392.

Kazdin, A. E. (1977). Assessing the clinical or applied significance of behavior change through social validation. *Behavior Modification, 1,* 427–452.

Koul, R. Schlosser, R. W., Corwin, M., & Sims, S. (1997, November). *Effects of speech output on graphic symbol learning.* Paper presented at the Annual Convention of the American Speech-Language and Hearing Association, Boston.

Law, M., & Baum, C. (1998). Evidence-based occupational therapy. *Canadian Journal of Occupational Therapy, 65,* 131–135.

Lauer, J. M., & Asher, J. W. (1988). *Composition research: Empirical designs.* New York: Oxford University Press.

Layton, T. L. (1988). Language training with autistic children using four different modes of presentation. *Journal of Communication Disorders, 21,* 333–350.

Levine, S. P., Gauger, J. R. D., Bowers, L. D., & Khan, K. J. (1986). A comparison of mouthstick and morse code text inputs. *Augmentative and Alternative Communication, 2,* 51–55.

Light, J. (1989). Toward a definition of communicative competence for individuals using augmentative and alternative communication systems. *Augmentative and Alternative Communication*, 5, 137–144.

Light, J., & Binger, C. (1998). *Building communicative competence with individuals who use augmentative and alternative communication*. Baltimore: Paul H. Brookes.

Light, J., Dattilo, J., English, J., Gutierrez, L., & Hartz, J. (1992). Instructing facilitators to support the communication of people who use augmentative communication systems. *Journal of Speech and Hearing Research*, 35, 865–875.

Lloyd, L. L., Fuller, D. R., & Arvidson, H. (1997). *Augmentative and alternative communication: A handbook of principles and practices*. Needham Heights, MA: Allyn & Bacon.

Lloyd-Smith, W. (1997). Evidence-based practice and occupational therapy. *British Journal of Occupational Therapy*, 60, 474–478.

Locke, & Mirenda, P. (1992). Roles and responsibilities of special education teachers serving on teams delivering AAC services. *Augmentative and Alternative Communication*, 8, 200–214.

Logeman, J. (2000). What is evidence-based practice and why should we care? *ASHA Leader*, 5(5), 3.

Lonigan, C. J., Elbert, J. C., & Johnson, S. B. (1998). Empirically supported psychosocial interventions for children: An overview. *Journal of Child Clinical Psychology*, 27, 138–145.

Millar, D., Light, J., & Schlosser, R. (2000). The impact of AAC on natural speech development: A meta-analysis. In *Proceedings of the 9th biennial conference of the International Society for Augmentative and Alternative Communication* (pp. 740–741). Washington, DC: ISAAC.

Mirenda, P. (1997). Supporting individuals with challenging behavior through functional communication training and AAC: A research review. *Augmentative and Alternative Communication*, 13, 207–225.

Mirenda, P., & Beukelman, D. R. (1987). A comparison of speech synthesis intelligibility with listeners from three age groups. *Augmentative and Alternative Communication*, 3, 120–128.

Mitchell, G. J. (1999). Evidence-based practice: Critique and alternative view. *Nursing Science Quarterly*, 12, 30–35.

Mizuko, M. (1987). Transparency and ease of learning of symbols represented by Blissymbols, PCS, and Picsyms. *Augmentative and Alternative Communication*, 3, 129–136.

Nussbeck, S. (2000). *Gestützte Kommunikation. Ein Ausdrucksmittel für Menschen mit geistiger Behinderung*. Göttingen, Germany: Hogrefe

Nutbeam, D. (1996). Improving the fit between research and practice in health promotion: Overcoming structural barriers. *Canadian Journal of Public Health*, 87, 18–23.

Olson, E. A. (1996). Evidence-based practice: A new approach to teaching the integration of research and practice in gerontology. *Educational Gerontology*, 22, 523–537.

Ottenbacher, K. (1990). Clinically relevant designs for rehabilitation research: The idiographic model. *American Journal of Physical and Medical Rehabilitation*, 69, 286–292.

Parsons, C. L., & La Sorte, D. (1993). The effect of computers with synthesized speech and no speech on the spontaneous communication of children with autism. *Australian Journal of Human Communication Disorders*, 21, 12–31.

Porter, P. B., & Schroeder, S. R. (1980). Generalization and maintenance of skills acquired in Non-Speech Language Initiation Program training. *Applied Research in Mental Retardation*, 1, 71–84.

Raghavendra, P. (2000). Evidence-based practice: Where are we in AAC? *Proceedings of the 9th biennial conference of the International Society for Augmentative and Alternative Communication* (pp. 742–743). Washington, DC: International Society for Augmentative and Alternative Communication.

Reid, D. H., & Hurlbut, B. (1977). Teaching nonvocal communication skills to multihandicapped retarded adults. *Journal of Applied Behavior Analysis*, 10, 591–603.

Remington, B., & Clarke, S. (1993). Simultaneous communication and speech comprehension. Part I: Comparison of two methods of teaching expressive signing and speech comprehension skills. *Augmentative and Alternative Communication, 9,* 36–48.

Robey, R. R., & Schultz, M. C. (1998). A model for conducting clinical-outcome research: An adaptation of the standard protocol for use in aphasiology. *Aphasiology, 12,* 787–810.

Rosenberg, W., & Donald, A. (1995). Evidence-based medicine: An approach to clinical problem solving. *British Medical Journal, 310,* 1122–1125.

Rotholz, D. A., Berkowitz, S. F., & Burberry, J. (1989). Functionality of two modes of communication in the community by students with developmental disabilities: A comparison of signing and communication books. *Journal of the Association for Persons with Severe Handicaps, 14,* 227–233.

Sackett, D. L., Richardson, W. S., Rosenberg, W., & Haynes, R. B. (1997). *Evidence-based medicine: How to practice and teach EBM.* New York: Churchill Livingstone.

Schlosser, R. W. (1999a). Comparative efficacy of interventions in augmentative and alternative communication. *Augmentative and Alternative Communication, 15,* 56–68.

Schlosser, R. W. (1999b). Social validation of interventions in augmentative and alternative communication. *Augmentative and Alternative Communication, 15,* 234–247.

Schlosser, R. W. (2002a). On the importance of being earnest about treatment integrity. *Augmentative and Alternative Communication, 18,* 36–44.

Schlosser, R. W. (2002b). *Roles of graphic symbols in concept formation.* Research in progress.

Schlosser, R. W. (2002c). *Evidence in augmentative and alternative communication (EVIDAAC).* Grant proposal in preparation.

Schlosser, R. W. (2001). Common pitfalls and solutions in designing and interpreting single-subject experiments. In S. von Tetzchner & J. Clibbens (Eds.), *Understanding the theoretical and methodological bases of augmentative and alternative communication* (pp. 112–118). Toronto: International Society for Augmentative and Alternative Communication.

Schlosser, R. W., Belfiore, P. J., Nigam, R., Blischak, D., & Hetzroni, O. (1995). The effects of speech output technology in the learning of graphic symbols. *Journal of Applied Behavior Analysis, 28,* 537–549.

Schlosser, R. W., Blischak, D., M., Belfiore, P. J., Bartley, C., & Barnett, N. (1998). The effects of synthetic speech output and orthographic feedback on spelling in a student with autism: A preliminary study. *Journal of Autism and Developmental Disorders, 28,* 319–329.

Schlosser, R. W., & Braun, U. (1994). Efficacy of AAC interventions: Methodologic issues in evaluating behavior change, generalization, and effects. *Augmentative and Alternative Communication, 10,* 207–223.

Schlosser, R. W., & Lee, D. (2000). Promoting generalization and maintenance in augmentative and alternative communication: A meta-analysis of 20 years of effectiveness research. *Augmentative and Alternative Communication, 16,* 208–227.

Schlosser, R. W., & Lloyd, L. L. (1993). Effects of initial element teaching in a storytelling context on Blissymbol acquisition and generalization. *Journal of Speech and Hearing Research, 36,* 979–995.

Schlosser, R. W., McGhie-Richmond, D., Blackstien-Adler, S., Mirenda, P., Antonius, K., & Janzen, P. (2000). Training a school team to integrate technology meaningfully into the curriculum: Effects on student participation. *Journal of Special Education Technology, 15,* 31–44.

Schlosser, R. W., & Sigafoos, J. (2002). Selecting graphic symbols for an initial request lexicon: An integrative review. *Augmentative and Alternative Communication, 18,* 102–123.

Schweigert, P., & Rowland, C. (1992). Early communication and microtechnology: Instructional sequence and case studies of children with severe multiple disabilities. *Augmentative and Alternative Communication, 8,* 273–286.

Scruggs, T. E., & Mastropieri, M. A. (1998). Summarizing single-subject research. *Behavior Modification, 22,* 221–243.

Sigafoos, J., Laurie, S., & Pennell, D. (1996). Teaching children with Rett syndrome to request preferred objects using aided communication: Two preliminary studies. *Augmentative and Alternative Communication, 12,* 88–96.

Tickle-Degnen, L. (1998). Using research evidence in planning treatment for the individual client. *Canadian Journal of Occupational Therapy, 65,* 152–159.

Tickle-Degnen, L. (2000). Teaching evidence-based practice. *American Journal of Occupational Therapy, 54,* 559–560.

Vaughn, B., & Horner, R. (1995). Effects of concrete versus verbal choice systems on problem behavior. *Augmentative and Alternative Communication, 11,* 89–92.

White, H. D. (1994). Scientific communication and literature retrieval. In H. Cooper & L. V. Hedges (Eds.), *The handbook of research synthesis* (pp. 41–70). New York: Russell Sage Foundation.

Wolf, M. M. (1978). Social validity: The case for subjective measurement, or how applied behavior analysis is finding its heart. *Journal of Applied Behavior Analysis, 11,* 203–214.

Yoder, P., & Layton, T. (1988). Speech following sign language training in autistic children with minimal verbal language. *Journal of Autism and Developmental Disabilities, 18,* 217–229.

Zarin, D. A., Seigle, L., Pincus, H. A., & McIntyre, J. S (1997). Evidence-based practice guidelines. *Psychopharmacology Bulletin, 33,* 641–646.

CHAPTER 13

Presymbolic Communication Intervention

Cecilia Olsson
ALA Research Foundation, Stockholm,
Sweden

Mats Granlund
ALA Research Foundation, Stockholm,
and Mälardalen University, Västerås,
Sweden

I. INTRODUCTION

This chapter examines the efficacy of communication intervention for persons who are functioning at a presymbolic level. Evidence-based practices (EBP) has been defined as "the integration of best and current research evidence with clinical/educational expertise and relevant stakeholder perspectives to facil-

The Efficacy of Augmentative and Alternative Communication

itate decisions for assessment and intervention that are deemed effective and efficient for a given direct stakeholder" (Schlosser & Raghavendra, 2003, p. 263). Regarding the evaluation of communication interventions for persons considered to be functioning at a presymbolic level, only a few research studies are available. Thus, it is difficult to review the intervention literature in relation to EBP. In a previous literature review on communication intervention for presymbolic communicators, Granlund and Olsson (1999) used an evaluation framework proposed by Simeonsson (1995), including the following three levels of certainty of change following intervention: (1) suggestive, (2) preponderant, and (3) conclusive. Within this framework, the levels of certainty of change are related to available information about different aspects of the intervention cycle. The aspects are the purpose and nature of the intervention, how ecologically valid the intervention is, the integrity of implementation and maintenance of prescribed intervention methods, how outcomes are documented, and whether outcomes and effects are associated with the intervention. Based on this framework, arguments in support of the following statements are provided: (1) goals related to interaction are more important than goals primarily focused on learning new communication skills, (2) intervention studies must contain information on how the intervention is personalized, and (3) more explicit interaction goals and methods for intervention must be developed.

To collect evidence on what can be considered best practices in augmentative and alternative communication (AAC), practitioners must define both the desired outcomes of intervention and of what the intervention consists. Goals lead to actions (or intervention approaches), and outcomes are the effects of those actions (Granlund, Blackstone, & Norris, 1998). Evidence for good practices can only be established after a value-based decision has been made about what can be considered a good outcome. A first major step in conducting outcomes evaluation, therefore, is to define clearly the desired outcomes of the intervention. It is important to note that the desired outcomes of intervention are never the only outcomes; however, they are the outcomes that should be measured (see also Chapter 3).

For presymbolic communicators, desired outcomes of intervention may vary from learning more complex communication skills to interacting with others in a mutually rewarding fashion. Desired outcomes vary dependent on stakeholder perspectives and questions asked (chapter 10). In most presymbolic communication intervention studies, it is the researcher who has decided the desired outcomes of intervention. In some studies, the goals set are socially validated by care providers who are asked whether they consider the goals as important or not. This is, however, not identical to having care providers formulate the problem or deciding the goal by themselves. Therefore it is important to review factors considered important for involving care providers in intervention decisions. Goals set for communication intervention are primarily focused on body function or communicative skills (Granlund & Olsson, 1999; Iacono, in press). The existing information on goals and methods for interventions focused on interaction between care providers and persons who function at a presymbolic level is scant. Some relevant information can be found by reviewing research evidence on interaction between infants and care providers or communication intervention for young children.

Thus, this chapter is structured around three questions. First, what is a good intervention outcome for persons who interact at a presymbolic level? Second, how are decisions made about what outcomes to prioritize in intervention? Third, what methods used in communication intervention are focused on interaction between presymbolic communicators and their partners?

II. WHAT IS A GOOD OUTCOME?

To develop effective communication interventions for persons who function at the presymbolic level, one must first clearly define both the desired outcomes of intervention and the nature of the intervention itself. Desired outcomes of communication intervention for presymbolic communicators can be classified according to the new classification of health status under development by the World Health Organization (2001). Communication disability is not an illness, disease, or disorder but a term describing a human condition characterized by functional limitations in expressing needs, feelings, and intent and difficulties in participating fully in information exchange and social relationships. In this classification, the outcome of communication intervention can be classified across four dimensions: (1) body function and structure,(2) activity, (3) participation, and (4) the extent to which environmental factors serve as barriers or facilitators. Although the content of communication intervention for presymbolic communicators could include changing body functions, the primary focus should be to intervene with activity limitations and restrictions in the participation in everyday life.

A. THEORIES OF COMMUNICATION AND GOALS FOR INTERVENTION

The dyadic interaction is probably the most salient situation for any kind of human development and should therefore be regarded with special interest in intervention programs for presymbolic communicators. For a communicative interaction to occur between any two persons, it is necessary for the receiver to perceive an action from the sender, to assign a meaning to this action, and to respond in accordance with the interpreted meaning. Many researchers assume that what is known about parent-infant interaction could also be applicable to desired outcomes of interventions targeting caregiver interactions with a person with profound multiple disabilities who is functioning at a presymbolic level. However, two concerns must be taken into consideration when using general theories of interaction between child and care provider as a basis for selecting goals for intervention with presymbolic communicators.

First, as Mahoney, Boyce, Fewell, Spiker, and Wheeden (1998) have pointed out, what we know from the literature as important features of the social interaction between parent and child is incompatible with how goals for communication intervention are commonly formulated. These programs tend to emphasise a directive approach with different types of instructional techniques to help the individual reach significant developmental milestones in language development or more complex communicative skills. This is not congruent with research on child development indicating that optimal child development and interaction are more associated with a parental style of adopted responsiveness. Second, it is debatable whether research findings from studies of early interaction between children who are normally developing and their caregivers are valid for planning and implementing interventions for persons functioning at a presymbolic level (McCollum & Hemmeter, 1997).

We argue that the desired outcome of intervention for presymbolic communicators is a mutually rewarding interaction with communication partners rather than the development of more complex communication skills per se. We cannot assume that factors supportive of optimal development in typically developing children are the same as those that will support mutually rewarding interaction for presymbolic communicators and their partners. Neither can we base interventions on preselected caregiver strategies derived from studies of normal child development and assume that these strategies will be effective in stimulating mutually rewarding interaction for presymbolic communicators and their partners. Research focused on mother-infant interaction tends to stress the importance of joint attention, mutual feelings of happiness, and repetitive structures (McCollum & McBride, 1997). However, even for "normal" children what is considered to be "good interaction" varies between cultures and within cultures depending on context (McCollum & McBride, 1997; Super & Harkness, 1999). The conclusion is that practices must be based on research that clearly states the purpose and nature of intervention. Is the intervention focused on desired changes in one of the partners or on optimizing the reward of the interaction for both partners? What are the unique features that create a functional communicative interaction in a unique dyad? An analysis of different concepts, definitions and perspectives may help us recognize the theoretical framework on which we build assumptions about desired outcomes and best intervention.

1. Interaction

Many terms and concepts are used to refer to the early presymbolic communication between a child and a caregiver, such as interaction, social interaction, interpersonal interaction, dyadic interaction, and communication. Sometimes they are used interchangeably, though they can also be regarded as different levels of specification of the kind of interaction illustrated in Figure 13.1.

The word "interaction" per se does not reveal anything other than the interplay of different variables, set of variables, or other phenomena affecting each other. Interactions are ongoing within the body, between actions performed by the individual, and between people participating in everyday contexts. There are always intrapersonal interactions at the body level, meaning that different phenomena or functions within the person are interacting. Several studies within the domain of communication have stated that certain subject characteristics, such as motor skills, intellectual development, and use of senses, interact and have an impact on the communicative ability of the person (Granlund, Olsson & Karlan, 1991; Guess, Rues, Roberts, & Siegel-Causey, 1993; Sonksen, Levitt & Kitzinger, 1984). Likewise, the provision of assistive technology for compensating functional limitations in vision, hearing, and motor functions may have an indirect impact on a person's interpersonal interaction with others (Butler, 1986; Schweigert & Rowland, 1992).

Other forms of interaction take place in conjunction with actions performed by the individual. One kind is between a person and an object—that is,

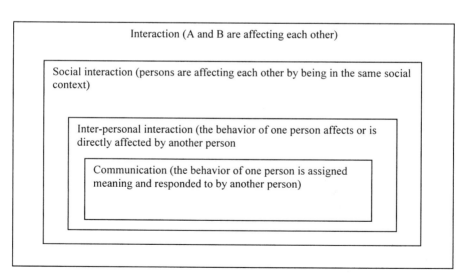

Figure 13.1 Interaction.

when a child plays with toys. Not only is the child affecting the toy, but the toy, in its shape and function, may also affect the child's preference for the toy as well as the frequency and manner with which the child manipulates it (Ivory & McCollum, 1999). The interaction between a person and his or her environment in broader terms can also be the focus of the analysis. If the environment is a social context, interaction is defined as *social interaction*. This specifies that a person is affected by and affects other persons. This can occur with no explicit contact, just by being in the same room or place. People behave differently when there is another person present compared to when they are all alone, even if the other person does not seem to take any notice of someone else's presence.

A third kind of interaction stipulates that the behavior of one person is directly related to the behavior of other persons. That is, they participate in *interpersonal interaction* or, if there are only two persons involved, *dyadic interaction*. Communication intervention for presymbolic communicators is mainly focused on interpersonal and dyadic interaction. Each of the interactions described affects an ongoing dyadic interaction. Evidence for best practices must meet the criteria of fidelity of intervention and include documentation of context, subject, and environmental features as thoroughly as possible. Furthermore, it must be possible to identify what interaction problem the intervention aims to address. According to Granlund and Sundin (1998), individuals who experience similar communication difficulties seem to have much in common with regard to intervention requirements regardless of the specific disabilities involved. Therefore, documentation of strategies used for problem identification must be regarded as very important for the ecological validity of an intervention (for further discussion on ecological validity, see Chapters 3 and 12).

2. How the Concept of Communication Is Defined

What definition of communication one chooses to adopt depends on the research question for a study (see also Chapter 4) or the intervention target group (Granlund & Olsson, 1999). A key issue in communication intervention for presymbolic communicators is the degree of importance assigned to intentionality. Communicative skills of a presymbolic communicator are often described as unintentional, preintentional, or intentional, indicating that the person is more or less aware that his or her behaviors are affecting another person (Goldbart, 1994; Ogletree, Wetherby, & Westling, 1992). It is argued that this classification of communicative intent is irrelevant for persons who function at a presymbolic level. Intent is an internal state of which conclusions are made from external representation—that is, behaviors. External evidence for intentions is taken from the behavior repertoire of normally developing persons. However, it is obvious that the absence of these observable features cannot in itself be taken as proof for unintentional communication by atypically developing persons (Granlund &

Olsson, 1999; Grove, Bunning, Porter, & Olsson, 1999). In a study of four young students with severe intellectual and multiple disabilities, Iacono, Carter, and Hook (1998) explored the applicability of published operational definitions of intentional communication. They found that very few of the participants' communicative behaviors met the formal criteria. With respect to the participants' physical and potential sensory impairments, they raise questions about the relevance of the operational definitions and indicate that there is a need to look further for other and maybe more individual indicators of intentional communication for this population.

From a broader perspective, there are many other intentions than the intent to communicate that guide a person's behavior. Human beings are by definition intentional systems, and there is always some kind of intention underlying any kind of behavior (Dennett, 1987). Even a highly developed person is not always aware of the message he or she is communicating. Furthermore, several intentions at different levels of awareness are most probably functioning at the same time within one communicative act and may also change during the process of communication (Stamp & Knapp 1990). It is possible to distinguish four levels of awareness of one's intention: (1) unawareness of any intent, (2) goal-intentional, (3) means-intentional, and (4) partner-intentional awareness.

a. Level 1: Unawareness of Any Intent

Ellis and Beatti, quoted by Goldbart (1994), defined communication as follows: "Communication occurs when one organism (the transmitter) encodes information into a signal which passes to another organism (the receiver) which decodes the signal and is capable of responding appropriately" (p. 16). It is a question of the intentions of the organism rather than of the mind. The body as a system is reacting, and the intention would then be to maintain or restore the balance of the system.

b. Level 2: Goal-Intentional Awareness

This level implies a possibility to direct one's own behavior toward a specific goal. It is a matter of a simple cause-effect chain, and there is only one target at a time, either a direction toward an object or toward another person. The intent can then be nonsocial when concerned with objects or events, or social when the goal is another person. Goldbart (1994) stressed that this is an important step in the child's development that has to be noticed by the environment if the communication is to develop further. Most researchers choose not to define the activity at this level of awareness as communication (e.g., Camaioni, 1993). Burgon, Le Poire, and Rosenthal (1995), however, stated that "communication is an inherently strategic, goal-oriented enterprise in which communicators often plan and enact behaviors designed to influence others" (p. 290). There are expectations of the environment and awareness that it is possible to influence the environment.

c. Level 3: Means-Intentional Awareness

At this level there is an awareness of the possibility to combine intentions toward a goal (an object or another person)—that is, to use a tool to achieve the goal. The tool can be an object as well as another person and with respect to cognitive development there is no difference (Camaioni, 1993). Yet for definitions of communication at this level of awareness, it is the awareness or use of the partner as a means that is essential (Bates, Benigni, Bretherton, Camaioni, & Volterra, 1979; Bretherton & Bates, 1979; Motley, 1986; Ogletree et al., 1992). At this level it is obvious that there is an awareness of one's intentions, and communication is often referred to as intentional communication.

d. Level 4: Partner-Intentional Awareness

There is a difference between using the partner as a means (level 3) and seeing the partner as someone who can understand one's own intentions (Camaioni, 1993). Furthermore, Camaioni distinguished between when the child uses the adult as a means to obtain an object and when the child uses the adult as an agent. Though it is not until the child can use an object to get the attention of the partner that Camaioni would call it a communicative intent. The communicative goal might be to get the partner to make inferences in a desired way or to create new conceptualizations (Stamp & Knapp, 1990, with reference to Winograd, 1977).

According to Stamp and Knapp (1990), scholars seem to agree on the following four statements: "(1) multiple levels or degrees of consciousness exist; (2) more than one intention can occur during the act of communicating; (3) communicative intentions can be linked to varying states of consciousness; and (4) both consciousness and intent may change during the process of communicating" (p. 283).

B. Definitions of Communication: Implications for Intervention

In studies concerning children with normal development, definitional issues do not have any implications for how the child is treated and interacted with. Children with normal development are treated as communicators long before they reach the criteria of the more narrow definitions stated earlier. In studies of persons with severe disabilities, definitional issues do have implications. A narrow definition of communication excludes presymbolic communicators from being regarded as communicators. Furthermore, communicative intent is often regarded as a necessary prerequisite to get access to interventions aiming at use of a symbol system. The application of operational criteria to intentional communication for persons with severe disabilities may cause underestimation as well as overestimation of a person's skill, which in turn may cause problems in getting access to appropriate interventions and services. This offers an argument for loosening the criteria for intentionality (Iacono *et al.*, 1998).

In several studies of presymbolic communicators the focus of the study has been on the person's use of intentional communicative behaviors in terms of different communicative functions and discourse roles, thus excluding a great proportion of the actual interaction being studied. That is, the focus has been on the individual's performance of communicative actions rather than on interaction between persons or on participation in social relationships. One frequently studied intentional function is that of behavior regulation, in which one partner serves as a means for the other partner to reach a goal. Behavior regulation typically consists of initiating or responding to requests, demands, or protests. Another function is social interaction, in which social contact/closeness with the partner in itself is the goal as in social routines, greetings, or attracting another person's attention to oneself. The third frequently studied function is joint attention where the goal is to share experiences of an object, an activity, or another kind of topic. It is characterized by comments and information sharing. Within these last two functions a person can have the role of initiating, or responding. It can also lead to an extended communication where maintaining the communication can be a discourse role. The communicative behaviors studied consists of motor activity such as eye gaze, facial expressions, body movements, gestures, pointing, or verbal activity such as vocalizations. In preverbal behaviors the manipulation of object and sequences of actions are also included.

Ogletree *et al.* (1992) assessed prelinguistic intentional communicative behaviors for 10 children with intellectual disabilities (age 6 to 12.5 years) in comparison to results of 10 children at comparable developmental level (11 to 14 months) without intellectual disabilities. Results showed that the two groups differed significantly in several aspects. The children had about the same rate of communication, but in normally developing children a larger proportion of the communicative acts had the function of joint attention whereas the children with intellectual disabilities, on the other hand, had a larger proportion of communicative acts serving a behavior regulation function. Children with intellectual disabilities initiated more and responded less than the normally developing children, who had a more even distribution of initiations and responses. The children with intellectual disabilities also used less sophisticated communicative behaviors, such as immature vocalizations, and did not, to the same extent as the other group, combine gestures and vocalizations. Also Cress, Shapley, Linke, Clark, Elliott, Bartels, and Aaron (2000), in a study of 30 children (mean age 18.6 months) with physical impairments, found that the children who showed intentional communication had less joint attention communication than typically developing children. One explanation is that children with physical impairments use fewer 3-point eye gaze shifts, which is an important indicator of intentional communication in this function until a more advanced communicative form is developed.

In another study of the use of communicative function and form, nine children (age 3 to 6.5 years) with severe multiple disabilities were observed in two different situations and quite different results were found (Olsson & Granlund, 1993; 1994). In contrast to the other studies referred to earlier, joint attention in this study was found to constitute the largest proportion of the communicative functions used. Among the discourse roles, initiations were lowest in frequency. The contrasting findings can, to a large extent, be explained by differences in the operationalizations of observed variables. In the study by Ogletree *et al.* (1992), only behaviors identified as intentional were recorded. Intentional behaviors were defined as motor/vocal acts directed toward the adult and response awaited. To determine that the act was directed toward the adult, the child needed to show at least one of the following behaviors: (1) give/show objects, (2) touch the adult, (3) use an isolated gesture or vocalization while looking at the adult, or (4) use a gesture paired with a vocalization while looking at the adult. In the study by Olsson and Granlund (1993), any behavior that the caregiver responded to was registered as a communicative act. One finding in that study was that a majority of the communicative behaviors exhibited by the children were below the criteria for being regarded as means intentional. These results indicate the importance of focusing interventions on participation and interpersonal interaction rather than on the performance of activities and communicative skills.

C. The Communicative Process as a Focus for Intervention

Communicative interaction involves at least two persons. Until today it has been common to view the communicative act between them as a linear model of discrete state units (Fogel, 1993b). The linear model consists of a message that is coded by a sender and then transmitted to a receiver who decodes it and is assumed to get the same message. Based on this model of discrete units as a framework, the main focus for assessment and intervention has been on the partners, such as the presymbolic communicator or the caretaker or in some cases a peer. Assessments and interventions have dealt with issues of coding, transmission, and decoding of a specific message.

The discrete unit model, however useful it may appear as a model, is an oversimplification of what is taking place in human interaction (Fogel, 1993b). Because several parallel intentions are involved in a communicative act and because intentions change over time, it is difficult to pinpoint the "true intention" or the "true message." Furthermore, Fogel (1993b) argued that both participants are involved in parallel activity where each can modify his or her own actions without waiting for a turn or to produce a discrete signal that makes it difficult to label one "sender" and "receiver." A communicative act then consists of the persons involved without assigning them a specific discourse role and several messages and intentions at different levels of awareness, transmitted with behaviors that are changeable during the process of transmission.

According to the model proposed by Fogel (1993a, 1993b), communication should be studied as a continuous process where the partners adapt to each other and mutually co-regulate their behaviors. Adapting the complexity of a dynamic system as a working model for practice will cause a lot of evidence problems. At present, no research based on this model can support evidence-based practices. Still, this model is proposed as a framework for communication intervention for persons who function at a presymbolic level. Very often the partner of a presymbolic communicator has to face the fact, "knowing *that* he or she wants to say something" but "not knowing *what* he or she wants to say." If communication is regarded as consisting of discrete units in a linear model, there is a risk that the communicative interaction will break down when there is an expectation of one true message and coding/decoding problems arise. If, on the other hand, the communicative act is regarded as a dynamic process, the assumption that the presymbolic partner has something "to say" will serve as the start of the process. Based on the assumption that there are several intentions and that there might be different messages that can be negotiated, several options to find at least one shared message become possible. With this view of communication the communicative competence or lack of competence cannot be related to one of the partners, rather it is within the dyad.

III. HOW ARE DECISIONS MADE ABOUT PRIORITIZING OUTCOMES?

In traditional intervention research, the desired outcomes are typically defined by the researcher in relation to their purposes with the research endeavor. Caretakers are often asked for their input on whether the preselected goal is relevant or not. It is known that goals are value laden. That is, goals always reflect the values of the stakeholders who set them. This means that the desired outcomes of different stakeholder groups may differ. It is argued that outcomes targeted for communication intervention are meant to have an impact on the lives of presymbolic communicators and their primary partners. Therefore, caregivers should actively participate in selecting the goals and the intervention approaches. Collaboration and consultation between the actors involved in intervention are necessary before making decisions about the desired outcomes of intervention. Most research studies and clinical reports on communication intervention for presymbolic communicators do not offer accounts of the decision-making process associated with desired outcomes of interventions (Granlund & Olsson, 1999). Thus, it is difficult to establish the degree to which the caretakers have participated in decision making and whether the intended effect is actually a desired outcome for the individual and/or for caregivers/partners (see Chapter 10 for further information on the process of assessing stakeholder perspectives through social validation).

A. The Intervention Process

The intervention process encompasses elements of initial screening, focused assessment, follow-up assessment, goal setting and designing methods, implementing intervention, and evaluating the effectiveness of an intervention (Bailey & Simeonsson, 1988). In this process, families and other caretakers participate in transactions with professionals. For this reason, the impact of intervention may begin as early as the initial screening, and both expected and unexpected outcomes of intervention will follow from each element added to the process (Björck-Åkesson, Granlund, & Simeonsson, 2000).

A central theme in intervention collaboration is assessment. According to Björck-Åkesson et al. (2000), at least seven purposes for assessment can be identified: (1) screening, (2) diagnosis, (3) classification and eligibility decisions, (4) projection of goals for intervention, (5) intervention planning, (6) program monitoring, and (7) evaluation of outcomes. The first four of these purposes are directly related to the person who functions at a presymbolic level, whereas the latter three may be of wider scope. With a communication intervention perspective, there are other purposes such as (1) mutual learning, (2) listing realistic goals for intervention, and (3) evaluating the results in terms of social relationships. These purposes presuppose an active role for caretakers in the assessment process. Thus, assessment methods are a part of the intervention and should include strategies for involving caretakers in every step of the intervention cycle.

Every phase in the assessment process must have a clear beginning and end (Simeonsson et al., 1996). How clearly marked an assessment phase is perceived to be is related both to the type of the phenomenon that is being assessed and how formal the assessment is. If a communication problem is defined in terms of a functional limitation of the body or an activity limitation, standardized tests of ability or criterion-referenced tests of skills are frequently used (Björck-

Åkesson *et al.*, 2000). The evaluation takes the form of experts measuring a presymbolic communicator's response to preset test items under set conditions. Here, caretakers tend to be passive recipients of information collected by professionals. In assessing participation in interpersonal interaction and social relationships, communicative competence is within the dyad. This excludes standardized tests from the assessment techniques to be used. Instead, interviews with caretakers or observations of interaction are the preferred techniques. The degree of formality of such assessment techniques will have an impact on the intervention effects of assessment. In formal assessment, the beginning and end of the information collection stage are clearly marked. This allows caretakers to have a more active learning experience; it also helps them to compare the actual assessment with expectations. As a result, it becomes easier for caretakers to discuss the conclusions reached from an assessment. In informal assessment, on the other hand, it is difficult for caretakers to determine that assessment is taking place or is completed. Therefore it becomes harder for caretakers to draw conclusions about the results of an assessment (Björck-Åkesson *et al.*, 2000). In communication intervention with presymbolic communicators, observations of naturally occurring interpersonal interaction are almost exclusively implemented as an informal assessment. There is a need to develop formal instruments for assessing interpersonal interaction in which caretakers can take an active role in collecting and interpreting information.

B. ASSESSMENT INSTRUMENTS

Goldbart (1994) described an attempt to formalize and make sense of the unique behaviors of children with severe disabilities using the instrument "Affective Communication Assessment" (ACA, devised by Coupe, Barton, Barber, Collins, Levy & Murphy, 1985). In this assessment, persons who are very familiar with the child interpret the child's reaction to different stimuli in interaction with caretakers. The components of the child's reaction are carefully recorded to provide information about the basis of the interpretation and offer data on the behavior repertoire of the child. In addition, the child's typical patterns and cluster of behaviors fairly regularly associated with a particular response are recorded. Then new stimuli are introduced to check the regularity of the response pattern and the interpretation. The ACA helps teachers and others to make sense of the child's idiosyncratic behaviors and provides systematic feedback that helps the child to experience an awareness of the possibilities to affect the environment. This kind of assessment, based on careful descriptions of what is actually going on with no restricted options set by the researcher, can be regarded as a good example of how the criteria of ecological validity and fidelity of implementation as well as outcome documentation are met.

Granlund and Olsson (1998) described a questionnaire in which parents/caretakers are asked to rate their current perceptions as well as their desires for change concerning their interaction with persons with profound multiple disabilities. Items cover areas such as "I know how to maintain my child's/the person's focus on a common theme" and "My child/the person knows how to direct my attention toward a certain object/action/person." The responder is asked to rate the degree to which the phenomenon occurred at the present time and the degree to which they would like the phenomenon to occur in the future on a scale from 1 = seldom to 5 = almost every time. The difference in ratings between the present situation and the desired situation is used as an index of the significance of an interaction problem. This may serve as an example of how the criterion of ecological validity is met in assessment and may form the basis for describing the purpose and nature of intervention.

Rowland and Schweigert (1993) have developed an instrument in which caretakers are asked to rate the communicative environment of children with profound multiple disabilities. Several concrete aspects of the environment are covered, and for each item the responder is asked to indicate if this aspect is considered in creating a communicative environment. In the rationale for the scale, it is stated that a positive answer to the questions indicates a more adapted communicative environment. Thus, the questions can be seen as implicit instructions aimed at changing the environment.

In summary, assessment tools in communication intervention for presymbolic communicators are a part of the intervention. They should be designed to help focus partners on interaction rather than isolated communicative skills, help partners to generate ideas for goals for intervention, and help partners to generate ideas for interaction intervention.

C. Goal Setting

In a study of 25 young children with profound multiple disabilities who communicated at a presymbolic level, Wilder (2000) used the Granlund and Olsson (1998) questionnaire to ask parents about their perceptions of interacting with their children. The results revealed a large variance both, in the parents' current perceptions of the interaction with the children and in the desires for change. Both current perceptions of interaction and desires for change had only weak to moderate statistical relationships with the children's abilities to express communicative functions as measured with the Early Social Communication Scales (Siebert & Hogan, 1982) adapted for use with children with profound multiple disabilities (Karlan, Granlund, & Ward, 1988). The result implies that interaction is a multidimensional phenomenon that, only to a certain degree, can be predicted by assessing communicative skills/performance of activities in the interaction partners. That is, interaction develops within the dyad and has to be measured within the dyad. For this reason, assessment questions must be framed in terms of interaction in order to facilitate the formulation of goals focused on interaction.

This interpretation is further supported by comparing results from Wilder's study with those reported by Stephenson and Dowrick (2000). They asked parents of children with disabilities about their priorities for communication skill intervention. Twenty skills within the area of requesting, refusing, getting attention, and socializing were discussed, rated for importance, and ranked. Results revealed that the skills "asking for objects," "objects to actions from others," "drawing attention to pain and discomfort," "maintaining interaction," and "rejecting objects or actions" were highly ranked. This is partly in contrast to Wilder's study of parents' perceptions of interaction. She used the index of the significance of an interaction problem (the difference between the current and the desired state) as her measure. The result revealed that the most significant problems were related to directing and maintaining the partner's attention to a common focus of interest (joint attention and maintaining interaction). Problems related to requesting and rejecting (behavior regulation) were rated significantly lower.

In conclusion, to support caretakers in setting goals related to interaction it is important to include methods explicitly focused on interaction in the assessment process. Further, the assessment materials used have to allow for and stimulate a high degree of caretaker involvement in the assessment process. Assessment needs to be considered a part of the intervention and not only a part of intervention planning.

IV. INTERVENTION METHODS FOCUSED ON INTERACTION

In interventions for presymbolic communicators focused on interaction, most methods used are indirect (Granlund & Olsson, 1999). The focus of the method is on changing the skills, attitudes, beliefs, and behaviors of the communicative partner or changing the physical context of the interaction. Learning occurs when the person who communicates on a presymbolic level gradually takes over the responsibility for initiating and maintaining the interaction. Theorists such as Vygotsky (1962), Fogel (1993b, p. 93), and Ware and Healey (1994, p. 10) have stressed the responsibility of the adult or the more skilled person in helping the child or the less skilled person to accomplish the process and reach a goal. Applied by Granlund and Olsson (1999) and Grove *et al.* (1999) to communication with presymbolic persons, the goal is to find out or construct a message or frame of reference that can be shared by both interacting partners. To fulfil this participation aim, the presymbolic communicator needs support from the adult or more skilled person, including "over interpretations" of behaviors as communicative acts. Also, necessary contextual adaptations must be made that allow and enable the presymbolic partner to fulfil his or her potential to contribute to the interaction.

A. ASSIGNING A MEANING

Communicating with presymbolic communicators often means that the communication partner has to be sensitive to what the individual does and act as if invited to a communicative activity. The actions of the presymbolic communicator are assigned a meaning. The difference between caregivers interacting at a presymbolic level with normally developing children and with persons who have disabilities is merely a question about how to interpret the meaning of the behavior of the presymbolic communicator. If one assumes that all behaviors have a message value, there is no activity that cannot be regarded as communicative. To what degree it leads to a communicative interaction depends not only on one of the partners but on both. Because persons at a presymbolic level may not have the same repertoire of behaviors as typically developing children, there is a need for the partner to adapt to other kinds of expressions (Iacono et al., 1998). This means that any behavior that can be interpreted as a communicative act needs to be responded to, not only behaviors that meet the criteria of being means-intentional. It also implies that to assess a communicative function, the behavior of the presymbolic communicator as well as the responses of the caregiver must be assessed. That is, how the behavior is interpreted and the resulting consequences are determining factors for what function to register. Probably caregivers of children with profound multiple disabilities act in about the same way when they attribute meaning to the activity of the child as caregivers do in the interaction with typically developing children. Caregivers of children with multiple disabilities must, to a higher degree, respond to behaviors that are not so obviously adult directed. Thus, they might need interventions focused on helping them to perceive and redefine the behaviors of the presymbolic communicator as communicative. This may be accomplished, for example, by actively participating in collecting and interpreting assessment information.

B. HOW TO "READ" THE PRESYMBOLIC COMMUNICATOR

For a communicative act to occur, there have to be behaviors that either convey a clear meaning or can be assigned a meaning. At a presymbolic level in persons with severe disabilities, there are limitations in the behavior repertoire, which cause ambiguity regarding the meaning of the behavior and the intentions of the person. In a study of 50 pairs of mothers and their 6-month-old babies, Weinberg, Gianio, and Tronick (1989) observed how the babies differed in their facial expressions of feelings and combination of behaviors depending on what they were relating to. They found that some facial expressions are more likely to appear together with certain behaviors than others and these form coherent affective action configurations, which communicate a set of differentiated messages to the caregivers. They could distinguish two different configurations depending on whether the child was directed toward a person or an object and two different configurations communicating an active or a more passive negative attitude toward an event. What often is interpreted and responded to as a message of a particular emotion consists of many different behaviors organized in a particular manner. Iacono et al. (1998), in their study of four children with multiple disabilities, found differences in behavior patterns depending on what function was communicated. Gestures alone or with vocalization tended to be interpreted as requests, whereas vocalizations and smiles tended to be interpreted as comments and responses. When communicating with a person at a presymbolic level, there probably is not one behavior but an organized configuration of behaviors that conveys a message to the environment. If a person with disabilities lacks one or more of the characteristics in a configuration, it will probably cause confusion about how to interpret the individual (Harding, 1983, Iacono et al., 1998). Thus, when a person with severe disabilities lacks the ability to use vocalizations, eye gazes, or motor control of arms and hands, it inevitably affects the caregiver's possibilities to use intuitively known strategies to "read" the person. Caretakers may require help to make sense of the idiosyncratic behaviors of presymbolic communicators. A starting point for such interventions may be the previously described ACA (Coupe et al., 1985).

C. INTERACTION PATTERNS

With the dyad as the focus for intervention, the methods implemented are aimed at changing discourse patterns, such as turn-taking patterns or modes of communication (Iacono et al., 1998; Ware & Healey, 1994). According to McCollum and Hemmeter (1997), the partners and the context define what should be considered a mutually rewarding interaction. The actual interaction between a person functioning at the presymbolic level and caretakers will vary depending on culture, situation, and caretaker (Granlund & Olsson, 1993; McCollum, & McBride, 1997). As a consequence, the interaction intervention must be individualized depending on partners. Each caretaker must identify his or her desires for change in interaction patterns. Thus, the intervention starts with assessing caretakers' perceptions of their current interaction with the presymbolic communicator. Many caretakers experience difficulties in maintaining interaction and in sharing the focus of attention with presymbolic communicators (Wilder, 2000).

Most intervention methods focusing on interaction patterns are based on providing feedback to caretakers on videotaped interaction sequences (e.g., Watson, 1994). The feedback must be based on interaction problems that were identified as significant by interaction partners. It is important that the focus of the feedback is on the dyad rather than on isolated communicative skills in the presymbolic communicator or the partner.

D. INFERENCES AND CHANGING THE CONTEXT

Meanings assigned to the behaviors of a presymbolic communicator are based on an interpretation of the information available, including the context, prior knowledge, and the interpreters' feelings and desires (Grove, et al., 1999; Olsson & Grove, 1998). The less conventional and structurally sophisticated the communicative form is, the more the partners have to rely on inference from other sources—for example, when a baby cries and the mother looks at the watch, finds out that it is bedtime, and interprets "Ah, you are crying because you are tired, let's have a nap."

How a person interprets and responds to the activity of another person is also a matter of what communicative function the activity is assumed to serve. Again, the less articulated the form is, the more variations there can be in the function of a certain behavior. The baby's crying can be an expression of a need, which gives it a behavior-regulating function. On the other hand, the crying can be a way to attract the partner's attention to oneself, which means that it serves the function of social interaction.

In communication between two persons, factors related to the persons as well as to the context are influencing the interaction. A communication intervention can focus on changing the context as a means for creating opportunities for specific kinds of interaction. Rowland and Schweigert (1993) described how they engaged caretakers in assessing aspects of the communicative environment of children with multiple disabilities. The assessment tool is designed to be reactive (to help people reflect on interaction patterns and contexts). The items in the schedule are framed in a manner so that they provide implicit instructions about environmental changes that are possible to make.

V. CONCLUSIONS

Intervention focused on interaction for persons who function at a presymbolic level needs to be focused on the dyad. That is, the overarching aim of

Table 13.1

Questions to be Asked about the Quality of Communication Intervention Outcomes for Presymbolic Communicators

The level of the desired outcome	The time frame of the effect
Skills and activities of the presymbolic communicator • Does the person use existing skills?	Short-term effects • Are goals set in terms of changes in participation reached? • Do the use of extant communication skills and assistive technology change as a function of intervention?
Interactional patterns and partner behaviors • Do interactional patterns change following from intervention? • What changes in pattern can be observed over time?	Long-term effects • Are ongoing changes in interactional patterns observed as a function of framing mutually rewarding interactions? • Are changes seen in social relationships?

interventions is to provide a basis for mutually rewarding interactions and full participation in social relationships for presymbolic communicators. To reach this goal, caretakers must be involved in all steps in the intervention circle including assessment and goal setting. The interventions must be focused on the dyad—that is, discourse patterns. It must also be personalized depending on the perceived needs of individual dyads. There is a need to combine these requirements from a temporal perspective. An intervention can be defined as the actions taken to reach the desired outcome. Clinical interventions rarely consist of a single intervention or a fixed treatment. Instead, interventions are better defined as "a menu of possibilities accompanied by a series of supports that facilitate [the] consumer's interaction with these possibilities" (Knapp, 1995, p. 7). A major challenge for communication intervention with presymbolic communicators, therefore, is to consider the impact of these possibilities, the series of supports that facilitate the interactions among the possibilities, and their interrelationships.

Table 13.1 illustrates the questions that can be asked in estimating the quality of communicative interventions for persons who communicate at a presymbolic level in relation to participation. Consensus around such quality indicators is a necessary requirement before EBP can be established.

As initially stated, only a limited number of intervention studies focus on communication intervention for presymbolic communicators that inform EBP. This chapter reviewed what can be inferred from the literature so far. The conclusions can serve as a framework both for future research and for implementations in practice. As a summary, Table 13.2 presents a list of preliminary indicators of "best practices" in interaction-focused research and interventions for persons functioning at a presymbolic level.

Table 13.2

Preliminary Indicators of "Best Practices" in Interaction-Focused Research and Interventions for Persons at a Presymbolic Level

Preliminary indicators of "best practices"	Intervention purpose and nature	Ecological validity	Implementation fidelity	Documentation	Design appropriateness
Intervention is aiming at mutually rewarding interaction for both partners rather than the development of more complex communication skills (Fogel, 1993b; Goldbart, 1994; Granlund & Olsson, 1998; McCollum & Hemmeter, 1997; Wilder, 2000).	X	X			X
Focus is on interpersonal interaction problems rather than performance and skill problems (Fogel, 1993b; Goldbart, 1994; Granlund & Olsson, 1998, 1999; Grove et al., 1999; McCollum & Hemmeter, 1997; Olsson & Grove, 1998; Wilder, 2000).	X	X			X
Intervention is focused on interaction problems identified as significant by caretakers rather than by the clinician/researcher (Goldbart, 1994; Granlund & Olsson, 1998; Watson, 1994; Wilder, 2000).	X				
Assessment of partners' adopted responsiveness rather than using a directive approach (Granlund & Olsson, 1999; Mahoney et al., 1998).	X	X			

318

A theoretical framework that is appropriate for presymbolic communicators with disabilities is used (Mahoney et al., 1998; McCollum & Hemmeter, 1997; Iacono et al., 1998).	x		
Concepts that are clearly defined and relevant for interaction with presymbolic communicators rather than a preestablished terminology within the wider field of communication are used (Granlund & Olsson, 1999; Grove et al., 1999; Iacono et al., 1998; Olsson & Granlund, 1993, 1994).	x	x	
Careful and detailed descriptions of the context in which interaction is studied are made (Granlund & Olsson, 1993; Rowland & Schweigert, 1993).		x	
Unique features for functional communication in unique dyads rather than preset variables are the focus for intervention (McCollum & McBride, 1997; Super & Harkness, 1999).			x
Assessment contains descriptions of what is actually going on rather than restricted options set by the researcher (Fogel, 1993b; Goldbart, 1994).			x
Goals for intervention set by caretakers not only accepted by caretakers (Granlund & Olsson, 1998, 1999; Stephenson & Dowrick, 2000; Wilder, 2000).		x	x

REFERENCES

Bailey, D. B., & Simeonsson, R. J. (1988). *Family assessment in early intervention.* New York: Merrill.

Bates, E., Benigni, L., Bretherton, I., Camaioni, L., & Volterra, V. (1979). *The emergence of symbols.* New York: Academic Press.

Björck-Åkesson, E., Granlund, M., & Simeonsson, R. (2000). Assessment philosophies and practices in Sweden. In M. Guralnick (Ed.), *Interdisciplinary clinical assessment of young children with developmental disabilities* (pp. 391–412). London: Paul H. Brookes.

Bretherton, I., & Bates, E. (1979). The emergence of intentional communication. In I. C. Uzgiris (Ed.), *Social interaction and communication during infancy* (pp. 81–100). San Francisco: Jossey-Bass.

Burgon, J. K., Le Poire, B. A., & Rosenthal, R. (1995). Effects of preinteraction expectancies and target communication on perceiver reciprocity and compensation in dyadic interaction. *Journal of Experimental Social Psychology, 31,* 287—321.

Butler, C. (1986). Effects of powered mobility on self-initiated behaviors of very young children with locomotor disability. *Developmental Medicine and Child Neurology, 28,* 325–332.

Camaioni, L. (1993). The development of intentional communication. A re-analysis. In J. Nadel & L. Camaioni (Eds.), *New perspectives in early communicative development* (pp. 82–96). London: Routledge.

Coupe, J., Barton, L., Barber, M., Collins, L., Levy, D., & Murphy, D. (1985). *Affective Communication Assessment.* Manchester, UK: Melland School.

Cress, C. J., Shapley, K. L., Linke, M. L., Clark, J., Elliott, J., Bartels, K., & Aaron, E. R. (2000). *Characteristics of intentional communication in young children with physical impairments.* Paper presented at the 8th biennial conference of the International Society for Augmentative and Alternative Communication (ISAAC), Washington, D.C., USA.

Dennett, D. C. (1987). *The intentional stance.* Cambridge, MA: MIT Press.

Fogel, A. (1993a). *Developing through relationships.* Chicago: University of Chicago Press.

Fogel, A. (1993b). Two principles of communication, Co-regulation and framing. In J. Nadel & L. Camaioni (Eds.), *New perspectives in early communicative development* (pp. 9–22). London: Routledge.

Goldbart, J. (1994). Opening the communication curriculum to students with PMLDs. In J. Ware (Ed.), *Educating children with profound and multiple learning difficulties* (pp. 16–22). London: David Fulton.

Granlund, M., Blackstone, S., & Norris, L. (1998). The outcome of communication intervention—defining outcomes. In E. Björck-Åkesson & P. Lindsay (Eds.), *Communication . . . Naturally* (pp. 203–216). Västerås, Sweden: Mälardalen University Press.

Granlund, M., & Olsson, C. (1993). Investigating communicative functions in profoundly retarded persons: A comparison of two methods of obtaining information about communicative behaviors. *Mental Handicap Research, 6,* 50–68.

Granlund, M., & Olsson, C. (1998). *Familjen och habiliteringen* (The family and the intervention services). Stockholm: Ala-Research Foundation.

Granlund, M., & Olsson, C. (1999). Efficacy of communication intervention for presymbolic communicators. *Augmentative and Alternative Communication, 15,* 1, 25–37.

Granlund, M., Olsson, C., & Karlan, G. R. (1991). Investigating the relationships among motor ability, cognitive ability and communication of persons with profound mental retardation. *Scandinavian Journal of Educational Research, 35,* 31–55.

Granlund, M., & Sundin, M. (1998). *Funktionalitet i mål och metoder* (Functionality and goal attainment). Stockholm, Sweden: Stiftelsen ALA.

Grove, N., Bunning, K., Porter, J., & Olsson, C. (1999). See what I mean: Interpreting the meaning of communication by people with severe and profound intellectual disabilities. Journal of Applied Research in Intellectual Disabilities, *12*(3), 190–203.

Guess, D., Rues, J., Roberts, S., & Siegel-Causey, E. (1993). *Extended analysis of behavioral state, environmental events, and related variables among students with profound disabilities.* Lawrence, KS: University of Kansas.

Harding, C. G. (1983). Setting the stage for language acquisition: Communication development in the first year. In R. M. Golinkoff (Ed.), *The transition from prelinguistic to linguistic communication* (pp. 93–113). Hillsdale NJ: Erlbaum.

Iacono, T., (in press). Evidence-based practice in AAC. In S. Reiley, A. Perry, & J. Douglas (Eds.), *Evidence-based practice in speech pathology.* London: Whurr.

Iacono, T., Carter, M., & Hook, J. (1998). Identification of intentional communication in students with severe and multiple disabilities. *Augmentative and Alternative Communication, 14,* 102–114.

Ivory, J. J., & McCollum, J. A. (1999). Effects of social and isolate toys on social play in an inclusive setting. *The Journal of Special Education. 32, 4,* 238–243.

Karlan, G., Granlund, M., & Ward, M. (1988). *Early Social Communication Scale adapted for children with profound multiple disabilities.* Unpublished manuscript, Purdue University.

Knapp, M. (1995). How shall we study comprehensive collaborative services for children and families? *Educational Research, 24,* 5–16.

Mahoney, G., Boyce, G., Fewell, R. R., Spiker, D., & Wheeden, C. A. (1998). The relationship of parent-child interaction to the effectiveness of early intervention services for at-risk children and children with disabilities. *Topics in Early Childhood Special Education, 18,* 1, 5–17.

McCollum, J. A., & Hemmeter, M. L. (1997). Parent-child interaction intervention when the children have disabilities. In M. J. Guralnick (Ed.), *The effectiveness of early intervention* (pp. 549–576). Baltimore: Paul H. Brookes.

McCollum, J., & McBride, S. (1997). Ratings of parent-infant interaction: Raising questions of cultural validity. *Topics in Early Childhood Special Education, 17,* 494–519.

Motley, M. (1986). *Consciousness and performance: The issue of communicative intention.* Paper presented at the Speech Communication Association Convention, Chicago, IL.

Ogletree, B. T., Wetherby, A. M., & Westling, D. L. (1992). Profile of the prelinguistic intentional communication behaviors of children with profound mental retardation. *American Journal of Mental Retardation, 97,* 186–196.

Olsson, C., & Granlund, M. (1993). *Förutsättningar och möjligheter—kommunikation hos barn med grava flerhandikapp* (Ability and possibility—communication among children with profound multiple disabilities). Stockholm: Stiftelsen ALA.

Olsson, C., & Granlund, M. (1994). Ability and possibility to communicate—a study of pre-school children with multiple disabilities. *Proceeding at the 6th biennial conference of the International Society for Augmentative and Alternative Communication (ISAAC),* Maastricht, The Netherlands.

Olsson, C., & Grove, N. (1998). Whose message?—Issues of inference in interpreting communicative intentions. *Proceedings at the 8th biennial conference of the International Society for Augmentative and Alternative Communication, (ISAAC),* Dublin, Ireland.

Rowland, C., & Schweigert, P. (1993). Analyzing the communicative environment to increase functional communication. *Journal of the Association for Persons with Severe Handicaps, 18,* 161–176.

Schlosser, R. W., & Raghavendra, P. (2003). Toward evidence-based practice in AAC. In R. W. Schlosser, *The Efficacy of Augmentative and Alternative Communication: Towards Evidence-Based Practice* (pp. 259–297). San Diego: Academic Press.

Schweigert, P., & Rowland, C. (1992). Early communication and micro-technology: Instructional sequence and case studies of children with severe multiple disabilities. *Augmentative and Alternative Communication, 8,* 273–286.

Siebert, J., & Hogan, A. (1982). *Procedures manual for the Early Social Communication Scale.* Unpublished manuscript, University of Miami.

Simeonsson, R. (1995). Intervention in communicative disability: Evaluation issues and evidence. In J. Roennberg & E. Hjelmquist (Eds.), *Communicative disability: Compensation and development* (pp. 79–96). Linkoping: Linkoping University Press.

Simeonsson, R., Huntington, G., McMillen, J., Haugh-Dodds, A., Halperin, D., Zipper, I., & Leskinen, M. (1996). Services for young children and their families: Evaluating the intervention cycle. *Infants and Young Children, 9,* 31–42.

Sonksen, P. M., Levitt, S., & Kitzinger, M. (1984). Identification of constraints acting on motor development in young visually disabled children and principles of remediation. *Child: Care, Health and Development, 10,* 273–286.

Stamp, G. H., & Knapp. M. L. (1990). The construct of intent in interpersonal communication. *Quarterly Journal of Speech, 76,* 282–299.

Stephenson, J., & Dowrick, M. (2000). Parent priorities in communication intervention for students with severe disabilities. *Education and Training in Mental Retardation and Developmental Disabilities, 35,* 25–35.

Super, C., & Harkness, S. (1999) The environment as culture in developmental research. In S. Friedman & T. Wachs (Eds.), *Measuring environment across the life span* (pp. 279–323). Washington, DC: American Psychological Association.

Ware, J., & Healey, I. (1994). Conceptualizing progress in children with profound and multiple learning difficulties. In J. Ware (Ed.), *Educating children with profound and multiple learning difficulties* (pp. 1–14). London: David Fulton.

Watson, J. (1994). Using interaction in the education of pupils with PMLDs: Intensive interaction, two case studies. In J. Ware (Ed.), *Educating children with profound and multiple learning difficulties* (pp. 126–149). London: David Fulton.

Weinberg, M. K., Gianino, A. F., & Tronick, E. Z. (1989). *Facial expressions of emotion and social and object oriented behavior are specifically related in 6-month-old infants.* Paper presented at the Society for Research in Child Development (SRCD) Biennial convention, Kansas City, MO.

World Health Organization (2001). *ICIDH-2: International classification of functioning, disability, and health—Final Draft.* Madrid: WHO.

Wilder, J. (2000). *Samspelet mellan föräldrar och barn med flera grava funktionsnedsättningar* (The interaction between parents and their children with profound multiple disabilities). Västerås, Sweden: Mälardalen University.

Winograd, T. (1977). A framework for understanding discourse. In P. A. Carpenter & M. A. Just (Eds.), *Cognitive Processes in Comprehension,* Hillsdale, NJ: Erlbaum.

Vygotsky, L. S. (1962). In E. Haufman & G. Vakar (Trans-eds.). *Thoughts and language.* Cambridge, MA: MIT Press.

CHAPTER 14

Strategies for Beginning Communicators

Jeff Sigafoos
Department of Special Education
University of Texas at Austin

Erik Drasgow
Department of Educational Psychology
University of South Carolina

Ralf Schlosser
Department of Speech-Language
  Pathology and Audiology
Northeastern University

The Efficacy of Augmentative and Alternative Communication

I. INTRODUCTION

Most children progress from beginning communicators to fluent speakers during their first 2 to 3 years of life. Unfortunately, individuals with developmental disabilities, physical disabilities, or both all too often fail to make this transition. Indeed, evidence from epidemiological surveys and assessment studies indicate that nearly all individuals with disabilities who require extensive to pervasive supports (Luckasson *et al.*, 1992) also have a severe communication impairment (Matas, Mathy-Laikko, Beukelman, & Legresley, 1985; Sigafoos & Pennell, 1995; Wing & Attwood, 1987). Such individuals appear unlikely to acquire any appreciable amount of speech and are therefore obvious candidates for augmentative and alternative communication (AAC).

In the absence of effective AAC intervention, many of these individuals are likely to remain at the beginning stages of communication and some may even develop challenging behaviors to fill the communicative void (Reichle, 1997). This situation may occur because communicative partners often find it difficult to interpret the communicative intent or purpose of the individual's existing behaviors (e.g., facial expressions, vocalizations, body movements, tantrums) due to the subtle, problematic, idiosyncratic, and often inconsistent nature of such "prelinguistic" or "nonsymbolic" acts (Sigafoos *et al.*, 2000a). To enhance the beginning communicator's development and facilitate his or her participation in society, AAC intervention is needed to establish alternative forms of communication that are more symbolic, age appropriate, and easier for communicative partners to interpret (Reichle, Halle, & Dragsow, 1998). Intervention is also needed to replace existing challenging behaviors with socially appropriate communicative alternatives (Mirenda, 1997). Prizant, Wetherby, and Rydell (2000) argued that although unconventional forms, including some problem behaviors, may be intentional and functional for the individual, the long-term goal of intervention should "focus on helping individuals acquire more conventional and socially acceptable forms to communicate" (p. 211).

But how would a practitioner go about helping beginning communicators acquire more conventional and socially acceptable forms of communication? What strategies are effective in teaching beginning communicators to use AAC? This chapter reviews the evidence concerning the efficacy of AAC intervention for beginning communicators. Our goal in reviewing this literature is to provide evidence-based recommendations for some of the many decisions faced by practitioners. After considering the characteristics of beginning communicators and evidence-based practice (EBP), the chapter is organized around the types of questions that a practitioner or other relevant stakeholder might ask when starting AAC interventions with beginning communicators.

II. BEGINNING COMMUNICATORS

Beukelman and Mirenda (1998, p. 265) outlined the characteristics of beginning communicators in relation to AAC intervention. Beginning communicators include individuals across the age range (i.e., young children to older adults). These individuals have a severe communication impairment associated with severe to profound levels of developmental, physical, or sensory disabilities such as cerebral palsy, mental retardation, autism, or deaf/blindness. As a result of their severe communication impairment, beginning communicators typically rely on prelinguistic or nonsymbolic forms of communication, such as informal gestures, undifferentiated vocalizations, eye contact, facial expressions, and body movements. As mentioned earlier, some beginning communicators may use various forms of challenging behavior (e.g., aggression, self-injury, tantrums) to communicate. This reliance on prelinguistic forms is problematic because these acts are difficult to interpret and it is also often unclear if such acts actually represent intentional communication (Beukelman & Mirenda, 1998; Sigafoos *et al.*, 2000b; Wetherby & Prizant, 1989).

It is apparent from the description by Beukelman and Mirenda (1998) that although beginning communicators share some general characteristics, this is by no means a homogeneous group. Still, the general characteristics of beginning communicators outlined by Beukelman and Mirenda have implications for the design of AAC interventions. Indeed, AAC practitioners who have not worked with this population before often find these characteristics so unique and the needs of beginning communicators so demanding that it becomes challenging to imagine the types of intervention goals and strategies that would be indicated. However, the aims of intervention for beginning communicators are in principle no different from those for other individuals who require AAC. It has been argued that the overall aim of AAC intervention is to provide a system of communication that will lead to increased communicative competence, which should, in turn, lead to improved social interactions and increased participation in society (Ferguson, 1994; Light & Binger, 1998).

On the other hand, it is often true that the initial specific goals for beginning communicators may be different in kind from other AAC candidates who have more advanced linguistic and cognitive skills. Initial goals for beginning communicators typically focus on the acquisition of functional communication skills such requesting and rejecting (Reichle, York, & Sigafoos, 1991). In this context, functional refers to AAC systems that enable the individual to participate more independently in these types of communicative exchanges across a range of partners and settings. In addition, newly acquired communication skills are more functional when they are fluent, spontaneous, generalized, and maintained after intervention has ended. The basic premise underlying this chapter is that adherence to the principles of EBP, including the implementation of empirically validated strategies, will enable practitioners to be more successful in achieving functional outcomes for beginning communicators.

III. IMPLEMENTATION OF EMPIRICALLY VALIDATED STRATEGIES

Suppose you have decided to start an AAC intervention by teaching an initial requesting response. Numerous strategies could be implemented in an attempt to achieve this goal (Sigafoos & Mirenda, 2002). However, a strategy demonstrated to be effective with a sample of beginning communicators in one or more well-designed research studies (i.e., an empirically validated strategy) may not necessarily work with other clients in everyday clinical practice. This potential discrepancy relates in part to the distinction between the ideal or optimal conditions that are described in some research studies versus the average or even substandard conditions that may be typical of everyday practice in the home, school, clinic, job setting, and community (see also Chapter 2).

In light of the potentially important differences between research and practice, it is helpful to assess the generality of strategies evaluated in applied intervention research before implementing those strategies with other beginning communicators in practice (see Chapter 3). One type of generality is called subject generality. Subject generality refers to the extent to which similar outcomes would be achieved when the strategy is used with a person who was not part of the research study. If the new individual shares many characteristics with the research participants—or if good results were reported across several studies that collectively included a range of individuals with differing characteristics— then the practitioner can perhaps be more confident that that strategy would likely work with his or her client.

Using empirically validated strategies that have worked with similar types of individuals is certainly an important part of EBP. But how does the practitioner know whether a particular individual is sufficiently similar to those described in a collection of research studies to warrant using the strategy evaluated in those studies? Even two beginning communicators with identical genetic syndromes will have unique experiences leading to many important differences that may influence the effectiveness of an intervention strategy. Practitioners must be able to individualize interventions, and this requires more than replicating empirically validated strategies in practice. It requires the ability to select, from an array of promising intervention options, a strategy or a package of strategies that is likely to produce the best outcome. It also requires the ability to modify instruction in light of the individual's potentially unique response to those strategies.

Consider the example of learning styles and autism. There is some evidence to suggest that children with autism are better at processing visual as opposed to auditory stimuli (Schopler & Mesibov, 1995). In addition, children with autism often show stimulus overselectivity (Koegel & Koegel, 1995), which means that they might attend to only one aspect of a complex stimulus or situation. So, for example, if the child's AAC system consisted of black and white line drawings affixed to a speech-generating device (SGD), the child might attend only to the drawings and not to the speech output. Indeed, one could speculate that the inclusion of speech output might even interfere with learning to use the line drawings for communication. Based on this evidence and logical reasoning, a clinician might predict that a communication board with line drawings alone would be a better option than a SGD for a child with autism. To complicate matters, however, some preliminary evidence suggests that auditory feedback in the form of speech output from a SGD might actually improve the efficacy of communication intervention for some individuals with autism (Schlosser, Blischak, Belfiore, Bartley, & Barnett, 1998). These latter results highlight the potential dangers in making predictions for any given individual based on certain shared general characteristics, such as a diagnosis of autism.

This does not mean that research on beginning communicators should not be used in clinical decision making. Rather it means that there is more to EBP than merely selecting a promising empirically validated strategy and then replicating it faithfully in the real world. It is certainly important for AAC interventions to be grounded in the principles of EBP for the reasons discussed throughout this text (see Chapters 2, 3, and 12). A big component of EBP is selecting strategies that have been empirically validated through research and implementing those strategies consistently, with adequate attention to treatment integrity (see Chapter 9). Not only are empirically validated strategies more likely to be effective (Gambrill, 1999), but the use of untested or unproven methods can often do more harm than good. Consider, for example, the many false claims of abuse arising from facilitated communication (Jacobson, Mulick, & Schwartz, 1995).

What more is there to EBP? In addition to the implementation of empirically validated strategies, there are at least three important factors related to EBP that practitioners should consider when starting an AAC intervention with a beginning communicator.

A. Individual Attributes

First, EBP is no doubt facilitated when practitioners take account of individual attributes. Various attributes and characteristics, such as the individual's visual acuity, degree of motor control, levels of alertness, impulsiveness, motivation, and preferences, might influence the outcomes of AAC intervention (Granlund & Blackstone, 1999). A child with severe physical limitations would not be a good candidate for the use of manual signs nor would line drawings be appropriate for a blind child. These are obvious examples of how individual attributes can affect clinician decisions, but less obvious examples can be imagined.

Consider, for example, that some learners may have a strong tendency to respond very quickly and before attending to the task demands. This pattern of responding is often called impulsiveness, and it typically leads to frequent incorrect responses. Duker, Van Doeselaar, and Verstraten (1993) have shown that a response delay strategy may be indicated in such cases. The individual is essentially made to wait before making a response. A related strategy involves repeating the verbal instruction that you want the individual to attend to before allowing the individual to make the response. Both strategies are designed to reduce impulsiveness and thereby promote more efficient learning (e.g., fewer trials to criterion, fewer errors).

When armed with assessment information of relevant individual attributes, such as a tendency toward making impulsive responses, the evidence-based practitioner is in a better position to select intervention strategies that are best suited to the individual. Individual assessment data thus become part of the practitioner's evidence base for designing the AAC intervention.

B. Data-Based Instruction

A second part of EBP is data-based instruction (see Chapter 12). Data-based instruction consists of using learner-generated performance data to evaluate the effects of intervention. Even careful implementation of an empirically validated strategy well suited to the attributes of a particular individual is no guarantee that the strategy will be effective. A practitioner therefore needs to collect data at the individual level to monitor the effects of the strategy on a regular basis (e.g., daily or weekly). Along these lines, the practitioner might make use of the single-subject experimental designs described in Chapter 6 to evaluate an individual's response to an intervention strategy (e.g., speed of acquisition, percentage of correct responses, error patterns). Individual performance data are used to decide whether (1) the intervention is working well enough to continue it, (2) the intervention is having negative effects and therefore needs to be stopped, or (3) some aspect of the strategy and its implementation needs to be modified for this individual in order to achieve better outcomes (e.g., Zhan & Ottenbacher, 2001).

C. BASIC PRINCIPLES AND MECHANISMS

A third aspect of implementing EBP is the need for a firm grounding in the basic principles and mechanisms that underlie empirically validated strategies. Implementing AAC is not like following a recipe in a cookbook or selecting a technique from a bag of tricks. The point was made eloquently by Linscheid (1999) who wrote:

> I am hopeful that the movement to determine empirically-validated treatments (techniques) does not move us toward placing more emphasis on the technique than on the operant and respondent learning principles on which the techniques are based. Developing the techniques for application is easy if you know the basic operant and respondent conditioning principles; modifying the techniques to fit the specific case is impossible if you do not. (p. 215)

In reviewing strategies that might be used with beginning communicators, it would therefore seem critical to determine not only what works for whom and under what conditions (Granlund & Blackstone, 1999), but also to understand the reasons why the strategy should work and what to do if it does not.

IV. CLINICAL AND EDUCATIONAL DECISIONS

This section presents and describes some of the major questions that practitioners working with beginning communicators might ask. For each decision point, the basic principles that appear critical to achieving a positive outcome will be extracted from the literature. The approach in the next section is decidedly principle based rather than strategy based. In the long run, this focus is more consistent with EBP.

A. ARE BEGINNING COMMUNICATORS READY FOR AAC?

Until about the mid-1980s, beginning communicators often were considered to be poor candidates for AAC because they almost invariably lacked one or more of the various readiness skills and cognitive abilities that were considered prerequisites to intervention (Beukelman & Mirenda, 1998). In addition, their cognitive and linguistic limitations were often perceived as simply too severe to enable them to benefit from AAC intervention. Some of these prerequisites included the ability to visually track a moving object or to match pictures to objects, as well as evidence of object permanence, means–ends, cause-effect, and communicative intentionality.

However, there appears to be little direct evidence to support the exclusion of beginning communicators from AAC intervention on the basis of deficits in readiness skills and cognitive abilities (Reichle & Karlan, 1985). This does not mean that the presence of certain readiness skills and cognitive abilities would not increase the efficacy of AAC intervention or influence what can be achieved during intervention. But does it mean that beginning communicators who lacked the presumed prerequisites could not learn functional communication skills given a well-designed AAC intervention?

One way to attempt to answer this question empirically would be to demonstrate convincingly that even individuals who lacked the supposed prerequisites (evidence of communicative intentionality, for example) were nonetheless still able to learn the targeted communication skills as a function of participating in AAC intervention. Along these lines, Stephenson and Linfoot (1996) provided an analysis of 13 intervention studies focused on teaching graphic mode AAC to learners with severe intellectual disabilities. Participants in each of the studies were classified as to whether they did or did not have communicative intent. In 7 of the 13 studies, there were participants who did not appear to have communicative intent, but who nonetheless acquired the targeted communication skills as a function of AAC intervention. These studies mainly focused on teaching beginning requesting skills, as in requesting access to preferred objects or activities, but a few studies also taught individuals to name or label objects.

This analysis suggests that the lack of communicative intent may not preclude an individual from learning to make requests and name objects using AAC. However, this conclusion needs to be interpreted with caution because in some studies it was not always clear whether participants had communicative intent or not. This difficulty stems from three main sources. First, the researchers did not always or fully assess communicative intentionality prior to intervention. This is understandable given that the principle aim of these studies was to evaluate the intervention and not to isolate the influence of communicative intentionality on intervention outcomes. Second, the determination of communicative intent based on participant descriptions in research studies would likely be difficult simply because these descriptions are typically not sufficiently detailed. Third, the definition and assessment of communicative intentionality is itself fraught with major conceptual and methodological problems (Zeedyk, 1996). This means that the same individual could be credited with communicative intent in one study, but not in another depending on the definitional criteria and the assessment protocols adopted in the study (see also Chapter 13 for the issue of intentionality).

In short, the case for or against prerequisites remains unproven and perhaps unprovable. Some might argue that if the individual learned to use AAC for functional communication, then he or she must have had the required prerequisites to begin with. Others could argue that a well-designed AAC intervention might actually facilitate the emergence of the very skills and abilities that are considered prerequisites. So to avoid the paralysis-by-analysis trap, the best answer to the question is yes: Beginning communicators are ready for AAC. This approach is ethically defensible, and it is the most proactive even if it cannot be proven. At any rate, there are many published intervention studies in this area (Sigafoos & Mirenda, 2002) to inspire clinicians who want to start an AAC intervention rather than waiting around for the beginning communicator to develop what may or may not be necessary prerequisites.

B. What AAC Mode and System Is Best for Beginning Communicators?

There does not seem to be any one best mode or system of AAC for beginning communicators as a whole. The evidence base contains numerous intervention studies in which beginning communicators have been taught to use various aided and unaided communication systems, including natural gestures, manual signs, photographs, line drawings, tangible object symbols, and SGDs (Drasgow, Halle, Ostrosky, & Harbers, 1996; Duker & Jutten, 1997; Reichle, Beukelman, & Light, 2002; Romski & Sevcik, 1996; Turnell & Carter, 1994). Several studies have compared various AAC systems and modes to determine if there might be a general advantage for one type of system or mode over another. Usually investigators have looked for advantages in terms of acquisition, generalization, and maintenance. For example, in selecting symbols for inclusion on a communication board, some evidence shows that in general the more iconic the symbol, the easier it will be for beginning communicators to learn (Hurlbut, Iwata, & Green, 1982). In addition, Sundberg (1993) listed several potential advantages for selecting manual signs as the initial communication modality for beginning communicators. These potential advantages include easier acquisition because some manual signs involve a simple motor response that can be physically prompted by clinicians if necessary. Manual signs are also highly portable. A potential disadvantage, however, is that communicative partners in many inclusive settings may not understand manual signs (Rotholz, Berkowitz, & Burberry, 1989).

Comparative analyses might be seen as the ideal basis for selecting AAC modes and systems. Johnston (1988), however, pointed out the difficulties of drawing inferences from comparative studies because of the potential problems that may arise in equating conditions and eliminating carryover effects when comparing two interventions. This apparent conflict is resolved by referring the reader to Chapters 7, 13, and 21, and noting that good comparison studies can minimize these potential conflicts (e.g., Schlosser, 1999). Thus, comparison studies that are well implemented may indeed be an excellent source for such decision making.

The potential limitations of comparison studies do not mean that an EBP approach to selecting AAC modes and systems is not possible. Although such decisions can and should depend to a large extent on the demands of the environment and characteristics of the individual (Reichle *et al.*, 1991), there remains scope for including an EBP approach as well. Recall how we argued earlier in this chapter that part of EBP involves using individual performance data to make decisions. When a practitioner is in doubt as to the best mode or system for an individual, then he or she could start to teach both. Not only might this lead to the successful use of multiple AAC modes and systems, which is itself beneficial, but over time evidence may accumulate as to the best mode or system for that individual (Sigafoos & Drasgow, 2001).

The "best mode" decision may include considering more than information about cost and acquisition, generalization, and maintenance. One additional important factor to consider is personal preference. Soto, Belfiore, Schlosser, and Haynes (1993) provided an example of how a practitioner might generate preference data. In this study, a 22-year-old man with severe intellectual disabilities was taught to use a picture-based communication board and a SGD to request desired items. After he learned to use both devices, he was allowed to choose between the two. When given the opportunity, this young man always chose to use the SGD. From his perspective, the SGD was the best AAC system. This study is limited because it involved only one person, but the results suggest that including preference data can contribute valuable information to selecting the best mode for an individual. Moreover, additional research is needed to evaluate the influence of preference on such other factors as generalization.

The basic principle underlying preference assessments of the type described by Soto *et al.* (1993) is to let the learner decide on the best mode and system for him or her. Of course, the individual would require a sufficient amount of comparable experience with each option to make an informed choice. After assisting the beginning communicator in selecting an AAC system or systems, the next question that a clinician might ask is, "What should I teach the person to do with this system?"

C. WHAT SHOULD I TEACH FIRST?

Emerging evidence suggests that the best outcomes are achieved when one focuses on teaching new AAC forms (e.g., manual signs, pointing to line drawings on a SGD) that match the communicative functions already expressed through existing prelinguistic acts (Wetherby, Warren, & Reichle, 1998). Well before the emergence of conventional gestures or spoken words, typically developing children indicate various communicative functions using prelinguistic behaviors. The first communicative functions to emerge among typically developing children are (1) rejecting, (2) requesting, and (3) commenting, usually in that same order (Bates, Camaioni, & Volterra, 1975; Carpenter, Mastergeorge, & Coggins, 1983).

Individuals with developmental disabilities who are at the beginning stages of communication may not necessarily express all of the early communication functions that would be observed in typically developing same-aged peers. In fact, the evidence suggests that beginning communicators tend to use their existing prelinguistic acts primarily for behavior regulation functions—that is, to reject or protest and to request objects and actions (Wetherby & Prizant, 1992). Other early communicative functions, such as commenting and requesting information, are rarely observed among beginning communicators with developmental disabilities. Even when more social functions are observed, such as greeting, these often appear to be ritualistic responses to specific situations, rather than truly social communicative acts.

Considered together, these two lines of evidence (i.e., observations from typical development and assessment of communicative function in persons with developmental disabilities) provide a compelling evidence-based argument for starting AAC intervention by teaching beginning communicators new ways to reject and request. The basic principle here is to begin AAC intervention by teaching new forms that match the existing communicative functions currently expressed by existing prelinguistic acts.

An important step in this approach is to first identify how the individual currently uses existing forms to reject and request (Brady & Halle, 1997). This means finding out not only what the person does to request (e.g., reaches for an object, stares at an object, leads an adult's hand to the object) and what the person does to reject (e.g., pushes objects away, turns head away, screams), but also the conditions under which these actions are more or less likely to occur. Consider this example involving Natalie, a 6-year-old girl with Rett syndrome. During a clinical assessment of her prelinguistic requesting acts, we found that she consistently reached for preferred objects, but only under certain conditions. Specifically, she was most likely to reach when preferred objects were held directly in front of her. If the very same objects were placed on the table in close view, she was less likely to reach for them.

This was useful information when starting her AAC intervention. We now knew what she would do in an attempt to gain access or request an object. We also knew the conditions under which she was most likely to do this. The next step then was to map a new and more symbolic form onto this existing requesting function so as to better represent the learner's intention (Ostrosky, Drasgow, & Halle, 1999; Prizant et al., 2000). Her intervention began with the practitioner offering preferred items by holding these directly in front of her. As she reached for the item, her outstretched hand was gently guided down to the table to press a BIGmack™ switch, which produced the recorded message "I want that." Each time she reached, she was prompted to press the switch. With each new reach, the amount of prompting was faded and she very quickly came to press the switch independently without first reaching for the object. When she had pressed the switch, she was given the offered item. Using these procedures, she learned to use the BIGmack™ switch to make requests within 20 minutes, a result that has been replicated with six additional beginning communicators (Sigafoos, 2000).

Similar techniques and principles form the basis for the Picture Exchange Communication System (PECS) (Bondy & Frost, 1994). With PECS, the practitioner waits for the individual to reach for an item. As the person reaches, the practitioner prompts the individual to pick up a picture or line drawing of that object and place it in the practitioner's open hand in exchange for the real object that the person was reaching for in the first place. PECS has proven to be an effective and efficient intervention for beginning communicators. Most beginning communicators master the initial exchange very quickly (Schwartz, Garfinkle, & Bauer, 1998). The success of the program appears to depend on ensuring that individuals come to the task with a strong inclination to reach for preferred objects. They are then taught a new form (exchanging a picture or line drawing) to replace reaching.

The assumption in this approach to intervention, and it is a good one, is that when people reach for an object, they are indicating a desire for that object. They are, in effect, requesting access to the object. Because the existing behavior (reaching) most likely indicates that the person is motivated to gain access to the object at that particular moment, this becomes the ideal time to prompt and reinforce the new requesting response. It is important to remember though that reaching is only one way that a person might indicate a motivation to request and other behaviors are of course more likely to be used to indicate a motivation to reject (push the item away, turn away, throw the item, etc.).

Once new AAC forms have been taught to match each function in the individual's preexisting and prelinguistic repertoire, the clinician can move on to increasing vocabulary. Too often it seems practitioners begin by teaching vocabulary. For example, the individual is shown a cup and taught to sign *cup*, shown a pen and taught to sign *pen*, shown a spoon and taught to sign *spoon*, and so on. Alternatively, interventionists often adopt a receptive labeling paradigm. With this paradigm, the individual is taught to point to the object named by the practitioner. The assumption with both of these labeling tasks is that once the individual has acquired a large labeling vocabulary it will be automatically available for use to request, reject, greet, and comment, or name, for example.

The evidence, however, shows this to be a bad assumption. These various communicative functions are quite independent (Lamarre & Holland, 1985). Teaching a beginning communicator to label a spoon or to understand the spoken word *spoon*, will in no way guarantee that this vocabulary will then be used to request when the individual is hungry and needs a spoon to eat, for example (Sigafoos, Doss, & Reichle, 1989). So instead of teaching a large labeling vocabulary or a large receptive vocabulary, our reading of the literature suggests that the efficacy of AAC intervention and the outcomes for beginning communicators are improved when practitioners begin by mapping new forms onto existing functions and then by beginning to expand the vocabulary. When starting an AAC intervention for beginning communicators, the best functions to target for mapping appear to be requesting and rejecting.

D. How Do I Teach Requesting?

There are a large number of intervention studies on teaching AAC to beginning communicators (Sigafoos & Mirenda, 2002). The majority of these studies have focused on teaching requesting. Requesting includes using AAC to gain and maintain access to preferred objects, activities, and actions, including requesting attention. Emerging from this vast literature are numerous empirically validated strategies for teaching beginning communicators to use AAC to request preferred or needed objects, activities, and actions (Sigafoos & Mirenda, 2002). From this literature, we have identified what appear to be the fundamental concepts underlying the effectiveness of these various intervention strategies and have translated these basic principles into five instructional steps that might prove helpful in guiding practice:

1. First, the new and more conventional response form that the person will be taught to indicate a request needs to be defined in objective and measurable terms. This is necessary so that practitioners will be able to know what response form is to be prompted and reinforced (see steps 4 and 5).

2. Once defined, the probability of acquisition appears to depend on the extent to which the new form is more efficient than the prelinguistic acts currently used by the beginning communicator to make requests (Horner & Day, 1991; Lim, Browder, & Sigafoos, 1998). This means that the new response form should be one that the leaner can perform quickly with little effort and one that social partners will be able to interpret readily and respond to reliably. It also means making sure the old form is no longer effective (see step 5).

3. Instruction needs to be implemented when the individual is motivated to request (Drasgow, Halle & Sigafoos, 1999). One way to do this is to offer

objects or activities that the individual wants or needs as determined by a preference assessment (Fisher et al., 1992; Lohrmann-O'Rourke & Browder, 1998). Another way to do this is to implement instruction when the individual signals an intent to request by reaching for, approaching, looking at, or perhaps even leading an adult's hand to an object. At these times, the practitioner would preempt the old form and prompt and reinforce the new form. Although this incidental teaching approach provides an effective context for teaching AAC skills, some individuals may not initiate very often, which could slow acquisition (Reichle et al., 1991). Instead of simply waiting for the individual to initiate, a practitioner can implement additional strategies to create the need for requesting and thereby increase the number of instructional opportunities. Sigafoos (1999) identified several empirically validated strategies for this purpose, including (a) withholding one or more preferred or needed items, (b) interrupting or blocking access to a preferred activity, (c) providing incomplete reinforcement such as only half of the pieces needed to assemble a toy, and (d) delayed assistance to create a need for the individual to request help.

4. During intervention, it is imperative to ensure that each instructional opportunity ends with the learner making the desired response. Of course it is important to remember that an instructional opportunity should occur only when the learner is in fact motivated to communicate. Opportunities to teach requesting occur in situations when the learner indicates in some way that he or she wants to gain or maintain access to a desired object or activity, such as by approaching an activity or reaching for an object. When it is clear that the individual is motivated to communicate, the practitioner's job is to ensure that the new response occurs and is reinforced. If the individual does not produce the new requesting response within a reasonable period (e.g., 10 seconds) or if the individual persists in using the old form, then the interventionist would prompt the desired response and preempt the old form using verbal, model, gesture prompts, or physical assistance as necessary. Over successive opportunities, these prompts would be faded to promote independence. Numerous prompting strategies have been used to teach requests to beginning communicators and guidelines have been developed for implementing and fading prompts (Duker, 1988; Reichle et al., 1991).

5. The final step is to provide positive reinforcement for the new requesting response. This involves providing the requested object, activity, or action contingent upon the individual making a request with the new response form. During the early stages of intervention, it is essential to ensure that the new form is reinforced immediately and consistently while the old form is not reinforced or extinguished. This differential reinforcement is perhaps the most powerful variable related to the efficacy of AAC intervention for beginning communicators. All effective interventions to teach requesting include it. No intervention is likely to be effective without it.

E. How Do I Teach Rejecting?

Compared to requesting, far fewer intervention studies have focused on teaching new AAC forms to achieve rejecting and protest functions. Still, a number of studies have demonstrated effective procedures for teaching rejecting and related skills to beginning communicators (e.g., Duker & Jutten, 1997; Hung, 1980; Reichle, Rogers, & Barrett, 1984; Sigafoos & Roberts-Pennell, 1999; Yamamoto & Mochizuki, 1988). From these studies, Sigafoos, O'Reilly, Drasgow, and Reichle (2002) extracted what appear to be the basic principles underlying the effectiveness of these strategies. It is perhaps not surprising that, to a large extent, these principles parallel those for teaching requesting:

1. The new and more conventional response form that the person will be taught to use to reject needs to be defined in objective and measurable terms.

2. The new rejecting form needs to be made more efficient than the prelinguistic acts currently used to indicate rejection.

3. Instruction should be implemented at times when the individual is clearly motivated to reject. The need to reject can be created by offering things that are nonpreferred and disliked. One should also use incidental teaching at times when the individual signals an intent to reject by, for example, pushing an item away, turning away, or perhaps simply refusing to accept an offered item. It is at these times that the practitioner would preempt the old form and prompt and reinforce the new form. The practitioner can also boost the number of instructional opportunities by arranging the environment to create the need to reject. Sigafoos and Roberts-Pennell (1999) did this by offering the wrong item after the child had made a choice from two items. Similar strategies have been used with success in other studies (Duker & Jutten, 1997; Yamamoto & Mochizuki, 1988).

4. To promote learning, the individual should be required to make the new desired response during each instructional opportunity, even if this means prompting the response. Again, instruction begins when the learner is motivated to reject (step 3), but once it begins it is important to make sure every learning opportunity ends with the beginning communicator making the desired response. During the early stages of intervention, it also helps to prevent errors by pre-empting or interrupting the old form and then prompting the new form. Over successive opportunities the learner is assisted to become more independent by fading the prompts.

5. The final step is to provide negative reinforcement for the new rejecting response. This involves taking away the rejected object or stopping the rejected activity contingent upon the individual producing the new response form. Again, the basic principle is to provide differential negative reinforcement.

The new form is reinforced immediately and consistently, whereas the old form is no longer reinforced or extinguished.

F. Can I Teach Other Communicative Functions?

A cursory review of the intervention literature would suggest that the answer to this question is a resounding yes. Various studies have taught beginning communicators to use AAC for various seemingly social communicative functions, as opposed to behavior regulation functions. Skills taught include naming or labeling objects (Cregan, 1993; Sigafoos *et al.*, 1989), commenting (Reichle, Barrett, Tetlie, & McQuarter, 1987), asking for information (Koegel, Camarata, Valdez-Menchaca, & Koegel, 1998), and conversational skills (Hunt, Alwell, & Goetz, 1988). However, a closer analysis of these studies suggests that while the skills taught might look like purely social communication, they may in fact function as general requests.

In the typical paradigm for teaching object labels, the beginning communicator is shown an object (e.g., spoon, cup, pencil) and asked, "What's this?" A correct response, which might consist of producing the corresponding manual sign or pointing to a line drawing of the object, is followed by verbal praise ("Yes, that's right. Good job."). If the child is incorrect or does not respond, a correct response is prompted and then reinforcement is provided. However, because beginning communicators with developmental disabilities are not typically motivated by praise alone, studies that have been effective in teaching labeling, commenting, and question asking have also included tangible reinforcement (food, drinks) to ensure acquisition. The need for tangible reinforcement is a potential problem. Is the child learning labels or is the child learning that there are lots of ways—that is, lots of manual signs—that can be used to gain access to preferred foods and drinks? The answer often shows up during generalization assessments. The child now walks around labeling things that are not present. Some might call this delayed echolalia or incorrect labeling, but what might really be happening is that the child is hungry or thirsty and is requesting food or drink.

So while the literature contains numerous studies on teaching other more social communicative functions to beginning communicators, it remains unclear whether or not these interventions are effective in teaching functions that are truly social and not already present in the child's repertoire. On the other hand, for individuals who already have these types of social communicative functions (e.g., commenting, greeting), the process of mapping new AAC forms onto these existing functions should be effective. The basic principles are no different from those described for mapping new forms onto existing requesting or rejecting functions.

Wetherby and Prizant (1989) referred to this mapping process as horizontal development. Vertical development, in contrast, involves expanding the functions represented by a new form. So, for example, if the child has learned new forms to request, vertical development would seek to establish these same new forms into comments. We are not aware of any studies that have demonstrated effective strategies for vertical development of communicative functions among beginning AAC users. This is obviously an area that would be ripe for research.

G. How Can I Ensure Appropriate Use of Newly Acquired Communication Skills?

When clinicians ask this question, they are usually thinking in broad terms. After the beginning communicator has acquired new AAC forms to map existing functions, a practitioner can start to build vocabulary, and implement strategies to ensure these newly acquired skills and vocabulary are used effectively under a range of conditions. This means that the individual should become very skilled or fluent in using the AAC system. In addition, the individual should be able to initiate communication without always having to be prompted by a communicative partner. Communicative acts also should be initiated under the right conditions, across a range of contexts, and with a range of communicative partners. In the literature, these various aspects of appropriate use are often referred to as (1) fluency, (2) spontaneity, (3) conditional use, and (4) generalization, respectively (Sigafoos & Mirenda, 2002). In this chapter this broad view is adopted, and each of these related objectives is considered part of the more general goal to ensure the appropriate use of newly acquired communication skills.

The literature has demonstrated a number of empirically validated strategies for promoting appropriate use of newly acquired AAC forms. Although there has been little empirical work on building fluency (McCook, Cipani, Madigan, & LaCampagne, 1988), there is a good evidence base of effective strategies for building spontaneity (Carter, 1992; Halle, 1987; Kaczmarek, 1990), developing conditional use (Reichle & Johnston, 1999; Sigafoos, 1998; Sigafoos & Drasgow, 2001), and, to some degree, promoting generalization (O'Neill, Faulkner, & Horner, 2000; see also Chapter 20; Schlosser & Lee, 2000). The results of these studies suggest that better outcomes are more likely when the following basic principles are incorporated into AAC intervention from the start:

1. Select a set of instructional exemplars that best represent the range of variation found in the natural environment. So, for example, if you are teaching a child to request preferred objects, it would make sense to identify a number

of preferred foods, beverages, toys, and so on and use these as referents during acquisition training.

2. To build fluency, beginning communicators need ample opportunities to practice their newly acquired AAC skills. This can be done by creating opportunities for the beginning communicator to use newly acquired AAC skills throughout the day, in a variety of contexts, and by using a variety of motivational techniques (Sigafoos, Kerr, Roberts, & Couzens, 1994).

3. Intervention should be implemented across a range of contexts and environments in which the new response forms are expected to occur. Doing so increases the likelihood of generalization (O'Neill, 1990). In line with point 1, instruction should occur across a range of current and future contexts and environments.

4. Drasgow et al. (1999) argued that acquisition and generalization might not occur because of motivational variables. For example, if the child does not produce a newly acquired AAC form when given the opportunity, it is often perceived as a lack of generalization. However, this scenario could occur if the child was not motivated to communicate at the time of the instructional opportunity. The efficacy of AAC intervention, in terms of acquisition and generalization, is improved when practitioners ensure that motivation exists during each and every opportunity.

5. Differential reinforcement is important for acquisition as well as generalization and maintenance. To ensure appropriate and continued use of newly acquired AAC forms, it would appear critical to ensure that only responses that represent good articulations of the desired form are reinforced. Old forms such as reaching or screaming are likely to intrude every now and then simply because the individual has no doubt had a longer history of using these forms in a variety of situations in comparison to the newly acquired forms. Therefore in addition to reinforcement for new forms, it is critical to ensure that communicative partners no longer respond to the old forms.

H. What about Maintenance?

Although point 5 briefly touched on maintenance, this is such an important issue that it warrants a closer look in this penultimate section of the chapter. Once a beginning communicator has acquired new AAC forms, practitioners obviously want to ensure that these new forms continue to be used over time. Unfortunately, providing evidence-based recommendations to maintain newly acquired AAC skills is a problem, because few intervention studies have included long-term follow-up measures (Light, 1999). Although studies now typically include short-term follow-up measures (e.g., 3, 6, or 12 months), there is a lack of research on the maintenance of AAC intervention effects past 1 year (Foxx,

1999). Still several existing studies (e.g., Foxx & Faw, 1990; Koegel, O'Dell, & Koegel, 1987; Stiebel, 1999) point to a number of promising strategies for promoting maintenance of newly acquired AAC forms (also see Chapter 20):

1. Foxx (1999) noted that setting stringent acquisition criteria (over-learning) during training might help to promote maintenance. Acquisition training in AAC interventions typically ends when the individual has reached some minimal criteria (e.g., 80% correct over three sessions). Although such minimal criteria may be sufficient to demonstrate the acquisition of new AAC forms, more stringent criteria provide the added practice that can build fluency and establish more durable responding.

2. Maintenance is more likely to occur when a range of communicative partners reinforces new AAC forms. It is therefore important to teach new AAC forms that are sufficiently precise and readily understood by both familiar and unfamiliar persons (Durand & Carr, 1992). A detailed message from a SGD with highly intelligible digitized speech (e.g., "I would like a small glass of orange juice") is more likely to be reinforced by unfamiliar listeners than if the same request was made using manual signs (Rotholz et al., 1989).

3. Because maintenance is more likely when the communicative attempts are consistently successful in producing reinforcement, it makes sense to ensure partners are taught how to reinforce new AAC forms. Although this will be ensured to a large extent by following the principle outlined in point 2, there may be some cases when partners will require explicit support so that they know when and how to reinforce the use of new AAC forms by beginning communicators.

4. Continued use of new AAC forms after acquisition training can be promoted by continuing to provide and create opportunities for communication. When the desired forms fail to occur during such opportunities, booster sessions in which the new forms are prompted and reinforced may be sufficient to reinstate correct responding.

5. Finally, it may be useful to think of AAC intervention for beginning communicators as a longitudinal process. As the individual develops and his or her circumstances change, there will no doubt be the need to expand and modify the AAC system. New vocabulary will need to be added, new modes taught, and existing modes updated. This means there will be a need for ongoing clinical involvement, which can provide the opportunity to assess and promote maintenance.

V. SUMMARY

Implementation of AAC has indeed produced meaningful outcomes for beginning communicators. The best results appear to occur when intervention focuses on teaching new and more efficient AAC forms to map existing functions. Although the intervention research has led to the development and empirical validation of numerous instructional strategies, effective implementation of these strategies requires a thorough grounding in the basic principles that underlie these strategies. The application of empirically validated strategies based on operant learning principles has led to a reliable and valid body of knowledge on how to effectively teach initial requesting and rejecting skills. Although appropriate use and maintenance remain somewhat elusive and underinvestigated, empirically validated strategies for addressing these challenges are emerging from the creative application of these same basic principles.

The evidence for teaching other more social communicative functions does not appear convincing at this time. When social functions, such as commenting, have been the target of intervention, the tangible reinforcers used to promote acquisition could mean that these new skills function as requests, not comments. This makes us question whether AAC intervention can in fact develop functions that are not already part of the person's prelinguistic repertoire. In a sense, this question is related to the old issue of prerequisites, but it is ultimately an empirical question that has yet to be fully addressed. Until more evidence is available, the best available evidence suggests that there is no viable reason to exclude beginning communicators from AAC intervention. The current evidence base is clearly sufficient to guide AAC interventions for beginning communicators. It is hoped that the effective implementation of EPB as outlined in this chapter will enable practitioners to assist beginning communicators in achieving many meaningful outcomes from AAC intervention. Additional research is needed to develop new and more effective interventions to increase the range of meaningful outcomes for beginning communicators.

REFERENCES

Bates, E., Camaioni, L., & Volterra, V. (1975). The acquisition of performatives prior to speech. *Merrill-Palmer Quarterly, 21,* 205–226.

Beukelman, D., & Mirenda, P. (1998). *Augmentative and alternative communication: Management of severe communication disorders in children and adults* (2nd ed.). Baltimore: Paul H. Brookes.

Bondy, A. S., & Frost, L. A. (1994). The Picture Exchange Communication System. *Focus on Autistic Behavior, 9,* 1–19.

Brady, N. C., & Halle, J. W. (1997). Functional analysis of communicative behavior. *Focus on Autism and Other Developmental Disabilities, 12,* 95–104.

Carpenter, R. L., Mastergeorge, A. M., & Coggins, T. E. (1983). The acquisition of communicative intentions in infants eight to fifteen months of age. *Language and Speech, 26,* 101–116.

Carter, M. (1992). A review of naturalistic communication training strategies for persons with severe handicaps: Implications for the development of spontaneity. *Australasian Journal of Special Education, 15,* 17–31.

Cregan, A. (1993). Sigsymbol system in multimodal approach to speech elicitation: Classroom project involving an adolescent with severe mental retardation. *Augmentative and Alternative Communication, 9*, 146–160.

Drasgow, E., Halle, J. W., Ostrosky, M. M., & Harbers, H. M. (1996). Using behavioral indication and functional communication training to establish an initial sign repertoire with a young child with severe disabilities. *Topics in Early Childhood Special Education, 16*, 500–521.

Drasgow, E., Halle, J., & Sigafoos, J. (1999). Teaching communication to learners with severe disabilities: Motivation, response competition and generalisation. *Australasian Journal of Special Education, 23*, 47–63.

Duker, P. C. (1988). *Teaching the developmentally handicapped communicative gesturing: A how-to-do book.* Lisse, The Netherlands: Swets & Zeitlinger.

Duker, P. C., & Jutten, W. (1997). Establishing gestural yes-no responding with individuals with profound mental retardation. *Education and Training in Mental Retardation, 32*, 59–67.

Duker, P. C., Van Doeselaar, C., & Verstraten, A. (1993). The effects of response delay on correct responding to instructions during communicative gesture training. *Education and Training in Mental Retardation, 28*, 327–332.

Durand, V. M., & Carr, E. G. (1992). An analysis of maintenance following functional communication training. *Journal of Applied Behavior Analysis, 25*, 777–794.

Ferguson, D. L. (1994). Is communication really the point? Some thoughts on interventions and membership. *Mental Retardation, 32*, 7–18.

Fisher, W., Piazza, C. C., Bowman, L. G., Hagopian, L. P., Owens, J. C., & Slevin, I. (1992). A comparison of two procedures for identifying reinforcers in persons with severe and profound disabilities. *Journal of Applied Behavior Analysis, 25*, 491–498.

Foxx, R. M. (1999). Long-term maintenance of language and social skills. *Behavioral Interventions, 14*, 135–146.

Foxx, R. M., & Faw, G. D. (1990). Long-term follow-up of echolalia and question answering. *Journal of Applied Behavior Analysis, 23*, 387–396.

Gambrill, E. (1999). Evidence-based clinical behavior analysis, evidence-based medicine and the Cochrane collaboration. *Journal of Behavior Therapy and Experimental Psychiatry, 30*, 1–14.

Granlund, M., & Blackstone, S. (1999). Outcome measurement in AAC. In F. T. Loncke, J. Clibbens, H. H. Arvidson, & L. L. Lloyd (Eds.), *Augmentative and alternative communication: New directions in research and practice* (pp. 207–227). London: Whurr.

Halle, J. W. (1987). Teaching language in the natural environment: An analysis of spontaneity. *Journal of the Association for Persons with Severe Handicaps, 12*, 28–37.

Horner, R. H., & Day, H. M. (1991). The effects of response efficiency on functionally equivalent competing behaviors. *Journal of Applied Behavior Analysis, 24*, 719–732.

Hung, D. W. (1980). Training and generalization of yes and no as mands in two autistic children. *Journal of Autism and Developmental Disorders, 10*, 139–152.

Hunt, P., Alwell, M., & Goetz, L. (1988). Acquisition of conversational skills and the reduction of inappropriate social interaction behaviors. *Journal of the Association for Persons with Severe Handicaps, 13*, 20–27.

Hurlbut, B. I., Iwata, B. A., & Green, J. D. (1982). Non-vocal language acquisition in adolescents with severe physical disabilities: Blissymbols versus iconic stimulus formats. *Journal of Applied Behavior Analysis, 15*, 241–258.

Jacobson, J. W., Mulick, J. A., & Schwartz, A. A. (1995). A history of facilitated communication. *American Psychologist, 50*, 750–765.

Johnston, J. M. (1988). Strategic and tactical limits of comparison studies. *The Behavior Analyst, 11*, 1–9.

Kaczmarek, L. A. (1990). Teaching spontaneous language to individuals with severe handicaps: A matrix model. *Journal of the Association for Persons with Severe Handicaps, 15*, 160–169.

Koegel, L. K., Camarata, S. M., Valdez-Menchaca, M., & Koegel, R. L. (1998). Setting generalization of question-asking by children with autism. *American Journal on Mental Retardation, 102,* 346–357.

Koegel, R. L., & Koegel, L. K. (Eds.). (1995). *Teaching children with autism: Strategies for initiating positive interactions and improving learning opportunities.* Baltimore: Paul H. Brookes.

Koegel, R. L., O'Dell, M. C., & Koegel, L. K. (1987). A natural language teaching paradigm for non-verbal autistic children. *Journal of Autism and Developmental Disorders, 17,* 187–200.

Lamarre, J., & Holland, J. G. (1985). The functional independence of mands and tacts. *Journal of the Experimental Analysis of Behavior, 43,* 5–19.

Light, J. C. (1999). Do augmentative and alternative communication interventions really make a difference?: The challenges of efficacy research. *Augmentative and Alternative Communication, 15,* 13–24.

Light, J. C., & Binger, C. (1998). *Building communicative competence with individuals who use augmentative and alternative communication.* Baltimore: Paul H. Brookes.

Lim, L., Browder, D. M., & Sigafoos, J. (1998). The role of response effort and motion study in functionally equivalent task designs and alternatives. *Journal of Behavioral Education, 8,* 81–102.

Linscheid, T. R. (1999). Commentary: Response to empirically supported treatments for feeding problems. *Journal of Pediatric Psychology, 24,* 215–216.

Lohrmann-O'Rourke, S., & Browder, D. M. (1998). Empirically validated methods to assess the preferences of individuals with severe disabilities. *American Journal on Mental Retardation, 103,* 146–161.

Luckasson, R., Coulter, D. L., Polloway, E. A., Reiss, S., Schalock, R. L., Snell, M. E., Spitalnik, D. M., & Stark, J. A. (1992). *Mental retardation: Definition, classification, and systems of support* (9th ed.). Washington, DC: American Association on Mental Retardation.

Matas, J., Mathy-Laikko, P., Beukelman, D., & Legresley, K. (1985). Identifying the nonspeaking population: A demographic study. *Augmentative and Alternative Communication, 1,* 17–31.

McCook, B., Cipani, E., Madigan, K., & LaCampagne, J. (1988). Developing requesting behavior: Acquisition, fluency, and generality. *Mental Retardation, 26,* 137–143.

Mirenda, P. (1997). Supporting individuals with challenging behavior through functional communication training and AAC: Research review. *Augmentative and Alternative Communication, 13,* 207–225.

O'Neill, R. E. (1990). Establishing verbal repertoires: Toward the application of general case analysis and programming. *The Analysis of Verbal Behavior, 8,* 113–126.

O'Neill, R. E., Faulkner, C., & Horner, R. H. (2000). The effects of general case training of manding responses on children with severe disabilities. *Journal of Developmental and Physical Disabilities, 12,* 43–60.

Ostrosky, M. M., Drasgow, E., & Halle, J. W. (1999). "How can I help you get what you want?" A communication strategy for students with severe disabilities. *Teaching Exceptional Children, 31,* 56–61.

Prizant, B. M., Wetherby, A. M., & Rydell, P. J. (2000). Communication intervention issues for children with autism spectrum disorders. In A. M. Wetherby & B. M. Prizant (Eds.), *Autism spectrum disorders: A transactional developmental perspective* (pp. 193–224). Baltimore: Paul H. Brookes.

Reichle, J. (1997). Communication intervention with persons who have severe disabilities. *Journal of Special Education, 31,* 110–136.

Reichle, J., Barrett, C., Tetlie, R., & McQuarter, R. (1987). The effect of prior intervention to establish generalized requesting on the acquisition of object labels. *Augmentative and Alternative Communication, 3,* 3–11.

Reichle, J., Beukelman, D., & Light, J. (Eds.). (2002). *Exemplary strategies for beginning communicators: Implications for AAC.* Baltimore: Paul H. Brookes.

Reichle, J., Halle, J., & Drasgow, E. (1998). Implementing augmentative communication systems. In A. M. Wetherby, S. F. Warren, & J. Reichle (Eds.), *Transitions in prelinguistic communication* (pp. 417–436). Baltimore: Paul H. Brookes.

Reichle, J., & Johnston, S. S. (1999). Teaching the conditional use of communicative requests to two school-aged children with severe developmental disabilities. *Language, Speech, and Hearing Services in Schools, 30*, 324–334.

Reichle, J., & Karlan, G. (1985). The selection of an augmentative system of communication intervention: A critique of decision rules. *Journal of the Association for Persons with Severe Handicaps, 10*, 146–156.

Reichle, J., Rogers, N., & Barrett, C. (1984). Establishing pragmatic discriminations among the communicative functions of requesting, rejecting, and commenting in an adolescent. *Journal of the Association for Persons with Severe Handicaps, 14*, 75–80.

Reichle, J., & Yoder, D. E. (1985). Communication board use in severely handicapped learners. *Language, Speech, and Hearing Services in Schools, 16*, 146–157.

Reichle, J., York, J., & Sigafoos, J. (Eds.). (1991). *Implementing augmentative and alternative communication: Strategies for learners with severe disabilities.* Baltimore: Paul H. Brookes.

Romski, M. A., & Sevcik, R. A. (1996). *Breaking the speech barrier: Language development through augmented means.* Baltimore: Paul H. Brookes.

Rotholz, D., Berkowitz, S., & Burberry, J. (1989). Functionality of two modes of communication in the community by students with developmental disabilities: A comparison of signing and communication books. *Journal of the Association for Persons with Severe Handicaps, 14*, 227–233.

Schlosser, R. W. (1999). Comparative efficacy of interventions in augmentative and alternative communication. *Augmentative and Alternative Communication, 15*, 56–68.

Schlosser, R. W., Blischak, D. M., Belfiore, P. J., Bartley, C., & Barnett, N. (1998). Effects of synthetic speech output and orthographic feedback on spelling in a student with autism: A preliminary study. *Journal of Autism and Developmental Disorders, 28*, 309–319.

Schlosser, R. W., & Lee, D. L. (2000). Promoting generalization and maintenance in augmentative and alternative communication: A meta-analysis of 20 years of effectiveness research. *Augmentative and Alternative Communication, 16*, 208–226.

Schopler, E., & Mesibov, G. B. (Eds.). (1995). *Learning and cognition in autism.* New York: Plenum Press.

Schwartz, I. S., Garfinkle, A. N., & Bauer, J. (1998). The Picture Exchange Communication System: Communication outcomes for young children with disabilities. *Topics in Early Childhood Special Education, 18*, 144–159.

Sigafoos, J. (1998). Assessing conditional use of graphic mode requesting in a young boy with autism. *Journal of Developmental and Physical Disabilities, 10*, 133–151.

Sigafoos, J. (1999). Creating opportunities for augmentative and alternative communication: Strategies for involving people with developmental disabilities. *Augmentative and Alternative Communication, 15*, 183–190.

Sigafoos, J. (2000, October). *Talking a new TACT: Technology assisted communication training for people with developmental disabilities.* Presentation at the 8th national joint conference of the National Council on Intellectual Disability and Australian Society for the Study of Intellectual Disability. Fremantle, Australia.

Sigafoos, J., Doss, L. S., & Reichle, J. (1989). Developing mand and tact repertoires in persons with severe developmental disabilities using graphic symbols. *Research in Developmental Disabilities, 10*, 183–200.

Sigafoos, J., & Drasgow, E. (2001). Conditional use of aided and unaided AAC: A review and clinical case demonstration. *Focus on Autism and Other Developmental Disabilities, 16*, 152–161.

Sigafoos, J., Kerr, M., Roberts, D., & Couzens, D. (1994). Increasing opportunities for requesting in classrooms serving children with developmental disabilities. *Journal of Autism and Developmental Disorders, 24*, 631–645.

Sigafoos, J., & Mirenda, P. (2002). Strengthening communicative behaviors for gaining access to desired items and activities. In J. Reichle, D. Beukelman, & J. Light (Eds.), *Exemplary practices for beginning communicators* (pp. 123–156). Baltimore: Paul H. Brookes.

Sigafoos, J., O'Reilly, M., Drasgow, E., & Reichle, J. (2002). Strategies to achieve socially acceptable escape and avoidance In J. Reichle, D. Beukelman, & J. Light (Eds.), *Exemplary strategies for beginning communicators: Implications for AAC* (pp. 157–186). Baltimore: Paul H. Brookes.

Sigafoos, J., & Pennell, D. (1995). Parent and teacher assessment of receptive and expressive language in preschool children with developmental disabilities. *Education and Training in Mental Retardation and Developmental Disabilities, 30*, 329–335.

Sigafoos, J., & Roberts-Pennell, D. (1999). Wrong-item format: A promising intervention for teaching socially appropriate forms of rejecting to children with developmental disabilities? *Augmentative and Alternative Communication, 15*, 135–140.

Sigafoos, J., Woodyatt, G., Keen, D., Tait, K., Tucker, M., Roberts-Pennell, D., & Pittendreigh, N. (2000a). Identifying potential communicative acts in children with developmental and physical disabilities. *Communication Disorders Quarterly, 21*, 77–86.

Sigafoos, J., Woodyatt, G., Tucker, M., Roberts-Pennell, D., & Pittendreigh, N. (2000b). Assessment of potential communicative acts in three individuals with Rett syndrome. *Journal of Developmental and Physical Disabilities, 12*, 203–216.

Soto, G., Belfiore, P. J., Schlosser, R. W., & Haynes, C. (1993). Teaching specific requests: A comparative analysis on skill acquisition and preference using two augmentative and alternative communication aids. *Education and Training in Mental Retardation, 28*, 169–178.

Stephenson, J., & Linfoot, K. (1996). Intentional communication and graphic symbol use by students with severe intellectual disability. *International Journal of Disability, Development and Education, 43*, 147–165.

Stiebel, D. (1999). Promoting augmentative communication during daily routines: A parent problem-solving intervention. *Journal of Positive Behavior Interventions, 1*, 159–169.

Sundberg, M. L. (1993). Selecting a response form for nonverbal persons: Facilitated communication, pointing systems, or sign language? *The Analysis of Verbal Behavior, 11*, 99–116.

Turnell, R., & Carter, M. (1994). Establishing a repertoire of requesting for a student with severe and multiple disabilities using tangible symbols and naturalistic time delay. *Australia and New Zealand Journal of Developmental Disability, 19*, 193–207.

Wetherby, A., & Prizant, B. (1989). The expression of communicative intent: Assessment guidelines. *Seminars in Speech and Language, 10*, 77–91.

Wetherby, A., & Prizant, B. (1992). Profiling young children's communicative competence. In S. Warren & J. Reichle (Eds.), *Causes and effects in communication and language intervention* (pp. 217–253). Baltimore: Paul H. Brookes.

Wetherby, A. M., Warren, S. F., & Reichle, J. (1998). *Transitions in prelinguistic communication.* Baltimore: Paul H. Brookes.

Wing, L., & Attwood, T. (1987). Syndromes of autism and atypical development. In D. Cohen & A. Donnellan (Eds.), *Handbook of autism and pervasive developmental disorders* (pp. 3–19). New York: John Wiley & Sons.

Yamamoto, J., & Mochizuki, A. (1988). Acquisition and functional analysis of manding with autistic children. *Journal of Applied Behavior Analysis, 21*, 57–64.

Zeedyk, M. (1996). Developmental accounts of intentionality: Toward integration. *Developmental Review, 16*, 416–461.

Zhan, S., & Ottenbacher, K. J. (2001). Single subject research designs for disability research. *Disability and Rehabilitation, 23*, 1–8.

CHAPTER 15

Selecting Graphic Symbols for an Initial Request Lexicon[1]

Ralf W. Schlosser
Department of Speech-Language Pathology and Audiology
Northeastern University

[1]Sections I and II were previously published as Schlosser, R. W., & Sigafoos, J. (2002). Selecting graphic symbols for an initial request lexicon: An integrative review. *Augmentative and Alternative Communication, 18,* 102–123. Some of the wording and terminology has been modified from the original article in order to maintain consistency within this book. The authors have the permission from the International Society for Augmentative and Alternative Communication to republish the article for the purposes of this monograph. Sections III and IV were developed for this chapter.

I. INTRODUCTION

Graphic symbols are often an effective mode of communication for many individuals who require alternatives to natural speech. During the initial stages of intervention, to establish augmentative and alternative communication (AAC), learners are often taught to select graphic symbols as a means of gaining and maintaining access to preferred items. The use of graphic symbols for these purposes is commonly referred to as requesting. Requesting is often targeted as an initial communicative objective because it (1) is among the earliest communicative functions to emerge in typically developing children, (2) provides the learner with a means to gain and maintain access to preferred objects and activities, and (3) enables the learner to exert some degree of control over the environment (Reichle, York, & Sigafoos, 1991). Considerable research has now shown that requesting can be taught as the initial communicative target during AAC intervention with beginning communicators and persons with developmental disabilities (see Chapter 14 and Sigafoos & Mirenda, 2002). When graphic symbols are taught as the means of requesting, the symbols selected might become part of a communication board or electronic communication aides.

Internationally, literally dozens of graphic symbol sets and systems are available (Franzkowiak, 1990; Fuller, Lloyd, & Stratton, 1997; vanBalkom & Welle Donker-Gimbrere, 1988). For the purpose of this chapter, we adopt the description of graphic symbols provided by Beukelman and Mirenda (1998). Beukelman and Mirenda classified graphic symbols as a form of aided communication that involves two-dimensional representations of objects, activities, or concepts. In many cases, the graphic symbols include a printed word descriptor, and in some cases, printed words and letters may be used without corresponding symbols as in a word or an alphabet board. Given the range of symbol sets and systems available, interventionists are faced with the difficult task of determining which type of symbols to implement when assisting beginning AAC users in the acquisition of an initial request lexicon.

Selection considerations may be theory based, research based, anecdote based or represent combinations of these three bases. Theory-based considerations are derived from one or more theoretical or conceptual perspectives and may be supported empirically. Theories, applicable to selecting graphic symbols for an initial request lexicon, have been drawn from psycholinguistics, cognitive processing, cognitive psychology, semiotics, and applied behavior analysis.

Research-based considerations are derived from evaluating the certainty of empirical evidence gathered through research or from factual information. Related to the purpose of this review, evidence related to two issues needs to be taken into account. First, what is the certainty of evidence of the studies available based on their self-stated purposes? There is a progression in terms of the certainty of evidence that was originally proposed by Simeonsson (1995) and adapted to AAC by several workers (Granlund & Olsson, 1999; Millar, Light, & Schlosser, 2000). This chapter uses an adapted version of these taxonomies. The levels of certainty of evidence vary from inconclusive to suggestive and from preponderant to conclusive (Appendix 15A). Second, how well does the research literature speak to those variables pertinent to the decision-making process in selecting graphic symbols for the goal of obtaining an initial request lexicon?

Anecdote-based considerations are derived from reasonable conjectures or grounded in anecdotal reports, clinical experience, intuition, reasoning, knowledge, practice wisdom, or learner accounts. Anecdote-based considerations may be published or they may circulate orally in the field. Because anecdotes may differ among interventionists and we have not engaged in a survey of these anecdotes, it would be presumptuous to conduct a review of these unpublished anecdotes in this chapter. Therefore, only published anecdotes will be incorporated where applicable. Although anecdote-based (and theory-based) considerations are not recommended for wholesale adoption, they do serve an important function. That is, when interventionists cannot wait until research becomes available, these considerations may be implemented at their discretion. In other words, empirical evidence from research alone is insufficient in directing graphic symbol selection for an initial request lexicon in practice; recourse to theory and anecdotes are essential in this process.

The purpose of this chapter is twofold. First, the existing research evidence is reviewed in terms of its certainty of evidence and the degree to which the research base may speak to those variables pertinent to the decision-making process in selecting graphic symbols for an initial request lexicon. The latter part of this chapter illustrates how evidence-based practice (EBP) may assist practitioners in selecting graphic symbols for an initial request lexicon.

II. SELECTION CONSIDERATIONS

The selection considerations reviewed in this chapter are drawn from theories that were deemed informative to the selection of graphic symbols for an initial request lexicon, namely from fields such as psycholinguistics, cognitive processing, cognitive psychology, semiotics, and applied behavior analysis. Thus, the selection considerations reviewed include the role of (1) iconicity and realism, (2) speech output, (3) spoken language comprehension of the referent, (4) concreteness of the referent, (5) the reinforcement value of the referent, and (6) correspondence. For each of these variables, theory-based selection considerations are reviewed first, followed by research pertaining to these theoretical notions.

A. Iconicity and Realism

1. Theory-Based Selection Considerations

The literature attributes great importance to iconicity and the "iconicity hypothesis" (Fristoe & Lloyd, 1979; Lloyd & Fuller, 1990). Iconicity has been defined from various perspectives. It has been portrayed, for example, as the relationship between symbol and referent (Harrell, Bowers, & Bacal, 1973; Lloyd & Fuller, 1990). Specifically, iconicity has been defined as the degree to which a symbol visually (i.e., physically) resembles its referent or some aspect of the referent (Lloyd & Fuller, 1990). To avoid the extrapolation that it is somehow the graphic symbol itself that determines the degree, to which resemblance with the referent is posited, the psycholinguistic definition of iconicity may be more suitable. That is, iconicity refers to any association that an individual forms between a symbol and its referent. This association may be based on a recognized physical link between the symbol and its referent or any idiosyncratic association made by the viewer (Robinson & Griffith, 1979). This definition differs from the earlier one in that it acknowledges that the relationship between symbol and referent are mediated by the learner through words such as "recognized" and "viewer." Most studies on iconicity and the iconicity hypothesis that are relevant to graphic symbol selection are based on either one of these definitions. According to the iconicity hypothesis, symbol-referent relations that are more iconic are supposedly easier to learn than those that are less iconic. If this hypothesis were verified, it would call for selecting iconic over opaque symbol-referent relations for initial request lexicons.

Stephenson and Linfoot (1995) argued that iconicity allows learners to aquire each symbol that represents one object and to generalize the concept that a symbol stands for the object it resembles. Sevcik, Romski, and Wilkinson (1991), on the other hand, argued that symbolic (i.e., opaque) representations provide freedom from image-based referents. This in turn is believed to increase the power of generalization by allowing learners to move beyond direct resemblance between the medium and its representation. Our reading of this discussion calls for the selection of iconic symbols based on the first argument and the selection of opaque symbols (especially over time) based on the second argument.

The field of psycholinguistics and semiotics can inform this theoretical discussion further. For instance, it has also been postulated that iconicity is culture bound, time bound, and experience bound (Brown, 1977; Gangkofer, 1990). Thus, the understanding of pictographs is not the result of the symbol's resemblance to its referent, but rather understanding occurs because people have learned to read the symbols. Gangkofer (1990) postulated several preconditions for reading pictographs based on a semiotic approach: (1) daily exposure to and experience with pictographs in a given society, (2) learning of codes that have been agreed upon in a given society (codes are based on a society's historic and cultural developments), (3) differentiating design of the symbols, (4) rule-governed development of pictographs, and the (5) cognitive construction of meaning. According to Gangkofer (1990), these postulations are supported by the culturally distinct interpretation of certain pictographs, the learned understanding of photographs and films, and the degree of abstractness attributed to paintings based on the learned code for its deciphering. Reichle (1991) provided an anecdotal account of a learner in support of the theoretical importance of iconicity being experience bound in general and exposure to line drawings in his environment in particular:[2]

> [O]ne learner with whom the author worked did as well discriminating among line drawings as he did discriminating among color photographs. This was puzzling until the learner's mother related that for the previous 3 years she had used line drawings of specific toys to indicate the content of various plastic storage containers. Over the course of several years, this learner had had thousands of teaching opportunities in matching line drawings to real referents, and had become a generalized line drawing matcher. (p. 49)

These postulations by Brown (1977) and Gangkofer (1990) are consistent with the semiotic perspective for AAC (Soto & Olmstead, 1993): Pierce describes the following three elements of a "sign" (here graphic symbol): the (1) representamen (i.e., the physical graphic), (2) referent (i.e., the object or what the symbol refers to), and the (3) interpretant (i.e., the signified or understood meaning). It is the notion of the interpretant that adds to our understanding of iconicity as a theoretical construct. The interpretant is postulated to mediate between the physical graphic and the referent in order to provide meaning. So the question arises, what constitutes the interpretant? This interpretant is believed to involve cultural presuppositions of the learner, a particular context, motivational factors, psychological characteristics, or the collective unconscious (Soto & Olmstead, 1993). Although some of these "components" are difficult to operationalize and it is unclear what their exact function might be in interpreting the physical graphic-referent relation, they do seem to encompass some of the constructs that might affect the role of iconicity in establishing an initial request lexicon. Some of these constructs to be discussed more clearly later in this chapter are spoken referent comprehension, concreteness of the referent, and the reinforcement value of the referent.

A theoretical concept that seems closely related to iconicity and the iconicity hypothesis is that of "realism." Researchers in cognitive psychology have

[2]Even though this is an anecdote-based consideration, it is included here with the theory-based considerations because it supports this theoretical aspect. In addition, it is the only published anecdote that the authors were able to identify and therefore does not warrant a separate subheading.

attributed considerable attention to realism, which can be defined as the extent to which graphic symbols realistically depict objects (Johnson, Paivio, & Clark, 1996). Theoretically, realism may be one instance of iconicity in that it specifies on what basis the link between symbol and object should be evaluated—that is, the realistic depiction of the object. In other words, the viewer forms a connection between the symbol and object on the basis of how realistic the object is depicted. Cognitive psychologists have hypothesized that more realistic graphic symbols yield faster object identification (i.e., labeling) than less realistic graphic symbols (Johnson et al., 1996). Whether or not "realism" may contribute to the acquisition of an initial requesting repertoire has not been a concern to researchers in cognitive psychology, but it may be important to researchers in AAC.

2. Research-Based Selection Considerations

To determine whether realism or iconicity plays a role in selecting graphic symbols for an initial request lexicon, studies that manipulate the degree of realism/iconicity shall be examined next.

a. Realism

Most studies on realism have been concerned with its effects on picture naming (i.e., labeling) rather than requesting. Johnson et al. (1996) reported on (1) a body of evidence which suggests that more realistic pictures of objects are identified faster than less realistic pictures of the same objects, (2) a second body of literature that indicates the opposite, and (3) a third line of work suggesting that realism may augment picture identification depending on task conditions. Overall, they conclude that the understanding of the effects of realism on naming is limited by the perceptual complexity of our dimension, the lack of an accepted metric for measuring realism (Levie, 1987), and the narrow range over which realism has generally been varied (e.g., comparisons of real objects with fairly detailed line drawings). In addition, it is important to keep in mind that the pictorial stimuli involved have not been drawn from the graphic symbol sets and systems typically used as part of AAC systems.

b. Iconicity

Research seemingly provides strong support for the iconicity hypothesis in individuals with various developmental disabilities, including persons with intellectual disabilities (Briggs, 1983; Forbus, 1987; Hern, Lammers, & Fuller, 1996; Mizuko & Reichle, 1989 [support for nouns only, but not for verbs and modifiers]; Nail-Chiwetalu, 1992), multiple disabilities (Hurlbut, Iwata, & Green,

1982), autism (Kozleski, 1991b), and receptive language delays (Burroughs, Albritton, Eaton, & Montague, 1990). In addition, the iconicity hypothesis is supported for persons without disabilities (Clark, 1981; Ecklund & Reichle, 1987; Fuller, 1997; Hayes, 1996; Luftig & Bersani, 1985a, 1985b; Mizuko, 1987; Shalit, 1991; Yovetich & Young, 1988) (see Table 15.1).

Table 15.1 reveals that these studies in support of iconicity generally used nouns, or if a few words of other classes were included they were not analyzed separately. Given that these findings apply only to the word class of nouns, they are relevant because initial request lexicons mostly include objects/activities as referents. Even activities, which could be portrayed through verbs, may be depicted via objects, which are part of the activity. For example, Kozleski (1991b) used "trampoline" for jump and "ball" to indicate the act of throwing. The informativeness of this research for purposes of this chapter, however, is limited in that the participants in this research were required to engage in a labeling response rather than a requesting function.

Therefore, the body of research on teaching an initial request repertoire using graphic symbols is examined next (Alwell, Hunt, Goetz, & Sailor, 1989; Angelo & Goldstein, 1990; Glennen & Calculator, 1985; Hunt, Alwell, Goetz, & Sailor, 1990; Hunt, Goetz, Alwell, & Sailor, 1986; Kozleski, 1991a, 1991b; Lim, Browder, & Sigafoos, 1998; Reichle, Barrett, Tetlie, & McQuarter, 1987; Reichle & Brown, 1986; Reichle & Johnston, 1999; Reichle, Lindamood, & Sigafoos, 1986; Roberts-Pennell & Sigafoos, 1999; Romski, Sevcik, & Pate, 1988; Rotholz, Berkowitz, & Burberry, 1989; Schwartz, Garfinkle, & Bauer, 1998; Sigafoos, Couzens, Roberts, Phillips, & Goodison, 1996; Sigafoos, Doss, & Reichle, 1989; Sigafoos, Laurie, & Pennell, 1996; Sigafoos & Meikle, 1995; Sigafoos & Reichle, 1992; Sigafoos, Reichle, Doss, Hall, & Pettitt, 1990; Soto, Belfiore, Schlosser, & Haynes, 1993; Van Acker & Grant, 1995) (see Table 15.2).

A review of Tables 15.1 and 15.2 indicates that we can draw from only *one* requesting study involving various graphic symbol sets/systems that are associated with varying degrees of iconicity (Kozleski, 1991a). Kozleski (1991a) found that each of their four students with autism required fewer trials to criterion in sets that are associated with a higher degree of iconicity than those sets associated with a lower degree of iconicity. Based on the suggestive evidence provided in this study, evidence-based practitioners may be well advised to consider more iconic symbols for an initial request lexicon, at least for students with autism.

As reviewed previously, on theoretical grounds it has been argued that iconic symbols delimit generalization beyond image-based referents (see Sevcik *et al.*, 1991). If that were so, it would guide evidence-based practitioners to select more opaque symbols in order to foster generalization. To argue in favor of selecting opaque symbol-referent relations, however, would require evidence that iconic symbol-referent relations prevent stimulus generalization, whereas opaque ones enhance stimulus generalization. Put another way, it would demand

Table 15.1

Studies Relevant to Examining the Iconicity Hypothesis★

Study	Study Type	Subjects	Symbols	Word Class (#)
Briggs (1983)	Iconicity hypothesis★	6 students with moderate to severe intellectual disabilities; mean age 11;9	PIC, Blissymbols, TO	*PIC*: V (3), I (1), A (1) *Bliss*: N (4), P (1); TO: N (2), V (2), P (1)
Burroughs, Albritton, Eaton, & Montague, (1990).	Iconicity hypothesis★	26 preschoolers with language delays; age range from 4; to 6;6	Rebus, Blissymbols	N (9), V (3), P (2), A (1)
Clark (1981)	Iconicity hypothesis★	36 nondisabled preschoolers; age range: 4;3–5;4	Carrier, Blissymbols, Rebus, TO	N (9), V (3), P (2), A (1)
Forbus (1987)	Iconicity hypothesis★	20 adults with severe intellectual disabilities; mental age from 3;7 to 5;9	Rebus, Blissymbols	N (5), V (3), P (2)
Fuller (1997)	Iconicity hypothesis; complexity	13 nondisabled adults, mean age 20;7; nondisabled preschoolers, mean age: 60 months.	Blissymbols (HTLC, HTHC)	N (29), V (8), A (2), AD (1)
Goossens' (1983)	Iconicity hypothesis	54 subjects with moderate intellectual disabilities; age range 16 years to 31.5 years	Blissymbols, Rebus, Manual signs	V (12)

RV	SRC	Task	MT	Results	Certainty
Not assessed	Not assessed	Labeling (auditory match-to-sample)	Board	PIC symbols were learned more readily followed by Blissymbols, and TO	Suggestive (no treatment integrity data)
Not assessed (considered to be of functional value in the oral vocabularies)	Not assessed (only general, PPVT-R)	Spoken labeling when presented with symbols	Board	Rebus symbols were recalled better than Blissymbols. Subjects showed greater improvements, however, with Blissymbols from pre- to posttest	Suggestive (no treatment integrity and interobserver agreement [IA] data)
Not assessed (considered functional in the oral vocabularies of subjects)	Not assessed (only general, PPVT-R)	Spoken labeling when presented with symbols	Board	Carrier, Rebus, and Bliss were learned better than TO; partially iconic systems (Bliss, Rebus) were learned more easily than the non-iconic Carrier; Rebus was learned more easily than Bliss	Suggestive (no treatment integrity and IA data)
Not assessed (considered to be of functional value in the vocabularies of subjects)	Not assessed	Labeling (auditory match-to-sample)	Board	Rebus symbols were learned better than Blissymbols across IQ and MA groups	Suggestive (no treatment integrity and IA data)
Not assessed (considered typical words for children between 54 and 66 months)	Not assessed (only general, PPVT-R)	Labeling (auditory match-to-sample)	Board	Translucency facilitated learning for both adults and children. Complexity appeared a factor only in the learning of low translucent children for children	Suggestive (no treatment integrity and IA data)
Not assessed (considered functional; amenable for requesting objects/action).	Not assessed (only general PPVT)	Labeling (visual match-to-sample)	Board	For subjects with memory constraints, learning followed this order: Blissymbols, manual signs, and Rebus. Persons	Suggestive (no treatment integrity and IA data)

(continues)

Table 15.1 (*continued*)

Study	Study Type	Subjects	Symbols	Word Class (#)
Hayes (1996)	Iconicity hypothesis; complexity	25 nondisabled elderly adults, age range 65 years and older	Blissymbols (I. HTLC, II. HTHC, III. LTLC, IV. LTHC)	*I*: N (8), V (2); *II*: N (9), V (1); *III*: N (7), V (1), A (1), P (1); *IV*: N (8), V (1), A (1)
Hern, Lammers, & Fuller (1996)	Complexity, Iconicity hypothesis	28 adults with intellectual disabilities and functional speech; mean age of 34.5 years	Blissymbols (I. HTLC, II. HTHC, III. LTLC, IV. LTHC)	*I*: N (8), V (1), A (1); *II*: N (8), V (1), A (1); *III*: N (6), V (1), A (3); *IV*: N (6), V (3), A (1)
Kozleski (1991a)	Iconicity hypothesis	4 students with autism; age range: 7;7 to 13;6	Photos, Rebus, Blissymbols, Premack, TO	N (2), V (1) per symbol type per subject
Luftig & Bersani (1985a)	Iconicity hypothesis	20 preschoolers; age range: 4;4 to 5;2	Blissymbols, TO	N (8), V (6), A (4), AD (1), PRO (1)
Luftig & Bersani (1985b)	Iconicity hypothesis	65 undergraduate students	Blissymbols (I. HTLC, II. HTHC, III. LTLC, IV. LTHC)	*I*: N (10), V (2), A (1), AD (1), PRE (1); *II*: N (11), V (3), A (1); *III*: N (9), V (2), AD (3), PRO (1); *IV*: N (6), V (4), A (4), AD (1)
Mizuko (1987)	Transparency; Iconicity hypothesis	36 nondisabled preschoolers, mean age of 37.5 mo.	Blissymbols, PCS, Picsyms	N (15), V (15), A (15)

RV	SRC	Task	MT	Results	Certainty
				without memory constraints also found Blissymbols most difficult	
Not assessed	Not assessed	Labeling (auditory match-to-sample)	Board	Translucency facilitated learning. Complexity levels (low and high) made no difference for either level of translucency	Suggestive (no treatment integrity and IA data)
Not assessed (functional and appropriate for the sample studied)	Not assessed (only general, RO-WPVT)	Labeling (auditory match to sample)	Board	Blissymbols high in iconicity were learned and retained to a greater degree than those low in iconicity. Symbols high in complexity were learned better than those low in complexity	Suggestive (no treatment integrity and IA data)
Yes (items of high interest value per observation, and indirect assessment	Not assessed (only general, SICD, below 3 years)	Requesting in response to "What to do you want? (visual match-to-sample)	Board	All students required fewer trials to criterion in sets that are associated with a higher degree of iconicity	Suggestive (no treatment integrity data)
Not assessed (functional for persons with disabilities)	Not assessed	Labeling (spoken) when presented with symbols/TO	Board	The Blissymbol learning group acquired the list significantly faster than did the TO group	Suggestive (no treatment integrity and IA data)
Not assessed	Not assessed	Labeling (spoken) when presented with symbols	Board	Blissymbols ranked high in translucency were learned significantly better than symbols ranked low in translucency	Suggestive (no treatment integrity and IA data)
Not assessed (frequency of occurrence)	Not assessed (only general, PPVT-R, age-appropriate)	Labeling (auditory match-to-sample)	Board	Regardless of word class (nouns, verbs, descriptors) PCS and Picsyms were more	Suggestive (no treatment integrity

(*continues*)

Table 15.1 (*continued*)

Study	Study Type	Subjects	Symbols	Word Class (#)
Mizuko & Reichle (1989)	Trans-parency; Iconicity hypothesis	21 speaking adults with intellectual disabilities; mean age 37;7	PCS, Picsyms, Blissymbols	N (15), V (15), A (15)
Nail-Chiwetalu (1991)	Iconicity hypothesis; complexity	34 students with moderate mental retardation, age range 8–10 years	Blissymbols	N (31), V (6), A (3)
Shalit (1991)	Iconicity hypothesis; Component composition and transparency	43 nondisabled high school students (Study 1); 35 nondisabled high school students (Study 2)	Blissymbols (HRHC); (LRLC) (Study 1 & 2)	N (23), V (1), L (1), A (4), P (1)
Yovetich & Young (1988)	Iconicity hypothesis; concreteness	20 university students; mean age of 21;9	Blissymbols (HRHC, HRLC, LRHC, LRLC)	Unknown

★Studies with this denotation do not meet strict scientific requirements to examine the iconicity hypothesis; that is, they did not predetermine iconicity values but inferred that learning differences across graphic symbol sets/systems are due to iconicity.
Key:
• RV = Reinforcement Value, SRC = Spoken Referent Comprehension, MT = Means to Transmit, Certainty = certainty of evidence
• HTLC = High Translucency Low Complexity, HTHC = High Translucency High Complexity, LTHC = Low Translucency High Complexity, LTLC = Low Translucency Low Complexity;

RV	SRC	Task	MT	Results	Certainty
				transparent and easier to learn than Blissymbols	data)
Not assessed (frequency of occurrence)	Not assessed (only general, PPVT-R between 2–5 yrs)	Labeling (auditory match-to-sample)	Board	PCS and Picsyms were found more transparent and easier to learn than Bliss with nouns; no differences in transparency or learning with verbs and descriptors	Suggestive (no treatment integrity data)
Not assessed	Not assessed (considered part of their receptive vocabulary or conception)	Labeling (auditory match-to-sample)	Board	More symbols were learned and retained in the HT condition, regardless of complexity. In the LT condition, complexity appeared to aid in learning and retention	Suggestive (no treatment integrity data)
Not assessed	Not assessed	Labeling (spoken response) (Study 1), rating of translucency (Study 2)	Board	Providing the component composition increased the transparency and translucency of compounds. HRHC symbols were easier to guess than LRLC symbols	Suggestive (no treatment integrity or IA data)
Not assessed	Not assessed	Labeling (spoken response)	Board	The guessability of a gloss was significantly affected by the dimension of representativeness	Suggestive (no treatment integrity or IA data)

• HRHC = High Representativeness High Concreteness, HRLC = High Representativeness Low Concreteness; LRHC = Low Representativeness High Concreteness; LRLC = Low Representativeness Low Concreteness
• PCS = Picture Communication Symbols, PIC = Picture Ideogram Communication Symbols, PPVT-R = Peabody Picture Vocabulary Test-Revised, SICD = Sequenced Inventory of Communication Development, TO = Traditional orthography
• A = Adjective, AD = Adverb, N = Noun, L = Locative, P = Preposition, PR0 = Pronoun, V = Verb

Table 15.2

Studies on requesting interventions in AAC involving graphic symbols[1]

Study	Subjects	RT	WC	RV	SRC	C	Symbols
Alwell et al. (1989)	2 students with severe disabilities	Generalized ("want") (Ana); Explicit ("object") (May-Lin)	N (Ana); N, V (May-Lin)	Preferred routines	Not assessed	N/A	TO (Ana); Photos (May-Lin)
Angelo & Goldstein (1990)	4 children with mild to moderate mental retardation	Explicit (for information)	who, what, where	Not reported	Not assessed	N/A	Rebuses
Glennen & Calculator (1985)	1 child with physical disabilities	Explicit	N	Preferred toys	Known words	Not tested	B & W line drawings
Hunt et al. (1986)	3 students with multiple and/or severe mental retardation	Explicit (want + object) (Everett), or ("object") (Monica, Nate).	N	Objects and events with high motivation for task completion	Not assessed	Not tested	Photos (Everett), line drawing (Monica), TO (Nate)
Kozleski (1991a)	4 students with autism	Explicit	N, V	Items of high interest value (i.e., food, objects, motor activities)	Not assessed (SICD, below 3 years)	Not tested	Photos, Rebus, Blissymbols, Premack, TO
Kozleski (1991b)	2 students with severe intellectual and physical disabilities	Explicit	N	Preferred leisure items	Not assessed	Yes	Photos (Polaroid)
Lim et al. (1998)	3 students with severe intellectual disabilities	Explicit (for assistance)	N	Preferred snack item	Not assessed	N/A	TO

Rationale for symbols	Means to transmit	Results	Certainty
No picture discrimination or matching skills (Ana); developed interest in photos and was able to discriminate (May-Lin)	Card on waistband (Ana); book (May-Lin)	The students learned to request items or events within interrupted behavior chain contexts and generalized to a variety of naturally occurring, out-of-routine contexts.	Conclusive
Not specified	Boards	The children learned to request information as a result of the pragmatic teaching strategy and generalized across partners and environments.	Suggestive (no treatment integrity data)
Not specified	Board	Spontaneous requests for toys increased and the child generalized his requesting to untrained symbols and untrained partners.	Inconclusive (pre-experimental design)
Not specified	Book (Everett, Nate), board (Monica)	The students were successfully taught to request items or events within four interrupted behavior chain contexts. Requests generalized to at least two other chains in which training had not yet occurred.	Conclusive
Types of symbols associated with varying degrees of iconicity (to examine the "iconicity hypothesis")	Boards	The students required fewer trials to criterion in sets that are associated with a higher degree of iconicity (compare with Hurlbut).	Suggestive (no treatment integrity data)
Subjects were able to match objects to photos; iconicity was believed to enhance learners' meaningful use	Board with buzzers & bulb (Oscar); board that activates speech output & flashing of a picture of item (Melissa)	Both students were able to initiate requests for high interest objects following an expectant time delay strategy intervention.	Inconclusive (major design flaws)
Not specified	Flashcard (condition a); flashcard in book (condition b)	The students learned to request assistance with opening a plastic bag. Mixed results were found for use of the efficient open-book pointing response with the less efficient closed book pointing response.	Conclusive

(continues)

Table 15.2 (*continued*)

Study	Subjects	RT	WC	RV	SRC	C	Symbols
Reichle & Brown (1986)	1 adult with autism	Explicit (want + object label)	N	Preferred food objects	Not assessed (only object labeling baseline)	Not tested	Rebus, PIC, TO ("want')
Reichle & Johnston (1999)	2 students with severe intellectual disabilities	Explicit (object label − Bill); Explicit (want + object label − Jake)	N	Preferred foods	Not assessed	Yes	PCS
Reichle *et al.* (1987)	1 student with autism	Generalized followed by object labeling	N	Preferred objects	Not assessed (only object labeling baseline)	N/A	TO ("want"); and Rebus-like symbols of objects
Roberts-Pennell & Sigafoos (1999)	1 young child with autism and severe intellectual disabilities	Generalized (more) (for more play)	"more"	Preferred play activity	Not assessed	N/A	Black and white line drawing ("more")
Romski *et al.* (1988)	4 adolescents and young adults with severe intellectual disabilities	Explicit	N	Preferred foods	Un-known words	Not tested	Lexigrams
Rotholz *et al.* (1989)	2 students with autism	Explicit	N	Preferred foods	Not assessed (only PPVT-R at 3.0 and 2.5)	N/A	PCS
Schwartz, Garfinkle, & Bauer (1998)	31 (Study 1) and 18 (Study 2) young children with developmental disabilities	Explicit (Phases 1–3); Generalized *and* explicit (Phase 4);	N	Preferred activities and materials	Not assessed	Phase 3 only	PCS (black & white; colored)

Rationale for symbols	Means to transmit	Results	Certainty
Not specified	Wallet	The learner requested and provided information during elicited generalization probes.	Inconclusive (pre-experimental design)
Matching proficiency	Wallet	Both students learned to request by pointing to graphic symbols when the preferred foods were distant, and to select the objects directly when the foods were in close proximity.	Inconclusive (pre-experimental design)
Not specified	Board	Results indicated that prior generalized request training did not influence acquisition or generalized use of object labels.	Conclusive
Parental preference	Board (affixed to table top)	Adam did not learn to use the symbol "more" to request a continuation of the play activity	Suggestive (no treatment integrity data)
Lexigrams permit the study of learning to communicate symbolically and provided equivalent symbol experience for all subjects at onset	Keyboard with visual illumination feedback	Results indicate that three of the four participants learned to use Lexigrams to request foods.	Inconclusive (pre-experimental design)
Not specified	Book	Results demonstrated successful communication in community settings by the students with communication books but not with signs.	Suggestive (no treatment integrity data)
Not specified	Flashcards to be exchanged or placed on a strip of laminated poster board	All children learned to request with adults and peers (Study 1). All children learned to request and some generalized to an untrained activity and untrained functions (Study 2).	Inconclusive (pre-experimental design)

(*continues*)

Table 15.2 (*continued*)

Study	Subjects	RT	WC	RV	SRC	C	Symbols
Sigafoos (1998)	1 student with autism and pervasive intellectual disabilities	Generalized ("want")	N	Preferred foods and toys	Not assessed	N/A	PCS (black and white for WANT)
Sigafoos *et al.* (1996)	2 children with multiple disabilities	Explicit and generalized	N	Preferred foods and drinks	Not assessed	Not tested	COMPIC, (color was added later)
Sigafoos, Doss, & Reichle (1989)	3 adults with severe to profound mental retardation	Tacts (Part I) followed by explicit (Part II)	N	Preferred foods & utensils	Not assessed	Not tested	PCS (Carol); line drawings (Dan); line drawings (Larry).
Sigafoos & Kook (1992)	1 adult with severe mental retardation	Explicit	N	Preferred objects	Not assessed	Yes	Color copies of product logos, etc.; PCS (black & white)
Sigafoos, Laurie, & Pennell (1996)	2 students with Rett Syndrome (Study I); 2 student with Rett Syndrome (Study II)	Generalized (Study I); Explicit (Study II)	N	Preferred objects	Not assessed	N/A (Study I); Yes (II)	Black and white line drawing (Study 1); Product logo (Study 2)
Sigafoos & Meikle (1995)	2 young children with autism	Explicit	N	Preferred leisure materials	Not assessed	Not tested	B & W line drawings
Sigafoos & Reichle (1992)	4 adults with multiple disabilities	Explicit vs. generalized	N	Preferred objects	Not assessed	Not tested	Rebus, PCS

Rationale for symbols	Means to transmit	Results	Certainty
Not specified	Board (flashcard)	The learner established conditional use of generalized requesting, defined as pointing to "WANT" "when preferred items were placed out of reach, but reaching directly for items that were within reach" (p. 133).	Inconclusive (pre-experimental design)
Not specified	Board (symbols placed on table)	Procedures were effective in teaching g generalized and explicit requests for food and drinks.	Suggestive (no treatment integrity data, and minor design flaws)
Not specified	Board	Results suggest that responses acquired as tacts do not readily occur as mands. "Spontaneous" manding was developed through a transfer of stimulus control procedure.	Suggestive (no treatment integrity data)
Not specified (possible reasons were considered in the discussion section)	Folder	Results suggest that correspondence did emerge after intervention, which required the learner to select the item requested.	Suggestive (no treatment integrity data)
Not specified (Study 1); "better suited to the needs of the child" (Study 2)	Board (Study 1, 2), Plate switch to activate music (Study 2, Milli)	Results of Study I indicated that one of two children learned to request preferred objects independently using a generalized request symbol. Children, who had failed with generalized requesting, learned to make explicit requests in Study II.	Preponderant (minor design flaws: only 1 replication)
Not specified	Board (symbols placed on table)	Both, the missing item-strategy and the interrupted behavior chain strategy evoked spontaneous requests with no significant differences in effectiveness or challenging behaviors.	Inconclusive (no treatment integrity data and major design flaws)
Not specified; symbols for both sets were rated equally in that they looked "some-what" like the actual items.	Folder	This study compared the effectiveness of explicit to more generalized requesting strategies in 4 adults with multiple disabilities. Correct requests	Conclusive

(continues)

Table 15.2 (*continued*)

Study	Subjects	RT	WC	RV	SRC	C	Symbols
Sigafoos, Reichle, Doss, Hall, & Pettitt (1990)	2 adults with severe mental retardation	Explicit	N	Utensils for preferred food items	Known words	Not tested	Black and white line drawings
Soto *et al.* (1993)	1 adult with profound mental retardation	Explicit ("I want" + object label)	N	Materials for preferred leisure and snack activities	Not assessed	Not tested	Sigsymbols
Stephenson & Linfoot (1995)	1 student with severe mental retardation	Explicit	N	Items he was known to consume or use	Some comprehended and some were not	Yes	COMPIC, and hand-drawn black and white symbols
Van Acker & Grant (1995)	3 students with Rett Syndrome	Explicit	N	Preferred & non-preferred food items	Not assessed	Not tested	Lexigrams

Notes:

[1] Some studies involved more students than listed in the table. The table includes only students who were taught using graphic symbols.

RT = Request Type, WC = Word Class, RV = Reinforcement Value, SRC = Spoken Referent Comprehension

N = Noun, V = Verb, PCS = Picture Communication Symbols, PIC = Picture Ideogram Communication Symbols, PPVT-R = Peabody Picture Vocabulary Test-Revised, SICD = Sequenced Inventory of Communication Development, TO = Traditional orthography, SGD = Speech Generating Device

evidence that persons have difficulty relating these graphic symbols to objects that differ from the training object along one or more dimensions (e.g., size, color, or shape). Unfortunately, data to that end are largely lacking. A few data are available and indicate that this is not so. The suggestive evidence study by Hurlbut *et al.* (1982) with students with multiple disabilities indicated stimulus generalization in both iconic and opaque symbol-referent formats. The role of

Rationale for symbols	Means to transmit	Results	Certainty
		increased as a function of intervention, with little consistent differences between strategies.	
Not specified	Wallet	Mands for two of three utensils emerged following tact intervention.	Suggestive (no treatment integrity data)
Existing manual sign repertoire, sign-linked Sigsymbols, and iconicity of pictographs	Board versus SGD	The participant learned explicit requests with a communication board *and* a SGD. He preferred, however, using the SGD.	Suggestive (no treatment integrity data)
Not specified	Board	The participant learned to request objects in a functional choice-making context.	Preponderant (minor design flaws: only 1 replication; settings and responses confounded)
ability to electronify (computer-based requesting system)	Computer-based SGD	Participants displayed increased item requesting when provided computer-based requesting instruction. Also, the participants discriminated between liked and disliked items above chance.	Suggestive (minor design flaws: only 1 replication; no treatment integrity and no inter-observer agreement data)

iconicity may be mediated by other variables as well. Therefore, it is essential that we review the evidence relative to the other derived theory-based considerations.

B. Speech Output

1. Theory-Based Selection Considerations

Dual coding theory (Paivio, 1986) may also add to the list of "components" that may function as an interpretant. Specifically, this theory suggests that iconicity may be mediated by how the message represented by the graphic symbol is transmitted. The availability of speech output, for example, may influence the iconicity of symbol-referent relations and how easy these relations are to learn.

2. Research-Based Selection Considerations

The role of different means to transmit on the acquisition of symbol-referent associations of varying degrees of iconicity has not been studied. Iconicity studies have used a communication board or folder. Although one of the requesting studies in Table 15.2 compared a speech-generating device (SGD) with a communication board with one young adult who had profound intellectual disabilities (Soto *et al.*, 1993), conclusions about the role of speech output cannot be drawn for at least two reasons. First, no data are available on the perceived iconicity of Sigsymbol-referent relations. Second, SGDs and boards differ along more variables than speech output alone (i.e., proprioceptive feedback, visual appearance) (see Schlosser, 1999). In another study, three students with profound intellectual disabilities, sensory, and physical disabilities were successfully taught the continuation of routine activities using switch-activated SGDs or calling devices (Gee, Graham, Goetz, Oshima, & Yoshioka, 1991). However, no graphic symbols were placed on the switches.

There is, however, some evidence of how the means to transmit affects the acquisition of opaque symbol-referent relations. The work of Romski and Sevcik (1992) indicates that persons with severe intellectual disabilities can acquire initial request lexicons and other communicative functions using Lexigrams when provided with speech output as part of the System for Augmenting Language. In the absence of a control condition (without speech output), the roles of the intervention as a causal change agent in general and the contribution of speech output in particular are unclear.

A subsequent study did employ a control condition without speech output (Schlosser, Belfiore, Nigam, Blischak, & Hetzroni, 1995). Using a *labeling* response, two out of three young adults with severe to profound intellectual disabilities did learn Lexigrams more efficiently with speech output than without it. The third participant reached criterion only in the speech output condition and failed to attain criterion without speech output. Thus, even though speech output was effective for this participant as well, efficiency comparisons could not be made for him. This study demonstrates that speech output contributes to the efficient learning of symbol-referent relations. Limitations of this study, for purposes of this chapter, are the use of a labeling response rather than a requesting response and the exclusive use of opaque symbols. To speak to the role of speech output and iconicity in establishing an initial request lexicon more clearly, research needs to systematically vary the presence of speech output (presence versus absence) along with the degree of iconicity (iconic versus abstract).

C. SPOKEN LANGUAGE COMPREHENSION OF THE REFERENT

1. Theory-Based Selection Considerations

From the postulated experience boundness of iconicity, Sevcik *et al.* (1991) deducted that learners who do not comprehend the spoken referent may not benefit from iconicity because they would be unable to perceive a similarity between the symbol and its referent. This finds support in the theoretical concept of equivalence relations from applied behavior analysis (Sidman & Tailby, 1982). Accordingly, learners that have a prior receptive understanding of the word may be able to learn a symbol-referent relation more efficiently than those who do not have this understanding (Clarke, 1987). In other words, preexisting receptive knowledge of the words corresponding to the symbols being taught (word-referent relations) may mediate the learning of symbol-referent relations (Remington, 1993).

2. Research-Based Selection Considerations

To examine whether learners may benefit from iconicity relative to their spoken referent comprehension, experiments require the use of two sets of word referents (known and unknown) along with two sets of symbol-referent relations (iconic, opaque). A review of Table 15.1 indicates that the majority of iconicity studies have relied on a general assessment of receptive vocabulary skills via standardized tests. Whereas it may be appropriate to assume that nondisabled subjects with age-appropriate receptive vocabulary skills have the receptive skills for the referents used (Sevcik *et al.*, 1991), the same assumption cannot be made for persons with disabilities. Nonetheless, in only one study was the receptive knowledge of the referents tested as part of their screening or preassessment protocol (Hurlbut *et al.*, 1982). Yielding suggestive evidence, this study indicated that students with multiple disabilities benefit more from iconic symbol-referent relations than opaque symbol-referent relations when the words are known. A possibly limiting factor for the generalizability of this study for purposes of this chapter is the use of a labeling response rather than a requesting response. Among the requesting studies (Table 15.2), only two assessed spoken referent comprehension (Sigafoos *et al.*, 1990; Stephenson & Linfoot, 1995). These, however, did not manipulate the degree of iconicity and thus bear little relevance to the issue at hand.

From Romski and Sevcik (1992), the field has gained descriptive post-hoc evidence regarding the role of receptive skills when learning to use opaque graphic symbols to request with SGDs. Low comprehenders seemed to learn to comprehend symbols before producing them. High comprehenders, in contrast, seemed to learn to comprehend and produce symbols simultaneously by using their extant receptive vocabulary knowledge of the word and transferring it to the symbols with which the word was paired. Initial experimental data support these descriptive data: a person with profound intellectual disabilities learned opaque symbol-referent relations (i.e., Lexigrams) more efficiently for known than for unknown words when using a SGD with the speech output turned on or off (Schlosser *et al.*, 1995). This study, however, also involved a labeling response rather than a requesting response.

In summary, suggestive evidence from one emerging body of research involves the manipulation of iconicity and the other involves the spoken language comprehension of the referent. Before these efforts are linked systematically within studies that teach requesting, only preliminary conclusions can be drawn at best: Knowing the word-referent relation seems to assist in learning opaque symbols, but it is unknown whether it would also help the learning of iconic symbols. Some persons benefit from iconicity for known words, but we do not know if they would also benefit if the words were unknown.

D. CONCRETENESS OF THE REFERENT

1. Theory-Based Selection Considerations

Concreteness is one of two prominent stimulus attributes in symbol processing based on dual coding theory. Concreteness has been defined "in terms of the ease with which the stimulus evokes an image of an object or objects" (Paivio, 1971, p. 59). Because initial request lexicons often tend to include symbols to request favorite objects or activities (Reichle & Sigafoos, 1991), the concreteness of the referent is applicable here. Naive learners are believed to learn symbols more readily for highly iconic symbol-referent relations when concrete referents are involved (Yovetich & Young, 1988). Concrete referents are also more likely to be found among iconic symbol-referent relations as opposed to opaque ones. This is because nouns (e.g., objects) lend themselves more to a graphic representation that is iconic than referents of other parts of speech such as verbs (Simone, 1995).

2. Research-Based Considerations

Pertinent research on this relationship would need to manipulate the referents' concreteness (high concrete, low concrete) and the degree of iconicity (iconic, opaque). Only one study has addressed whether the learner may benefit more from iconicity if the referents are concrete rather than abstract. Yovetich and Young (1988) examined the role of representativeness (R) and concreteness (C) on the guessability of Blissymbols in nondisabled college students using a labeling response. Representativeness is a concept that is functionally similar to iconicity (Fuller & Stratton, 1992). Blissymbol-referent pairs rated high in R and C (HRHC) were correctly named more often than those high in R, but low in C (HRLC). HRLC symbol-referent pairs were labeled more often correctly than LRHC symbol-referent pairs. This was taken to indicate that the accuracy with which a symbol is labeled is related more to the degree of iconicity than to the concreteness of the label of that item.

Before drawing any definite conclusions for purposes of this chapter, future work is needed with persons with disabilities and other symbol set/systems using a requesting response. The only requesting study from Table 15.2 that bears some preliminary relevance and suggestive evidence involves exclusively concrete referents, but varying degrees of iconicity (Kozleski, 1991a). As mentioned earlier, highly iconic symbols were more readily acquired than less iconic ones.

E. Reinforcement Value of the Referent

1. Theory-Based Selection Considerations

An initial requesting repertoire provides a direct benefit to the learner by allowing her to access those types of reinforcement that require the mediation of another (Sigafoos & Reichle, 1992; Skinner, 1957). The learner is provided with the object/event specified by the symbol selected. This suggests that as long as the receipt of a referent is reinforcing, the type of symbol in relation to its referent (i.e., iconicity as it is widely understood) may be of lesser or no importance. Thus, operant theory in general and its assumptions about the role of the reinforcement value of the referent in particular may bear different implications than those discussed earlier. Reichle (1991) illustrated this possibility eloquently for manual signs:

> Although translucency of a sign has been shown to influence the rate at which it is acquired, it may not be the single most important factor. The reinforcing value of an item might have a greater effect on the rate at which the corresponding gesture is acquired. That is, a candy bar represented by an opaque gesture might be more easily acquired than a highly guessable gesture for water. (p. 54)

For learners to use the graphic symbols successfully, the receipt of the referent must not only be reinforcing, but also the learner's access to the referent must be more efficient than competing behaviors such as presymbolic forms and challenging behaviors. In addition, the selection of the symbol must be functionally equivalent to these competing behaviors (Horner & Day, 1991; Reichle & Wacker, 1993). For as long these conditions are met, the type of symbol introduced may be of less import.

2. Research–Based Selection Considerations

Pertinent research on this relationship would need to manipulate the reinforcement value of the referent (preferred, nonpreferred) and the degree of iconicity (iconic, opaque). In the majority of iconicity studies (Table 15.1), however, little or no attention has been given to the reinforcement values of referents. Hurlbut et al. (1982), for example, taught graphic symbol sets/systems associated with varying degrees of iconicity in a study that produced suggestive evidence. It is unclear, however, whether or not the objects were preferred. Other considerations, such as age appropriateness or functionality (e.g., Goossens', 1984), seem to have dominated the referent selection process. Kozleski's (1991a) suggestive evidence study, however, may provide some preliminary leads in this direction. Four students with autism were taught to request objects/activities with three graphic symbol sets/systems associated with varying degrees of iconicity. The students preferred the food items, common objects, and the motor activities for which symbols were introduced. Whether the students comprehended the spoken referents for which the symbols were introduced is unknown. All students reached criterion with fewer trials in symbols associated with higher degrees of transparency rather than lower transparency as determined in another experiment (see Mirenda & Locke, 1989). Thus, at least in students with autism, iconicity seems a relevant secondary consideration even when reinforcing referents are involved. The evidence produced, however, is merely suggestive given the minor flaws in design (a multiple-baseline design with only two tiers) and the absence of interobserver agreement data for both independent and dependent variables.

In summary, the relation between iconicity and reinforcement value of the referent is still largely unknown. Kozleski's (1991a) suggestive evidence that iconicity is still a relevant selection consideration even when preferred referents are involved partially questions the earlier presented theoretical argument that iconicity may be of lesser or no importance for as long as the learner perceives the receipt of a requested object as reinforcing. It is still unknown whether iconicity would have had a similar or a lesser effect when referents with a low reinforcement value had been involved. Thus, it remains possible that iconicity plays less of a role when introducing symbols for highly reinforcing referents. The study by Van Acker and Grant (1995), involving girls with Rett syndrome, suggests that the reinforcement value does seem to play a role with opaque symbol-referent relations. Each of the girls requested preferred foods above chance levels and nonpreferred foods below chance levels. The role of the reinforcement value is unfortunately unknown for iconic symbol-referent relations. So we seem to have suggestive evidence for some pieces of the puzzle and only for students from the autistic spectrum disorder. The field would benefit from knowing all the pieces and in particular how they interact for students with autistic spectrum disorder and students with other developmental disabilities. Clearly, future research needs to systematically manipulate the reinforcement values and the degree of iconicity.

F. Correspondence

1. Theory-Based Selection Considerations

A number of authors suggested that correspondence is crucial in the development of a requesting repertoire (Reichle, Sigafoos, & Piché, 1989; Sigafoos & Kook, 1992; Stephenson & Linfoot, 1995). The term "correspondence" is generally used to refer to a correspondence between "doing and saying" or "saying and doing" (Stokes, Osnes, & Chambers DaVerne, 1993). "Do-say" suggests that a learner has taken an object and when later asked what it was, the learner can accurately report. In requesting using AAC, the "say-do" notion of correspondence is more relevant because learners typically first ask (i.e., "say") and then get (i.e., "do") the item. Here, correspondence suggests that the learner selected the item that corresponded to the prior symbol selected. In other words, evidence-based practitioners want to ensure that when a learner selects a symbol that the symbol represents the item this learner really wanted. For example, if the child points to the symbol of *doll*, does she then select the doll from an array of toys? So if the child points to the symbol of *doll* and is then given a choice between a doll and a truck, correspondence is said to occur if the child selects the doll and a lack of correspondence is said to occur if the child takes the truck. If learners are not required to select the item requested, it is unclear whether or not a correspondence between requesting and selecting has been established during intervention. In many cases, the initial lexicon may work against correspondence because all of the initial symbols represent preferred items. Selecting any symbol from the set is therefore likely to result in the individual receiving a preferred item. Under these conditions, the lack of correspondence is perhaps less of a critical issue from the individual's perspective. Why bother to carefully and deliberately scan the array of symbols before making a request when touching any symbol is likely to bring reward? Although this strategy may seem efficient, it is however counterproductive in the long run in that the individual may not learn how to make explicit requests when she or he really wants or needs a specific item. Because correspondence between requesting and selecting may not occur automatically when an initial request lexicon has been acquired (Reichle *et al.*, 1989), additional intervention strategies may be needed to establish the correspondence between requesting and selecting. On theoretical grounds, there is considerable debate as to which intervention strategy might be most beneficial toward that end.

Sigafoos and Kook (1992), for example, described an intervention for developing a correspondence between requesting and selecting preferred items that involved requiring the learner to select the item corresponding to his prior request. When the learner pointed to symbol A, for example, he was given the opportunity to choose between items A and B. Initially, the learner showed a lack of correspondence in that he would often choose the nonmatching referent. An error correction procedure was used to teach correspondence between requesting and selecting. During error correction, he was prevented from taking a nonmatching referent and prompted to select the matching referent. This strategy was effective in developing the appropriate correspondence between requesting and selecting. In the Sigafoos and Kook (1992) study, all of the graphic symbols in the learner's initial lexicon represented preferred items, so any request was likely to lead to reinforcement. If the initial lexicon consists only of symbols representing preferred items, then the need for and benefit of request-select correspondence may be less compelling. One implication of this analysis for selecting graphic symbols for an initial request lexicon is that perhaps the array of choices should include nonpreferred items. This would possibly create an added incentive for discriminated symbol use and facilitate correspondence training.

Duker, Dortmans, and Lodder (1993) have taken a slightly different approach toward correspondence training. They argued that correspondence also involves accepting the item that corresponds to a prior request *and* refusing a nonmatching referent. These authors noted that, following a request via manual signs (e.g., *I want eat*), one adolescent and five young adults would often accept a nonmatching referent such as a drink. This observation suggested that the participants' requests were not corresponding to the real items represented by their manual signs. The solution was to teach a repetition strategy. This involved teaching them to repeat the original sign when presented with the wrong item as a way of rejecting the wrong item. Put another way, the functions of requesting and rejecting were introduced concurrently.

In a related study, Sigafoos and Roberts-Pennell (1999) described a similar approach for teaching correspondence to two children with developmental disabilities. After the children made a request, they were given either the matching item or a nonmatching referent (i.e., the wrong item). Prior to intervention, the children would often accept the wrong item. During intervention, the children were taught to reject the wrong item using either a natural headshake gesture "no" or by using a SGD with the prerecorded message "No thanks. I want the other one." Both children learned to use this rejecting response when offered the wrong item, which in turn implies that they had also acquired a one-to-one correspondence between their prior requests and receipt of a specific item.

There appears to be a variation between correspondence training as studied by Sigafoos and Kook (1992) and correspondence training as studied by Duker *et al.* (1993) and Sigafoos and Roberts-Pennell (1999). The difference seems to rest with the person controlling access to the array of items. In the first study, it is the learner who has free access to an array of objects. In the other two studies, it is the partner who delivers an object. Because learners in their daily lives are typically confronted with both types of situations (i.e., free access or restricted access), both variations of correspondence training appear to be relevant to ensure successful requesting.

The testing for correspondence is crucial for ensuring that requesting was successfully trained. For it is only when learners demonstrate correspondence that their requests are functioning as requests for specific items (Sigafoos & Kook, 1992). Correspondence testing, however, appears more applicable when the learner is taught an *explicit* request as opposed to a *generalized* request. Typically, generalized requesting involves the learner choosing an object from an array of objects following the indication of a general request such as *want*. Therefore, the evidence-based practitioner has difficulty knowing whether the learner really wanted the object chosen. Some limited level of correspondence, however, may be addressed if the interventionist includes both preferred and less preferred items in the choice array. Because it is assumed and implied, however, that the learner knows what she wanted, it may not be necessary or applicable to test for correspondence when teaching generalized requesting.

2. Research-Based Selection Considerations

Intervention studies that have focused on teaching an initial graphic mode request lexicon typically do not require the individual to select the item requested. More specifically, this review of these requesting studies (Table 15.2) reveals that correspondence has been tested in only three studies (Kozleski, 1991a; Sigafoos & Kook, 1992; Stephenson & Linfoot, 1995) as opposed to eight studies without correspondence testing and five studies where correspondence training was not applicable (i.e., taught generalized requests). Considering that correspondence has been established as a necessary evaluation component for ensuring the acquisition of requesting, studies without this component cannot ensure with certainty that requests were truly under the functional control of a corresponding consequence. Put another way, correspondence should be viewed as one dependent variable for the acquisition of requesting in addition to the requesting variable itself.

When the learner is taught an explicit request using the first conceptualization reviewed earlier, access needs to be provided to an array of objects, and correspondence is demonstrated when the child selects the object depicted with the symbol. When the learner is taught an explicit request using the second conceptualization reviewed earlier, the learner needs to be given the wrong object. Correspondence is demonstrated when the child rejects the offer of the wrong item and repeats the original request. It is important that evidence-based practitioners build correspondence into the definition of what constitutes a successful request.

Because the theoretical constructs of both iconicity and realism speak directly to the relation between symbol and referent, it is plausible that these concepts may affect correspondence, which also involves the symbol (i.e., "say") and the referent ("do"). To date there has been no research that has investigated the extent to which the iconicity and realism of graphic symbols affect the correspondence between requesting and selecting (see Tables 15.1 and 15.2). Common sense might suggest that the more iconic and realistic the symbol-referent relation, then the more likely learners will demonstrate a correspondence between requesting and selecting referents. Sigafoos and Kook (1992) suggested, for example, that it may be easier to obtain a correspondence between requests and object selections with graphic symbols (as opposed to manual signs) because it is possible to select symbols that bear a high resemblance with the preferred items; graphic symbols are also static and remain present once select, and they could therefore serve as a visual prompt for selecting the corresponding item. On the other hand, other variables, such as spoken referent comprehension, reinforcer values, and preferences for symbol referents and for the competing choices may influence correspondence and mitigate the influence of iconicity and realism. Suffice it to say at this point that research is needed to address these issues so that these empirical data could be used for guiding theory development and implications for practice.

G. Summary and Conclusions

The purpose of the first section was to integrate theory and research concerning the selection of graphic symbols for an initial request lexicon. Implications for further research are articulated, and where the evidence permitted, general suggestions for practice are offered.

1. Directions for Future Research

Some strides have been made toward an understanding of how some of the identified key variables influence the selection of graphic symbols for an initial request lexicon. The certainty of this evidence, however, is often not conclusive due to limitations in experimental design (see Chapter 6), treatment integrity (see Chapter 9), or interobserver agreement of the dependent variable. Thus, many of these studies need to be replicated in such a manner that the evidence renders more conclusive findings.

One of the shortcomings of the current body of studies, for our purposes, is the manipulation of only two key variables in relation to one another or, alternatively, only one variable with the level of the other variable kept constant (see Table 15.3). This has allowed only a glimpse into the more complex world of graphic symbol selection for an initial request lexicon. Future research needs to examine the intricate relations among all relevant key variables. Framing research questions around clinical questions that are guided by relevant theory may help move more quickly in this direction.

Based on this review, research in the following areas needs to be conducted to improve our understanding of this complexity. One line of work may examine the role of iconicity (opaque versus iconic) on requesting referents of varying reinforcement status (preferred, nonpreferred). Another focus of research may be directed toward the effects of iconicity (opaque versus iconic) on requesting referents that are receptively known by the learner versus referents that are unknown. A third line of work may evaluate the role of iconicity in requesting referents that are concrete versus those that are abstract. Fourth, research should investigate whether symbols of varying degrees of iconicity for referents yield differential requesting depending on the whether messages are transmitted with or without speech output. Evidence of correspondence is not a requirement to show symbol discrimination, but it is a requirement to ensure functional requesting. Learners might be able to demonstrate discrimination in that they always point to the symbol for drink versus truck, for example, when these are placed in different locations. An item bias would reveal such discrimination. Correspondence becomes important when moving beyond general requests to explicit requests. Here, to ensure functional use of explicit symbols, interventionists should monitor whether correspondence between saying and doing has been established. In other words, evidence of correspondence is essential; otherwise learners remain at a level where they are only making general requests, as if each and every symbol meant "want."

The notion of realism as a specific instance of iconicity offers another viable avenue of future research with the potential to inform the selection of graphic symbols. Many line drawings rely on representations that are stylized to varying degrees (Schlosser, 1997). Thus, the question becomes how these stylized representations affect the perceived degree to which the graphic realistically depicts the object. Studies need to be conducted to gather realism data on the various graphic symbol sets and systems to facilitate comparison with available iconicity data. In addition, studies on the effects of realism on the acquisition of symbol-referent relations should be conducted analogous to those investigating the iconicity hypothesis. Should these studies yield that realism is sufficiently different from iconicity, studies examining the intricate relations between realism and other key variables, described earlier, would be warranted.

Table 15.3

Key Variables in Studying Graphic Symbol Selection for an Initial Request Repertoire

Study	Reinforcement value		Iconicity		Spoken Referent Comprehension		Concreteness of referent		Means to transmit	
	Preferred	Nonpreferred	Iconic	Opaque	Known	Unknown	Concrete	Abstract	Speech output	No speech output
Alwell et al. (1989)—Ana	■		■				■			■
Alwell et al. (1989)—May-Lin	■			■			■			■
Angelo & Goldstein (1990)			■					■		■
Briggs (1983)			■	■						■
Burroughs et al. (1990)			■	■						■
Forbus (1987)			■	■						■
Fuller (1987)			■	■						■
Glennen & Calculator (1985)	■		■	■	■		■			■
Goossens' (1983)			■	■						■
Hayes (1996)			■	■						■
Hern et al. (1996)			■	■						■
Hunt et al. (1986)	■		■				■			■

Hurlbut et al. (1982)

Kozleski (1991a)

Kozleski (1991b)

Lim et al. (1998)

Luftig & Bersani (1985a)

Luftig & Bersani (1985b)

Mizuko (1987)

Mizuko & Reichle (1989)

Nail–Chiwetalu (1991)

Reichle & Brown (1986)

Reichle et al. (1987)[1]

Reichle & Johnston (1997)

Roberts–Pennell & Sigafoos (1999)

Romski et al. (1988)

Rotholz et al. (1989)

Schwartz et al. (1998)

(continues)

Table 15.3 (*continued*)

Study	Reinforcement value		Iconicity		Spoken Referent Comprehension		Concreteness of referent		Means to transmit	
	Preferred	Nonpreferred	Iconic	Opaque	Known	Unknown	Concrete	Abstract	Speech output	No speech output
Shalit (1991)				■						■
Sigafoos (1998)	■		■							■
Sigafoos et al. (1996)	■		■				■			■
Sigafoos et al. (1989)	■		■				■			■
Sigafoos & Kook (1992)	■		■				■			■
Sigafoos et al. (1996)	■		■				■			■
Sigafoos & Meikle (1995)	■		■				■			■
Sigafoos & Reichle (1992)	■		■	■			■			■
Sigafoos et al. (1990)	■		■	■	■		■		■	
Soto et al. (1993)	■		■				■		■	■
VanAcker & Grant (1995)		■	■				■		■	
Yovetich & Young (1988)							■	■		■

2. General Implications for Clinical Practice

This first part of this chapter addressed the question "What graphic symbols should we select for an initial request lexicon in beginning communicators?" through an integrative review of theory and research and, where applicable, anecdotal considerations. Given the limitation in the existing research base, both in terms of the certainty of evidence and the lack of research into the interplay of variables pertinent to this question, the implications for practice are necessarily limited. Table 15.4 offers a summary of *preliminary* practice recommendations along with supporting research. In the spirit of EBP, these recommendations are put into perspective using the earlier described certainty of evidence indicators and by describing the scope of their application. Evidence that is marked "suggestive" should be viewed cautiously until these studies are replicated and elevated to more certain levels of evidence. The "scope of application" column is intended to provide evidence-based practitioners with a frame of reference for legitimately applying these recommendations to specific clinical situations. In applying these implications for decision making with specific learners, practitioners should integrate these preliminary findings with their clinical or educational expertise (e.g., concerning direct symbol assessment and teaching of requesting) and an assessment of relevant stakeholder perspectives (e.g., the learner's symbol preferences) (see Chapter 12).

In integrating the findings for a specific learner, evidence-based practitioners are also encouraged to go beyond the typical engagement with iconicity in selecting graphic symbols to encompass other potentially pertinent variables such as spoken referent comprehension, the reinforcement value of the referent, the concreteness of the referent, and the potential benefits of using speech output. Evidence-based practitioners are further encouraged to build correspondence testing into the evaluation protocol for measuring the learning of an initial requesting repertoire. The next section provides an example for applying the preliminary recommendations from this review to a specific learner using the EBP steps outlined in Chapter 12.

III. SELECTING GRAPHIC SYMBOLS: AN EBP PROCESS ILLUSTRATION

The steps involved in implementing EBP in AAC as described in Chapter 12 include the following: (1) asking an answerable question, (2) selecting evidence sources, (3) executing the search strategy, (4) examining the evidence, (5) applying the evidence, (6) evaluating the application of the evidence, and (7) disseminating the findings. Prior to asking the actual answerable question (also known as the "foreground" question) it may sometimes be necessary to ask "background" questions.

Table 15.4

Selecting Graphic Symbols for an Initial Request Lexicon: Preliminary Practice Recommendations

Preliminary practice recommendations	Supporting research evidence	Certainty of evidence	Scope of recommendation
Select iconic rather than opaque symbols for referents that are concrete	Students with autism required fewer trials to criterion in iconic sets than sets that are less iconic for concrete referents (Kozleski, 1991a).	Suggestive	Applies to students with autism using boards and preferred items of unknown spoken referent comprehension status
Select iconic rather than opaque symbols when introducing symbols for preferred referents	Students with autism required fewer trials to criterion in iconic sets than sets that are less iconic for preferred referents (Kozleski, 1991a).	Suggestive	Applies to students with autism using boards and preferred items of unknown spoken referent comprehension status
When introducing opaque symbols, select referents that are preferred rather than nonpreferred	Three girls with Rett Syndrome requested preferred foods above chance levels compared to non-preferred foods below chance (Van Acker & Grant, 1995).	Suggestive	Applies to girls with Rett Syndrome using a computer-based requesting system with animated graphics and touch-sensitive screen requesting preferred and non-preferred foods

A. THE PROCESS PERTAINING TO THE *BACKGROUND* QUESTION

Background questions demand general knowledge about direct stakeholders as a group. Naturally, first evidence sources are sought for the background question; the foreground question becomes relevant only if the answer to the background question is affirmative or at least hopeful.

1. Asking a Well-Built Question

As indicated in Chapter 12, the question to be asked needs to be well-built and facilitate a systematic search of the relevant evidence. This step is extremely important to the process because the nature of the question will determine the direction of the other steps involved. The selection of graphic symbols for an initial request lexicon pertains to the second role identified in the "Knowledge and Skills" document of ASHA (2002)—"determining AAC methods, components, and strategies to maximize functional communication by individuals." An appropriate background question to the selection of graphic symbols for an initial request lexicon might be the following:

Do learners with developmental disabilities acquire an initial request lexicon using graphic symbols?

2. Selecting Evidence Sources

The next step involves selecting evidence sources that bear relevance to this question. Obviously, the first section of this chapter will end up as our primary source, but for educational purposes it is important to illustrate other possible evidence sources. A typical approach would be first to consult AAC texts with a focus on learners with developmental disabilities (Reichle *et al.*, 1991; Romski & Sevcik, 1992). In addition, it may be helpful to consult (1) recent conference proceedings of the International Society for Augmentative and Alternative Communication (ISAAC) and related organizations such as the American Association on Mental Retardation (AAMR), the American Speech-Language and Hearing Association (ASHA), and others; (2) various databases; and the (3) annual indices of recent volumes and the CD-ROM (Vols. 1–13; Vols. 14–17) of *Augmentative and Alternative Communication*.

3. Executing the Search Strategy

Initially, the evidence-based practitioner may want to determine whether there are any published systematic reviews. Reviews have the advantage for the practitioner that someone else has already gone through the process of synthesizing the information in some shape or form. In the absence of a review, the practitioner would need to go through this painstaking process with very little time at hand for doing so.

Preferably, the evidence-based practitioner would be seeking any meta-analyses of requesting studies in AAC, due their excellent ranking in the hierarchy of evidence (see Chapters 11 and 12). If meta-analyses or other systematic reviews were identified, one could quickly locate those requesting studies, if any, involving learners with developmental disabilities and graphic symbols. In an attempt to locate such reviews, I first looked up "requesting" in the index of the text by Reichle *et al.* (1991). This yields the key word "request(s)" and the key words "in graphic mode" one level below that. A quick review of this section yields no references to meta-analyses, systematic reviews, or any efficacy studies. Therefore, I went back to the index to consult other promising key words under "request(s)" and found "explicit versus generalized requests." This yields references to several studies in which graphic symbols were introduced as the mode for requesting (i.e., Reichle & Brown, 1986; Reichle *et al.*, 1989; Romski *et al.*, 1988; Sigafoos *et al.*, 1989; Sigafoos *et al.*, 1990). Understandably, the references are somewhat dated given the text's publication year of 1991. Nonetheless, they represent a good starting point. Still, reviews could have been published after 1991. So the next logical step is to consult various databases (ERIC, PsycInfo, CINHAL) using key words such as "reviews" *and* "augmentative communication." Although ERIC yields several reviews, none of them directly pertain to the topic at hand. PsycInfo and CINHAL resulted in a narrative review by Stepenson and Linfoot (1996); they reviewed literature that explains how "pictures" (i.e., graphic symbols) come to be used as symbols for the objects they stand for. Although several requesting studies were reviewed in this paper, these studies had been located already through other means.

Although *Augmentative and Alternative Communication* is indexed in CINHAL, it is worthwhile to handsearch this journal because of potential differences in natural language terms and controlled vocabulary terms used in the database (see also Chapter 11). A search of the CD-ROM for Volumes 1 to 13 of *Augmentative and Alternative Communication* revealed no additional references for requesting studies. The words "requesting" and "beginning communicators" appeared in a review article by Mirenda and Mathy-Laikko (1989), but no other references resulted from an ancestry search of their bibliography. A handsearch of recent annual indices from Volumes 14 to 17 using the terms yielded.

Next, recent conference proceedings were consulted including the CD-ROM of the 2000 ISAAC biennial conference and the proceedings of the 2001 Annual Meeting of the AAMR. The former yielded no further evidence concerning this question, but the latter resulted in a presentation by Schlosser and

Sigafoos (2002) titled "Selecting Graphic Symbols for an Initial Request Lexicon: An Integrative Review." Although I obviously knew about this prior to searching, the point here is to demonstrate how an evidence-based practitioner may have located this review. Anyhow, this presentation is the basis of the first section of this chapter.

Through the co-author of this presentation and resulting article (Schlosser & Sigafoos, 2002), this author learned of a review conducted by Sigafoos and Mirenda (2002) on strategies for beginning communicators. An evidence-based practitioner could have located this same information by searching relevant Web sites of prominent publishers in the AAC field for recent titles in preparation or by visiting the exhibit halls of relevant conferences. Frequently, these publishers present tables of contents of texts in preparation or texts that were recently released.

In summary, the integrative review presented in the first section of this chapter should represent a good starting point for evaluating the available evidence, considering that the focus of the paper was on requesting via the graphic symbol mode. Therefore, we would expect that all requesting studies using graphic symbols should be included, along with those identified through other means such as the text by Reichle *et al.* (1991) and the chapter by Sigafoos and Mirenda (2002). Table 15.2 offers a summary of requesting studies using the graphic symbol mode, yielding numerous studies. Thankfully, all studies identified in Reichle *et al.* (1991) are represented in this table. Further, all studies identified in Sigafoos and Mirenda (2002) as teaching requesting via the graphic symbol mode (Kozleski, 1991a; Lim *et al.*, 1998; Reichle & Brown, 1986; Roberts-Pennell & Sigafoos, 1999; Romski *et al.*, 1988; Sigafoos, 1998; Sigafoos & Meikle, 1995) were included in Table 15.2 as well.

4. Examining the Evidence

The next step involves a critical examination of the evidence in support of learners with developmental disabilities being able to successfully acquire an initial request lexicon via graphic symbols? Each of the identified requesting studies will be evaluated using the guiding questions pertaining to internal validity (i.e., design, treatment integrity, interobserver agreement of dependent measure, social validity) and external validity (i.e., design, ideal-typical generality, subject generality, social validity) described in Chapter 12. Please note that not every study was evaluated in terms of all of these EBP indicators, for some of these indicators function as preconditions for others. For example, if the internal validity for the objective outcomes were inconclusive, there would be little point to evaluating the social validity of the study. Therefore Table 15.5 only lists those studies (of Table 15.2) with a certainty of evidence rated as preponderant or conclusive in terms of internal validity.

Table 15.5

Studies on Requesting Interventions Involving Graphic Symbols with Preponderant or Conclusive Certainty of Evidence[1]

Study	Subjects	Type of request taught	Word class	Reinforcement value	Spoken referent comprehension	Correspondence
Alwell et al. (1989)	2 students with severe disabilities	Generalized ("want") (Ana); Explicit ("object") (May-Lin)	"want"—N (Ana); N, V (May-Lin)	Routines in which students displayed moderate distress when interrupted and consistently attempted to complete	Not assessed	N/A
Angelo & Goldstein (1990)	4 children with mild to moderate intellectual disabilities	Explicit requests for information	who (persons), what (objects), where (locations)	Not reported	Not reported	
Hunt et al. (1986)	3 students with multiple and/or severe intellectual disabilities	Explicit ("want" + object) (Everett) or ("object") (Monica, Nate).	N	Objects or events that represented high motivation for task completion	Not assessed	Not tested
Lim et al. (1998)	3 students with severe intellectual disabilities	Explicit request for assistance	N	Preferred snack item	Not assessed	N/A

Symbols	Rationale for symbol selection	Means to transmit	Results	Certainty of Evidence	Social Validity
TO (Ana); Photographs (May-Lin)	Ana: no picture discrimination or matching skills; May-Lin: developed interest in photographs and was able to discriminate	Card attached to waistband (Ana); Communication book (May-Lin)	The students were successfully taught to request items or events within interrupted behavior chain contexts and generalized to a variety of naturally occurring, out-of-routine contexts.	Conclusive	Procedures (i.e., routines to be used for interruption) were validated by teaching staff and parents)
Rebuses	Not specified	Communication boards	The children learned to request information as a result of the pragmatic teaching strategy and generalized this skill across partners and environments.	Preponderant	Outcomes were validated: 10 graduate students perceived significant differences when viewing before-and-after training tapes
Photographs (Everett), line drawing (Monica), TO (Nate)	Not specified	Communication book (Everett, Nate), Communication board (Monica)	Three students with severe disabilities were successfully taught to request items or events within four interrupted behavior chain contexts. Requests generalized to at least two other chains in which training had not yet occurred.	Conclusive	Procedures: Sequences were selected with consultation of teachers
TO	Not specified	Flashcard (condition a); flashcard in communication book (condition b)	The students learned to request assistance with opening a plastic bag. Mixed results were found for use of the efficient open-book pointing response with the less efficient closed book pointing response.	Conclusive	Procedures: Teachers rated the response effort of each task design

(continues)

Table 15.5 (*continued*)

Study	Subjects	Type of request taught	Word class	Reinforcement value	Spoken referent comprehension	Correspondence
Reichle et al. (1987)	1 student with autism	Generalized followed by object labeling	N	Preferred objects	Not assessed (only object labeling baseline: "what's this?" in presence of objects & symbols)	N/A
Sigafoos & Reichle (1992)	4 adults with multiple disabilities	Explicit vs. generalized	N	Preferred objects	Not assessed	Not tested
Stephenson & Linfoot (1995)	1 student with severe intellectual disabilities	Explicit	N	Items he was known to consume or use	Yes—assessed (some were comprehended and some were not; the status of each referent was not reported)	Yes

[1]Some studies involved more students than listed in the table. The table includes only students who were taught using graphic symbols.

Table 15.5 indicates that learners of varying ages (school-age students and adults) and types of developmental disabilities (i.e., mild, moderate to severe intellectual disabilities, multiple disabilities, and autism) have successfully learned to request via a variety of graphic symbols (i.e., COMPIC, Picture Communication Symbols, hand-drawn black and white line drawings, other line drawings, photographs, Rebus, traditional orthography). The evidence to that effect is at a pre-

Symbols	Rationale for symbol selection	Means to transmit	Results	Certainty of Evidence	Social Validity
Traditional orthography ("want"); and Rebus-like symbols of objects	Not specified	Communication board	Results indicated that prior generalized request training did not influence acquisition or generalized use of object labels.	Conclusive	Not assessed
Rebus, PCS	Not specified; symbols for both sets were rated equally in that they looked "somewhat" like the actual items.	Communication folder	This study compared the effectiveness of explicit to more generalized requesting strategies in 4 adults with multiple disabilities. Correct requests increased as a function of intervention, with little consistent differences between strategies.	Conclusive	Methods: Interventionists validated the preferred status of objects
COMPIC, and hand-drawn black and white symbols	Not specified	Communication board	The participant learned to request nine objects in a functional choice-making context.	Preponderant (minor flaws in design-multiple probe across only 2 settings; confounding of changes in setting and responses)	Not assessed

ponderant or conclusive level of certainty. Although several studies have assessed the social validity of various *procedural aspects* (e.g., preference assessment, response effort, sequence of activities) to be used, in only one study was the social significance of the requesting outcomes assessed—graduate students perceived significant differences between before-and-after tapes, confirming the primary data (Angelo & Goldstein, 1990).

In conclusion, the background question "Do learners with developmental disabilities acquire an initial request lexicon using graphic symbols?" can be answered in the affirmative. The outcomes in these studies, however, have not been evaluated sufficiently by relevant stakeholder groups. The next step involves the application of the evidence.

5. Applying the Evidence

Before proceeding to the foreground question concerning what research evidence might tell the practitioner about the selection of the type of graphic symbols, the practitioner would meet with relevant stakeholders to discuss the findings. This will allow the practitioner to determine whether to further explore empirical support for certain graphic symbols over others or whether to seek options other than graphic symbols. Because the learner for whom the foreground question is posed is 7 years old, plausible relevant stakeholders are the parents and the elementary school teacher. The practitioner would meet with the parents and the teacher to share the findings from the review of the evidence. In sharing the findings, the practitioner would state that there is "good" database evidence in support of using graphic symbols for an initial request lexicon for children with developmental disabilities such as their child. The practitioner may continue by saying that several studies support this conclusion and that this is remarkable given that the AAC field is still young. This would provide a context for the findings from the review. Usually, the practitioner might add, the research base may produce one or two studies on the same phenomenon. The practitioner would caution, however, that the research to date has not asked parents whether they were in agreement with the data indicating the success of using graphic symbols for requesting. On a positive note, teachers validated the teaching procedures used in some of these studies. This tells the evidence-based practitioner that other people who knew the participants in these studies found the way the teaching was conducted acceptable. In summary, the practitioner would propose that graphic symbols seem to be a viable avenue for the child and solicit feedback and input from the parents and teacher as to how they feel about this possibility.

Perhaps both the parents and the teacher are in agreement, but have numerous questions and concerns about how to get started. For example, the teacher might want to know whether it is best to start with teaching requests for objects, activities, information, or social closeness? The mother might wonder whether it is necessary to use the same graphic symbols at home, even though she perfectly understands her child's presymbolic forms of communicating requests? For questions such as these, the team may find the evidence-based principles outlined in Chapter 14 helpful in guiding further decision making. This chapter focuses on the types of graphic symbols the team may wish to explore using for this 7-year-old child. Because we are primarily interested in the foreground question, the two remaining steps in typically implementing EBP (evaluating the application of the evidence and disseminating the findings) may be omitted for the background question.

B. THE PROCESS PERTAINING TO THE *FOREGROUND* QUESTION

Now that the background question has been answered in the affirmative, we can proceed with the EBP process as it pertains to the actual question of interest, the foreground question.

1. Asking a Well-Built Question

The following is an example of a well-built foreground question related to the selection of graphic symbols for an initial request lexicon:

> For Glen, a 7-year-old boy with developmental disabilities (i.e., autism)—who is a beginning communicator with intact vision and hearing in an inclusive classroom, supported by an aide, and living at home with his mother—what types of graphic symbols are most beneficial toward establishing an initial request lexicon?

As is obvious from this example, this questions contains at least the following essential components: it (1) describes the direct stakeholder and his capabilities relevant to the clinical problem (a 7-year-old child with developmental disabilities who is a beginning communicator—see Chapter 14 for characteristics of beginning communicators), (2) explains the direct stakeholder's current (and possibly future) environment and relevant other stakeholders (i.e., an inclusive classroom with support from a teacher's aide and the home with support from his mother), (3) makes explicit the clinical or educational problem to be solved (i.e., what types of graphic symbols should be selected because they are most beneficial), and (4) specifies the expected clinical/educational outcomes (i.e., establishing an initial request lexicon). "Foreground" questions such as this one ask for specific knowledge and skills about managing direct stakeholders or relevant other stakeholders.

2. Selecting Evidence Sources and Executing the Search Strategy

In terms of selecting evidence sources and executing the search strategy, the efforts of the evidence-based practitioner will be limited due to the preliminary work that went into answering the background question. The integrative review of requesting studies using graphic symbols, conducted earlier in the chapter, provides the practitioner with the best information available today. Meta-analysis or other quantitative reviews on this topic are in preparation but are not yet available. Therefore, the practitioner has to rely on this narrative review. Because those requesting studies that communicate a high degree of certainty have already been identified, Table 15.5 is the first evidence source awaiting examination. Additionally, Table 15.4, which posited preliminary practice recommendations for selecting graphic symbols for an initial request lexicon, shall be consulted.

3. Examining the Evidence

Studies in Table 15.5 demonstrate that successful requesting outcomes can be yielded with a variety of graphic symbols, including COMPIC, Picture Communication Symbols, hand-drawn black and white line drawings, other line drawings, photographs, Rebus, and traditional orthography. Unfortunately, this positive evidence provides little insight into selecting one type of graphic symbol over others because the variables relevant to our foreground question were not manipulated in these studies; their respective purposes differed from our clinical question.

Table 15.4, on the other hand, was specifically created to compile those requesting study that would inform graphic symbol selection. The reason that none of the studies of this table is included in Table 15.5 has to do with their lower level of certainty (i.e., suggestive). In absence of more certain evidence, this is the best and most current evidence available. Based on the work of Kozleski (1991a), which happened to be conducted with children of the same diagnosis as Glen (i.e., autism), it may be beneficial to select iconic rather than opaque symbols if the referents for which the symbols are introduced are concrete and preferred.

Further, the evidence-based principles derived in Chapter 14 suggest that teaching requesting is successful when taught for *preferred* objects and activities as opposed to objects and activities the learner is indifferent about: "Instruction needs to be implemented when the individual is motivated to request (Drasgow, Halle, & Sigafoos, 1999). One way to do this is to offer objects or activities that the individual wants or needs as determined by a preference assessment (Lohrmann-O'Rourke, & Browder, 1998)" (p. 20). In all likelihood, the child will already have presymbolic means to request these preferred referents so that new forms (i.e., graphic symbols) can be mapped onto these existing forms (see Chapters 13 and 14). Preferred objects and activities also constitute *concrete* referents, meeting the second circumstance posited in Table 15.4 that calls for selecting iconic symbols.[3]

---

[3]The study by VanAcker and Grant (1995) is not relevant here because it only applies to opaque symbols.

4. Applying the Evidence

The evidence-based practitioner would then share the findings, albeit limited, with the relevant stakeholders (parents, teacher, teacher's aide), listen to their reactions and feedback, and together develop a course of action. It is important for the practitioner to highlight the preliminary nature of this *suggestive* evidence. The practitioner may also share with the stakeholders that children who understand the word referents of the objects/activities *have been hypothesized* to benefit more from symbols that are iconic than children who do not understand the word referents (Sevcik *et al.*, 1991). The practitioner suggests that we could test Glen's receptive speech related to the objects identified in the preference assessment and only select those that he does understand for teaching requesting. Even though this is highly exploratory, this may increase chances that the iconic symbols will be indeed successful for Glen.

Both the parents and the elementary school teacher felt comfortable with the receptive vocabulary assessment and exploring the use of iconic graphic symbols such as Picture Communication Symbols (Johnson, 1994). One of the available symbol assessment protocols is initiated to gather additional data (Franklin, Mirenda, & Phillips, 1994) before proceeding with the use of Picture Communication Symbols.

5. Evaluating the Application of the Evidence

Given the preliminary nature of the suggestive evidence used in this situation to help direct a clinical/educational course of action, the practitioner recommends that data be collected to determine whether the graphic symbols work for Glen. The stakeholders concur with the practitioner, and together they develop a protocol for teaching requesting and for monitoring the effectiveness under typical conditions. As far as a protocol for teaching is concerned, the practitioner may ask other clinical questions (e.g., what teaching strategies seem effective?) beyond the scope of this chapter. The interested reader may consult Chapter 14 for the evidence-based suggestions provided for teaching an initial request lexicon. As for monitoring the effectiveness of Picture Communication Symbols, the team agrees that data need to be collected on Glen's requesting behavior, including levels of prompting, spontaneous requesting, and correspondence. Previously, it was demonstrated how important it is to measure whether the learner is able to select the corresponding object after a symbol is selected.

To assist the team with evaluating the application of the evidence under typical conditions, the team decides to use goal attainment scaling (Schlosser, 2002). Goal attainment scaling is a method for evaluating individual progress toward unique goals and involves seven steps (Kiresuk, Smith, & Cardillo, 1994): (1) specify a set of goals; (2) assign a weight for each goal according to priority;

Table 15.6

Glen's Goals for Requesting Using Graphic Symbols along with Goal Attainment Levels

Goal Attainment Levels	Goal. Requesting preferred objects and activities via graphic symbols
BEST EXPECTED OUTCOME (+2)	Requests preferred objects and activities *spontaneously* (i.e., unprompted objects are *not* visible) and displays correspondence in school (with teacher aide *and* teacher) and at home (with mother) using graphic symbols.
MORE THAN EXPECTED OUTCOME (+1)	Requests preferred objects and activities *spontaneously* (i.e., unprompted object are *not* visilbe) and displays correspondence in school (with teacher aide *and* teacher)
EXPECTED OUTCOME (0)	Requests preferred objects and activities and displays correspondence in school (with teacher aide *and* teacher) after *natural prompts* (e.g., an array of 4 objects is visible) using graphic symbols (A)
LESS THAN EXPECTED OUTCOME (−1)	Requests preferred objects and activities and displays correspondence in school with the teacher aide following *verbal and gestural prompts*
WORST EXPECTED OUTCOME (−2)	Requests preferred objects and activities in school with the teacher aide only following *verbal, gestural, and physical prompts*, but is inconsistent with correspondence (I)

I = Initial performance, A = Attained performance.

(3) specify a continuum of possible outcomes (worst expected outcome [−2], less than expected outcome [−1], expected outcome [0], more than expected outcome [+1], and best expected outcome [+2]); (4) determine current or initial performance; (5) intervene for a specified period; (6) determine performance attained on each objective; and (7) evaluate extent of attainment.

Typically, such a matrix includes several goals, which occupy as many columns as there are goals. For the purposes of this chapter, however, "requesting preferred objects and activities" will be used as the only goal. Together, the team develops a matrix with the continuum of possible outcomes (see Table 15.6).

Next, the team determines Glen's current or initial performance. Typically, the initial or current level of performance should commensurate with the worst expected outcome. If Glen were to attain the worst expected outcome, following intervention, this would render no progress as a result of intervention.[4] After a predetermined period of intervention, say 3 months, the team will revisit the matrix to determine the level of attainment. In this case, Glen attains the

---

[4]With individuals who have progressive disorders, it would be advisable to start at −1 (less than expected outcome) to afford the potential to capture a decline in performance.

expected outcome level (0). Thus, it can be concluded that the graphic symbols selected (i.e., Picture Communication Symbols) seem to be effective for Glen as a mode for requesting preferred objects and activities. For more detailed information concerning goal attainment scaling, the reader may want to consult Schlosser (2002). An alternative to the use of goal attainment scaling is the use of an appropriate single-subject experimental design as described in Chapter 6. A multiple-probe design across sets of objects and activities might lend itself to evaluating the effectiveness of using iconic graphic symbols for requesting preferred objects and activities.

6. Disseminating the Findings

The last step, where EBP comes full circle so to speak, involves the dissemination of the findings. In Chapter 12, this step was added to the existing steps typically discussed in the literature on EBP. The practitioner would share her experiences in going through this process and its outcomes so that future evidence-based practitioners can learn from the information and researchers become aware of the gaps in the knowledge base for purposes of implementing EBP. Related to the topic at hand, researchers should be made aware of the current gaps in the research base for informing practitioners about what types of graphic symbols might be more beneficial than others. Although this potential research-directing function of EBP related to selecting graphic symbols for an initial request function was already evident in the conclusions of the first section (see Section II. G. 1), it is worthwhile to share experiences pertaining to other clinical questions with the community of researchers and practitioners alike. The journal of *Augmentative and Alternative Communication* features a section titled "Intervention Notes." This might represent an excellent forum for submitting this type of work. Other clinically oriented journals, such as the *Clinics in Communication Disorders* or the *American Journal of Speech-Language Pathology* may be appropriate target journals as well.

IV. SUMMARY AND CONCLUSIONS

The first section of this chapter reviewed the existing research evidence in terms of its certainty of evidence and the degree to which the research base may speak to those variables pertinent to the decision-making process in selecting graphic symbols for an initial request lexicon. Although a considerable body of requesting studies has been produced, its certainty of evidence is often compromised by the lack of adequate designs, given their self-stated purpose, or the lack of treatment integrity data. Many of these studies need to be replicated taking into account adequate measures for increasing the certainty of results. Further, the informativeness of this body of research for selecting graphic symbols for an initial request lexicon has been found limited because variables that are deemed relevant (e.g., preference status of referents, spoken referent comprehension, iconicity, speech output) have not been systematically manipulated in this research. This latter review-generated result is not as much a criticism of these individual studies. After all, their self-stated purposes differed from the purpose of this review and the clinical questions posed in the second section of the chapter. It is therefore not surprising that the evidence-based practice recommendations for selecting graphic symbols for initial request lexicon, derived in the second section of this chapter, were rather limited. Nonetheless, describing the process of EBP for the background question and the foreground question for this topic allowed the author to illustrate the potential of EBP for informing the shaping of a research agenda.

REFERENCES

Alwell, M., Hunt, P., Goetz, L., & Sailor, W. (1989). Teaching generalized communicative behaviors within interrupted behavior chain contexts. *Journal of the Association for Persons with Severe Handicaps*, *14*, 91–100.

Angelo, D. H., & Goldstein, H. (1990). Effects of a pragmatic teaching strategy for requesting information by communication board users. *Journal of Speech and Hearing Disorders*, *55*, 231–243.

Beukelman, D., & Mirenda, P. (1998). *Augmentative and alternative communication: Management of severe communication disorders in children and adults* (2nd ed.). Baltimore: Paul H. Brookes.

Briggs, T. R. (1983). *An investigation of the efficiency and effectiveness of three nonvocal communication systems with severely handicapped students*. Unpublished doctoral dissertation, Georgia State University, Atlanta.

Brown, R. (1977). Why are signed languages easier to learn than spoken languages? Part two. *Bulletin of the American Academy of Arts and Sciences*, *32*, 25–44.

Burroughs, J., Albritton, E., Eaton, B., & Montague, J. (1990). A comparative study of language delayed preschool children's ability to recall symbols from two symbol systems. *Augmentative and Alternative Communication*, *6*, 202–206.

Clark, C. (1981). Learning words using traditional orthography and the symbols of Rebus, Bliss, and Carrier. *Journal of Speech and Hearing Disorders*, *46*, 191–196.

Clarke, S. (1987). *An evaluation of the relationship between receptive speech and manual sign language with mentally handicapped children*. Unpublished doctoral thesis, University of Southampton, Southampton, UK.

Drasgow, E., Halle, J., & Sigafoos, J. (1999). Teaching communication to learners with severe disabilities: Motivation, response competition and generalisation. *Australasian Journal of Special Education*, *23*, 47–63.

Duker, P. C., Dortmans, A., & Lodder, E. (1993). Establishing the manding function of communicative gestures with individuals with severe/profound mental retardation. *Research in Developmental Disabilities*, *14*, 39–49.

Ecklund, S., & Reichle, J. (1987). A comparison of normal children's ability to recall symbols from two logographic systems. *Language, Speech, and Hearing Services in Schools*, *18*, 34–40.

Forbus, S. S. (1987). *A comparative study of the ease of learning Rebus and Bliss symbols by severely mentally retarded adults.* Unpublished master's thesis, University of Arkansas at Little Rock, Little Rock, AK.

Franklin, N. K., Mirenda, P., & Phillips, G. (1994). Comparisons of five symbol assessment protocols with nondisabled preschoolers and learners with severe disabilities. *Augmentative and Alternative Communication, 12,* 73–77.

Franzkowiak, T. (1990). Kommunizieren mit grafischen Symbolen: Eine Bestandsaufnahme. In H. Brügelmann & H. Balhorn (Ed.), *Das Gehirn, sein Alfabet und andere Geschichten* (pp. 178–184). Konstanz, Germany: Faude.

Fristoe, M., & Lloyd, L. (1979). Effects on learning of instructed use of manual signs. *ASHA, 21,* 792.

Fuller, D. (1997). Effects of translucency and complexity on the associative learning of Blissymbols by cognitively normal children and adults. *Augmentative and Alternative Communication, 12,* 40–47.

Fuller, D. R., Lloyd, L. L., & Schlosser, R. W. (1996, August). *What do we know about graphic AAC symbols, and what do we still need to know about them?* Paper presented at the ISAAC Research Symposium, Vancouver, BC, Canada.

Fuller, D., Lloyd, L., & Stratton, M. (1997). Aided AAC symbols. In L. L. Lloyd, D. R. Fuller, & H. H. Arvidson (Eds.). *Augmentative and alternative communication: A handbook of principles and practices* (pp. 48–79). Needham Heights, MA: Allyn & Bacon.

Fuller, D. R., & Stratton, M. M. (1992). Representativeness versus translucency: Different theoretical backgrounds, but are they really different concepts? A position paper. *Augmentative and Alternative Communication, 7,* 51–58.

Gangkofer, M. (1990). Bilder lesen muss man lernen: Grundschüler deuten BLISS-Symbole. In H. Brügelmann & H. Balhorn (Eds.), *Das Gehirn, sein Alfabet und andere Geschichten* (pp. 169–177). Konstanz, Germany: Faude.

Gee, K., Graham, N., Goetz, L., Oshima, G., & Yoshioka, K. (1991). Teaching students to request the continuation of routine activities by using time delay and decreasing physical assistance in the context of chain interruption. *Journal of the Association for Persons with Severe Handicaps, 16,* 154–167.

Glennen, S. L., & Calculator, S. N. (1985). Training functional communication board use: A pragmatic approach. *Augmentative and Alternative Communication, 1,* 134–142.

Goossens', C. (1984). The relative iconicity and learnability of verb referents differentially represented by manual signs, Blissymbols, and Rebus symbols: An investigation with moderately retarded individuals (Doctoral dissertation, Purdue University, 1983). *Dissertation Abstracts International, 45,* 809A.

Granlund, M., & Olsson, C. (1999). Efficacy of communication intervention for presymbolic communicators. *Augmentative and Alternative Communication, 15,* 25–37.

Harrell, M., Bowers, J. W., & Bacal, J. P. (1973). Another stab at meaning: Concreteness, iconicity, and conventionality. *Speech Monographs, 40,* 199–207.

Hayes, C. L. (1996). *The effects of translucency and complexity on the acquisition of Blissymbols by cognitively normal elderly individuals.* Unpublished master's thesis, University of Arkansas at Little Rock.

Hern, S. L., Lammers, J., & Fuller, D. R. (1996). *The effects of translucency, complexity, and other variables on the acquisition of Blissymbols by institutionalized individuals with mental retardation.* Unpublished manuscript, University of Arkansas.

Horner, R. H., & Day, H. M. (1991). The effects of response efficiency on functionally equivalent competing behaviors. *Journal of Applied Behavior Analysis, 24,* 719–732.

Hunt, P., Alwell, M., Goetz, L., & Sailor, W. (1990). Generalized effects of conversation skill training. *Journal of the Association for Persons with Severe Handicaps, 15,* 250–260.

Hunt, P., Goetz, L., Alwell, M., & Sailor, W. (1986). Using an interrupted behavior chain strategy to teach generalized communication responses. *Journal of the Association for Persons with Severe Handicaps, 11*, 196–204.

Hurlbut, B., Iwata, B., & Green, J (1982). Non-vocal language acquisition in adolescents with severe physical disabilities: Blissymbol versus iconic stimulus formats. *Journal of Applied Behavior Analysis, 15*, 241–258.

Johnson, C. J., Paivio, A., & Clark, J. M. (1996). Cognitive components of picture naming. *Psychological Bulletin, 120*, 113–139.

Johnson, R. (1994). *The Picture Communication Symbols Combination.* Solana Beach: Mayer-Johnson Co.

Kiresuk, T., Smith, A., & Cardillo, J. (1994), *Goal attainment scaling: Applications, theory, and measurement.* London: L Erlbaum.

Kozleski, E. (1991a). Expectant delay procedure for teaching requests. *Augmentative and Alternative Communication, 7*, 11–19.

Kozleski, E. (1991b). Visual symbol acquisition by students with autism. *Exceptionality, 2*, 173–194.

Levie, W. H. (1987). Research on pictures: A guide to the literature: In D. M. Willows & H. A. Houghton (Eds.). *The psychology of illustration: Vol. 1. Basic research* (pp. 1–50). New York: Springer.

Lim, L., Browder, D. M., & Sigafoos, J. (1998). The role of response effort and motion study in functionally equivalent task designs and alternatives. *Journal of Behavioral Education, 8*, 81–102.

Lloyd, L., & Fuller, D. (1990). The role of iconicity in augmentative and alternative communication symbol learning. In W. Fraser (Ed.), *Key issues in mental retardation research* (pp. 295–306). London: Routledge.

Lohrmann-O'Rourke, S., & Browder, D. M. (1998). Empirically validated methods to assess the preferences of individuals with severe disabilities. *American Journal on Mental Retardation, 103*, 146–161.

Luftig, R., & Bersani, H. (1985a). An initial investigation of translucency, transparency, and component complexity of Blissymbolics. *Journal of Childhood Communication Disorders, 8*, 191–209.

Luftig, R., & Bersani, H. (1985b). An investigation of two variables influencing Blissymbol learnability with nonhandicapped adults. *Augmentative and Alternative Communication, 1*, 32–37.

Millar, D., Light, J., & Schlosser, R. (2000). The impact of AAC on natural speech development: A meta-analysis. In *Proceedings of the 9th biennial conference of the International Society for Augmentative and Alternative Communication* (pp. 740–741). Washington, DC: ISAAC.

Mirenda, P., & Locke, P. (1989). A comparison of symbol transparency in nonspeaking persons with intellectual disabilities. *Journal of Speech and Hearing Disorders, 54*, 131–140.

Mirenda, P., & Mathy-Laikko, P. (1989). Augmentative and alternative communication applications for persons with congenital communication disorders: An introduction. *Augmentative and Alternative Communication, 5*, 3–13.

Mizuko, M. (1987). Transparency and ease of learning of symbols represented by Blissymbols, PCS, and Picsyms. *Augmentative and Alternative Communication, 3*, 129–136.

Mizuko, M., & Reichle, J. (1989). Transparency and recall of symbols among intellectually handicapped adults. *Journal of Speech and Hearing Disorders, 54*, 627–633.

Nail-Chiwetalu, B. (1992). The influence of symbol and learner factors on the learnability of Blissymbols by students with mental retardation. (Doctoral dissertation, Purdue University, 1991). *Dissertation Abstracts International, 53*, 1125A.

Paivio, A. (1971). *Imagery and verbal processes.* Toronto, Canada: Holt, Rinehart, & Winston.

Paivio, A. (1986). *Mental Representations: A Dual-Coding Approach.* New York: Oxford University Press.

Reichle, J. (1991). Defining the decisions involved in designing and implementing augmentative and alternative communication systems. In J. Reichle, J. York, & J. Sigafoos (Eds.), *Implementing augmentative and alternative communication: Strategies for Learners with Severe Disabilities* (pp. 39–60). Baltimore: Paul H. Brookes.

Reichle, J., Barrett, C., Tetlie, R., & McQuarter, R. (1987). The effect of prior intervention to establish generalized requesting on the acquisition of object labels. *Augmentative and Alternative Communication, 3*, 3–11.

Reichle, J., & Brown, L. (1986). Teaching the use of a multi-page direct selection communication board to an adult with autism. *Journal of the Association for Persons with Severe Handicaps, 11,* 68–73.

Reichle, J., & Johnston, S. S. (1999). Teaching the conditional use of communicative requests to two school-age children with severe developmental disabilities. *Language, Speech, and Hearing Services in Schools, 30,* 324–334.

Reichle, J., Lindamood, L., & Sigafoos, J. (1986). The match between reinforcer class and response class: Its influence on communication intervention strategies. *Journal of the Association for Persons with Severe Handicaps, 11,* 131–135.

Reichle, J., & Sigafoos, J. (1991). Establishing an initial repertoire of requesting. In J. Reichle, J. York, & J. Sigafoos (Eds.). *Implementing augmentative and alternative communication: Strategies for learners with severe disabilities* (pp. 89–114). Baltimore: Paul H. Brookes.

Reichle, J., Sigafoos, J., & Piché, L. (1989). Teaching an adolescent with blindness and severe disabilities: A correspondence between requesting and selecting preferred objects. *Journal of the Association for Persons with Severe Handicaps, 14,* 75–80.

Reichle, J., & Wacker, D. (1993). *Communicative alternatives to challenging behavior: Integrating functional assessment and intervention strategies.* Baltimore: Paul H. Brookes.

Reichle, J. York, J., & Sigafoos, J. (1991). *Implementing augmentative and alternative communication: Strategies for Learners with severe disabilities.* Baltimore: Paul H. Brookes.

Remington, B. (1993). Augmentative and alternative communication and behavior analysis: A productive partnership? *Augmentative and Alternative Communication, 10,* 3–13.

Roberts-Pennell, D., & Sigafoos, J. (1999). Teaching young children with developmental disabilities to request more play using the behaviour chain interruptions strategy. *Journal of Applied Research in Intellectual Disabilities, 12,* 100–112.

Robinson, J. H., & Griffith, P. L. (1979). On the scientific status of iconicity. *Sign Language Studies, 25,* 297–315.

Romski, M., & Sevcik, R. (1992). Developing augmented language in children with severe mental retardation. In S. Warren & J. Reichle (Eds.), *Causes and effects in communication and language intervention* (pp. 113–131). Baltimore: Paul H. Brookes.

Romski, M. A., Sevcik, R. A., & Pate, J. L. (1988). Establishment of symbolic communication in persons with severe retardation. *Journal of Speech and Hearing Disorders, 53,* 94–107.

Rotholz, D., Berkowitz, S., & Burberry, J. (1989). Functionality of two modes of communication in the community by students with developmental disabilities: A comparison of signing and communication books. *Journal of the Association for Persons with Severe Handicaps, 14,* 227–233.

Schlosser, R. W. (1997). Nomenclature and category levels in graphic symbols, Part II: The role of similarity in categorization. *Augmentative and Alternative Communication, 13,* 14–29.

Schlosser, R. W. (1999). Comparative efficacy of interventions in augmentative and alternative communication. *Augmentative and Alternative Communication, 15,* 56–68.

Schlosser, R. W. (2002). *Measuring outcomes in speech-language pathology through goal attainment scaling.* Manuscript under review.

Schlosser, R. W., Belfiore, P., Nigam, R., Blischak, D., & Hetzroni, O. (1995). The effects of speech output technology in the learning of graphic symbols. *Journal of Applied Behavior Analysis, 28,* 537–549.

Schlosser, R. W., Lloyd, L. L., & McNaughton, S. (1997). Graphic symbol selection in research and practice: Making the case for a goal driven process. In E. Bjorck-Åkesson & P. Lindsey (Eds.).

"Communicating . . . Naturally"—Theoretical and Methodological Issues in Augmentative and Alternative Communication (pp. 126–141). Proceedings of the Fourth ISAAC Research Symposium, Vancouver, Canada. Västerås: Mälardalen University Press.

Schlosser, R. W., & Sigafoos, J. (2002). Selecting graphic symbols for an initial request lexicon: An integrative review *Augmentative and Alternative Communication, 18,* 102–123.

Schwartz, I. S., Garfinkle, A. N., & Bauer, J. (1998). The Picture Exchange Communication System: Communicative outcomes for young children with disabilities. *Topics in Early Childhood Special Education, 18,* 144–159.

Sevcik, R., Romski, M., & Wilkinson, K. (1991). Roles of graphic symbols in the language acquisition process for persons with severe cognitive disabilities. *Augmentative and Alternative Communication, 7,* 161–170.

Shalit, A. (1991). *A microcomputer-based synthesis of Blissymbols from key components to facilitate language acquisition in severely disabled people.* Unpublished doctoral dissertation, University of Cape Town, Cape Town, South Africa.

Sidman, M. (1988). *Tactics of scientific research: Evaluating experimental data in psychology.* Boston: Authors Cooperative.

Sidman, M., & Tailby, W. (1982). Conditional discrimination vs. matching-to-sample: An expansion of the testing paradigm. *Journal of the Experimental Analysis of Behavior, 37,* 5–22.

Sigafoos, J. (1998). Assessing conditional use of graphic mode requesting in a young boy with autism. *Journal of Developmental and Physical Disabilities, 10,* 133–151.

Sigafoos, J., Couzens, D., Roberts, D., Phillips, C., & Goodison, K. (1996). Teaching requests for food and drink to children with multiple disabilities in a graphic communication mode. *Journal of Developmental and Physical Disabilities, 8,* 247–262.

Sigafoos, J., Doss, S., & Reichle, J. (1989). Developing mand and tact repertoires in persons with severe developmental disabilities using graphic symbols. *Research in Developmental Disabilities, 10,* 183–200.

Sigafoos, J., & Kook, A. M. (1992). Obtaining a correspondence between requesting and selecting preferred objects. *Developmental Disabilities Bulletin, 20,* 1–12.

Sigafoos, J., Laurie, S., & Pennell, D. (1996). Teaching children with Rett syndrome to request preferred objects using aided communication: Two preliminary studies. *Augmentative and Alternative Communication, 12,* 88–96.

Sigafoos, J., & Meikle, B. (1995). A comparison of two procedures for increasing spontaneous requests in children with autism. *European Journal on Mental Disability, 2,* 11–24.

Sigafoos, J., & Mirenda, P. (2002). Strengthening communicative behaviors for gaining access to desired items and activities. In J. Reichle, D. Beukelman, & J. Light (Eds.). *Exemplary practices for beginning communicators* (pp. 123–156). Baltimore: Paul H. Brookes.

Sigafoos, J., & Reichle, J. (1992). Comparing explicit to generalized requesting in an augmentative communication mode. *Journal of Developmental and Physical Disabilities, 4,* 167–188.

Sigafoos, J., Reichle, J., Doss, S., Hall, K., & Pettitt, L. (1990). "Spontaneous" transfer of stimulus control from tact to mand contingencies. *Research in Developmental Disabilities, 11,* 165–176.

Sigafoos, J., & Roberts-Pennell, D. (1999). Wrong-item format: A promising intervention for teaching socially appropriate forms of rejecting to children with developmental disabilities? *Augmentative and Alternative Communication, 15,* 135–140.

Simeonsson, R. (1995). Intervention in communicative disability: Evaluation issues and evidence. In J. Roennberg & E. Hjelmquist (Eds.), *Communicative disability: Compensation and development.* Linkoping: Linkoping University Press.

Simone, R. (1995). *Iconicity in language.* Amsterdam, Netherlands/Philadelphia, PA: John Benjamins.

Skinner, B. F. (1957). *Verbal behavior.* Englewood Cliffs, NJ: Prentice Hall.

Soto, G., Belfiore, P., Schlosser, R., & Haynes, C. (1993). Teaching specific requests: A comparative analysis on skill acquisition and preference using two AAC aids. *Education and Training in Mental Retardation, 28,* 169–178.

Soto, G., & Olmstead, W. (1993). A semiotic perspective for AAC. *Augmentative and Alternative Communication, 9,* 134–141.

Stephenson, J., & Linfoot K. (1995). Choice-making as a natural context for teaching early communication board use to a ten-year-old boy with no spoken language and severe intellectual disability. *Australian and New Zealand Journal of Developmental Disabilities, 20,* 263–286.

Stephenson, J., & Linfoot, K. (1996). Pictures as communication symbols for students with severe intellectual disability. *Augmentative and Alternative Communication, 12,* 244–255.

Stokes, T., Osnes, P. G., & Chambers DaVerne, K. (1993). Communicative correspondence and mediated generalization. In J. Reichle & D. P. Wacker (Eds.), *Communicative alternatives to challenging behavior: Integrating functional assessment and intervention strategies* (pp. 299–315). Baltimore: Paul H. Brookes.

Van Acker, R., & Grant, S. (1995). An effective computer-based requesting system for persons with Rett syndrome. *Journal of Childhood Communication Disorders, 2,* 31–38.

van Balkom, H., & Welle Donker-Gimbrere, M. (1988). *Kiezen voor communicatie: een handboek over communicatie van mensen met een motorische of meervoudige handicap [Choosing for communication: A handbook about the communication of motoric and multiply handicapped children].* Nykerk, Netherlands: Intro.

Yovetich, W., & Young, T. (1988). The effects of representativeness and concreteness on the "guess-ability" of Blissymbols. *Augmentative and Alternative Communication, 4,* 35–39.

Appraisal of Evidence Levels

In determining the certainty of evidence of a study, take into account the relative weight of each variable and contingent relationships among variables. Inter-observer agreement (IA) of the independent variable (IV) (a.k.a. treatment integrity) is as important as that of the dependent variable (DV); and, a strong design without IA renders the study suggestive.

INCONCLUSIVE:

Establishes that certain graphic symbol acquisition outcomes are *not* plausible. The study's flaws preclude any conclusions that symbol acquisition is the result of the IV:

- Exhibits *fatal* design flaws (irrespective of IA–DV *or* IV).

SUGGESTIVE:

Certain graphic symbol acquisition outcomes are plausible, and are within the realm of possibility:

- *Minor design flaws* with *inadequate* IA (DV and/or IV); *or*
- *Strong* design with *inadequate* IA (DV *and/or* IV).

PREPONDERANT:

Certain graphic symbol acquisition outcomes are not only possible, but also they are more likely to have occurred than they have not:

- *Minor design flaws* in with *adequate (or better)* IA (DV *and* IV).

CONCLUSIVE:

Certain graphic symbol acquisition outcomes are undoubtedly the result of the IV:

- *Strong* design along with *adequate (or better)* IA (DV *and* IV).

CHAPTER 16

Effects of AAC on Natural Speech Development[1]

Ralf W. Schlosser
Department of Speech-Language Pathology and Audiology
Northeastern University

I. INTRODUCTION
II. HYPOTHESES ON THE RELATION OF
   AAC AND SPEECH DEVELOPMENT
III. WHAT DOES THE RESEARCH TELL
   US?
   A. Findings from the Research Synthesis by
      Millar *et al.* (2002)
   B. The Millar *et al.* (2002) Synthesis and
      Jackson's (1980) Criteria
IV. DECIDING ON WHETHER TO USE
   AAC: AN EBP ILLUSTRATION
   A. Asking an Answerable Question
   B. Selecting Evidence Sources and Executing
      the Search Strategy
   C. Examining the Evidence
   D. Applying the Evidence
   E. Evaluating the Application of the Evidence
   F. Disseminating the Findings
V. IMPLICATONS FOR FUTURE
   RESEARCH
   A. Design Issues
   B. Measurement Issues
VI. CONCLUSIONS

[1]The writing of this chapter was made possible through support from a Distinguished Switzer Fellowship (H133F010010) from the National Institute on Disability and Rehabilitation Research.

I. INTRODUCTION

Parents and other family members of children with little or no functional speech are often concerned about the impact of introducing augmentative and alternative communication (AAC) into their child's natural speech development. Understandably, the parents are worried the use of AAC implies that professionals have given up on speech development. Once practitioners are aware of this concern, they typically ensure parents that graphic symbols or manual signs are part of a multimodal system, which includes the use of natural speech models by communication partners. Moreover, practitioners try to emphasize that it is important for the child to communicate through whatever appropriate modes are available, whether they are graphic, manual sign, gestures, or natural speech. Although some parents may be less concerned after these important conversations take place, these concerns may not go away completely.

If practitioners could point to some well-controlled research studies which demonstrated that AAC intervention causes no detriment to natural speech development, parents and other stakeholders may be feel less apprehensive toward exploring the use of AAC. Therefore, in this chapter (1) the existing research evidence on the effects of AAC intervention on natural speech development is reviewed, (2) an evidence-based practice (EBP) application concerning the use of AAC relative to natural speech development is illustrated; and (3) directions for future research are offered. Before pursuing the review of the existing research base, theoretical arguments that may inform the relation of AAC and natural speech development are discussed.

II. HYPOTHESES ON THE RELATION OF AAC AND SPEECH DEVELOPMENT

Most theoretical accounts have viewed the role of AAC intervention on natural speech development as facilitative. Lloyd and Kangas (1994), for example, argued that an introduction of AAC might reduce the pressure for producing speech and allow the learner to focus on communication and thereby indirectly enhance speech production. Romski and Sevcik (1992) suggested that synthetic speech output might play a role in the emergence of expressive spoken language skills in learners with severe intellectual disabilities. This hypothesis is based on the assumption that "the consistency of the synthetic speech output preserves dimensions of the auditory signal that permit the listener to segment the stream of speech more easily" (Romski & Sevcik, 1993, p. 283). Romski and Sevcik (1996) also suggested that it may be the immediacy and consistency of synthetic speech output that encourages imitation and production of natural speech. Along a similar vein, Blischak (1999) hypothesized that synthetic speech output may activate or strengthen the phonologic code, which may then focus the child's attention on the phonologic characteristics of the words, thereby contributing to increased natural speech production. Others have approached the role of AAC intervention for natural speech development from applied behavior analysis perspectives based on principles such as automatic reinforcement and functional equivalence.

The phenomenon of automatic reinforcement (Skinner, 1957), for example, purports to explain the facilitative role of AAC intervention on natural speech development (Mirenda, in press). Accordingly, if an AAC mode (aided or unaided) is presented together with the spoken word as neutral stimuli (e.g., COOKIE + "cookie") and these are followed by a reinforcer (i.e., a cookie), both the use of the AAC mode and the spoken word (or approximations thereof) would automatically increase in frequency (Mirenda, in press). Clarke, Remington, and Light (1986) have approached natural speech development within simultaneous communication training from a functional equivalence framework. Simultaneous communication involves the pairing of spoken words with manual signs in teaching expressive signing. Accordingly, for a child to acquire expressive speech, the child should be able to (1) imitate the words involved in training and (2) attend to both spoken words and pictures during training. Only under these conditions, will spoken word stimuli control spoken word responses, and spoken words and corresponding pictures will be established as functionally equivalent.

Although these theories postulate a facilitative effect of AAC, some authors have suggested that AAC might hinder speech. The argument is that the children might prefer to use AAC due to its perceived ease of use compared to speech (Dowden & Marriner, 1995; Glennen & DeCoste, 1997). The next section reviews the research evidence. Among other issues, it will explore whether the available data might support one or the other theoretical positions.

III. WHAT DOES THE RESEARCH TELL US?

In 1987, Udwin conducted a review of the experimental adequacy of AAC intervention studies. One of his conclusions reads as follows: "A further criticism concerns the claims made in many training studies about accompanying improvements in speech output [natural speech development; added by this author], social interaction, and other behavioral indices. These reports are typically anecdotal, lack adequate control procedures and reliable assessments to back them up" (p. 21). Whether or not the state on this issue has changed for the better will be the focus of this section. To answer this question, this author will draw from a recently completed research synthesis on the effects of AAC intervention on natural speech development (Millar, Light, & Schlosser, 2000). First, the results will be presented, followed by an analysis of the review in terms of Jackson's

(1980) seven criteria for a systematic review (see Chapter 11). Instead of relying on the conference proceedings, the information reported here is based on a draft manuscript (Millar, Light, & Schlosser, 2002).

A. FINDINGS FROM THE RESEARCH SYNTHESIS BY MILLAR ET AL. (2002)

A total of 24 studies with a total of 58 participants met the criteria for inclusion. Only a synopsis shall be presented in narrative form. For detailed information, the reader may consult the original source once it becomes available. The majority of participants ($n = 27$, 47%) had a diagnosis of mental retardation (Angelo & Goldstein, 1990; Barrett & Sisson, 1987; Clarke et al., 1986; Clarke, Remington, & Light, 1988; Cregan, 1993; Francis & Williams, 1983; Gibbs & Carswell, 1991; Iacono & Duncum, 1995; Kouri, 1988; Pecyna, 1988; Remington & Clarke, 1993; Sanchez-Fort, Brady, & Davis, 1995; Sisson & Barrett, 1984) or autism ($n = 16$, 28%) (Benaroya, Wesley, Ogilvie, Klein, & Meaney, 1977; Bondy & Frost, 1994; Bonta & Watters, 1983; Casey, 1978; Fulwiler & Fouts, 1976; Hinerman, Jenson, Walker, & Peterson, 1982; Kouri, 1988; Salvin, Routh, Foster, & Lovejoy, 1977).

Most of the studies included unaided approaches such as manual signing ($n = 18$, 75%), whereas only a few studies used aided approaches ($n = 4$, 17%) (Angelo & Goldstein, 1990; Bondy & Frost, 1994; Goossens', 1989; Pecyna, 1988) or mixed approaches ($n = 4$, 8%) (Cregan, 1993; Iacono & Duncum, 1995). Among those studies involving aided approaches, only one study used an AAC system with speech output (Iacono & Duncum, 1995). Thirteen studies included a discrete trial or confrontational naming type of intervention format, eight included a more naturally occurring format, and three used a combination of the two approaches.

The gains in natural speech were coded for the highest quality studies per individual treatments and participants. The studies with the highest quality were all at the "suggestive" certainty of evidence level (i.e., Barrett & Sisson, 1987; Clarke et al., 1986; Conaghan, Singh, Moe, Landrum, & Ellis, 1992; Kouri, 1988; Linton & Singh, 1984; Sisson & Barrett, 1984). No studies were coded at the certainty of evidence level of "conclusive." For definitions of levels of evidence, see Section III. B.

Of the 58 participants, no conclusion was possible for 41 participants, due to significant or fatal flaws in the internal validity of the design, reliability of the dependent variable, or treatment integrity (Angelo & Goldstein, 1990; Benaroya et al., 1977; Bondy & Frost, 1994; Bonta & Watters, 1983; Casey, 1978; Clarke et al., 1988; Conaghan et al., 1992; Cregan, 1993; Francis & Williams, 1983; Fulwiler & Fouts, 1976; Gibbs & Caswell, 1991; Hinerman et al., 1982; Iacono

& Duncum, 1995; Kouri, 1988; Pecyna, 1988; Remington & Clarke, 1993; Salvin *et al.*, 1977; Sanchez-Fort *et al.*, 1995; von Tetzchner, 1984).

Of the remaining 17 participants, 14 (82%) showed an increase in speech productions (Barrett & Sisson, 1984 [2 of 2 participants]; Clarke *et al.*, 1986 [1 of 1 participant]; Conaghan *et al.*, 1992 [3 of 6 participants]; Kouri, 1988 [3 of 5 participants]; Linton & Singh, 1984 [2 of 4 participants]; Sisson & Barrett, 1984 [4 of 4 participants]). No change in natural speech was observed for three (18%) of the participants. Most of the gains in natural speech were measured in terms of number of words (9 subjects) whereas fewer relied on the number of vocalizations of single words or phrases (5 subjects).

In summary, the review by Millar *et al.* (2002) suggests that based on the studies with suggestive evidence, the majority of participants improved their natural speech as a result of AAC intervention. Although three participants failed to show any improvements, it is important to point out that none of the participants decreased their natural speech productions. The review also indicated that a large number of studies were flawed in terms of methodology and therefore they provide somewhat limited information for evidence-based practitioners. Thus, based on this synthesis, it seems safe to conclude that AAC intervention does not hinder or hamper speech development. In fact, with a suggestive certainty AAC intervention increases natural speech production for the majority of individuals with developmental disabilities.

B. THE MILLAR *ET AL.* (2002) SYNTHESIS AND JACKSON'S (1980) CRITERIA

Jackson (1980) postulated seven criteria that need to be met for a review to be considered systematic. Each of these criteria will be applied to the effort by Millar *et al.* (2002). The first criterion states that the topic has to be carefully defined and delimited. Millar *et al.* (2002) included studies using an experimental (e.g., single-subject design) or a descriptive research design (e.g., case study). The study needed to provide documentation of an AAC intervention, defined as the compensation of spoken or written communication through unaided or aided systems (Lloyd, Fuller, & Arvidson, 1997) and documentation of speech functioning during or following AAC intervention. Studies addressing the recovery of natural speech by individuals following an acquired disability were not included. The participants' speech needed to be inadequate to meet daily communication needs. Individuals with hearing impairments were only considered if the hearing impairment was secondary to another disability.

Second, previous reviews need to be described and distinguished. Millar *et al.* (2002) clearly distinguished their effort from a previous review by Silverman

(1995). Based on a review of more than 100 published reports, Silverman concluded, "the use of augmentative and alternative communication seems to facilitate speech (i.e., increase verbal output) in some children and adults" (p. 34). Millar *et al.* (2002) identified a number of shortcomings concerning this review (see also Chapter 11 for methods to review the literature), including a heavy reliance on unpublished reports, missing citations, outdated references, and inaccurate conclusions. These shortcomings, which were also perpetuated through repeated citations in commonly used AAC texts and articles (e.g., Dowden & Marriner, 1995; Glennen & DeCoste, 1997), set the stage for the current more systematic synthesis effort.

Third, procedures for obtaining studies must be detailed for a review to be systematic. A three-pronged search strategy aimed to locate studies between 1975 and 1998. First, it included electronic searches of various databases (e.g., PsycINFO, ERIC, MEDLINE) using key words such as "nonspeaking," "nonvocal," "augmentative communication," "speech production," and "speech development." In addition, handsearches of approximately 45 journals were performed. Finally, ancestral searches of references from studies that met the selection criteria were conducted.

Fourth, the degree to which the studies share the same dependent and independent variables must be reported. The independent variable needed to be an AAC intervention as defined in the criteria for inclusion (noted earlier). All studies shared "speech functioning" as their dependent variable. The specific measurement of speech functioning was intentionally defined to accommodate a variety of dependent measures such as intelligibility, number of vocalizations, and so forth.

Fifth, the criteria used to arrive at judgments of effectiveness should be stated. Outcome measures were coded for each participant when possible. Effect sizes were calculated for group designs, and the percentage of nonoverlapping data was calculated for single-subject experimental designs. For data series with certainty of evidence levels (discussed later) coded as conclusive, preponderant, or suggestive, changes in each participant's speech were determined as an increase, decrease, or no change. In addition to these outcomes measures, the increases or decreases in speech were quantified. For example, an intervention may have resulted in a gain of 10 words or a loss of 2 words following intervention.

Sixth, the covariation of study outcomes with study characteristics must be examined. Study characteristics included the (1) goal of the study, (2) type of research design, (3) type of AAC system, (4) instructional approach, (5) duration of the intervention, (6) type of AAC measure, (7) interobserver agreement of the AAC measure, (8) speech development design, (9) speech measurement type, (10) speech measurement technique (e.g., confrontational naming tasks), (11) interobserver agreement of speech measures, (12) participant's disability, (13) cognitive level, (14) age, (15) gender, and (16) level of certainty of evidence. This hierarchy is similar to the one presented in Chapter 15 of this text. It consists of four levels: conclusive, preponderant, suggestive, and inconclusive. Conclusive evidence establishes that the natural speech outcomes for the participant were undoubtedly the result of the AAC intervention (i.e., the internal validity of the design, interobserver agreement for the dependent variable, and treatment integrity were all strong). Preponderant evidence establishes that the natural speech outcomes were more likely to have occurred as a result of the AAC intervention (i.e., the design was strong, and there were minor flaws in the interobserver agreement for the dependent variable or treatment integrity). Suggestive evidence establishes that the natural speech outcomes were plausible as the result of the AAC intervention (i.e., minor flaws in the internal validity of the design, and/or minor flaws in the interobserver agreement of the dependent variable, or treatment integrity; or fatal flaws in treatment integrity and interobserver agreement), and inconclusive evidence suggests that the flaws in the study preclude any statements concerning natural speech outcomes. For participants with certainty of evidence levels coded as conclusive, preponderant, or suggestive, changes in each participant's speech were determined as an increase, decrease, or no change. As with outcomes, changes in each participant's speech were determined for individual comparisons. In addition, the increases or decreases in speech were quantified (e.g., gain of 10 words following intervention, loss of 2 words following intervention). Changes in speech were indeterminable for participants with certainty of evidence levels coded as inconclusive. The covariation of study outcomes with study characteristics was not examined statistically. Rather, the authors used the study characteristic "certainty of evidence" to determine which was the best evidence and presented it as such. This is consistent with a best-evidence approach to meta-analysis (Slavin, 1986) (see also Chapter 11).

Last, the conclusions of the synthesis need to be supported with the data from the studies reviewed. Millar *et al.* (2002) did not overstate their findings in light of the overall poor methodological quality of the original data. The best-evidence approach (Slavin, 1986) encourages the mindful reporting of effectiveness data depending on the methodological quality of the evidence. Thus, the conclusions drawn were in line with the data.

IV. DECIDING ON WHETHER TO USE AAC: AN EBP ILLUSTRATION

The steps involved in implementing evidence-based practice (EBP) in AAC as described in Chapter 12 include (1) asking an answerable question, (2) selecting evidence sources, (3) executing the search strategy, (4) examining the evidence, (5) applying the evidence, (6) evaluating the application of the evidence, and (7) disseminating the findings.

A. Asking an Answerable Question

As indicated in Chapter 12, the question to be asked needs to be answerable through a systematic search of the relevant evidence. The question pertains to the following role identified in the "Knowledge and Skills" document of the American Speech-Language and Hearing Association (2002): "determining AAC methods, components, and strategies to maximize functional communication by individuals." The following is an example of an answerable question related to natural speech development:

> Charlie is a 4-year-old child with severe intellectual disability, secondary to Down syndrome. He is unable to meet his daily communication needs through natural speech. However, he has recently learned to imitate some sounds such as "mama," "dada," "quack-quack," and "bye-bye." He does not use these sounds spontaneously to express communicative functions. Charlie's family and his service providers in his early intervention program anticipate many of his needs, or they attempt to read some of his presymbolic behaviors such as pointing and gesturing. Charlie's parents have been hoping that he is just a late talker who will eventually speak. After 2 years of living with that hope, however, they have reached a point where they are willing to reevaluate this approach. Although they are interested in exploring other forms of communication, they have serious concerns about Charlie's potential for learning to use speech should he begin to use other forms of communication. So the parents are interested in finding an answer to the following question: Would the use of AAC modes benefit Charlie's natural speech development? His parents would like Charlie to be a better communicator through whatever appropriate means, and they want him to improve his speech as well.

This question contains the essential components. That is, the components (1) describe the direct stakeholder and his capabilities relevant to the clinical problem (a 4-year-old child with severe intellectual disabilities who is currently communicating through presymbolic means—see Chapter 14 for characteristics of beginning communicators), (2) explain the direct stakeholder's current and future environment and relevant other stakeholders (i.e., early intervention program, home environment, parents, early intervention service providers), (3) make explicit the clinical or educational problem to be solved (i.e., whether the introduction of an AAC system would hinder his natural speech development), and (4) specify the expected clinical/educational outcomes (i.e., become a better communicator while improving his speech).

B. Selecting Evidence Sources and Executing the Search Strategy

As argued in Chapter 12, evidence-based practitioners should first seek syntheses of research rather than attempting to synthesize individual studies. Thus, the practitioner would engage in a database search using key words such as "augmentative communication," and "alternative communication" and combine them with the key words "review," "synthesis," or "meta-analysis." A search on ERIC, Psycinfo, and Medline yielded several reviews, but none of them focused on natural speech development as an outcome variable. The review by Millar *et al.* (2000) cannot be retrieved through these databases because the paper, based on the conference presentation, has not been published yet. The only way to gain access to this systematic review is to search the CD-ROM of the Proceedings of the 2000 Biennial Conference of the International Society of Augmentative and Alternative Communication. Once this has been obtained, the evidence-based practitioner could write to the author to request a draft version of the write-up. Readers here have the benefit of having access to the synopsis presented earlier.

The review by Millar *et al.* (2002) met all of Jackson's (1980) criteria. Therefore, it should be considered a systematic review or meta-analysis. Meta-analyses rank higher than narrative reviews in terms of the design hierarchy of evidence (see Chapter 12). Because this synthesis included studies up to 1998, it is important to supplement this review with individual studies that may have been published between 1999 and 2002. An ERIC search yields studies by Blischak (2000), DiCarlo, Stricklin, Banajee, and Reid (2002), and Mirenda, Wilk, and Carson (2000), which may be of relevance.

C. Examining the Evidence

1. The Evidence Related to AAC and Natural Speech Development

a. Examining the Evidence Gained from the Meta-analysis

In terms of the hierarchy of evidence proposed in Chapter 12, the review by Millar *et al.* (2002) represents a meta-analysis, primarily of single-subject experimental research. As such, it is ranked higher than any narrative reviews would be on this topic.

As indicated earlier, however, none of the studies reviewed by Millar *et al.* (2002) were at a conclusive level of evidence. There were, however, four studies at a suggestive level of evidence. This level of evidence indicates that speech outcomes were plausible as a result of the AAC intervention than not. For the purposes of this answerable question, the suggestive level represents the best evidence. Given that Charlie has a diagnosis of intellectual disabilities, the evidence-based practitioner is particularly interested in studies that included participants with intellectual disabilities. The four studies involved seven participants with intellectual disabilities (Barrett & Sisson, 1987; Clarke *et al.*, 1986; Kouri, 1988; Sisson & Barrett, 1984). Table 16.1, which summarizes the results from these

Table 16.1

Summary of Evidence on AAC Intervention and Natural Speech Development for the Clinical Question Stated in this Chapter

Study	Purpose of study	Participant (age)	Outcomes (PND[a])	Speech gains	Level of evidence
Barrett & Sisson (1987)	To compare oral, simultaneous communication, and modified simultaneous communication in terms of expressive speech or signing of sentence parts and sentences	J (5;3)	T1a: 81 T1b: 33 T2a: 41 T2b: 58	+3 words +2 words +2 words +1 word	Suggestive
		M (13)	T1a: 65 T1b: 11 T2a: 78 T2b: 67	+1 word +1 word +1 word +2 words	Suggestive
Kouri (1988)	To determine the effects of simultaneous communication on language behaviors	B. V. (2;10)	T1: 71 T2: 94	+5 words +36 words	Suggestive
Sisson & Barrett (1984)	To compare oral versus simultaneous communication in terms of vocal or signed sentence imitation	E (7)	T1: 100 T2: 100 T3: 100	+4 words +3 words +2 words	Suggestive
		M (8;1)	T1: 100 T2: 98 T3: 100	+4 words +4 words +4 words	Suggestive
		T (4;8)	T1: 100 T2: 97 T3: 100	+4 words +3 words +3 words	Suggestive
Clarke et al. (1986)	To compare known with unknown words in terms of expressive signing, receptive speech, and expressive speech	M. (6)	Not possible to calculate	+32% known words +32% unknown words	Suggestive

[a]Percentage of nonoverlapping data.

studies at the suggestive level, indicates that the mean percentage of nonoverlapping (PND) data ranged from 11 to 100, with a mean PND of 78.6. Based on the effectiveness criteria described in Chapter 11, a mean PND corresponds to treatments that are considered "fairly effective." In other words, the AAC interventions used in these studies are fairly effective in promoting natural speech development. It is interesting to note that two of the three studies involved comparisons between at least two treatments with some of the variation in PND accounted for by the different treatments (e.g., Barrett & Sisson, 1987). Other studies, however, report very homogenous findings across treatments (Clarke *et al.*, 1986; Kouri, 1988; Sisson & Barrett, 1984). The gains in the number of words produced ranged from 1 word to 5 words, with the exception of one participant in the study by Kouri (1988), who gained 36 words in treatment 2.

In summary, from this meta-analysis the following implications can be drawn for the answerable question at hand:

- AAC intervention does not hinder natural speech development.
- AAC intervention enhances natural speech development.
- Based on suggestive evidence, AAC interventions studied are limited to those using manual signing.
- Gains in natural speech were relatively modest, but need to be viewed within the context of how many words the learner spoke prior to the intervention.
- Observed gains in natural speech development were not within functional communication situations.

b. Examining the Evidence Gained from Other Studies

Several more recent studies were identified that may speak to the main answerable question (Blischak, 1999; DiCarlo *et al.*, 2002; Mirenda *et al.*, 2000). It turns out, however, that these studies focused on individuals with autism. In fact, none of these studies involved individuals with intellectual disabilities as their only diagnosis. As such, their relevance may be limited because individuals with autism may be presented with different characteristics (e.g., Mirenda, in press; Schlosser & Blischak, 2001). Therefore, it is not necessary to evaluate the certainty of evidence from these studies for the question at hand.

One of the summary points from the meta-analysis emphasized the focus on manual signing as the AAC system. In anticipation of the next step (applying the evidence), it may be relevant to explore whether there is any other research on the effects of aided AAC use on natural speech development with people with intellectual disabilities. Research on the effects of aided AAC use on natural speech development has not kept up with the application of aided AAC use in practice. The 2-year longitudinal study conducted by Romski and Sevcik (1996) appears to be the only available research at this time. They reported improvements in natural speech intelligibility in 13 youths with moderate to severe intellectual disabilities (two participants also had a diagnosis of autism) as a result of a treatment package involving a speech-generating device (SGD) as part of the System for Augmenting Language (SAL) (see also Chapter 19). These results are encouraging and represent the only longitudinal evidence toward natural speech development for people with intellectual disabilities. In terms of the hierarchy of the evidence proposed in Chapter 12, however, this evidence is at a level that is commensurate with case studies (see Chapter 19). In summary, preliminary evidence suggests that the use of SGDs within the System for Augmenting Language may enhance the intelligibility of natural speech in learners with moderate to severe intellectual disabilities.

Charlie has made recent gains in the vocal imitation of several words. Several authors have hypothesized that the ability to imitate vocally may be a predictor of natural speech development as a result of AAC intervention (Carr & Dores, 1981; Clarke *et al.*, 1988; Romski & Sevcik, 1992; Schepis, Reid, Fitzgerald, Faw, Van Den Pol, & Welty, 1982; Yoder & Layton, 1988). Three studies, involving manual signing, reported post-hoc evidence that participants with good vocal imitation skills improved in natural speech, whereas participants without vocal imitation skills did not (Carr & Dores, 1981; Clarke *et al.*, 1988; Schepis *et al.*, 1982). Of course, post-hoc evidence is speculative and of somewhat limited value for the evidence-based practitioner. The only prospective study, involving a group design, supported this hypothesis for manual signing (Yoder & Layton, 1988). This study, however, involved individuals with autism as participants. Thus, it is unclear whether these results would generalize to people with intellectual disabilities.

This leaves us with two post-hoc studies involving manual signing with five learners with severe intellectual disabilities between the ages of 5;5 years and 9;9 years (Clarke *et al.*, 1988). Study I indicated that the only two of the four participants who improved in terms of expressive speech during simultaneous communication training were those who showed reliable vocal imitation skills of the words involved in training. The participant in study II was 12;1 years old and showed no changes in expressive speech, consistent with his poor vocal imitation performance. In addition to the post-hoc nature of these findings, the studies lacked treatment integrity data but were otherwise well controlled (see Chapter 21). In summary, the data at this point are very speculative but seem to suggest that vocal imitation skills contribute to natural speech development in learners with severe intellectual disabilities who receive simultaneous communication training.

D. Applying the Evidence

The evidence-based practitioner would then share the findings from the preceeding lists with Charlie's parents as well as the service providers in his early intervention program who, in addition to Charlie himself, are the relevant stakeholders in this case. The question raised can be answered as follows: There is no evidence that indicates the use of AAC hinders natural speech development, and there is suggestive evidence that the use of manual signing facilitates natural speech development; the evidence that aided AAC use facilitates natural speech development is, at this point, inconclusive.

In addition to this information, the practitioner would also highlight that the primary aim of AAC is to compensate for the lack of functional speech through whatever combination of modalities necessary for Charlie to be competent in communicating his needs, feelings, wants, and desires. These modalities may include manual signing, gestures, finger-spelling, pointing, graphic symbols, SGDs, communication boards, computers, and residual natural speech. In other words, the practitioner would emphasize that the primary aim of AAC is not the development of natural speech, even though natural speech would continue to be used by communication partners as augmented input and encouraged as output by Charlie. Along these lines, the practitioner would also point out that even though the evidence for promoting natural speech is stronger for manual signing, there are other considerations that may delimit the utility of manual signing, such as the lack of intelligibility with many communication partners.

The practitioner would listen to any questions, concerns, or comments Charlie's parents or the service providers may have about the evidence presented and try to answer accordingly. Should the parents and the service providers be inclined to pursue AAC further with Charlie, the practitioner would recommend an assessment of what skills Charlie brings to the AAC task and his current and future environments (Beukelman & Mirenda, 1998; Glennen & DeCoste, 1997). Should Charlie's parents and service providers be less than convinced about the evidence presented for natural speech development as a result of AAC intervention, the practitioner would need to be respectful of this view. Perhaps the practitioner could reiterate the importance for Charlie to be able to communicate (regardless of the mode or combination of modes used). The practitioner would reemphasize that Charlie's ability to communicate appeared to be one of their motivations for exploring AAC.

E. Evaluating the Application of the Evidence

If it is decided to pursue AAC further with Charlie, it would be prudent to monitor the effectiveness of the AAC system. To do so, the team should develop goals that are reflective not only of meeting Charlie's communication needs but also his natural speech development. Perhaps the team can explore the use of goal attainment scaling to measure progress toward individualized goals (see Schlosser, 2002).

F. Disseminating the Findings

The last step involves the dissemination of the findings. The practitioner and the other stakeholders would share their experiences in going through this process and its outcomes so that future evidence-based practitioners and other stakeholders can learn from the information and researchers become aware of the gaps in the knowledge base for purposes of implementing EBP. Chapter 12 provides ideas for possible publication outlets.

V. IMPLICATIONS FOR FUTURE RESEARCH

The synthesis by Millar et al. (2002) provides a starting point for discussing future research directions. These directions are organized in terms of (1) design issues and (2) measurement issues.

A. Design Issues

Millar et al. (2002) noted that the majority of studies reviewed did not aim to investigate the effects of AAC interventions on natural speech development. Rather, the interest in speech development often appeared to be an afterthought. This is reflected in the use of the designs chosen to evaluate this issue. Although the designs chosen to evaluate the acquisition of AAC are often valid (see Chapter 6), when it comes to evaluating the effects of AAC intervention on natural speech development, the designs chosen are often weak. For example, the "single post treatment probe design" is not an adequate design to unequivocally attribute the level of natural speech development to the AAC intervention. These design concerns are analogous to the research on promoting generalization and maintenance, where the designs for evaluating generalization and maintenance effectiveness often do not allow for an unequivocal demonstration of the functional relation between acquisition and generalization or maintenance (see Chapters 6 and 20). For assistance in choosing an appropriate design, the reader may wish to consult Chapter 6, Section III. B. In summary, at least two things need to take place if the field is to advance its understanding of the effects of AAC intervention on natural speech development. First, the research question needs to focus on natural speech development. Second, the design chosen needs to allow for an unequivocal demonstration that natural speech development is the result of AAC intervention.

B. Measurement Issues

1. Operational Definitions for Measuring Change

As Table 16.2 indicates, studies examining the effects of AAC intervention on natural speech development have used a wide variety of operational definitions for measuring change. Given these differences in the data set, it becomes paramount to identify the dimensions that might need to be considered in measuring natural speech development in learners using AAC. One of these aspects relates to the type of change that is being observed. The majority of the studies with operational definitions examined the *intelligibility* of vocal behaviors. Some authors treated intelligibility as a binary variable, whereby intelligibility was given when a word was considered correct (e.g., Conaghan *et al.*, 1992). Although increases in the production of correctly vocalized words are highly desirable, some learners' progress might be subtler. Thus, future investigators may want to consider including a second measure that has the potential to capture these smaller improvements in intelligibility. Here, some sort of intelligibility rating scale might be useful (see the next section).

2. Rating Scales for Measuring Intelligibility

At least two rating scales purport to measure the degree of intelligibility of natural speech: the Overall Speech Intelligibility Rating Scale (Koegel, Camarata, Koegel, Ben-Tall, & Smith, 1998) and the Intelligibility Rating Scale (Romski, Plenge, & Sevcik, 1988).

a. The Overall Speech Intelligibility Rating Scale

This is a 6-point Likert scale ranging from 0 to 5: (0) = not intelligible, very difficult to understand; (1) mostly not intelligible, requires much strain to understand; (2) sometimes intelligible, requires some strain to understand; (3) sometimes intelligible, requires minimal strain to understand; (4) mostly intelligible, usually does not require strain to understand; and (5) very intelligible, easy to understand. This scale has been used in a study focused on increasing speech intelligibility in children with autism who were more vocal than children typically encountered in AAC intervention (Koegel *et al.*, 1998). Pre- and post-ratings of language samples were made by listeners who were unfamiliar with the children and naïve to the experimental conditions and hypotheses. To eliminate order effects and experimenter drift, the observers viewed the tapes in random order. Because the results indicated improvements in intelligibility, this study offers initial data in support of the validity of the scale for its identi-

Table 16.2

Operational Definitions (and Their Appraisal) of Natural Speech Measures and Appraisal of Dependent Measures in Selected Studies

Study	Operational definitions of natural speech measures	Appraisal of definition	Appraisal of dependent measure
Angelo & Goldstein (1990)	"A *nonboard request* was any unprompted gesture or conventional spoken word that was interpreted as an information request based on context within the delay" (p. 234) "A *no response* was any unrelated gestural or vocal/verbal response, or total absence of response within the delay. An unintelligible verbalization was also scored as a no response" (p. 234)	Neither definition permits one to distinguish vocal from gestural responses	Not reflected in dependent measure (only pointing to graphics)
Barrett & Sisson (1987)	"[C]orrect vocalization was scored if articulation was clear enough to afford reliable recognition of the word or words trained" (p. 406).	Intelligibility criterion (i.e., if recognized)	Confounded: Vocalized and signed responses are intermixed
Barrera & Sulzer-Azaroff (1983)	"[V]ocal responses were coded into the following categories: (a) clear, spontaneous, complete vocal, (b) either unclear, prompted, or incomplete vocal, (c) complete spontaneous gestural, and (d) either incomplete or prompted gestural" (p. 384)	Intelligibility, spontaneity, and completeness mixed up	Confounded: Percentage of correct vocal and gestural responses per word/session (Fig. 1); vocal responses were separated from gestural responses (Fig. 2)
Barrera et al. (1980)	No definition	N/A	Confounded: number of words successfully spoken or signed
Benaroya, et al. (1977)	No definition	N/A	N/A
Bondy & Frost (1994)	No definition	N/A	N/A
Bonta & Watters (1983)	No definition	N/A	N/A

(*continues*)

Table 16.2 (*continued*)

Study	Operational definitions of natural speech measures	Appraisal of definition	Appraisal of dependent measure
Casey (1978)	"Communicative behavior was defined as . . . (c) any verbal response that was solicited; and (d) any verbal response that was spontaneously generated" (p. 49)	Unclear; for example, were vocal approximations counted?	Mean proportions of (a) communicative behavior (confounded) (b) solicited verbalizations (c) spontaneous verbalizations
Conaghan, et al. (1992)	"Vocalizations were scored as correct if the trainer could recognize the participant's vocal response"	The trainer knows the target words and in all likelihood, would accepted vocal approximations of the target word	Vocalizations and signed responses were separated
	"The procedure was similar to that used for sign production except that an audiotape of the subjects' vocalizations was assessed" (p. 188)	More stringent measure	
Linton & Singh (1984)	"A vocalization was scored as correct if the target word was intelligible and approximated the correct sound of the word" (p. 558)	Intelligibility by experimenter	Vocalizations and signed responses were separated

fied purpose. Future research should explore the usefulness of this scale with learners using AAC.

b. The Intelligibility Rating Scale

The Intelligibility Rating Scale (Romski *et al.*, 1988) was developed more specifically for learners with intellectual disabilities using AAC who typically do not demonstrate evidence of extant connected speech. The scale is reliable and provides an 8-point rating of single word intelligibility: (0) no response; (1) a word response that is unintelligible and undifferentiated from other vocal responses and is clearly not an attempt to produce the target word; (2) a word response that is unintelligible and is differentiated from other responses but is clearly not an attempt to produce the target word; (3) a word response that is unintelligible, although at least one phoneme is correct, syllabification is indicated correctly, or the response is clearly recognizable as an attempt at the target word; (4) a word response that is "semi-intelligible" to an experienced listener; (5) a word response that is intelligible with multiple articulation errors; (6) a response that is intelligible with one articulation error; and (7) a word response that is completely intelligible.

To date, the Intelligibility Rating Scale has been applied as an outcome measure in at least one study (Romski, Sevcik, Robinson, & Wilkinson, 1990). Twelve youths with severe to profound intellectual disabilities participating in the SAL longitudinal study were presented with elicited probes on three occasions: at baseline (T1), after one school year (T2), and at the end of the second school year (T3). Specifically, participants were presented with photographs depicting each symbol on their display and asked, "What is this?" Spontaneous responses, defined as responses without further prompting or models, were audiotaped. If the participants did not respond within 10 seconds, a model was provided and the participant was asked to repeat the model (e.g., "cookie, say cookie"). Using the scale, audiotaped samples were rated by an independent speech-language pathologist. A second speech-language pathologist rated 15% of the samples, which resulted in an interrater agreement of .95. Intelligibility results indicate that 7 of the 12 participants increased the proportion of words that were rated as intelligible. The median rating of intelligibility of spontaneous responses increased from 1.75 during baseline to 2.0 at T2 and to 2.5 at T3.

3. Considering the Stringency of the Test

Changes in natural speech development may have different implications depending on who is used to evaluate these changes. An experimenter evaluating the vocal productions of the participants represents a rather lenient test of intelligibility. In all likelihood, the experimenter will know what words to expect and therefore may rate the participants' vocal productions as very intelligible. An experimenter may even accept vocal approximations as correct responses (e.g., "kaka" for "cracker") if the operational definition allows for this to occur (e.g., Schwartz, Garfinkle, & Bauer, 1998). On the other hand, someone who is unfamiliar with the participant and unfamiliar with the words or phrases for which AAC modes were introduced may rate intelligibility rather low—a more stringent intelligibility test. In addition to the factors of the familiarity of the listener with the participant and knowledge of the referents for which AAC modes are taught, the amount and type of other context supplied to the listener may also be of relevance. Future researchers and evidence-based practitioners need to be cognizant of these issues when designing studies or when evaluating research, respectively.

4. Is the Speech Related to the AAC Mode?

Related to the operational definition of changes in natural speech development is the issue whether to count only the speech that is related to the manual sign referents or the graphic symbol referents. There is no absolute correct answer to this question, as long as it is specified in the definition. It would appear that the answer to the question should be based on the researcher's hypothesis. The hypothesis that the consistency of synthetic speech output that encourages imitation and production of natural speech (Romski & Sevcik, 1993), for example, would call for the recording of natural speech that is related to the AAC mode—that is, the synthetic speech output that is being imitated. If, on the other hand, the hypothesis is that AAC intervention results in generalized natural speech development, analyses of natural speech recordings need to go beyond just those vocalizations that pertain to referents for which symbols were introduced.

5. Dependent Measures

Millar *et al.* (2002) noted that for the majority of the studies reviewed, natural speech development was not their primary focus. This lack of focus is evident in numerous studies where the dependent measure involved some combination of modalities, including natural speech but not limited to natural speech (see Table 16.2). This confounding is not a flaw in and of itself, but when one is trying to discern the effects of AAC intervention on natural speech development it is paramount that a dependent measure is used that is solely devoted to measuring natural speech development.

VI. CONCLUSIONS

In this chapter (1) the existing research evidence on the effects of AAC intervention on natural speech development was reviewed, (2) an EBP application concerning the use of AAC relative to natural speech development was illustrated, and (3) directions for future research were offered. In terms of the first objective, it seems safe to conclude that AAC intervention does not hinder speech development. In fact, based on the studies with suggestive evidence, the majority of participants showed improvements in natural speech. Although the field has made progress since Udwin's (1987) observations, moving from inconclusive evidence to suggestive evidence in selected studies, it is noteworthy that there were no studies at the preponderant or conclusive level of evidence—the level most suitable for shaping EBP. This, together with the large number of inconclusive studies, suggests that speech development continues to be viewed as an afterthought. Given the importance of this issue for many families, leaving room for doubt for these families bears the danger that this issue might become a powerful deterrent to the timely introduction of AAC. Thus, it is high time that sound studies with the potential for conclusive evidence be conducted; the studies need to be designed to examine the effects of AAC intervention on natural speech development. Such research is particularly needed with aided symbols and systems, including nonelectronic communication boards and SGDs.

Clearly, research on the effects of AAC intervention on natural speech development has lagged behind the current prominence of aided AAC symbols and systems over manual signing in recent decades. It is fair to say that little research in this area is driven by hypotheses as to why AAC intervention should facilitate or hinder natural speech development. As such, the existing research contributes little to our understanding of the underlying mechanisms behind natural speech facilitation through AAC intervention. Studies should be conducted that systematically test each of these hypotheses. For example, to test the automatic reinforcement hypothesis, one would need to compare one intervention with spoken input together with augmented input to a second intervention with augmented input without spoken input. The intervention with spoken input should result in increased natural speech development, whereas the intervention without spoken input should not result in increased natural speech development. It would also be in the interest of the AAC field to promote research on predictors of natural speech development. It has been suggested that the vocal imitation skills of the learner may be such a predictor. Identifying predictor variables would permit practitioners to make better prognoses for families who are concerned about their child's speech development.

Finally, it is essential that any observed gain in natural speech development be put into perspective as far as its magnitude or impact is concerned. What does it mean, for example, when a participant in a study gained two words? It could be that the participant speaks two words intelligibly after AAC intervention, which were unintelligible prior to intervention. More specificity, however, is needed to put this gain into better perspective. Some probing questions that may be useful to ask of natural speech gains reported in research are the following: (1) Are the words intelligible to familiar or unfamiliar partners? (2) Are the words used to express communicative functions? (3) Could the words stand by themselves without any other AAC modes accompanying them, or do they only become intelligible when accompanied by gestures and other AAC modes? Questions such as these help put research findings concerning natural speech gains into perspective for families and other stakeholders. Moreover, such questions help us to avoid overstating expected gains to families and other stakeholders.

REFERENCES

American Speech-Language-Hearing Association. (2002, April 16). *Augmentative and alternative communication: Knowledge and skills for service delivery.* ASHA Leader, 7 (Suppl. 22), 97–106.

Angelo, D. H., & Goldstein, H. (1990). Effects of a pragmatic teaching strategy for requesting information by communication board users. *Journal of Speech and Hearing Disorders, 55,* 231–243.

Barrera, R. D., Lobato-Barrera, D., & Sulzer-Azaroff, B. (1980). A simultaneous treatment comparison of three expressive language training programs with a mute autistic child. *Journal of Autism and Developmental Disorders, 10,* 21–37.

Barrera, R. D., & Sulzer-Azaroff, B. (1983). An alternating treatment comparison of oral and total communication training programs with echolalic autistic children. *Journal of Applied Behavior Analysis, 16,* 379–394.

Barrett, R. P., & Sisson, L. A. (1987). Use of the alternating treatments design as a strategy for empirically determining language training approaches with mentally retarded children. *Research in Developmental Disabilities, 8,* 401–412.

Benaroya, S., Wesley, S., Ogilvie, H., Klein, L. S., & Meaney, M. (1977). Sign language and multisensory input training of children with communication and related developmental disorders. *Journal of Autism and Childhood Schizophrenia, 7,* 23–31.

Beukelman, D., & Mirenda, P. (1998). *Augmentative and alternative communication: Management of severe communication disorders in children and adults* (2nd ed.). Baltimore: Paul H. Brookes.

Blischak, D. M. (1999). Increases in natural speech production following experience with synthetic speech. *Journal of Special Education Technology, 14,* 47–57.

Bondy, A. S., & Frost, L. A. (1994). The picture exchange communication system. *Focus on Autistic Behavior, 9,* 1–19.

Bonta, J. L., & Watters, R. G (1983). Use of manual signs by developmentally disordered speech-deficient children in delayed auditory-to-picture matching-to-sample. *Analysis and Intervention in Developmental Disabilities, 3,* 295–309.

Carr, E., & Dores, P. (1981). Patterns of language acquisition following simultaneous communication with autistic children. *Analysis and Intervention in Developmental Disabilities, 1,* 1–15.

Casey, L. O. (1978). Development of communicative behavior in autistic children: A parent program using manual signs. *Journal of Autism and Childhood Schizophrenia, 8,* 45–59.

Clarke, S., Remington, B., & Light, P. (1986). An evaluation of the relationship between receptive speech skills and expressive signing. *Journal of Applied Behavior Analysis, 19,* 231–239.

Clarke, S., Remington, B., & Light, P. (1988). The role of referential speech in sign learning by mentally retarded children: A comparison of total communication and sign-alone training. *Journal of Applied Behavior Analysis, 21,* 419–426.

Conaghan, B. P., Singh, N. N., Moe, T. L., Landrum, T., & Ellis, C. R. (1992). Acquisition and generalization of manual signs by hearing-impaired adults with mental retardation. *Journal of Behavioral Education, 2,* 175–203.

Cregan, A. (1993). Sigsymbol system in a mulimodal apprach to speech elicitation: Classroom project involving an adolescent with severe mental retardation. *Augmentative and Alternative Communication, 9,* 146–160.

DiCarlo, C., Stricklin, S., Banajee, M., & Reid, D. (2002). Effects of manual signing on communicative verbalizations by toddlers with and without disabilities in inclusive classrooms. *Journal of the Association for Persons with Severe Handicaps, 26,* 1201–1226.

Dowden, P., & Marriner, N. (1995). Augmentative and alternative communication: Treatment principles and strategies. *Seminars in Speech and Language, 16,* 140–156.

Francis, V., & Williams, C. (1983). The effects of teaching British sign language to mentally handicapped, non-communicating children. *British Journal of Mental Subnormality, 28,* 18–28.

Fulwiler, R. L., & Fouts, R. S. (1976). Acquisition of American Sign Language by a noncommunicating autistic child. *Journal of Autism and Childhood Schizophrenia, 6*, 43–51.

Gibbs, E. D., & Carswell, L. E. (1991). Using total communication with young children with Down syndrome: A literature review and case study. *Early Education and Development, 2*, 306–320.

Glennen, S. L., & DeCoste, D. (1997). *Handbook of augmentative and alternative communication*. San Diego, CA: Singular.

Goossens', C. (1989). Aided communication intervention assessment: A case study of a child with cerebral palsy. *Augmentative and Alternative Communication, 5*, 14–26.

Hinerman, P. S., Jenson, W. R., Walker, G. R., & Peterson, P. B. (1982). Positive practice overcorrection combined with additional procedures to each signed words to an autistic child. *Journal of Autism and Developmental Disorders, 12*, 253–263.

Iacono, T. A., & Duncum, J. E. (1995). Comparison of sign alone and in combination with an electronic communication device in early language intervention: Case study. *Augmentative and Alternative Communication, 11*, 249–259.

Jackson, G. B. (1980). Methods for integrative reviews. *Review of Educational Research, 50*, 438–460.

Koegel, R. L., Camarata, S., Koegel, L. K., Ben-Tall, A., & Smith, A. E. (1998). Increasing speech intelligibility in children with autism. *Journal of Autism and Developmental Disorders, 28*, 241–251.

Kouri, T. A. (1988). Effects of simultaneous communication in a child-directed treatment approach with preschoolers with severe disabilities. *Augmentative and Alternative Communication, 4*, 222–232.

Linton, J. M., & Singh, N. N. (1984). Acquisition of sign language using positive practice overcorrection. *Behavior Modification, 8*, 553–566.

Lloyd, L. L., Fuller, D. R., & Arvidson, H. H. (1997). *Augmentative and alternative communication: A handbook of principles and practices*. Needham Heights, MA: Allyn & Bacon.

Lloyd, L. L., & Kangas, K. (1994). Augmentative and alternative communication. In G. H. Shames, E. H. Wiig, & W. A. Secord (Eds.), *Human communication disorders* (4th ed.), (pp. 606–657). New York: Merrill/Macmillan.

Millar, D., Light, J., & Schlosser, R. (2000). The impact of AAC on natural speech development: A meta-analysis. In *Proceedings of the 9th biennial conference of the International Society for Augmentative and Alternative Communication* (pp. 740–741). Washington, DC: ISAAC.

Millar, D. C., Light, J. C., & Schlosser, R. W. (2002). *The impact of augmentative and alternative communication on natural speech development: A research review*. Manuscript in preparation.

Mirenda, P. (in press). Toward functional augmentative and alternative communication for students with autism: Manual signs, graphic symbols, and voice output communication aids. *Language, Speech, and Hearing Services in Schools*.

Mirenda, P., Wilk, D., & Carson, P. (2000). A retrospective analysis of technology use patterns in students with autism over a five-year period. *Journal of Special Education Technology, 15*, 5–16.

Pecyna, P. M. (1988). Rebus symbol communication training with a severely handicapped preschool child: A case study. *Language, Speech, and Hearing Services in Schools, 19*, 128–143.

Remington, B., & Clarke, S. (1993). Simultaneous communication and speech comprehension. Part II. Comparison of two methods of overcoming selective attention during expressive sign training. *Augmentative and Alternative Communication, 9*, 49–60.

Romski, M. A., Plenge, T., & Sevcik, R. A. (1988). *Intelligibility Rating Scale*. Unpublished manuscript, Georgia State University.

Romski, M. A., & Sevcik, R. A. (1992). Developing augmented language in children with severe mental retardation. In S. F. Warren & J. Reichle (Eds.), *Causes and effects in communication and language intervention* (pp. 113–131). Baltimore: Paul H. Brookes.

Romski, M. A., & Sevcik, R. A. (1993). Language comprehension: Considerations for augmentative and alternative communication. *Augmentative and Alternative Communication, 9*, 281–285.

Romski, M. A., & Sevcik, R. A. (1996). *Breaking the speech barrier*. Baltimore: Brookes.

Romski, M. A., Sevcik, R. A., Robinson, B., & Wilkinson, K. (1990, November). *Intelligibility and form changes in the vocalizations of augmented communicators.* Paper presented at the annual meeting of the American Speech-Language-Hearing Association, Seattle. WA.

Salvin, A., Routh, D. K., Foster, R. E., & Lovejoy, K. M. (1977). Acquisition of modified American Sign Language by a mute autistic child. *Journal of Autism and Childhood Schizophrenia, 7,* 359–371.

Sanchez-Fort, M. R., Brady, M. P., & Davis, C. A. (1995). Using high-probability requests to increase low-probability communication behavior in young children with severe disabilities. *Education and Training in Mental Retardation and Developmental Disabilities, 30,* 151–165.

Schepis, M. M., Reid, D. H., Fitzgerald, J. R., Faw, G. D., Van Den Pol, R. A., & Welty, P. A. (1982). A program for increasing manual signing by autistic and profoundly retarded youth within the daily environment. *Journal of Applied Behavior Analysis, 15,* 363–379.

Schlosser, R. W. (2002). *Using goal attainment scaling to measure outcomes in speech-language pathology.* Manuscript under review.

Schlosser, R. W., & Blischak, D. M. (2001). Is there a role for speech output in interventions for persons with autism? A review. *Focus on Autism and Other Developmental Disabilities, 16,* 170–178.

Schwartz, I., Garfinkle, A., & Bauer, J. (1998). The Picture Exchange Communication System: Communicative outcomes for young children with disabilities. *Topics in Early Childhood Special Education, 18,* 144–159.

Silverman, F. H. (1995). *Communication for the speechless* (3rd ed.). Boston: Allyn & Bacon.

Sisson, L. A., & Barrett, R. P. (1984). An alternating treatments comparison of oral and total communication training with minimally verbal, mentally retarded children. *Journal of Applied Behavior Analysis, 17,* 559–566.

Skinner, B. F. (1957). *Verbal Behavior.* Englewood Cliffs, NJ: Prentice Hall.

Slavin, R. E. (1986). Best-evidence synthesis: An alternative to meta-analytic and traditional reviews. *Educational Researchers, 15,* 5–11.

Udwin, O. (1987). Analysis of the experimental adequacy of alternative and augmentative communication training studies. *Child Language Teaching and Therapy, 3,* 18–39.

von Tetzchner, S. (1984). Facilitation of early speech development in a dysphatic child by used of signed Norwegian. *Scandinavian Journal of Psychology, 25,* 265–275.

Yoder, P. J., & Layton, T. L. (1988). Speech following sign language training in autistic children with minimal verbal language. *Journal of Autism and Developmental Disorders, 18,* 217–229.

CHAPTER 17

Application of Current Literacy Theory, Efficacy Research, and Clinical Practice to AAC Users

Doreen M. Blischak
University of Florida
Department of Communication Sciences
and Disorders

Aimee Gorman
University of Florida
Department of Communication
Sciences and Disorders

Linda J. Lombardino
University of Florida
Department of Communication Sciences
and Disorders

I. INTRODUCTION

One of my favorite high school teachers designed a specialized typing course to meet the needs of his orthopedically handicapped students. Boy, did that class ever change my life. The teacher accepted nothing but perfection. Writing has ended up to be my most effective means of communication (Johnson, 2000, p. 50).

This quote by augmentative alternative communication (AAC) user Peg Johnson underscores the importance of literacy development for individuals with little or no functional speech. Indeed, it is true for all that skilled reading and writing are critical for full participation in post-20th-century technologically

The Efficacy of Augmentative and Alternative Communication

driven cultures. We depend on literacy for access to an ever-increasing flood of information in order to advance ourselves educationally, socially, and economically. Yet what do we currently know about literacy? We know that (1) reading is a skill that must be taught explicitly, and (2) it requires the ability to make neural connections between pronunciation patterns and letter sequences, the verbal memory to maintain these patterns, and the ability to access them rapidly. We also know that the majority of reading deficits are due to inadequate exposure to orthography and that a smaller number of problems are due to neurologically based processing differences that hinder the rapid and accurate identification of single words. In some cases, reading deficits result from the interaction of these two important ingredients.

The fact remains, however, that most children learn to read and write to an acceptable degree in schools in which a vast array of teaching methods are used. Many other children and adults with reading difficulties have benefited from improved methods of identification and remediation. Thus, the critical job of educators and those in related professions is to identify those children at risk for reading difficulties and initiate an effective intervention program—one that is guided by evidence-based practice (EBP) (see Chapter 12).

How do these twin issues of typical reading development and treatment of reading difficulties relate to individuals who use AAC? Answering this timely question is what we attempt to accomplish in this chapter through discussion of models of typical reading development, identification and treatment of children at risk for reading disability, and research to date involving literacy assessment and intervention with individuals who use AAC.

II. LITERACY DEVELOPMENT AND DISABILITY

A. MODELS OF LITERACY DEVELOPMENT

Basic to any approach to assessment and intervention is reference to an underlying theoretical model that guides the selection of goals and methods. Proposed models of literacy development tend to fall into one of two categories: developmental and connectionist. Developmental models (e.g., Chall, 1983; Ehri, 1995; Frith, 1985) emphasize stages that children pass through as they progress from emergent literacy skills such as scribbling and decoding environmental print to becoming fluent readers of age-level text. Connectionist models (e.g., Seidenberg & McClelland, 1989), on the other hand, emphasize the interaction among modular processing units (e.g., phonological, orthographic) that allow for access to the meaning of text.

Ehri's descriptive developmental model proposes that reading development may be described in terms of four overlapping stages:

- Prereading/emergent reading: Children "read" logos or familiar words based on salient visual cues.
- Decoding: Reading reflects knowledge of grapheme-phoneme correspondence.
- Fluency: Automatic reading.
- Reading to learn: The reading process becomes secondary to the purpose of reading.

Seidenberg and McClelland (1989) proposed a connectionist model that posits four separate modules responsible for the storage and retrieval of phonological, orthographic, and semantic information during reading and spelling. Parallel processing that takes place among these four modules allows for efficient reading of both familiar and unfamiliar content. The orthographic module activates when a word is seen and the sequence of its graphemes is activated. The phonological module is activated when the pronunciation of the word is automatically recognized and when phonemic analysis is necessary to decode an unfamiliar word. The semantic module connects pronunciation with meaning and the context module continuously refines primitive word meanings to account for the context in which the word appears. Although the orthographic (visual) and phonological (auditory) modules form the foundation of this model, all four work together to send and receive information to and from each other. Each module also has interconnected sets of units. For example, the more familiar the reader is with a word, the stronger the connection between the orthographic pattern of the word and its pronunciation stored in the reader's memory.

For additional information regarding models of literacy development, the reader is invited to explore texts from leading experts in the field of reading and reading disability, such as Adams (1990), Blachman (1997), Ehri (1995), and Pumfrey and Reason (1991). An excellent overview of early reading development research may be found in Snow, Scarborough, and Burns (1999).

B. GUIDING PRINCIPLES

Given what is currently known about literacy development, a list of principles for guiding assessment and intervention may be developed:

- Reading involves phonemic decoding, automatic word recognition, and comprehension, whereas writing requires formulation (utterance construction) and encoding (spelling) (e.g., Bourassa & Treiman, 2001; Scott, 1999).
- Reading and writing are complex, multicomponent learned skills that require interaction of both top-down (emphasis on content, use)

and bottom-up (emphasis on form) processes (e.g., Pumfrey & Reason, 1991).

- Throughout literacy development, one process may be emphasized more than another until the ultimate goal of fluent reading with comprehension is attained (e.g., Ehri, 1991).
- Literacy development depends on a strong foundation in oral language, including vocabulary, utterance, conversation, and narrative development (e.g., Catts & Kamhi, 1999; Snow et al., 1999).
- Literacy development in alphabetic languages requires metalinguistic skills such as phonological awareness, the knowledge that spoken words may be divided into smaller units (syllables, sounds), and the understanding that these units may be represented by orthographic symbols (i.e., alphabetic letters) (e.g., Adams, 1990).
- Literacy development takes place within a cultural/familial environment and reflects the values, language, and communication patterns of that group (e.g., Galda, Cullinan, & Strickland, 1993).
- Literacy development is enhanced by observation of others using print, opportunities to interact with print in a variety of forms (e.g., storybook reading, scribbling), appropriate instruction, and opportunities to practice (e.g., Adams, 1990; Snow et al., 1999).
- Literacy development may be hindered by both intrinsic (e.g., sensory, linguistic, neurological) and extrinsic factors (e.g., reduced opportunities, inappropriate instruction) (e.g., Eckert, Lombardino, & Leonard, 2001; Leonard et al., 2001; Smith & Blischak, 1997).

C. WHAT ARE READING DISABILITIES?

Reading disabilities are characterized by difficulty reading at the level expected for one's grade, age, sociocultural background, and intellectual abilities. There are different causes for reading disabilities: sensory or motor deficits, lack of appropriate instruction, severe language learning disabilities, or a specific reading disability (i.e., developmental dyslexia). Aaron and Joshi (1992) described different profiles, depending on the nature of the reading disability. Patterns are typically identified by examining specific oral and written language skills, including the following: listening comprehension, nonword decoding, word identification, and reading comprehension. Children with reading disabilities who have developmental delays show deficits in all areas. Children with a *language learning disability* typically show better decoding skills than reading and listening comprehension. Children with a *specific reading disability* (often used synonymously with developmental dyslexia) have decoding deficits, normal listening comprehension, and relatively good reading comprehension skills.

D. Children at Risk for Reading Disability

1. Identification

Difficulty with phonological awareness has become widely accepted as one of the primary predictors of reading disability (Adams, 1990; Goswami & Bryant, 1990; Scarborough, 1998; Snow *et al.*, 1999; Wagner & Torgesen, 1987). However, several other predictors of reading disability were described in Scarborough's (1998) extensive review of predictive studies. At the preschool level, moderately good predictors of later reading skill include measures of infant achievement and aptitude, expressive and receptive vocabulary and syntax, and pronunciation accuracy. At school entry, the best reading readiness predictors include letter naming, invented spelling, and concepts of print, including knowledge of word boundaries and sound-letter associations. During this same period, predictors of later reading success include oral language skills such as confrontation naming, sentence/story recall, general language index, and phonological awareness.

Some of the strongest predictors of reading skill at the kindergarten level come from combining measures such as letter naming and phonological awareness (Scarborough, 1998). With a goal of establishing the most reliable indices for early reading screening, O'Connor and Jenkins (1999) conducted an extensive study of predictors of reading disability by administering the word identification and word attack tests from the *Woodcock Reading Mastery Test-Revised* (Woodcock, 1987) three times to three cohorts of children from early kindergarten to late first grade. O'Connor and Jenkins (1999) reported two noteworthy findings with strong clinical implications for early identification of reading disability. Best predictors varied slightly according to time at which the children were examined. The best predictors in early kindergarten were tasks of syllable deletion, rapid naming, and phoneme segmentation. In late kindergarten and in early first grade, the best predictors were rapid naming, phoneme segmentation, and sound repetition. Further, the later the measures were administered (i.e., early first grade versus late kindergarten), the more accurate they were in identifying the children who were at risk.

2. Intervention

In a recent publication on early reading intervention, Abbott and Berninger (1999) delineated four skills that are critical for the beginning stages of reading: (1) orthographic knowledge in the form of letter names, recognition of letters in words, and writing letters; (2) phonological awareness in terms of segmenting the spoken word into phonemes; (3) knowledge of the alphabetic principle in order to integrate letter and phoneme knowledge; and (4) application of the alphabetic principle in recognizing familiar words and decoding unfamiliar words.

Table 17.1

Major Components of the Orton-Gillingham method (Gillingham & Stillman, 1998)

- Visual and auditory phonogram drills
- Reading and spelling regular and irregular vowel teams
- Reading and spelling root words and suffixes
- Reading phonetically controlled texts
- Learning basic syllable types
- Learning common spelling rules (i.e., doubling consonants)
- Learning rules for syllabication

Table 17.2

Major Components of the Lindamood Individualized Phoneme Sequencing Program (LIPS) (Lindamood & Lindamood, 1998)

- Identifying and classifying consonant and vowel sounds by manner of production
- Tracking phonemes in words using mouth pictures and colored blocks
- Reading and spelling mono- and multisyllabic words
- Using suffix patterns in reading and spelling
- Developing sight word reading and spelling
- Reading phonetically controlled texts

These basic skills have been taught successfully to young children who have not acquired the phonemic and orthographic knowledge needed to decode print and to older children who still present with weak foundations in reading skills. Some excellent sources for working with children at this level are *Road to the Code* by Blachman, Ball, Black, and Tangel (2000) and *Phonemic Awareness in Young Children* by Adams, Foorman, Lundberg, and Beeler (1998).

Berninger *et al.* (2002) recently argued for the use of integrated explicit instruction in other structural dimensions of written language for older children who are faced with reading more complex syllabic structures on a regular basis. Both the *Orton-Gillingham* method (Gillingham & Stillman, 1998) and many other adaptations of the original Orton method (Cox, 1984; Orton, 1976; Slingerland, 1971) are ideally suited for this type of instruction. The *Lindamood®* *Individual Phoneme Sequencing Program* (*LIPS*) (Lindamood & Lindamood, 1998) is the most comprehensive approach available for teaching reading and spelling patterns. A brief outline of the components of these methods can be found in Tables 17.1 and 17.2.

III. LITERACY ASSESSMENTS IN INDIVIDUALS WHO USE AAC

A. ISSUES

Although persons who use AAC may attain high levels of literacy (e.g., Fried-Oken & Bersani, 2000) it is an unfortunate reality that many AAC users do not become competent readers and writers (e.g., Berninger & Gans, 1986a; Light, Stoltz, & McNaughton, 1996). As with typically speaking individuals, it is unlikely that a single underlying deficit may account for literacy difficulties in AAC users. Intrinsic factors such as sensory impairment, intellectual disability, language impairment, or reading disability may hinder literacy development in some individuals who use AAC. Extrinsic factors such as reduced opportunities to interact with print and low expectations may affect literacy development to an even greater degree (Koppenhaver & Yoder, 1993; Light & Smith, 1993). Intervention, then, is designed to decrease the effects of both intrinsic and extrinsic factors by providing supports (e.g., amplification, corrective lenses) and services (e.g., education, speech-language therapy) based on a thorough and reliable assessment of an AAC user's skills, needs, environments, and opportunities (Smith & Blischak, 1997).

When assessing skills as complex as those involved in reading and writing, the assessment team may face a seemingly insurmountable array of obstacles. The first of these involves one of the most challenging aspects of AAC: assessment of underlying linguistic and metalinguistic abilities, which is typically accomplished through observation of spoken responses. A thorough literacy assessment also involves directly assessing reading performance, which also requires spoken responses, particularly in the early stages of reading (e.g., Berninger & Gans, 1986b). For most AAC users, however, it is only through communication via graphic methods that behaviors that typically require spoken responses may be observed (e.g., alphabet knowledge, word recognition, and sentence construction).

A second complication arises when the examiner provides task adaptations or allows the AAC user to respond using familiar alternative modes. Each adaptation has the potential to introduce confounding variables by adding or reducing task demands, thereby altering the original nature of the task. For example, an AAC user may be asked to perform phoneme segmentation. Using written letters instead of spoken responses requires alphabet knowledge as well as additional visual and cognitive effort (i.e., phoneme-grapheme correspondence). Conversely, assessing single-word reading by having the individual point to a named word from a closed set, rather than reading the word aloud, changes a word identification task to the easier one of word recognition (Blischak, 1994; Vandervelden & Siegel, 2001).

Overriding these task-specific issues are two related questions: (1) To what extent is a developmental model appropriate for individuals who, because of intrinsic and extrinsic differences (including AAC use), are not developing "typically"? (2) Should methods and tasks used to assess literacy in speaking individuals be used with individuals with little or no functional speech? These issues are, as of yet, unresolved (see Koppenhaver, 2000). Until research findings challenge our present approaches, we may, in the words of Rhea Paul "take suggestions from typical development, test them, and learn from the experiment" (1997, p. 143). Conventional wisdom and clinical judgment would also tell us to select assessments that require the fewest adaptations, assess skills using more than one method, interpret all results with caution, and continuously reassess both the individual's progress and the assessment methods (see also Johnson-Martin, Wolters, & Stowers, 1987). This leads us to examine available research to support the use of particular assessment methods with individuals who use AAC.

B. Research

Many published papers in the field of AAC have presented data regarding the assessment of literacy and its component skills (i.e., intrinsic factors) in groups of AAC users. For example, Foley and Pollatsek (1999), Hjelmquist, Sandberg, and Hedelin (1994), Sandberg (2001), Sandberg and Hjelmquist (1996), and Vandervelden and Siegel (1999) examined literacy abilities in relation to metalinguistic skills such as phonological awareness and utterance construction. Such an approach is currently emphasized in the field of reading disabilities, which regards such metalinguistic abilities as essential for and predictive of reading and spelling abilities. However, few have attempted to examine and report the validity and reliability of the assessment methods themselves. In a recent publication, Vandervelden and Siegel (2001) examined their prior research and sought to determine the appropriateness of the alternative assessment of phonological processing with AAC users. In their study, school-aged AAC users and a comparison group of typically developing children were given a variety of phonological processing and reading tasks. Vandervelden and Siegel (2001) concluded that their assessment protocol was appropriate for AAC users but that future research is needed with different groups of AAC users and to further explore issues such as short-term memory demands. The authors also called for research into using these types of assessments to develop intervention strategies across ability levels.

Identification of extrinsic barriers that restrict access to literacy experiences and materials has also been the subject of several descriptive studies. Light and colleagues investigated parental and teacher expectations, as well as interactions surrounding story reading between preschool AAC users and their mothers (Light, Binger, & Smith, 1994; Light & McNaughton, 1993; Light & Smith, 1993).

Overall, these studies found that adults had lower expectations regarding literacy development in children with severe speech and physical impairments and that these children had fewer opportunities to actively engage in literacy activities. In another vein, Koppenhaver, Evans, and Yoder (1991) surveyed literate adult AAC users in an effort to determine factors that contributed to their literacy development. Respondents described growing up in homes and schools where access to literacy materials and experiences were frequent and actively encouraged.

Several other descriptive studies are worth noting. McGinnis and Beukelman (1989) collected samples of written assignments from elementary-aged students in order to suggest a functional vocabulary for AAC users who participate in the regular education curriculum. Smith, Thurston, Light, Parnes, and O'Keefe (1989) also investigated the written language by analyzing writing samples of six AAC users produced via word processing. These descriptive studies not only contribute to our knowledge base regarding the written language needs of AAC users, but also reflect adherence to state-of-the art assessment procedures, in which assessment of both individual skills and environments as well as the environments of typically developing peers are important components.

Although these assessment studies have provided valuable information regarding identification of intrinsic and extrinsic factors that affect literacy development, it is imperative that our field move forward in the continued development of appropriate, valid, and reliable assessment methods. It is only through effective assessment that appropriate intervention goals, methods, and means of documenting progress may be targeted. Clearly, much work remains to be done in the area of literacy assessment. We now examine the research base involving literacy intervention for individuals who use AAC.

IV. LITERACY INTERVENTION WITH AAC USERS

A. Case Studies

Case studies that carefully document successful intervention certainly have their place in an evolving research base. Although lack of experimental control prevents the drawing of conclusions regarding the efficacy of described interventions (see Chapters 2, 3, and 12), case studies provide a wealth of material from which to design and implement empirical research regarding effective intervention strategies.

A relatively large and diverse number of case studies have described literacy intervention techniques for individuals with a broad range of congenital and acquired disabilities such as aphasia, cerebral palsy, intellectual disabilities, sensory impairments, and traumatic brain injury. Intervention has addressed issues such as the following:

- Contributing factors to literacy development, such as interaction with print and use of voice output technology (Blischak, 1995; Erickson, Koppenhaver, Yoder, & Nance, 1997; Hedrick, Katims, & Carr, 1999; Katims, 1996; Smith, 1992);
- Reading acquisition (Bellon, Ogletree, & Harn, 2000; Ottem, 2001; Ratcliff & Little, 1996; Thorley, Ward, Binepal, & Dolan, 1991)
- Technology applications, such as alphabet learning and text production (Armstrong & MacDonald, 2000; DeRuyter & Donoghue, 1989; Glennen, Sharp-Bittner, & Tullos, 1991; Hsieh & Luo, 1999; Hux, Rankin-Erickson, Manasse, & Lauritzen, 2000; King & Hux, 1995; Kubota *et al.*, 2000; Light, Beesley, & Collier, 1988; Light, Roberts, Dimarco, & Greiner, 1998; Newell, Arnott, Booth, & Beattie, 1992; Schutz-Muehling & Beukelman, 1990; Steelman, Pierce, & Koppenhaver, 1993; Vanderheiden & Smith, 1989)

In general, these case studies have reflected developmental models, in which literacy intervention procedures incorporated instructional methods used by peers. Recurring intervention themes in these case studies included addressing both top-down and bottom-up strategies, developing spoken language and AAC concurrently, teaching metalinguistic skills, and reducing the effects of intrinsic and extrinsic barriers to literacy development. The application of assistive technology to support both literacy participation and acquisition was included in the majority of the described cases, with emphasis on the need to design appropriate individualized methods for maximal independence. Thus, these well-documented cases of literacy success have provided hypotheses that lend themselves well to the development of controlled treatment efficacy research.

B. Empirical Research

Empirical research involves controlled application of levels of an independent variable to quantify its effect on the dependent variable(s). Experimental procedures are typically replicated within or across participants to increase confidence in obtained results. Empirical research may be divided into two broad design categories: single-subject experimental designs and group designs.

1. Single-Subject Experimental Designs

Single-subject experimental designs constitute a type of empirical research in which one or more treatments are provided to and compared within one individual (see also Chapter 6). Data are collected and displayed across time to demonstrate change in the dependent variable(s). Treatment efficacy can then be demonstrated with a greater degree of confidence than with case studies. Single-subject experimental research is particularly applicable to the low incidence, widely diverse population of AAC users (Bedrosian, 1995). Issues of generalizability may be resolved by replicating the research protocol across several participants and studies.

a. Spelling

By their nature, single-subject experiments address fairly narrow research questions, in contrast to the broad themes evident in case studies. For example, four published studies have evaluated methods of spelling instruction for individuals with physical or multiple disabilities. First, Koppenhaver and Yoder (1989) used a multiple-baseline design with two 13-year-old with physical disabilities students. Results indicated that use of a strategy in which the learner looked at a word, visualized and said the word, then wrote it was superior to a strategy employing memorization and fill-in-the-blank practice. Subsequently, McNaughton and Tawney (1993) compared two methods of spelling instruction, copy-write-compare and student-directed cueing, with two adult AAC users. Both methods were found to be effective in increasing spelling skills. Then, in 1996, Stromer, Mackay, Howell, and McVay demonstrated the efficacy of computer-based instruction for improving spelling abilities in two adults with intellectual disabilities and hearing loss. Schlosser, Blischak, Belfiore, Bartley, and Barnett (1998) provided three different combinations of synthetic speech and orthographic feedback during spelling instruction for a 10-year-old boy with autism. Although all three conditions were effective in improving spelling, provision of synthetic speech (present in two conditions) resulted in more efficient spelling acquisition. Results from these studies, taken as a whole, indicate that, as with typically developing individuals, different methods of spelling instruction may successfully support spelling acquisition. To date, no particular diagnostic procedures have been developed to differentiate learner characteristics that lend themselves better to one procedure over another.

b. Storybook Reading

Another important issue that has been investigated via single-subject experimental research has been participation in interactive storybook reading by young children who use AAC. Bedrosian (1999) described two single-subject experimental studies in which interventions were designed to increase participants' expressive communication through use of low-tech AAC (i.e., communication boards, switch-activated tape player) and facilitator training. Both methods were demonstrated to be effective for children with cerebral palsy. Research by Koppenhaver, Erickson, Harris, McLellan, and Skotko, and Newton (2001) supported the efficacy of these intervention methods in a study in which girls with Rett syndrome increased both quality and quantity of symbolic communication during an intervention program that featured low-tech AAC (i.e., simple speech-generating devices [SGDs], graphic symbols) along with parent training during storybook reading.

Despite its obvious advantage over case studies, single-subject experimental research appears to be rarely utilized in literacy intervention research in the field of AAC. This is indeed unfortunate, considering how desperately the field is in need of efficacy studies (Koppenhaver, 2000). Use of single-subject experimental designs is a feasible method of providing experimental control and lending support for the use of particular intervention methods, particularly for a population as diverse as that of persons who use AAC.

2. Group Designs

Group empirical research involves application of an independent variable (i.e., treatment) to a group of participants (see also Chapter 7). One or more comparison groups that receive a different treatment (or no treatment in the case of a control group) are also used. Data are typically subjected to statistical analysis to determine the effect(s) of the independent variable on the dependent variable(s).

a. Technology for Text Production

A relatively large number of group studies have investigated various aspects of technology used for production of written text, such as keystroke savings (e.g., Higginbotham, 1992; Lanspa, Wood, & Beukelman, 1997) and speech recognition (e.g., Coleman & Myers, 1991; Ferrier, Shane, Ballard, Carpenter, & Benolt, 1995; Thomas-Stonell, Kotier, Leeper, & Doyle, 1998). Studies such as these are useful in guiding the selection of technology as a tool in literacy development. However, because studies of this type involve investigation of aspects of the tools themselves, rather than effects of technology use itself on literacy development, they will not be reviewed here.

b. Graphic Symbol Use

Few group studies demonstrating effective literacy intervention for individuals who use AAC have been published. On one occasion, literacy emerged as a secondary effect in a longitudinal study conducted by Romski and Sevcik (1996). Adolescents with intellectual disabilities used SGDs upon which Lexigrams (arbitrary graphic symbols) and the printed word had been placed. It was found that during the period of functional SGD use, some participants demonstrated recognition of the printed words, without the accompanying Lexigram. Although it has been repeatedly demonstrated that pairing a picture with a printed word generally interferes with word recognition, participants in Romski and Sevcik's research nevertheless developed some ability to recognize these words. Pufpaff, Blischak, and Lloyd (2000) have argued that it is likely that for these participants, orthography was the more meaningful portion of the graphic display and thus eventually overshadowed the simpler, but ultimately less familiar Lexigram.

The effect of graphic symbol use on literacy development has received a good deal of attention in the AAC field (e.g., Bishop, Rankin, & Mirenda, 1994; Blischak & McDaniel, 1995; McNaughton, 1993; McNaughton, & Lindsay, 1995; Rankin, Harwood, & Mirenda, 1994). From these discussions, important questions arise. To paraphrase McNaughton (1993), what effects might the use of graphic symbols have on literacy development? Does graphic symbol use create a "radically different developmental experience" (p. 60) for children who use them as their primary mode of communication? Unfortunately, the types of graphic symbols and methods for using them in combination with print that are most effective in promoting literacy acquisition have yet to be determined. It appears that little in the field of AAC has changed since Beukelman and Mirenda's (1998) lament:

> AAC specialists have been investigating the relationship between graphic symbols and literacy learning. A central question in this area is whether individuals can transfer the processes and abilities developed through the use of graphic symbols to the tasks of reading (and writing) (Bishop *et al.*, 1994). Unfortunately, as of 1998, no research existed that could help us to better understand this relationship. Nonetheless, interventionists routinely use the graphic symbols with which some AAC users communicate as a means to foster these individuals' literacy development. (p. 374)

c. Phonologic Awareness

One group intervention study regarding literacy development in children with little or no functional speech was published by Blischak (1999). In this small *n* study, two groups of preschool and young school-aged children received individual phonological awareness instruction in the form of rhyming stories and games. One group of children used graphic symbols for participating in the activities, whereas the other used graphic symbols with synthetic speech output. Unfortunately, statistical differences between the groups were not realized in terms of phonological awareness, although the natural speech production of children in the synthetic speech group increased (see Chapter 16).

In spite of the lack of evidence to support various clinical approaches and methods, practitioners and caregivers must forge ahead and provide intervention based on the best evidence to date. As Mirenda and Erickson (2000) have proposed in regard to our "lack of definitive knowledge," we should "utilize a balanced approach that incorporates all of the processes that are known to be involved in successful literacy learning" (p. 356). An attempt to implement such a balanced approach is described in the following case example.

C. Case Example

The case example of Michael, initially presented by Blischak (1998), described a clinical team's examination of a preschool child's literacy development as an integral part of his speech, language, and communication development through AAC use. Of particular interest to the team was the extent to which intervention targeted development of all five components of language as well as literacy learning. Table 17.3 provides a description of Michael's background, therapy goals, and activities.

When examining Michael's goals, it appeared that speech-language and AAC intervention reflected current best practices in communication disorders. Michael was encouraged to express one- and two-word utterances utilizing both unaided and aided AAC methods. Natural speech was encouraged, though production of specific phonemes was not yet targeted. Michael had the opportunity for both individual and small-group interaction to provide functional age- and

Table 17.3

Case Example: Michael

Background
- 4.6 years of age
- Severe expressive speech-language delay and mild developmental delay
- Early intervention since the age of 3 with ongoing parent involvement

Current Intervention
- Individual speech-language and occupational therapy two times weekly
- Attendance at small group speech-language preschool program two times weekly

Semester Goals: Five Components of Language
- Phonology: Produce/imitate single word approximations
- Semantics: Produce gestures or manual signs/point to graphic symbols of objects, actions, social utterances (e.g., *hi*, *mine*).
- Syntax: Imitate production of two-word combinations using speech, sign, or graphic symbols
- Morphology: Not targeted
- Pragmatics: use speech, signs, graphic symbols, or SGD to express various functions

Semester Goals: Literacy Development
- Recognize first name in print
- Recognize and name alphabet letters

Activities
Play, snack, art, games and story time in individual and small group settings

developmentally appropriate communicative contexts. His mother actively participated in his treatment by observing therapy sessions and using AAC methods at home.

In regard to literacy, Michael's goals reflected a fairly traditional approach: work on alphabet recognition and production prior to beginning kindergarten. Unfortunately, missing were goals that addressed other emergent literacy skills. It appeared that Michael's intervention team expected that alphabet learning along with exposure to literacy experiences such as storybook reading were sufficient to prepare him for a lifetime of literacy. However, studies cited throughout this chapter suggest that Michael's active participation in these activities was likely to be severely limited unless vigorous efforts were made to identify and target literacy goals and provide needed adaptations. Further, although alphabet instruction may foster the development of phonological and phoneme-grapheme awareness, a thorough assessment should be completed to determine Michael's metalinguistic strengths and needs.

How might Michael's team have addressed these unmet literacy needs? Suggestions for EBP regarding literacy intervention in AAC, even today, are currently insufficient. Thus, Michael's team's best option was to follow the suggestion advocated earlier in this chapter: provide intervention consistent with what is known about typical literacy development, with individualized adaptations that promote Michael's independent participation. Suggestions for addressing Michael's unmet literacy needs include the following:

Increase Phonologic Awareness
- Assess Michael's awareness of rhyme, sound blending and segmenting, and phoneme-grapheme correspondence.
- Provide intervention with AAC adaptations such as line drawings, magnetic letters, computer software.

Increase Active Participation in Storybook Reading
- Assess Michael's ability to independently access books and other sources of print; assess his ability to participate in storybook reading one-on-one and in small groups.
- Provide opportunities and adaptations for independent access to books, including computer-based books; expand current graphic symbol/SGD messages to include those that typically developing children produce during storybook reading, such as questions/answers and comments.

Construct and Retell Narratives
- Provide pictures, orthography, and computer software to assist Michael in constructing and repeating simple narratives of actual events and stories.

Produce Print in a Variety of Forms

- Incorporate with work on phonologic awareness, speech sound production, narratives, and occupational therapy, using adapted computer software and hardware as needed.

Continue Parent Involvement

- Encourage parent contribution to assessment and goal setting.
- Model techniques for eliciting and reinforcing desired responses.
- Provide parent with materials and activities for home use.

V. FUTURE RESEARCH

This chapter examined discussion of typical reading development, current intervention practices in the field of reading disabilities, issues surrounding literacy assessment and intervention, and a review of the limited research involving aspects of literacy intervention with individuals who use AAC. Although case studies predominate in the AAC literature related to literacy, both they and the research studies cited reflect a theme that has reappeared throughout the chapter: application of current trends in literacy theory and treatment to intervention for individuals who use AAC. However, without research that examines the effects of the use of current literacy intervention approaches *with AAC methods*, sufficient evidence to guide our interventions is incomplete. As illustrated in the case of Michael, it is imperative that practitioners in the field of AAC move beyond assumptions, inadequate assessments, unmet areas of development/need, and untested methods to fully address the literacy needs of all individuals who use AAC.

A challenge to both researchers and evidence-based practitioners, then, is to engage in collaborative research (e.g., Apel, 2001; Blischak & Cheek, 2000) to advance our knowledge and provide evidence to support best practices across all areas of literacy assessment and intervention. Delineation and discussion of the vast array of potential research issues and questions could easily be a chapter in and of itself. For that reason, the following list is not intended to be comprehensive. Instead, it is designed to cover some of the major areas of potential and to-be-continued research in the AAC field. The reader is invited to expand this list and contribute additional issues and ideas.

Emergent Literacy

- What are the effects of using graphic symbols during storybook interactions?
- Are storybook interactions enhanced by use of speech output?
- What are the effects of using speech output during solitary book experiences?

- What are the effects of use of assistive technology on storybook interactions (e.g., books on tape, mechanical page turners, storybook software)?
- What types of technology promote early scribbling/writing experiences?
- Do opportunities to actively participate in emergent literacy experiences via AAC enhance later-developing literacy abilities?

Phonologic Awareness

- What are the most valid and reliable methods of assessing phonologic awareness abilities in persons who use AAC?
- What are the effects of using speech output on development of phonologic awareness? On development of phoneme-grapheme correspondence?
- Does development of phoneme-grapheme correspondence enhance later-developing literacy abilities?

Word Recognition

- What are the most valid and reliable methods of assessing word recognition skills in persons who use AAC?
- What are the effects of early graphic symbol use on word recognition? Of speech output?
- Which types of graphic symbols promote word recognition?

Narrative Construction

- What are the effects of using graphic symbols on narrative construction? Of speech output?

Writing/Text Production

- What are the effects of various text input methods on spelling and composition (e.g., scanning, prediction)?
- What are the effects of speech output on spelling, composition, and editing?

REFERENCES

Aaron, P. G., & Joshi, R. M. (1992). *Reading problems: Consultation and remediation.* New York: Guilford Press.

Abbott, S. P., & Berninger, V. W. (1999): It's never too late to remediate: Teaching word recognition to students with reading disabilities in grades 4–7. *Annals of Dyslexia, 49,* 223–250.

Adams, M. J. (1990). *Beginning to read: Thinking and learning about print.* Cambridge, MA: MIT Press.

Adams, M. J., Foorman, B. R., Lundberg, I., & Beeler, T. (1998). *Phonemic awareness in young children: A classroom curriculum.* Baltimore: Paul H. Brookes.

Apel, K. (2001). Developing evidence-based practices and research collaborations in school settings. *Language, Speech, and Hearing Services in Schools, 32,* 149–152.

Armstrong, L., & MacDonald, A. (2000). Aiding chronic written language expression difficulties: A case study. *Aphasiology, 14,* 93–108.

Bedrosian, J. L. (1995). Limitations in the use of nondisabled subjects in AAC research. *Augmentative and Alternative Communication, 11,* 6–10.

Bedrosian, J. L. (1999). Efficacy research issues in AAC: Interactive storybook reading. *Augmentative and Alternative Communication, 15,* 45–55.

Bellon, M. L., Ogletree, B. T., & Harn, W. E. (2000). Repeated storybook reading as a language intervention for children with autism: A case study on the application of scaffolding. *Focus on Autism and Other Developmental Disabilities, 15,* 52–58.

Berninger, V., Abbott, R., Abbott, S., Graham, S., & Richards, T. (2002). Reading and writing: Connections between language by hand and language by eye. *Journal of Learning Disabilities, 15,* 39–56

Berninger, V. W., & Gans, B. M. (1986a). Assessing word processing capability of the nonvocal, nonwriting. *Augmentative and Alternative Communication, 2,* 56–63.

Berninger, V. W., & Gans, B. M. (1986b). Language profiles in nonspeaking individuals of normal intelligence with severe cerebral palsy. *Augmentative and Alternative Communication, 2,* 45–50.

Beukelman, D. R., & Mirenda, P. (1998). Literacy development of AAC users. In *Augmentative and alternative communication* (2nd ed., pp. 355–390). Baltimore, MD: Paul H. Brookes.

Bishop, K., Rankin, J. L., & Mirenda, P. (1994). Impact of graphic symbol use on reading acquisition. *Augmentative and Alternative Communication, 10,* 113–125.

Blachman, B. A. (1997). *Foundations of reading acquisition and dyslexia: Implications for early intervention.* Mahwah, NJ: Erlbaum.

Blachman, B. A., Ball, E. W., Black, R., Tangel, D. M. (2000). *Road to the code program for young children.* Baltimore: Paul H. Brookes.

Blischak, D. M. (1994). Phonologic awareness: Implications for individuals with little or no functional speech. *Augmentative and Alternative Communication, 10,* 245–254.

Blischak, D. M. (1995). Thomas the writer: Case study of a child with severe physical, speech, and visual impairments. *Language, Speech, and Hearing Services in Schools, 26,* 11–20.

Blischak, D. M. (1998, October). *Language issues in augmentative and alternative communication: Covering all the bases?* Presentation at the Crossroads Conference on Communicative Disorders. Purdue University, West Lafayette, IN.

Blischak, D. M. (1999). Increases in natural speech production following experience with synthetic speech. *Journal of Special Education Technology, 14,* 44–53.

Blischak, D. M., & Cheek, M. (2000). "A lot of work keeping everything controlled": A class research project. *American Journal of Speech-Language Pathology, 10,* 10–16.

Blischak, D. M., & McDaniel, M. A. (1995). Effects of picture size and placement on memory for written words. *Journal of Speech and Hearing Research, 38,* 1356–1362.

Bourassa, D., & Treiman, R. (2001). Spelling development and disability: The importance of linguistic factors. *Language, Speech, and Hearing Services in Schools, 32,* 172–181.

Catts, H., & Kamhi, A. (Eds.) (1999). *Language and reading disabilities.* Needham Heights, MA: Allyn & Bacon.

Chall, J. S. (1983). *Stages of reading development.* New York: McGraw-Hill.

Coleman, C. L., & Myers, L. S. (1991). Computer recognition of the speech of adults with cerebral palsy and dysarthria. *Augmentative and Alternative Communication, 7,* 34–42.

Cox, A. (1984). *Alphabetic phonics: Structures and techniques.* Cambridge, MA: Education Publishing Service.

DeRuyter, F., & Donoghue, K. A. (1989). Communication and traumatic brain injury: A case study. *Augmentative and Alternative Communication, 5,* 49–54.

Eckert, M., Lombardino, L., & Leonard, C. (2001). Planar asymmetry tips the phonological playground and the environment raises the bar. *Child Development, 72,* 988–1002.

Ehri, L. C. (1991). The development of reading and spelling in children: An overview. In M. Snowling & M. Thomson (Eds.), *Dyslexia: Integrating theory and practice* (pp. 63–79). London: Whurr.

Ehri, L. C. (1995). Phases of development in learning to read words by sight. *Journal of Research in Reading, 18*, 116–125.

Erickson, K. A., Koppenhaver, D. A., Yoder, D. E., & Nance, J. (1997). Integrated communication and literacy instruction for a child with multiple disabilities. *Focus on Autism and Other Developmental Disabilities, 12*, 142–150.

Ferrier, L. J., Shane, H. C., Ballard, H. F., Carpenter, T., & Benoit, A. (1995). Dysarthric speakers' intelligibility and speech characteristics in relation to computer speech recognition. *Augmentative and Alternative Communication, 11*, 165–174.

Foley, B. E., & Pollatsek, A. (1999). Phonological processing and reading abilities in adolescents and adults with severe congenital speech impairments. *Augmentative and Alternative Communication, 15*, 156–174.

Fried-Oken, M., & Bersani, H. A. (Eds.) (2000). *Speaking up and spelling it out.* Baltimore: Paul H. Brookes.

Frith, U. (1985). Beneath the surface of developmental dyslexia. In K. E. Patterson, J. C. Marshall, & M. Colheart (Eds.), *Surface dyslexia.* London: Routledge & Kegan Paul.

Galda, L., Cullinan, B., & Strickland, D. (1993). *Language, literacy and the child.* London: Harcourt Brace Jovanovich College Publishers.

Gillingham, A., & Stillman, B. W. (1998). *The Gillingham manual.* Cambridge, MA: Educators Publishing Service.

Glennen, S. L., Sharp-Bittner, M. A., & Tullos, D. C. (1991). Augmentative and alternative communication training with a nonspeaking adult: Lessons from MH. *Augmentative and Alternative Communication, 7*, 240–247.

Goswami, U., & Bryant, P. (1990). *Phonological skills and learning how to read.* East Sussex, Britain: Erlbaum.

Hedrick, W. B., Katims, D. S., & Carr, N. J. (1999). Implementing a multimethod, multilevel literacy program for students with mental retardation. *Focus on Autism and Other Developmental Disabilities, 14*, 231–239.

Higginbotham, D. J. (1992). Evaluation of keystroke savings across five assistive communication technologies. *Augmentative and Alternative Communication, 8*, 258–272.

Hjelmquist, E., Sandberg, A. D., & Hedelin, L. (1994). Linguistics, AAC, and metalinguistics in communicatively handicapped adolescents. *Augmentative and Alternative Communication, 10*, 169–182.

Hsieh, M., & Luo, C. (1999). Morse code typing training of an adolescent with cerebral palsy using microcomputer technology: Case study. *Augmentative and Alternative Communication, 15*, 216–221.

Hux, K., Rankin-Erickson, J. L., Manasse, N., & Lauritzen, E. (2000). Accuracy of three speech recognition systems: Case study of dysarthric speech. *Augmentative and Alternative Communication, 16*, 186–196.

Johnson, P. L. (2000). If I do say so myself. In M. Fried-Oken & H. A. Bersani, Jr. (Eds.), *Speaking up and spelling it out* (pp. 47–55). Baltimore: Paul H. Brookes.

Johnson-Martin, N. M., Wolters, P., & Stowers, S. (1987). Psychological assessment of the nonvocal, physically handicapped child. *Physical and Occupational Therapy in Pediatrics, 7*, 23–38.

Katims, D. S. (1996). The emergence of literacy in elementary students with mild mental retardation. *Focus on Autism and Other Developmental Disabilities, 11*, 147–157.

Koppenhaver, D. A. (2000). Literacy *in* AAC: What should be written on the envelope we push? *Augmentative and Alternative Communication, 16*, 270–279.

Koppenhaver, D. A., Erickson, K. A., Harris, B., McLellan, J., Skotko, B. G., & Newton, R. A. (2001). Storybook-based communication intervention for girls with Rett syndrome and their mothers. *Disability and Rehabilitation, 23*, 149–159.

Koppenhaver, D. A., Evans, D. A., & Yoder, D. E. (1991). Childhood reading and writing experiences of literate adults with severe speech and motor impairments. *Augmentative and Alternative Communication, 7*, 20–32.

Koppenhaver, D. A., & Yoder, D. E. (1989). Study of a spelling strategy for physically disabled augmentative communication users. *Communication Outlook, 19*, 10–12.

Koppenhaver, D. A., & Yoder, D. E (1993). Classroom literacy instruction for children with severe speech and physical impairments (SSPI): What it is and what might be. *Topics in Language Disorders, 13*, 1–15.

Kubota, M., Sakakihara, Y., Uchiyama, Y., Nara, A., Nagata, T., Nitta, H., Ishimoto, K., Oka, A., Horio. K., & Yanagisawa, M. (2000). New ocular movement detector system as a communication tool in ventilator-assisted Werdnig-Hoffman disease. *Developmental Medicine & Child Neurology, 42*, 61–64.

Lanspa, A., Wood, L. A., & Beukelman, D. R. (1997). Efficiency with which disabled and nondisabled students locate words in cue windows: Study of three organizational strategies—freuency of word use, word length, and alphabetic order. *Augmentative and Alternative Communication, 13*, 117–124.

Leonard, C. M., Eckert, M., Lombardino, L., Oakland, T., Kranzler, J., Mohr, C., King, W., & Freeman, A. (2001). Anatomical risk factors for phonological dyslexia. *Cerebral Cortex, 11*, 148–157.

Light, J., Beesley, M., & Collier, B. (1988). Transition through multiple augmentative and alternative communication systems: A three-year case study of a head injured adolescent. *Augmentative and Alternative Communication, 4*, 2–14.

Light, J., Binger, C., & Smith, A. K. (1994). Story reading interactions between preschoolers who use AAC and their mothers. *Augmentative and Alternative Communication, 10*, 255–268.

Light, J., & McNaughton, D. (1993). Literacy and augmentative communication (AAC): The expectations and priorities of parents and teachers. *Topics in Language Disorders, 13*, 33–46.

Light, J. C., Roberts, B., Dimarco, R., & Greiner, N. (1998). Augmentative and alternative communication to support receptive and expressive communication for people with autism. *Journal of Communication Disorders, 31*, 153–180.

Light, J., & Smith, A. K. (1993). Home literacy experiences of preschoolers who use AAC systems and of their nondisabled peers. *Augmentative and Alternative Communication, 9*, 10–25.

Light, J., Stoltz, B., & McNaughton, D. (1996). Community-based employment: Experiences of adults who use AAC. *Augmentative and Alternative Communication, 12*, 215–228.

Lindamood, P., & Lindmood, P. (1998). *The Lindamood® phoneme sequencing program for reading, spelling, and speech.* Austin, TX: Pro-Ed.

McGinnis, J. S., & Beukelman, D. R. (1989). Vocabulary requirements for writing activities for the academically mainstreamed student with disabilities. *Augmentative and Alternative Communication, 5*, 183–191.

McNaughton, S. (1993). Graphic representational systems and literacy learning. *Topics in Language Disorders, 13*, 58–75.

McNaughton, S., & Lindsay, P. (1995). Approaching literacy with AAC graphics. *Augmentative and Alternative Communication, 11*, 212–228.

McNaughton, D., & Tawney, J. (1993). Comparison of two spelling instruction techniques for adults who use augmentative and alternative communication. *Augmentative and Alternative Communication, 9*, 72–82.

Mirenda, P., & Erickson, K. A. (2000). Augmentative communication and literacy. In A. M. Wetherby & B. M. Prizant (Eds.), *Autism spectrum disorders* (pp. 333–367). Baltimore: Paul H. Brookes.

Newell, A. R., Arnott, J. L., Booth, L., & Beattie, W. (1992). Effect of the "PAL" word prediction system on the quality and quantity of text generation. *Augmentative and Alternative Communication, 8*, 304–311.

O'Connor, R. E., & Jenkins, J. R. (1999). Prediction of reading disabilities in kindergarten and first grade. *Scientific Studies of Reading, 3*, 159–197.

Orton, J. (1976). *A guide to teaching phonics*. Cambridge, MA: Educators Publishing Service.

Ottem, E. (2001). Use of pictographic-articulatory symbols to promote alphabetic reading in a language-impaired boy: Case study. *Augmentative and Alternative Communication, 17*, 52–60.

Paul, R. (1997). Facilitating transitions in language development for children using AAC. *Augmentative and Alternative Communication, 13*, 141–148.

Pufpaff, L. A., Blischak, D. M., & Lloyd, L. L. (2000). Effects of modified orthography on the identification of printed words. *American Journal on Mental Retardation, 105*, 14–24.

Pumfrey, P. D., & Reason, R. (1991). *Specific learning difficulties: Challenges and responses*. Berks, England: NFER-Nelson.

Rankin, J. L., Harwood, K., & Mirenda, P. (1994). Influence of graphic symbol use on reading comprehension. *Augmentative and Alternative Communication, 10*, 269–281.

Ratcliff, A., & Little, M. (1996). A conversation based barrier task approach to teach sight-word vocabulary to a young augmentative communication system user. *Child Language Teaching and Therapy, 12*, 128–135.

Romski, M. A., & Sevcik, R. A. (1996). *Breaking the speech barrier: Language development through augmented means*. Baltimore: Paul H. Brookes.

Sandberg, A. D. (2001). Reading and spelling, phonological awareness, and working memory in children with severe speech impairments: A longitudinal study. *Augmentative and Alternative Communication, 17*, 11–26.

Sandberg, A. D., & Hjelmquist, E. (1996). Phonological awareness and literacy abilities in nonspeaking preschool children with cerebral palsy. *Augmentative and Alternative Communication, 12*, 138–153.

Scarborough, H. S. (1998). Early identification of children at risk for reading disabilities: Phonological awareness and some other promising predictors. In B. K. Shapiro, P. J. Accardo, & A. Capute (Eds.), *Specific reading disability: A view of the spectrum* (pp.75–120). Timonium, MD: York Press.

Schlosser, R. W., Blischak, D. M., Belfiore, P. H., Bartley, C., & Barnett, N. (1998). Effects of synthetic speech output and orthographic feedback on spelling in a student with autism: A preliminary study. *Journal of Autism and Developmental Disorders, 28*, 309–319.

Schutz-Muehling, L. D., & Beukelman, D. R. (1990). An augmentative and alternative writing system for a college student with fibrositis: A case study. *Augmentative and Alternative Communication, 7*, 250–255.

Scott, C. (1999). Learning to write. In H. Catts & A. Kamhi (Eds.), *Language and reading disabilities*. Needham Heights, MA: Allyn & Bacon.

Seidenberg, M. S., & McClelland, J. L. (1989). A distributed, developmental model of words recognition and naming. *Psychological Review, 96*, 523–568.

Slingerland, B. (1971). *A multi-sensory approach to language arts for specific language disability children*. Cambridge, MA: Educators Publishing Service.

Smith, A. K., Thurston, S., Light, J., Parnes, P., & O'Keefe, B. (1989). The form and use of written communication produced by physically disabled individuals using microcomputers. *Augmentative and Alternative Communication, 5*, 115–124.

Smith, M. M. (1992). Reading abilities of nonspeaking students: Two case studies. *Augmentative and Alternative Communication, 8*, 57–66.

Smith, M. M., & Blischak, D. M. (1997). Literacy. In L. L. Lloyd, D. R. Fuller, & H. H. Arvidson (Eds.), *Augmentative and alternative communication* (pp. 414–444). Needham Heights, MA: Allyn & Bacon.

Snow, C. E., Scarborough, H. S., & Burns, M. S. (1999). What speech-language pathologists need to know about early reading. *Topics in Language Disorders, 20*, 48–58.

Steelman, J. D., Pierce, P. L., & Koppenhaver, D. A. (1993). The role of computers in promoting literacy in children with severe speech and physical impairments (SSPI). *Topics in Language Disorders, 13*, 76–88.

Stromer, R., Mackay, H. A., Howell, S. R., & McVay, A. A. (1996). Teaching computer-based spelling to individuals with developmental and hearing disabilities: Transfer of stimulus control to writing tasks. *Journal of Applied Behavior Analysis, 29,* 25–42.

Thomas-Stonell, N., Kotier, A., Leeper, H. A., & Doyle, P. C. (1998). Computerized speech recognition: Influence of intelligibility and perceptual consistency on recognition accuracy. *Augmentative and Alternative Communication, 14,* 51–56.

Thorley, B., Ward, J., Binepal, T., & Dolan, K. (1991). Communicating with printed words to augment signing: Case study of a severely disabled deaf-blind child. *Augmentative and Alternative Communication, 7,* 80–87.

Vanderheiden, G. C., & Smith, R. O. (1989). Application of communication technologies to an adult with a high spinal cord injury. *Augmentative and Alternative Communication, 5,* 62–66.

Vandervelden, M. C., & Siegel, L. S. (1999). Phonological processing and literacy in AAC users and students with motor speech impairments. *Augmentative and Alternative Communication, 15,* 191–211.

Vandervelden, M. C., & Siegel, L. S. (2001). Phonological processing in written word learning: Assessment for children who use augmentative and alternative communication. *Augmentative and Alternative Communication, 17,* 37–51.

Wagner, R. K., & Torgesen, J. K. (1987). The nature of phonological processing and its causal role in the acquisition of reading skills. *Psychological Bulletin, 101,* 192–212.

Woodcock, R. (1987): *Woodcock Reading Mastery Tests—Revised.* Circle Pines, MN: American Guidance Service.

CHAPTER 18

Efficacy of AAC Intervention in Individuals with Chronic Severe Aphasia

Rajinder Koul
Department of Communication
Disorders
Texas Tech University Health
Sciences Center

Melinda Corwin
Department of Communication
Disorders
Texas Tech University Health
Sciences Center

I. INTRODUCTION

One of the most significant recent advances in improving the communicative abilities of individuals with acquired brain injury has been the development of augmentative and alternative communication (AAC) methods—that is, techniques, strategies, and symbols for augmenting or replacing natural speech or writing (Lloyd, Fuller, & Arvidson, 1997). A review of past research suggests that AAC is being increasingly used to facilitate and enhance the communicative abilities of individuals with a range of acquired communication disorders (e.g., Bertoni, Stoffel, & Weniger, 1991; Beukelman & Mirenda, 1998; Coelho & Duffy, 1987; Funnell & Allport, 1989; Gardner, Zurif, Berry, & Baker, 1976; Garrett, Beukelman, & Low-Morrow, 1989; Garrett & Kimelman, 2000; Glass, Gazzaniga, & Premack, 1973; Helm-Estabrooks, Fitzpatrick, & Barresi, 1982; Hermann, Reichle, Lucius-Hoene, Wallesch, & Johannsen-Horbach, 1988; Koul, Arvidson, & Pennington, 1997; Koul & Harding, 1998; Kraat, 1990; Lane & Samples, 1981; Lasker, Hux, Garrett, Moncrief, Eischeid, 1997; McCall, Shelton, Weinrich, &

Cox, 2000; Naeser, Palumbo, Baker, & Nicholas, 1994; Ross, 1979; Sawyer-Woods, 1987; Skelly, 1979; Trunzo-Rahbar, 1980; Waller & Newell, 1997; Weinrich, 1991; Weinrich, Boser, & McCall, 1999). This chapter provides an overview of the current repertoire of AAC options available for individuals with aphasia. Specifically, it focuses on evaluating the literature on the efficacy of AAC intervention in individuals with chronic severe or global aphasia.

II. APHASIA

Aphasia is a language impairment resulting from damage to certain areas of the brain that are responsible for the interpretation and formulation of language. It is estimated that approximately 80,000 people acquire symptoms of aphasia every year in the United States (National Institute on Deafness and Other Communication Disorders, 1997). The foremost cause of aphasia is a cerebrovascular accident (i.e., stroke). According to the U.S. Department of Health and Human Services (1995), approximately 550,000 people have strokes each year. The risk of stroke doubles after the age of 55, and two-thirds of all strokes occur in people over 65 years old (National Institute on Neurological Disorders and Stroke, 1999). Every year, approximately 180,000 individuals in the United States require nursing home care as a result of a stroke (National Stroke Association, 1991). A significant number of these individuals need AAC intervention during their stay in intensive and long-term care units. Other reported causes of aphasia include intracranial tumors, infections, toxicities, and traumatic brain injury.

In most individuals with aphasia some degree of spontaneous recovery of language function occurs in 3 to 6 months after the incurrence of the brain lesion. However, substantial individual variations are observed during the recovery process (Geschwind, 1985). Some individuals may completely recover their natural language capabilities, whereas others are unable to demonstrate significant recovery of their natural language abilities despite intensive traditional speech-language intervention. This chapter focuses primarily on individuals with aphasia for whom the ability to use natural language is severely and permanently impaired. Such individuals may gain significantly from AAC intervention.

A number of distinct aphasia profiles have led to the development of several classification schemes devoted to differential diagnosis of aphasia subtypes (e.g., Goodglass & Kaplan, 1983; Kertesz, 1982; Porch, 1981; Schuell, 1965). A classification system, which was specifically tailored to guide the AAC intervention in aphasia, was put forth by Garrett and Beukelman (1992). Their classification scheme differentiates individuals with aphasia on the basis of severity of aphasia, communication needs, and communication participatory patterns. Several studies have employed Garrett and Beukelman's (1992) model to facilitate communication through AAC intervention with varying degrees of success (Cress & King, 1999; Fox, Sohlberg, & Fried-Oken, 2001; Lasker et al., 1997).

There are two aphasia subtypes that frequently require some type of AAC intervention: chronic severe Broca's aphasia and global aphasia. Individuals with global aphasia usually demonstrate severe impairment in all four natural language modalities (speaking, comprehension, reading, and writing). Expressive speech of individuals with chronic severe Broca's aphasia is typically characterized as non-fluent and is composed of few effortful unintelligible words with awkward intervening pauses. According to Garrett and Beukelman's (1992) categorization of aphasia subtypes, individuals with global aphasia fall predominantly in the category of "basic choice communicators," and those who exhibit severe chronic Broca's aphasia can be mainly classified as "controlled situation communicators." Traditional aphasia treatment techniques involving linguistic skill retraining have been largely unsuccessful in individuals with global aphasia or chronic severe Broca's aphasia (Nicholas & Helm-Estabrooks, 1990).

III. AAC INTERVENTION AND APHASIA

Graphic symbols such as line drawings, pictographs, visual input communication, cutout paper symbols, and less transparent symbol systems like Blissymbolics have often been used as an alternative form of communication in individuals with severe aphasia (e.g., Glass *et al.*, 1973; Johannsen-Hornbach, Cegla, Mager, & Schempp, 1985; Lane & Samples, 1981; Nishikawa, 1980; Ross, 1979; Sawyer-Woods, 1987; Trunzo-Rahbar, 1980). In addition to graphic symbols, manual signs and gestures have also been used to facilitate communication in individuals with severe aphasia (Herman *et al.*, 1988; Kelsch, 1979; Rao & Horner, 1979; Skelly, 1979). Results suggest that individuals with severe aphasia are able to acquire, with varying degrees of success, graphic symbols, manual signs, and gestures (Coelho, 1982; Funnell & Allport, 1989; Helm-Estabrooks *et al.*, 1982). However, their ability to use these alternative forms of communication outside structured treatment contexts has been limited. This lack of generalization is because of inadequate emphasis given to factors such as communication partner training, participatory patterns, and communicative needs of individuals demonstrating aphasia (Garrett & Beukelman, 1992). A mere replacement of natural language with a graphic symbol, manual sign, or computer-based AAC system will not facilitate the functional communication skills of individuals with severe or global aphasia.

A. THEORETICAL FRAMEWORK FOR AAC INTERVENTION IN APHASIA

The theory of multiple profile of symbolic capacities in aphasia proposes that deficits in aphasia are limited to processing linguistic symbols. This theory suggests that a range of performance can be observed in individuals with aphasia across symbol systems. Individuals with aphasia, as a result of left hemisphere lesions, tend to identify pictures and line drawings with greater ease than written words (Gainotti, Silveri, & Sena, 1989; Goldstein, Canavan, & Polkey, 1988; Wapner & Gardner, 1981). Koul and Lloyd (1998) compared the performance on recognition of graphic symbols by individuals with aphasia, individuals with right-hemisphere brain damage, and neurologically normal adults. Their results indicated that individuals with aphasia and normal adults do not differ significantly in the recognition of graphic symbols. These studies suggest that individuals with aphasia are capable of representing objects, events, and states through graphic symbols. In addition, several studies suggest that the right temporal lobe does play a substantial role in acquisition, memory, and retention of abstract as well as iconic drawings (Cermak & Tarlow, 1978; De Renzi & Lucchelli, 1993; Jones-Gotman & Milner, 1978). The ability of the right hemisphere to process graphic symbols suggests that AAC intervention strategies need to capitalize on the untapped capabilities of undamaged areas of the brain. Further, in contrast to natural spoken language, the production of "sentences" using graphic symbols does not require complex morphosyntactic, phonetic, or articulatory processing. The absence of such complex processing demands suggests that it may be relatively easier to acquire and use graphic symbols for communication than natural language symbols.

B. Conceptualizing the Efficacy of AAC Interventions in Aphasia

Formal language rehabilitation programs have a long history in treatment of speech and language impairments in individuals with aphasia (Lyon, 1992; National Institute on Deafness and Other Communication Disorders, 1991). Like other areas of rehabilitation, however, there is a dearth of reliable and valid efficacy and outcome data. This chapter applies concepts proposed in this text (see Chapters 2 and 3) to evaluate the efficacy of AAC intervention in aphasia as presented in the literature. In Chapter 2, efficacy was defined as an all-encompassing term that includes "effectiveness," "efficiency," and "effects" (see also Calculator, 1991; Kendall & Norton-Ford, 1982; Olswang, 1990; Rosen & Proctor, 1981; Schlosser & Braun, 1994). Effectiveness is the desired change in the dependent variable (e.g., ability to spontaneously initiate requests) as a result of manipulation of an independent variable (e.g., using a speech-generating device [SGD] in functional communicative settings). Efficiency is the comparison of the relative effectiveness of two or more treatment techniques on one or more criteria variables (e.g., rate of acquisition). The efficiency of a treatment can only be determined after its effectiveness has been established. Effects may be conceptualized as the breaking down of a treatment package into its component parts and linking the component parts to changes in the dependent variable. Rosen and Proctor (1981) proposed three effects: intermediate, instrumental, and ultimate. Intermediate effects are linked to those treatment components that facilitate positive changes in the dependent variable (i.e., treatment goal). For example, adequate size and arrangement of graphic symbols and written words on a SGD display for an individual with severe Broca's aphasia and visual field defects can enhance acceptance as a means of communication. Instrumental effects are changes that occur as an offshoot of treatment intervention. These offshoots may not be expected but are welcome consequences of intervention. For example, if acceptance of SGDs as a means of communication enhances oral production of simple sentences in an individual with severe Broca's aphasia, then acceptance of SGDs serves as an instrumental effect. When the objectives of an intervention program are met (i.e., desired changes in the dependent variable are empirically observed and measured), then ultimate effects are achieved. Achievement of ultimate effects leads to termination of the treatment program. For example, if the ultimate objective of a treatment program is achieved by enabling an individual with global aphasia to use a SGDs independently, effectively, and efficiently across communicative settings and partners, then the treatment program may be terminated. Additionally, all of the studies reviewed in this chapter will be evaluated in terms of internal, external, and social validity. Examining an AAC intervention study along these three dimensions will allow the authors to make extrapolations as to the strength of the efficacy data obtained from that study and to inform evidence-based practice.

C. AAC Intervention Approaches

This section provides an overview of the two major AAC options available for individuals with aphasia. Additionally, their efficacy is evaluated by analyzing the data currently available for each of the intervention approaches.

1. Technologically Based AAC Intervention Approaches

With the rapid proliferation of AAC technologies in the 1990s, a number of graphic symbol software programs or dedicated devices (e.g., DynaVox, produced by DynaVox Systems; Vanguard by Prentke Romich Company; and Gus Multimedia Speech System by Gus Communications, Inc.) have become available for individuals with severe or global aphasia. However, a computer-based visual input communication (C-VIC) system has been most frequently used by researchers to evaluate the ability of individuals with chronic severe Broca's aphasia or global aphasia to acquire and use an alternative form of communication (e.g., Boser & Weinrich, 1998; McCall, Shelton, Weinrich, & Cox, 2000;

Shelton, Weinrich, McCall, & Cox, 1996; Weinrich, Boser, McCall, & Bishop, 2001; Weinrich, McCall, Shoosmith, Thomas, Katzenberger, & Weber, 1993; Weinrich, McCall, Weber, Thomas, & Thornburg, 1995; Weinrich, Shelton, McCall, & Cox, 1997). The C-VIC uses iconic and animated graphic symbols that allow an association between a symbol and its referent. Symbols can be combined to produce complete expressions. Vocabulary in C-VIC is organized into various categories that are related to parts of speech such as proper nouns, common nouns, verbs, modifiers, prepositions, and grammatical mood markers (Weinrich, 1992). A participant may select one of the categories such as verbs, which results in an explosion into several subcategories and the process may be repeated until the target symbol is located. This target symbol can be dragged into a communication space on the computer screen and displayed along with other symbols for conversational purposes. C-VIC was specifically developed and promoted to provide an alternative modality of communication for individuals with aphasia. In contrast to C-VIC, commercially available graphic symbol software programs (e.g., Talking Screen by Words+, and GUS Multimedia Speech System by Gus Communications, Inc.) and dedicated communication devices (e.g., Dynavox by DynaVox Systems and Liberator by Prentke Romich Company) were not developed as disorder specific. These software programs or dedicated devices are generally promoted as systems that may meet the communicative needs of individuals with severe speech and language impairments.

The Talking Screen, GUS, and dedicated communication devices such as the Dynavox present symbols in a dynamic display format using a similar menu-driven program. This format allows symbols to be presented across multiple screens in a logical sequence. For example, a participant may select one of the superordinate categories (e.g., vehicles) in the first screen, which will result in an explosion into several subordinate categories (car, truck, jeep, etc.) on the second screen, and further click "car" in the second screen to chose the brand name (Ford, Honda, etc.) on the third screen. The screens are designed in a manner so that each symbol is displayed in a separate grid. The total number of symbols that can be displayed on each screen is determined by factors such as the participant's cognitive, linguistic, motor, and visuo-perceptual skills and size of the monitor. Each symbol can be programmed to produce a spoken message. For example, a symbol for Coke may be programmed to produce the message "I'd like some Coke." Further, some symbols, which represent referents in categories such as pronouns, prepositions, and function words, can be programmed to produce instant speech (i.e., name of the referent). Examples of some of those symbols are YES, NO, BETWEEN, and YOU. Additionally, symbols selected across several screens can be stored and combined to produce syntactically correct simple as well as complex sentences. A participant may select "I" from one screen, "want" from the second screen, and "coffee" from the third screen to produce the message "I want coffee." These software programs and dedicated devices can be accessed via a mouse or an adapted switch or through scanning and produce high-quality synthetic speech upon selection of a symbol or sequence of symbols.

2. Efficacy of Technologically Based AAC Intervention Approaches

Studies involving technologically based AAC intervention with individuals with chronic aphasia are relatively limited in number. Table 18.1 presents a concise summary of relevant studies. In general, results with C-VIC and other computer-based graphic symbol communication systems have indicated that individuals with chronic severe Broca's aphasia or global aphasia are able to access, identify, manipulate, and combine graphic symbols to produce simple phrases and sentences (Goodenough-Trepagnier, 1995; Koul & Harding, 1998; Steele, Weinrich, Wertz, Kleczewska, & Carlson, 1989). Further, improvement in oral production of sentences and generalization to untrained behaviors as a result of C-VIC training has been reported as well (Weinrich *et al.*, 1995; Weinrich *et al.*, 1999).

Additionally, data also indicate that symbols for nouns are identified and produced with a higher degree of accuracy than symbols for other grammatical classes (Koul & Harding, 1998; Weinrich, 1991; Weinrich, Steele, Carlson, Kleczewska, Wertz, & Baker, 1989). Specifically, the greater difficulty in processing even animated C-VIC verbs may indicate that verb processing deficits seen in individuals with Broca's or global aphasia may transcend the modality (i.e., visual/verbal) in which symbols are presented (Weinrich, 1992). Finally, substantial variability in performance demonstrated by individuals with aphasia within studies precludes any prediction of the performance of individuals with chronic Broca's or global aphasia on computer-based AAC systems.

Although substantial data are available on the effectiveness of the C-VIC system, the clinical implications are limited because most of the studies were designed to understand the underlying nature of the aphasia deficit, not to test its veracity as a functional AAC system (e.g., Weinrich *et al.*, 1999; Weinrich *et al.*, 2001). Further, substantial data available on C-VIC are based on case study methodology. Case studies, by their very nature, can neither rule out threats to internal validity nor be used to make a determination about external validity (see Chapters 3, 6, and 12). In summary, available data on the effectiveness of C-VIC as an AAC system are weak. Future research that employs single-subject experimental designs or quasi-experimental group methodology is recommended to determine the effectiveness of C-VIC as a viable AAC system.

In addition to C-VIC, data are also available on more generic graphic-symbol-based communication systems. Koul and Harding (1998) evaluated the ability of five individuals with chronic severe or global aphasia to identify and produce graphic symbols using a Talking Screen software program that turns a microcomputer into an electronic communication device. The participants ranged

Table 18.1

Summary of technologically based AAC Intervention Studies Conducted with Individuals with Severe and Global Aphasia

Authors	Number of participants and age ranges	Aphasia type and severity	Goals/research questions	AAC system	Research design	Results	Efficacy
Boser & Weinrich (1998)	n = 1 65 years	Severe Broca's	To determine whether an individual with severe aphasia can produce, generalize, and maintain correct tense morphology	C-VIC[a]	Case study	Significant improvement (p < .01) from baseline scores; generalization to untrained morphology and maintenance observed for a period of 1 year	Demonstrated treatment effectiveness, observed ultimate and instrumental effects (i.e., generalization within and across behaviors)
Koul & Harding (1998)	n = 5 57–75 years	Three severe chronic Broca's and two global	To determine whether individuals with aphasia can identify symbols from different grammatical categories and combine those symbols to produce simple sentences	TS[b]	Multiple baseline design	Participants were able to identify graphic symbols and produce sentences using those symbols with varying degrees of accuracy; higher identification accuracy was observed for noun symbols in comparison to symbols from other grammatical classes	Demonstrated treatment effectiveness; ultimate effects observed to varying degrees
Koul, Oetzel, Corwin,	n = 3 63–73 years	Severe Broca's	To determine whether individuals with aphasia can produce sentences	DCD[c]	Multiple baseline design	Performance on sentence production task varied across	Demonstrated treatment effectiveness;

456

Study	n / Age	Deficit	Research question	Treatment	Study type	Results	Effects
& Nigam (2001)			of increasing syntactical complexity			participants. However, all participants were able to produce two- and three-word constructions with higher degree of accuracy	observed ultimate effects that varied across subjects; instrumental effects observed (i.e., generalization to untrained sentences)
McCall, Shelton, Weinrich, & Cox (2000)	n = 1 57 years	Global	Does training with C-VIC improve natural language abilities?	C-VIC	Case Study	No improvement observed in spoken language skills, although subject demonstrated ability to comprehend and produce sentences in C-VIC	No treatment effectiveness observed
Naeser, Palumbo, Baker, & Nicholas (1994)	n = 7 43–65 years	Global	Relationship between BASA scores and response to C-VIC training	C-VIC	Group Study	Participants who performed better on C-VIC training had a total BASA raw score of at least 26 and a score of at least 7 on the auditory comprehension subtest of BASA	Demonstrated treatment effectiveness to varying degrees; instrumental effects observed (i.e., ability to independently communicate using C-VIC)
Rostron, Ward, & Plant (1996)	n = 1	Severe apraxia and aphasia	Can an individual with severe aphasia use the software to produce single symbols and symbol combinations in functional communicative situations?	Easy Speaker[a]	Case Study	Participants identified and produced single symbols but did not use the software program in functional communication situations	Demonstrated weak ultimate effects; no instrumental effects observed

(continues)

Table 18.1 (*continued*)

Authors	Number of participants and age ranges	Aphasia type and severity	Goals/research questions	AAC system	Research design	Results	Efficacy
Shelton, Weinrich, McCall, & Cox (1996)	$n = 3$ 51–75 years	Global	Can individuals with global aphasia comprehend and produce C-VIC single words and sentences?	C-VIC	Case Study	Participants produced C-VIC sentences using various syntactic structures, although all had significant difficult in appropriate use of verbs	Demonstrated treatment effectiveness; ultimate effects observed to varying degrees
Weinrich, Boser, & McCall (1999)	$n = 1$ 65 years	Severe nonfluent aphasia	Can an individual with severe non-fluent aphasia trained in C-VIC produce correct verb tenses in a sentence completion task presented in verbal and written modes?	C-VIC	Case Study	C-VIC training was effective in assisting the participant to produce complete past-tense marked English across verbal and written modes; however, no generalization to untrained verbs was observed	Demonstrated treatment effectiveness; ultimate effects observed
Weinrich, Boser, McCall, & Bishop (2001)	$n = 2$ 68–71 years	Severe nonfluent	n subjects with chronic nonfluent aphasia comprehend and produce English passive sentences orally and using C-VIC	C-VIC	Case Study	Both participants produced and comprehend C-VIC passive sentences with high degree of accuracy; however, only one participant demonstrated ability to produce and comprehend sentences orally	Demonstrated treatment effectiveness to varying degrees; ultimate effects observed in one subject

Study	n / Age	Aphasia type	Research question	Device	Design	Results	Conclusions
Weinrich, McCall, Weber, Thomas, & Thornburg (1995)	n = 2 44–53 years	Severe chronic Broca's	Can training of locative prepositional phrases and S-V-O-sentences using C-VIC improve verbal production of those structures?	C-VIC	Case Study	Significant improvement demonstrated in oral and C-VIC production of prepositional phrases and sentences	Demonstrated treatment effectiveness; ultimate effects observed
Weinrich, Shelton, McCall, & Cox (1997)	n = 3 48–63 years	Severe chronic Broca's	Can individuals with aphasia use C-VIC to produce multisentence productions after training on single sentence production task?	C-VIC	Case Study	C-VIC training effective in improving multisentence productions	Only two subjects demonstrated treatment effectiveness; ultimate effects observed in varying degrees in two subjects
Weinrich, Steele, Carlson, et al. (1989)	n = 1 57 years	Global	Can individual with global aphasia comprehend reversible prepositional phrases as a result of C-VIC training?	C-VIC	Multiple baseline design	Participant comprehended prepositions in C-VIC with approximately 90% accuracy; his performance on C-VIC was better than his performance on identical tasks in printed English	Demonstrated treatment effectiveness; ultimate effects observed

[a] C-VIC = Computerized visual input communication.
[b] TS = Talking screen.
[c] DCD = Dedicated communication device.
[d] Easyspeaker = Graphic symbol software for Windows.

in age from 57 to 75 years. Analysis of results using a multiple-baseline design (see Chapter 6) indicated that all participants acquired the basic skills necessary to access and manipulate the symbol software program. Further, symbols for nouns were identified correctly with a higher degree of accuracy across participants compared to symbols from other grammatical categories. The performance on the symbol production task varied across participants. The most commonly observed errors on the production task were inaccurate selection of symbols for verb referents. The percentage of correct sentences produced by participants ranged from 30% to about 81%.

Koul, Oetzel, Corwin, and Nigam (2001) demonstrated the ability of individuals with severe Broca's aphasia to produce grammatically complex sentences using a dedicated communication device and a set of 119 graphic symbols. They used a multiple-baseline design across behaviors replicated across three participants (see Chapter 6) to assess the effects of treatment on sentence production. The use of a multiple-baseline design to evaluate the effectiveness of two different computer-based graphic symbol communication systems (Koul & Harding, 1998; Koul et al., 2001) enhances the internal validity of their data. However, the generality of their data is limited because of the limited number of replications and lack of data on social validity.

Rostron, Ward, and Plant (1996) described the use of a computer-based graphic symbol software (EasySpeaker for windows) by an individual with severe apraxia and aphasia. The vocabulary in the EasySpeaker software is organized in the same manner (i.e., semantic hierarchical fashion) as the Talking Screen or the Dynavox. Treatment consisted of activities designed to facilitate the use of software at home for 4 weeks. Vocabulary was programmed so that the participant was able to converse with his family members. Results indicated that although the individual with aphasia was able to operate the device and select the requested symbol or symbol combinations, he did not use it in functional communication situations at home.

Using an Introtalker, a SGD with digitized speech and 27 Minspeak icons, Beck and Fritz (1998) investigated the ability of five individuals with Broca's aphasia and five individuals with Wernicke's aphasia to learn iconic encoding for concrete and abstract messages. Results indicated that a significantly greater number of iconic codes for concrete messages were learned in contrast to abstract messages. Results also showed that individuals with Wernicke's aphasia had significantly greater difficulty in learning iconic codes for abstract messages than individuals with Broca's aphasia. These results suggest that although individuals with chronic severe aphasia can learn and use symbols, their ability to learn symbols and messages is reduced as the concreteness or iconicity of symbols or messages decreases.

In summary, results based on C-VIC as well as other computer-based graphic symbol communication systems indicate that individuals with severe chronic Broca's or global aphasia demonstrate superior performance on high-technology AAC systems compared to their natural languages. However, there is a paucity of data on their ability to translate this superior performance to functional communication situations. Thus, it is imperative that clinicians be cautious in recommending dedicated communication devices or other computer-based AAC systems to individuals with aphasia until they have made substantial clinical observations as to the effectiveness of a high-technology AAC system.

3. No-Technology AAC Intervention Approaches

Communicative options that do not involve speech output but still require the individual with aphasia to use some type of external aid have been called "no-technology" options. These include partner-assisted, strategy-user, and independent access systems (Lasker, 2001).

a. The Partner-Assisted Option

The Partner-Assisted option, also referred to as written-choice communication, involves the communicative partner selecting simple and familiar contexts, identifying communication topics of interest, and initiating interaction (Garrett & Beukelman, 1995, 1998). The partner provides the individual with aphasia with written word choices to point to in response to questions. Because this method involves cued rather than free recall, it may facilitate responses from persons with chronic severe or global aphasia. The effectiveness of the written-choice communication strategy, however, is to a large extent dependent on the residual reading abilities of an individual. Individuals with global aphasia demonstrate impairments in all auditory-based language modalities and thus may not benefit from the written-choice communication strategy. An example of interaction using the standard written-choice strategy is as follows:

Communicative Partner: Which soap opera did you watch yesterday? [Writes in large block letters while simultaneously saying:

DAYS OF OUR LIVES
THE YOUNG AND THE RESTLESS
ALL MY CHILDREN
AS THE WORLD TURNS]
AAC User: [Points to DAYS OF OUR LIVES]
Communicative Partner: Oh, right. That one's at 12:30. I missed it. Who did Sheila have an affair with? [writes in large block letters while simultaneously saying:
  BEAU
  OSCAR

JAMES
VICTOR]
AAC User: Him [points to JAMES]
Communicative Partner: Oh my gosh, and Sheila's husband found out?
AAC User: [nods head]
Communicative Partner: Who told him? [writes in large
block letters while simultaneously saying:
MRS. JONES
SALLY
RON
NONE OF THE ABOVE]
AAC User: Oh, yes. [points to SALLY]
Communicative Partner: Where were they when she told him?
[writes in large block letters while simultaneously saying:
SALLY'S HOUSE
JAMES' HOUSE
RESTAURANT
NONE OF THE ABOVE]
AAC User: [points to RESTAURANT]
Communicative Partner: Oh, I'll bet he was devastated.
AAC User: [nods head]

b. The Strategy-User Option

The strategy-user option involves the individual using alternative modes or strategies, such as gestures, drawing, or writing, to assist in conveying messages. A real-life example is as follows:

Communicative Partner: What did you do this weekend?
AAC User: [using the nondominant hand, writes JOHN (husband's name) on a piece of paper, then makes the gesture for shooting a gun].
Communicative Partner: You and John went hunting?
AAC User: [shakes head; points to written word JOHN,
then points to herself and sketches a trailer/camper]
Communicative Partner: Oh, only John went hunting.
You stayed in the trailer, huh?
AAC User: [nods head]
Communicative Partner: Did John shoot anything?
AAC User: [nods head; draws two horizontal ovals on paper]
Communicative Partner: Are those animals?
AAC User: [nods head]
Communicative Partner: So he shot two animals . . .

AAC User: [writes DE on paper]
Communicative Partner: Oh, deer?
AAC User: [nods head]

c. The Independent Accesser Option

The independent accesser option involves the use of stored information systems, such as a communication board or book or a remnant book. A communication board or book contains pictures or written words to which the individual with aphasia has visual and manual (pointing) access. The items/topics may be divided by category and placed on a single piece of cardboard or plastic, in a small notebook or wallet, or in a large three-ring binder. The pictures/words may be generic or personalized. Some examples of categories and items for a generic board/book are as follows:

Wants/Needs	Feelings	Hygiene Items
Drink	Tired	Toothbrush
Food	Hungry	Comb
Remote Control	Cold	Soap
Bathroom	Hot	Washcloth

A personalized communication board/book typically includes more personal categories/items in addition to generic ones. Example categories and items in a personalized communication board/book are as follows:

Friends	Restaurants	Family
Bob and Elizabeth	Gardski's Loft	Larry
Bill and Karen	Mi Tio's	Lucy
Renee	Orlando's Italian Restaurant	Ken
Frank	Mesquite's Barbeque	Connie

A remnant book can serve as an additional personalized supplement to a communication book. It contains actual items that reflect an individual's recent experiences, such as ticket stubs, church bulletins, and family event photographs, so it must be regularly updated. An example interaction using a remnant book is as follows:

AAC User: [points to a photograph of herself and her grandson in front of several old, restored cars]
Communicative Partner: Did you and Ben go to a car show?
AAC User: [nods head and points to ticket stub that says, 'Classic Auto Show; Saturday, June 23]

Communicative Partner: Oh, on Saturday. That sounds like fun. What are your favorite restored models?
AAC User: [points to a cutout magazine picture of a 1957 Chevy]
Communicative Partner: Wow, a '57 Chevy! That's one of my favorites too.

4. Efficacy of No-Technology AAC Intervention Approaches

The no-technology AAC intervention approaches range from techniques that are modeled on the communication participation model (e.g., Fox *et al.*, 2001) to those in which individuals with chronic Broca's or global aphasia were trained to acquire and use graphic symbols such as pictographs, line drawings, and translucent symbol systems such as Blissymbolics (Bliss, 1965) without the aid of technology (e.g., Funnell & Allport, 1989).

Lasker *et al.* (1997) evaluated the relative effectiveness of three different written-choice communication strategies in enhancing efficiency and quality of communication for three individuals with severe chronic aphasia. Results indicated that the performance varied across participants. Specifically, for a participant with severe Wernicke's aphasia, accuracy scores for a standard written-choice communication condition were superior to auditory-only and visual-only conditions. In contrast, for a participant with severe expressive and moderate receptive aphasia and for another participant with Broca's aphasia, accuracy scores on the standard written choice-communication condition did not differ from the scores obtained for auditory-only and visual-only conditions. Unfortunately, the design used a BC-B/C-BC design whereby one feedback mode component each was taken away from baseline (BC) in an alternating treatment phase (B alternated with C) before BC was reintroduced along with the use of the same stimuli across B and C conditions. This design does not rule out sequence or carryover effects. Therefore, the internal validity of this study needs to be viewed with caution (see Chapter 20).

Garrett *et al.* (1989) described the effectiveness of a multimodal communication system (i.e., word dictionary, alphabet card, information pocket, breakdown resolution clues, conversational control strategies, and natural communication) in an individual with Broca's aphasia. Their results indicated that there were more conversational turns, conversational initiations, and communication acts, and fewer communication breakdowns in the posttreatment condition. Cress and King (1999) supported these findings and reported that multimodality AAC strategies were effective in improving the functional communication of two individuals with primary progressive aphasia without dementia.

Using an alternating treatments design, Fox *et al.* (2001) investigated the effects of conversational topic choice on outcomes of AAC intervention in three individuals with Broca's aphasia. Participants were assigned to two conditions: choice topic and nonchoice topic. Choice topics were topics of high interest for participants and nonchoice topics were assigned by the investigators. In general, results obtained were variable. One participant demonstrated greater use of AAC symbols (i.e., personal photographs, color photographs from magazines, and line drawings with word labels) for choice topics. In contrast, the remaining two participants did not demonstrate a difference in the use of AAC symbols between conditions. The internal validity of this study is enhanced as adequate data on treatment integrity as well as dependent variable reliability are reported. Variability in the results, however, precludes any statements about generality. Further, an interesting aspect of this study was the collection of social validity data on satisfaction ratings across choice topic and nonchoice topic conditions from conversational partners and participants.

Ward-Lonergan and Nicholas (1995) evaluated the ability of an individual with global aphasia to communicate effectively through drawing. The treatment was composed of tasks that ranged from simply copying of pictures to drawing complex pictures from memory. Results indicated that the posttreatment drawings were rated as much more recognizable by a naive judge than pretreatment drawings. His pretreatment drawings as reported by authors were sketchy and lacked details. Although this study lacked internal and external validity, the authors provided descriptive information about the effective use of drawings by their participant in his home environment.

Although there is ample empirical evidence that individuals with chronic severe aphasia can acquire and use pictographs, line drawings, and symbol systems such as Blissymbols (e.g., Lane & Samples, 1981; Nishikawa; 1980; Ross, 1979; Sawyer-Woods, 1987) in structured treatment contexts, no generalization data are available as to the use of these graphic symbols in communicative situations outside the training contexts. Further, most of these studies have employed a case study design and thus lack internal validity. In contrast, Koul and Lloyd (1998) used a group design to investigate the ability of individuals with global aphasia and moderate aphasia to acquire transparent, translucent, and opaque Blissymbols. Results indicated that individuals with aphasia as well as the matched controls did not differ significantly in acquiring and retaining single Blissymbols. Further, the iconicity of symbols played a significant role in symbol acquisition and retention. Although, Koul and Lloyd's (1998) study did demonstrate internal validity, the external validity is somewhat limited because of the nature of the experimental task (i.e., paired-associate learning).

In general, the current state of knowledge with respect to the efficacy of no-technology AAC intervention indicates that although the goals of the intervention are met, the variability in results within and across studies (e.g., Lasker *et al.*, 1997) precludes any conclusions as to the generality of the results. A positive aspect of available research on no- technologically based AAC intervention approaches in contrast to technologically based approaches is the relatively more frequent use of research designs with the potential to enhance the internal validity of the studies. Future research also needs to concentrate on issues related to the social validation of treatment goals, procedures, and outcomes by relevant stakeholders (see Chapter 10).

IV. SUMMARY AND CONCLUSIONS

This chapter presented a critical review the efficacy of two distinct options for AAC intervention in individuals with severe and global aphasia. The current state of knowledge on whether AAC intervention works for individuals with aphasia is adversely affected not only because of the short supply of data but also because most of the available data are seriously compromised due to internal validity concerns. However, the following preliminary implications can be extrapolated from the current data.

- In the experimental context, both technologically based and no-technology based AAC intervention options seem to be effective (i.e., data indicate that the dependent variable changes as a result of the experimental treatment or training).
- Individuals with chronic severe Broca's and global aphasia seem to perform better on tasks that involve graphic symbols in comparison to tasks that involve natural language.
- Individuals with global aphasia and severe Broca's aphasia are able to use computer-based graphic symbol communication systems to access, manipulate, and combine symbols to produce sentences and phrases in experimental contexts.
- Variability of results within and across studies indicates that predictions about the effectiveness of AAC intervention for individuals with aphasia cannot be made.
- Although some descriptive information is available that indicates the use of AAC techniques and strategies in real-life functional contexts, there is no empirical evidence to support these strategies.
- AAC intervention that involves multiple modalities and is based on the communication participation model seems to enhance communicative effectiveness and efficiency of individuals with aphasia.

It is extremely important for effective clinical practice, as well as public policy, that sound efficacy data be available on AAC intervention with individuals with aphasia. It is suggested here that single-subject experimental designs, using both direct and systematic replications, are an appropriate and practical methodology to use for evaluating the efficacy data of individuals with aphasia. Hence, future research needs to move beyond case studies to the use of controlled designs to evaluate the effects of treatment.

REFERENCES

Beck, A. R., & Fritz, H. (1998). Can people who have aphasia learn iconic codes? *Augmentative and Alternative Communication, 14,* 184–195.

Bertoni, B., Stoffel, A., & Weniger, D. (1991). Communicating with pictographs: A graphic approach to the improvement of communicative interactions. *Aphasiology, 5,* 341–353.

Beukelman, D. R., & Mirenda, P. (1998). *Augmentative and alternative communication: Management of severe communication disorders in children and adults* (2nd ed.). Baltimore: Paul H. Brookes.

Bliss, C. K. (1965). *Semantography: Blissymbolics* (2nd ed.). Sydney, Australia: Semantography Publications.

Boser, K. I., & Weinrich, M. (1998). Functional categories in agrammatic production: Evidence for access to tense projections. *Brain and Language, 65,* 207–210.

Calculator, S. N. (1991). Evaluating the efficacy of AAC intervention for children with severe disabilities. In J. Brodin & E. Björck-Åkesson (Eds), *Methodological issues in research in augmentative and alternative communication* (pp. 22–31). Proceedings from the First ISAAC Research Symposium. Stockholm: The Swedish Handicap Institute.

Cermak, L. S., & Tarlow, S. (1978). Aphasic and amnestic patients' verbal vs. nonverbal retentive abilities. *Cortex, 14,* 32–40.

Coelho, C. (1982). *An investigation of sign acquisition and use by severe chronic aphasia subjects.* Unpublished doctoral dissertation, University of Connecticut.

Coelho, C., & Duffy, R. J. (1987). The relationship of the acquisition of manual signs to severity of aphasia: A training study. *Brain and Language, 31,* 328–345.

Cress, C. J., & King, J. M. (1999). AAC Strategies for people with primary progressive aphasia without dementia: Two case studies. *Augmentative and Alternative Communication, 15,* 248–259.

De Renzi, E., & Lucchelli, F. (1993). The fuzzy boundaries of apperceptive agnosia. *Cortex, 29,* 187–215.

Fox, L. E., Sohlberg, M. M., & Fried-Oken, M. (2001). Effects of conversational topic choice on outcomes of augmentative communication intervention for adults with aphasia. *Aphasiology, 15,* 171–200.

Funnell, E., & Allport, A. (1989). Symbolically speaking: Communicating with Blissymbols in aphasia. *Aphasiology, 3,* 279–300.

Gainotti, G., Silveri, M. C., & Sena, E. (1989). Pictorial memory in patients with right, left and diffuse brain damage. *Journal of Neurolinguistics, 4,* 479–495.

Gardner, H., Zurif, E., Berry, T., & Baker, E. (1976). Visual communication in aphasia. *Neuropsychologia, 14,* 275–292.

Garrett, K. L., & Beukelman, D. R. (1992). Augmentative communication approaches for persons with severe aphasia. In K. M. Yorkston (Ed.), *Augmentative communication in the medical setting* (pp. 245–338). Tucson, Arizona: Communication Skills Builders.

Garrett, K. L., & Beukelman, D. R. (1995). Changes in the interaction patterns of an individual with severe aphasia given three types of partner support. In M. Lemme (Ed.), *Clinical aphasiology* (pp. 237–251). Austin, TX: PRO-ED.

Garrett, K. L., & Beukelman, D. R. (1998). Adults with severe aphasia. In D. R. Beukelman & P. Mirenda (Eds.), *Augmentative and alternative communication: Management of severe communication disorders in children and adults* (2nd ed., pp. 465–499). Baltimore: Paul H. Brookes.

Garrett, K. L., Beukelman, D. R., & Low-Morrow, D. (1989). A comprehensive augmentative communication system for an adult with Broca's aphasia. *Augmentative and Alternative Communication*, *5*, 55–61.

Garrett, K. L., Kimelman, M. D. Z. (2000). AAC and aphasia: Cognitive-linguistic considerations. In D. R. Beukelman, K. M. Yorkston, & J. Reichle (Eds.), *Augmentative and alternative communication for adults with acquired neurologic disorders* (pp. 339–374). Baltimore: Paul H. Brookes.

Geschwind, N. (1985). Mechanisms of change after brain lesions. In R. Nottebohm (ed.), *Annals of the New York Academy of Sciences, Vol 457: Hope for a New Neurology* (pp. 1–11). New York: Academy of Sciences.

Glass, A., Gazzaniga, M., & Premack, D. (1973). Artificial language training in global aphasics. *Neuropsychologia*, *11*, 95–103.

Goldstein, L. H., Canavan, A. G. M., & Polkey, C. E. (1988). Verbal and abstract designs paired associate learning after unilateral temporal lobectomy. *Cortex*, *24*, 41–52.

Goodenough-Trepagnier, C. (1995). Visual analogue communication: An avenue of investigation and rehabilitation of severe aphasia. *Aphasiology*, *9*, 321–341.

Goodglass, H., & Kaplan, E. (1983). *Boston diagnostic examination for aphasia*. Philadelphia, PA: Lea & Febiger.

Helm-Estabrooks, N., Fitzpatrick, P., & Barresi, B. (1982). Visual action therapy for global aphasia. *Journal of Speech and Hearing Disorders*, *47*, 385–389.

Hermann, M., Reichle, T., Lucius-Hoene, G., Wallesch, C. W., & Johansen-Horbach, H. (1988). Nonverbal communication as a compensatory strategy for severely nonfluent aphasics—a quantitative approach. *Brain and Language*, *33*, 41–54.

Johannsen-Hornbach, H., Cegla, B., Mager, U., & Schempp, B. (1985). Treatment of chronic global aphasia with a nonverbal communication system. *Brain and Language*, *24*, 74–82.

Jones-Gotman, M., & Milner, B. (1978). Right temporal lobe contribution to image-mediated verbal learning. *Neuropsychologia*, *16*, 61–71.

Kelsch, J. E. (1979). *Amer-Ind recognition in patients with Aphasia*. Unpublished master's thesis, Purdue University.

Kendall, P., & Norton-Ford, J. (1982). Therapy outcome research methods. In P. Kendall & J. Butcher (Eds.), *Handbook of research methods in clinical psychology* (pp. 429–460). New York: John Wiley and Sons.

Kertesz, A. (1982). *Western aphasia Battery*. New York: Grune & Stratton.

Koul, R. K., Arvidson, H., & Pennington, G. (1997). Intervention for persons with acquired disorders. In L. L. Lloyd, D. Fuller, & H. Arvidson (Eds.), *Augmentative and alternative communication: A handbook of principles and practices* (pp. 340–366). Boston: Allyn & Bacon.

Koul, R. K., & Harding, R. (1998). Identification and production of graphic symbols by individuals with aphasia: Efficacy of a software application. *Augmentative and Alternative Communication*, *14*, 11–23.

Koul, R. K., & Lloyd, L. L. (1998). Comparison of graphic symbol learning in individuals with aphasia and right hemisphere brain damage. *Brain and Language*, *62*, 394–421.

Koul, R. K., Oetzel, S., Corwin, M., & Nigam, R. (2001). Production of visual syntax by individuals with severe Broca's aphasia. *The ASHA Leader*, *6*, 115.

Kraat, A. W. (1990). Augmentative and alternative communication: Does it have a future in aphasia rehabilitation? *Aphasiology*, *4*, 321–338.

Lane, V. W., & Samples, J. M. (1981). Facilitating communication skills in adult aphasics: Application of Blissymbolics in a group setting. *Journal of Communication Disorders*, *14*, 157–167.

Lasker, J. (2001, May). *AAC strategies for adults with aphasia: From picture boards to touch screens*. Paper presented at the Annual Convention of Georgia Speech-Hearing-Language Association, Atlanta, GA.

Lasker, J., Hux, K., Garrett, K. L., Moncrief, E. M., & Eischeid, T. J. (1997). Variations on the written choice communication strategy for individuals with severe aphasia. *Augmentative and Alternative Communication*, *13*, 108–116.

Lloyd, L. L., Fuller, D. R., & Arvidson, H. (1997). Augmentative and alternative communication: A handbook of principles. Needham Heights, MA: Allyn & Bacon.

Lyon, J. (1992). Communication use and participation in life for adults with aphasia in natural settings: The scope of the problem. *American Journal of Speech-Language Pathology*, *1*, 7–14.

McCall, D., Shelton, J. R., Weinrich, M., & Cox, D. (2000). The utility of computerized visual communication for improving natural language in chronic global aphasia: Implications for approaches to treatment in global aphasia. *Aphasiology*, *14*, 795–826.

Naeser, M. A., Palumbo, C. L., Baker, E. H., & Nicholas, M. L. (1994). CT scan lesion site analysis in severe aphasia: Relationship to no recovery of speech and treatment with the nonverbal computer-assisted visual communication program (C-VIC). *Seminars in Speech and Language, 15*, 53–70.

National Institute on Deafness and Other Communication Disorders (1991). *Aphasia treatment: Current approaches and research opportunities*. Bethesda, MD: NIH

National Institute on Deafness and Other Communication Disorders (1997). *Aphasia,* NIH Pub. No. 97–4257.

National Institute on Neurological Disorders and Stroke (1999). *Stroke: Hope through research*, NIH Pub. No 99–2222.

National Stroke Association (1991). The scope of stroke. *Clinical Updates*, *1*, 1–3.

Nicholas, M., & Helm-Estabrooks, N. (1990). Aphasia. *Seminars in Speech and Language: The Efficacy of Speech-Language pathology Intervention*, *11*, 135–144.

Nishikawa, L. K. (1980). *Blissymbolics as an augmentative communication tool for adults with expressive aphasia*. Unpublished master's thesis, Loma Linda University.

Olswang, L. B. (1990). Treatment efficacy: The breadth of research. In L. B. Olswang, C. K. Thompson, S. F. Warren, & N. J. Minghetti (Eds.), Treatment efficacy research in communication disorders. *Proceedings of the American Speech-Language-Hearing Foundation's National Conference on Treatment Efficacy* (pp. 99–103). San Antonio, TX: ASHA.

Porch, B. E. (1981). *Porch index of communicative ability* (3rd ed.). Palo Alto, CA: Consulting Psychologists Press.

Rao, P., & Horner, J. (1979). Gesture as a deblocking modality in a severe aphasic patients. In R. Brookshire (Ed.), *Clinical aphasiology* (pp.180–187). Minneapolis, MN: BRK.

Rosen, A., & Proctor, E. (1981). Distinctions between treatment outcomes and their implications for treatment evaluation. *Journal of Consulting and Clinical Psychology*, *49*, 418–425.

Ross, A. J. (1979). A study of the application of Blissymbols as a means of communication for a young brain damaged adult. *British Journal of Disorders of Communication*, *14*, 103–109.

Rostron, A., Ward, S., & Plant, R. (1996). Computerized augmentative communication devices for people with dysphasia: design and evaluation. *European Journal of Disorders of Communication*, *31*, 11–30.

Sawyer-Woods, L. (1987). Symbolic function in a severe non-verbal aphasic. *Aphasiology*, *1*, 287–290.

Schlosser, R. W., & Braun, U. (1994). Efficacy of AAC interventions: Methodologic issues in evaluating behavior change, generalization, and effects. *Augmentative and Alternative Communication*, *10*, 207–223.

Schuell, H. M. (1965). *The Minnesota Test for Differential Diagnosis of Aphasia*. Minneapolis, MN: University of Minnesota Press.

Shelton, J. R., Weinrich, M., McCall, D., & Cox, D. M. (1996). Differentiating globally aphasic patients: Data from in-depth language assessments and production training using C-VIC. *Aphasiology*, *10*, 319–342.

Skelly, M. (1979). *AmerInd gestural code based on universal American Indian hand talk*. New York: Elsevier.

Steele, R., Weinrich, M., Wertz, R., Kleczewska, M., & Carlson, G. (1989). Computer-based visual communication in aphasia. *Neuropsychologia, 27*, 409–426.

Trunzo-Rahbar M. J. (1980). *Assessment of the Bliss symbol communication system in adult aphasics with severe oral and verbal apraxia*. Unpublished master's thesis, Wichita State University.

U.S. Department of Health and Human Services. (1995). *Post-stroke rehabilitation.* Rockville, MD: U.S. Department of Health and Human Services.

Waller, A., & Newell, A. F. (1997). Towards a narrative-based augmentative communication system. *European Journal of Disorders of Communication, 32,* 289–306.

Wapner, W., & Gardner, H. (1981). Profiles of symbol-reading skills in organic patients. *Brain and Language, 12,* 303–312.

Ward-Lonergan, J. M., & Nicholas, M. (1995). Drawing to communicate: A case report of an adult with global aphasia. *European Journal of Disorders of Communication, 30,* 475–491.

Weinrich, M. (1991). Computerized visual communication as an alternative communication system and therapeutic tool. *Journal of Neurolinguistics, 6,* 159–176.

Weinrich, M. (1992). "Agrammatic" production in chronic global aphasia. *NIDCD Monograph, 2,* 135–145.

Weinrich, M., Boser, K. I., & McCall, D. (1999). Representation of linguistic rules in the brain: Evidence from training an aphasic patient to produce past tense verb morphology. *Brain and Language, 70,* 144–158.

Weinrich, M., Boser, K. I., & McCall, D., & Bishop, V. (2001). Training agrammatic subjects on passive sentences: Implications for syntactic deficit theories. *Brain and Language, 76,* 45–61.

Weinrich, M., McCall, D., Shoosmith, L., Thomas, K., Katzenberger, K., & Weber, C. (1993). Locative prepositional phrases in severe aphasia. *Brain and Language, 45,* 21–45.

Weinrich, M., McCall, D., Weber, C., Thomas, K., & Thornburg, L. (1995). Training on an iconic communication system for severe aphasia can improve natural language production. *Aphasiology, 9,* 343–364.

Weinrich, M., Shelton, J. R., McCall, D., & Cox, D. M. (1997). Generalization from single sentence to multisentence production in severely aphasic patients. *Brain and Language, 58,* 327–352.

Weinrich, M., Steele, R., Carlson, G. S., Kleczewska, M., Wertz, R. T., & Baker, E. (1989). Processing of visual syntax by a globally aphasic patient. *Brain and Language, 36,* 391–405.

CHAPTER 19

Roles of Speech Output in AAC

An Integrative Review

Ralf W. Schlosser
Department of Speech-Language
  Pathology and Audiology
Northeastern University

Doreen M. Blischak
Department of Communication
  Sciences and Disorders
University of Florida

Rajinder K. Koul
Department of Communication
Sciences and Disorders
Texas Tech University

I. **Introduction**
II. **Roles of Speech Output for (Potential) Communication Partners**
   A. Intelligibility
   B. Comprehension
   C. Attitudes
   D. Communicative Competence
   E. Communicative Behavior
III. **Roles of Speech Output for the Learner**
   A. Graphic Symbol Learning
   B. Requesting
   C. Other Communicative Functions and Social Regulation Functions
   D. Learner Preference
   E. Challenging Behaviors
   F. Natural Speech Production
   G. Comprehension
   H. Literacy
IV. **Roles of Speech Output for the Learner-Partner Dyad**
V. **Deciding on the Use of Speech Output: An EBP Illustration**
   A. Asking a Well-Built Question
   B. Selecting a Evidence Sources and Executing the Search Strategy

I. INTRODUCTION

Whereas in the 1970s, augmentative and alternative communication (AAC) consisted primarily of manual signs, during the past two decades, several aided AAC options such as nonelectronic communication boards became available. Speech-generating devices (SGDs) (also known as voice output communication aids [VOCAs]), along with their corresponding software (e.g., talking word processors), represent one of the most recent additions to the current repertoire of AAC options. Unlike communication boards or typical word processors, SGDs and SGD software provide auditory stimuli via speech output as an added component. This speech output may be recorded (analog or digital) or synthesized (Lloyd, Fuller, & Arvidson, 1997). Analog speech refers to the arrangement of electromagnetic particles on tape that represent the entire pattern of sound waves (e.g., standard tape recorders and cassette tapes). Digitized speech represents sampled segments of sound waves that have been stored in binary code in the microchip (e.g., computers or SGDs). Synthesized speech may be defined as speech that is artificially produced (e.g., by electronic means rather than by the human vocal tract). Soon after SGDs and SGD software became available, studies into their effectiveness began to be published and continue to be published to date.

Speech output has been studied in at least two ways. First, speech output may be part of a larger treatment package. For example, one study aimed to increase functional use of an SGD within a task-specific context (McGregor, Young, Gerak, Thomas, & Vogelsberg, 1992). Second, speech output has also been isolated as an independent variable to study its specific impact. For example, three adults with severe to profound intellectual disabilities were taught to point to Lexigrams under two conditions: with the synthetic speech output turned on and with the speech output turned off (Schlosser, Belfiore, Nigam, Blischak, & Hetzroni, 1995).

Practitioners, who are faced with the difficult task of matching appropriate communication systems to individuals with disabilities and their environments desperately seek research-based evidence for their recommendations to third-party payers. Often these funding agencies ask questions concerning the benefits of more costly devices that provide speech output over less expensive nonelectronic communication systems. Although evidence-based practitioners may be able to support their recommendations with individual studies, it is difficult to draw definite conclusions or recommendations on the basis of individual studies alone (see Chapter 11). To draw more firm and more credible conclusions, it is necessary to synthesize the literature. In this chapter the extant knowledge base concerning the effects of speech output on learners, communication partners, and learner-partner dyads is synthesized and directions for future research are offered. This narrative synthesis is then used as the basis for an illustration in evidence-based practice (EBP) related to decision making involving speech output.

II. ROLES OF SPEECH OUTPUT FOR (POTENTIAL) COMMUNICATION PARTNERS

To date, the research on speech output has focused primarily on the effects on communication partners. Partner-oriented effects of speech output may pertain to intelligibility, comprehension, preferences, attitudes, communicative competence, and interactions.

A. INTELLIGIBILITY

Ralston, Pisoni, and Mullennix (1989) defined intelligibility as the listener's ability to recognize phonemes and words when they are presented in isolation. Schmidt-Nielson (1990) refers to speech intelligibility as a measure that provides an index of the lower bounds of perceptual performance for a given SGD, when no higher-level linguistic context is provided. Overall these definitions describe intelligibility as the ability of an individual to comprehend synthetic speech at a fundamental level based on the characteristics of the acoustic output.

An examination of studies that compared synthetic and natural speech revealed that nondisabled individuals identify and respond to natural speech stimuli more accurately and quickly than synthetic stimuli (Hoover, Reichle, Van Tasell, & Cole, 1987; Koul & Allen, 1993; Logan, Greene, & Pisoni, 1989; Mirenda & Beukelman, 1987, 1990; Mitchell & Atkins, 1989; Pisoni, 1981; Ralston, Pisoni, Lively, Greene, & Mullennix, 1991). The percentage intelligibility for the high-quality synthesizers such as DECtalk in a single-word intelligibility task has ranged from 81.7% correct with an open-response format (Mirenda & Beukelman, 1987) to 96.7% correct with a closed-response format (Greene, Manous, & Pisoni, 1984). In contrast, word intelligibility scores for natural speech have ranged from 97.2% with an open response format to 99% with a closed response format (Logan et al., 1989). Similar results have been obtained for sentence tasks with accuracy scores ranging from 99% for meaningful sentences presented via natural speech to 96% for sentences presented via DECtalk synthesizer (Mirenda & Beukelman, 1987). For anomalous sentences, accuracy scores ranged from 97.7% for natural speech to 78.7% for synthetic speech (Pisoni & Hunnicutt, 1980). Additionally, several investigators have used more sensitive test paradigms such as sentence verification latency to detect differences in natural and high-quality synthetic speech. These tests have revealed consistently shorter response times for natural speech than for synthetic voices (Manous, Pisoni, Dedina, & Nusbaum, 1985; Ralston et al., 1991). Further, response times for high-quality synthesizers such as DECtalk were shorter than those for less intelligible synthesizers such as Votrax or Infovox (Manous et al., 1985; Raghavendra & Allen, 1993). Comprehension is another partner-oriented effect of speech output.

B. COMPREHENSION

Kintsch and van Dijk (1978) described comprehension as a process by which the listener constructs a coherent mental representation of the meaningful information contained in a passage and relates this representation to previously or currently available information in memory. Comprehension of synthetic speech involves recognizing the stimuli presented and then performing higher-level processing to obtain meaning. Short-term memory processes play a central role in perception and comprehension of both natural and synthetic speech. Comprehension may be measured successively or simultaneously. Successive measures involve testing the comprehension of stimulus materials soon after presentation while simultaneous measures involve testing comprehension as it occurs.

1. Word and Sentence Comprehension in Nondisabled Persons

A substantial number of studies have examined the effects of training or practice on the comprehension of synthetic speech by nondisabled individuals (e.g., Greenspan, Nusbaum, & Pisoni, 1988; McNaughton, Fallon, Tod, Weiner, & Neisworth, 1994; Rounsefell, Zucker, & Roberts, 1993; Schwab, Nusbaum, & Pisoni, 1985; Venkatagiri, 1994). The nondisabled individuals were not actual communication partners of AAC users, but they may possess some of the characteristics of communication partners. These studies examined the effects of practice on various qualities of synthesizers and stimulus complexities.

Schwab et al. (1985) and Greenspan et al. (1988) studied the effects of repeated exposure to synthetic speech on the comprehension of synthetic words and sentences. They used a low-quality synthesizer (i.e., Votrax Type-n-Talk TTS synthesizer) to present stimuli. Both studies analyzed the effects of repeated exposure on words (i.e., Phonetically Balanced and Modified Rhyme Test stimuli) and on sentences (i.e., Harvard psychoacoustic sentences and Haskins Laboratories semantically anomalous sentences). Whereas Schwab et al. (1985) studied the practice effect on only novel words and sentences, Greenspan *et al.* (1988) addressed the effects of practice on both novel and repeated stimuli. Their results indicated that repeated exposure to synthetic speech results in significant improvement in its comprehension. Additionally, Schwab *et al.* (1985) found a decreased response latency after synthetic speech exposure. In a follow-up study 6 months later, they also found that participants had maintained the knowledge they gained from participating in the experiment.

Rounsefell *et al.* (1993) studied the effects of training through repeated exposure to synthetic speech versus no training on the comprehension of synthetic speech produced by three synthesizers, ranging from least intelligible (i.e., Echo II) to most intelligible (i.e., DECtalk). Testing only for novel sentences, Rounsefell *et al.* (1993) found a significant increase in the comprehension of synthetic speech for all three synthesizers following training. McNaughton *et al.* (1994) studied the effects of training with novel and repeated synthetic stimuli on the comprehension of synthetic speech in children and adults. The Echo II and DECtalk synthesizers produced the stimuli. Results indicated that accuracy scores improved significantly after training for both the Echo II and DECtalk synthesizers and for both novel and repeated stimuli. Further, both groups demonstrated significant improvement between the first and the last of the five listening sessions. Significantly more repeated stimuli were understood in contrast to novel stimuli across the two synthesizers.

Venkatagiri (1994) observed the effects of training over a 3-day period on sentences produced by the Echo II synthesizer. He found a significant improvement in comprehension of synthetic speech across 3 days. His subjects demonstrated greater improvements in comprehension from day 1 to day 2 of training, with smaller improvements from day 2 to day 3. This latter smaller improvement in comprehension was attributed to a possible ceiling effect. Additionally, he demonstrated that synthesized short sentences, consisting of two to seven words, were not easier to comprehend than synthesized long sentences made up of two short sentences joined with a conjunction. In summary, repeated listening to synthetic speech improves its comprehension in nondisabled individuals. The magnitude of the comprehension, however, depends on the quality of the synthesizer, the complexity of the task and stimuli, and the type of training.

2. Discourse Comprehension in Nondisabled Persons

A series of studies by Higginbotham and his colleagues investigated the effects of synthetic speech output variables on discourse comprehension by nondisabled listeners (Higginbotham & Baird, 1995; Higginbotham, Drazek, Kowarsky, Scally, & Segal, 1994; Higginbotham, Scally, Lundy, & Kowarsky, 1995). Based on Kintsch (1988), discourse comprehension was defined, in these studies, as the listener's ability to construct a representation of discourse that allows for the performance of various mental operations, such as recall and inference making (Higginbotham *et al.*, 1994).

Higginbotham *et al.* (1994) studied the effects of voice quality (DECtalk II, Echo Plus) and presentation rate (normal, slow) on the discourse comprehension of university students and staff listening to texts of varying length, complexity, and familiarity of content. Findings indicated that listeners summarized texts produced by DECtalk significantly better than those produced by Echo Plus. Also, listeners summarized slowly presented texts significantly better than those presented at a normal presentation rate and summarized history texts better than science texts. No differences were found for text length or text complexity variables. Interaction analyses also suggested that at slow presentation rates, text complexity had little effect on a listener's text summarization abilities. However, at a normal presentation rate, subjects' summarization ability declined as a function of text complexity.

Studies comparing discourse presented in natural and synthetic speech with typically developing individuals have found that comprehension accuracy is dependent on the quality of the synthesizer (Higginbotham *et al.*, 1994; Paris, Gilson, Thomas, & Silver, 1995; Ralston *et al.*, 1991). Ralston *et al.* (1991) observed that Votrax, a low-quality synthesizer, was significantly inferior to natural speech on a comprehension task. In contrast, Paris *et al.*'s (1995) data indicated that there were no significant differences between comprehension scores for high-quality synthesizer (i.e., DECtalk) and natural speech.

Although no significant difference has been observed between DECtalk and natural speech (e.g., Logan *et al.*, 1989; Mirenda & Beukelman, 1987, 1990), there are several factors that can adversely affect the outcome of comprehension. Paris *et al.* (1995) found that when task difficulty was increased, comprehension accuracy of synthetic speech was inferior to natural speech. Higginbotham *et al.* (1994) observed that the rate of presentation and text complexity also had an effect on interpretation of the discourse. A slower rate of presentation (10 seconds of silence between words) produced more accurate summaries of discourse. However, at a normal speech presentation rate, summarization abilities for even high-quality synthesizers such as DECtalk declined as a function of task complexity.

C. ATTITUDES

1. Effects of AAC Systems on Attitudes

Several studies have examined the effects of AAC systems on attitudes (see Table 19.1 for a summary). Gorenflo and Gorenflo (1991), for example, studied the attitudes of undergraduate students enrolled in an introductory psychology class toward six experimental conditions. The conditions consisted of a combination of "augmentative communication technique" (unaided, communication board with alphabet and a SGD [laptop computer with Votrax]) and information (no additional information versus additional information about the nonspeaking individual). Three videotapes were prepared that depicted a nonspeaking male with physical disabilities interacting with a nondisabled female. Results revealed that subjects expressed more favorable attitudes on the Attitudes Towards Nonspeaking Persons (ATNP) scale when provided with the additional information. Also, attitudes improved with the sophistication of the "augmentative communication technique." In other words, undergraduate students rated an AAC system package more favorably if it included synthetic speech output compared to an AAC system packages without speech output.

Blockberger, Armstrong, O'Connor, and Freeman (1993) examined the attitudes of elementary students toward a same-aged AAC user engaged in conversations under three conditions: (1) unaided, (2) communication board with alphabet, and (3) SGD (Epson HX-20 with Real Voice–female version). The responding students were drawn from classrooms that neither included a child with little or no functional speech nor included a child with an obvious physical disability. Three videotapes, one per condition, were prepared showing a scripted conversation (based on an actual, natural conversation that had occurred between the two) between a nonspeaking girl and a speaking adult female. The girl was an attractive child enrolled in a regular class in a different school district. Females, better readers, and children who had experience with persons with disabilities displayed more positive attitudes on the Chedoke-McMaster Attitudes toward Children with Handicaps (CATCH) scale. The attitudes, however, did not vary for different AAC systems. These results seem contradictory to those obtained by Gorenflo and Gorenflo (1991). Yet these differences in findings may be explained by a number of differences across the two studies. In addition to the necessary differences in population (i.e., variables pertaining to subjects, person with disabilities, and partners), there are also differences in variables related to the script, independent variable, dependent variable (e.g., CATCH versus ATNP), and procedures.

Beck and Dennis (1996) studied the attitudes of fifth-grade students toward a 13-year old boy with cerebral palsy engaged in a conversation under two conditions: (1) combination of gesturing, verbalizing, and pointing to an alphabet board; and (2) a combination of gesturing, verbalizing, and an SGD (i.e., with Smoothtalker™). Results on the CATCH indicated no differences in attitudes by condition. Significant differences in attitudes were found, however, in terms of the respondents' school (more favorable scores for integrated schools than for nonintegrated schools) and the respondents' gender (more favorable scores for females). Even though the conditions studied were both multimodal, unlike those studied by Blockberger et al. (1993), these results appear fairly consistent with

Table 19.1

Attitude Studies Involving Speech Output

Key variables	Subvariables	Studies			
		Gorenflo et al. (1994)	Blockberger et al. (1993)	Gorenflo & Gorenflo (1991)	Beck & Dennis (1996)
Subjects	Sample and type	284 student majoring in education who were enrolled in a required introductory special education course	249 elementary school students	151 undergraduate students enrolled in an introductory psychology class	186 fifth-grade students
	Familiarity with person depicted	No	No	No	No
	Experience with disabled persons	None had taken a special education course before; experience unknown	Seventy-five percent had child with disability in their school; 40% females and 36% males had a friend with disabilities; 32% males and 20% females had played with a person with a disability in the past week; all schools subscribed to a policy of integration	Not reported	83 students attended a school that included children with disabilities; none had a disability themselves; 87% reported that they have a friend who is disabled and that they played with that friend within the last week (= School 1—integrated); remaining 103 School 2—nonintegrated)
Person with disabilities	Gender and age of person depicted	Female (26 years)	Female (9 years)	Male (22 years)	Male (13 years)
	Disability	None (simulated; no physical disability was simulated)	Nonspeaking, spastic diplegia	Nonspeaking, quadriparetic spastic cerebral palsy	Nonspeaking, flaccid cerebral palsy
	Ambulation	Manual wheelchair	Not reported	Powered wheelchair	Manual wheelchair
	Familiarity with independent variables	Familiar with various AAC devices	Familiar with unaided and electronic techniques, not with alphabet board; this was taught separately	No experience	Experience with SGD

Partner	Gender and age	Female (26 years)	Female adult	Female adult (23 years)	Female adult
	Experience with AAC users	None, naïve	Familiar with the three AAC techniques	No experience in interacting with AAC users	Speech-language pathologist who had been working with the boy
	Familiarity with person with disability	Naïve	Familiar	Not reported	Familiar
	Naivete to research question	Naïve	Not reported	Naive	Not reported
Script	Nature of dialogue	Social dialogue between two acquaintances that met after an undetermined though prolonged duration; all initiations came from natural speaker; same script across conditions	Based on an actual, natural conversation that had occurred between a clinician and the nonspeaking girl; same script across conditions	To reflect a broad range of communicative functions; each participant elicited same number of affirmative responses, exchanges, descriptive statements, and informative statements; same script across conditions	No structured script was used in an attempt to keep the conversation as natural as possible
Independent and dependent variables	Independent	Four synthetic voice conditions: (a) ArticR65B male voice (AVM), (b) Smoothtalker 3.0 male voice, (c) RealVoice female, (d) DECtalk "Beautiful Betty" female	Three AAC techniques: (a) unaided (sign language), (b) aided nonelectronic (alphabet board), (c) aided electronic (Epson HX-20 with Real Voice [female])	Combination of AAC technique and information: (a) unaided (own voice + gestures + facial expressions) – presence, (b) unaided (own voice + gestures + facial expressions) – absence, (c) alphabet board – presence, (d) alphabet board – absence, (e) computer-based SGD – presence, (f) computer-based SGD – absence	Two AAC techniques: (a) combination of gesturing, verbalizing, and pointing to an alphabet board, (b) combination of gesturing, verbalizing, and SGD

(continues)

Table 19.1 (continued)

		Studies			
Key variables	Subvariables	Gorenflo et al. (1994)	Blockberger et al. (1993)	Gorenflo & Gorenflo (1991)	Beck & Dennis (1996)
	Intelligibility of speech output	Varying degrees from high to low	High	Low	High
	Means to select across conditions	Direct selection	Direct selection	Direct selection	Direct selection
	Assignment to independent variables	Subjects were randomly assigned to conditions with the provision that there were no differences in terms of gender, age, marital status, and past contact with nonspeaking persons and voice synthesizers	Classes were randomly assigned to one of three videotapes; not stratified for any demographics (reported to have influenced results; see below)	Subjects were randomly assigned to the six experimental conditions	Each subgroup was randomly assigned to the experimental condition
	Dependent	ATNP	CATCH	ATNP	CATCH
Procedures	Instruction to subjects	"You will be seeing a short videotape in which two people are having a conversation. One person is seated in a wheelchair and is using a communication device. She is unable to speak as a result of a car accident she was involved in approximately 3 years ago" (p. 66).	"On this tape you'll see a conversation between a girl named M. and me. M is going to talk to me by using sign language (or … using this talking computer or using this alphabet board)" (p. 245).	"You will be seeing a short videotape in which two people are having a conversation. One of the persons is in a wheelchair and is using his own voice to communicate [unaided condition], using an alphabet letter board to aid or augment his communication [alphabet board condition]; using a computerized communication	"We are doing a survey to find out a little bit about boys and girls your age and about what you know and think about handicapped children. You may have a handicap or you may know somebody who is handicapped. … Today I will show you a videotape of a boy who has difficulty speaking. To help him talk, he uses something called

	aid that has a voice synthesizer to aid or augment his communication [VOCA condition]. Half of the subjects were given the information sheet to read which contained factual information about the nonspeaking person's physical disability, social activities, and academic and employment status" (p. 22).		augmentative communication. That means that he can't speak like you and I can; he needs something else to help him be able to talk. In this tape, you will see him as he talks with his classroom teacher" (p. 86).
Viewing of devices	A tan box concealed the actual SGD	The partner held up the device when introducing the conditions; this faded out and the image of the child and partner faded in	Not reported
Results	Main research question	More favorable attitudes for voices that are "easier to listen to"	No differences in attitudes between groups of different AAC techniques	More favorable attitudes when provided with additional information regarding the nonspeaking individual; attitudes also increased with the sophistication of AAC technique	No differences for AAC technique
	Other questions	Gender-appropriate voice did not produce more favorable attitudes than gender-inappropriate voice	More positive attitudes by females, better readers, and children with experiences with disabilities	N/A	Significant differences in terms of school (integrated versus nonintegrated) and gender (more favorable scores for females)

the earlier study. Perhaps, this parallel is due to fairly high consistency across the two studies in terms of variables pertaining to the script, independent variable, dependent variable, or procedures. Relative to differences in findings compared to Gorenflo and Gorenflo (1991), the same observations apply as noted for Blockberger *et al.* (1993).

Evidence-based practitioners are interested in selecting AAC systems that result in more favorable attitudes by communication partners toward learners. The existing literature, however, offers little unequivocal assistance in that respect. Whereas two studies suggest that the type of AAC system does not make a difference (Beck & Dennis, 1996; Blockberger *et al.*, 1993), one study indicates that AAC system packages, which include synthetic speech output, are rated more favorably than AAC system packages without speech output.

It is evident that this area of research is very much in its infancy in that we are only beginning to grasp the role of AAC systems, if any, in shaping the attitudes of potential communication partners. Future research endeavors should strive to engage in systematic replications of previous studies, changing only one variable at a time rather than continuing the current path of changing multiple variables at a time (see Table 19.1). Proceeding along these lines would result in more useful data for clinical decision making. Further, it would be helpful to study the role of speech output by isolating it as an independent variable while keeping other variables constant. The studies thus far have measured initial attitudes upon first exposure by potential partners. How do the attitudes of partners change over time from initial first exposure to increased familiarity through repeated interactions? Questions such as this one warrant systematic study.

In evaluating the role of attitudinal research for clinical decision making, it should be kept in mind that attitudes may not necessarily predict behavior (Hegde, 1994). For example, partners who may display favorable attitudes toward a learner may not necessarily behave accordingly. Thus, it would also seem important to examine whether speech output affects the *behaviors* displayed by partners. For instance, do partners initiate more conversations with learners as a result of access to speech output (see Schepis & Reid, 1995)? Once speech output has been selected, does it differentially affect attitudes of potential partners depending on the synthesizer type applied or the specific communicative purpose for which speech output is used? As exemplified by the few studies reviewed next, we have only a limited understanding of these issues.

2. Effects of Synthesizer Intelligibility on Attitudes

Gorenflo, Gorenflo, and Santer (1994) studied the effects of synthesized speech intelligibility on attitudes of students majoring in education at a Midwestern university. Four videotapes were prepared that depicted a female AAC user having a conversation with a speaking female without disability. Subjects were randomly assigned to four voice conditions: (1) AritcR65B male voice, (2) Smoothtalker 3.0 male voice, (3) RealVoice female voice, and (4) DECtalk "Beautiful Betty" female voice. Results indicated that attitudes, as measured with the ATNP, were more favorable when the synthetic voice is more intelligible. Gender-appropriate voice, however, did not produce more favorable attitudes than gender-inappropriate voice.

This positive relationship between intelligibility and attitudes makes intuitive sense because the more favorable attitudes are for persons with voices that are easier to listen to. Based on this research, along with research on preferences, clinicians may be inclined to select devices with highly intelligible synthesized speech over less intelligible speech as a matter of rule. A number of caveats, however, need to be considered before adopting such a strategy. First, university students majoring in education are not exactly representative of the general population of laypeople. Second, the person with disability depicted in the videotape may or may not have similar characteristics (gender, age, diagnosis, etc.) as the client on the practitioner's caseload. Thus, the generality of these findings to other segments of the general population of potential partners and other learners using AAC is yet to be studied. Third, other considerations may be competing with the goal of promoting positive attitudes. For example, less intelligible synthesized speech may produce greater comprehension in the learner (see "spoken language comprehension"). So the clinician will need to weigh the benefits to the learner relative to those of the partner. The lack of attitudinal differences for gender-appropriate versus gender-inappropriate voice suggests that clinicians should follow the preferences of the learner rather than prescriptive notions of gender. This clinical implication is again within the confines of the limited generality discussed earlier.

3. Attitudes Toward Using a SGD for Telephoning

Nakamura and colleagues studied the attitudinal effects of using speech output for the purpose of communicating via telephone. This work differs from the attitude research reviewed earlier because it evaluates the attitudes of actual communication partners rather than potential partners. Nakamura and Arima (1991) (as reported in Nakamura, Arima, Sakamoto, & Toyota, 1993) studied listener attitudes toward using an SGD for telephoning by two adult AAC users with cerebral palsy. The first task involved the phoning of public organizations to ask for their business hours. The second task required calling university students at home, while they were out, and asking a family member when the student is returning. Participants were unable to obtain an answer from 5 of the 33 public organizations called and from 8 of the 46 private residences called. Many listeners felt anxious or uneasy responding to the SGD with synthesized speech. Some listeners felt the device was deceptive and mechanical. Participants felt that "it was stressful to place calls by voice synthesizer" because, as one participant put it, "I always presuppose negative attitudes of the listeners" (p. 252). The different phone use patterns between the two AAC users (in terms of message content and response lag) resulting in different listener impressions suggested that listeners' attitudes might be influenced by strategies of telephone use.

In a follow-up study, Nakamura *et al.* (1993) examined the attitudes toward using an SGD for telephoning as a function of (1) the time lag of responses and (2) explanation of caller's disability. Mostly undergraduate students and their parents, siblings, and friends served as participants. A speakerphone, a microcomputer, and a text-to-speech unit with an intelligibility (mean percentage of correct responses) of 83.2 were used (i.e., ASCII AVM-10, male voice). The experimenter called the participant and asked for the phone number of another friend. If the participant was not at home, the experimenter asked whomever took the call when the subject would return. The time lag of responses (nondelay and 3-second delay) and the explanation of the talker's situation (natural voice explanation [NVE], artificial voice explanation [AVE], and nonexplanation [NOE]) were experimentally controlled. Introductory explanations of the talker's situation were found effective in improving the impressions of listeners as measured by an informal questionnaire about impressions toward using the telephone. Moreover, there were significant differences among the three explanation groups with the NEV producing less listener anxiety than AVE and NOE, and AVE producing less anxiety than NOE. Results also indicated that female participants had more positive impressions than the male participants did. There was no difference in terms of time lag of response.

Although these findings show that using the phone with speech output can create uneasiness and anxiety in listeners, they also indicated that, when preparing the listener with an introductory statement, listeners do display more favorable attitudes. Thus, practitioners may want to proactively assist the learner in learning how to use an introductory statement in conversing over the phone.

D. COMMUNICATIVE COMPETENCE

1. Effects of Using SGDs in Conversation under Various Conditions

Several studies examined perceptions of potential partners concerning the communicative competence of learners using an SGD. Bedrosian, Hoag, Calculator, and Molineux (1992) studied the perceived communicative competence of a simulated learner using an SGD with digitized speech output in terms of (1) message length (single word versus phrases), (2) expanded repetition by the communication partner in response to learner messages (presence versus absence), and (3) rater background (naive versus familiar). Results indicated a significant interaction effect involving rater background and message length. The learner was perceived as more competent when using phrases than when using single-word messages. When using single-word messages, the learner's competence was rated higher by the naive adults than by the clinicians. In a reanalysis of the same data set obtained by Bedrosian *et al.* (1992), Hoag, Bedrosian, Johnson, and Molineux (1994) studied the effects of the same conditions only pertaining to the social aspect of communicative competence. Regardless of rater background (naive, familiar), message length was found to affect the ratings of the learner's perceived amount of participation, management of partner attention, and degree of social ease.

2. Effects of Speech Output Type

In a follow-up study, Hoag and Bedrosian (1992) studied the perceptions of communicative competence by naive raters of a simulated learner using a SGD in terms of (1) type of speech output (digitized versus synthesized), (2) message length, and (3) expanded repetition by the partner. A significant main effect was found only for message length; conversational conditions with phrases were ranked higher than single-word messages. This finding differs from Bedrosian *et al.* (1992) and was attributed to differences in sample size. In discussing the lack of differences between speech output type, these authors considered the high intelligibility of the synthesizer selected (i.e., Smoothtalker 3.0 male), and the partners responding to the learner's messages regardless of speech output type.

This research shows that perceived communicative competence of learners using SGDs can be influenced by how the learner uses the system, at least in terms of message length. Whether or not the type of speech output (digitized versus synthesized) or the intelligibility of synthesized speech (high versus low) do in deed impact communicative competence ought to be studied further. Partner responses to messages from the learner may differ (unless it is controlled in the experiment), depending on the type of speech output and degree of intelligibility. This in turn may influence raters' impressions of learners' communicative competence. In addition, it would be interesting to study the effects of speech output as an independent variable on perceived communicative competence. Is a learner, using a device with speech output (an SGD), going to be rated more competent than the same learner is using a device without speech output?

E. COMMUNICATIVE BEHAVIOR

Schepis and Reid (1995) studied the effects of a treatment package involving speech output on staff communicative interactions with Megan, a 23-year-old woman with a diagnosis of profound intellectual disabilities, spastic quadriplegia, and visual impairments. The treatment package consisted of subject pretraining, staff training in the operational aspects of the device, and access to the SGD (Mega Wolf™) during intervention. During pretraining, the young woman was trained in discrete trial format to activate the SGD, which was programmed to output requests for preferred items, by pressing the photograph of the item. Also, several group home staff members listened to the speech output to determine the intelligibility; they expressed no difficulty understanding the output. Staff training in operational aspects of the device included verbal and written information on how to place the SGD on Megan's wheelchair tray top, how to turn the SGD on and off, how to find the page containing the item requests, and how to store the device. During this session, Megan was also demonstrated the use of the device. A multiple probe design across two time periods (with one serving as the control) and settings was used to evaluate the effects. Results indicated that staff interactions with Megan increased substantially during intervention in both settings and were maintained during the follow-up periods, which occurred 98 days and 83 days later, respectively. Moreover, there were no changes in staff behavior during the control condition.

Due to small *n*, these results are preliminary and require replication. They do, however, suggest the potential power of mere access to an SGD, considering that the learner received only minimal pretraining and the partners received only training in the operational aspects of the device. That is, they did not receive any instruction on how to foster interaction through their own behavior. These are encouraging findings for clients such as Megan in group home settings and adult education classrooms who often rely on idiosyncratic gestures, manual signs, or unintelligible vocalizations.

III. ROLES OF SPEECH OUTPUT FOR THE LEARNER

Roles of speech output for the learner may pertain to graphic symbol learning, requesting, other communicative functions and social regulation functions, learner preference, challenging behaviors, natural speech production, comprehension, and spelling. Research within each of these areas will be reviewed in the following section.

A. Graphic Symbol Learning

For many individuals, graphic symbols are a low-tech necessity as a means to communicate about various referents. To do so it is essential that these individuals are able to associate symbols with their word referents. SGDs are reported to have advantages over nonelectronic communication boards due to the provision of additional auditory stimuli in the form of synthesized speech presented as (1) an antecedent stimulus (Romski & Sevcik, 1993) and (2) a consequence stimulus (Romski & Sevcik, 1988). Although students with severe intellectual disabilities acquired graphic symbols when taught with SGDs (Romski & Sevcik, 1992a, 1992b), other studies report similarly successful effects using AAC systems without synthetic speech, including computer-keyboard systems (Romski, Sevcik, & Pate, 1988) and communication boards (Hurlbut, Iwata, & Green, 1982). Given the expense of SGDs and the scarcity of comparative research on the effects of the presence or absence of synthetic speech on learner behavior, studies into the effects of added synthesized speech on the learning of graphic symbols becomes paramount.

Schlosser *et al.* (1995) examined the effects of added auditory stimuli in the form of synthesized speech on the learning of arbitrary graphic symbols. As such, speech output was studied as an independent variable. Three young adults with severe to profound intellectual disabilities were taught to point to Lexigrams when presented with the verbal cue "Point to _____," a 0-second delay model of the correct symbol (i.e., simultaneous prompting), and were provided with corrective feedback. The participants were taught Lexigrams under two conditions: one group of Lexigrams was trained with speech output (SPEECH), and a matched group of Lexigrams was taught without speech output (NO SPEECH). Each group of Lexigrams was divided into four sets of Lexigrams, which were sequentially trained to criterion in each condition. In the SPEECH condition, a SuperWolf™ was used with the synthesized speech (i.e., Votrax) turned on. In the NO SPEECH condition, the same device was used, but the speech output was turned off. This allowed the researchers to equate the conditions, except for the presence or absence of speech output, including the physical appearance and provision of proprioceptive feedback that would otherwise distinguish an SGD from a nonelectronic communication board. All three participants reached criterion when they were provided with speech output. Although two participants also reached criterion when not provided with speech output, the addition of speech output resulted in more efficient learning and a decreased error rate. Thus, the findings suggest that the provision of synthesized speech output contributes to the efficient acquisition of graphic symbols in young adults with severe to profound intellectual disabilities.

This study provides promising support for the use of AAC systems with speech output (as input *and* feedback) in promoting the learning of arbitrary symbols for known words in young adults with severe to profound intellectual disabilities. It is yet to be determined, however, whether these findings have generality beyond the learning parameters of this study or beyond the type of participants used in this experiment. Directions for some of these parameters shall be provided as follows.

The findings were obtained with a synthesizer of low intelligibility (i.e., Votrax). Schlosser *et al.* (1995) hypothesized that symbol learning may be enhanced even further with a synthesizer high in intelligibility because it is closer to natural speech. Further, it is unknown whether speech output also enhances the learning of symbols that bear a stronger relationship to their referent— symbols that are high in translucency or iconic. In this study, the symbols were arbitrary in nature. Because practitioners are faced with the dilemma that both kinds of symbols are prominent not only in the repertoire of symbol options in AAC, but also within a learner's selected graphic symbol set or system, future research is of imminent importance.

The symbols introduced in AAC intervention are not always for referents that a student comprehends when present with the spoken word. On occasion, learners with severe intellectual disabilities may be introduced to a symbol without comprehending the referents. That is, the referent will eventually be comprehended through the symbol. Romski and Sevcik (1993) grouped their participants receiving an AAC treatment package involving speech output into "high comprehenders" and "low comprehenders" on a post-hoc basis. They suggested that comprehension of spoken words for which symbols are taught might facilitate transfer to paired symbols. Experimental data from one of the three participants in Schlosser *et al.* (1995) lend some initial support to this hypothesis. Half of Carl's (one of the participants) target words consisted of words he did not comprehend. Results of the SPEECH condition suggested that teaching symbols for comprehended spoken words were found consistently more efficient those than for words not comprehended. Because Carl did not reach criterion in the NO SPEECH condition, comparison to the SPEECH condition could not be made. Clearly, the role of spoken word comprehension in graphic symbol learning with and without speech output instruction warrants further research before any implications for clinical practice may be drawn.

Synthesized speech may be provided as a consequence to the learner's key activation (i.e., feedback) or as an antecedent through the partner's key activation (also known as augmented input or aided language stimulation) (Goossens' & Crain, 1986; Romski & Sevcik, 1988). Researchers and expert clinicians encourage partners to provide augmented input as an intervention strategy due to its proposed benefits to the learner (Beukelman & Mirenda, 1998; Goossens' & Crain, 1986; Romski & Sevcik, 1988, 1993). Yet only 10% of partners' overall spoken communicative utterances directed to nonspeaking children with intellectual disabilities have been found to include augmented input (Sevcik, Romski, Watkins, & Deffebach, 1993). Therefore, it becomes crucial to examine the effects of speech output under learning conditions with and without augmented input.

Participants in the Schlosser *et al.* (1995) study received synthesized speech in the SPEECH condition and no speech in the NO SPEECH condition. This allowed the contrast of the effects of receiving synthesized speech (as in using an SGD) with the effects of *not* receiving speech (as in using a nonelectronic communication board). What if the communication partners were to provide the necessary input and feedback via natural speech? Blischak, Schlosser, and Miller (2000) have studied this issue to determine whether it is the nature of the speech signal that makes a difference, rather than the mere quantity of input and feedback. In part 1 of the their study, three adults with intellectual disabilities were taught to recognize graphic symbols with the addition of an equal number of natural (investigator-produced) or synthetic (device-produced) speech productions. Symbol learning was most effective and efficient in the synthetic speech condition. In part 2, two of the original three participants again learned to recognize graphic symbols. This time, both natural and synthetic speech, were produced by an SGD. Again, graphic symbol learning was most efficient in the synthetic speech condition. This suggests that it is not just the amount of additional feedback but the type of speech that is relevant for graphic symbol learning with synthetic speech output being more efficient than natural speech.

B. REQUESTING

Requesting serves an important function, especially for beginning communicators (see Chapter 15 and Reichle & Sigafoos, 1991). Several studies examined the effectiveness of treatment packages involving speech output on requesting (DiCarlo & Banajee, 2000; Dyches, 1998; Romski & Sevcik, 1996; Schepis, Reid, & Behrman, 1996; VanAcker & Grant, 1995).

1. Effectiveness of Treatment Packages

Dyches (1998) studied the effects of coincidental instruction of activating a switch connected to a loop tape with digitized speech to request a drink by four children with autism and severe disabilities. It was concluded that each of the four students increased the number of requests. A close examination of the graphic data, however, does not allow us to share the same conclusion. Also, the study contains a number of methodological flaws, including the use of different dependent measures in baseline and intervention, inappropriate design, no treatment integrity data, and the lack of controlling the number of obligatory contexts. This makes it difficult to draw any conclusions based on this study.

In their longitudinal work with 13 primary and secondary school-age youngsters with moderate to severe intellectual disabilities, Romski and Sevcik (1992a, 1996) investigated the effects of the System of Augmenting Language (SAL) on symbol acquisition and use. The System of Augmenting Language consists of the following components: (1) an SGD with synthesized speech available for use in natural communicative environments is provided; (2) appropriate and initially limited arbitrary symbol (i.e., Lexigrams) vocabularies are provided, with the printed English word above each symbol; (3) children are encouraged, although not required, to use the device; (4) communication partners are taught to use the device to augment their speech input to the child with symbol input; and (5) ongoing resource and feedback mechanisms are provided. Results indicate that, through the SAL, the youngsters successfully learned to request using an SGD. These results are preexperimental due to the specific design used and do not permit adequate control of maturation and history as threats to internal validity.

DiCarlo and Banajee (2000) evaluated the effects of a least-to-most prompting strategy during snack activity on the use of an SGD with digitized speech output to request attention or objects in two young children with developmental delays and no functional speech. Using a multiple baseline design across two participants, the data indicated that the treatment package was successful in increasing requesting using the SGD in both children. Moreover, requests through less intelligible modes decreased during the intervention, suggesting an inverse functional relation with SGD use. Unfortunately, these data are rendered inconclusive due to a lack of treatment integrity data and a major design flaw. In terms of design, the SGD was made available only during the intervention phase, thereby precluding an adequate control of novelty effects. The participants may have engaged in more requesting behavior because the SGD was something out of the ordinary rather than because of the characteristics inherent in an SGD.

VanAcker and Grant (1995) examined the effects of a computer-based SGD for teaching requests in three girls with Rett syndrome. Teaching involved computer-animated graphics and touch-sensitive input using an Amiga computer with a built-in synthesizer. All three girls displayed increased item requesting and learned to differentially request liked and disliked foods as a result of the treatment package involving speech output.

Schepis et al. (1996) used a graduated guidance and time delay procedure to teach three adults with profound intellectual and physical impairment to request preferred items and activities with an SGD and synthetic speech output. Training included the provision of the verbal prompt (e.g., "Meg, show me what you would do if you wanted chocolate milk") immediately followed by the least amount of physical guidance necessary to assist the participant in activating the SGD for the requested item. Once activated correctly, the participants received the item requested. After two consecutive prompts, a time delay procedure was implemented. Any attempts for an incorrect activation were blocked and redirected through verbal instruction (e.g., "Meg, show me chocolate milk") and physical guidance. A multiple probe design across items and participants indicated that each of the participants learned to request the items in response to the training procedure. Probes in the training setting as well as other nontraining settings, including other communication partners, indicated that the participants effectively requested items and activities in functional contexts. The perspectives of 14 individuals unfamiliar with the participants were gathered to study the social validity of the participant's communication with the SGD and without the SGD. During this phase, one of the participants moved to a device with digitized speech output for reasons not reported. The stakeholders surveyed included laypersons from the community as well as professionals from the participants' place of work. Following 20-minute observations, individuals completed a Likert scale to rate the ease or difficulty in understanding the participants' communication and the helpfulness of the SGD. Results supported the functional utility of the SGD.

In each of these studies, speech output was provided as part of a larger treatment package. Practitioners who are seeking to promote requesting in youngsters with moderate to severe intellectual disability may consider using SAL with its specified components while keeping in mind the preliminary nature of the findings (Romski & Sevcik, 1996). Practitioners seeking to promote differential requesting in girls with Rett syndrome may find the package by VanAcker and Grant (1995) useful. Future research may be directed to replicate these findings using more intelligible synthetic speech as part of the treatment package. It is imperative that researchers study the relative benefits of using a fairly structured approach (Schepis *et al.*, 1996; VanAcker & Grant, 1995) as opposed to more naturalistic approaches (e.g., Romski & Sevcik, 1996) to request training. Because the results of these studies can only speak to the effectiveness of the treatment package as a whole rather than to its individual components, future research needs to be designed to isolate the effects of speech output on requesting.

2. Effectiveness of the Presence versus Absence of Speech Output

At least two studies have compared the effectiveness of AAC systems with speech output to those without speech output in terms of requesting. One study compared the effects of an SGD to a communication board on requesting materials for a leisure activity by a young adult with profound mental retardation (Soto, Belfiore, Schlosser, & Haynes, 1993). The communication board and the SGD were found equally effective, although the participant demonstrated a clear preference for the SGD postintervention (see Section III. D. on Preferences).

Doss, Locke, Johnston, Reichle, Sigafoos, Charpentier, and Foster (1991) conducted two experiments comparing the effectiveness and efficiency of various AAC systems in terms of ordering meals in a fast-food restaurant. In the first experiment, a nonelectronic communication wallet was compared with an SGD (i.e., a Light Talker™ with an Echo speech synthesizer). Effectiveness was defined as the number of times the clerk requested clarifications. Efficiency was defined as the time it took to order a meal. With both AAC systems, the participant was successful in requesting the desired foods. Even though the SGD was found less efficient and effective than the wallet, these results were discussed as possibly due to (1) uncontrolled changes in the setting, (2) a low intelligibility speech synthesizer, or (3) the fewer number of sources of information to attend to with the wallet. In a follow-up experiment, they compared a (1) nonelectronic communication wallet, (2) an SGD (i.e., RealVoice^{TM}) with a printer, (3) a RealVoice^{TM} without a printer, and (4) an SGD (i.e., ALLTALK^{TM}) with digitized speech. No significant differences were found across AAC systems in terms of the number of clarifications needed by the clerk. That is, the participant successfully requested food items regardless of the AAC system. However, the wallet was found more efficient than the RealVoice^{TM} with printer, and the ALLTALK^{TM} was more efficient than the RealVoice^{TM}. There were no differences between the RealVoice^{TM} with and without a printer, and between the wallet and the ALLTALK. Compared to the less intelligible RealVoice^{TM}, digitized speech decreased the time required to place an order to some extent but not enough to compete with the wallet. Whether or not the SGD was provided with printed output did not seem to make a difference in terms of efficiency. This suggests that the partners did not rely on written output to interpret the messages from the user.

Although the studies by Soto *et al.* (1993) and Doss *et al.* (1991) require direct and systematic replications due to small *n* and the use of nondisabled subjects, respectively, they do offer preliminary implications for practice. First, it shows that the selection of AAC systems may not be an absolute (i.e., "systems with speech output are more effective"). Rather it appears to be mediated by the specific context (e.g., setting, and partner) in which the system is expected to be used. Devices without speech output may work just as well under circumstances described in these studies. As argued by Doss *et al.* (1991), it could be that in some situations speech output represents an unnecessary or even distracting source of information for the partner. Thus, practitioners need to ask themselves whether speech output may be beneficial given the context (see also the evidence-based practice illustration in this chapter, Section V).

Because the AAC systems compared in both studies differed not only in terms of speech output, the lack of differences cannot be attributed to the presence or absence of speech output alone (see "graphic symbol learning" section). Any single other difference or any combination of these differences could have been responsible. Studies that isolate the presence of speech output as an independent variable are needed to evaluate its relative contribution in promoting requesting. Such studies are currently under way with beginning communicators (Schlosser, Blischak, Sigafoos, Ferrier, & Manuel, 2001–2003). At the same time, we need to see more studies that examine how speech output interacts with other AAC system features such as print output (Doss *et al.*, 1991) and other context variables or instructional variables. For example, in both experiments by Doss *et al.* (1991), the participants presented so-called introductory cards (e.g., "Hi! I don't talk." I will use this device to place my order) before using each of the AAC systems to proceed with the order. It is essential that we begin to study how speech output interacts with various instructional strategies such as the use of introductory cards.

C. Other Communicative Functions and Social Regulation Functions

1. Effects of a Treatment Package

McGregor *et al.* (1992) successfully taught a 20-year-old student with physical disabilities to express the following variety of communicative functions using an SGD (TouchTalker™) within the task-specific context of computer data entry: "please, come here" (request for assistance), "something is wrong" (comment), "may I please have more work" (request for materials), "I would like to take a break" (request to escape), and "I am finished" (comment). The effectiveness was evaluated through a multiple baseline design across settings. During baseline, the SGD was made available and readied for the data entry task. However, no specific instructions were provided concerning the communicative use of the SGD. In a staggered fashion, a preinstruction phase (review of task-related message keys) was followed by natural environment teaching and sequential withdrawal of preinstruction to induce maintenance.

2. Communication Board versus an SGD

Healy (1994) compared an SGD (Scan Wolf™) with a communication board on the frequency of learner-initiated conversations and responses to initiations of others in three school settings. Stephen, a 17-year-old with an intellectual disability and cerebral palsy, participated in this study. A multiple baseline design across settings was used to evaluate the impact of using the SGD. Vocabulary selection and organization occurred prior to baseline. Prior to baseline, Stephen also received training to establish an appropriate access method and to familiarize himself with operational aspects. The SGD was introduced sequentially in each setting following a baseline with the communication board. Results indicated an increase in the frequency of initiations by Stephen and an increase in responses to others following the introduction of the SGD across settings, while the use of other nonvocal modalities was maintained. Unfortunately, this work contains numerous shortcomings, which makes it difficult to place much confidence in the positive data yielded. One of the most striking problems is the comparison of "apples" (communication board) in baseline and "oranges" (SGD) in intervention. Given the purpose of this study, the SGD should have been made available during baseline without instruction. This would have allowed for an adequate control of novelty effects. Second, from the description of "was introducing systematically" it is unclear what the actual intervention procedures were, making it difficult to determine what treatment package actually caused the changes to occur. Finally, Stephen used a different method of access during baseline (direct selection) and in intervention (scanning).

D. LEARNER PREFERENCE

To date we have very little research on the preferences of learners relative to the presence or absence of speech output. In the study by Soto *et al.* (1993), Sam, a young adult with profound intellectual disabilities, was taught to request high-interest materials with an SGD and a nonelectronic communication board to perform a leisure activity. The preference assessment was conducted following intervention in both conditions. Essentially, he was presented with both AAC systems and asked to choose the one he would like to work with in a given session. Sam almost always preferred the SGD.

These findings are interesting for more than one reason, but particularly because they provide clinicians with social validation data (Schlosser, 1999). These data could provide clinicians with additional decision-making guidelines for prescribing AAC systems when an evaluation indicates that both AAC systems are equally effective (as was the case here). From this study, however, it is unclear whether Sam preferred the SGD over the communication board because of speech output or its different physical appearance, its provision of proprioceptive feedback, or any combination of these three. The evidence-based practitioner may be satisfied with knowing that the package as a whole was preferred. To complicate things further, without a preference baseline it is unclear whether Sam developed these preferences as a result of being exposed to both AAC systems or whether he had these preferences to begin with.

Future research should isolate speech output as the independent variable in preference assessments by holding other variables constant (i.e., proprioceptive feedback, physical appearance). Also, the inclusion of preference pretests would increase our understanding of how learners develop preferences given their exposure to various AAC systems. Interestingly, research on preferences and speech output has typically concerned itself with *partner* preferences (see Section II). That is, research has solicited the preferences of partners related to the type of speech output (i.e., natural versus synthetic) and the appropriateness of age and gender issues in speech output. There is no plausible rationale as to why the same preference issues should not be studied with learners as well.

E. Challenging Behaviors

The role of speech output has also begun to be explored as part of the functional communication training (FCT) approach to the treatment of challenging behaviors such as self-injurious behaviors. FCT involves the assessment of the communicative function of a behavior and the teaching of an alternative communicative response to serve that same function (Durand, 1990). See Mirenda (1997) and Schlosser (1997) for reviews on FCT applications in AAC. If a person's challenging behavior is maintained by escape from difficult tasks, for example, that person may be taught to request assistance or a break. If successful, this person will increase request behavior while decreasing the challenging behaviors that served this very same escape function. Although FCT is clearly related to the previous section on requesting, it is the teaching of requesting with the primary aim of replacing challenging behaviors that warrants separate attention.

1. SGDs and Functional Communication Training

Durand (1993) evaluated the effects of FCT using SGDs to replace challenging behaviors in three individuals with severe disabilities and little or no functional speech. SGDs (i.e., IntroTalker™ with digitized speech, Wolf™ with synthesized speech) were selected because they were believed to increase the recognizability of the participants' responses over manual signs. The participants were successfully taught to request escapes, tangibles, or attention using their SGDs rather than their challenging behaviors. Thus, using SGDs that provide speech output in teaching requests may play an important role in facilitating the effectiveness of FCT. Although it seems plausible to assume that the use of SGDs increases the ability of partners to recognize the request made, direct comparisons with aided AAC systems that do not provide speech output (e.g., boards) and unaided AAC systems (i.e., manual signs) have not been made.

In a follow-up study, Durand (1999) extended these results with five students with severe disabilities to evaluate whether these SGDs can be used successfully with untrained community members in novel community settings following training in the classroom. Following a functional assessment, each of the students was taught with FCT to use an IntroTalker™ with digitized speech to express the functions that seemingly maintained their challenging behaviors. A multiple baseline design across students was used to evaluate the effectiveness of the intervention. Concurrently to the multiple baseline design, generalization was evaluated by assessing performance in novel settings with novel partners in the community. Results replicate previous FCT studies and indicated that the students successfully used their SGD to express the communicative functions maintaining their challenging behavior. Whereas appropriate communication increased, challenging behaviors decreased. More important, though, this study demonstrates that the students successfully recruited maintaining stimuli from untrained partners in their communities. Durand (1999) hypothesized that the speech output from SGDs may have facilitated the responsiveness of the partners because the students' communicative behavior was immediately recognizable. This author further hypothesized that the immediate speech output may have served as a conditioned stimulus that bridged the delay between a student's request and a partner's response. Both of these hypotheses offer interesting directions for future research.

2. SGDs and Response Efficiency

Whether or not the replacement behavior can successfully address the function of the challenging behavior depends on the efficiency of the alternative response (Horner & Day, 1991). In other words, from the learner's perspective the replacement behavior must be "as good a deal" as the challenging behavior. Three variables have been demonstrated to affect the efficiency of a response: the (1) physical effort required to perform the response, (2) the schedule of reinforcement, and (3) the time delay between presentation of the discriminative stimulus for a target response and delivery of the reinforcer for that response (Horner & Day, 1991). In terms of "physical effort," an alternative response must require the expenditure of fewer calories than the challenging behavior if it is to compete with the challenging behavior. To be efficient, the schedule of reinforcement must be such that it takes fewer alternative response emissions to gain access to the reinforcer than it takes emissions of challenging behavior. For example, if a child needs to activate a key on an SGD five times before obtaining the requested break, it may be more efficient for the child to continue with the challenging behavior that yields the desired break after only one occurrence. Finally, the alternative response must yield faster access to the desired reinforcer than the challenging behavior in order to be efficient and competitive. These three variables have been demonstrated to influence the effectiveness of FCT primarily with manual signs and nonelectronic communication systems such as flash cards (Horner & Day, 1991). With SGDs, however, only "physical effort" has been studied as an independent variable.

In a study involving one person who exhibited aggression, an SGD was programmed in two different ways to examine the role of response efficiency: the participant needed to either spell out a complete message or select a pre-stored message (Horner, Sprague, O'Brien, & Heathfield, 1990). Selecting the pre-stored message was found to be more efficient in competing with the challenging behavior, supporting the hypothesis that physical effort contributes to response efficiency.

SGDs or other electronic signaling devices may also maximize the schedule of reinforcement and reduce the delay between the response and access to a reinforcer. A worker who runs out of materials, for example, may request assistance even if the supervisor is across the room. Steege *et al.* (1990) selected a battery-operated tape recorder to teach an individual with escape-motivated problem behavior to activate "stop." They argued that the activation of pretaped messages may be made as assertive as needed by adjusting the volume whereas signs could go unnoticed or may be ignored. Reporting a similar rationale, Wacker *et al.* (1990) selected a loop tape with a recorded message ("I am tired of rocking, somebody give me something to do?") to allow one of their participants to appropriately leave an activity.

The preliminary study on the role of physical effort (Horner *et al.*, 1990) suggests that SGDs need to be programmed so that they reduce unnecessary physical effort in order to be more efficient than challenging behaviors. With SGDs, physical effort may also come into play when choosing devices for ease of key activation. Whereas boards and the like require merely a pointing response, SGDs vary in the degree of effort required to activate keys with some SGDs allowing for adjustment of the physical effort. Durand (1993), for example, selected an IntroTalker™ rather than a SuperWolf™ for one of the participants because its activation required less physical effort. To date, the effects of varying degrees of physical effort required for key activation of pre-stored messages have not been examined within FCT. Extrapolating from basic research on the effects of physical effort on choice behavior (by varying the pressure required to depress a response key), subjects do seem to make more choices when having to engage in less physical effort (basic research cited by Durand, 1990).

With persons who are taught to request attention, SGDs may indeed maximize the schedule of reinforcement and reduce time delay in comparison to either boards or manual signs because the partner does not need to face the individual in order to receive and respond to the request. This may be crucial in classroom situations where teachers cannot face a particular student all the time because attention needs to be distributed among many students. When communication boards are used, O'Neill and Reichle (1993) recommend the use of a separate response to obtain the partner's attention, such as activating a buzzer before emitting a more complete response. As of now, however, these recommendations have not undergone systematic evaluation.

In summary, the use of speech output with SGDs shows considerable potential in helping replace challenging behaviors when applied within FCT. Considerable work, however, remains to be done to help us understand the exact role of speech output. To do so, those systems that do offer speech output need to be systematically compared with those that do not provide speech output. We also need to conduct studies that examine how speech output interacts with other variables pertinent to the efficiency of an alternative communicative response such as physical effort for key activation, schedule of reinforcement, and time delay.

F. Natural Speech Production

Whether AAC interventions in general enhance or hinder natural speech production has been a long-standing issue of debate. Even before the AAC field emerged with its own identity, this issue engaged some authors in discussions concerning the benefits of acquiring signing skills for vocal behaviors (Hopper & Helmick, 1977). A recent meta-analysis of studies concerned with the impact of AAC intervention on natural speech production revealed that the majority of studies examined the role of manual signs on speech production (Millar, Light, & Schlosser, 2000). There is very little research on the effects of aided AAC systems in general and on the effects of speech output in particular. There are, however, a few studies that provide valuable directions for future research as well as initial implications for practice.

1. Effectiveness of Treatment Packages

Dyches (1998) monitored the number of verbalizations in one participant with autism in a study concerned with the effects of coincidental instruction in activating a switch connected to a loop tape with digitized speech to request a drink. Verbalizations were defined as "verbalizing the desire to have a drink; this included verbal approximations (e.g., 'pah' for 'pop'), words (e.g., 'drink') and sentences or phrases (e.g., 'I want a drink')" (p. 154). Results do not indicate any changes in the number of verbalizations as a result of intervention. As reviewed earlier, however, this study is flawed in numerous ways making it difficult to draw valid conclusions.

Referring to an earlier study (Romski, Sevcik, Robinson, & Wilkinson, 1990), Romski and Sevcik (1992b) reported improvements in the natural speech intelligibility of youths with moderate or severe intellectual disabilities after the use of an SGD as part of SAL over a 2-year period. According to Romski and Sevcik (1993), this report suggests that synthetic speech output may play a role in the emergence of expressive spoken language skills, particularly for persons who exhibit difficulties processing the natural speech signal. They speculate that while the initial intelligibility may be different from natural speech, the consistency of the synthetic speech output may preserve dimensions of the auditory signal that permit the listener to segment the stream of speech more easily. Romski and Sevcik (1996) also suggested that it may be the immediacy and consistency of synthetic speech output that encourages imitation and production of natural speech.

2. Effectiveness of the Presence versus Absence of Speech Output

To date, we are aware of only two studies that attempted to isolate speech output as an independent variable in determining its effect on natural speech production (Blischak, 1999; Parsons & La Sorte, 1993). Blischak (1999) examined changes in natural speech production in two groups of preschoolers and young school-aged children with severe speech impairments as a result of two different phonologic awareness instruction methods. One group received instruction with graphic symbols alone, whereas the other group received graphic symbols with DECtalk synthetic speech. Even though the differences obtained only approached statistical significance, the changes were quite noteworthy. The children in the Graphic Symbols group declined in the production of natural speech from 25.42% to 12.08% following instruction, whereas the children in the Synthetic Speech group increased natural speech production from 19.67% to 39.33%. To explain these findings, Blischak (1999) discussed a number of plausible hypotheses, including those reviewed earlier. Also, she speculated that synthetic speech output may have activated or strengthened the phonologic code, which may have served, then, to focus the child's attention to the phonologic characteristics of the words, thereby contributing to increased natural speech production. Although preliminary due to small n, more studies of this nature are needed before we begin to understand these promising suggestive effects of speech output on natural speech production.

Parsons and La Sorte (1993) studied the effects of synthetic speech output (i.e., Echo IIb) from computer-based SGDs on spontaneous utterances in six children with autism. Prior to the onset of this study, these children demonstrated the ability to produce speech without necessarily demonstrating functional speech. The frequency of spontaneous utterances served as the dependent measure, and the computer with the speech synthesizer turned on or off served as the independent variable. Spontaneous utterances "were defined as any spoken verbalization initiated by the subject or the subject's verbal response to a question asked by the computer" (p. 17). They used both additive designs (A-B-BC-B-BC) and reductive/subtractive designs (A-BC-B-BC) to examine the role of additional speech output. Some of the participants were assigned to the additive design, whereas others were assigned to the reductive design in an attempt to control for order effects. With the additive design, speech output was added to a computer following the B phase. With the reductive design, speech output was removed following the BC phase. Results indicated that intervention without speech output produced no change in the frequency of spontaneous utterances. When speech output was added, however, the frequency of spontaneous utterances increased. Although promising, these results may be compromised by the design used in that these authors relied on across-subjects control of order effects rather than within-subject control, which is more typical in single-subject experimental designs. Although across-subject control of order effects is not a flaw in and of itself, it is this author's position that it becomes a flaw when the n is too small (e.g., an $n = 3$ per condition) given the n standards of between-group designs. By using across-subject control, the standards of between-group designs are applicable. To confirm these encouraging findings, it would be helpful to replicate the study using within-subject control of order effects (see also Chapter 6).

To learn about the specific role of speech output (i.e., not the treatment package including speech output), it is essential that more studies be designed wherein the provision of speech output is isolated as the independent variable to assess its effect on natural speech production. With the exception of the two studies reviewed, such research is scant. Even though these studies need to be replicated with a larger number of subjects (Blischak, 1999) or replicated using appropriate within-subject control of order effects (Parsons & LaSorte, 1993), they do offer indications of the suggestive positive impact of speech output on natural speech production. This, along with the absence of any evidence suggesting that speech output may hinder natural speech production, provides evidence-based practitioners with some preliminary support in consultations with relevant stakeholders. Parents may be concerned that their child will not improve in their natural speech production once an artificial method of speech output is introduced.

In preparing future studies, researchers may benefit from previous and current syntheses of AAC interventions. Udwin (1987), for example, concluded: "A further criticism concerns the claims made in many training studies about accompanying improvements in speech output [natural speech production]. . . . These reports are typically anecdotal, lack adequate control procedures and reliable assessments to back them up" (p. 21). More than two decades later, a meta-analysis of AAC intervention studies focusing on effects in natural speech development showed that this research continues to be methodologically weak (Millar *et al.*, 2000). This makes it impossible to draw any firm conclusions concerning the role of AAC intervention on natural speech production in general and speech output on natural speech production in particular. It appears though as if natural speech production has been thought of as a "collateral effect" of AAC intervention (e.g., Abrahamsen, Romski, & Sevcik, 1989) rather than a primary effect. This perception may have translated into a lack of focus on this variable as far as research design is concerned. By pointing out methodological shortcomings, these syntheses can be invaluable for the design of future experiments on the role of speech output on natural speech production (interested readers are encouraged to consult this reading and Chapter 16). In conclusion, using the words of Romski and Sevcik (1993), "in a time when artificial speech technology is advancing rapidly, it is critical to examine this topic as part of the AAC intervention process" (p. 283).

G. Comprehension

Speech output may also play a role in facilitating natural speech comprehension. Romski and Sevcik (1993) hypothesized that because of the consistency of synthetic speech output, the dimensions of the auditory signal may be better preserved. This in turn may permit learners to segment the stream of speech more easily aiding their comprehension. The two routes to augmented language learning identified by Romski and Sevcik (1992a) and reviewed earlier give initial credence to the role of extant speech comprehension skills brought to the AAC language learning task. Whether or not, however, exposure to synthetic speech may also improve natural speech comprehension skills, as hypothesized, has not been studied to date.

1. Word and Sentence Comprehension

There is very little research regarding the comprehension of synthetic speech and the effects of practice on comprehension by learners with intellectual disabilities. Koul and Hanners (1997), for example, compared the performance of a group of learners with mild to moderate intellectual disabilities ($n = 10$) with a matched control ($n = 10$) group on word recognition and sentence verification tasks. One highly intelligible text-to-speech system (i.e., DECtalk) and another relatively less intelligible system (i.e., RealVoice) presented synthetic speech stimuli. The performance of learners with intellectual disabilities was found significantly poorer than that of nondisabled learners on a sentence verification task. Also a trend toward longer response latencies for sentences verified correctly was observed for learners with mild to moderate intellectual disabilities in comparison to nondisabled individuals. No significant difference, however, was observed between learners with intellectual disabilities and nondisabled individuals on a relatively easier word identification task. Additionally, data revealed that DECtalk male and female synthetic voices were significantly superior to RealVoice synthesizer across groups. Post-hoc analyses on practice effects indicated a significant interaction between synthetic voice and tasks. The different types of voices employed in this study, however, confounded the practice effect observed.

2. Discourse Comprehension

Willis, Koul, and Paschall (2000) studied post-perceptual discourse comprehension in 12 learners with mild to moderate intellectual disabilities. Results revealed a nonsignificant trend toward superior comprehension accuracy scores for DECtalk (i.e., a high quality synthesizer) compared to RealVoice and MacinTalk (i.e., relatively lower quality synthesizers). Further, the type of comprehension errors made in a task with synthetic speech was identical to those in a task with natural speech. This indicates that strategies used to decipher information by individuals with intellectual disabilities do not differ across natural and synthetic forms of speech. Another unpublished study by Dahle and Goldman (1990) indicated that individuals with intellectual disabilities exhibit significantly slower response latencies for synthetic speech than do nondisabled children and children with learning disabilities. Although the above mentioned studies provide us with important preliminary data, their generalizability is limited by the small number of subjects in each of the studies.

H. Literacy

Table 19.2 offers a synopsis of relevant studies on the effects of speech output on literacy outcomes such as spelling, phonological awareness, reading, and writing. The effects of speech output on each of these outcome areas are discussed separately in the sections that follow.

1. Spelling

The role of communication technology in promoting spelling has received little empirical attention (Foley, 1993; Steelman, Pierce, & Koppenhaver, 1993). SGDs and SGD software for word processing provide visual displays or speech output, which allow for additional visual and auditory feedback for the learner. Feedback has been defined as any stimuli presented following the performance that bears a relationship to some aspect of the performance. In technology-based instruction, feedback has been specified as any message or display that the technology presents to the learner after a response (Sales, 1993). In spelling instruction with SGDs and SGD software such as word processors, feedback may thus be defined as any stimuli presented to the learner following the selection of a letter or word, including print feedback via the visual display mode or speech feedback via speech output. It is yet unknown what feedback conditions are more effective and efficient in maximizing the support received in spelling through these devices. This is important to determine because these students are known to experience severe difficulties in producing accurate spellings (Koppenhaver & Yoder, 1992). Feedback conditions are essentially composed of feedback modes and feedback levels.

For students with cerebral palsy and severe speech impairments, McNaughton and Tawney (1993) incorporated speech and print feedback for each letter and word as part of their successful teaching of spelling. Their study, however, was aimed at comparing two methods of spelling instruction, rather than at the isolation of the effects of speech and print feedback. Research that manipulates the presence and absence of feedback modes in SGDs and word processors while monitoring their effects on spelling is scarce with persons who rely on AAC. This dearth of research is especially surprising in the case of autism because attempts to promote communication through the written word have met with some success (LaVigna, 1977). Moreover, reports suggest that computer-assisted communication systems with speech and print feedback are compatible with autistic cognitive styles and processing preferences (e.g., Heimann, Nelson, Tjus, & Gillberg, 1995). These reports, however, were again not intended to provide sufficient experimental control to isolate speech and print feedback.

a. Supporting Spelling through Beneficial Feedback Modes

To begin to fill this dearth of research on the role of communication technology in spelling, Schlosser, Blischak, Belfiore, Bartley, and Barnett (1998) taught Martin, a 10-year-old nonspeaking student with autism, to spell words under three feedback mode conditions using an SGD: (1) SPEECH, (2) PRINT, and (3) SPEECH + PRINT. In each condition, feedback was provided for each letter selected and word entered. Using an adapted alternating treatments design, results indicate that Martin reached criterion in each condition. He spelled target words, however, more efficiently in the SPEECH condition, followed by SPEECH + PRINT by itself. In discussing plausible explanations for these findings, the literature on the development of spelling and phonologic awareness skills offers some clarification. Cataldo and Ellis (1988) purported that in the early stages of development, spelling is primarily a phonologic process (i.e., auditory-speech) as opposed to an orthographic process (i.e., visual-print). Thus, synthetic speech feedback could potentially assist a beginning speller in forming letter-sound association. Due to an $n = 1$ in this preliminary study, Schlosser and Blischak (2002b) have since replicated this study with four more learners with autism. The only procedural difference between the preliminary study and this replication was the provision of fingerspelled input to Martin in all three conditions. In the replication, no such input was provided to the learners. All of the learners reached criterion in each of the conditions, with the exception of Carl who did not reach criterion in the PRINT condition by the time summer break caused researchers to terminate the teaching. In addition, three of the four learners (Scott, Fred, and Justin) reached criterion first in the PRINT or SPEECH + PRINT condition. For two of these learners there was either no difference or only 1 session difference between PRINT and SPEECH + PRINT. The fourth learner, Carl, first attained criterion in the SPEECH + PRINT condition followed by SPEECH and PRINT. Because the findings from Martin did not replicate, explanations were discussed that could account for these differences. The use of fingerspelled input in the first study is an obvious procedural difference between the two studies that is a worthwhile point of discussion. Possibly, the SPEECH condition was so efficient because Martin obtained visual input in each condition and therefore did not need to rely as much on print feedback from the visual display. Martin's observed use of fingerspelled rehearsal when entering a letter into the keyboard (i.e., he made the shape of a letter and then proceeded to activate this letter key while holding this very same shape) would lend some post-hoc support to this

Table 19.2

Studies on the Role of Speech Output for the Development of Literacy Skills

Study	Subjects	Design	Speech output	Locus of Control	Independent variable
Barron *et al.* (1992)	66 nondisabled children (mean age of 5;7 years)	Between-group design with semi-random assignment + control group	Synthetic (DECtalk)	Software-directed	Phonological awareness training with three feedback modes: • Speech • Speech-print • Speech-print (semantic control)
Blischak (1999)	9 preschoolers and young elementary students with severe speech impairment (4;4–7 years)	Within-subject pretest-posttest design	Synthetic (DECtalk)	Software-directed	Phonological awareness instruction focused on rhyme instruction under two conditions: • Graphic symbols • Graphic symbols and speech
Borgh & Dickson (1992)	48 nondisabled children (mean age of 8;1 years and 10;11 years, respectively)	Within-subject cross-over design	Synthetic (Votrax)	• Software-directed feedback • Learner-directed repetition of feedback	Writing of stories on the word processor with two feedback modes providing feedback at sentence-level and text-level: • Speech • No speech

Dependent variables	Dependent measures	Results
Phonological awareness	• Oddity rhyming score • Phoneme deletion score	Learners with low letter-sound knowledge showed gains in rhyming compared to the control, irrespective of whether they received print feedback or not. Thus, speech output seems to help with rhyming. Only learners with high letter-sound knowledge, who were given print feedback, showed gains in phoneme deletion compared to the control group. Thus, speech output by itself does not help phoneme deletion.
• Rhyme detection • Rhyme oddity • Rhyme production • Natural speech production	• Rhyme detection score • Rhyme oddity score • Rhyme production score • Percentage of natural speech production	Results indicated no differences in rhyming scores between the condition with and without speech output. In neither condition did the children improve in rhyme detection. Children in the speech condition significantly improved in rhyme oddity from 31% to 38%, but that was close to chance levels. These children also improved in terms of rhyme production from 17% to 28% without reaching significance.
• Length • Editing • Quality • Motivation • Audience awareness	• Number of keystrokes • Number of keystrokes in the final story version • Number of sentences • Keystroke data (changes in reentered sentences) • Primary Trait System • Q-sort ranking of stories • Interview responses	Results indicate that more editing was performed under the "speech" condition than the "no speech" condition. Further, the speech condition was found related to more editing at the sentence level rather than the story level. In terms of social validation, most of the participants enjoyed writing more when the computer "talked." No other significant differences were noted.

(continues)

Table 19.2 (*continued*)

Study	Subjects	Design	Speech output	Locus of Control	Independent variable
Farmer, Klein, & Bryson (1992)	14 students with reading disabilities (mean age = 15;8 years)	Within-subjects design	Synthetic (DECtalk)	Learner-directed feedback (students needed to tag words)	Presenting of stories with two feedback modes at the word-level: • Speech • No speech
Heimann et al. (1995)	7 children with infantile autism (range from 7;8 to 13;8 years); 3 of the learners also had intellectual disabilities	One-group pretest posttest design	Digitized (i.e., prerecorded)		A communication and literacy treatment package that featured a multimedia computer program along with teacher-child dialogue
Koke & Neilson (1987)	3 adults with physical disabilities and little or no functional speech (16 to 22 years)	Single-subject ABA-design	Synthetic (Votrax)	Software-directed (i.e., automatic for letters and words); Learner-directed (entire text)	Feedback mode at the letter and word level: • Print with speech • Print without speech
Lewis, Graves, Ashton, & Kieley (1998)	132 students with learning disabilities (12;3 years) plus a comparison group of 132 general education	Pretest-posttest control group design with random assignment to groups	Synthetic (DECtalk)	Learner-directed	Writing with word processing under four conditions and one control condition: • Keyboarding instruction • An alternative keyboard • Word prediction (WP)

Dependent variables	Dependent measures	Results
• Comprehension • Word recognition • Enthusiasm • Proposed reading time per week	• Mean percentage of comprehension questions answered correctly • Mean percentage of words read correctly • Mean time to read tagged words • Questionnaire responses	Results indicate no significant differences in comprehension between the two conditions. Further, there were no differences in word recognition across conditions. There were also no differences across conditions in terms of the time it took to read tagged words. Social validation data indicated considerable enthusiasm for the "speech" condition.
• Reading • Phonological awareness	• Flashcard A (sentences), C (words), and Umesol (words) • Phonological awareness test • Vocabulary test • Sentence-test mode	Strong gains in reading and phonological awareness for four of the children.
Spelling within elicited composition	• Final errors • Number of letter-level changes • Word-level changes • Changes unrelated to auditory feedback	Speech feedback resulted in a positive influence on spelling accuracy, as indicated by an increase in final errors and a decrease in the total number of changes made when auditory feedback was withdrawn. Withdrawal of speech feedback had no effect on the number of letter-level and unrelated changes, but did result in a decrease in word-level changes made.
• Writing speed • Writing quality • Writing accuracy • Attitude toward writing (social validation)	• Writing speed: speed probes for text entry • Writing quality: the Story Quality Scale and the Expository Quality Scale • Writing accuracy: mechanics errors, spelling errors, and	The WPS group showed the most significant decrease in speed compared to handwriting. The availability of speech with word prediction slows down writing with word prediction. There was no difference in accuracy between WP and

(continues)

Table 19.2 (*continued*)

Study	Subjects	Design	Speech output	Locus of Control	Independent variable
	students				• Word prediction with speech output (hear word choices) (WPS) • Handwriting (control)
Lovett *et al.* (1994)	17 speaking children with neurological impairments and 5 speaking children with developmental dyslexia (mean age of 9.8 years)	Between-group design with random assignment	Synthetic (DECtalk)	Software-directed (i.e., automatic feedback)	Feedback levels: • Letter-sound (b was pronounced "buh") • Onset-rime ("tr" and "ain" for "train") • Whole-word • Control (math)
McArthur (1998)	5 students with learning disabilities (9 to 10 years)	Single-subject multiple baseline design combined with a withdrawal design	Synthetic (Smooth-talker)	Learner-directed	Feedback mode: • Word-level and paragraph speech feedback and word prediction
Olson *et al.* (1986)	Children with reading disabilities	Within-group design	Synthetic (DECtalk)		Feedback mode: • Print and speech • Print only
Raskind & Higgins (1995)	33 college students with learning disabilities (mean age of 24;9 years)	Within-group design	Synthetic ("Sound-proof")	Learner-directed (choice of speech feedback [yes/no] and level)	Feedback by word, line, sentence, or paragraph: • Synthetic speech • Natural speech • No assistance

Dependent variables	Dependent measures	Results
	syntax errors • Attitudes: adaptation of Estes Attitudes Scale	WPS. However, WPS made significantly fewer spelling errors during the posttest compared to the pretest. There was no differences were found between WPS and WP in terms of quality and attitudes.

• Word
  identification
• Spelling
	• Number of target words
	  identified
	• Number of target words
	  spelled correctly	

• Legibility
• Spelling
• Writing
  accuracy
• Writing speed
	• Proportion of legible
	  words
	• Proportion of correctly
	  spelled words
	• Correct word sequences
	• Legible word sequences
	• Words written/minute
	  (i.e., composing rate)
	• Length of entries
		The *combination* of synthetic speech and word prediction had a strong effect on the legibility and spelling accuracy of dialogue journal entries for four of the five learners

• Word decoding • Comprehension		With speech feedback the learners decoded words more readily and improved comprehension of the stories. The children liked working with speech feedback.

• Proofreading
  (i.e., error
  detection)
	• Total errors detected
	• Capitalization errors
	  detected
	• Usage errors detected
	• Spelling errors detected
	• Typographical errors
	  dected
		Students found more significantly more total errors, capitalization errors, and usage errors in the synthetic speech condition than the other two conditions. A higher percentage of spelling and typographical errors were found for speech synthesis than read aloud condition, but these were not significant.

(continues)

Table 19.2 (*continued*)

Study	Subjects	Design	Speech output	Locus of Control	Independent variable
Reitsma (1988)	72 speaking first-grade students (mean age of 7.2 years)	Between-group design with random assignment to conditions	Analog (i.e., recorded)	Learner-directed in reading-along and speech-select conditions	Feedback modes at the word level: (a) Guided-reading (b) Reading-along ("talking book") (c) Speech-select ("learner-directed retrieval of spoken word forms") (d) Control
Schlosser et al. (1998)	1 learner with autism and no functional speech (10 years)	Single-subject adapted alternating treatments design	Synthetic (DECtalk)	Software-directed (i.e., automatic feedback)	Feedback modes (letter and word level): • Print • Speech • Speech-print
Schlosser & Blischak (2002a)	4 learners with autism and no functional speech	Single-subject adapted alternating treatments design	Synthetic (DECtalk)	Software-directed (i.e., automatic feedback)	Feedback modes (letter and word level): • Print • Speech • Speech-print
Wise (1992)	56 children in first grade and 56 children in second grade divided in two groups of low and average reading ability		Synthetic (DECtalk)	Learner-directed	Feedback level (orthographic and speech): • Whole-word (e.g., reader) • BOSS type syllables (e.g., read/er), • Onset-rime subsyllables

Dependent variables	Dependent measures	Results
		They were significant in comparison to the no assistance condition. In summary, the use of speech outperformed the other proofreading conditions in seven out of nine error categories—four of them at significant levels.
• Reading accuracy • Reading speed	• Mean number of reading errors • Mean reading time on sample of 20 words • Standardized Reading Achievement Test	Both, the guided-reading and speech-select conditions were effective in promoting reading fluency. There were no differences in accuracy although the tendency of the data was in the same direction as fluency. No differences were found on the standardized test.
Spelling	• Percentage of words spelled correctly • Percentage of correct letter sequences	Although the learner reached criterion and maintained performance in each condition, the provision of speech feedback alone and in combination with print feedback resulted in more efficient spelling than print feedback alone.
Spelling	• Percentage of words spelled correctly • Percentage of correct letter sequences	
Reading-word decoding		Whole-word feedback and BOSS syllable feedback proved to be the most helpful for first and second graders with low and average reading ability. Onset-rime was somewhat less helpful on multisyllabic words for the younger and low reading groups. For monosyllabic

(*continues*)

Table 19.2 (*continued*)

Study	Subjects	Design	Speech output	Locus of Control	Independent variable
					(e.g., r/ead/er) • Grapheme-phoneme units (e.g., r/ea/d/er)
Wise (1987)	20 nondisabled children in second grade	Within-group design	Synthetic (DECtalk)	Learner-directed	Feedback level (orthographic and speech): • Syllabic division based on Spoehr and Smith (1973) (e.g., rea/der) • Syllabic division based on BOSS' rules (e.g., read/er)
Wise et al. (1989)	37 children (mean age of 10;1 years); ••	Between-group design with control group	Synthetic (DECtalk)	Learner-directed	Feedback level (orthographic and speech): • Whole-word (e.g., reader) • BOSS type syllables (e.g., read/er), • Onset-rime subsyllables (e.g., r/ead/er)
Wise et al. (1990)	20 nondisabled children in first grade	Within-group design	Synthetic (DECtalk)	Learner-directed	Feedback level (orthographic and speech): • Onset-rime (e.g., d/ish, c/lap) • Other (e.g., di/sh, cla/p)

hypothesis. Future research is needed to clarify whether fingerspelled rehearsal can productively replace print feedback from visual displays.

Until this is clarified, the results from the four learners taken together with Martin's results appear to yield two distinct patterns of how learners with autism may benefit from speech and print feedback by SGDs. One type of learner appears to benefit more from print feedback either by itself or in combination

Dependent variables	Dependent measures	Results
		words, onset-rime was as effective as whole-word feedback. Grapheme-phoneme segmentation aided word learning the least across groups.
Reading-word decoding		BOSS segmentation was more effective than the other syllabic division condition.
• Word recognition; reading comprehension • Phonological decoding • Phonological awareness in language • Intelligence quotient (IQ)	• PIAT score for word recognition • PIAT score for reading comprehension • PIAT score for spelling • Number of words read correctly • Percent of nonwords read correctly • Percent correct • WISC-R Full Scale IQ • Ratio of targeting frequency	Learners with segmented feedback demonstrated impressive pretest to posttest gains in phonological decoding compared to small gains in the whole-word feedback and control conditions.
Reading-word decoding		Results indicated significant advantages in posttest recognition for words that were segmented at the onset-rime boundary (e.g., d/ish).

with speech feedback. The data of Scott, Fred, and Justin are indicative of this pattern. Another type of learner appears to benefit more from speech feedback either by itself (Martin) or in combination with print feedback (Carl). Unfortunately, predictors that would allow the evidence-based practitioner to make a data-based decision in to which group of learners a given individual may fall are not available. Therefore, Schlosser and Blischak (2002a) argued that the implementation of an individualized assessment protocol might be most suitable for determining how to best support the spelling of learners with autism through the most beneficial feedback modes.

Other studies have examined the role of feedback modes in learners with physical disabilities and learners with learning disabilities. Koke and Neilson (1987), for instance, studied the effects of two feedback modes on spelling during elicited composition in three adults with physical disabilities and little or no functional speech. In one condition, the participants received print feedback and in the other condition they also received synthetic speech feedback. Although the findings showed improvements in spelling accuracy in the print plus speech feedback condition, this study is plagued with methodologic shortcomings, which question the internal validity of these findings. MacArthur (1998) used a multiple-baseline design combined with a withdrawal design to study the effects of whole-word speech feedback combined with word prediction on spelling in five children with learning disabilities. The *combination* of synthetic speech and word prediction had a strong effect on the spelling accuracy of dialogue journal entries for four of the five learners.

In summary, research on identifying beneficial feedback modes with speech output by itself or in combination with print feedback is in a beginning phase. To date, little information can be gleaned from these few studies other than that these is a need for individualized assessment protocols.

b. Supporting Spelling with Speech Output at Beneficial Feedback Levels

Determining the most efficacious feedback modes is not the only issue that warrants the attention of evidence-based practitioners. SGDs and word processors can be programmed so that speech feedback can be provided least at three levels: after each letter is entered, after each word is entered, or both. Thus, it becomes important to determine which levels best support the spelling performance of learners. The previously discussed studies with learners with autism provided feedback for each letter entered and following the completion of a word (Schlosser *et al.*, 1998; Schlosser & Blischak, 2002a). Although this study does shed some initial light onto the role of different feedback modes when feedback is provided at the level of both, for each letter and for each word, it does not speak to the relative efficacy of various feedback levels. Such research is currently being planned in children with severe speech and physical impairments (Schlosser & Blischak, 2002b). Lovett, Barron, Forbes, Cuksts, and Steinbach (1994) did compare various feedback levels but found no significant differences in terms of spelling performance in children with neurological impairments or developmental dyslexia (see Table 19.2). Comparable studies are needed with AAC users. Until such evidence becomes available, evidence-based practitioners may need to determine the level of feedback on a case-by-case basis through an individualized assessment protocol.

2. Phonological Awareness

The effects of speech output on phonological awareness are largely unknown. Two studies, however, offer some initial evidence. Barron, Golden, Selden, Tait, Marmurek, and Haines (1992) engaged a group of nondisabled children in phonological awareness training with speech output (SPEECH), speech and print feedback (SPEECH-PRINT-1), or speech and print feedback under semantic control (SPEECH-PRINT-2). Learners with low letter-sound knowledge showed gains in rhyming compared to the control group, irrespective of whether or not they received print feedback. Thus, speech output seems to help with rhyming. Only learners with high letter-sound knowledge who were given print feedback showed gains in phoneme deletion compared to the control group. Thus, speech output by itself does not help with phoneme deletion.

Blischak (1999) implemented phonologic awareness instruction in two conditions with nine preschoolers and elementary students with severe physical and speech impairments. One condition involved graphic symbols and the other condition involved graphic symbols and synthetic speech output. Although the condition with speech output yielded improvements in rhyme oddity and rhyme detection, these changes failed to reach statistical significance. Blischak (1999) argued that perhaps the length of the intervention program was too short and contributed to the small increments in improvements. Practical implications for the role of speech output on phonological awareness are premature given the current state of research evidence. Although both of the studies seem to support a facilitative role for speech output in fostering phonological awareness, one of these studies used nondisabled children and the effects from the other study were statistically not significant. Thus, future research is needed to examine this relationship further.

In addition to feedback modes, it is also of interest to determine the levels of feedback most beneficial for supporting phonologic awareness. Research, however, is scant in this area. A study by Olson and Wise (1992) compared different feedback levels (whole-word, syllable, and onset-rime) in terms of their effects on phonologic awareness in speaking children with reading disabilities. Although no differences were found for feedback levels, the learner's pretest phonological awareness score was the strongest predictor for gains in phonological decoding and word decoding. Studies into supporting phonological awareness through beneficial feedback levels are needed with AAC users so practitioners are in a better position to optimize existing software.

3. Reading

Reading may involve a variety of skills including decoding/recognition (of words, letters, and other segmented levels), comprehension (of words, sentences, and passages), and proofreading (to identify and correct errors). Performance on these skills may be measured via accuracy or speed. As indicated in Table 19.2, a considerable number of studies have examined the effects of speech feedback modes on reading (Espin & Sindelar, 1988; Farmer, Klein, & Bryson, 1992; Olson, Foltz, & Wise, 1986; Raskind & Higgins, 1995; Reitsma, 1988) and the effects of feedback levels on reading (Elbro, Rasmussen, & Spelling, 1996; Lovett et al., 1994; Olson & Wise, 1992; Spaai, Reitsma, & Ellermann, 1991; Wise, 1987, 1992; Wise, Olson, Anstett, Andrews, Terjak, Scheider, Kostuch, & Kriho, 1989; Wise, Olson, & Treiman, 1990).

Feedback modes may include auditory feedback via speech (digitized, synthetic, natural) or visual feedback via highlighted text. In reading tasks, however, visual feedback is different from print feedback received during spelling. In reading tasks the text is already in front of the reader and does not have to be entered. Therefore, the notion of print feedback does not apply. Rather, it is the highlighting of orthographic wholes or of segments, which provides the visual computer feedback that is relevant. This may be referred to as *orthographic feedback*.

Studies on feedback modes compared the provision of speech versus no speech (Espin & Sindelar, 1988; Farmer et al., 1992; Reitsma, 1988), the provision of speech along with orthographic feedback versus speech by itself (Olson et al., 1986), or synthetic speech versus natural speech (Raskind & Higgins, 1995). Two studies found no differences for feedback modes (Farmer et al., 1992; Reitsma, 1988) whereas three studies did find that the provision of speech feedback assisted in proofreading (Espin & Sindelar, 1988; Raskind & Higgins, 1995) and word decoding (Olson et al., 1986).

Studies on feedback levels typically manipulated the level of feedback for both orthographic and speech feedback. The following feedback levels have been studied: whole-word, letter, onset-rime subsyllables, BOSS-type syllable, and grapheme-phoneme. With the exception of two studies reviewed in Table 19.2 (Elbro et al., 1996; Wise et al., 1990), all others compared different level of segmented feedback with whole-word feedback. Studies in this latter group yielded mostly an advantage for segmented feedback over whole-word feedback (Lovett et al., 1994; Olson & Wise, 1992; Wise et al., 1989). The exception is the study by Spaai et al. (1991), which found whole-word feedback more effective than grapheme-phoneme feedback, and the study by Wise et al. (1990), which found whole-word feedback as effective as the BOSS-syllable feedback.

Given that none of the reading studies reviewed in Table 19.2 were conducted with AAC users, it becomes difficult to apply any of these findings to individuals who use AAC. Clearly, studies with AAC users are needed to answer critical questions such as the following: What feedback modes (speech, orthographic, or both) are most beneficial to support reading? At what levels should word processors be programmed to supply orthographic and speech feedback?

What is the role of learner-directed versus software-directed feedback? Are there any predictors for certain levels and modes of feedback? These are several of the pressing questions that need to be tackled before we understand how speech output can support reading skills in learners using AAC.

4. Writing

Writing is another important literacy skill that may be affected by speech output. Only two studies among the studies reported in Table 19.2 examined the effects of speech output on various writing-related skills. Lewis, Graves, Ashton, and Kieley (1998) compared the use of word prediction by itself and word prediction with speech output (i.e., the learner was able to listen to the word choices) in terms of writing speed, writing quality, writing accuracy, and attitudes in students with learning disabilities. Although there were no differences in writing accuracy, writing quality, and attitudes toward writing, speech output was found to slow down the writing process for these learners. Borgh and Dickson (1992) studied the effects of speech feedback versus no speech feedback on writing length, writing quality, editing, motivation, and audience awareness in nondisabled students. Results indicated that learners did more editing when they received speech feedback. In terms of social validation, most of the participants enjoyed writing more when the computer "talked." No other significant differences emerged.

These studies offer only a glimpse into the role of speech output as a potential writing facilitator in AAC users. Given that many AAC users write using word processors with speech output, it becomes crucial to find out whether speech output does promote writing, and if so, at what feedback level. Some of the many unanswered questions are the following: What are the effects of speech feedback and/or print feedback during the writing process on writing speed, accuracy, quality, editing, and learner perceptions (e.g., enthusiasm)? What are the effects of the learner being able to listen to the word choices from word prediction on editing and writing accuracy? How does speech output during writing interact with word prediction? What are the differences, if any, between software-directed and learner-directed provision of speech feedback? At what level should speech or print feedback (letter, word, sentence, paragraph, and text) be provided to be most efficacious for writing?

IV. ROLES OF SPEECH OUTPUT FOR THE LEARNER-PARTNER DYAD

Little research has evaluated changes in the dyad as a result of speech output by monitoring both learner and partner behavior. Schepis, Reid, Behrmann, and

Sutton (1998), for example, evaluated the effects of SGD use combined with naturalistic teaching procedures for increasing the communicative interactions of four children with autism (age 3 to 5 years) and their support personnel during classroom routines. This intervention program featured staff training, which consisted of several components. First, the experimenter conducted a 30- to 45-minute training session with classroom staff that focused on one target child and a classroom routine selected for intervention. During this session, the experimenter and staff discussed the child's preferences and the type of messages that would provide the most useful responses in terms of frequency of use and communicative functions. In addition, they collectively chose a graphic representation for each message, and the staff was instructed in SGD operation and procedures. Last, the experimenter provided spoken and written presentations outlining the main components of naturalistic teaching procedures in relation to SGD use for a target child and routine. The effectiveness of the interventions was evaluated using a multiple probe design across two participants in two routines and across two participants in one routine. During baseline, students did not have access to an SGD during targeted activities. During intervention, SGDs with digitized speech output were made available. Dependent measures included those pertaining to child behavior and classroom staff behavior. Child behavior was defined as the child being in close proximity of another person and directing a communicative response to that person. Child communication categories included (1) child-to-child communication, (2) physically guided SGD, (3) word vocalization, (4) nonword vocalization, and (5) gesture. Classroom staff communicative behavior was defined as any intelligible verbalization, other than verbal prompts to communicate, directed toward a target child. Results indicated increases in child communicative behavior and classroom staff communicative behavior as a result of introducing an SGD through naturalistic teaching. In addition, the use of modes other than the SGD (e.g., gestures) did not decrease as a result of introducing the SGD. Teachers' ratings of children's SGD communication, as well as ratings of a person unfamiliar with the children, provided social validation support for the contextual appropriateness of SGD use. Unfortunately, the study failed to control for possible novelty effects due to exposure to the SGD only during intervention. Therefore it becomes difficult to attribute changes in the dependent measures to the treatment involving the SGD rather than the mere novelty of the SGD.

In summary, the effects of speech output have been reviewed in terms of their effects on (potential) communication partners, learners, and learner-partner dyads. In the next section, this narrative review is used as the basis for decision making related to the use of speech output in practice guided by principles of EBP.

V. DECIDING ON THE USE OF SPEECH OUTPUT: AN EBP ILLUSTRATION

The steps involved in implementing EBP in AAC as described in Chapter 12 include (1) asking a well-built question, (2) selecting evidence sources, (3) executing the search strategy, (4) examining the evidence, (5) applying the evidence, (6) evaluating the application of the evidence, and (7) disseminating the findings.

A. ASKING A WELL-BUILT QUESTION

As indicated in Chapter 12, questions need to be well-built to facilitate a systematic search of the relevant evidence. This step is extremely important to the process because the nature of the question will determine the direction of the other steps involved. The selection of graphic symbols for an initial request lexicon pertains to the second role identified in the "Knowledge and Skills" document of the American Speech-Language and Hearing Association (2002): "determining AAC methods, components, and strategies to maximize functional communication by individuals."

The following is an example of a foreground question related to the use of speech output:

> Cassandra is a 14-year-old beginning communicator with profound intellectual disabilities who is in the beginning of her transition from school into community settings. Currently, she has been successfully using presymbolic means to communicate basic needs and wants in the school setting, but the school team has found her communicative attempts are not always recognizable to laypersons such as cashiers in fast-food restaurants, grocery clerks in supermarkets, and staff at the bowling ally. To prepare Cassandra to be more intelligible in community settings, the team is considering the use of aided communication for an initial request lexicon. Specifically, the team is asking the following question: Should we introduce Cassandra to an SGD rather than a nonelectronic communication board or wallet?

This question contains the essential components needed in order to be well-built. The components (1) describe the direct stakeholder and his or her capabilities relevant to the clinical problem (a 14-year old female with profound intellectual disabilities who is currently communicating through presymbolic means; see Chapter 15 for characteristics of beginning communicators), (2) explain the direct stakeholders' current and future environments and relevant other stakeholders (i.e., the focus is on community settings with laypeople), (3) make explicit the clinical or educational problem to be solved (i.e., whether or not to introduce an aided communication system that offers speech output), and (4) specify the expected clinical/educational outcomes (i.e., establishing an initial request lexicon).

B. Selecting Evidence Sources and Executing the Search Strategy

Before going through the process of selecting evidence sources and executing the search strategy, it helps to describe the type of studies ideally suited to speak to the practical question. Studies comparing requesting in individuals with profound intellectual disabilities in community settings with and without speech output would be ideal. As argued in Chapter 12, evidence-based practitioners should first seek syntheses of research rather than attempting to synthesize individual studies. Thus, the practitioner would engage in a database search using keywords such as *speech output* and *voice output communication aids* and combine those with the key words *review, synthesis,* or *meta-analysis*. An ERIC and Psycinfo search yields two narrative reviews on speech output (Lancioni, O'Reilly, & Basili, 2001; Schlosser & Blischak, 2001). In addition, the integrative review conducted earlier in the chapter as well as the review of comparative efficacy studies in Chapter 21 will be used. The review by Schlosser and Blischak (2001) is not relevant to Cassandra because its focus is on learners with autism. As argued in that review, learners with autism may be presented with characteristics that may differentially affect decisions as to whether speech output should be used.

The review by Lancioni *et al.* (2001) is relevant because one of its two foci is on speech output systems used with people with severe/profound intellectual disabilities or multiple disabilities. At least those studies that include persons with severe to profound intellectual disabilities are possibly of relevance to the question at hand. They grouped studies into those that include one or a few messages on the SGD (Dattilo & Camarata, 1991; Durand, 1993, 1999; Locke & Mirenda, 1988; Mathy-Laikko, Iacono, Ratcliff, Villarruel, Yoder, & Vanderheiden, 1989; Schepis & Reid, 1995; Schepis *et al.*, 1996) and those that involve a larger number of messages (i.e., Adamson, Romski, Deffebach, & Sevcik, 1992; Schepis *et al.*, 1998; Soto *et al.*, 1993). The study by Schepis *et al.* (1998) involves young children with autism and is therefore excluded from this process for the same reasons discussed earlier for the review by Schlosser and Blischak (2001). The dependent measures evaluated in a number of studies included communicative functions other than requesting per se or other dependent variables (Adamson *et al.*, 1992; Dattilo & Camarata, 1991; Mathy-Laikko *et al.*, 1989; Schepis & Reid, 1995) or used designs that are preexperimental (i.e., Adamson *et al.*, 1992; Locke & Mirenda, 1988; Romski & Sevcik, 1996). Therefore, these studies shall not be considered further for the question at hand.

The review conducted in this chapter yields several studies that may be of relevance to the question. Specifically, those studies reviewed under the headings "requesting" and "graphic symbol learning" are possibly applicable. The studies on requesting as an outcome variable were grouped into those that investigated speech output as part of a treatment package (DiCarlo & Banajee, 2000; Dyches, 1998; Romski & Sevcik, 1996; Schepis et al., 1996; VanAcker & Grant, 1995) and studies that compared the use of AAC systems with speech output and without speech output (e.g., Doss et al., 1991; Soto et al., 1993). The studies by Dyches (1998) and VanAcker and Grant (1995) involve students from the Autistic Spectrum Disorder; they are excluded on those grounds. The study by Doss et al. (1991) is directly relevant as far as the question of using speech output in community settings (i.e., ordering fast food in a restaurant) is concerned. Unfortunately, the study involves a nondisabled individual who simulated a customer who is nonspeaking. Therefore this study shall be provisionally included. Several other studies meet our initial screening (DiCarlo & Banajee, 2000; Schepis et al., 1996).

Among the studies reviewed under the heading of "graphic symbol learning," both studies are relevant (Blischak et al., 2000; Schlosser et al., 1995). Although graphic symbol learning is not the same as using the graphic symbols communicatively to express a request, learning to associate symbols with referents is an important skill for moving someone like Cassandra from communicating via presymbolic means to communicating via symbolic means.

C. EXAMINING THE EVIDENCE

The studies identified in the previous section may be grouped into three tiers of relevance. The first tier includes studies that compare requesting instruction with SGDs to requesting instruction with AAC systems without speech output (i.e., Doss et al., 1991; Soto et al., 1993). These studies speak directly to the question of whether to introduce Cassandra to a device with speech output or a system without speech output. The second tier includes studies that compare SGDs with AAC systems without speech output in terms of graphic symbol learning (Blischak et al., 2000; Schlosser et al., 1995). Although graphic symbol learning bears some relevance to establishing requesting behavior through aided symbols, it is several steps removed from the communicative use of symbols to express requests. As such, they can only lend some indirect support to the decision-making process. The third tier includes studies in which participants were introduced to an SGD as part of a treatment package during requesting instruction following baseline (DiCarlo & Banajee, 2000; Durand, 1993, 1999; Schepis et al., 1996). Although these studies can speak to the effectiveness of introducing an SGD as part of an intervention package, they cannot answer whether an intervention with a nonelectronic device would have also yielded effective and perhaps more efficient results.

Studies in each of these tiers were evaluated in terms of their certainty of evidence along with other pertinent variables such as participants, design (including control of novelty effects through adequate baseline procedures), treatment integrity, and interobserver agreement. The certainty ratings were derived by following the procedures outlined in Chapter 16, except that baseline procedures were also considered as part of evaluating the ability of the design to rule out threats to internal validity. As noted earlier, when evaluating the effects of SGDs it becomes important to minimize novelty effects as a threat to internal validity. Novelty effects may be minimized by allowing access to the SGD already during baseline. In some of the studies, the SGD was only made available during intervention, making it difficult to rule out effects due to the novelty of the device.

The two studies most relevant to the question offer suggestive evidence that SGDs appear equally effective in communicating requests as nonelectronic communication boards or wallets. In fast-food restaurants, which is one of the community settings relevant to Cassandra, the low-tech wallet was more efficient than SGDs. Thus, it appears that direct care staff in group home settings, adult education programs, and cashiers in fast-food restaurants are more efficient listeners without speech output. It has been argued that the speech output perhaps adds another layer of processing demands on the listener, which may not be necessary (e.g., Doss *et al.*, 1991). In addition to the listener, however, the decision-making process should also take into account the needs of the learner. Related to the learners, it is important to realize that neither of the participants in these studies was at a presymbolic level at the onset of the study. The participant in Soto *et al.* (1993) had several manual signs in his communicative repertoire, and the participant in Doss *et al.* (1991) was nondisabled, simulating an AAC user. Therefore, they brought to the tasks a different skill than Cassandra. Cassandra still needs to learn that symbols represent certain referents, and this is where the studies in the second tier of relevance come in (Blischak *et al.*, 2000; Schlosser *et al.*, 1995). Both of these studies support the efficiency of additional auditory input, and feedback from speech output assists learners with severe to profound intellectual disabilities to associate symbols with referents. Based on this evidence relative to Cassandra's learner characteristics, it would seem important to use a device with speech output.

The majority of studies in tier 3 indicate, with suggestive to conclusive certainty, that SGDs can be successfully introduced to teach requesting in a variety of settings, including classrooms, vocational sites, and, most important for this question, community settings. In particular, the second study by Durand (1999) supports the use of speech output in community settings such as the local candy store, the shopping mall, and the movie theater. Durand (1999) hypothesized that the use of speech output made the learners' responses more recognizable. Because no comparisons were made with other AAC systems, however, it is difficult to ascertain whether communication wallets would have been effective as well or perhaps even more efficient.

Had Cassandra already been operating at a symbolic level, the selection of a wallet or other nonelectronic communication system would have been the more defensible choice. Taking into account, however, the characteristics of the learner, partner, and the context of Cassandra relative to those in the studies reviewed, it would seem important to select a device that offers speech output. Such a device may allow her to learn to associate graphic symbols with referents more quickly (i.e., moving from presymbolic to symbolic communication) while increasing the recognizability of her output to laypersons in community settings. Some laypersons in some community settings may not be sufficiently literate to read the gloss on a nonelectronic display or wallet. This becomes crucial when the graphic symbols cannot be deciphered despite the context. If it is decided that a device with speech output is to be used, the next question pertains to the type of speech output. Should it be digitized or synthetic speech output? In the only relevant direct comparison between the two types of speech output, Doss *et al.* (1991) offered suggestive evidence that digitized speech output is more efficient than synthetic speech output. In addition to this suggestive evidence from research, the practitioner would also consider other objective advantages and disadvantages of digitized versus synthetic speech output. Here a narrative review paper on this topic is applicable (Blischak, Schlosser, & Efros, 2002). SGDs with digitized speech output, for example, are generally easily programmed, can be individualized to the learner's age, gender, and language dialect, and offer natural prosody and intonation. Each of these considerations supports the use of digitized speech output. On the other hand, synthetic speech output is always the same and thus is very consistent, whereas digitized speech may vary even if the same speaker is used for recording. This consistency may not be all that important for the listeners in the various community settings because they will vary from one of Cassandra's visits to the next. Therefore, these listeners would not benefit from repeated listening experiences in order to increase the intelligibility of the speech signal (e.g., McNaughton *et al.*, 1994).

D. Applying the Evidence

The practitioner would then share the findings with the relevant stakeholders (parents, teacher, teacher's aide, and selected laypersons), listen to their reactions and feedback, and together develop a course of action. If the stakeholders agree to explore an SGD with digitized speech output, the practitioner might emphasize the need to develop a nonelectronic backup system in case the SGD fails. With little extra effort, a nonelectronic wallet could be developed using the same graphic symbols as on the SGD.

E. Evaluating the Application of the Evidence

Especially given the suggestive nature of the evidence used in this situation to help direct a clinical/educational course of action, the practitioner recommends that data be collected to determine whether the SGD is working for Cassandra. Given that a wallet has been developed, the practitioner might even want to encourage the team to collect data with both systems, analogous to an alternating treatments design, and draw conclusions based on this direct comparison with Cassandra. Should that ideal procedure prove difficult to implement, data could be collected on the effectiveness of the SGD only.

In either case, the practitioner and the stakeholder together develop a protocol for teaching requesting and for monitoring the effectiveness under typical conditions. As far as a protocol for teaching is concerned, the practitioner may ask other clinical questions beyond the scope of this chapter (e.g., what teaching strategies seem effective?). The interested reader may consult Chapter 14 for the excellent evidence-based suggestions provided for teaching an initial request lexicon.

F. Disseminating the Findings

The last step, where EBP comes full circle so to speak, involves the dissemination of the findings. In Chapter 12, this step was added to the existing steps typically discussed in the literature on EBP. The practitioner would share experiences in going through this process and its outcomes so that future evidence-based practitioners can learn from the information and researchers become aware of the gaps in the knowledge base for purposes of implementing EBP. Chapters 12 and 16 provide ideas for possible publication outlets.

VI. CONCLUSIONS

This narrative review provided the basis for the evidence-based practice illustration toward the end of this chapter. As discussed extensively in Chapter 11, narrative reviews rank lower than more systematic reviews in terms of the hierarchy of evidence. Until such systematic reviews are implemented, this represents the best and most current evidence and will have to do for now. Meta-analyses on the effects of speech output on learners and partners are currently being planned (Schlosser & Blischak, 2002c).

Nonetheless, from this review it is clear that speech output has changed aided communication and outcome areas related to communication. Yet researchers in the field are only beginning to understand exactly how aided communication has been affected and what outcomes have been changed. Undoubtedly, great strides have been made to determine some of the effects of speech output on communication partners, the learner, and the learner-partner dyad. Within each of these major research areas, however, the surface has only been scratched. Future research has to be conducted to further our sometimes superficial understanding of the outcome areas identified. Moreover, there may be other potential outcomes that have yet to be conceptualized and studied. As far as learner effects are concerned, for instance, it would be interesting to evaluate whether speech output promotes subvocal rehearsal or inner speech in persons with little or no functional speech? Subvocal rehearsal is considered an important skill in the development of literacy. Further, it would be important to learn about the effects of speech output on participation patterns in inclusive classrooms, and there may be other learner effects in need of further exploration. The reader has probably several potential partner effects or learner-partner dyad effects in mind that require further study.

Researchers and evidence-based practitioners who are concerned with the effects of speech output ought to be cognizant of the role of potential novelty effects related to speech output. Very little is to be gained from research that fails to rule out (or at the very least minimize) novelty as a potential reason for superior efficacy results over devices without speech output. Practitioners are more interested in moving beyond the effects of novelty and the initial excitement over new technology to effects that are more enduring. In addition to the need for more studies into the effects of speech output as an independent variable, it is also essential that researchers study how speech output interacts with other device-related variables such as visual feedback and word prediction, and other variables such as various treatment packages and contexts. As far as type of speech output, it is evident that most studies to date have dealt with synthetic speech rather than digitized speech. With the proliferation of devices that offer digitized speech and the often held beliefs in the superiority of digitized speech, it becomes paramount that researchers study the relative differences between these types of speech output. Only then will the field obtain a thorough understanding of the relative strengths and weaknesses of each type of speech output, which in turn can lead to evidence-based decision making. Last but not least, more research needs to be directed toward identifying the predictors of success with speech output. These predictor variables may be learner characteristics or features of the environment. Such information would allow practitioners to prescribe speech output for learners with certain characteristics and avoid speech output for those that do not meet these characteristics.

REFERENCES

Abrahamsen, A. A., Romski, M. A., & Sevcik, R. A. (1989). Concomitants of success in acquiring an augmentative communication system: Changes in attention, communication, and sociability. *American Journal on Mental Retardation, 93*, 475–496.

Adamson, L. B., Romski, M. A., Deffebach, K., & Sevcik, R. A. (1992). Symbol vocabulary and the focus of conversations: Augmenting language development for youth with mental retardation. *Journal of Speech and Hearing Research, 35,* 1333–1343.

American Speech-Language-Hearing Association. (2002, April 16). Augmentative and alternative communication: Knowledge and skills for service delivery. *Asha Leader, 7* (*Suppl. 22*), 97–106.

Barron, R. W., Golden, J. O., Seldon, D. M., Tait, C. F., Marmurek, H. H. C., & Haines, L. P. (1992). Teaching prereading skills with a talking computer: Letter-sound knowledge and print feedback facilitate nonreaders' phonological awareness training. *Reading and Writing: An Interdisciplinary Journal, 4,* 179–204.

Beck, A. R., & Dennis, M. (1996). Attitudes of children toward a similar-aged child who uses augmentative communication. *Augmentative and Alternative Communication, 12,* 78–87.

Bedrosian, J., Hoag, L., Calculator, S., & Molineux, B. (1992). Variables influencing perceptions of the communicative competence of an adult augmentative and alternative communication system user. *Journal of Speech and Hearing Research, 35,* 1105–1113.

Beukelman, D. R., & Mirenda, P. (1998). *Augmentative and alternative communication: Management of severe communication disorders in children and adults* (2nd ed). Baltimore: Paul H. Brookes.

Blischak, D. M. (1999). Increases in natural speech production following experience with synthetic speech. *Journal of Special Education Technology, 14,* 47–57.

Blischak, D. M., Schlosser, R. W., & Efros, D. (2002). *Selection and use of speech output for communication and learning: What does the research tell us?* Manuscript in preparation.

Blischak, D. M., Schlosser, R. W., & Miller, M. (2000, November). *Effects of natural vs. synthetic speech on graphic-symbol learning.* Poster presented at the annual convention of the American Speech-Language and Hearing Association (ASHA), Washington, DC.

Blockberger, S., Armstrong, R. W., O'Connor, A., & Freeman, R. (1993). Children's attitudes toward a nonspeaking child using various augmentative and alternative communication techniques. *Augmentative and Alternative Communication, 9,* 243–250.

Borgh, K., & Dickson, W. P. (1992). The effects on children's writing of adding speech synthesis to a word processor. *Journal of Research on Computing in Education, 24,* 533–544.

Cataldo, S., & Ellis, N. (1988). Interactions in the development of spelling, reading, and phonological skills. *Journal of Research in Reading, 11,* 86–109.

Dahle, A., & Goldman, R. (1990, November). *Perception of synthetic speech by normal and developmentally disabled children.* Paper presented at the annual convention of the American Speech-Language-Hearing Association, Seattle, WA.

Dattilo, J., & Camarata, S. (1991). Facilitating conversation through self-initiated augmentative communication treatment. *Journal of Applied Behavior Analysis, 24,* 369–378.

DiCarlo, C. F., & Banajee, M. (2000). Using voice output devices to increase initiations of young children with disabilities. *Journal of Early Intervention, 23,* 191–199.

Doss, L. S., Locke, P. A., Johnston, S. S., Reichle, J., Sigafoos, J., Charpentier, P. J., & Foster, D. J. (1991). Initial comparison of the efficiency of a variety of AAC systems for order meals in fast food restaurants. *Augmentative and Alternative Communication, 7,* 256–265.

Durand, V. M. (1990). *Severe behavior problems: A functional communication training approach.* New York: Guilford Press.

Durand, V. M. (1993). Functional communication training using assistive devices: Effects on challenging behavior and affect. *Augmentative and Alternative Communication, 9,* 168–176.

Durand, V. M. (1999). Functional communication training using assistive devices: Recruiting natural communities of reinforcement. *Journal of Applied Behavior Analysis, 32,* 247–267.

Dyches, T. T. (1998). Effects of switch training on the communication of children with autism and severe disabilities. *Focus on Autism and Other Developmental Disabilities, 13,* 141–162.

Elbro, C., Rasmussen, I., & Spelling, B. (1996). Teaching reading to disabled readers with language disorders: A controlled evaluation of synthetic speech feedback. *Scandinavian Journal of Psychology*, *37*, 140–155.

Espin, C. A., & Sindelar, P. T. (1988). Auditory feedback and writing: Learning disabled and nondisabled students. *Exceptional Children*, *55*, 45–51.

Farmer, M. E., Klein, R., & Bryson, S. E. (1992). Computer-assisted reading: Effects of whole-word feedback on fluency and comprehension in readers with severe disabilities. *Remedial and Special Education*, *13*, 50–60.

Foley, B. E. (1993). The development of literacy in individuals with severe congenital speech and motor impairments. *Topics in Language Disorders*, *13*, 16–31.

Goossens', C., & Crain, S. (1986). *Augmentative communication intervention resource*. Lake Zurich, IL: Don Johnston Development Equipment.

Gorenflo, C. W., & Gorenflo, D. W. (1991). The effects of information and agumentative communication technique on attitudes toward nonspeaking individuals. *Journal of Speech and Hearing Research*, *34*, 19–34.

Gorenflo, C. W., Gorenflo, D. W., & Santer, S. A. (1994). Effects of synthetic voice output on attitudes toward the augmented communicator. *Journal of Speech and Hearing Research*, *37*, 64–68.

Greene, B. G., Manous, L. M., & Pisoni, D. B. (1984). Perceptual evaluation of DECtalk: A final report on version 1.8. In *Research on speech perception progress report no. 10*. Bloomington, IN: Speech Research Laboratory, Psychology Department, Indiana University.

Greenspan, S. L., Nusbaum, H. C., & Pisoni, D. B. (1988). Perceptual learning of synthetic speech produced by rule. *Journal of Experimental Psychology*, *3*, 421–433.

Healy, S. (1994). The use of a synthetic speech output communication aid with a youth having severe developmental disability. In K. Linfoot (Ed.), *Communication strategies for people with developmental disabilities: Issues from theory and practice* (pp. 156–176). Baltimore: Paul H. Brookes.

Hegde, M. N. (1994). *Clinical Research in Communicative Disorders: Principles and Strategies*. San Diego, CA: Singular.

Heimann, M., Nelson, K. E., Tjus, T., & Gillberg, C. (1995). Increasing reading and communication skills in children with autism through an interactive multimedia computer program. *Journal of Autism and Developmental Disorders*, *25*, 459–480.

Higginbotham, D. J., & Baird, L. (1995). Discourse analysis of listeners' summaries of synthesized speech passages. *Augmentative and Alternative Communication*, *11*, 101–112.

Higginbotham, D. J., Drazek, A. L., Kowarsky, K., Scally, C., & Segal, E. (1994). Discourse comprehension of synthetic speech delivered at normal and slow presentation rates. *Augmentative and Alternative Communication*, *10*, 191–202.

Higginbotham, D. J., Scally, C. A., Lundy, D. C., & Kowarsky, K. (1995). Discourse comprehension of synthetic speech across three augmentative and alternative communication (AAC) output methods. *Journal of Speech and Hearing Research*, *38*, 889–901.

Hoag, L., & Bedrosian, J. (1992). Effects of speech output type, message length, and reauditorization on perceptions of the communicative competence of an adult AAC user. *Journal of Speech and Hearing Research*, *35*, 1363–1366.

Hoag, L., Bedrosian, J., Johnson, D., & Molineux, B. (1994). Variables affecting perceptions of social aspects of the communicative competence of an adult AAC user. *Augmentative and Alternative Communication*, *10*, 129–137.

Hoover, J., Reichle, J., Van Tasell, D., & Cole, D. (1987). The intelligibility of synthesized speech: Echo II versus Votrax. *Journal of Speech and Hearing Research*, *30*, 425–431.

Hopper, C., & Helmick, R. (1977). Nonverbal communication and the severely handicapped: Some considerations. *AAESPH Review*, *2*, 47–53.

Horner, R. H., & Day, H. M. (1991). The effects of response efficiency on functionally equivalent competing behaviors. *Journal of Applied Behavior Analysis, 24,* 719–732.

Horner, R. H., Sprague, J. R., O'Brien, M., & Heathfield, L. (1990). The role of response efficiency in the reduction of problem behaviors through functional equivalence training: A case study. *Journal of the Association for Persons with Severe Handicaps, 15,* 91–97.

Hurlbut, B., Iwata, B., & Green, J. (1982). Non-vocal language acquisition in adolescents with severe physical disabilities: Blissymbol versus iconic stimulus formats. *Journal of Applied Behavior Analysis, 15,* 241–258.

Kintsch, W. (1988). The role of knowledge in discourse comprehension: A construction-integration model. *Psychological Review, 95,* 163–182.

Kintsch, W., & Van Dijk, T. A. (1978). Towards a model of text comprehension and production. *Psychological Review, 85,* 363–394.

Koke, S., & Neilson, J. (1987). *The effects of auditory feedback on the spelling of nonspeaking physically disabled individuals.* Unpublished master's thesis, University of Toronto, Toronto.

Koppenhaver, D. A., & Yoder, D. E. (1992). Literacy issues in persons with severe speech and physical impairments. In R. Gaylord-Ross (Ed.), *Issues and research in special education* (Vol. 2, pp. 156–201). New York: Columbia University, Teachers College Press.

Koul, R. K., & Allen, G. D. (1993). Segmental intelligibility and speech interference thresholds of high-quality synthetic speech in presence of noise. *Journal of Speech and Hearing Research, 36,* 790–798.

Koul, R. K., & Hanners, J. (1997). Word identification and sentence verification of two synthetic speech systems by individuals with intellectual disabilities. *Augmentative and Alternative Communication, 13,* 99–107.

Lancioni, G. E., O'Reilly, M. F., & Basili, G. (2001). Use of microswitches and speech output systems with people with severe/profound intellectual or multiple disabilities: A literature review. *Research in Developmental Disabilities, 22,* 21–40.

LaVigna, G. W. (1977). Communication training in mute, autistic adolescents using the written word. *Journal of Autism and Childhood Schizophrenia, 7,* 135–149.

Leong, C. K. (1992). Enhancing reading comprehension with text-to-speech (DECtalk) computer system. *Reading and Writing: An Interdisciplinary Journal, 4,* 205–217.

Lewis, R. B., Graves, A. W., Ashton, T. M., & Kieley, C. L. (1998). Word processing tools for students with learning disabilities: A comparison of strategies to increase text entry speed. *Learning Disabilities Practice, 13,* 95–108.

Lloyd, L. L., Fuller, D. R., & Arvidson, H. (1997), *Augmentative and alternative communication: A handbook of principles and practices.* Needham Heights, MA: Allyn & Bacon.

Locke, P. A., & Mirenda, P. (1988). A computer-supported communication approach for a child with severe communication, visual, and cognitive impairments: A case study. *Augmentative and Alternative Communication, 4,* 15–22.

Logan, J. S., Greene, B. G., & Pisoni, D. B. (1989). Segmental intelligibility of synthetic speech produced by rule. *Journal of the Acoustical Society of America, 86,* 566–581.

Lovett, M. W., Barron, R. W., Forbes, J. E., Cuksts, B., & Steinbach, K. A. (1994). Computer speech-based training of literacy skills in neurologically impaired children: A controlled evaluation. *Brain and Language, 47,* 117–154.

MacArthur, C. A. (1998). Word processing with speech synthesis and word prediction Effects on the dialogue journal writing of students with learning disabilities. *Learning Disabilities Quarterly, 21,* 151–166.

Manous, L. M., Pisoni, D. B., Dedina, M. J., & Nusbaum, H. C. (1985). *Comprehension of natural and synthetic speech using a sentence verification task.* (Research on Speech Perception, Progress Report No. 11). Bloomington, IN: Indiana University.

Mathy-Laikko, P., Iacono, T., Ratcliff, A., Villarruel, F., Yoder, D., & Vanderheiden, G. (1989). Teaching a child with multiple disabilities to use a tactile augmentative communication device. *Augmentative and Alternative Communication, 5*, 249–256.

McGregor, G., Young, J., Gerak, J., Thomas, B., & Vogelsberg, R. T. (1992). Increasing functional use of an assistive communication device by a student with severe disabilities. *Augmentative and Alternative Communication, 8*, 243–250.

McNaughton, D., Fallon, D., Tod, J., Weiner, F., & Neisworth, J. (1994). Effects of repeated listening experiences on the intelligibility of synthesized speech. *Augmentative and Alternative Communication, 10*, 161–168.

McNaughton, D., & Tawney, J. (1993). Comparison of two spelling instruction techniques for adults who use augmentative and alternative communication. *Augmentative and Alternative Communication, 9*, 72–73.

Millar, D., Light, J. L., & Schlosser, R. W. (2000). *The impact of augmentative and alternative communication on natural speech development: A meta-analysis.* In proceedings of the 9th biennial conference of the International Society for Augmentative and Alternative Communication (pp. 740–741). Washington, DC: ISAAC.

Mirenda, P. (1997). Supporting individuals with challenging behavior through functional communication training and AAC: A research review. *Augmentative and Alternative Communication, 13*, 207–225.

Mirenda, P., & Beukelman, D. R. (1987). A comparison of speech synthesis intelligibility with listeners from three age groups. *Augmentative and Alternative Communication, 5*, 84–88.

Mirenda, P., & Beukelman, D. R. (1990). A comparison of intelligibility among natural speech and seven speech synthesizers with listeners from three age groups. *Augmentative and Alternative Communication, 6*, 61–68.

Mitchell, P. R., & Atkins, C. P. (1989). A comparison of the single word intelligibility of two voice output communication aids. *Augmentative and Alternative Communication, 5*, 84–88.

Nakamura, K., & Arima, M. (1991). Communication aid no koukateki riyouni kansuru shinrigakuteki kenkyuu [Psychological study concerning the effective use of a communication aid]. In T. Takamatsu (Ed.), *Kouseishou heisei 2 nendo shin-shinshougai kenkyu takamatuhan chousa houkokushop* (pp. 242–246). [Report of Japanese Ministry of Health and Welfare: Studies on persons with mental and physical disabilities (Takamatsu research group) in 1991.] Tokyo: Japanese Ministry of Health and Welfare.

Nakamura, K., Arima, M., Sakamoto, A., & Toyota, R. (1993). Telephoning with a voice output device: Listener reactions. *Augmentative and Alternative Communication, 9*, 251–258.

Olson, R., Foltz, G., & Wise, B. (1986). Reading instruction and remediation with the aid of computer speech. *Behavior Research Methods, Instruments, and Computers, 18*, 93–99.

Olson, R. K., & Wise, B. (1992). Reading on the computer with orthographic and speech feedback: An overview of the Colorado remediation project. *Reading and Writing: An Interdisciplinary Journal, 4*, 107–144.

O'Neill, R. E., & Reichle, J. (1993). Addressing socially motivated challenging behavior by establishing communicative alternatives: Basics of a general-case approach. In J. Reichle & D. P. Wacker (Eds.), *Communicative alternatives to challenging behavior: Integrating functional assessment and intervention strategies* (pp. 205–235). Baltimore: Paul H. Brookes.

Paris, C. R., Gilson, R. D., Thomas, M. H., & Silver, N. C. (1995). Effect of synthetic voice on intelligibility of speech comprehension. *Human Factors, 37*, 335–340.

Parsons, C. L., & La Sorte, D. (1993). The effect of computers with synthesized speech and no speech on the spontaneous communication of children with autism. *Australian Journal of Human Communication Disorders, 21*, 12–31.

Pisoni, D. B. (1981). Speeded classification of natural and synthetic speech in a lexical decision task. *Journal of the Acoustical Society of America, 70*, S98.

Pisoni, D. B., & Hunnicutt, S. (1980). Perceptual evaluation of MITalk: The MIT unrestricted text-to-speech system. *Proceedings of the International Conference on Acoustics, Speech and Signal Processing* (pp. 572–575). New York: IEEE.

Raghavendra, P., & Allen, G. D. (1993). Comprehension of synthetic speech with three text–to–speech systems using a sentence verification paradigm. *Augmentative and Alternative Communication, 9,* 126–133.

Ralston, J. V., Pisoni, D. B., Lively, S. E., Greene, B. G., & Mullennix, J. W. (1991). Comprehension of synthetic speech produced by rule: Word monitoring and sentence-by-sentence listening times. *Human Factors, 33,* 471–491.

Ralston, J. V., Pisoni, D. B., & Mullennix, J. W. (1989). Comprehension of synthetic speech produced by rule. *Research on speech perception progress report no. 15* (pp. 77–132). Bloomington, IN: Speech Research Laboratory, Psychology Department, Indiana University.

Raskind, M. H., & Higgins, E. (1995). Effects of speech synthesis on the proofreading efficiency of postsecondary students with learning disabilities. *Learning Disabilities Quarterly, 18,* 141–158.

Reichle, J., & Sigafoos, J. (1991). Establishing an initial repertoire of requesting. In J. Reichle, J. York, & J. Sigafoos (Eds.), *Implementing augmentative and alternative communication: Strategies for learners with severe disabilities* (pp. 89–114). Baltimore: Paul H. Brookes.

Reitsma, P. (1988). Reading practice for beginners: Effects of guided reading, reading-while listening, and independent reading with computer-based speech feedback. *Reading Research Quarterly, 23,* 219–235.

Romski, M. A., & Sevcik, R. A. (1988). Augmentative and alternative communication systems: Considerations for individuals with severe intellectual disabilities. *Augmentative and Alternative Communication, 4,* 83–91.

Romski, M. A., & Sevcik, R. A. (1992a). Augmentative language comprehension and augmentative communication. *Proceedings of the consensus validation conference on augmentative and alternative communication* (pp. 49–55). Washington, DC: The National Institute on Disability and Rehabilitation Research.

Romski, M. A., & Sevcik, R. A. (1992b). Developing augmented language in children with severe mental retardation. In S. F. Warren & J. Reichle (Eds.), *Causes and effects in communication and language intervention* (pp. 113–131). Baltimore: Paul H. Brookes.

Romski, M. A., & Sevcik, R. A. (1993). Language comprehension: Considerations for augmentative and alternative communication. *Augmentative and Alternative Communication, 9,* 281–285.

Romski, M. A., & Sevcik, R. A. (1996). *Breaking the speech barrier.* Baltimore: Paul H. Brookes.

Romski, M. A., Sevcik, R. A., & Pate, J. L. (1988). Establishment of symbolic communication in persons with severe retardation. *Journal of Speech and Hearing Disorders, 53,* 94–107.

Romski, M. A., Sevcik, R. A., Robinson, B., & Wilkinson, K. M. (1990, November). *Intelligibility and form changes in the vocalizations of augmented communicators.* Presentation at the annual convention of the American Speech-Language-Hearing Association. Seattle, WA.

Rounsefell, S., Zucker, S. H., & Roberts, T. G. (1993). Effects of listener training on intelligibility of augmentative and alternative speech in the secondary classroom. *Education and Training in Mental Retardation, 12,* 296–308.

Sales, G. C. (1993). Adapted and adaptive feedback in technology-based instruction. In J. V. Dempsey & G. C. Sales (Eds.), *Interactive instruction and feedback* (pp. 159–175). Englewood Cliffs, NJ: Educational Technology.

Schepis, M. M., & Reid, D. H. (1995). Effects of a voice output communication aid on interactions between support personnel and an individual with multiple disabilities. *Journal of Applied Behavior Analysis, 28,* 73–77.

Schepis, M. M., Reid, D. H., & Behrmann, M. M. (1996). Acquisition and functional use of voice output communication by persons with profound multiple disabilities. *Behavior Modification, 20,* 451–468.

Schepis, M. M., Reid, D. H., Behrmann, M. M., & Sutton, K. A. (1998). Increasing communicative interactions of young children with autism using a voice output communication aid and naturalistic teaching. *Journal of Applied Behavior Analysis, 31*, 561–578.

Schlosser, R. W. (1997). Communication-based approaches to problem behavior: AAC considerations in intervention development. In L. L. Lloyd, D. R. Fuller, & H. Arvidson (Eds.), *Augmentative and alternative communication: A handbook of principles and practices (445–473)*. Needham Heights, MA: Allyn & Bacon.

Schlosser, R. W. (1999). Social validation of interventions in augmentative and alternative communication. *Augmentative and Alternative Communication, 15*, 234–247.

Schlosser, R. W., Belfiore, P. J., Nigam, R., Blischak, D., & Hetzroni, O. (1995). The effects of speech output technology in the learning of graphic symbols. *Journal of Applied Behavior Analysis, 28*, 537–549.

Schlosser, R. W., & Blischak, D. M. (2001). Is there a role for speech output in interventions for persons with autism? A review. *Focus on Autism and Other Developmental Disabilities, 16*, 170–178.

Schlosser, R. W., & Blischak, D. M. (2002a). *The effects of print and speech feedback from speech generating devices on spelling in learners with autism*. Manuscript under review.

Schlosser, R. W., & Blischak, D. M. (2002b). *The effects of feedback levels from speech generating devices on writing and spelling in learners with severe speech and physical impairments*. Research in preparation.

Schlosser, R. W., & Blischak, D. M. (2000c). *The effects of speech output in augmentative and alternative communication: A meta-analysis*. Research in progress.

Schlosser, R. W., Blischak, D. M., Belfiore, P. J., Bartley, C., & Barnett, N. (1998). The effects of synthetic speech output and orthographic feedback on spelling in a student with autism: A preliminary study. *Journal of Autism and Developmental Disorders, 28*, 319–329.

Schlosser, R. W., Blischak, D. M., Sigafoos, J., Ferrier, L. J., & Manuel, S. (2001–2003). *The role of speech output technology for beginning communicators*. Grant in Progress, CFDA 84.327A Steppingstones of Technology Innovation for Students with Disabilities.

Schmidt-Neilson, A. (1990). Intelligibility testing for speech technology. In R. W. Bennett, A. K. Syrdal, & S. L. Greenspan (Eds.), *Behavioral aspects of speech technology: Theory and applications*. Boca Raton, FL: CRC, 4.

Schwab, E. C., Nusbaum, H. C., & Pisoni, D. B. (1985). Some effects of training on the perception of synthetic speech. *Human Factors, 27*, 395–408.

Sevcik, R. A., Romski, M. A., Watkins, R. V., & Deffebach, K. P. (1993). *A descriptive analysis of augmented linguistic input to nonspeaking children with mental retardation*. Unpublished manuscript, Georgia State University.

Soto, G., Belfiore, P. J., Schlosser, R. W., & Haynes, C. (1993). Teaching specific requests: A comparative analysis on skill acquisition and preference using two augmentative and alternative communication aids. *Education and Training in Mental Retardation, 28*, 169–178.

Spaai, G. W. G., Reitsma, P., & Ellermann, H. H. (1991). Effects of segmented and whole-word sound feedback on learning to read single words. *Journal of Educational Research, 84*, 204–213.

Steege, M. W., Wacker, D. P., Cigrand, K. C., Berg, W. K., Novak, C. G., Reimers, T. M., Sasso, G. M., & DeRaad, A. (1990). Use of negative reinforcement in the treatment of self-injurious behavior. *Journal of Applied Behavior Analysis, 23*, 459–467.

Steelman, J. D., Pierce, P. L., & Koppenhaver, D. A. (1993). The role of computers in promoting literacy in children with severe speech and physical impairments (SSPI). *Topics in Language Disorders, 13*, 76–88.

Udwin, O. (1987). Analysis of the experimental adequacy of alternative and augmentative communication training studies. *Child Language Teaching and Therapy, 3*, 18–39.

VanAcker, R., & Grant, S. H. (1995). An effective computer-based requesting system for persons with Rett syndrome. *Journal of Childhood Communication Disorders, 16*, 31–38.

Venkatagiri, H. S. (1994). Effect of sentence length and exposure on the intelligibility of synthesized speech. *Augmentative and Alternative Communication, 10,* 96–104.

Wacker , D. P., Steege, M. W., Northrup, J., Sasso, G., Berg, W., Reimers, T., Cooper, L., Cigrand, K., & Donn, L. (1990). A component analysis of functional communication training across three topographies ofsevere behavior problems. *Journal of Applied Behavior Analysis, 23,* 417–429.

Willis, L., Koul, R. K., & Paschall, D. P. (2000). Discourse comprehension of synthetic speech by individuals with mental retardation. *Education and Training in Mental Retardation and Developmental Disabilities, 35,* 106–114.

Wise, B. (1987). *Word segmentation in computerized reading instruction.* Unpublished doctoral dissertation, University of Colorado at Boulder.

Wise, B. (1992). Whole words and decoding for short-term learning: Comparisons on a "talking-computer" system. *Journal of Experimental Child Psychology, 54,* 147–167.

Wise, B., Olson, R. K., Anstett, M., Andrews, L., Terjak, M., Schneider, V., Kostuch, J., & Kriho, L. (1989). Implementing a long-term computerized remedial reading program with synthetic speech feedback. *Behaviour Research Methods, Instruments, and Computers, 21,* 173–180.

Wise, B., Olson, R. K., & Treiman, R. (1990). Subsyllabic units in computerized reading instruction: Onset-rime vs. Post-vowel segmentation. *Journal of Experimental Child Psychology, 24,* 1–19.

CHAPTER 20

Evidence-Based Strategies for Promoting Generalization and Maintenance

Ralf W. Schlosser
Department of Speech-Language
 Pathology and Audiology
Northeastern University

David Lee
Department of Educational
 and School Psychology
 and Special Education
Penn State University

I. INTRODUCTION

Individuals who use augmentative and alternative communication (AAC) have been observed to demonstrate difficulty generalizing newly acquired skills to contexts other than those involved in training (Calculator, 1988). Due to this observed difficulty with generalization, interest in AAC has shifted from determining what types of strategies produce changes in targeted communicative behavior to determining the strategies that produce generalizable and lasting changes (Calculator, 1988; Light, 1999; Reichle & Sigafoos, 1991; Schlosser & Braun, 1994). This shift is consistent with recent changes in the field of communication disorders at large (Hughes, 1985; Spradlin, 1989) and related fields such as special education and applied behavior analysis (Baer, Wolf, & Risley, 1987; Fox,

The Efficacy of Augmentative and Alternative Communication

1989; Haring, 1988; Rutherford & Nelson, 1988; Scruggs & Mastropieri, 1994; Stokes & Osnes, 1988; White *et al.*, 1988). Authors across these fields agree that generalization and maintenance must be actively promoted through the application of appropriate strategies from the onset of the intervention process rather than merely assessed post facto. Also, different implications must be drawn if generalization or maintenance occurs (or fails to occur) as a function of doing nothing (i.e., "train and hope") as opposed to applying a strategy (e.g., "train sufficient exemplars"). It therefore becomes vital to systematically identify strategies that effectively promote generalization and maintenance. That is, maintenance and generalization must become not only major dependent variables, but also the strategies used to promote maintenance and generalization must be examined as crucial independent variables (Stokes & Osnes, 1988).

II. STATUS OF THE EXISTING EVIDENCE BASE

Such an examination was the purpose of a recent synthesis of 51 single-subject experimental AAC intervention studies published between 1976 and 1995—that is, the authors aimed to determine which strategies are effective in promoting generalization and maintenance (Schlosser & Lee, 2000). Results from this synthesis revealed, however, that the breadth of strategies available has been largely untapped and "train and hope" approaches continue to be overused. To be exact, "train and hope" was used in 91.2% of all data series (Schlosser & Lee, 2000). In fact, strategies such as "train sufficient exemplars," "sequential modification," "modification of the environment," "train to generalize," "indiscriminable contingencies," "reinforce unprompted generalization," and "mediate generalization" were not used at all in this data set. This post facto evaluation of generalization is in sharp contrast to best practices proposed for AAC intervention (Calculator, 1988; Reichle, 1997; Reichle & Sigafoos, 1991; Schlosser & Braun, 1994). In addition, a large number of studies used generalization or maintenance designs that do not lend themselves to an unequivocal demonstration of generalization or maintenance effectiveness. This unfortunate practice rendered an analysis into the relative effectiveness of various strategies premature as well. For appropriate design strategies for generalization and maintenance, see Chapter 6.

Given this status of the evidence base, it is premature to herald individual strategies as the most effective strategies. More appropriately, this calls for training of evidence-based practitioners and researchers alike in (1) the breadth of available strategies, (2) how these strategies may be incorporated into treatment planning, and (3) evaluation procedures to empirically validate the efficacy of the various strategies. In this chapter the repertoire of strategies and their potential role in intervention planning and implementation is illustrated through vignettes of published examples.

III. STRATEGIES TO PROMOTE GENERALIZATION AND MAINTENANCE

Strategies to promote generalization may be applied individually—that is, one at a time—or combined using multiple strategies. First, the spectrum of available single strategies is described before moving onto the use of combined strategies.

A. SINGLE STRATEGIES

Single strategies for promoting generalization and maintenance may be grouped into those affecting (1) settings, (2) consequences, (3) antecedents, and (4) others. Table 20.1 presents an overview of strategies associated with

Table 20.1

Strategies to Promote Generalization[a]

Strategies affecting settings
- Natural settings ✓
- Sequential modification
- Modification of the environment

Strategies affecting consequences
- Introduce to natural maintaining contingencies ✓
- Indiscriminable contingencies
- Train to generalize
- Reinforce unprompted generalization

Strategies affecting antecedents
- Program common stimuli ✓
- Train sufficient exemplars
- Multiple exemplars ✓
- General case programming

Other strategies
- Train loosely
- Mediate generalization
- Functional equivalence training (N/A)

[a]Taken from Schlosser and Braun (1994). The strategies listed and the definitions thereof (see Appendix B) were derived from readings of recent generalization literature (e.g., Calculator, 1988; Carr, 1988; Chadsey-Rusch & Halle, 1992; Haring, 1988; Stokes & Osnes, 1988; White et al., 1988).

✓ These strategies were represented in the synthesis of AAC interventions studies (Schlosser & Lee, 2000).

N/A Communication-based approaches to problem behavior were not included in Schlosser and Lee (2000).

these four groupings along with an indication as to whether a given strategy has been represented in original research as reviewed by Schlosser and Lee (2000).

1. Strategies Affecting Settings

It is essential that acquired communication skills can be used in multiple settings if they are to be truly useful for it is rare that communicative functions are tied to only one setting. For instance, a child may want to comment on a book during story reading time in school and before going to sleep at home. Alternatively, a child may want to make choices in the school cafeteria, during story time in school, at the fast-food restaurant, and in the toy store. Thus, it becomes critical to explore ways for promoting generalization across settings. At least three strategies have been documented in the literature, which are aimed at promoting setting generalization: (1) training in natural settings, (2) sequential modification, and (3) modification of the environment.

a. Training in Natural Settings

Training in natural settings was one of the few strategies represented in the synthesis of generalization and maintenance studies (Schlosser & Lee, 2000). With this strategy, the training or generalization occurs in a setting where the response can be normally expected to occur. That is, training is conducted directly in at least one type of setting in which the skill will be used. Generalization is then probed in other nontraining settings. To understand some concepts more readily, it may help to first envision how intervention with the opposite strategy (i.e., training in a contrived setting) would look like. One of the authors remembers a visit to a state institution where the administration proudly showed the visitors a simulated "cafeteria" where, so the administration believed, the residents could safely learn to place an order, deal with money, and practice people skills before applying these skills in the community. This approach ignores the fact that many social and nonsocial stimuli differ between the simulated cafeteria and the actual cafeteria in the community, including noise level, familiarity of the sales clerk with people with disabilities, and furniture, to name but a few. These differences may make it very difficult for some people with severe disabilities to generalize to the natural environment. Therefore, the strategy "train in natural settings" assumes that it would be more effective to go straight into the community and teach these skills while probing for generalization in other community settings. An example from the published intervention literature follows. For other examples, the reader may consult studies such as those by Alwell, Hunt, Goetz, and Sailor (1989) and Schepis and Reid (1995).

> Three high school students with severe disabilities were taught to initiate and maintain a conversation independently with a communication book. Instruction occurred across a variety of school settings with several regular education students serving as communication partners. Conversation initiation and turn-taking skills generalized to opportunities in other settings (Hunt, Alwell, Goetz, & Sailor, 1990).

b. Sequential Modification

Sequential modification may be thought off as a sequence of "train and hope" applied to different settings. Training is provided in one setting, and generalization is probed in other settings. If necessary, training is conducted sequentially in more and more settings until generalization to all desired settings is observed. In general, the methodology is as follows: training in setting 1, no generalization in setting 2, training in setting 2, no generalization in setting 3, training in setting 3, and so on. This strategy does not seem to stipulate whether or not the training settings need to be a natural setting or a contrived setting. Even though there are similarities, there is a difference between a typical train and hope approach to generalization and sequential modification. The difference is that in a typical train and hope approach, training would not be conducted in successively more settings until generalization is observed. The authors were unable to locate a published AAC example using sequential modification. Therefore a fictitious example was developed instead.

> A student with severe intellectual disabilities needed training in using a speech-generating device (SGD) for everyday conversation in the cafeteria, playground, and at home before generalizing to all remaining settings of interest. A second student only required training in two situations before generalizing.

c. Modification of the Environment

This third strategy affecting settings refers to the modification of environments to both decrease inappropriate behaviors and increase appropriate behaviors in different settings. If the features in the environment that naturally maintain inappropriate behavior are discontinued or limited in some way, then the inappropriate behavior should decrease in frequency. Appropriate behavior in non-training settings may be increased through the following modification strategies: (1) arranging the physical environment so that there is a need for a communication skill to occur (e.g., Sigafoos, 1999), (2) reducing anticipation of the child's needs and provision of desired objects on the part of the instructor (Calculator, 1988), and (3) reducing the use of prompts without giving a chance for the subject to perform (Halle, Baer, & Spradlin, 1981).

> The missing-item format involves the withholding of one or more items needed to complete or engage in a preferred activity (Sigafoos, 1999). At the point in

an activity when the item is needed, the learner is required to request the missing item through an appropriate communicative response. The instructor supplies prompting on an as-needed basis. It is possible that generalization of the same requesting response in other settings is facilitated without the provision of prompts.

2. Strategies Affecting Consequences

Strategies affecting consequences include (1) introducing the learner to naturally maintaining consequences, (2) teaching the learner to recognize indiscriminable contingencies, (3) training the learner to generalize, and (4) reinforcing unprompted generalization.

a. Introducing Naturally Maintaining Consequences

This strategy refers to bringing the learner into contact with naturally occurring contingencies. This may be accomplished by teaching the learner to actively recruit reinforcers available in the environment or teaching behaviors or functional skills that are likely to come into contact with reinforcing consequences in natural settings not directly programmed during intervention. For example, a learner may be taught to actively solicit feedback by asking, "How am I doing?" This attention likely serves as a positive reinforcer. An example of teaching functional skills that are likely to come into contact with reinforcing consequences in natural settings is provided next. For other examples of this strategy, the reader may consult the work of other researchers such as Gobbi, Cipani, Hudson, and Lapenta-Neudeck (1986); Rotholz, Berkowitz, and Burberry (1989); and Locke and Mirenda (1988).

> Three teens with multiple disabilities were taught to use graphic symbols to request objects. Generalization was encouraged by using objects in training that would be regularly encountered outside instruction, making sure the boys always carried their communication boards and that someone would always be present to provide any requested items (Hurlbut, Iwata, & Green, 1982).

This selection of objects, which would be regularly encountered outside instruction, clearly fits the strategy of naturally maintaining contingencies. The other components of these procedures, however, warrant some commentary. Teaching the boys to carry their communication boards is not part of this generalization strategy per se, but a function of using an aided AAC system as opposed to an unaided system. To make this strategy with an aided system work, the boys needed to be sure to carry their board or else they had no intelligible way of communicating their requests. The last component, making sure that someone always is present to provide a requested item, is not part of this generalization strategy either. In fact, one may argue that the consistent presence of someone contradicts the term "natural contingencies"; at the very least, it is not realistic to expect that there is always going to be someone to acknowledge requests of the items. This procedural component is necessitated when introducing a pointing-based aided system such as the communication board as opposed to an exchange-based aided system such as the Picture Exchange Communication System (Bondy & Frost, 1994) or an unaided approach such as manual signing. As discussed in Chapter 14, the Picture Exchange Communication System is possibly effective because an exchange can only take place when someone is present. Thus, the learner does not need to be taught to recruit the attention of a communication partner before making the request. This is not to say, however, that Hurlbut *et al.* (1982) should have introduced manual signs or the Picture Exchange Communication System instead of the communication board. Rather, this highlights important instructional considerations when introducing a learner to naturally maintaining contingencies with pointing-based systems. Perhaps, this approach would be more successful if the learners were taught to first draw attention from a communication partner, such as by using a buzzer or by fading out the presence of communication partners.

b. Recognizing Indiscriminable Contingencies

With this strategy, consequences are programmed so that the learner is unable to discriminate when and in what settings a response will be reinforced, as under intermittent schedules of reinforcement or under schedules of delayed reinforcement. In general, resistance to extinction (generalization over time) is the theoretical basis for this approach. As such, this strategy appears to be uniquely suited to promote maintenance rather than generalization. Unfortunately, this strategy was not represented in the data set of the meta-analysis (Schlosser & Lee, 2000) nor could we find a published AAC example elsewhere. Perhaps, the following fictitious example, adapted from Fowler and Baer (1981), may stimulate interest in this technique so that researchers and evidence-based practitioners may begin to explore its merits.

> Two learners who use AAC and two nondisabled peers always maintained their interaction skills better when verbal praise and teacher feedback was provided after progressively greater delays, rather than immediately following each behavior.

c. Training to Generalize

With this strategy, reinforcement during intervention occurs only for performing some generalized instance of the target skill. Performing a previously reinforced version of a response is no longer reinforced. Thus, in the beginning of the intervention cycle, a reinforcer is delivered when the learner performs targeted skills. After some time into the intervention cycle, the instructor only reinforces the nontargeted skills. The underlying logic of this strategy is based on the assumption that the performance of the generalized behavior is susceptible to reinforcement. Thus, by providing reinforcement only for generalized responses, the learner is more likely to produce these responses—the learner is "trained to generalize." The following example of the train to generalize strategy is applied to a study by Nigam (1999), who taught three children with intellectual disabilities the acquisition and generalized production of two-term semantic relationships using a matrix-training strategy and the mand-model procedure. A multiple-baseline design across sets of action-object combinations with generalization probes of untrained combinations was used to evaluate the production of graphic symbol combinations. Two of the participants learned the early syntactic-semantic rule of combining action-object symbols and demonstrated generalization to untrained action-object combinations.

> Three students with intellectual disabilities were taught action-object combinations using graphic symbols. In the beginning, the selection behavior of students was reinforced only for the combinations targeted during intervention. Later into the training program, reinforcers were delivered only if the students correctly produced untrained action-object combinations. Correct production of taught combinations was no longer reinforced (adapted from Nigam, 1999).

d. Reinforcing Unprompted Generalization

Sometimes generalization will occur without any reason that can be readily discerned at that time. If this happens, the reinforce unprompted generalization strategy calls for the provision of reinforcement for this spontaneous or unprompted display of generalization. In other words, unprompted generalization is reinforced like any other target behavior. Even though this strategy is similar to the train to generalize strategy, there are at least two important differences. First, in the train to generalize strategy, reinforcement is reserved for the generalized behavior, whereas with this strategy both target and generalized behaviors are reinforced. Second, the reinforce unprompted generalization strategy appears to be applicable outside the teaching and testing context, whereas the train to generalize strategy is restricted to the reinforcement of generalized behavior within the confines of a given context. The following hypothetical example illustrates the reinforce unprompted generalization strategy:

> Three students were taught to request materials for a leisure activity using an SGD. On occasion, one of the students requested materials for which he had not been taught the graphic symbol. The instructor reinforced this spontaneous generalization by providing the requested item.

3. Strategies Affecting Antecedents

Strategies affecting antecedents include (1) programming common stimuli, (2) training sufficient exemplars, (3) training multiple exemplars, and (4) general case instruction.

a. Programming Common Stimuli

This strategy involves the selection of a salient, but not necessarily task-related, stimulus from the situation to which generalization is desired and including that stimulus in the training program. Common stimuli may be physical or social in nature. The availability of physical stimuli (e.g., furniture) during both intervention and generalization situations may serve as a discriminative function because they assume a salient role in intervention. Available common social stimuli may also have discriminative properties to facilitate generalization. For example, the presence of the peers (from the situation to which generalization is desired) might trigger generalization.

> Three girls with Rett syndrome were trained by a teacher to use a computer-based SGD system to request food items during snack time in the classroom. Generalization across settings and persons was tested in a different setting (i.e., the lunchroom or the home) by nondisabled peers and the participants' mothers, respectively. The equipment to be used during generalization was programmed as common stimuli as it was consistent across intervention and generalization phases (Van Acker & Grant, 1995).

b. Training Sufficient Exemplars

This strategy is similar to "sequential modification." Whereas sequential modification is concerned with settings, this strategy is concerned with stimuli. Stimuli exemplars are sequentially added to the training program and generalization is consistently monitored. The adding of exemplars continues until generalization to all related stimuli occurs. Anderson and Spradlin (1980) offered an example of this strategy from the field of applied behavior analysis. In their study, an adolescent with severe disabilities was taught to name objects, and probed with other objects from the same class. Some objects required only a single exemplar to produce generalized naming, while other objects required five exemplars before generalization occurred. The following fictitious example illustrates the potential application of this strategy in AAC interventions.

> A student with severe disabilities was taught to request objects (e.g., cups) and was probed with other objects from the same class (e.g., different cups). Some objects required only a single exemplar to produce generalized requesting, whereas other objects required five exemplars before generalization occurred.

c. Training Multiple Exemplars

Several examples of the stimulus or response class (e.g., several examples of plural usage) to which generalization is desired are trained concurrently. Whereas the train sufficient exemplars strategy involves the sequential introduction of stimuli, this strategy involves concurrent training of multiple exemplars. Some-

times, negative training exemplars are used to teach correct responses in generalization contexts. This strategy was successfully applied by Hunt *et al.* (1990) as
follows:

> Three high school students with severe disabilities were taught to initiate
> and maintain a conversation independently with a communication book. Instruction
> occurred with several nondisabled students serving as partners across a variety of school
> settings. Initiation and turn-taking skills generalized to opportunities with partners not
> included in the instructional sessions.

d. General Case Instruction

According to Horner, Sprague, and Wilcox (1982), there are six basic steps
to general case instruction: (1) define the instructional universe, (2) define the
range of variation within that universe, (3) select examples from the universe for
use in teaching and testing, (4) sequence teaching examples, (5) teach the examples, and (6) test with the generalization examples.

With general case instruction, the universe to which generalization is
desired is analyzed and representative examples of positive stimuli (stimuli in the
presence of which the skill should be used), negative stimuli (stimuli in the presence of which the skill should not be used), and irrelevant stimuli (stimuli that
should not affect skill use but might inappropriately do so) are selected for training. The idea is to assess various settings for common elements and then teach
them to the common denominator. This is by far the most systematic generalization strategy, and it is therefore heralded as the most effective strategy by
researchers in the field of severe disabilities (Chadsey-Rusch & Halle, 1992;
O'Neill, 1990; O'Neill, Faulkner, & Horner, 2000) and the AAC field (Feely &
Johnston, 2000; Reichle, 1997; Reichle & Johnston, 1999). In the AAC field, this
strategy has received only limited attention as far as its application in research is
concerned (Reichle & Johnston, 1999) and was absent from the data set reviewed
by Schlosser and Lee (2000). The following published example illustrates the use
of general case instruction:

> Two students with severe disabilities were taught to request desired items by
> (1) touching a graphic symbol when the item was out of reach (*positive stimuli*) and
> (2) reaching for the items when they were in close proximity (*negative stimuli*).
> Generalization across untrained activities including untrained items was monitored
> (Reichle & Johnston, 1999).

Feely and Johnston (2000) illustrated the importance of teaching both
positive and negative exemplars in research completed by one of the authors. Five
young children were taught to request access to preferred items using graphic
symbols. During baseline, probes were conducted to evaluate pre-intervention
performance with positive stimuli (i.e., opportunities in which it was appropriate
to emit the requesting response), with negative stimuli (i.e., opportunities in which

it was inappropriate to perform the requesting response—the item was in close proximity and accessible), and irrelevant stimuli (i.e., opportunities where it was unclear whether or not the response should be emitted). Initially, the children were taught only with the positive stimuli while generalization to negative and irrelevant stimuli was continuously monitored. It turns out that three of the five learners generalized well based on the teaching of positive stimuli only. Up to this point, this is very similar to the strategy of teaching multiple exemplars discussed earlier. After all, with the multiple exemplar strategy, only positive exemplars are selected. However, two learners failed to acquire a generalized response. Specifically, they performed the requesting response when the item was directly in front of them. As a result of this failure to generalize, the two students were directly taught to refrain from selecting the graphic symbol and self-select the item. Subsequently, these two learners generalized well to nontraining stimuli. From this research it seems appropriate to extrapolate that some learners may benefit from the systematic teaching of the universe to which generalization is desired (i.e., general case instruction), whereas other learners might generalize based on a multiple exemplar strategy.

These examples are illustrations of general case instruction whereby learners were introduced to positive stimuli and negative stimuli. Sometimes, however, it may be essential to show learners how to communicate when confronted with irrelevant stimuli as described in the following fictitious example:

> Three students with severe disabilities using a multimodal AAC system, consisting of manual signing and a communication display, were taught with whom to use manual signs and with whom to rely on the communication display. They were taught with representative examples of *positive stimuli* (i.e., familiar partners who are known to understand sign), *negative stimuli* (i.e., strangers), and *irrelevant stimuli* (familiar partners representing people who have known the students for various periods of time). Generalization to stimuli that were not part of training were tested.

4. Other Strategies

Finally, there is a group of strategies that cannot be readily assigned to any of the previous groups of strategies. It includes (1) training loosely, (2) mediating generalization, and (3) functional equivalence training.

a. Training Loosely

Settings, cues, prompts, materials, response definition, and other features of the teaching situation are purposely varied to avoid a ritual, highly structured, invariant program, which might inhibit generalization. This would include making antecedents less discriminable by purposefully introducing variety into the conditions of instruction so the person will not readily identify performance with a particular set of conditions or circumstances. This strategy is somewhat difficult to fathom, but as a general guideline, the train loosely strategy establishes "structure within chaos." In other words, the variations are not an accident but are premeditated. Typically, authors would claim that they have applied this approach if a generalization strategy was not identified a priori for a given study. Perhaps, the following hypothetical example will illustrate this approach:

> In teaching a beginning communicator to request objects and activities, the experimenter varied not only the objects and activities, but also the use of strategies to create opportunities for requesting (e.g., missing-item) and the application of the least-to-most prompting hierarchy. In terms of strategies, the missing-item format would be used sometimes, and the interrupted chain strategy would be used at other times. In terms of the prompting hierarchy, the level of intrusiveness of prompts would be varied and the length of pause time increased.

b. Mediating Generalization

This strategy involves introducing a physical stimulus or the teaching of a secondary behavior to help a learner remember or figure out how and when to generalize. Self-mediated physical stimuli are maintained and transported by the learner, such as the use of a sequence chart. Students may be taught how to self-instruct via a picture sequence. This self-instruction skill may then be used for other activities. Wacker and Berg (1983) used this approach with five adolescents with moderate or severe intellectual disabilities who were taught to self-instruct task completion using a picture sequence. The learners then used the self-instruction skill to generalize completion of a new task with a new picture sequence card. This example was adapted to AAC as follows:

> The three students with severe disabilities who were taught when to use manual signing via general case instruction (noted earlier) were also taught to follow a picture checklist. This picture chart was designed to assist the students in making an appropriate decision as to whether or not to use manual signing with partners who were not part of training.

c. Functional Equivalence Training

Functional equivalence training involves the teaching of an alternate response class that serves the same function as the original response class in order to induce response generalization. Although the response classes may be quite distinct topographically (e.g., verbal and motor classes of behavior), they function similarly in that they elicit the same reinforcers. This strategy is prominent in communication-based approaches to problem behavior, an example of which is presented as follows (Durand, 1993).

> Michelle's problem behavior was determined to serve an escape and attention-getting function. Using an SGD, she was taught to request "I want to be with the group" rather than engaging in problem behavior.

Functional equivalence training, however, is not limited to the management of problem behavior. Functional equivalence training also bears importance when the evidence-based practitioner wishes to replace an existing communication mode with another mode that is believed to be more conventional or more readily understood by communication partners. This may be the case when moving a child, who is a beginning communicator, from presymbolic to symbolic modes (see Chapter 14). An example of this application of functional equivalence training is provided as follows:

> Natalie, a learner with Rett syndrome, was observed to request preferred objects directly in front of her by reaching toward them. The intervention goal was to map a new form onto this prelinguistic requesting function. As she reached for the item, her outstretched hand was gently guided down to the table to press a BIG-mack™ switch, which produced the recorded message "*I want that*." Each time she reached, she was prompted to press the switch. With each new reach, the amount of prompting was faded and she very quickly came to press the switch independently without first reaching for the object. When she had pressed the switch, she was given the offered item (Sigafoos, 2000).

In the preceding example, the reaching for the object and the depressing of the switch were functionally equivalent in providing Natalie access to preferred objects. The effectiveness of the generalization strategy hinges on the response efficiency of the alternative response (Horner & Day, 1991). Response efficiency needs to be a major consideration for interventionists when planning for response generalization via functional equivalence training. To compete with problem behaviors or existing prelinguistic communicative forms, the alternative response needs to be more efficient in terms of the following variables: (1) the physical effort required to perform the response (the calories of energy expended), (2) the schedule of reinforcement (i.e., the number of appropriate responses required to yield reinforcement), and (3) the time delay between presentation of the discriminative stimulus for a target response and delivery of the reinforcer for that response (Horner & Day, 1991; Horner, Sprague, O'Brien, & Heathfield, 1990; Lim, Browder, & Sigafoos, 1998).

B. COMBINED STRATEGIES

The single strategies described here may also be combined to promote generalization and maintenance. Similar to the use of single strategies, the use of multiple strategies was underexamined in the data set reviewed by Schlosser and Lee (2000). An exception was the study by Hunt, Alwell, and Goetz (1991):

Even though Hunt *et al.* (1991) used a combination of "train in the natural environment" and "multiple exemplars" to promote generalization to other settings and partners, they noticed that generalization was limited until they also involved some partner training. This illustrates the transactional nature of the interaction process.

The use of combined strategies may be essential when the intervention targets generalization across multiple dimensions, as is the case in the previous example. Hunt *et al.* (1991) targeted generalization across settings and generalization across partners. These interventionists had the option of addressing both dimensions through a single strategy such as the train loosely strategy or to consider multiple strategies such as the train in the natural environment strategy to promote generalization across settings and the multiple exemplars strategy to promote generalization to other partners.

IV. INTEGRATING STRATEGIES INTO INTERVENTION PLANNING

If researchers and evidence-based practitioners are to utilize the preceding information in a meaningful manner, it is essential that these strategies be incorporated into intervention planning. For efficacy researchers, the intervention planning process entails formulating a research question (see Chapter 4), selecting an adequate experimental design (see Chapters 6 to 8), and determining and implementing procedures (see Chapter 12). Intervention planning for the practitioner typically involves goal setting, ensuring accountability, and delivering instruction (Zangari & Kangas, 1997). Some of the phases involved in research parallel those in practice such as goal setting and formulating a research question. Therefore, they will be discussed together.

A. Determine Where You Want to Go

To promote generalization and maintenance from the onset of intervention through the application of appropriate strategies, goals and objectives need to be written that reflect these desired outcomes. In school settings, the following statement summarizes the beliefs of some practitioners pertaining to goals: "If its not written in the Individual Education Plan, it won't get done." So if we want to ensure that generalization and maintenance are promoted from the onset, expectations for generalization and maintenance need to be made explicit in the goals and objectives themselves.

Based on the work of several authors (Mirenda, Iacono, & Williams, 1990; Rainforth, York, & MacDonald, 1992), Zangari and Kangas (1997) established eight criteria to guide practitioners in developing AAC goals. Accordingly, any targeted AAC goal should meet one or more of these criteria: (1) maintain health and vitality, (2) enhance participation in current and future integrated environments, (3) increase social integration (especially with peers), (4) have frequent or multiple applications across environments and activities, (5) be essential for further development, (6) be a priority for the client, (7) be a family priority, (8) be a priority of significant people in the target environment. Criterion 4 opens the door for stating goals that integrate generalization expectations. An example toward that end is provided by Calculator and Jorgenson (1994, p. 71):

> **Goal:** Within real-life situations such as choosing food in the lunchroom, selecting books in the library, or picking friends to be on his team in gym, Josh will make a choice among three offerings.

> **Objective:** When presented with a natural cue and a gestural prompt across various settings (e.g., the server asking him what he wants for hot lunch, and if he doesn't choose the server pointing to the various choices), Josh will point to a choice (from among three) within the time limit given other students. This will be measured by observations across at least three settings and by interviewing peers and teachers.

This goal and objective emphasizes the importance of choice making being applicable across a variety of settings (i.e., the lunchroom, library, and gym) and various communication partners (i.e., the server in the lunchroom, the librarian, and peers in the gym). As such, this goal and objective sets the stage for inducing generalization via the use of appropriate strategies. Even though the goal and objective do not explicitly state there is an expectation for generalization, one can assume that the evidence-based practitioner will want to avoid having to teach the choice-making skill in each of these situations. Rather, the practitioner is likely going to look out for opportunities to maximize instructional efficiency by programming for generalization across settings and partners. To do so, the practitioner will have to consult available strategies and determine which ones to use (see the following discussion).

Similar to the setting of goals in practice, efficacy researchers formulate research questions (see Chapter 4). If generalization or maintenance are to be proactively induced, they have to be considered when formulating a research question. A typical research question related to the preceding goal may read as follows: What are the effects of milieu teaching on choice making in a child with little or no functional speech? This question does not demand any exploration of generalization or maintenance. In fact, it only requires the researcher to evaluate the effects of an intervention in terms of behavior change—that is, the taught behavior of choice making in the situation in which it was taught. If generalization, for example, is indeed desired, a more fruitful research question might read as follows: What are the effects of milieu teaching on choice making in trained situations and generalization to untrained situations? That way, it is clear that generalization is a focus of this investigation and needs to be taken into account in all phases of intervention planning such as choosing an appropriate design (see the following discussion). Other workers have taken this one step further and advocated that generalization or maintenance strategies become independent variables themselves and need to be investigated as such (Stokes & Osnes, 1988). A research question along these lines might read as follows: What are the effects of introducing a learner to naturally maintaining contingencies on choice making in training and nontraining situations?

B. Ensure the Source of Generalization/ Maintenance Outcomes

If generalization or maintenance are indeed a desired outcome, appropriate steps need to be taken that allow evidence-based practitioners and researchers alike to evaluate whether these outcomes have been attained. In practice, the area of outcomes measurement has received increasing attention in recent years. This section is not intended to summarize outcomes measurement issues in general. For information about and discussion of outcomes measurement, the reader may consult any of the following references: Granlund & Blackstone (1999) or Schlosser (in press). For the purposes of this chapter, accountability is possible when data are being collected not only on the acquisition of a target behavior, but also on its maintenance after training is discontinued or when the behavior generalized to untrained conditions. Practitioners who, for example, use goal attainment scaling to measure outcomes (see Schlosser, 2002) need to develop scales not only for the acquisition and maintenance of targeted behaviors, but also for generalized responding. Practitioners may also want to consider collecting direct data such as observations *and* indirect data such as interviews from relevant stakeholders to document the extent of generalization and maintenance. Ultimately, accountability is only ensured when threats to internal validity for generalization and maintenance outcomes are minimized. To do so, evidence-based practitioners need to select adequate designs that allow them to attribute observed generalization/maintenance outcomes to the AAC intervention rather than to extraneous variables. Chapter 6 offers a complete appraisal of the various design options available to those who employ single-subject experimental designs.

C. Implement Instruction

Generalization or maintenance strategies need to be implemented as part of other instructional procedures (Zangari & Kangas, 1997). Relative to the previously stated objective for Josh, generalization strategies could be used as part of milieu teaching procedures. In the example, it is important to realize that the settings and communication partners in this example are systematically linked to one another. The librarian goes with the library, the server with the lunchroom, and so on. Therefore, any strategy to be used cannot rely on varying only one dimension at a time (e.g., only the setting). Among the available strategies, a combination of training in natural settings and sequential modification seems to be a plausible solution. It would make sense to pursue training in a setting where choice making is expected to be performed (i.e., the lunchroom) rather than in a simulated environment. During training in a natural setting, the interventionist would most likely provide additional prompts beyond those offered naturally by the respective communication partners. Using time delay, these prompts would be gradually faded so that the choice-making response is brought under the control of the natural prompts. Sequential modification would call for the probing of generalized choice making in nontraining settings such as the library and the gym. Should Josh fail to provide a choice-making response in the library and gym, the evidence-based practitioner would teach choice making in the library next and probe in the gym, and so on. An alternative to sequential modification, which is essentially a sequence of the train and hope strategy, would be to train in multiple settings before probing for generalization, analogous to the multiple exemplar strategy used for various stimuli.

To ensure that the generalization or maintenance strategies are implemented as planned, treatment integrity checks need to be conducted for those procedural steps just like for the other instructional procedures. If, for example, the multiple exemplars strategy is used to teach choice making in multiple settings, the interventionist would want to make sure that the learner was indeed presented with choice-making opportunities in multiple settings according to the treatment plan. For further discussion on treatment integrity, the reader may consult Chapter 9.

V. SUMMARY

A host of strategies have been purported to promote generalization or maintenance of behavioral interventions. In AAC, a synthesis revealed that these strategies have been severely underutilized. The few studies in which such strategies were employed often failed to demonstrate unequivocally that generalization/maintenance outcomes are the result of AAC intervention. In light of the current evidence base, it is premature to recommend one strategy over another. Instead it is critical that evidence-based practitioners and researchers alike are aware of the range of these strategies and begin to build them into intervention planning. This chapter was intended to be useful toward that end. General case instruction appears to be the most comprehensive strategy and holds considerable promise, which it is hoped will be realized as more databased applications in AAC become available.

REFERENCES

Alwell, M., Hunt, P., Goetz, & Sailor, W. (1989). Teaching generalized communicative behaviors within interrupted behavior chain contexts. *Journal of the Association for the Severely Handicapped, 14,* 91–100.

Anderson, S. R., & Spradlin, J. E. (1980). The generalized effects of productive labeling training involving common object classes. *Journal of the Association for the Severely Handicapped, 5,* 143–157.

Baer, D. M., Wolf, M. M., & Risley, T. R. (1987). Some still current dimensions of applied behavior analysis. *Journal of Applied Behavior Analysis, 20,* 313–327.

Bondy, A. S., & Frost, L. A. (1994). The Picture Exchange Communication System. *Focus on Autistic Behavior, 9,* 1–19.

Calculator, S. N. (1988). Promoting the acquisition and generalization of conversational skills by individuals with severe disabilities. *Augmentative and Alternative Communication, 4,* 94–103.

Calculator, S. N., & Jorgenson, C. M. (Eds.) (1994). *Including students with severe disabilities in schools* (pp. 183–214). San Diego, CA: Singular.

Carr, E. G. (1988). Functional equivalence as a mechanism of response generalization. In R. H. Horner, G. Dunlap, & R. L. Koegel (Eds.). *Generalization and maintenance: Life-style changes in applied settings* (pp. 221–241). Baltimore: Paul H. Brookes.

Chadsey-Rusch, J., & Halle, J. (1992). The application of general case instruction to the requesting repertoires of learners with severe disabilities. *Journal of the Association for Persons with Severe Handicaps, 17,* 121–132.

Durand, V. M. (1993). Functional communication training using assistive devices: Effects on challenging behavior and affect. *Augmentative and Alternative Communication, 9,* 168–176.

Feely, K., & Johnston, S. (2000). Addressing generalization in AAC interventions. *Proceedings of ISAAC 2000, The Ninth Biennial Conference of the International Society for Augmentative and Alternative Communication* (pp. 38–39). Washington, DC: ISAAC.

Fowler, S., & Baer, D. M. (1981). Do I have to be good all day? The timing of delayed reinforcement as a factor in generalization. *Journal of Applied Behavior Analysis, 14,* 13–24.

Fox, L. (1989). Stimulus generalization of skills and persons with profound mental handicaps. *Education and Training in Mental Retardation, 24,* 219–229.

Gobbi, L., Cipani, E., Hudson, C., & Lapenta-Neudeck, R. (1986). Developing spontaneous requesting among children with severe mental retardation. *American Journal on Mental Deficiency, 24,* 357–363.

Granlund, M., & Blackstone, S. (1999). Outcomes measurement in AAC. In F. Loncke, J. Clibbens, H. H. Arvidson, & L. L. Lloyd (Eds.), *AAC: New directions in research and practice* (pp. 207–227). London: Whurr.

Halle, J. W., Baer, D. M., & Spradlin, J. E. (1981). An analysis of teachers' generalized use of delay in helping children: A stimulus control procedure to increase language use in handicapped children. *Journal of Applied Behavior Analysis, 14,* 389–409.

Haring, N. G. (1988). A technology for generalization. In N.G. Haring (Ed.), *Generalization for students with severe handicaps—Strategies and solutions* (pp. 5–11). Seattle, WA:. University of Washington Press.

Horner, R. H., & Day, H. M. (1991). The effects of response efficiency on functionally equivalent competing behaviors. *Journal of Applied Behavior Analysis, 24,* 719–732.

Horner, R. H., Sprague, J. R., O'Brien, M., & Heathfield, L. T. (1990). The role of response efficiency in the reduction of problem behaviors through functional equivalence training: A case study. *Journal of the Association for Persons with Severe Handicaps, 15,* 91–97.

Horner, R. H., Sprague, J. R., & Wilcox, B. (1982). General case programming for community activities. In B. Wilcox & G. T. Bellamy (Eds.), *Design of high school programs for severely handicapped students* (pp. 61–98). Baltimore: Paul H. Brookes.

Hughes, D. L. (1985). Measurement of generalization. In D. L. Hughes (Ed.), *Language treatment and generalization—A clinician's handbook* (pp. 15–36). San Diego, CA: College-Hill Press.

Hunt, P., Alwell, M., & Goetz, L. (1991). Establishing conversational exchange with family and friends: Moving from training to meaningful communication. *Journal of Special Education, 25,* 305–319.

Hunt, P., Alwell, M., Goetz, L., & Sailor, W. (1990). Generalized effects of conversation training. *Journal of the Association for Persons with Severe Handicaps, 15,* 250–260.

Hurlbut, B. I., Iwata, B. A., & Green, J. D. (1982). Nonvocal language acquisition in adolescents with severe physical disabilities: Blissymbol versus iconic stimulus formats. *Journal of Applied Behavior Analysis, 15,* 241–257.

Light, J. C. (1999). Do augmentative and alternative communication interventions really make a difference?: The challenges of efficacy research. *Augmentative and Alternative Communication, 15,* 13–24.

Lim, L., Browder, D. M., & Sigafoos, J. (1998). The role of response effort and motion study in functionally equivalent task designs and alternatives. *Journal of Behavioral Education, 8,* 81–102.

Locke, P. A., & Mirenda, P. (1988). A computer-supported communication approach for a child with severe communication, visual, and cognitive impairments: A case study. *Augmentative and Alternative Communication, 4,* 15–22.

Mirenda, P., Iacono, T., & Williams, R. (1990). Communication options for persons with severe and profound disabilities: State of the art and future directions. *Journal of the Association for Persons with Severe Handicaps, 15,* 2–31.

Nigam, R. (1999). *Acquisition and generalization of two-term semantic relationships by children who use augmentative and alternative communication.* Unpublished doctoral dissertation, Purdue University, West Lafayette, IN.

O'Neill, R. E. (1990). Establishing verbal repertoires: Toward the application of general case analysis and programming. *The Analysis of Verbal Behavior, 8,* 113–126.

O'Neill, R. E., Faulkner, C., & Horner, R. H. (2000). The effects of general case training of manding responses on children with severe disabilities. *Journal of Developmental and Physical Disabilities, 12,* 43–60.

Rainforth, B., York, J., & MacDonald, C. (1992). *Collaborative teams for students with severe disabilities: Integrating therapy and educational services.* Baltimore: Paul H. Brookes.

Reichle, J. (1997). Communication intervention with persons who have severe disabilities. *The Journal of Special Education, 31,* 110–134.

Reichle, J., & Johnston, S. S. (1999). Teaching the conditional use of communicative requests to two school-aged children with severe developmental disabilities. *Language, Speech, and Hearing Services in Schools, 30,* 324–334.

Reichle, J., & Sigafoos, J. (1991). Establishing spontaneity and generalization. In J. Reichle, R. J. York, & J. Sigafoos (Eds.), *Implementing augmentative and alternative communication: Strategies for learners with severe disabilities* (pp. 157–172). Baltimore: Paul H. Brookes.

Rotholz, D. A., Berkowitz, S. F., & Burberry, J. (1989). Functionality of two modes of communication in the community by students with developmental disabilities. *Journal of the Association for Persons with Severe Handicaps, 14,* 227–233.

Rutherford, R. B., & Nelson, C. M. (1988). Generalization and maintenance of treatment effects. In J. Witt, S. N. Flintt, & F. M. Gresham (Eds.). *Handbook of behavior therapy in education* (pp. 277–324). New York: Plenum.

Schepis, M. M., & Reid, D. H. (1995). Effects of a voice output communication aid on interactions between support personnel and an individual with multiple disabilities. *Journal of Applied Behavior Analysis, 28,* 73–77.

Schlosser, R. W. (2002). *Measuring outcomes in speech-language pathology through goal attainment scaling.* Manuscript under review.

Schlosser, R. W. (in press). Outcomes measurement in augmentative and alternative communication. In D. R. Beukelman, J. Reichle, & J. Light (Eds.), *Communicative competence in augmentative and alternative communication.* Baltimore: Paul H. Brookes.

Schlosser, R. W., & Braun, U. (1994). Efficacy of AAC interventions: Methodologic issues in evaluating behavior change, generalization, and effects. *Augmentative and Alternative Communication, 10*, 207–223.

Schlosser, R. W., & Lee, D. (2000). Promoting generalization and maintenance in augmentative and alternative communication: A meta-analysis of 20 years of effectiveness research. *Augmentative and Alternative Communication, 16*, 208–227.

Scruggs, T. E., & Mastropieri, M. A. (1994). The effectiveness of generalization training: A quantitative synthesis of single subject research. In T. E. Scruggs & M. A. Mastropieri (Eds.), *Advances in learning and behavioral disabilities* (Vol. 8, pp. 259–280). Greenwich, CT: JAI.

Sigafoos, J. (1999). Creating opportunities for augmentative and alternative communication: Strategies for involving people with developmental disabilities. *Augmentative and Alternative Communication, 15*, 183–190.

Sigafoos, J. (2000, October). *Talking a new TACT: Technology assisted communication training for people with developmental disabilities.* Presentation at the 8th national joint conference of the National Council on Intellectual Disability and Australian Society for the Study of Intellectual Disability. Fremantle, Australia.

Spradlin, J. E. (1989). Model of generalization. In L. V. McReynolds & J. E. Spradlin (Eds.), *Generalization strategies in the treatment of communication disorders* (pp. 132–146). Toronto, Canada: Decker.

Stokes, T. F., & Osnes, P. G. (1988). The developing technology of generalization and maintenance. In R. H. Horner, G. Dunlap, & R. L. Koegel (Eds.), *Generalization and maintenance: Life-style changes in applied settings* (pp. 5–20). Baltimore: Paul H. Brookes.

Van Acker, R., & Grant, S. H. (1995). An effective computer-based requesting system for persons with Rett syndrome. *Journal of Childhood Communication Disorders, 16*, 31–38.

Wacker, D. P., & Berg, W. L. (1983). The effects of picture prompts on the acquisition of complex vocational tasks by mentally retarded adolescents. *Journal of Applied Behavior Analysis, 16*, 417–433.

White, O. R., Liberty, K. A., Haring, N. G., Billingsley, F. F., Boer, M., Burrage, A., Connors, R., Farman, R., Federochak, G., Leber, B. D., Liberty-Laylin, S., Miller, S., Opalski, C., Phifer, C., & Sessoms, I. (1988). Review and analysis of strategies for generalization. In N. G. Haring (Ed.), *Generalization for students with severe handicaps—Strategies and solutions* (pp. 15–51). Seattle, WA: University of Washington Press.

Zangari, C., & Kangas, K. (1997). Intervention principles and procedures. In L. L. Lloyd, D. R. Fuller, & H. Arvidson (Eds.). *Augmentative and alternative communication: A handbook of principles and practices* (pp. 235–253). Needham Heights, MA: Allyn & Bacon.

CHAPTER 21

Comparative Efficacy Studies Using Single-Subject Experimental Designs

How Can They Inform Evidence-Based Practice?

Ralf W. Schlosser
Department of Speech-Language Pathology and Audiology
Northeastern University

I. **Introduction**
II. **What Do We Know?**
   A. Method of the Review
   B. Results of the Narrative Review
III. **Simultaneous Communication or Sign Alone: An EPB Illustration**
   A. Asking Well-Built Questions
   B. The Primary Question: Selecting Evidence Sources and Executing the Search Strategy
   C. The Primary Question: Examining the Evidence
   D. The Primary Question: Applying the Evidence
   E. The Secondary Question: Selecting Evidence Sources and Executing the Search Strategy
   F. The Secondary Question: Examining the Evidence
   G. The Secondary Question: Applying the Evidence
   H. Evaluating the Application of the Evidence
   I. Disseminating the Findings
IV. **Conclusions: The Role of Comparison Studies for EBP**
   A. Evaluating the Evidence from Comparison Studies
   B. How Can Comparison Studies Inform EBP?

I. INTRODUCTION

Typically, efficacy research seeks to evaluate the efficacy of one particular intervention. For example, a researcher may want to evaluate whether the Picture Exchange Communication System (PECS) is effective for teaching children with autism to communicate basic needs (e.g., Schwartz, Garfinkle, & Bauer, 1998). Once it has been demonstrated that individual interventions are efficacious in their own right, practitioners are often interested in knowing whether another approach might be even more efficacious. After all, there is rarely just one intervention option for teaching a skill in augmentative and alternative communication (AAC). The practitioner seeking to teach requesting to children with autism, for example, may be interested in knowing whether an approach that involves pointing to graphic symbols (e.g., the System for Augmenting Language, Romski & Sevcik, 1996; and Chapter 8) may be more effective than using the exchange that is part of PECS. This is just one of many scenarios that could be illuminated through comparative efficacy studies. Evidence-based practitioners may also need to decide between (1) a gestural mode and a graphic mode, (2) a graphic mode and traditional orthography, (3) scanning method A and scanning method B, (4) direct instruction and activity-based intervention, and (5) speech-generating devices and nonelectronic communication boards (Schlosser, 1997). Evidence from comparison studies is deemed especially helpful to inform these decision-making scenarios. As with other intervention research, evidence-based practitioners are encouraged to first seek out systematic reviews of evidence. Thus, this chapter first provides a narrative review of comparative efficacy studies using single-subject experimental designs. Next, the evidence-based practitioner is presented with an illustration as to how this narrative review can be used to answer a clinical or educational question. Last, the chapter examines how comparative studies such as those reviewed here can inform evidence-based practice in general.

II. WHAT DO WE KNOW?

A. METHOD OF THE REVIEW

This section reviews comparative efficacy studies using the process of a narrative review to inform evidence-based practice (EBP). It is understood that this narrative review needs to be supplemented or replaced with a meta-analysis at a later point.

1. Inclusion Criteria

To be included in this review, the studies had to use single-subject experimental designs commonly used to compare the efficacy of more than one intervention (see Chapters 6 and 12). Group studies were excluded (e.g., Kahn, 1977, 1981). In addition, the intervention needed to be within the realm of AAC, defined as "an area of clinical practice that attempts to compensate (either temporarily or permanently) for the impairment and disability patterns of persons with severe expressive communication disorders (i.e., people with severe speech-language and writing impairments)" (American Speech-Language-Hearing Association, 1989, p. 107).

Studies were drawn from an article on methodological issues in comparative efficacy evaluation, in which the author offered a synopsis of comparison studies involving single-subject experimental designs (Schlosser, 1999). In addition, the database of 50 studies involving single-subject experimental designs included in a recent meta-analysis (Schlosser & Lee, 2000), and the master file of those that failed to meet the specific criteria for inclusion in that review were searched for comparison studies.

2. Coding Categories

Each of the included studies were reviewed in terms of several methodological criteria deemed essential for determining the certainty of the evidence stemming from comparison studies (Schlosser, 1999; see also Chapter 6). Only an abbreviated summary shall be provided here. The reader may consult the coding manual in Appendix 21A for detailed information. The studies were coded in terms of the following categories: (1) the participants are not biased toward a particular condition due to previous experiences; (2) the design offers adequate control of sequence effects and carryover effects; (3) the design allows for within-subject replication of effects; (4) carryover effects/sequence effects are further minimized through procedural safeguards; (5) a learning criterion was set; (6) a teaching criterion was set; (7) the equivalence of instructional sets is demonstrated and based on current knowledge of contributing factors to equivalency; (8) treatments are randomly assigned to instructional sets; (9) the functional independence of sets is demonstrated; (10) interobserver agreement data for the dependent measure(s) are adequate for the particular target behaviors; (11) treatment integrity is comparable across conditions; (12) procedures are held constant except for to be examined differences across conditions; (13) effectiveness of conditions is demonstrated unequivocally through the attainment of a learning criterion; and (14) efficiency comparisons are based on attainment of an a priori learning criterion for all conditions compared.

3. Analysis

Although quantitative scores were yielded for each of the studies, no summary statistics were generated for purposes of this chapter. A meta-analysis on this topic is currently in the planning stage, and quantitative results will be made available upon its completion (Schlosser & Sigafoos, 2002). The quantitative data generated were, however, used as a basis for the narrative review offered in Tables 21.1 to 21.3, particularly for the appraisal of the certainty of evidence generated from each of the reviewed studies.

B. Results of the Narrative Review

A summary of the narrative review is provided for unaided approaches (Table 21.1), aided approaches (Table 21.2), and comparisons of unaided with aided approaches (Table 21.3). Each of the reviewed studies is summarized in terms of the following categories: (1) group (based on a common intervention theme), (2) author(s), (3) intervention definition, (4) participants, (5) design, (6) results, and (7) appraisal of certainty.

1. Review of Studies Involving Unaided Approaches

The long-standing history of unaided approaches is reflected in the more prominent role of comparisons among unaided efficacy evaluations. A total of 23 studies were identified and reviewed. In a large number of studies, marked group 1 in Table 21.1, the effects of simultaneous communication versus sign-alone training or traditional speech training were investigated (e.g., Barrera, Lobato-Barrera, & Sulzer-Azaroff, 1980; Barrett & Sisson, 1987; Brady & Smouse, 1978; Clarke, Remington, & Light 1988; Remington & Clarke, 1983; Sisson & Barrett, 1984; Wells, 1981; Wherry & Edwards, 1983).

Barrera *et al.* (1980), for example, found simultaneous communication to be most efficient. Remington and Clarke (1983), however, raised the possibility that this finding may have been due to differences in stimuli sets. Although the training stimuli were "familiar object(s) from the child's environment" (p. 24), pretesting on receptive knowledge of the word referents was not implemented. It is therefore possible, they argue, that simultaneous communication was more efficient because the child could have learned the sign simply by translating a previously acquired verbal referent rather than an unknown referent. In their study, therefore, Remington and Clarke (1983) compared the effects of simultaneous communication versus sign-alone training on expressive signing and receptive knowledge of *known* target words in two children with autism. One child had no functional speech, whereas the other had some spoken imitation skills.

Results indicated that both conditions were equally effective and efficient in terms of the rate of expressive sign acquisition. Although the nonspeaking child failed to increase receptive understanding of the words in either condition, the imitative child improved receptive understanding in the simultaneous signing condition. With the exception of Wherry and Edwards (1983) and Remington and Clarke (1983), these studies generally support the effectiveness and efficiency of simultaneous communication over sign-alone training or oral training in terms of expressive signing, receptive speech, and natural speech development. Although the certainty of many of the studies is compromised as listed in Table 21.1, the finding appears sufficiently robust across seven studies.

The second group of studies, marked group 2 in Table 21.1, concerned itself with studying the conditions under which simultaneous communication works more effectively or efficiently. One study, for example, examined whether simultaneous communication works better when introducing manual signs for known words or for unknown words (Clarke, Remington, & Light, 1986). Results indicated that simultaneous communication is more efficient in terms of expressive signing when the signs are introduced for known words rather than for unknown words. Only one of the three students improved in terms of expressive speech for both known and unknown words. A body of four studies evaluated how to maximize simultaneous communication training. This involved the study of modifying its procedures as follows: (1) overtraining (i.e., "extensive sign training"), (2) pretraining of receptive skills (i.e., "mediated sign training," "receptive-expressive order") or expressive skills (i.e., "expressive-receptive order"), and (3) mixing some oral-only trials into simultaneous communication (i.e., "differential sign training") (Remington & Clarke, 1993a, 1993b; Watters, Wheeler, & Watters, 1981). Depending on the study, extensive sign training was either more or equally effective as mediated sign training; across studies, extensive sign training was more efficient than mediated sign training for expressive signing. Stimulus overselectivity, which precluded the acquisition of speech comprehension, could not be overcome through either of these instructional strategies (Remington & Clarke, 1993a). Because of these continued problems, a subsequent study involved yet another variation of simultaneous communication procedures in an effort to remedy stimulus overselectivity. That is, differential sign training was designed as a method whereby simultaneous communication is intermixed with some trials of oral-only. This was deemed to shift the overselective attention of the learners from the visual stimuli (i.e., manual signs) to the auditory stimuli (i.e., word referents). The studies in this group summarized thus far are fairly homogeneous as far as the participants are concerned. The remaining study by Watters *et al.* (1981) is related in terms of the interventions studied but different in its focus on children with autism.

A third group consists of one study that is somewhat related to group 1 yet sufficiently different to warrant its own grouping. Carr, Pridal, and Dores

Table 21.1

Comparative Studies Using Single-Subject Experimental Designs: Unaided Approaches

Group	Study	Purpose	Interventions defined	Participants	Design
	Barrera, Lobato-Barrera, & Sulzer-Azaroff (1980)	To compare oral, sign-alone, and simultaneous communication in terms of expressive speech	(a) *Oral*: teaching referent speech directly (b) *Sign-alone*: omits referent speech and only presents the signs (c) *Simultaneous communication*: simultaneous signing and speaking the name of the referent	One boy with autism ($4\frac{1}{2}$ years) and no functional speech	AATD replicated across two sets
	Barrett & Sisson (1987)	To compare oral, simultaneous communication, and modified simultaneous communication in terms of expressive speech or signing of sentence parts and sentences	(a) *Oral*: teaching referent speech directly (b) *Simultaneous communication*: simultaneous signing and speaking the name of the referent (c) *Modified simultaneous communication*: as above, but requiring only a vocal response	Two children with moderate intellectual disabilities and severe emotional or behavior disorders (5;3 years; 13 years)	AATD with multiple probe design
	Brady & Smouse (1978)	To compare oral, sign-alone, and simultaneous communication in terms of receptive speech	Presented with object and discriminative stimulus, modeling and guiding through action: (a) *Oral*: vocal ("tap block") (b) *Sign-alone*: signed (c) *Simultaneous communication*: vocal + signed	One child with autism (6;4 years)	ATD with most effective treatment in the third phase
	Clarke, Remington, & Light (1988) —Study 1	To compare simultaneous communication with sign-alone training for receptively known words in terms of sign acquisition and expressive speech	Concurrent teaching of signs across conditions (a) *Simultaneous communication*: simultaneous signing and speaking the name of the referent (b) *Sign-alone training*: omits referent speech and only presents the signs	Four students with severe intellectual disabilities (5;5 years to 9;9 years)	AATD with multiple probe design across subjects (Study 1)
1	Clarke et al. (1988)— Study 2	To compare simultaneous communication with	As in study 1	One student with severe intellectual	AATD with multiple probe across signs

Results	Appraisal of certainty
Simultaneous communication was found more effective than oral and sign-alone training in yielding expressive word acquisition.	Both, sequence and carryover effects were controlled with the design and procedural safeguards. The sets were equated in terms of relevant variables through informal means based on an inadequate recognition of variables contributing to learning difficulty (i.e., receptive status of referents). Although a learning criterion was used, it was set only for the first condition. This precluded comparisons in terms of efficiency. The lack of treatment integrity makes it impossible to attribute the findings to the independent variable. This is further compounded by counting of signed and vocal responses together in the graphs, which makes it difficult to discern the specific changes.
For Jake, simultaneous communication facilitated 100% mastery while the other two conditions resulted in less substantial gains. Modified simultaneous communication was slightly more effective than the oral condition. Jake reached criterion only in simultaneous communication. For Moe, the oral condition was more effective than modified simultaneous communication and simultaneous communication. Moe attained criterion only in the oral and modified conditions, indicating that oral was more efficient.	The AATD combined with a multiple probe design permitted control of sequence and carryover effects and within-subject replication. Counterbalancing further minimized sequence effects. The sets of sentences were equated through informal means based on a complete recognition of variables contributing to spoken and signed learning difficulty. A learning criterion was established, but not attained in all conditions. Therefore, only limited efficiency comparisons were legitimate for one participant. Interobserver agreement data were high and comparable across conditions. Treatment integrity data were not reported, which diminishes the certainty of evidence of an otherwise well conducted study.
The student learned to perform the requested action best when trained through simultaneous communication, followed by sign-alone and the oral condition. Upon reaching the teaching criterion, simultaneous communication was applied only.	An ATD with the same words and objects in both conditions does not rule out that carryover effects may have influenced the findings. Order effects were controlled through counterbalancing. It is unclear whether the learner had receptive knowledge of the individual object and color labels prior to the study. The lack of treatment integrity data and interobserver agreement data for the dependent measure call into question the reliability of data collection and treatment implementation.
Both conditions were effective across students in that learning criterion was reached for both sets. In terms of efficiency, the learners required fewer trials to reach criterion in simultaneous communication than in the sign-alone condition. The two participants who improved in terms of expressive speech were those who showed reliable vocal imitation skills on the words involved in training.	Mandy may have been biased toward simultaneous communication training whereas the others received previous instruction in sign-alone training in previous research. The superior results attained for simultaneous communication training refute this bias at least for 3 of the children. Both, sequence and carryover effects were controlled with the design and procedural safeguards. The sets were equated through objective and factual means based on a complete recognition of factors contributing to sign acquisition. The lack of treatment integrity data calls into question the correct application of treatments and therefore the source of the obtained results.
Mick reached criterion only in the simultaneous condition (in the 32nd session). In the sign-alone training, he still had not	Mick may have been biased toward simultaneous communication due to participation in a previous study (Clarke *et al.*, 1986), which indicated that unknown words were controlled primarily

(continues)

Table 21.1 (*continued*)

Group	Study	Purpose	Interventions defined	Participants	Design
		sign-alone training for receptively known words for sign acquisition and expressive speech		disabilities (12;1 years)—lower functioning than in study 1	
	Remington & Clarke (1983)	To compare simultaneous communication training with sign-alone training on expressive sign labeling and speech comprehension	(a) *Simultaneous communication*: as above (b) *Sign-alone*: omits referent speech	Two students with autism (10 years and 15 years); 1 student also had severe intellectual disabilities	AATD with a multiple probe design across signs
	Sisson & Barrett (1984)	To compare oral versus simultaneous communication in terms of spoken or signed sentence imitation	(a) *Oral*: vocal stimuli (b) *Simultaneous communication*: vocal + signed stimuli	Three children with mild or severe intellectual disabilities and severe behavior disorders (4, 7, and 8 years)	AATD with multiple probe design across sentence pairs; the more effective procedure was used in the third phase
	Wells (1981)	To compare oral versus simultaneous communication on word articulation	(a) *Simultaneous communication*: as above (b) *Oral*: oral musculature exercise and vocal imitation	Three young adults with severe intellectual disabilities (18, 25, and 26 years)	AATD

Results	Appraisal of certainty
reached criterion in the 85th session. Only when the simultaneous communication condition was applied did change occur. Stimulus control assessments showed control of expressive signing by both visual and vocal stimuli. No changes in expressive speech were observed, consistent with his poor vocal imitation performance.	by vocal stimuli. The superior results obtained for simultaneous communication training refute this bias. Both, sequence and carryover effects were controlled with the design and procedural safeguards. The sets were equated through objective and factual means based on a complete recognition of factors contributing to sign acquisition. The lack of treatment integrity data calls into question the correct application of treatments and therefore the source of the obtained results. Further, the lack of interobserver agreement data makes the reliability of the recorded data uncertain.
Both simultaneous communication and sign-alone training were effective in that both learners attained the learning criterion for expressive signing. Although both learners required fewer trials and sessions to criterion with sign-alone training than with simultaneous communication, the differences were not statistically significant. John, who was able to imitate verbally, showed improvements in receptive knowledge of signs taught via simultaneous communication. Stimulus control analyses indicated that John's signing was under the control of both auditory and visual stimuli whereas Diane's signing was controlled only by visual stimuli.	Both, sequence and carryover effects have been minimized through the use of an AATD and procedural safeguards. In addition, the within-subject replication of effects strengthens the internal validity of the findings. Sets of signs were equated using objective methods based on a complete recognition of variables contributing to learning difficulty. Both sets were trained to a learning criterion resulting in sound efficiency comparisons. The lack of treatment integrity data diminishes the certainty of evidence from an otherwise well conducted study.
For two participants, Eli and Mick, simultaneous communication resulted in 100% mastery, whereas the oral condition yielded no gains (Eli) or small gains (Mick). Thus, simultaneous communication was more effective than oral communication. Once the yet unlearned sentences were trained with simultaneous communication, criterion was reached rapidly for them as well. For Tyco, both conditions were equally effective.	Both, sequence and carryover effects were minimized through the design and procedural safeguards such as counterbalancing. In addition, the within-subject replication of effects strengthens the internal validity of the results. The sets were equivalent using objective methods based on an accurate acknowledgment of pertinent variables. Problematic is the use of two different dependent measures across conditions: in the simultaneous communication condition, the learners were required to vocalize and sign whereas in the oral condition, the learners simply had to vocalize. This raises questions concerning the comparability of the conditions. The authors state that treatment integrity was monitored, but data were not supplied.
Results indicated that simultaneous communication yielded more effective word articulation than traditional speech training across participants.	The design, along with procedural safeguards (e.g., randomizing the order) minimized sequence and carryover effects. Sets of stimuli were equated based on an incomplete understanding of what contributes to learning; while the word sets were equated for some factors (not for receptive status) through informal means (reinforcement value) and factual means (developmental period of acquisition), the sign sets were not equated. Data on sign acquisition were not offered making it difficult to evaluate whether it is signed input or manual sign learning that contributed to better articulation. Conclusions are compromised by the lack of treatment integrity data.

(continues)

Table 21.1 (*continued*)

Group	Study	Purpose	Interventions defined	Participants	Design
	Wherry & Edwards (1983)	To compare oral, sign-alone, and simultaneous communication in terms of receptive speech (for various parts of speech), expressive speech, and eye contact	(a) *Oral*: as above (b) *Sign-alone*: as above (c) *Simultaneous* communication: as above	One child with autism (5 years old)	AATD
2	Clarke, Remington, & Light (1986)	To compare known words with unknown words in simultaneous communication training in terms of expressive signing, receptive speech, and expressive speech	(a) *Known words*: words that were receptively known (b) *Unknown words*: words that were receptively unknown	Three students with severe intellectual disabilities (11;3 years, 11;2 years, and 6 years)	AATD
	Remington & Clarke (1993a)— Study I	To compare extensive sign training with mediated sign training on acquisition of expressive signing and speech comprehension and reduction of stimulus overselectivity	(a) *Extensive sign training*: overtraining expressive signing in simultaneous communication with a reduced reinforcement schedule (see also Remington & Clarke, 1983) (b) *Mediated sign training*: training receptive speech functions prior to simultaneous communication	Four students with severe mental retardation (10 years to 12 years)	AATD with a multiple probe design across signs
	Remington & Clarke (1993a)— Study II			Two students with severe intellectual disabilities (5;9 years; 4;1 years)	AATD with multiple probe design across subjects
	Remington & Clarke (1993b)	To compare differential sign training with extensive sign training on expressive signing	(a) *Extensive sign training*: overtraining expressive signing in simultaneous communication with a reduced reinforcement schedule	Five children with severe intellectual disabilities (4 to 11 years); 3 children had	AATD with multiple probe design across signs

Results	Appraisal of certainty
Cumulative frequencies indicated more correct receptive speech responses for the sign-alone condition (21) followed by the simultaneous communication condition (16) and the oral condition (14.5). Statistically, the differences were nonsignificant. There were no changes in vocalizations between baseline and intervention. Although increases in eye contact were noted, they were statistically not significant.	The AATD offered the potential to minimize sequence and carryover effects. Procedural safeguards such as counterbalancing allowed for control of order effects. Although the three sets were randomly assigned to the three teachers no efforts were made to equate the sets. Thus, it is difficult to rule out that the sets were equally difficult to begin with. Even though a learning criterion was stated it appears that the target forms were not trained up to criterion. The lack of treatment integrity data further diminishes the certainty of evidence.
All students learned signs for known words faster and retained them better than sings for unknown words. Only Mandy improved her receptive speech with unknown words. Students were tested on expressive speech gains for known words, while Mandy was also tested on unknown words. Only Mandy improved her expressive speech, both, with known and unknown words. Only Mandy failed to show overselective attention during the stimulus control tests, and she was the only one whose receptive speech improved.	An AATD, along with procedural safeguards, allowed for the control of sequence and carryover effects. The sets were equated through objective and factual means based on a complete recognition of factors contributing to sign acquisition. The use of a learning criterion in both conditions facilitated legitimate efficiency comparisons. Unfortunately, the time-series data were collapsed into pre- and posttests bar graphs. This precludes a productive visual inspection of the data. The lack of treatment integrity data calls into question the correct application of the treatment.
All four children met criterion in the extensive condition, but only two children also reached criterion in the mediated condition as well. For these two children, the extensive condition was more efficient than the mediated condition in terms of trials-to-criterion for sign acquisition. Overtraining in simultaneous communication (i.e., extensive training) was not sufficient to remove stimulus overselectivity and permit speech comprehension to develop.	Both, sequence and carryover effects have been minimized with the design and procedural safeguards. In addition, the within-subject replication of effects in Study I strengthens the internal validity of the findings. The matching of sets was done through objective methods based on a complete recognition of factors contributing to learning difficulty. Further, variability across sets was minimized by going through a sign imitation training prior to the comparison. Efficiency comparisons in Study I were possible only for 2 of the children who had reached the learning criterion in both conditions. Multiple treatment interference, partially stemming from involvement in a previous experiment, was discussed as a potential reason for the 2 children who did not reach criterion in the Mediated conditions.
Both children reached criterion in both conditions, indicating that both methods were effective. Both children required fewer trials to criterion in the extensive condition, which rendered this method more efficient. The extensive condition, however, failed to overcome overselectivity and thus to facilitate speech comprehension.	In Study II, both children reached criterion in both conditions, allowing for legitimate efficiency comparisons. The lack of treatment integrity data in both studies diminishes the certainty of evidence from an otherwise well conducted pair of studies.
All children reached criterion in both conditions, indicating that expressive sign training and differential sign training were effective. Four children took fewer trials to criterion in the extensive condition than in the differential condition. The fifth child	Both, sequence and carryover effects were minimized through the use of an AATD and procedural safeguards. In addition, the within-subject replication of effects strengthens the internal validity of the findings. The matching of sets was done through objective methods based on a complete recognition of factors contributing to learning difficulty. Further, variability across sets

(continues)

Table 21.1 (*continued*)

Group	Study	Purpose	Interventions defined	Participants	Design
		and overcoming selective attention	(b) *Differential sign training*: Mixing simultaneous communication with trials where the referent word was the only cue	Down syndrome	
	Watters, Wheeler, & Watters (1981)	To compare two orders for training expressive and receptive sign use with simultaneous communication	(a) *Receptive-expressive order*: Receptive skills are taught first followed by expressive skills (b) *Expressive-receptive order*: expressive skills are taught first followed by receptive skills	Four children with autism (11;11 years, 10;9 years, 16 years, and 12; 10 years)	AATD with generalization probes; two signs at a time were trained simultaneously, 1 in each order
3	Carr, Pridal, & Dores (1984)	To compare receptive speech alone-training versus receptive sign-alone training in terms of receptive label discriminations (sign and speech)	(a) *Receptive speech-alone* (b) *Receptive sign-alone*	Ten children with autism: 6 poor verbal imitators (mean = 10 years); 4 good imitators (mean = 11 years)	ATD replicated across two groups of children
4	Conaghan, Singh, Moe, Landrum, & Ellis (1992)	To compare directed rehearsal, alone and combined with positive reinforcement with a no-training control condition, on expressive sign agent-action combinations and vocalizations	(a) *Directed rehearsal*: repetitions of the correct response contingent on errors (b) *Directed rehearsal plus positive reinforcement*: as above plus social and primary reinforcement for each correctly signed phrase (c) *No training*: control condition	Six adults with moderate to profound intellectual disabilities and hearing impairments	AATD
	Linton & Singh (1984)	To compare directed rehearsal alone, directed rehearsal plus positive reinforcement, and a no-training control condition on expressive signing and spoken language	(a) *Directed rehearsal*: repetitions of the correct response contingent on errors (b) *Directed rehearsal plus positive reinforcement*: as above plus positive reinforcement for correct responses (c) *No training*: control condition	Four adults with mild to profound intellectual disabilities and hearing impairments (18, 41, 59, and 67 years)	AATD

Results	Appraisal of certainty

reached criterion in both conditions at the same time. Improvements in speech comprehension and selective attention were only observed in the differential sign condition.

was minimized by going through a sign imitation training prior to the comparison. Efficiency comparisons were possible for all participants. The lack of treatment integrity data diminishes the certainty of evidence from an otherwise well conducted study.

Both orders were effective because all children reached criteria in both orders. In terms of efficiency, many more trials were required in the receptive-expressive order than the expressive-receptive order. Also, expressive signing required more trials when it followed receptive training and receptive training required fewer trials when it followed expressive training. Although some generalization was noted from expressive to receptive use, no generalization occurred for the opposite order. Per stimulus control analysis, the sign yielded more control than the spoken word.

Even though one word in each pair was taught in different conditions, using an AATD, it is not reported whether the specific order across sessions was counterbalanced. Also, there was no apparent attempt to equate the pairs for signing or word difficulty. Unfortunately, the acquisition trials to criterion were collapsed across sessions instead of reporting time-series data. Further, baseline data are provided neither in numeric nor in graphic form. This makes it difficult to attribute differences in the conditions to the orders in which the signs were introduced. Data are collapsed across sessions rather than displayed in time-series format. Conclusions are further compromised by the lack of interobserver agreement and treatment integrity data.

All six children in the poor verbal imitator group mastered the sign discriminations, but five of these children failed criterion with the speech discriminations. All four children in the good verbal imitator group reached criterion in both conditions, and there was no statistical difference in terms of trials to criterion.

An ATD with the same words and objects in both conditions does not rule out carryover effects. Sequence effects were controlled through randomization of objects and conditions. The use of a teaching criterion along with a learning criterion is noteworthy as it permitted legitimate efficiency comparison. The lack of treatment integrity data, however, calls into question the correct application of the treatment. In addition, time-series data are not displayed. This prevents a visual analysis of the data.

Although directed rehearsal was more effective than the no-training control condition, the method was even more effective when combined with positive reinforcement. Results also showed excellent generalization by all participants across novel phrases, settings, and trainers but variable levels to another response mode. In addition, increased levels in vocalizations were found across most participants and conditions, especially pronounced when directed rehearsal was combined with positive reinforcement.

Both, sequence effects and carryover effects were controlled with the design and adequate procedural safeguards. Although the sets of sign-combinations were equated through informal means, this process was based on an incomplete recognition of contributing factors to sign acquisition. Treatment integrity data were provided, albeit only in rudimentary form (i.e., only for the accuracy of sign production).

All participants learned new signs in each of two training conditions. However, the addition of positive reinforcement was more effective than directed rehearsal alone with three participants. For the fourth participant, the conditions were equally effective. No learning took place in the control condition. In terms of vocalizations, two participants spoke all words correctly while there was no change with the third participant and some improvement with the fourth participant.

Both, sequence and carryover effects have been minimized through the use of this design and other procedural safeguards. Sets were equated through informal methods only, based on an incomplete recognition of factors contributing to sign production and spoken word production. A learning criterion was set but observed only for the first condition that reached it. This precluded efficiency comparison. Treatment integrity data were lacking, calling into question the certainty of the evidence.

(continues)

Table 21.1 (*continued*)

Group	Study	Purpose	Interventions defined	Participants	Design
	Goodman & Remington (1993)	To compare sign-specific reinforcement with nonspecific reinforcement in terms of expressive signing	Simultaneous communication was used in both conditions (a) *Specific reinforcement*: the learner gets what she asked for (i.e., as in a request) (b) *Nonspecific reinforcement*: the learner received social praise (i.e., as in labeling)	Four children with severe intellectual disabilities (4;5 years to 6;11 years)	AATD
5	Duker & Moonen (1986)	To compare complete versus incomplete presentation of requested objects and activities in terms of expressive spontaneous signing	Least-to-most prompting and simultaneous were used in both conditions (a) *Complete presentation*: a sign for eating a cookie was followed by the whole cookie (b) *Incomplete presentation*: a sign for eating a cookie was followed by initially presenting a part $(\frac{1}{4})$ of a cookie	Three students with severe to profound intellectual disabilities due to Down syndrome (12, 14, and 10 years)	ATD with MBD across participants
	Duker, Kraaykamp, & Visser (1994)	To compare complete versus incomplete presentation of requested objects and activities in terms of expressive spontaneous signing	Least-to-most prompting and simultaneous communication were used in both conditions (as in Duker & Moonen, 1986)	Three students with profound intellectual disabilities (12, 15, and 15 years)	ABABB'BB' replicated across participants
	Bennett, Gast, Wolery, & Schuster (1986)	To compare progressive time delay and the system of least prompts in terms of expressive signing	(a) *Progressive time delay*: increasing delay beginning from 0 sec up to 10 sec (b) *System of least prompts*: four levels within a prompt hierarchy beginning with the least intrusive and ending with the most intrusive prompts	Three students with moderate to severe intellectual disabilities and hearing impairments; one student was also deaf-blind (14 to 17 years)	PTD
6	Dalrymple, & Feldman (1992)	To compare prompting strategies with and without directed rehearsal with a no-training control condition on	(a) *Sequential prompting (SP)*: gradual increase in the amount of prompting within a trial (b) *SP with directed rehearsal (DR)*: SP plus	Ten youth and adults with moderate to severe intellectual disabilities	AATD; students 1–5 received SP/DR, SP, and NT; students 6–10 received GG/DR, GG,

Results	Appraisal of certainty
All four children reached the learning criterion in both conditions, indicating that sign-specific reinforcement was as effective as nonspecific reinforcement. In terms of efficiency, all but one of the children required fewer trials to reach criterion in the sign-specific condition.	The design chosen along with counterbalancing minimizes sequence and order effects. Considerable care was taken to equate sets both objectively and in terms of other factors contributing to learnability of signs and referents. The use of a learning criterion in both conditions permitted legitimate efficiency comparisons. The most significant weakness in this otherwise well-conducted study is the lack of formal treatment integrity data.
Spontaneous signing increased across the three students as a result of the least-to-most prompting. The incomplete presentation of requested objects and activities yielded more spontaneous signing than the complete presentation.	Despite procedural safeguards such as random allocation of the presentation mode, the design (with the same manual signs for both conditions) does not control for carry-over effects. Unfortunately, the data on the two presentation modes were collapsed into pre- and post-treatment bar graphs rather than integrated with the MBD in a time-series format. A learning criterion or teaching criterion was not established. In addition, the lack of treatment integrity calls into question the accurate application of the treatment.
All three learners increased their signed requests during intervention and decreased their requests when the intervention was withheld again. After the intervention was reinstated, signed requests increased again.	The design used does not permit the control of sequence effects and therefore it is difficult to determine whether the results obtained were due to the independent variable or the particular order in which it was manipulated. In addition, there may have been carryover effects at work given that the same materials were used in baseline and intervention phases. Phase changes were predetermined, minimizing reactivity and bias. The lack of treatment integrity calls into question the accurate application of treatment.
Both teaching methods were found effective in teaching expressive sign labels with the students because criterion was reached across sets and conditions. Progressive time delay was more efficient with two students and equally efficient with the third student in terms of sessions to criterion, opportunities to respond to meet criterion, errors to criterion, and direct instructional time.	Both, sequence and carryover effects were controlled with a PTD; sequence effects were also controlled through procedural safeguards such as counterbalancing. The sets of signs were equated through informal means, based on an incomplete recognition of contributing factors to sign acquisition. A learning criterion was used appropriately; each of the sign pairs was trained to criterion. This allowed for legitimate efficiency comparisons. Noteworthy is the within-subject replication and across-subject replication of effects along with the collection of treatment integrity data. These data suggest perfect implementation of the independent variable.
Even though four students (two each in SP and GG) reached the learning criterion, they failed to sign only in the presence of the object. Due to this lack of stimulus control their data were eliminated from further analyses (three of these students had a hearing loss). Of the remaining	The design along with randomized order across sessions controlled for sequence and order effects. The strength of this study are as follows: (a) its consistent results replicated across several participants and two types of prompting, (b) a no-training control condition, (c) the use of learning and teaching criteria (affording legitimate efficiency comparisons), and (d) the random

(continues)

Table 21.1 (*continued*)

Group	Study	Purpose	Interventions defined	Participants	Design
		expressive signing	repetitions of the correct response contingent on errors (c) *Graduated guidance (GG)*: starting with the most intrusive prompt and then gradually lightening assistance within and across trials (d) *GG with DR* (e) *No training (NT)*	some had additional hearing losses	and NT
	Iacono & Parsons (1986)	To compare physical shaping and imitation in terms of receptive signing	(a) *Physical shaping*: shaping the signs following a prompt hierarchy (b) *Imitation*: modeling the sign following a prompt hierarchy	Three students with profound intellectual disabilities (11;8 years, 15 years, and 13;8 years)	AATD with the more effective condition applied in the last phase
7	Sigafoos & Meikle (1995)	To compare the missing-item format with the interrupted behavior chain strategy in terms of spontaneous manual sign requests and challenging and stereotypical behaviors	(a) *Missing-item format*: an item is unavailable until the learner makes an appropriate request (b) *Interrupted behavior change*: the learner is interrupted in the midst of an ongoing activity; continuation is contingent on the learner making an appropriate request	Two students with autism (8 and 5 years)—only phase 1 involved manual signs	ATD replicated across three sets (only the one set involved manual signs) (without a baseline)

(1984) compared sign–alone training with speech–alone training on receptive signing and receptive speech in students with autism. Unlike the group 1 studies, this study did not employ simultaneous communication. Rather, the participants were grouped into "good verbal imitators" and "poor verbal imitators." It turns out that both conditions were effective and equally efficient with the good verbal imitators, whereas the sign–alone training was the only effective condition with the poor verbal imitators.

Another set of studies, marked group 4, compared the differential effects of introducing manual signs with and without positive reinforcement as part of the treatment package in 10 individuals with intellectual disabilities and hearing impairments (Conaghan, Singh, Moe, Landrum, & Ellis, 1992, Linton &

Results	Appraisal of certainty
students (with exception of one student), DR increased accuracy, reduced speed, and enhanced generalization (across trainers, objects, and settings) in both SP and GG for five of the six students. In terms of total instruction time, DR was more efficient than the control condition for three of the four students. Direct-care staff and trainers preferred the use of DR.	assignment of participants to conditions. There are, however, significant shortcomings as well, which delimit the certainty of the evidence. Most debilitating is the lack of treatment integrity data and the use of informal methods for equating sets based on an incomplete recognition of contributing factors to sign acquisition.
Results indicated that physical shaping was effective across the three participants in terms of receptive labeling of signs, whereas imitation was not effective. Once physical shaping was applied to the yet unlearned signs in the last phase, improvements were noted in those signs as well.	An AATD was used and provided the potential for the control of sequence effects and order effects. Counterbalancing of conditions was used as well to control for sequence effects. The equivalence of the signs across conditions was not assessed, making it difficult to attribute the findings to the treatment conditions. In addition, the participants were biased against the imitation condition, as they had not demonstrated any learning in a previous experiment using imitation. A teaching criterion was established to allow the termination of treatment. Treatment integrity data were not reported.
Results indicated that both conditions were equally effective in increasing spontaneous requesting. Removing the needed item (interrupted behavior chain) was not associated with any more [or less] challenging behavior or stereotypical behavior than withholding a needed item [missing-item format].	Even though the participants previously learned the requests (prompted) needed for this study using a condition more closely associated with the interrupted behavior chain strategy, results refute such a bias. The same sets of objects and symbols were used across conditions, which may have resulted in carryover effects. Procedural safeguards (e.g., counterbalancing), however, minimized order effects. A learning criterion was not set. Although interobserver agreement data were satisfactory, the lack of treatment integrity data question the adherence to the treatment protocol as intended. Also, because there was no baseline it is difficult to attribute the observed changes to the interventions.

Singh, 1984). Both of these studies support the effectiveness of adding positive reinforcement to directed rehearsal in terms of sign acquisition (Conaghan *et al.*, 1992; Linton & Singh, 1984) and natural speech development (Conaghan *et al.*, 1992). In the Linton and Singh (1984) study, the effects of the various training conditions on vocalizations were mixed.

In a fifth group of studies, researchers evaluated the effects of different types of reinforcement on expressive signing (Duker, Kraaykamp, & Visser, 1994; Duker & Moonen, 1986; Goodman & Remington, 1993). Goodman and Remington (1993), for instance, compared the effects of two reinforcement strategies on expressive signing in four children with severe intellectual disabilities. In the first condition, nonspecific reinforcement was provided—that is, participants received a reinforcer unrelated to the visual referents for the signs produced. This type of reinforcement is typically used when teaching labeling. In the second condition, specific reinforcement was provided—that is, participants received the visual referent for the signs produced. This type of reinforcement is consistent with the teaching of requesting where the learner gets what he or she asks for (see Chapter 14). Although both conditions were effective, the specific reinforcement strategy produced faster acquisition of expressive signing than the nonspecific strategy for three of the subjects. Thus, it appears that requesting is more powerful than labeling if the goal is for the learner to associate manual signs with referents. The other two studies were concerned with the manipulation of the amount of reinforcement rather than the type of reinforcement in learners with severe to profound intellectual disabilities (Duker *et al.*, 1994; Duker & Moonen, 1986). Specifically, the studies indicated that an incomplete presentation of a requested item increases the frequency of spontaneous signed requests compared to complete presentations of referents.

The sixth group of studies involved comparisons of various prompting strategies in terms of expressive signing (Bennett, Gast, Wolery, & Schuster, 1986; Dalrymple & Feldman, 1992) or receptive signing (Iacono & Parsons, 1986). Each of the studies compared different prompting strategies or the role of directed rehearsal combined with prompting strategies. Therefore, it is difficult to draw any overarching conclusions across these studies. The last group involves only one study, comparing the missing-item strategy with the interrupted behavior chain strategy in terms of spontaneous requests, challenging behaviors, and stereotypical behaviors in two children with autism (Sigafoos & Meikle, 1995). Results indicated that both strategies were effective in promoting requesting and replacing challenging behaviors and stereotypical behaviors.

2. Review of Studies Involving Aided Approaches

Given the relatively more recent history of aided AAC approaches, the number of comparative studies ($n = 20$) is less but almost comparable to those identified for unaided approaches (see Table 21.2). The first group of studies involved comparisons of various instructional strategies (Berkowitz, 1990; McNaughton & Tawney, 1993; Sigafoos & Meikle, 1995; Sigafoos & Reichle, 1992). Because not even two of the studies compared the same interventions it is difficult to see any overarching patterns in these data. Oliver (1983), who compared the effects of various instructional formats, tackled a related yet different issue. This is the only study that was located on this particular topic.

Group 3 involved three studies comparing the effectiveness or efficiency of various graphic symbol sets and systems (Brady & McLean, 1996; Hurlbut, Iwata, & Green, 1982; Kozleski, 1991). The studies by Hurlbut *et al.* (1982) and Kozleski (1991) are in agreement that iconic graphic symbol sets and systems are learned more readily in terms or labeling and requesting than less iconic graphic symbol sets and systems. The Brady and McLean (1996) study involved a comparison of two arbitrary symbol sets/systems—Lexigrams, which are nonphonetic, and traditional orthography, which is phonetic. The Lexigrams were effectively learned in a match-to-sample task whereas the participants never reached the learning criterion with orthography.

Group 4 includes only one study concerned with a comparison of various display types for organizing vocabulary on speech-generating devices (SGDs) (Reichle, Dettling, Drager, & Leiter, 2000). Since the advent of dynamic displays this has become a somewhat controversial issue among practitioners, researchers, and manufacturers. In light of this debate, more studies need to be conducted to examine this issue further.

Group 5 contains three studies addressing means for selecting symbols. Horn and Jones (1996), for example, compared a scanning technique with direct selection in one child with cerebral palsy. The other two studies looked into the role of variables that affect efficiency in selecting symbols. Belfiore, Lim, and Browder (1993) examined the effects of physical distance between two symbols that need to be combined through direct selection. Lim, Browder, and Sigafoos (1998) investigated the role of high versus low physical effort needed to access a "Help" symbol in order to communicate a request for assistance.

Group 6 consists of two studies examining the effects of various presentation modes on answering questions with the written choice strategy in older adults with aphasia (Lasker, Hux, Garrett, Moncrief, & Eischeid, 1997) or on accepting food items by an adult with autism (Vaughn & Horner, 1995). Whereas the results of the first study were somewhat mixed, the Vaughn and Horner (1995) clearly indicated that the mode does make a difference. Group 7 is represented by only one study. Fox, Moore Sohlberg, and Fried-Oken (2001) studied whether it makes a difference for individuals with aphasia if the conversation topic is chosen by them or by others in terms of communication aid use. Although all participants noted greater satisfaction when communicating about choice-topics, they did not necessarily use the communication aid more with choice topics than with nonchoice topics.

In Group 8 three studies share the common focus of investigating the effects of speech output in comparison to training without speech output (Parsons & La Sorte, 1993; Schlosser, Belfiore, Nigam, Blischak, & Hetzroni, 1995; Schlosser, Blischak, Belfiore, Bartley, & Barnett, 1998). More favorable results were found in conditions where the speech output was present in terms of spelling, graphic symbol learning, and spontaneous spoken utterances. Finally, group 9 contains two studies that evaluate the relative effects of nonelectronic communication boards versus SGDs (Soto, Belfiore, Schlosser, & Haynes, 1993) or SGD software (VanAcker & Grant, 1995). In the Soto et al. (1993) study, both an SGD

Table 21.2

Comparative Studies Using Single–Subject Experimental Designs: Aided Approaches

Group	Study	Purpose	Interventions defined	Participants	Design
1	Berkowitz (1990)	To compare delayed-prompting with fading-of-prompts in training discrimination of graphic symbols typically used on communication boards	(a) *Delayed prompting* (b) *Fading-of-prompts*	Four students with autism (12;3 years to 20;10 years)	AATD
	McNaughton & Tawney (1993)	To compare two instructional techniques on the acquisition and retention of spelling vocabulary	(a) *Copy-write-compare (CWC)*: learner copies a correct model of the word twice before spelling the word independently (b) *Student-directed cueing (SDC)*: learner makes a first attempt of the word before being shown a model of the correct spelling	Two adults with cerebral palsy (26 years and 22 years)	AATD
	Sigafoos & Meikle (1995)	To compare the missing-item format with the interrupted behavior chain strategy for increasing requests and minimizing challenging and stereotypical behaviors	(a) *Missing-item format*: an item is unavailable until the learner makes an appropriate request (b) *Interrupted behavior chain*: the learner is interrupted in the midst of an ongoing activity; continuation is contingent upon an appropriate request	Two students with autism (8 years, 8 years, and 5 years)	ATD replicated across 3 sets (without a baseline)
	Sigafoos & Reichle (1992)	To compare explicit to generalized requesting on successful requests with graphic symbols	(a) *Explicit request*: teaching to point to an explicit symbol (e.g., OREO) (b) *Generalized request*: teaching to point to a generalized symbol (e.g., COOKIE)	Four adults with multiple disabilities (22, 31, 31, and 36 years)	AATD with multiple probe design across object sets
2	Oliver (1983)	To compare group versus individual training formats on receptive identification of Blissymbols	(a) *Group I*: same symbols for everyone (b) *Group II*: different symbols for everyone (c) *Individual*: one-to-one (d) *No-treatment control*	Three adults with moderate to severe intellectual disabilities (23, 24, 25 years)	AATD combined with an MBD (the second tier was the control condition)

Results	Appraisal of certainty
All four students reached the learning criterion in both conditions, indicating that both prompting techniques were effective. In terms of efficiency, delayed-prompting required fewer trials to criterion and caused fewer errors to criterion than the fading of prompts.	The design minimized sequence and carryover effects. Procedurally, the authors used counterbalancing of sets across subjects rather than within-subject solutions. The equation of sets across conditions was based solely on pretest performance without regard to contributing factors to learning potential (the specific symbols and referents used were not reported). This is the study's greatest weakness. Its strengths are treatment integrity data and the training to a learning criterion in both conditions. This afforded legitimate efficiency comparisons.
Both methods were found effective with both participants in that an equal number of words were acquired across conditions (seven and eight words each for Linda and Wendy, respectively) when the teaching criterion came into effect. Maintenance probes indicate superior performance for the SDC condition across participants. In terms of efficiency, Linda required fewer mean number of learning trials to criterion in the CWC condition, whereas the pattern is reversed for Wendy (differences are minimal).	Both, sequence and carryover effects were minimized through the design and procedural safeguards. Linda may have been biased toward the CWC condition due to experiences with a similar approach prior to the study. Sets were equated through both objective and factual methods, based on an incomplete recognition of factors contributing to spelling difficulty (e.g., number of syllables, and grade level). A learning criterion was set for individual words rather than for the sets as a whole. Nonetheless, combined with a teaching criterion, efficiency comparisons were legitimate. The lack of treatment integrity and interobserver agreement data calls into question the certainty of the evidence.
Results indicated that both conditions were equally effective in increasing spontaneous requesting. Removing the needed item (interrupted behavior chain) was not associated with any more [or less] challenging behavior or stereotypical behavior than withholding a needed item [missing-item format].	Even though the participants previously learned the requests (prompted) needed for this study using condition more closely associated with the interrupted behavior chain strategy, results refute such a bias. The same sets of objects and symbols were used across conditions, which may have resulted in carryover effects. Procedural safeguards (e.g., counterbalancing), however, minimized order effects. A learning criterion was not set. Although interobserver agreement data were satisfactory, the lack of treatment integrity data question the adherence tot he treatment protocol. Also, because there was no baseline it is difficult to attribute the observed changes to the interventions.
Correct requesting responses increased as a function of intervention. However, there were little consistent advantages for one type of requesting strategy over the other. An analysis of error patterns suggested that while the participants learned reliable discriminations among the graphic symbols across object sets, establishing conditional discriminations within each set proved difficult.	The design minimized both sequence and carryover effects. A mixed order minimized sequence effects further. In addition, the within-subject replication of effects strengthens the internal validity of the findings. The sets were equated through objective methods reflecting an accurate recognition of variables contributing to learning difficulty. A learning criterion was not set. Treatment integrity data were strong indicating that the protocol was followed as intended.
Results indicated either equivalent or faster acquisition in group training (when the same symbols were taught to each learner of the group) than in individual training.	Both, sequence and carryover effects have been minimized through the use of an AATD and other procedural safeguards such as counterbalancing. The sets of symbols across conditions, however, have been equated only in terms of parts of speech and not for other relevant variables contributing to symbol learning such as receptive status of the referent and iconicity. A teaching criterion was employed to move from the alternating treatments

(continues)

Table 21.2 (*continued*)

Group	Study	Purpose	Interventions defined	Participants	Design
	Brady & McLean (1996)	To compare Lexigrams and traditional orthography in terms of arbitrary symbol learning	Using match-to-sample procedures to teach: (a) *Lexigrams*: nonphonetic arbitrary symbols (b) *Traditional orthography*: phonetic arbitrary symbols	Four adults with severe intellectual disabilities (28, 30, 31, and 31 years)	ABC/ACB
3	Hurlbut, Iwata, & Green (1982)	To compare Blissymbols with Rebus-like line drawings on the acquisition of labeling, spontaneous use, stimulus generalization, and response generalization of communication board skills	(a) *Blissymbols* (b) *Rebus-like colored line drawings*	Three students with multiple disabilities (14 to 18 years)	AATD
	Kozleski (1991)	To compare various graphic symbol sets and systems in terms of requesting	(a) Blissymbolics (b) Premack tokens (c) Traditional orthography (d) Rebus (e) Photopictorial	Four students with autism (7;10 years to 13;6 years)	MBD across subjects with multiple interventions introduced in counterbalanced order across subjects
4	Reichle, Dettling, Drager, & Leiter (2000)	To compare three types of displays on the response accuracy and latency in matching photographs to graphic symbols	(a) *Fixed*: all symbols on one page (b) *Dynamic active*: each symbol on one page linked to as second page (c) *Dynamic passive*: two pages linked by a "go to" symbol	One student with severe intellectual disabilities (16 years)	ATD
	Horn & Jones (1996)	To compare scanning and direct selection in terms	(a) *Inverse circular scanning*: a switch is activated continuously	One child with cerebral palsy	ATD

Results	Appraisal of certainty
	phase to implementing individual training across symbol sets. The lack of treatment integrity and interobserver agreement data calls into question the certainty of the evidence.
Each of the participants, except BD, reached the learning criterion for matching Lexigrams to objects. None of the participants reached the learning criterion with traditional orthography so training was implemented until the discontinue criteria was met. Thus, Lexigrams were more effective than traditional orthography.	The design employed the same objects in both conditions making it difficult to minimize carryover effects. Counterbalancing of conditions across participants does not rule out sequence effects either. Noteworthy is the setting of a learning criterion and a teaching criterion. The lack of interobserver agreement data and treatment integrity further diminishes the certainty of the evidence, already compromised by a poor design.
Both Blissymbols and Rebus-like line drawings were effective across students in terms of acquisition. Maintenance effectiveness, however, was superior for items trained with the iconic Rebus-like line drawings. Students required about four times as many trials to learn Blissymbols than the line drawings. In terms of stimulus generalization, all students averaged higher scores on Rebus-like line drawings. Similarly, all students yielded better response generalization with Rebus-like line drawings than with Blissymbols. As far as spontaneous use is concerned, Blissymbol use was restricted to previously trained symbols, whereas Rebus-like symbol use consisted partially of transfers from previously trained Blissymbols.	An AATD along with procedural safeguards permitted the control of sequence and carryover effects. Even though the students were possibly biased toward Blissymbols, the results in favor of Rebus-like line drawings suggest that this was not the case. Unfortunately, the sets of symbols were not equated for referent-related variables within each subject but rather across subjects in that one subject received the other symbol set for the same referents as the other subject. The authors argue that the consistency in results minimize existing differences, if any, in difficulty in the sets. Noteworthy is the use of a learning criterion across conditions, legitimate efficiency comparisons, and multiple dependent measures such as learner preferences, generalization, and maintenance. The lack of treatment integrity data diminishes the certainty of evidence from an otherwise well conducted study.
All four students required fewer trials to criterion in sets that are associated with a higher degree of iconicity.	The design used relies on across-subject control of sequence effects and for equating sets of stimuli. Within the limitations of this method, sequence effects were controlled reasonably well. The sets were equated through informal means based on an incomplete understanding of contributing factors (e.g., receptive status was not assessed). Treatment integrity data were not reported and thus compromise the conclusions from this study. Finally, it is difficult to attribute differences to iconicity because no apriori manipulation of iconicity occurred.
Response time was the fastest and accuracy was the greatest for the fixed and dynamic active display types. These differences became more evident after distractor symbols were added in phase 3.	An ATD with the same symbols in both conditions does not rule out that carryover effects have influenced the findings. Procedural safeguards such as counterbalancing were used to minimize sequence effects. A teaching criterion was in place as a legitimate way to change from Phase 1 to Phase 2, and Phase 2 to 3. The term "efficiency" was evoked without a learning criterion. The lack of treatment integrity data diminishes the certainty of the evidence.
Direct selection was used more effectively than inverse circular scanning in terms of response accuracy, acquisition rate, and response time. The	An ATD with the same symbols in both conditions does not rule out carryover effects. It is unclear whether sequence effects were controlled even though the sessions for each condition

(continues)

Table 21.2 (*continued*)

Group	Study	Purpose	Interventions defined	Participants	Design
		of response accuracy, acquisition rate (i.e., type of adult prompting assistance), and response time	to rotate the arrow until the switch is released to stop the arrow when the desired location is reached (b) *Direct selection*: head-mounted optical pointer	(4 years)	
5	Belfiore, Lim, & Browder (1993)	To compare high and low indices of difficulty on the response duration of head movements across defined tasks such as sequencing two symbols with a head pointer	Evaluated stimulus distance, while holding width constant and vice versa: (a) Low index of difficulty (b) High index of difficulty	One adult with severe multiple disabilities (56 years)	ATD with reversal components (the more effective treatment was applied in the last phase)
	Lim, Browder, & Sigafoos (1998)	To compare the use of pointing to a "help" card with opening a booklet and pointing to the "help" symbol in order to request assistance when attempting access to preferred foods	Three task designs (open bag, clipped bag, twist-tie bag): (a) *High efficient alternative response*: pointing to a "help" card (b) *Less efficient alternative response*: opening a booklet and pointing to "help"	Three students with severe intellectual disabilities (12, 13, and 16 years)	Multi-element sequential design combined with MBD across subjects
6	Lasker, Hux, Garrett, Moncrief, & Eischeid (1997)	To compare the written choice strategy under two presentation modes on response accuracy to questions regarding a set of pictures used during conversation	(a) *Visual*: choices were shown but not read aloud (b) *Auditory*: choices were not written but indicated by hyphens and numbers; the choices were read aloud (c) *Standard*: baseline	Three adults with severe aphasia secondary to stroke (82, 50, and 70 years)	BC-B/C-BC; one component each of baseline (BC) was taken away in an alternating treatment phase (B alternated with C) before BC was reintroduced
	Vaughn & Horner (1995)	To compare choices offered and requests made verbally with choices offered and requests made verbally plus photos in terms of acceptance of food items	(a) *Verbal only*: choices were offered verbally or the participant was asked to indicate his preferences verbally (b) *Picture plus verbal*: after making verbal choices the participant was asked to point to photos	One young adult with autism (21 years)	ABAB

Results	Appraisal of certainty
authors hypothesized that off-task and attention fatigue issues seemed to play a role in establishing this finding.	were conducted on alternating days. Finally, the lack of treatment integrity data does not permit any conclusions as to whether the performance was due to the respective selection techniques. On a positive note, a learning criterion was used for both conditions (even though it was attained in only one condition).
Across intervention phases, the participant required less time to sequence symbols and to complete the paint task when presented with the lower index of difficulty and more time when presented with the higher index of difficulty. There were no significant differences between the tasks when the lower index of difficulty was applied to both in the final intervention phase.	The design minimized sequence and carryover effects. Procedurally, the authors counterbalanced the presentation of tasks within each pair, and pairs of tasks across sessions and phases. The equivalence of the tasks was demonstrated through objective baseline testing. Although both teaching and learning criteria were not employed, this is not as consequential given that the authors were interested in measuring the duration of the response rather than the accuracy of the response. Unfortunately, treatment integrity data are missing. This may not be as crucial given that the independent variable involved the one-time variation of a physical variable rather than several verbal directives.
Each of the participants requested assistance mostly when presented with the tied bag rather than the opened bag or clipped bag. There were no discernable differences, however, between pointing to the "help" card versus opening the booklet and to the "help" symbol.	The design permitted control of sequence effects for tasks. Functional analyses ensured that the task designs were indeed functionally equivalent and the learners were motivated by access to the preferred foods. The design, however, failed to control for sequence effects for the functionally equivalent alternative responses because pointing to the "help" symbol was introduced before opening the booklet and no attempts for counterbalancing were made. Neither a learning criterion nor a teaching criterion was set. Interobserver agreement and treatment integrity data were collected.
Two of the participants performed equally well in each of the conditions, including baseline. Thus, no effects were shown. The third participant performed best during the initial baseline (standard condition), followed by visual-only, and auditory-only. In the second baseline, performance returned to the original baseline level.	Sequence and carryover effects were not minimized with the design used (same stimuli across sets). Even though conditions were alternated it is unclear whether counterbalancing was used. A learning criterion was not set, precluding comparisons in terms of efficiency. On a positive note, treatment integrity data indicate a high level of adherence to the treatment protocol. This, however, cannot remedy the shortcomings caused by the design used.
The participant accepted more food items in the conditions where the choices were made with the photographs than verbally. Results suggest that the aided choices were more representative of the participant's preferences.	The design does not rule out sequence effects; it is unclear whether the "picture plus verbal" condition was more effective than "verbal only" due to an artifact of the order in which the conditions were introduced. Moreover, carryover effects cannot be ruled out because the same array of food items was used in both conditions. Although treatment integrity was reported to be 100%, the authors acknowledge that during the reversal phase, the procedures were not followed as planned.

(continues)

Table 21.2 (*continued*)

Group	Study	Purpose	Interventions defined	Participants	Design
7	Fox, Moore Sohlberg, & Fried-Oken (2001)	To compare conversational topics chosen by the participants versus topics selected by someone else in terms of conversational use of communication folders	(a) *Choice topics*: topics chosen by the participants (b) *Nonchoice topics*: topics chosen by someone else	Three adults with severe aphasia (49, 77, and 83 years)	AATD
	Parsons & La Sorte (1993)	To compare the effects of synthetic speech output versus no speech output on spontaneous spoken utterances	(a) *With speech output*: the synthesizer was turned on (b) *Without speech output*: the synthesizer was turned off	Six students with autism (4;8 to 6; 8 years)	A–B–BC–B–BC/ A–BC–B–BC (additive- subtractive interactional designs)
8	Schlosser, Belfiore, Nigam, Blischak, & Hetzroni (1995)	To compare the effects of speech output to a control condition without speech output on expressive graphic symbol learning	Graphic symbols were taught through simultaneous prompting in two conditions: (a) *VOCA*: the synthesizer of the SGD was turned on allowing for auditory input and feedback (b) *Non-VOCA*: the synthesizer of the SGD was turned off	Three young adults with severe to profound intellectual disabilities (25, 25, and 24 years)	PTD
	Schlosser, Blischak, Belfiore, Bartley, & Barnett (1998)	To compare the effects of spelling instruction under three feedback conditions: auditory, visual, and auditory- visual	Words were taught in three feedback modes: (a) *Auditory*: the synthesizer of SGD was turned on (b) *Visual*: liquid crystal display (LCD) was available (c) *Auditory-visual*: the synthesizer was on and LCD available	One student with autism (10 years old)	AATD
9	Soto, Belfiore, Schlosser, &	To compare a SGD with a	(a) *VOCA*: teaching requests using a SGD	One young adult with	ATD with multiple

Results	Appraisal of certainty
One of the participants demonstrated greater symbol use for answering questions with choice topics when interacting with the experimenter and in probes with unfamiliar partners. No consistent differences were found for the other two participants. In terms of commenting, two participants commented more when conversing about choice topics than nonchoice topics. No consistent differences were found for commenting during generalization probes with unfamiliar partners. All participants displayed greater satisfaction with choice topics used for training. Two unfamiliar partners ranked the interactions on nonchoice topics more enjoyable.	The design allowed for the potential to control sequence and carryover effects. Conditions were counterbalanced to minimize sequence effects. No attempt, however, appeared to be made for equating the symbols/photos and the questions used to elicit responses across conditions in terms of variables that contribute to symbol learning/use and answering questions, respectively. Data were collapsed across sessions for each week, making it difficult to analyze the true variability of the data. The absence of a baseline adds further difficulty in attributing performance to either intervention. Neither a learning criterion nor a teaching criterion was set. Treatment integrity data were collected on the procedures for assessing the choice status of the topics, but not for other procedures.
Results indicated that intervention without speech output produced no change in the frequency of spontaneous utterances. When speech output was added, however, the frequency of spontaneous utterances increased.	The design does not permit sufficient control of order effects because it uses counterbalancing of treatment order across participants rather than within a participant. Three students per order are not a sufficient sample size even though the participants were randomly allocated to the order. Further, it is unclear whether the participants were exposed to the same stimuli in both conditions, making it difficult to rule out carryover effects. A teaching criterion was applied and permitted legitimate changes to the next phase. A learning criterion was not posted. The lack of treatment integrity data calls into question the certainty of the evidence.
Two learners reached criterion in both conditions, indicating that both VOCA and non-VOCA were effective. For the third learner, only the VOCA condition was effective in that learning criterion was not reached in the non-VOCA condition. Maintenance results showed no differences between conditions. For the two participants who did reach criterion in both conditions, the VOCA condition required fewer sessions to criterion and training errors to criterion. Findings suggest that auditory stimuli contribute to efficient acquisition of graphic symbols.	Both, sequence and carryover effects have been minimized through the design along with procedural safeguards. In addition, the within-subject replications across sets enhance the internal validity of the findings. The sets were equated both through factual and objective methods. Efficiency comparisons were only made for those 2 participants who reached the learning criterion in both conditions. An apriori teaching criterion would have allowed a more unbiased termination of treatment for the third participant. Treatment integrity data were strong and comparable across conditions in this well-conducted study.
The participant reached criterion and maintained performance in each of the conditions, indicating that the conditions were equally effective in terms of spelling acquisition. The provision of speech output alone (auditory) and in combination with orthographic feedback (auditory-visual) resulted in more efficient spelling acquisition than orthographic feedback (visual) alone.	Both, sequence and carryover effects have been minimized through the design along with procedural safeguards. The sets were equated both through factual and objective methods. Efficiency comparisons were legitimately made based on the achievement of the learning criterion across conditions. Treatment integrity data were strong and comparable across conditions.
The participant reached the learning criterion with both devices across settings, suggesting that both	Sequence and carryover effects cannot be ruled because of the design (i.e., the same symbols and objects across conditions).

(continues)

Table 21.2 (*continued*)

Group	Study	Purpose	Interventions defined	Participants	Design
	Haynes (1993)	communication board in terms of the acquisition of explicit requests and preferences	(b) *Non-VOCA*: teaching requests using a communication board	profound intellectual disabilities (22 years)	baseline design across settings
	Van Acker & Grant (1995)	To compare requesting via a communication board and a computer-based system with speech output using preferred and disliked objects	(a) Computer-based animated requesting system: (b) *VOCA*: the synthesizer of SGD is turned on (c) *Non-VOCA*: the synthesizer is turned off (baseline) (d) *Preferred objects*: objects were liked by the learners (e) *Disliked objects*: objects were disliked by the learners	Three students with Rett syndrome (11;7 years, 6;8 years, and 5;2 years)	Changing conditions MBD across behaviors

and a communication board were found equally effective in terms of requesting for a young adult with profound intellectual disabilities. In the VanAcker and Grant (1995) study, an increase in requesting was noted when a computer was used with SGD software compared to a baseline condition similar to a nonelectronic communication board.

3. Review of Studies Involving Aided and Unaided Approaches

The research base involving both aided and unaided approaches is more recent and as of yet less substantive (see Table 21.3) than for aided approaches or unaided approaches alone. Nonetheless, a few studies are available (Iacono & Duncum, 1995; Iacono, Mirenda, & Beukelman, 1993; Rotholz, Berkowitz, & Burberry, 1989; Sundberg & Sundberg, 1990).

One group of studies has been comparing unaided with aided approaches (Rotholz *et al.*, 1989; Sundberg & Sundberg, 1990). Both of these studies involved manual signing and communication boards/books, which are accessed through direct selection. The study by Rotholz *et al.* (1989) found the communication

Results	Appraisal of certainty
conditions were effective. Interestingly, the two conditions were also equally efficient in that they met criterion with the same sessions in both settings. Later the participant showed a stronger preference for the VOCA condition. The learner successfully generalized the use of the SGD to different settings and communication partners.	Procedural safeguards, however, have been put into place to possibly minimize these threats. Attainment of the learning criterion in both conditions legitimized efficiency comparisons. The preference results are inconclusive in absence of a preference baseline. The generalization results cannot be attributed to intervention unequivocally due to the design used. The lack of treatment integrity data reduces the certainty of evidence further.
All three learners increased requesting over baseline (similar to a nonelectronic board condition) when provided with computer-based instruction with speech output. Two of the learners met the learning criterion for all trained Lexigrams representing preferred objects, whereas the third student acquired only one of the initial three Lexigrams. Each of the learners discriminated between preferred and disliked objects in that the preferred objects were requested more frequently.	The design along with the lack of procedural safeguards do not rule out order effects neither in terms of the comparison between no-speech plus static graphics (baseline) and speech output and animated graphics (intervention) nor in terms of preferred and disliked objects. The sets of preferred and disliked objects were equated randomly as far as the assignment of Lexigrams to objects is concerned. They were not equated, however, in terms of the number of preferred and disliked objects. Conclusions are further compromised by the lack of treatment integrity data. Interobserver agreement data were not collected because the computer recorded the data automatically.

book to be more effective than manual signing. The study by Sundberg and Sundberg (1990) indicated that for three participants, manual signing and pointing to symbols on a board were both effective (the fourth participant attained criterion with manual signs only), but manual signing was more efficient for two of the three participants (for the third participant, the board was slightly more efficient than manual signing). In interpreting these seemingly discrepant findings across the two studies, the evidence-based practitioner needs to take into account the appraisal of the certainty of evidence as well as differences in participants, in the communicative functions being taught, and the settings across these studies.

The second group of studies compared the use of unaided approaches to combined approaches, consisting of unaided approaches plus SGDs (Iacono *et al.*, 1993; Iacono & Duncum, 1995). Essentially, the two studies were concerned with evaluating what would happen if an SGD were added to the use of simultaneous communication. Even though both studies involved young children with intellectual disabilities and similar dependent measures, no clear pattern has emerged from the data.

Table 21.3

Comparative Studies Using Single-Subject Experimental Designs: Aided versus Unaided Approaches

Group	Authors	Purpose	Interventions defined	Participants	Design
1	Rotholz, Berkowitz, & Burberry (1989)	To compare manual signing with a communication book in terms of successful requesting in a fast-food restaurant	(a) *Manual signing*: baseline condition (b) *Communication book*: training condition	Two students with autism (17 and 18 years)	ABAB with a multiple baseline design across subjects
	Sundberg & Sundberg (1990)	To compare manual signing with graphic symbols in terms of accuracy for tacts and intraverbals, rate of acquisition, and generalization to correspondence	(a) *Topography-based verbal behavior (TB)*: manual signing (b) *Selection-based verbal behavior (SB)*: graphic symbols accessed via direct selection	Four adults with mild to moderate intellectual disabilities (33, 40, 46, and 50 years)	B-C/C-B design
2	Iacono & Duncum (1995)	To compare simultaneous communication versus simultaneous communication with a speech-generating device (SGD) in terms of the number of words/word combinations produced	(a) *Simultaneous communication*: speech and manual sign (b) *Simultaneous communication plus SGD*: speech, manual sign, and SGD	One child with Down syndrome (2;8 years)	ATD replicated across two activities with the more effective condition applied in the last phase
	Iacono, Mirenda, & Beukelman (1993)	To compare simultaneous communication versus simultaneous communication with an SGD in teaching the expressive use of two-word semantic combinations	(a) *Simultaneous communication*: speech and manual sign (b) *Simultaneous communication plus SGD*: speech, manual sign, and SGD	Two young children with mild or moderate intellectual disabilities	AATD with multiple baseline design across two-word semantic relations

Results	Appraisal of certainty

Both students yielded no successful requests during baseline (manual signing) and reached 100% successful requests during the first B phase (book). During the second A phase (manual signing), performance returned to 0% and increased to 100% in the last B phase (book). For John, the mean number and range of requests per session were 2 (1–3) for the first signing phase, 2.2 (1–4) for the first book phase, 1 (1) for the second signing phase, and 2 (1–4) for the second book phase. For Sam, the mean number and range of requests per session were .9 (0–3) for the first signing phase, .75 (0–1) for the first book phase, 1 (1) for the second sign phase, and 1.6 (1–3) for the second book phase.

The ABAB design does not rule out sequence effects; it is unclear whether the book itself was more effective than signing or whether this was merely an artifact of the order in which the conditions were introduced. Second, without a baseline in the book condition, it is difficult to attribute the changes to the intervention. In addition, during 3 of the 4 phase changes, the learners displayed more requests in the book condition than in the signing condition. Because an intelligible request is a precondition for the listener to interpret the request correctly (to count as a successful request—for the dependent measure), it cannot be ruled out that the differences across conditions were due to the higher number of requests in the book condition. In other words, if one requests more, one might be more successful. Interobserver agreement data were supplied for both conditions and determined to be comparable. The lack of treatment integrity data diminishes the certainty of evidence.

For tacts (i.e., pointing to a symbol or making a sign when shown an object) and intraverbals (i.e., pointing to a symbol or making a sign when an object name was spoken), Gary, Dan, and Eric reached criterion across conditions, suggesting that both conditions were effective. Mary never reached criterion on the SB tact and was not trained on the intraverbal. In terms of efficiency, Gary and Dan required more trials in the SB than in the TB condition, whereas for Eric, SB was slightly more efficient than TB (112 versus 116 trials). Correspondence results, defined as pointing to an object when presented with the name, were equivocal across participants.

None of the participants had prior experiences with either manual signing or graphic symbols, ruling out bias toward conditions. Significant threats to internal validity result from both sequence and order effects due to design flaws and the use of the same word referents across conditions. The performance of one of the participants, Eric, actually documented the presence of an order effect. Moreover, the absence of a baseline makes it difficult to attribute changes to the intervention. Similarly, the lack of treatment integrity data calls into question whether the conditions were implemented as intended.

The participant produced more words or word combinations (in any modality) in the condition with signs, speech, and the SGD rather than the condition without the SGD. An overall analysis of the modality used by the participant yielded that the SGD was used most often, despite the fact that there were more opportunities to use sign.

The design, using the same vocabulary and scripts across conditions, does not allow for sufficient control of carryover effects. Procedural steps such as counterbalancing were used to minimize sequence effects. Noteworthy is the use of a teaching criterion to terminate treatment. Also, interobserver agreement data and treatment integrity data, reported per condition, strengthen the certainty of the evidence. The procedures in the sign and speech condition, however, were applied somewhat more stringently.

Results were mixed in that one of the learners showed no differences between conditions (both were effective) whereas the other child learned more effectively in the condition involving unaided *and* aided modes. Generalization production (with a wider array of response options) to nonteaching sessions occurred for all structures taught to the first child without differences across conditions. The second child only generalized those combinations taught in the first set.

An AATD along with procedural safeguards permitted the control of sequence and carryover effects. Participants may have been biased toward the "unimodal" condition because simultaneous communication was used in their classroom. Results, however, refute this possible bias. Even though only comprehended combinations and symbols, which the learners could match to the objects, were included, the equivalence of conditions is not clearly established and reported. The generalization performances need to be viewed cautiously in absence of a generalization baseline. Strong treatment integrity data suggest that the treatment was implemented as planned.

III. SIMULTANEOUS COMMUNICATION OR SIGN ALONE: AN EBP ILLUSTRATION

The steps involved in implementing EBP in AAC include (1) asking a well-built question, (2) selecting evidence sources, (3) executing the search strategy, (4) examining the evidence, (5) applying the evidence, (6) evaluating the application of the evidence, and (7) disseminating the findings (see Chapter 12).

A. ASKING ANSWERABLE QUESTIONS

The questions need to be answerable through a systematic search of the relevant evidence. The questions posed here pertain to the following role identified in the "Knowledge and Skills" document of the American Speech-Language and Hearing Association (2002)—"determining AAC methods, components, and strategies to maximize functional communication by individuals." The following are examples of questions related to the introduction of manual signing:

> Olivia is a 5-year-old child with severe intellectual disabilities and concomitant mild hearing loss who is currently attending an integrated kindergarten program. She is unable to meet her daily communication needs through natural speech and communicates primarily through presymbolic means. Her kindergarten peers have difficulty interpreting some of her presymbolic communicative behaviors. Olivia's fine motor ability is excellent, including the dexterity in her fingers. Next year, Olivia will be entering first grade in an elementary school. Her family and clinician are interested in exploring the possibility of introducing Olivia to manual signing. Although there seems to be agreement that manual signing may be a good option to explore, there is less of an agreement as to how manual signing should be introduced. Specifically, everyone is wondering whether to use simultaneous communication, sign-alone, or a hybrid as a method for teaching manual singing for expressive use. Once the main approach has been decided, the stakeholders are also interested in other strategies that might facilitate the learning and use of manual signing.

This scenario indicates that there are actually two clinical or educational problems to be solved. The first one, which shall be referred to as the primary question, is concerned with selecting the main approach for introducing manual signing between simultaneous communication and sign-alone training. A decision concerning this question is a necessary but not sufficient step toward the teaching of manual signs. That is why a secondary question is posed to explore other strategies that may examine the learning and use of manual signing.

To be precise, these questions contain the essential components necessary in order to be well-built. The components (1) describe the direct stakeholder and his or her capabilities relevant to the clinical problem (a 5-year-old child with severe intellectual disabilities who is currently communicating through presymbolic means; see Chapter 14 for characteristics of beginning communicators), (2) explain the direct stakeholders' current (i.e., integrated kindergarten program) and future environments (i.e., elementary school) and relevant other stakeholders (family, clinician, preschool teacher, elementary school teacher) (3) make explicit the clinical or educational problems to be solved (i.e., whether to teach manual signs through simultaneous communication, sign-alone, or a hybrid method; what other strategies may facilitate manual signing), and (4) specify the expected clinical/educational outcomes (i.e., to be able to use manual sign expressively).

B. The Primary Question: Selecting Evidence Sources and Executing the Search Strategy

In absence of a meta-analysis or other systematic synthesis, the evidence-based practitioner would rely on the studies summarized in narrative form in Table 21.1. This table includes studies that compared unaided approaches. In terms of the hierarchy of evidence proposed in Chapter 12, the review in Table 21.1 ranks lower than individual single-subject experimental studies. Therefore, one could use the table as a starting point for identifying individual single-subject experiments that are relevant. After all, individual single-subject experiments rank higher than a narrative review. For the purposes of this answerable question, the group 1 studies appears to be most relevant. There are two studies that compare simultaneous communication with sign-alone training with children who have severe intellectual disabilities (Clarke et al., 1988). The certainty of the evidence of these two studies is examined in the next section.

C. The Primary Question: Examining the Evidence

The first study by Clarke et al. (1988) clearly indicated that simultaneous communication was more efficient than sign-alone training for four learners with severe intellectual disabilities. The one learner in the second study by Clarke et al. (1988) only reached criterion with simultaneous communication and not with sign-alone. Both of these studies had strong designs using equated sets of stimuli; their only shortcoming was the lack of treatment integrity data (studies I and II) or interobserver agreement data (study II). Thus, the evidence-based practitioner cannot be sure whether the treatment was applied as intended, rendering the certainty of evidence as suggestive.

D. The Primary Question: Applying the Evidence

The evidence-based practitioner would then share the findings from the examination of evidence concerning the primary question with all relevant stakeholders. Given the suggestive evidence, the stakeholders agree to pursue simultaneous communication as the major approach for introducing Olivia to manual signs:

> Simultaneous communication will be used as the primary approach for introducing manual signing to Olivia.

This decision was partially influenced by the suggestive yet robust findings from other studies in group 1, which were in favor of simultaneous communication with populations other than people with intellectual disabilities. The next step calls for the selection of evidence sources for the secondary question.

E. The Secondary Question: Selecting Evidence Sources and Executing the Search Strategy

Several studies in group 2 appear to be relevant because they concerned themselves with studying the conditions under which simultaneous communication works more effectively or efficiently. For example, Clarke *et al.* (1986) examined whether simultaneous communication works better when introducing manual signs for known words or for unknown words. Three studies evaluated how to maximize simultaneous communication training through (1) overtraining (i.e., "extensive sign training"), (2) pretraining of receptive skills (i.e., "mediated sign training," "receptive-expressive order") or expressive skills (i.e., "expressive-receptive order"), and (3) mixing some oral-only trials into simultaneous communication (i.e., "differential sign training") (Remington & Clarke, 1993a, 1993b).

The study by Carr *et al.* (1984), group 3, does not apply here because neither of the two interventions compared involved simultaneous communication. The two studies in group 4 are not relevant because their focus was on the role of reinforcement, when combined with directed rehearsal. For this research to bear relevance, the studies would have required a comparison of simultaneous communication with and without directed rehearsal or positive reinforcement. The studies in group 5, however, are all informative for answering the secondary question because they looked into the role of different types of reinforcement on expressive signing during simultaneous communication in students with severe to profound intellectual disabilities. Goodman and Remington (1993) compared nonspecific reinforcement (i.e., the learner received a reinforcer unrelated to the visual referent) to specific reinforcement (the learner received the visual referent for the signs produced). The other two studies (Duker *et al.*, 1994; Duker & Moonen, 1986) were concerned with the manipulation of the amount of reinforcement rather than the type of reinforcement in learners with severe to profound intellectual disabilities. The studies by Bennett *et al.* (1986) and Dalrymple and Feldman (1992) in group 6 are pertinent because they involved comparisons of various prompting strategies or the role of directed rehearsal in terms of expressive signing in participants with mental retardation and some degree of hearing loss. Olivia is not a passive communicator. Therefore, the strategies compared by Sigafoos and Meikle (1995) do not apply in her case.

F. The Secondary Question: Examining the Evidence

Clarke *et al.* (1986) offered suggestive evidence that simultaneous communication is more efficient when introducing signs for referents that are receptively known as opposed to signs that are unknown. Apparently, knowing the referents allows the learner to map a sign onto what he or she already knows and therefore requires fewer learning trials. Based on this study with learners very similar to Olivia, it is recommended that

Manual signs should be first introduced for referents that Olivia knows.

The two studies by Remington and Clarke (1993a) found suggestive evidence that simultaneous communication was more efficient when the signs were overtrained rather than preteaching the receptive knowledge of the referents for which manual signs are introduced. Although intriguing, this finding is not applicable. The manual signs to be introduced will only be for known words; thus preteaching is not necessary. The comparison of overtraining simultaneous communication with mixing some oral-only trials into simultaneous communication ("differential sign training"), however, does bear relevance (Remington & Clarke, 1993b). In terms of expressive signing, this study yielded suggestive evidence that overtraining was more efficient than mixing some oral trials into simultaneous communication. Improvements in speech comprehension and selective attention, however, were only noted with differential sign training. Because Olivia does not appear to have difficulty with speech comprehension and selective attention, this may not be important. Thus, based on this evaluation it is suggested that

Manual signs should be overtrained rather than merely trained to acquisition.

In a study yielding suggestive evidence, Goodman and Remington (1993) showed that providing the learner with the visual referent (i.e., object) for the signs produced (as in requesting) was more efficient than providing the learner with a reinforcer unrelated to the visual referent. The learners were comparable to Olivia in terms of classification and chronological age. The studies reviewed thus far had relied on providing reinforcers unrelated to the visual referent. Although signing was expressive in these studies, it served merely as a labeling function or no communicative function. The study suggests that it is more efficient if

> Manual signs are introduced to serve a requesting function.

The studies by Duker and Moonen (1986) and Duker *et al.* (1994) suggest that when teaching manual signs as requests, it appears more effective to deliver only incomplete portions of the requested items. Unfortunately, an appraisal of these studies renders them inconclusive. The study by Bennett *et al.* (1986) renders conclusive evidence that progressive time delay is a more efficient prompting strategy than the system of least prompts. Although the students were older than Olivia, they were similar in terms of classification of intellectual disabilities and hearing loss. None of the other studies reviewed thus far involved learners with hearing loss. Bennett *et al.* (1986) did not teach a requesting function so it is unclear whether the results would generalize to the teaching of requesting. With some degree of caution it is therefore recommended that, if prompting is necessary,

> Manual signs should be prompted using progressive time delay.

The study by Dalrymple and Feldman (1992) suggests that directed rehearsal, when combined with prompting, generates more efficient expressive signing than prompting without directed rehearsal. Unfortunately, the evidence of this study is inconclusive and does not permit any recommendations.

G. THE SECONDARY QUESTION: APPLYING THE EVIDENCE

The evidence-based practitioner would then share the findings from the examination of evidence concerning the secondary question with all relevant stakeholders. There is suggestive evidence or conclusive evidence for all the recommendations provided earlier. These are summarized as follows:

- Manual signs should be first introduced for referents that Olivia knows (supported by suggestive evidence).
- Manual signs should be overtrained rather than merely trained to the acquisition criterion (supported by suggestive evidence).
- Manual signs should be introduced to serve a requesting function (supported by suggestive evidence).
- Manual signs should be prompted, when necessary, using progressive time delay (supported by conclusive evidence).

The practitioner would discuss these recommendations and try to come to a consensus about each of them. There may be other evidence sources beyond the comparative studies reviewed in this chapter that could provide additional insights into instructional approaches to introduce manual signing. For example, the literature on using milieu teaching and script-based learning may offer suggestions for introducing manual signs within functional contexts (e.g., Sack, McLean, McLean, & Spradlin, 1992). Although the evidence-based practitioner would consult this literature, this is beyond the scope of this chapter.

H. Evaluating the Application of the Evidence

If it is decided to pursue simultaneous communication with Olivia, it would be prudent to monitor the effectiveness of manual signing for Olivia in meeting his communication needs. The team should develop goals that are reflective of Olivia's communication needs. Perhaps, the team can explore the use of goal attainment scaling to measure progress toward individualized goals (see Schlosser, 2002).

I. Disseminating the Findings

As discussed in previous EBP illustrations, the last step involves the dissemination of the findings. The practitioner and the other stakeholders would share their experiences in going through this process and its outcomes so that future evidence-based practitioners and other stakeholders can learn from the information and researchers can become aware of the gaps in the knowledge base for purposes of implementing EBP. Chapter 12 provides ideas for possible publication outlets.

IV. CONCLUSIONS: THE ROLE OF COMPARISON STUDIES FOR EBP

A. Evaluating the Evidence from Comparison Studies

1. Comparison Designs and the EBP Hierarchy

Due to their ubiquitous role in EBP, comparative single-subject experimental designs received their special place within the design hierarchy proposed in Chapter 12. As discussed in Chapter 6, there are designs that lend themselves more readily than others for drawing valid conclusions about the relative efficacy of two or more interventions. The parallel treatments design (PTD) ranks highest because it allows for intrasubject replications across equated sets by combining an adapted alternating treatment design (AATD) with the features of a multiple-probe design. This intrasubject replication has the potential to enhance the internal validity of a comparison. The PTD is closely followed by the AATD, which allows for the creation of equal but independent sets and thereby minimizes threats to internal validity such as carryover effects. The traditional alternating treatments design (ATD) follows the adapted version of the same design because the same sets are used for each treatment; this causes concern about carryover effects. The ABACA/ACABA design offers counterbalancing of the order of treatments, but it is less suitable than any of the previously mentioned designs because the counterbalancing occurs across rather than within subjects (i.e., one order assigned to participant 1 and the other to participant 2). Finally, the A-B-BC-B-BC/A-BC-B-BC design suffers from the same problems as the aforementioned design. ABAB designs are not suitable for a comparison of two interventions because one of the conditions is presented as a baseline, which causes serious concerns about order effects.

2. Other Factors to Consider

As discussed extensively in Chapter 12, there are methodological issues to consider other than design when evaluating the certainty of research evidence such as treatment integrity and the reliability of the dependent measures. In addition to the variables that are relevant for all intervention research, comparative single-subject experimental designs are presented with other issues that influence the certainty of evidence. The appraisal of studies in Tables 21.1 to 21.3, following the coding categories in Appendix 21A, clearly demonstrated the importance of procedural safeguards, the equating of instructional sets based on current knowledge of factors contributing to learning difficulty, and legitimate bases for arriving at effectiveness and efficiency comparisons. These additional variables add to the burden of evidence-based practitioners and researchers alike. As the following section will demonstrate, this additional effort is well worth it given the role of comparative efficacy studies for EBP.

B. How Can Comparison Studies Inform EBP?

Although it is essential for any evolving field to first establish the effectiveness of a *particular* intervention (i.e., "is this intervention working?"), Schlosser (1999) argued that there are at least two sets of reasons for comparing the efficacy of two or more interventions[1] (i.e., "which intervention is working better?").

---

[1]Comparison studies in this chapter refer to the comparison of at least two interventions. It is acknowledged, however, that other types of comparisons, such as comparisons of the effects of one intervention on participants displaying two different characteristics (e.g., Carr, Pridal, & Dores, 1984), provide valuable contributions as well.

These reasons include the current state of the AAC field and increased accountability in health care and education. Concerning the current state of the field, the AAC field has reached a sufficient database, at least in selected areas, to permit the study of comparisons among interventions. That is, individual interventions have been demonstrated to be effective in their own right, thus providing the perfect opportunity to conduct comparative studies (examples of such areas were provided in Section II.)

In terms of accountability of health care systems and education, comparative efficacy evaluations provide databased arguments for choosing one intervention over another intervention. Comparisons are made not only in terms of whether one intervention works as well as the other in producing behavior change, generalization, and maintenance (effectiveness), but also in terms of efficiency (e.g., rate of learning, error rate, cost). In times of scarce resources, efficiency seems to be the most crucial index of efficacy. Increasingly, practitioners are being required to document rationales for the decisions they make in general and the interventions they support in particular. Because comparative efficacy evaluations provide data concerning the efficacy of at least two interventions in direct comparison, they can be invaluable for the practitioner to engage in the principles of EBP. In the introduction section of this chapter, a few scenarios were mentioned that require "the integration of best and current research evidence with clinical/educational expertise and relevant stakeholder perspectives to facilitate decisions for assessment and intervention that are deemed effective and efficient for a given direct stakeholder" (Chapter 12, p. 9). Evidence from comparison studies are especially helpful for tackling such choice scenarios involving target behaviors for which there is an array of intervention options and when it is difficult for the team to choose one over the other.

Evidence-based practitioners are encouraged to seek systematic reviews first, rather than having to engage in a search and appraisal of individual studies. Systematic reviews such as meta-analyses (see Chapter 11) generate "effect sizes" for individual interventions, which are then compared to determine what types of interventions are more effective than others. Although such data are extremely helpful to the evidence-based practitioner, it needs to be kept in mind that the reviewer rather than researchers of original studies generated these comparisons. Comparative efficacy studies, on the other hand, offer *direct* comparisons of two or more interventions or conditions within the same experiment. In other words, these comparisons are not review generated but study generated. A systematic review of comparative studies is the optimal source for the evidence-based practitioner because it affords a synthesis of study-generated comparisons across numerous studies. Ideally, this review should be implemented using meta-analytic techniques for the reasons specified in Chapter 11. Until the findings from such a review become available, the narrative review presented in this chapter should provide preliminary insights and valuable information for the practitioner.

REFERENCES

American Speech-Language-Hearing Association (1989). Competencies for speech-language pathologists providing services in augmentative communication. *ASHA, 31,* 107–110.

American Speech-Language-Hearing Association. (2002, April 16). Augmentative and alternative communication: Knowledge and skills for service delivery. *ASHA Leader, 7 (Suppl. 22),* 97–106.

Barrera, R. D., Lobato-Barrera, D., & Sulzer-Azaroff, B. (1980). A simultaneous treatment comparison of three expressive language training programs with a mute autistic child. *Journal of Autism and Developmental Disorders, 10,* 21–37.

Barrett, R. P., & Sisson, L. A. (1987). Use of an alternating treatments design as a strategy for empirically determining language training approaches with mentally retarded children. *Research in Developmental Disabilities, 8,* 401–412.

Belfiore, P. J., Lim, L., & Browder, D. M. (1993). Increasing the efficiency of instruction for a person with severe disabilities: The applicability of Fitt's law in predicting response time. *Journal of Behavioral Education, 3,* 247–258.

Bennett, D. L., Gast, D. L., Wolery, M., & Schuster, J. (1986). Time delay and system of least prompts: A comparison in teaching manual sign production. *Education and Training of the Mentally Retarded, 21,* 117–129

Berkowitz, S. (1990). A comparison of two methods of prompting in training discrimination of communication book pictures by autistic students. *Journal of Autism and Developmental Disorders, 20,* 255–262.

Brady, D. O., & Smouse, A. D. (1978). A simultaneous comparison of three methods of language training with an autistic child: An experimental single case analysis. *Journal of Autism and Childhood Schizophrenia, 8,* 271–279.

Brady, N. C., & McLean, L. K. (1996). Arbitrary symbol learning by adults with severe mental retardation: Comparison of lexigrams and printed words. *American Journal of Mental Retardation, 100,* 423–427.

Carr, E., Pridal, C., & Dores, P. (1984). Speech versus sign comprehension in autistic children: Analysis and prediction. *Journal of Experimental Child Psychology, 37,* 587–597.

Clarke, S., Remington, B., & Light, P. (1986). An evaluation of the relationship between receptive speech skills and expressive signing. *Journal of Applied Behavior Analysis, 19,* 231–239.

Clarke, S., Remington, B., & Light, P. (1988). The role of referential speech in sign learning by mentally retarded children: A comparison of total communication and sign-alone training. *Journal of Applied Behavior Analysis, 21,* 419–426.

Conaghan, B. P., Singh, N., Moe, T. L., Landrum, T. J., & Ellis, C. R. (1992). Acquisition and generalization of manual signs by hearing-impaired adults with mental retardation. *Journal of Behavioral Education, 2,* 177–205.

Dalrymple, A. J., & Feldman, M. A. (1992). Effects of reinforced directed rehearsal on expressive sign language by persons with mental retardation. *Journal of Behavioral Education, 2,* 1–16.

Duker, P. C., Kraaykamp, M., & Visser, E. (1994). A stimulus control procedure to increase requesting with individuals who are severely/profoundly intellectually disabled. *Journal of Intellectual Disability Research, 38,* 177–186.

Duker, P. C., & Moonen, X. M. (1986). The effect of two procedures on spontaneous signing with Down's syndrome children. *Journal of Mental Deficiency Research, 30,* 355–364.

Fox, L. E., Moore Sohlberg, M., & Fried-Oken, M. (2001). Effects of conversational topic choice on outcomes of augmentative communication intervention for adults with aphasia. *Aphasiology, 15,* 171–200.

Goodman, J., & Remington, B. (1993). Acquisition of expressive signing: Comparison of reinforcement strategies. *Augmentative and Alternative Communication, 9,* 26–35.

Horn, E. M., & Jones, H. A. (1996). Comparison of two selection techniques used in augmentative and alternative communication. *Augmentative and Alternative Communication, 12,* 23–31.

Hurlbut, B. I., Iwata, B. A., & Green, J. D. (1982). Nonvocal language acquisition in adolescents with severe physical disabilities: Blissymbol versus iconic stimulus formats. *Journal of Applied Behavior Analysis, 15,* 241–257.

Iacono, T., & Duncum, J. E. (1995). Comparison of sign alone and in combination with an electronic communication device in early language intervention: Case study. *Augmentative and Alternative Communication, 11,* 249–259.

Iacono, T., Mirenda, P., & Beukelman, D. R. (1993). Comparison of unimodal and multimodal AAC techniques for children with intellectual disabilities. *Augmentative and Alternative Communication, 9,* 83–94.

Iacono, T., & Parsons, C. (1986). A comparison of techniques in teaching signs to the intellectually disabled using an alternating treatments design. *Australian Journal of Human Communication Disorders, 14,* 23–34.

Kahn, J. V. (1977). A comparison of manual and oral language training with mute retarded children. *Mental Retardation, 15,* 21–23.

Kahn, J. V. (1981). A comparison of sign and verbal language training with nonverbal retarded children. *Journal of Speech and Hearing Research, 46,* 113–119.

Kozleski, E. B. (1991). Visual symbol acquisition by students with autism. *Exceptionality, 2,* 173–194.

Lasker, J., Hux, K., Garrett, K. L., Moncrief, E. M., & Eischeid, T. J. (1997). Variations on the written choice communication strategy for individuals with severe aphasia. *Augmentative and Alternative Communication , 13,* 108–116.

Lim, L., Browder, D. M., & Sigafoos, J. (1998). The role of response effort and motion study in functionally equivalent task designs and alternatives. *Journal of Behavioral Education, 8,* 81–102.

Linton, J. M., & Singh, N. N. (1984). Acquisition of sign language using positive practice overcorrection. *Behavior Modification, 8,* 553–566.

McNaughton, D., & Tawney, J. (1993). Comparison of two spelling instruction techniques for adults who use augmentative and alternative communication. *Augmentative and Alternative Communication, 9,* 72–82.

Oliver, P. R. (1983). Effects of teaching different tasks in group versus individual training formats with severely handicapped individuals. *TASH Journal, 8,* 79–91.

Parsons, C. L., & La Sorte, D. (1993). The effect of computers with synthesized speech and no speech on the spontaneous communication of children with autism. *Australian Journal of Human Communication Disorders, 21,* 12–31.

Reichle, J., Dettling, E. E., Drager, K. D. R., & Leiter, A. (2000). Comparison of correct responses and response latency for fixed and dynamic displays: Performance of a learner with severe developmental disabilities. *Augmentative and Alternative Communication, 16,* 154–163.

Remington, B., & Clarke, S. (1983). Acquisition of expressive signing by autistic children: An evaluation of the relative effects of simultaneous communication and sign-alone training. *Journal of Applied Behavior Analysis, 16,* 315–328.

Remington, B., & Clarke, S. (1993a). Simultaneous communication and speech comprehension. Part I: Comparison of two methods of teaching expressive signing and speech comprehension skills. *Augmentative and Alternative Communication, 9,* 36–48.

Remington, B., & Clarke, S. (1993b). Simultaneous communication and speech comprehension. Part II: Comparison of two methods of overcoming selective attention during expressive sign training. *Augmentative and Alternative Communication, 9,* 49–60.

Romski, M. A., & Sevcik, R. A. (1996). *Breaking the speech barrier: Language development through augmented means.* Baltimore: Paul H. Brookes.

Rotholz, D. A., Berkowitz, S. F., & Burberry, J. (1989). Functionality of two modes of communication in the community by students with developmental disabilities. A comparison of signing and communication books. *Journal of the Association for Persons with Severe Handicaps, 14,* 227–233.

Sack, S. H., McLean, L. S., McLean, J. E., & Spradlin, J. E. (1992). Effects of increased opportunities within scripted activities on communication rates of individuals with severe retardations. *Behavioral Residential Treatment*, 7, 235–257.

Schlosser, R. W. (1997, November). *"Which AAC intervention works better?" Methodologic issues in comparative efficacy evaluations*. Invited paper presented at the panel "Efficacy Research Issues in Augmentative and Alternative Communication" at the annual convention of the ASHA, Boston, MA.

Schlosser, R. W. (1999). Comparative efficacy of interventions in augmentative and alternative communication. *Augmentative and Alternative Communication*, 15, 56–68.

Schlosser, R. W. (2002). Using goal attainment scaling to measure outcomes in speech-language pathology. Manuscript under review.

Schlosser, R. W., Belfiore, P. J., Nigam, R., Blischak, D., & Hetzroni, O. (1995). The effects of speech output technology in the learning of graphic symbols. *Journal of Applied Behavior Analysis*, 28, 537–549.

Schlosser, R. W., Blischak, D. M., Belfiore, P. J., Bartley, C., & Barnett, N. (1998). The effects of synthetic speech output and orthographic feedback on spelling in a student with autism: A preliminary study. *Journal of Autism and Developmental Disorders*, 28, 319–329.

Schlosser, R. W., & Lee, D. (2000). Promoting generalization and maintenance in augmentative and alternative communication: A meta-analysis of 20 years of effectiveness research. *Augmentative and Alternative Communication*, 16, 208–227.

Schlosser, R. W., & Sigafoos, J. (2003). Augmentative and alternative communication for persons with development disabilities. A meta-analysis of comparative efficacy studies. Research in progress.

Schwartz, I. S., Garfinkle, A. N., & Bauer, J. (1998). The Picture Exchange Communication System: Communication outcomes for young children with disabilities. *Topics in Early Childhood Special Education*, 18, 144–159.

Sigafoos, J., & Meikle, B. (1995). A comparison of two procedures for increasing spontaneous requests in children with autism. *European Journal on Mental Disability*, 2, 11–24.

Sigafoos, J., & Reichle, J. (1992). Comparing explicit to generalized requesting in an augmentative communication mode. *Journal of Developmental and Physical Disabilities*, 4, 167–188.

Sisson, L. A., & Barrett, R. P. (1984). An alternating treatments comparison of oral and total communication training with minimally verbal retarded children. *Journal of Applied Behavior Analysis*, 17, 559–566.

Soto, G., Belfiore, P. J., Schlosser, R. W., & Haynes, C. (1993). Teaching specific requests: A comparative analysis on skill acquisition and preference using two augmentative and alternative communication aids. *Education and Training in Mental Retardation*, 28, 169–178.

Sundberg, C. T., & Sundberg, M. L. (1990). Comparing topography-based verbal behavior with stimulus selection-based verbal behavior. *The Analysis of Verbal Behavior*, 8, 31–41.

Van Acker, R., & Grant, S. H. (1995). An effective computer-based requesting system for persons with Rett syndrome. *Journal of Childhood Communication Disorders*, 16, 31–38.

Vaughn, B., & Horner, R. H. (1995). Effects of concrete versus verbal choice systems on problem behavior. *Augmentative and Alternative Communication*, 11, 89–92.

Watters, R. G., Wheeler, L. J., & Watters, W. E. (1981). The relative efficiency of two orders for training autistic children in the expressive and receptive use of manual signs. *Journal of Communication Disorders*, 14, 273–285.

Webster, C. D., McPherson, H., Sloman, L., Evans, M. A., & Kuchar, E. (1973). Communicating with an autistic boy by gestures. *Journal of Autism and Childhood Schizophrenia*, 3, 337–346.

Wells, M. E. (1981). The effects of total communication versus traditional speech training on word articulation in severely mentally retarded individuals. *Applied Research in Mental Retardation*, 2, 323–333.

Wherry, J. N., & Edwards, R. P. (1983). A comparison of verbal, sign, and simultaneous systems for the acquisition of receptive language by an autistic boy. *Journal of Communication Disorders*, 16, 201–216.

Definitions—AAC Comparison Studies Coding Manual

Dear Coder,

This manual contains operational definitions for those variables that are not self-evident or self-explanatory. Please consult this manual while coding any experiments. Questions or needed clarifications should be directed to the first author.

Participant—Bias

The participants are not biased toward a particular condition due to previous experiences.

1—Not biased
The participant description does not reveal any reason to believe that the subject may respond more favorably to one of the interventions due to prior exposure or history with a particular intervention. In particular, bias toward the intervention that is hypothesized to be most efficacious is problematic.

2—Possibly biased
The participant description does not allow the reader to rule out entirely that the participants may be biased toward one of the interventions. This may be the case when participant descriptions fail to describe the participants' experiences with each intervention prior to the study.

3—Biased
The participant description documents that the participants are biased toward one of the interventions based on prior experiences with or documented preferences concerning a treatment.

Design—Sequence Effects

Various comparative designs afford varied control of sequence effects. The ABAB design, for example, does not control for sequence effects because the intervention always follows the baseline.

1—Minimized
The design permits that sequence effects are minimized or controlled.

2—Cannot be ruled out
The design cannot rule out sequence effects.

Design—Carryover Effects

Various comparative designs afford varied control of carryover effects. An ATD (using the same stimuli with each intervention) does not rule out carryover effects.

1—Minimized

The design permits that carryover effects are minimized or controlled.

2—Cannot be ruled out

The design cannot rule out carryover effects.

Design—Within-Subject Replication

The comparative design affords within-subject replication. Both the PTD and the AATD/ATD combined with an MBD/MPD afford this opportunity. The PTD differs from the ATD combined with an MBD/MPD because the former includes maintenance probes on previously acquired sets whereas the latter does not.

1—Yes

The design does allow within-subject replication.

2—No

The design does not allow within-subject replication.

Procedural Safeguards

Carryover effects or sequence effects may be minimized through adequate procedural safeguards such as counterbalancing of conditions across sessions or days, randomizing the sequence, inserting an adequate time interval between conditions, enhancing discriminability of conditions through verbal and nonverbal means, and so forth.

1—Minimized

The procedural safeguards are adequate to minimize carryover and sequence effects.

2—Cannot be ruled out

The procedural safeguards are inadequate and therefore cannot rule out carryover and sequence effects.

Learning Criterion

An a priori learning criterion serves important functions for determining the relative effectiveness and efficiency of conditions.

1—Yes—All

An apriori learning criterion was set for all instructional sets of the conditions under study. Training was continued until criterion was reached in each of the conditions.

2—Yes—First

An apriori learning criterion was set as it applies only to that condition which attains the criterion first on its instructional set. Training is terminated once criterion is reached in that condition.

3—Yes—Per Stimuli

An a priori learning criterion was set as it applies only to each stimulus (e.g., spelling word) rather than per instructional set. Training is terminated with the help of an additional teaching criterion. This may result in a differential number of words learned across conditions.

4—No

An a priori learning criterion was not set.

Teaching Criterion

An a priori teaching criterion serves important functions for determining the termination of treatment and possibly the effectiveness and efficiency of interventions.

1—Yes

An a priori teaching criterion was set.

2—No

An a priori teaching criterion was not set.

Demonstrated Equivalence

1—N/A

The equivalence of sets is not relevant (as in an ATD or ABAB involving the same stimuli).

2—Yes (within participant)

The equivalence of sets is demonstrated within the same participant using any of the methods 2–8 of the next category.

3—Yes (across participants)

The equivalence of sets is demonstrated only across participants (see method 6 of the next category).

4—No

The equivalence of sets is not demonstrated.

5—Not reported

The equivalence of sets is not reported (e.g., it is unclear whether there are different sets per condition).

Equivalence Methods

If the equivalence of sets is demonstrated (marked 2 or 3 in previous question), a variety of methods may have been used, including those that are (1) informal, (2) factual, or (3) objective.

1—N/A
As with an ATD or ABAB using the same stimuli across conditions.

2—Informal
The equivalence of sets is demonstrated based on informal methods such as consultation of experts.

3—Factual
The equivalence of sets is demonstrated based on factual methods. Factual methods are derived from a logical analysis of the universe of potential stimulus items (e.g., mean length of words).

4—Objective
The equivalence of sets is demonstrated based on objective methods. Objective methods typically rely on observations of performance with instructional sets prior to intervention and include interobserver agreement data.

5—Objective *and* learning difficulty
The equivalence of sets is demonstrated based on objective methods through pretest performance. In addition, the authors present data that demonstrate equivalence in terms of learning difficulty or potential using pertinent contributing factors.

6—Across subjects through counterbalancing
The equivalence of sets is demonstrated by counterbalancing stimuli across subjects.

7—Random allocation
The stimuli were randomly assigned to the conditions as a method for equating sets.

8—Combined (factual/informal)
A combination of factual and informal methods is used for different variables.

9—No
The equivalence of sets is not documented.

Equivalence: Knowledge at Time of Study

Is the equivalence of sets demonstrated through an understanding of current knowledge of contributing factors at the time the study was completed?

1—N/A
The equivalence of sets is not relevant or has not been demonstrated at all.

2—Yes
The equivalence of sets is based on knowledge of contributing factors that is *current* at the time of study.

3—No
The equivalence of sets is based on knowledge of contributing factors that is *outdated* at the time of study.

Equivalence: Knowledge at Time of Review

Is the equivalence of sets demonstrated through an understanding of current knowledge of contributing factors?

1—N/A

The equivalence of sets is not relevant or has not been demonstrated at all.

2—Yes

The equivalence of sets is based on knowledge of contributing factors that is *current* at the time of review/examination.

3—No

The equivalence of sets is based on knowledge of contributing factors that is *outdated* at the time of review/examination.

Random Assignment

Are instructional sets randomly assigned to the treatments?

1—N/A

Assignment of sets to treatments is not relevant by virtue of the design used.

2—Yes

Sets are randomly assigned to treatments.

3—No

Sets are not randomly assigned to treatments.

Functional Independence

1—N/A

The independence of sets is not relevant because only one set is used (i.e., ATD).

2—Yes

The functional independence of sets is demonstrated (through logical reasoning).

3—No

The functional independence of sets is *not* demonstrated.

Interobserver Agreement

1—Not assessed

Interobserver agreement was not assessed.

2—Assessed only across conditions

Interobserver agreement was assessed, but only by presenting means and ranges across conditions.

3—Assessed and comparable

Interobserver agreement was assessed per condition and is comparable across conditions.

4—Not comparable

Interobserver agreement was assessed but is not comparable across conditions.

Treatment Integrity

1—Not assessed
Treatment integrity was not assessed.

2—Assessed only across conditions
Treatment integrity was assessed but only by presenting means and ranges across conditions.

3—Assessed and comparable
Treatment integrity was assessed and is comparable across conditions.

4—Not comparable
Treatment integrity was assessed but is not comparable across conditions.

Effectiveness

1—Attainment of learning criterion—All
The effectiveness of all conditions is demonstrated through the attainment of an apriori learning criterion.

2—Attainment of learning criterion—First
The effectiveness of one of the conditions is demonstrated through the attainment of an apriori learning criterion.

3—Visual analysis or teaching criterion
The effectiveness of conditions is demonstrated through a visual analysis of intervention performances relative to baseline performances (rather than the attainment of a learning criterion). This may or may not be accompanied by the attainment of a teaching criterion.

4—Not demonstrated
The effectiveness of conditions is not established.

Efficiency

1—N/A
The efficiency of conditions is not applicable because a learning criterion was not attained in each condition.

2—Learning criterion
The efficiency of conditions is determined based on the attainment of a learning criterion in each condition.

3—Teaching criterion
The efficiency of conditions is determined based on the attainment of a teaching criterion in each condition.

4—Learning criterion or teaching criterion
The efficiency of conditions is determined based on the attainment of a learning criterion or teaching criterion (in each condition), whichever came first.

5—Other
The efficiency of conditions is determined through means other than those defined above.

CHAPTER 22

Epilogue

Ralf W. Schlosser

Department of Speech-Language Pathology and Audiology
Northeastern University

I. INTRODUCTION

In Section I of this book, we conceptualized efficacy research and set the foundations for the validity of efficacy research. In Section II, the reader was exposed to (1) various design methodologies for studying and synthesizing the efficacy of interventions in augmentative and alternative communication (AAC) (e.g., single-subject experimental research) and (2) strategies for enhancing the trustworthiness of the research record, including asking appropriate research questions, carefully describing research participants, ensuring the fidelity of treatment implementation, and evaluating the social validity of outcomes, methods, and goals. The chapters in Section III of this text represent exemplars of how evidence from efficacy research may be used in selected content areas to engage in evidence-based practice (EBP). Multiple exemplars assist practitioners in gener-

The Efficacy of Augmentative and Alternative Communication

alizing the skills needed for EBP. Undoubtedly, other content areas could have served as exemplars, such as the effects of communication-based approaches on challenging behaviors or the effects of iconicity on symbol learning. Perhaps these and other areas of study will be added in a subsequent edition. This text focused on the efficacy of AAC interventions. Therefore, references to EBP are primarily restricted to decisions surrounding treatment implementation and treatment selection. It is acknowledged, however, that many other decision-making areas in AAC could benefit from EBP, including issues pertaining to assessment, vocabulary selection, and vocabulary organization to name but a few (for other decision-making areas, see the recent "Knowledge and Skills" document by ASHA, 2002).

II. INSIGHTS GAINED FROM EXPERIENCES WITH THE EBP PROCESS

In working on several process illustrations on EBP, a number of insights became apparent. This section describes each of these insights and posits directions for future work toward EBP.

A. EVALUATING RESEARCH EVIDENCE IS A DIALECTICAL PROCESS

First, although the framework described in Chapter 12 appears to follow a logical, step-by-step progression from the evaluation of internal validity to external validity, in practice this process is less sequential and more dialectical. In fact, this author found himself first asking an external validity question such as "Are the participants similar to my direct stakeholder?" When the answer was affirmative, the author found himself going back to the study and proceeded to evaluate its internal validity. When the answer was negative, the study did not need to be evaluated further. Thus, the process has much more of a back-and-forth movement than anticipated based on the developed framework.

B. EVIDENCE-BASED PRACTICE HAS TO BE A CYCLICAL PROCESS

After working through the process illustrations, it became clear that the last two steps in the EBP process—that is, evaluating EBP and the dissemination of findings—are absolutely essential for moving the field forward. Bennett and

Glaziou (1997) stated that evaluation leads to more questions, which need to be answered through subsequent research, and the cycle starts anew. If practitioners and other stakeholders were to share with the field what type of research evidence they needed to inform their decision making, these issues could be formalized into researchable questions and pursued in future research. Chapter 15 is a case in point. The research on the selection of graphic symbols for an initial request lexicon is not yet sufficiently focused on relevant variables to inform EBP in a more fruitful way. This example illustrates the research-directing function of EBP, which Bennett and Bennett (2000) also emphasized. On the other hand, if the formulation of research questions is not informed by the results of EBP endeavors, there is a clear danger that research becomes less and less relevant to practitioners and other stakeholders. Hoagwood, Burns, Kiser, Ringeisen, and Schoenwald (2001) go one step further and argue that future intervention research needs to take into account the fit between the intervention and the later context of delivery in practice. To illustrate this point, the earlier example about studying the effects of augmented input shall be considered. Under optimal conditions, researchers may wish to study the effects of augmented input on graphic symbol learning when input provided 100% of utterances directed to the learner. In daily practice, however, it has been estimated that only 10% of utterances directed to the learner include augmented input. Thus, intervention development needs to attend to such differences resulting from service delivery issues at the outset of intervention development rather than viewing them as "nuisance variables" that need to be controlled (Hoagwood *et al.*, 2001). The model described in Chapter 2 can be of help toward that end. Such changes in efficacy research are absolutely necessary if the field is to hope, as Hoagwood *et al.* (2001) put it, "that evidence-based practices do not gather too much dust on academic shelves" (p. 1187).

C. Evidence-Based Practice Can Be a Time-Consuming Process

Evaluating research evidence can be a time-consuming process. Because the field cannot afford not to use EBP, it is essential that this issue be taken seriously. Otherwise this issue could become a prominent deterrent or barrier to EBP use. A dual-pronged approach is necessary. Agencies and employers need to acknowledge that it costs more time to employ EBP than it does to provide services without consulting the evidence. Therefore, time needs to be built into the schedule if practitioners want to be able to go through the EBP process. At the same time, researchers, in collaboration with practitioners, need to take measures to facilitate the relatively speedy evaluation of evidence. These measures may take various forms. For example, more good-quality systematic reviews, in particular meta-analyses, need to be undertaken in numerous topic areas that are of interest to practitioners. Chapter 11 discussed criteria and strategies for producing and evaluating systematic syntheses. Such systematic reviews of the literature save an incredible amount of time for the evidence-based practitioner who is otherwise faced with the daunting task of having to first locate these individual studies and then evaluate and synthesize the information. While there is no real shortage of reviews in the AAC field (see Chapter 11), there is a dearth of high-quality reviews. The British-based National Health Services Centre for Reviews and Dissemination at the University of York (www.york.ac.uk/inst/crd/welcome.htm) houses the Database of Abstracts of Reviews of Effectiveness (DARE). This database includes reviews of high methodological quality published since September 1996. Each review is analyzed using specified criteria as to what constitutes a high-quality review. When one conducts a search for "augmentative and alternative communication," only the following entry is listed:

> Promoting generalization and maintenance in augmentative and alternative communication: A meta-analysis of 20 years of effectiveness research. [Abstract 146993] Database of Abstracts of Reviews of Effectiveness, available http://nhscrd.york.ac.uk/online/dare/20008778.htm. Abstract of Promoting generalization and maintenance in augmentative and alternative communication: A meta-analysis of 20 years of effectiveness research. Schlosser R. W., & Lee, D. (2000). *Augmentative and Alternative Communication, 16,* 208–227.

Part of the reason for this meager yield may be that DARE does not cover all relevant journals in which AAC research is published. Even then, however, the field should strive for more high-quality reviews, which may get listed in DARE. The database provides a structured abstract based on the review from the staff of the Centre for Reviews and Dissemination. The structured abstract for the previous entry is provided here as an example.

Document 146993
Promoting generalization and maintenance in augmentative and alternative communication: a meta-analysis of 20 years of effectiveness research.
Schlosser R W, Lee D L. AAC: Augmentative and Alternative Communication 2000; 16(4): 208–226.

This record is a structured abstract written by CRD reviewers. The original has met a set of quality criteria. Since September 1996 abstracts have been sent to authors for comment. Additional factual information is incorporated into the record. Noted as (A:. . . .).

Authors' objectives
To determine the effectiveness of interventions in augmentative and alternative communication (AAC) with particular emphasis on strategies that induce generalisation and/or maintenance.

Type of intervention
Treatment.

Specific interventions included in the review

The training of AAC (defined as an "area of clinical practice that attempts to compensate for the impairment and disability patterns of persons with severe expressive communication disorders"), serving a communicative function such as requesting.

The following prompt intervention strategies were included: mand/model; least to most intrusive; time delay; most to least intrusive; stimulus fading; graduated guidance; response shaping/successive approximation; and other or combination.

Experiments using match-to-sample procedures, discrimination, memory aids, recipe cards, and schedule boxes were excluded, as were interventions focussing on motor compliance and natural speech development (unless secondary to primary dependent measure of AAC). Communication-based approaches to challenging behaviours were also excluded.

Participants included in the review

Persons (adults and children) with severe expressive communication disorders. The following classifications were included: mental retardation (mild/moderate); mental retardation (severe/profound); multiple disabilities; physical disability; autism; mental retardation; and autism (other/combination).

Persons whose only disability was due to a hearing impairment were not included.

Outcomes assessed in the review

Behaviour change, generalisation and maintenance.

Study designs of evaluations included in the review

Single-subject experimental designs which used a time-series format with graphically displayed data. Group experiments were excluded.

What sources were searched to identify primary studies?

Databases were searched including the Educational Resources Information Centre (ERIC), PsycLIT, Psychological Abstracts, and Dissertation Abstracts International, using "appropriate natural-language terms," controlled-vocabulary terms and journal names. Forty-six journals were handsearched between 1976 and 1995, as well as the reports "AAC Theses and Dissertations" and "Master's and Doctoral Theses Update." Footnote chasing was used as a third technique, and the reference lists of retrieved articles were also checked.

Criteria on which the validity (or quality) of studies was assessed

The authors used predefined "rigid" quality indicators (see Other Publication of Related Interest no.1) in order to assess study quality. The criteria addressed issues relating to study design, interobserver agreement, procedural integrity, and availability of data to calculate the PND/POD (percentage of nonoverlapping data/percentage of overlapping data).

How were decisions on the relevance of primary studies made?

The second author and a trained expert in single-subject research and AAC evaluated each article independently of each other to determine whether an article should be included. Differences were reconciled through discussion. Agreement for inclusion was also determined between the second author and an independent rater.

How were judgements of validity (or quality) made?

The authors do not state how papers were assessed for validity or how many of the reviewers performed the validity assessment.

How were the data extracted from primary studies?

The second author and a trained research assistant independently extracted and coded the studies. Inter-rater agreement for 32 data series was 100% for all variables except PND intervention (91%).

Coding categories were as follows: study number; subject number; age; classification; intervention target; and prompt intervention strategy.

Each experimental phase was coded as follows: setting; instructional; AAC system; intervention design; generalisation design; maintenance design; generalisation and maintenance strategies; generalisation dimensions; procedural integrity data; procedural integrity in percent; interobserver agreement; interobserver agreement in percent; baseline characteristics; and PND intervention (IPND), PND generalisation using intervention baseline as comparison (GPND-IB), PND generalisation using generalisation baseline as a comparison (GPND-GB), POD maintenance using the intervention phase as a comparison (MPOD), and PND maintenance using the intervention baseline as a comparison (MPND).

Number of studies included in the review

Fifty studies, involving 232 data series, were included.

How were the studies combined?

The percentage of nonoverlapping data (PND) (requires the calculation of nonoverlap between baseline and successive intervention phases) (see Other Publications of Related Interest no.2) was used to combine studies of intervention effectiveness, generalisation effectiveness and maintenance effectiveness.

To integrate studies in terms of maintenance effectiveness, the percentage of overlapping data (POD) was also used by calculating the percentage of maintenance data points within or above the last three intervention data points.

How were differences between studies investigated?

Studies were grouped in the following categories: intervention; generalisation; and maintenance.

Results of the review

Interobserver agreement was 100% for inclusion of studies.

Fifty single-subject experimental studies, including 232 comparisons of experimental phases, reported quantitative outcome measures. Interventions were effective in terms of behaviour change, generalisation, and, to a lesser degree, maintenance.

Using predefined quality indicators to arrive at a best evidence data set (57 intervention studies, 7 generalisation studies and 1 maintenance study met all of the requirements), interventions remained effective in changing behaviour, whereas generalisation and maintenance data could not be interpreted due to the small number of studies.

Was any cost information reported?

No.

Authors' conclusions

This synthesis indicates that AAC interventions are effective in terms of behaviour change, generalisation, and, to a lesser degree, maintenance. This represents an important finding, considering these times of increased accountability and scarce resources. When predetermined quality indicators were applied to yield a more restricted data set, interventions remained effective in changing behaviour, whereas generalisation and maintenance data could not be interpreted due to the small n.

CRD commentary

The review addressed a well-defined question and the literature search was very thorough. Study selection was performed independently by two or more authors, thereby reducing the risk of bias. Study quality was assessed but was not used in the final analysis as the authors decided that not enough generalisation and maintenance data met the criteria. Details of individual studies pooled in this review were not presented in the text, only the bibliographic information is listed in an appendix. The statistical methods were well described and seem to be appropriate for calculating the effect sizes of single-subject data. The authors also discuss the limitations of the method they chose to use (% non-overlapping data). It is not clear whether pooling of all the different interventions was appropriate or not. Also, participants ranged from 5 years to over 25 years and had a range of disabilities.

Overall, this was a fairly good review and the authors' conclusions appear to follow on from the results.

What are the implications of the review?

Practice: The authors state that the lack of sufficient evidence data along with the prominence of "train and hope" approaches calls for training of clinical researchers and clinicians in the breadth of available strategies and training as to how these strategies may be incorporated into treatment procedures.

Research: The authors state that more care needs to be taken in selecting appropriate designs for evaluating generalisation and maintenance effectiveness while considering the range of available strategies for promoting generalisation and maintenance.

Other publications of related interest

1. Slavin RE. Best-evidence synthesis: An alternative to meta-analytic and traditional reviews. Educational Researchers 1986;15:5–11.

2. Scruggs TE, Mastropieri MA, Casto G. The quantitative synthesis of single subject research methodology: Methodology and validation. Remedial and Special Education 1987;8:24–33.

Subject index terms

Subject indexing assigned by CRD:

Autistic-Disorder; Communication-Disorders; Language-Disorders; Learning-Disorders; Mental-Retardation

Country code

United States

Review funding body

Office of Special Education Programs, US Department of Education, grant number CFDA 84 023E

Address for correspondence
Mr. R. W. Schlosser, Department of Speech-Language Pathology and Audiology, Northeastern University, 151B Forsyth, Boston, MA 02115, USA.

Accession number and database entry date
20008778 30092001

The URL of this record is: http://nhscrd.york.ac.uk/online/dare/20008778.htm

The evidence-based practitioner can review this structured abstract and then decide whether or not it is appropriate to read the entire article for more detailed information.

The evaluation of original research studies by someone other than the evidence-based practitioner may function as another time-saving measure. A number of fields now have evidence-based practice journals, such *Evidence-Based Medicine* (www.evidencebasedmedicine.com), *Evidence-Based Health Care* (www.hbuk.co.uk/journals/ebhc/), *Evidence-Based Mental Health* (http://ebmh. bmjjournals.com/), and *Evidence-Based Nursing* (www.evidencebasednursing. com/). These journals provide reviews of original research that is selected based on practical applicability or soundness of the evidence. The journal *Evidence-Based Nursing*, for example, has expert commentators put every article into a clinical context and draw out the key research findings. Its aim is to provide access to the best research related to nursing. Currently, evidence-based practitioners do not have access to such a journal in the AAC field specifically and broader related fields such as special education or communication disorders in general. The AAC field may or may not be large enough to accommodate a secondary journal devoted to the review of original AAC research published in numerous primary journals (e.g., "Evidence-Based Augmentative and Alternative Communication"). On the other hand, AAC is being published in more than 40 journals, which makes it extremely difficult to keep abreast of AAC intervention research. In fact, much of AAC intervention research is not published in *Augmentative and Alternative Communication*, but rather in other journals. A secondary journal would do a tremendous service toward timely access to appraised evidence. At this point, the journal *Augmentative and Alternative Communication* has enlisted individuals, so-called abstract reviewers, who review other journals for AAC content. Once located, abstracts of located AAC content get reprinted verbatim in the journal. Although this practice this does draw the attention of the readership to AAC research published elsewhere, it cannot replace an evaluation of the practical relevance and certainty of evidence of these studies.

D. THE ROLE OF STAKEHOLDERS IS PARAMOUNT

From the EBP process illustration exemplars provided in Section III of this book, it is clear that the evidence-based practitioner is confronted with a range of scenarios; for some clinical/educational questions, there is a solid research base (e.g., Chapter 14, "Strategies for Beginning Communicators"), and for others, the research evidence is in its infancy (e.g., Chapter 17, "Literacy"). Thus, the role that research evidence can and should play will vary with the specific question at hand and the weight of clinical/educational expertise varies with it. When there is little research to guide practice, for example, there needs to be greater use of practitioner expertise and reasoning (Bennett & Bennett, 2000; Naylor, 1995). Dynamic assessment, for example, may need to take a more active role.

The EBP process illustrations in Section III of this text were hypothetical and constructed by the respective authors. In these examples, the stakeholders' perspectives were portrayed to be consistent with those of the practitioner during the application of the evidence step of the EBP process. Although this allowed the successful uptake of research evidence in EBP to be illustrated, it is somewhat contrived and does not show the range of possible scenarios as far as the uptake of research is concerned. In practice, there will be situations where direct stakeholders disagree with the research evidence and make decisions that contradict the research evidence. Some voices have raised concerns that the research evidence has been declared the authority in the name of EBP and therefore dominates over the stakeholder's authority: "Declaring evidence the authority diminishes the client's authority and his or her right to seek information in unique ways and to decide what is possible in light of individual circumstances" (Mitchell, 1999, p. 31)

Such warnings have to be taken very seriously, and such perceived presuppositions of EBP need to be questioned. The definition of EBP put forth in Chapter 12 calls for an "*integration of* [italics added] best and current research evidence with clinical/educational expertise and relevant stakeholder perspectives to facilitate decisions for assessment and intervention that are deemed effective and efficient for a given direct stakeholder" (p. 263). The word "integration" means *joining* or *synthesis* and neither implies equality nor domination of any of the cornerstones of the decision-making process. It certainly does not mean that research evidence has authority over stakeholder perspectives, and it should not be interpreted as such. Stakeholder perspectives need to be valued perspectives regardless of available research evidence or the role of clinical/educational expertise. Stakeholders need to be put in the position of making informed choices as to what they wish to pursue in light of the best and current research evidence and recommendations based on clinical/educational expertise. Because it is the direct stakeholder and relevant other stakeholders who will be most affected by whatever decisions are being made, it is only fitting that the final decision is the prerogative of the stakeholders. The more knowledge and skills the stakeholders have in terms of interpreting or understanding research evidence, the less they have to rely on the practitioner's reading of the evidence. However, even if the stakeholders have to rely fully on the practitioner to synthesize the research evidence, the final decision should rest with the relevant stakeholders.

E. Training Practitioners in the Skills Needed to Engage in EBP

Another issue that became clear is the need for practitioners to be trained in the skills necessary for EBP. An important initial skill is to be able to frame a clinical/educational question that is answerable through an evaluation of the literature (Sackett, Richardson, Rosenberg, & Haynes, 1997). This is not as easy as it seems and, although Section III of this text provides instructions (see Chapter 12) and numerous examples of clinical/educational questions, practitioners require explicit training on how to formulate these questions. In this monograph, we attempted to formulate clinical/educational questions that are very specific by describing a particular direct stakeholder with whom assistance is being sought for decision making. Not all questions, however, need to be that specific. In fact, Chapter 14 includes more general questions such as "How do I teach requesting to beginning communicators?"—a direct stakeholder is not specified. Here, the research evidence being sought is more general, calling for the identification of effective teaching principles. The point is that both kinds of questions are legitimate in EBP. The reader may also find it helpful to consult the work of Rosen and Teesson (2001) on "The Well-Built Clinical Question" method or the Web site on Evidence-Based Practice Internet Resources hosted by McMaster University (www-hsl.mcmaster.ca/ebm/).

Another important set of skills pertains to the ability to search for evidence in an efficient manner. Tutorials are needed to assist existing practitioners as well as practitioners-to-be in the mechanics of searching for AAC evidence. This is a challenging and sometimes daunting task given that the literature is scattered across so many journals. However, insights into the coverage of various databases will go a long way toward accomplishing a more comprehensive search for AAC evidence. MEDLINE, for example, does not cover the journal *Augmentative and Alternative Communication*. Specialty databases such as DARE and the Cochrane Collaboration would seem to be a better first step compared to general databases. Unfortunately, at this time AAC content is not well represented in these databases. Chapters 11 and 12 provide several helpful suggestions for conducting searches.

Once the evidence is identified, practitioners need to appraise the evidence. This requires skills in research methodology and issues pertaining to internal and external validity. Over the years, this author has developed several appraisal checklists (see Chapters 6, 9, and 11; Schlosser, 1999, 2002) mostly related to the evaluation of single-subject experimental designs and systematic reviews. More such critical appraisal checklists are necessary, and they need to be field-tested by practitioners to determine their utility and to revise them if necessary.

Skills training in the evaluation of evidence must take a dual-pronged approach including both continuing education for existing practitioners and preservice education for future practitioners. Do existing classes on AAC, clinical procedures, or research methods/designs in special education programs and speech-language pathology programs prepare the practitioner-to-be sufficiently to think and act like an evidence-based practitioner? Surveys are needed to determine the extent to which existing preservice programs prepare its students for EBP.

III. THE FUTURE OF EFFICACY RESEARCH: TOWARD EBP

Efficacy research has been one of the primary recent concerns in the AAC field. Although great strides have been made, progress is necessary and attainable. To move forward in terms of producing stronger research evidence, several processes are necessary, including the asking appropriate research questions (Chapter 4), providing better descriptions of participants (Chapter 5), giving more thoughtful selection to research designs (Chapters 6 through 8), ensuring the integrity of treatments (Chapter 9), and evaluating the social validity of interventions (Chapter 10). Efficacy research is not useful unless it finds its way into daily practice. EBP can serve as a vehicle to do just that (see Chapter 12). Uptake of research evidence, however, is not automatic just because the evidence is available (see Hoagwood *et al.*, 2001). To increase uptake of research evidence, a number of steps need to be taken, including an increased availability of high-quality systematic reviews (see Chapter 11 and Section II), more efficacy research that takes into account the exigencies of daily service delivery issues by moving from research under ideal conditions to research under more typical conditions (see Chapter 2), training of practitioners in the skills necessary for EBP (see Section II. above), feeding results of EBP efforts back into research (see Chapters 12, 15, 17, and 18, and Section II), recognizing that direct stakeholders are the ultimate judges in EBP (see below), and putting systems in place to make the evaluation of research evidence more time efficient (see Section II). This is by no means a complete list, but it is a start toward evidence-based practice in AAC.

REFERENCES

American Speech-Language-Hearing Association (2002, April 16). Augmentative and alternative communication: Knowledge and skills for service delivery. *ASHA Leader, 7 (Suppl. 22),* 97–106.

Bennett, S., & Bennett, J. W. (2000). The process of evidence-based practice in occupational therapy: Informing clinical decisions. *Australian Occupational Therapy Journal, 47,* 171–180.

Bennett, J. W., & Glaziou, P. (1997). Evidence-based practice. What does it really mean? *Disease Management Health Outcomes, 1,* 277–280.

Hoagwood, K., Burns, B. J., Kiser, L., Ringeisen, H., & Schoenwald, S. K. (2001). Evidence-based practice in child and adolescent mental health services. *Psychiatric Services*, *52*, 1179–1189.

Mitchell, G. J. (1999). Evidence-based practice: Critique and alternative view. *Nursing Science Quarterly*, *12*, 30–35.

Naylor, C. D. (1995). Grey zones of clinical practice: some limits to evidence-based medicine. *Lancet*, *345*, 840–842.

Rosen, A., & Teesson, M. (2001). Does case management work? The evidence and the abuse of evidence-based medicine. *Australian and New Zealand Journal of Psychiatry*, *35*, 731–746.

Sackett, D. L., Richardson, W. S., Rosenberg, W., & Haynes, R. B. (1997). *Evidence-based medicine: How to practice and teach EBM*. New York: Churchill Livingstone.

Schlosser, R. W. (1999). Comparative efficacy of interventions in augmentative and alternative communication. *Augmentative and Alternative Communication*, *15*, 56–68.

Schlosser, R. W. (2002). On the importance of being earnest about treatment integrity. *Augmentative and Alternative Communication*, *18*, 36–44.

INDEX